CompTIA A+® Guide: Essentials

Third Edition
(Exam 220-701)

Mike Meyers'

CompTIA A+® Guide: Essentials

Third Edition
(Exam 220-701)

Mike Meyers

New York   Chicago   San Francisco
Lisbon   London   Madrid   Mexico City   Milan
New Delhi   San Juan   Seoul   Singapore   Sydney   Toronto

The McGraw·Hill Companies

Cataloging-in-Publication Data is on file with the Library of Congress

Sponsoring Editor
TIMOTHY GREEN

Editorial Supervisor
JODY MCKENZIE

Project Manager
ARUSHI CHAWLA

Acquisitions Coordinator
MEGHAN RILEY

Developmental Editor
LAURA STONE

Technical Editor
CHRISTOPHER A. CRAYTON

Copy Editor
BILL MCMANUS

Proofreader
PAUL TYLER

Indexer
WORDCO INDEXING SERVICES, INC.

Production Supervisor
JAMES KUSSOW

Composition
GLYPH INTERNATIONAL

Illustration
GLYPH INTERNATIONAL

Art Director, Cover
JEFF WEEKS

McGraw-Hill books are available at special quantity discounts to use as premiums and sales promotions, or for use in corporate training programs. To contact a representative, please e-mail us at bulksales@mcgraw-hill.com.

Mike Meyers' CompTIA A+® Guide: Essentials, Third Edition (Exam 220-701)

Copyright © 2010 by The McGraw-Hill Companies. All rights reserved. Printed in the United States of America. Except as permitted under the Copyright Act of 1976, no part of this publication may be reproduced or distributed in any form or by any means, or stored in a database or retrieval system, without the prior written permission of publisher, with the exception that the program listings may be entered, stored, and executed in a computer system, but they may not be reproduced for publication.

All trademarks or copyrights mentioned herein are the possession of their respective owners and McGraw-Hill makes no claim of ownership by the mention of products that contain these marks.

1 2 3 4 5 6 7 8 9 0   WDQ WDQ   1 0 9 8 7 6 5 4 3 2 1 0

ISBN: Book p/n 978-0-07-173871-2 and CD p/n 978-0-07-173872-9
of set 978-0-07-173873-6

MHID: Book p/n 0-07-173871-1 and CD p/n 0-07-173872-X
of set 0-07-173873-8

Information has been obtained by McGraw-Hill from sources believed to be reliable. However, because of the possibility of human or mechanical error by our sources, McGraw-Hill, or others, McGraw-Hill does not guarantee the accuracy, adequacy, or completeness of any information and is not responsible for any errors or omissions or the results obtained from the use of such information.

McGraw-Hill is an independent entity from CompTIA. This publication and CD-ROM may be used in assisting students to prepare for the CompTIA A+ exams. Neither CompTIA nor McGraw-Hill warrants that use of this publication and CD-ROM will ensure passing any exam. CompTIA is a registered trademark of CompTIA in the United States and/or other countries.

The logo of the CompTIA Authorized Quality Curriculum Program and the status of this or other training material as "Authorized" under the CompTIA Authorized Curriculum Program signifies that, in CompTIA's opinion, such training material covers the content of the CompTIA's related certification exam. CompTIA has not reviewed or approved the accuracy of the contents of this training material and specifically disclaims any warranties of merchantability or fitness for a particular purpose. CompTIA makes no guarantee concerning the success of persons using any such "Authorized" or other training material in order to prepare for any CompTIA certification exam.

Avast Home Edition appears courtesy of ALWIL Software, a.s., ©ALWIL
Spybot-S&D appears courtesy of Spybot, ©Safer Networking, Ltd.
CCleaner appears courtesy of Piriform Ltd., ©Piriform
FreeMeter appears courtesy of David Bowman
Ultimate Boot CD appears courtesy of Victor Chew

■ About the Author

Mike Meyers, lovingly called the "AlphaGeek" by those who know him, is the industry's leading authority on CompTIA A+ certification. He is the president and co-founder of Total Seminars, LLC, a provider of PC and network repair seminars, books, videos, and courseware for thousands of organizations throughout the world. Mike has been involved in the computer and network repair industry since 1977 as a technician, instructor, author, consultant, and speaker. Author of numerous popular PC books and videos, including the best-selling *CompTIA A+ Certification All-in-One Exam Guide*, Mike is also the series editor for the highly successful *Mike Meyers' Certification Passport* series, the *Mike Meyers' Computer Skills* series, and the *Mike Meyers' Guide to* series, all published by McGraw-Hill. As well as writing, Mike has personally taught (and continues to teach) thousands of students, including U.S. senators, U.S. Supreme Court justices, the United Nations, every branch of the U.S. Armed Forces, most branches of the Department of Justice, hundreds of corporate clients, academic students at every level, prisoners, and pensioners.

E-mail: michaelm@totalsem.com
Facebook: Mike Meyers (Houston, TX)
Twitter/Skype/most instant messaging clients: desweds
Web forums: www.totalsem.com/forums

About the Editor in Chief

Scott Jernigan wields a mighty red pen as Editor in Chief for Total Seminars. With a Master of Arts degree in Medieval History, Scott feels as much at home in the musty archives of London as he does in the warm computer glow of Total Seminars' Houston headquarters. After fleeing a purely academic life, he dove headfirst into IT, working as an instructor, editor, and writer. Scott has edited and contributed to dozens of books on computer literacy, hardware, operating systems, networking, and certification. His latest book is *Computer Literacy—Your Ticket to IC^3 Certification*. Scott co-authored the best-selling *CompTIA A+ Certification All-in-One Exam Guide* and the *Mike Meyers' A+ Guide to Managing and Troubleshooting PCs* (both with Mike Meyers). He has taught computer classes all over the United States, including stints at the United Nations in New York and the FBI Academy in Quantico.

About the Technical Editor

Christopher A. Crayton (MCSE, MCP+I, CompTIA A+, CompTIA Network+) is an author, technical editor, technical consultant, security consultant, and trainer. Formerly a computer and networking instructor at Keiser College (2001 Teacher of the Year), Chris has also worked as network administrator for Protocol and at Eastman Kodak Headquarters as a computer and network specialist. Chris has authored several print and online books on topics ranging from CompTIA A+ and CompTIA Security+ to Microsoft Windows Vista. Chris has provided technical edits and reviews for many publishers, including McGraw-Hill, Pearson Education, Charles River Media, Cengage Learning, Wiley, O'Reilly, Syngress, and Apress.

Peer Reviewers

Thank you to the reviewers, past and present, who contributed insightful reviews, criticisms, and helpful suggestions that continue to shape this textbook.

Donat Forrest
Broward County Community College
Pembroke Pines, FL

Brian Ives
Finger Lakes Community College
Canadaigua, NY

Farbod Karimi
Heald College
San Francisco, CA

Tamie Knaebel
Jefferson Community College
Louisville, KY

Keith Lyons
Cuyahoga Community College
Parma, OH

Winston Maddox
Mercer County Community College
West Windsor, NJ

Rajiv Malkan
Montgomery College
Conroe, Texas

Randall Stratton
DeVry University
Irving, TX

Scott Sweitzer
Indiana Business College
Indianapolis, IN

Thomas Trevethan
CPI College of Technology
Virginia Beach, VA

■ Acknowledgments

Scott Jernigan, my Editor in Chief at Total Seminars and boon companion on many an evening, worked his usual magic pulling together this latest edition. My thanks, amigo!

My acquisitions editor, Tim Green, kept me on target to get this book done. Seriously. Who else could motivate me to work on the book while on vacation in Key West, Florida? The sun, the surf, the silliness…all dashed away by a phone call. But I'm not bitter, just happy the book is done and Tim will quit yelling at me.

To Chris Crayton. You went so far beyond the call of technical editor that you should have your very own unique title, like *über technical editor king*! Thank you for helping make this book happen.

To Ed Dinovo. Your contributions of words and ideas helped build this book into a much better work than it could have been without you. Thank you very much.

To Alec Fehl. You did an outstanding job on this new book, and it is always a pleasure working with you.

My in-house photographer and fellow geek, Michael Smyer, contributed in many ways. His gorgeous photographs grace most pages. His tirelessness in challenging me technically on almost every topic both irritated and frustrated me, but the book is much better because of it. Excellent work, Michael.

Ford Pierson, my in-house editor and illustrator, brought outrageous wit and skill to his contributions throughout the book. Plus he has a killer instinct in Counter-Strike that makes the gaming sessions all the better. Great job, Ford.

Aaron Verber came in at the last minute with his red pen to help with page proofs, showing a careful eye that Scott will adore. I look forward to many more projects with you, lad.

On the McGraw-Hill side, the crew once again demonstrated why McGraw-Hill is the best in show as a publisher. With excellent work and even better attitude, this book went smoothly together.

Laura Stone reprised her role as developmental editor for this edition, keeping me on my toes for every detail, fact, illustration, screen shot, and photograph—all this while bouncing the newly born and very cute Maleah on one knee. Laura, you're amazing and a joy to work with. Thanks!

To the copy editors, page proofers, and layout folks—Bill McManus, Paul Tyler, WordCo Indexing Services, Inc., Amarjeet Kumar, and all the folks at Glyph International—superb work in every facet. Thank you for being the best.

■ *To Intel, for making great CPUs—and to AMD, for keeping Intel on the ball.*

—Mike Meyers

ABOUT THIS BOOK

Important Technology Skills

Information technology (IT) offers many career paths, leading to occupations in such fields as PC repair, network administration, telecommunications, Web development, graphic design, and desktop support. To become competent in any IT field, however, you need certain basic computer skills.

Mike Meyers' CompTIA A+® Guide: Essentials builds a foundation for success in the IT field by introducing you to fundamental technology concepts and giving you essential computer skills.

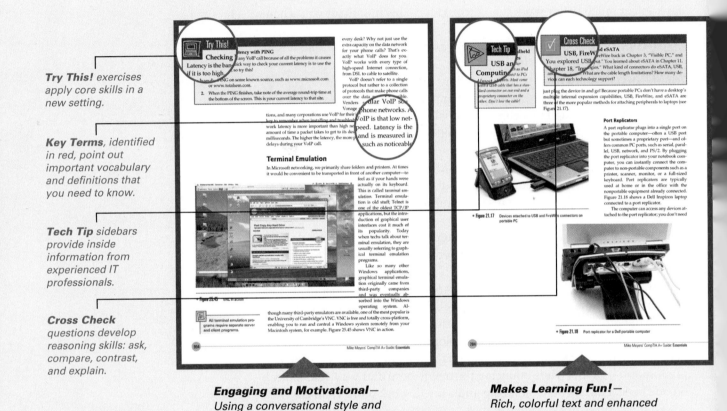

Try This! *exercises apply core skills in a new setting.*

Key Terms, *identified in red, point out important vocabulary and definitions that you need to know.*

Tech Tip *sidebars provide inside information from experienced IT professionals.*

Cross Check *questions develop reasoning skills: ask, compare, contrast, and explain.*

Engaging and Motivational—
Using a conversational style and proven instructional approach, the author explains technical concepts in a clear, interesting way using real-world examples.

Makes Learning Fun!—
Rich, colorful text and enhanced illustrations bring technical subjects to life.

Proven Learning Method Keeps You on Track
Mike Meyers' CompTIA A+® Guide: Essentials *is structured to give you comprehensive knowledge of computer skills and technologies. The textbook's active learning methodology guides you beyond mere recall and, through thought-provoking activities, labs, and sidebars, helps you develop critical-thinking, diagnostic, and communication skills.*

Effective Learning Tools

This pedagogically rich book is designed to make learning easy and enjoyable and to help you develop the skills and critical-thinking abilities that will enable you to adapt to different job situations and troubleshoot problems.

Mike Meyers' proven ability to explain concepts in a clear, direct, even humorous way makes these books interesting, motivational, and fun.

Chapter Review sections provide concept summaries, key terms lists, and lots of questions and projects.

Notes, Tips, and **Warnings** create a road map for success

Full-color photographs help you identify and recognize key PC components.

Offers Practical Experience—
Tutorials and lab assignments develop essential hands-on skills and put concepts in real-world contexts.

Robust Learning Tools—
Summaries, key terms lists, quizzes, essay questions, and lab projects help you practice skills and measure progress.

Each chapter includes:

- **Learning objectives** that set measurable goals for chapter-by-chapter progress

- **Try This!, Cross Check,** and **Tech Tip** sidebars that encourage you to practice and apply concepts in real-world settings

- Plenty of full-color **photographs** and **illustrations** that provide clear, up-close pictures of the technology, making difficult concepts easy to visualize and understand

- **Notes, Tips,** and **Warnings** that guide you through difficult areas

- **Highlighted Key Terms, Key Terms lists,** and **Chapter Summaries** that provide you with an easy way to review important concepts and vocabulary

- **Challenging End-of-Chapter Quizzes** that include vocabulary-building exercises, multiple-choice questions, essay questions, and on-the-job lab projects

CONTENTS AT A GLANCE

CONTENTS

Appendix B

■ **About the CD** 652

■ **Glossary** 655

■ **Index** 693

I started writing computer books for the simple reason that no one wrote the kind of books I wanted to read. The books were either too simple (Chapter 1, "Using Your Mouse") or too complex (Chapter 1, "TTL Logic and Transistors"), and none of them provided a motivation for me to learn the information. I believed that there were geeky readers just like me who wanted to know *why* they needed to know the information in a computer book.

Good books motivate readers to learn what they are reading. For example, if a book discusses binary arithmetic but doesn't explain why I need to learn it, that's not a good book. Tell me that understanding binary makes it easier to understand how a CPU works or why a megabyte is different from a million bytes—then I get excited, no matter how geeky the topic. If I don't have a good motivation to do something, then I'm simply not going to do it (which explains why I haven't jumped out of an airplane!).

In this book, I teach you why you need to understand the technology that runs almost every modern business. You'll learn to build and fix computers, exploring every nook and cranny, and master the art of the PC tech. In the process, you'll gain the knowledge you need to pass the CompTIA A+ Essentials exam.

Enjoy, my fellow geek.

—Mike Meyers

The logo of the CompTIA Authorized Quality Curriculum (CAQC) program and the status of this or other training material as "Authorized" under the CompTIA Authorized Quality Curriculum program signifies that, in CompTIA's opinion, such training material covers the content of CompTIA's related certification exam.

The contents of this training material were created for the CompTIA A+® Essentials exam (Exam 220-701), covering CompTIA certification objectives that were current as of August 2009.

CompTIA has not reviewed or approved the accuracy of the contents of this training material and specifically disclaims any warranties of merchantability or fitness for a particular purpose.

CompTIA makes no guarantee concerning the success of persons using any such "Authorized" or other training material in order to prepare for any CompTIA certification exam.

■ How to Become CompTIA Certified

This training material can help you prepare for and pass a related CompTIA certification exam or exams. In order to achieve CompTIA certification, you must register for and pass a CompTIA certification exam or exams.

In order to become CompTIA certified, you must:

1. Select a certification exam provider. For more information please visit http://www.comptia.org/certifications/testprep/ testingcenters.aspx.

2. Register for and schedule a time to take the CompTIA certification exam(s) at a convenient location.

3. Read and sign the Candidate Agreement, which will be presented at the time of the exam(s). The text of the Candidate Agreement can be found at http://www.comptia.org/certifications/testprep/policies/ agreement.aspx.

4. Take and pass the CompTIA certification exam(s).

For more information about CompTIA's certifications, such as its industry acceptance, benefits or program news, please visit www.comptia.org/ certification.

CompTIA is a not-for-profit information technology (IT) trade association. CompTIA's certifications are designed by subject matter experts from across the IT industry. Each CompTIA certification is vendor-neutral, covers multiple technologies and requires demonstration of skills and knowledge widely sought after by the IT industry.

To contact CompTIA with any questions or comments, please call (1) (630) 678 8300 or email questions@comptia.org.

INSTRUCTOR AND STUDENT WEB SITE

For instructor and student resources, check out www.MeyersEssentials .com. Students will find the chapter quizzes from the end of each chapter, and teachers can access instructor support materials.

■ Additional Resources for Teachers

Resources for teachers are provided via an Online Learning Center that maps to the organization of this textbook. This site includes the following:

- Answer keys to the end-of-chapter quizzes from this textbook
- Answer keys to the *Mike Meyers' CompTIA A+® Guide: Essentials Lab Manual, Third Edition (Exam 220-701)* lab activities
- Instructor's Manual that contains learning objectives, classroom preparation notes, instructor tips, and a lecture outline for each chapter
- Engaging PowerPoint slides on the lecture topics (including full-color artwork from this book)
- Access to EZ Test online and test files that enable you to generate a wide array of tests. EZ Test features automatic grading, hundreds of practice questions, and a variety of question types and difficulty levels, enabling you to customize each test to maximize student progress
- LMS cartridges and other formats may also be available upon request; contact your sales representative

The Path of the PC Tech

"Of everything I've learned during my stint at Maximum PC, one lesson reigns supreme: The PC is what we make of it."

—GEORGE JONES, *MAXIMUM PC*

In this chapter, you will learn how to

- **Explain the importance of gaining skill in managing and troubleshooting PCs**

- **Explain the importance of CompTIA A+ certification**

- **Describe how to become a CompTIA A+ Certified Technician**

Computers have taken over the world, or at least many professions. Everywhere you turn, a quick dig beneath the surface sawdust of construction, the grease of auto mechanics, and the hum of medical technology reveals one or more personal computers (PCs) working away, doing essential jobs. Because the PC evolved from novelty item to essential science tool to everyday object in a short period of time, there's a huge demand for a workforce that can build, maintain, troubleshoot, and repair PCs.

The Importance of Skill in Managing and Troubleshooting PCs

The people who work with computers—the **Information Technology (IT)** workforce—do such varied jobs as design hardware, write computer programs that enable you to do specific jobs on the PC, and create small and large groupings of computers—**networks**—so people can share computer resources. IT people built the Internet, one of the most phenomenal inventions of the 20th century. IT people maintain the millions of computers that make up the Internet. Computer technicians (or **PC techs**, as those of us in the field call each other) make up the core of the IT workforce. Without the techs, none of the other stuff works. Getting workers with skill in building, maintaining, troubleshooting, and fixing PCs is essential for success for every modern business.

In the early days of the personal computer, anyone who used a PC had to have skills as a PC tech. The PC was new, buggy, and prone to problems. You didn't want to rely on others to fix your PC when the inevitable problems arose. Today's PCs are much more robust and have fewer problems, but they're also much more complex machines. Today's IT industry, therefore, needs specialized workers who know how to make the machines run well.

Every profession requires specialized skills. For the most part, if you want to *get* or *keep* a job that requires those specialized skills, you need some type of **certification** or license. If you want a job fixing automobiles, for example, you get the *Automotive Service Excellence* (*ASE*) certification. If you want to perform companies' financial audits, you get your *Certified Public Accountant* (*CPA*) certification.

Nearly every profession has some criteria that you must meet to show your competence and ability to perform at a certain level. Although the way this works varies widely from one profession to another, all of them will at some point make you take an exam or series of exams. Passing these exams proves that you have the necessary skills to work at a certain level in your profession, whether you're an aspiring plumber, teacher, barber, or lawyer.

If you successfully pass these exams, the organization that administers those exams grants you certification. You receive some piece of paper or pin or membership card that you can show to potential clients or employers. This certification gives those clients or employers a level of confidence that you can do what you say you can do. Without this certification, either you will not find suitable work in that profession or no one will trust you to do the work.

The Importance of CompTIA A+ Certification

Microcomputers were introduced in the late 1970s, and for many years PC technicians did not have a universally recognized way to show clients or employers that they know what to do under the hood of a personal computer. Sure, vendor-specific certifications existed, but the only way to get them was to get a job at an authorized warranty or repair facility first and then get the certification. Not that there's anything wrong with vendor-specific training; it's just that no single manufacturer has taken enough market share to make IBM training, for example, something that works for any job. (Then there is always that little detail of getting the job first before you can be certified....)

The software/networking side of our business has not suffered from the same lack of certifications. Due to the dominance of certain companies at one time or another (for example, Microsoft and Cisco), the vendor-specific certifications have provided a great way to get and keep a job. For example, Microsoft's *Microsoft Certified Systems Engineer* (*MCSE*) and Cisco's *Cisco Certified Internetwork Expert* (*CCIE*) have opened the doors for many.

But what about the person who runs around all day repairing printers, repartitioning hard drives, upgrading device drivers, and assembling systems? What about the PC hobbyists who want to be paid for their skills? What about the folks who, because they had the audacity to show that they knew the difference between CMOS and a command prompt, find themselves with a new title such as PC Support Technician or Electronic Services Specialist? On the other hand, how about the worst title of them all: "The Person Who Doesn't Get a Nickel Extra but Who Fixes the Computers"? CompTIA A+ certification fills that need.

What Is CompTIA A+ Certification?

CompTIA A+ certification is an industry-wide, vendor-neutral certification program developed and sponsored by the **Computing Technology Industry Association (CompTIA)**. The CompTIA A+ certification shows that you have a basic competence in supporting microcomputers. You achieve this certification by taking two computer-based, multiple-choice examinations. The tests cover what technicians should know after nine months of full-time PC support experience. CompTIA A+ certification enjoys wide recognition throughout the computer industry. To date, more than 800,000 technicians have become CompTIA A+ certified, making it the most popular of all IT certifications.

Who Is CompTIA?

CompTIA is a nonprofit industry trade association based in Oakbrook Terrace, Illinois. It consists of over 20,000 members in 102 countries. You'll find CompTIA offices in such diverse locales as Amsterdam, Dubai, Johannesburg, Tokyo, and São Paulo.

CompTIA provides a forum for people in these industries to network (as in meeting people), represents the interests of its members to the government, and provides certifications for many aspects of the computer industry. CompTIA sponsors A+, Network+, Security+, and other certifications. CompTIA works hard to watch the IT industry and constantly looks to provide new certifications to meet the ongoing demand from its membership. Check out the CompTIA Web site at **www.comptia.org** for details on the other certifications you can obtain from CompTIA.

Virtually every company of consequence in the IT industry is a member of CompTIA. Here are a few of the biggies:

Adobe Systems	AMD	Best Buy	Brother International
Canon	Cisco Systems	CompUSA	Fujitsu
Gateway	Hewlett-Packard	IBM	Intel
Kyocera	McAfee	Microsoft	NCR
Novell	Panasonic	Sharp Electronics	Siemens
Symantec	Toshiba	Total Seminars, LLC (that's my company)	Plus many thousands more

CompTIA began offering CompTIA A+ certification back in 1993. When it debuted, the IT industry largely ignored CompTIA A+ certification. Since that initial stutter, however, the CompTIA A+ certification has grown to become the de facto requirement for entrance into the PC industry. Many companies require CompTIA A+ certification for all of their PC support technicians, and the CompTIA A+ certification is widely recognized both in the United States and internationally. Additionally, many other certifications recognize CompTIA A+ certification and use it as credit toward their certifications.

The Path to Other Certifications

Most IT companies—big and small—see CompTIA A+ certification as the entry point to IT. From CompTIA A+, you have a number of certification options, depending on whether you want to focus more on hardware and operating systems or move into network administration (although these aren't mutually exclusive goals). The following three certifications are worth serious consideration:

- CompTIA Network+ certification
- Microsoft Certified Professional certifications
- Cisco certifications

CompTIA Network+ Certification

If you haven't already taken the CompTIA Network+ certification exam, make it your next certification. Just as CompTIA A+ certification shows you have solid competency as a PC technician, **CompTIA Network+ certification** demonstrates your skills as a network technician, including understanding of network hardware, installation, and troubleshooting. CompTIA's Network+ certification is a natural step for continuing toward your Microsoft or Cisco certifications. Take the CompTIA Network+: it's your obvious next certification.

Microsoft Certified Professional Certifications

Microsoft operating systems control a huge portion of all installed networks, and those networks need qualified support people to make them run. **Microsoft Certified Professional** certifications are a natural next step after the CompTIA certifications. They offer a whole slew of tracks and exams,

CompTIA A+ is the entry point to IT, though definitely not the only route for learning about computers and having certifications to prove that knowledge. Several certifications cover computer literacy or digital literacy, the phrase that means "what every person needs to know about computers to survive in the 21st century." The most popular computer literacy certification is Certiport's IC^3 certification that tests on general computer knowledge; office productivity applications, such as Word and PowerPoint; and Internet applications such as Web browsing and e-mail.

CompTIA has a pre–CompTIA A+ exam (*not* a certification), called the *CompTIA Strata IT Technology exam,* that's geared a bit more to a user preparing to become a tech. It's designed to check basic knowledge levels for people getting into IT.

ranging from simple specializations in Windows Vista to numerous Microsoft Certified IT Professional (MCITP) certifications and beyond. You can find more details on Microsoft's learning Web site at www.microsoft .com/learning/en/us/certification/cert-overview.aspx.

Cisco Certification

Let's face it, Cisco routers pretty much run the Internet and most intranets in the world. A *router* is a networking device that controls and directs the flow of information over networks, such as e-mail messages, Web browsing, and so on. Cisco provides five levels of certification for folks who want to show their skills at handling Cisco products, such as the **Certified Cisco Network Associate (CCNA)**, plus numerous specialty certifications. See the Cisco certification Web site here for more details: www.cisco.com/web/learning/ le3/learning_career_certifications_and_learning_paths_home.html.

■ How Do I Become CompTIA A+ Certified?

You become CompTIA A+ certified, in the simplest sense, by taking and passing two computer-based, multiple-choice exams. No prerequisites are required for taking the CompTIA A+ certification exams (although there's an assumption of computer literacy, whether or not you have one of the computer literacy certifications). There is no required training course and no training materials to buy. You *do* have to pay a testing fee for each of the two exams. You pay your testing fees, go to a local testing center, and take the tests. You immediately know whether you have passed or failed. By passing both exams, you become CompTIA A+ certified. There are no requirements for professional experience. You do not have to go through an authorized training center. There are no annual dues. You pass; you're in. That's it. Now for the details.

> Previously, CompTIA offered a basic exam and then a choice of three different second exams. CompTIA reverted to the simpler two-exam format in 2009.

The Basic Exam Structure

CompTIA names the two exams introduced in 2009 as **CompTIA A+ 220-701 (Essentials)** and **CompTIA A+ 220-702 (Practical Application)**. It's common to refer to these two exams as the 2009 exams to differentiate them from older CompTIA exams. Although you may take either of the two exams first, I recommend taking the Essentials followed by the Practical Application. The Essentials exam concentrates on understanding terminology and technology, how to do fundamental tasks such as upgrading RAM, and basic Windows operating system support. The Practical Application exam builds on the Essentials exam, concentrating on advanced configuration and troubleshooting.

Both of the exams are extremely practical, with little or no interest in theory. All questions are multiple choice or "click on the right part of the picture" questions. The following is an example of the questions you will see on the exams:

Your laser printer is printing blank pages. Which item should you check first?

    A. Printer drivers

    B. Toner cartridge

    C. Printer settings

    D. Paper feed

The correct answer is B, the toner cartridge. You can make an argument for any of the others, but common sense (and skill as a PC technician) tells you to check the simplest possibility first.

The 2009 exams use a regular test format in which you answer a set number of questions and are scored based on how many correct answers you give, rather than the adaptive format used in years past. These exams have no more than 100 questions each. (Both exams have 100 questions each at the time of this writing.)

Be aware that CompTIA may add new questions to the exams at any time to keep the content fresh. The subject matter covered by the exams won't change, but new questions may be added periodically at random intervals. This policy puts stronger emphasis on understanding concepts and having solid PC-tech knowledge rather than trying to memorize specific questions and answers that may have been on the tests in the past. Going forward, no book or Web resource will have all the "right answers" because those answers will change constantly. Luckily for you, however, this book does not just teach you what steps to follow in a particular case but also explains how to be a knowledgeable tech who understands *why* you're doing those steps, so that when you encounter a new problem (or test question), you can work out the answer. Not only will this help you pass the exams, you'll also be a better PC tech!

To keep up to date, we monitor the CompTIA A+ exams for new content and update the special Tech Files section of the Total Seminars Web site (www.totalsem.com) with new articles covering subjects we believe may appear on future versions of the exams.

Windows-Centric

The CompTIA A+ exams are exclusively centered on the Microsoft Windows operating systems you would expect at a workstation or home. There are no Linux questions. There are no Macintosh OS X questions. You won't be asked about any version of Windows Server or Windows Mobile (used on smartphones and PDAs). Objectives in both exams clearly focus on the following operating systems:

- Windows 2000 Professional
- Windows XP Professional
- Windows XP Home
- Windows XP Media Center
- Windows Vista Home
- Windows Vista Home Premium
- Windows Vista Business
- Windows Vista Ultimate

Windows 7

CompTIA has the darnedest luck when it comes to the timing of new CompTIA A+ exams compared to releases of new Windows versions. CompTIA released the previous CompTIA A+ exams back in 2006, about four months before Microsoft released Windows Vista. It seems that once again CompTIA is caught missing a new operating system. Just a few months after CompTIA announced the 2009 updates to the CompTIA A+, Microsoft unveiled the next version of Windows: Windows 7.

Assuming CompTIA stays true to form, the chances of Windows 7 making it onto this version of the CompTIA A+ are very small. Adding Windows 7 is a major undertaking that would require CompTIA to change their clearly defined exam objectives. Don't worry about Windows 7. Structurally it is identical to Windows Vista. Even Microsoft has stated that Windows 7 is "a refined version of Windows Vista." If you know Vista, you will know Windows 7—and CompTIA isn't going to ask you about Windows 7 until the next update, probably around 2012.

Essentials (Exam 220–701)

The questions on the CompTIA A+ Essentials exam fit into one of six objectives. The number of questions for each objective is based on the percentages shown in Table 1.1.

The Essentials exam tests your knowledge of computer components, expecting you to be able to identify just about every common device on PCs, including variations within device types. Here's a list:

- Floppy drives
- Hard drives
- Optical drives
- Solid state drives
- Motherboards
- Power supplies
- CPUs
- RAM
- Monitors
- Input devices, such as keyboards, mice, and touchscreens

- Video and multimedia cards
- Network and modem cards
- Cables and connectors
- Heat sinks, fans, and liquid cooling systems
- Laptops and portable devices
- Printers
- Scanners
- Network switches, cabling, and wireless adapters
- Biometric devices

Table 1.1	Essentials (Exam 220-701) Objectives and Percentages	
Domain		**Percentage**
1.0 Hardware		27%
2.0 Troubleshooting, Repair, and Maintenance		20%
3.0 Operating Systems and Software		20%
4.0 Networking		15%
5.0 Security		8%
6.0 Operational Procedure		10%

The Essentials exam tests your ability to install, configure, and maintain all the standard technology involved in a personal computer. You need to be able to install and set up a hard drive, for example, and configure devices in Windows 2000, Windows XP, and Windows Vista. You have to understand drivers. You have to know your way around Windows and understand the tasks involved in updating, upgrading, and installing the operating systems. You need to know the standard diagnostic tools available in Windows—not only so you can fix problems, but also so you can work with higher-level techs to fix things.

You're tested on your knowledge of computer security, including identifying, installing, and configuring security hardware and software. You need to know security tools and diagnostic techniques for troubleshooting. You're not expected to know everything, just enough to be competent.

Finally, the Essentials exam puts a lot of emphasis on operational procedures, such as safety and environmental issues and also communication and professionalism. You need to know how to recycle and dispose of computer gear properly. You have to understand and avoid hazardous situations. The exam tests your ability to communicate effectively with customers and coworkers. You need to understand professional behavior and demonstrate that you have tact, discretion, and respect for others and their property.

This book covers the 220-701 exam, but many of the concepts and information you'll learn here will help you on the 220-702 exam as well. However, while there is bound to be some overlap of topics between the two exams, there is plenty of information on the 702 exam that is not covered in this book, so be sure to keep studying for that exam once you're finished with this book!

Practical Application (Exam 220-702)

The CompTIA A+ 220-702 exam covers four objectives. Table 1.2 lists the objectives and percentages.

The Practical Application exam covers the same hardware and software as Essentials, but with a much more hands-on approach to determining the appropriate technology for a situation—running diagnostics and troubleshooting—rather than identification of hardware or operating system utilities. The exam tests your knowledge of computer components and programs so you can make informed recommendations to customers. You need to understand how all the technology should work, know the proper steps to figure out why something doesn't work, and then fix it.

The first domain, Hardware, provides a stark example of the difference in focus between the exams. Essentials talks about identifying names,

Table 1.2	Practical Application (Exam 220-702) Objectives and Percentages	
Domain	**Percentage**
1.0 Hardware	38%
2.0 Operating Systems	34%
3.0 Networking	15%
4.0 Security	13%

purposes, and characteristics of various devices. The Practical Application exam, in contrast, goes into more depth, placing you in real-world scenarios where you must decide what to do. Every sub-objective in the Hardware objective starts with "Given a scenario" and then asks you to do something. Objective 1.1 says, for example, "Given a scenario, install, configure and maintain personal computer components." Objective 1.2 says, "Given a scenario, detect problems, troubleshoot and repair/replace personal computer components." The other objectives follow suit.

Another big difference between the two exams is the treatment of the Operating Systems and Software objective in the Essentials exam versus Operating Systems in the Practical Application exam. Essentials tests you on how to use Windows and how to recognize the components, features, and basic utilities of the operating systems. The Practical Application exam goes much deeper. You need to understand intimately how to use the command line to manage the operating systems. You're expected to know all sorts of disk structures and run all the major disk management tools. Finally, the Practical Application exam grills you on operating system recovery tools and techniques so you can help customers get back up and running quickly.

> Even though the Practical Application exam does not specifically cover operational procedures, expect some questions about ethics, proper behavior in the workplace, ways to communicate with customers to get the most information in troubleshooting situations, and more.

How Do I Take the Exams?

Two companies, **Prometric** and **Pearson VUE**, administer the CompTIA A+ testing. There are thousands of Prometric and Pearson VUE testing centers across the United States and Canada, and the rest of the world. You may take the exams at any testing center. Both Prometric and Pearson VUE offer complete listings online of all available testing centers. You can select the closest training center and schedule your exams right from the comfort of your favorite Web browser:

www.prometric.com
www.vue.com

Alternatively, in the United States and Canada, call Prometric at 800-776-4276 or Pearson VUE at 877-551-PLUS (7587) to schedule the exams and to locate the nearest testing center. International customers can find a list of Prometric and Pearson VUE international contact numbers for various regions of the world on CompTIA's Web site at www.comptia.org.

You must pay for the exam when you call to schedule. Be prepared to sit on hold for a while. Have your Social Security number (or international equivalent) and a credit card ready when you call. Both Prometric and Pearson VUE will be glad to invoice you, but you won't be able to take the exam until they receive full payment.

If you have special needs, both Prometric and Pearson VUE will accommodate you, although this may limit your selection of testing locations.

How Much Does the Exam Cost?

The cost of the exam depends on whether you work for a CompTIA member or not. At this writing, the cost for non-CompTIA members is $168 (U.S.) for each exam. International prices vary, but you can check the CompTIA Web site for international pricing. Of course, the prices are subject to change without notice, so always check the CompTIA Web site for current pricing.

Very few people pay full price for the exam. Virtually every organization that provides CompTIA A+ training and testing also offers discount **vouchers**. You buy a discount voucher and then use the voucher number instead of a credit card when you schedule the exam. Vouchers are sold per exam, so you'll need two vouchers to take the two CompTIA A+ exams. Total Seminars is one place to get discount vouchers. You can call Total Seminars at 800-446-6004 or 281-922-4166, or get vouchers via the Web site: www.totalsem.com. No one should ever pay full price for CompTIA A+ exams.

How to Pass the CompTIA A+ Exams

The single most important thing to remember about the CompTIA A+ certification exams is that CompTIA designed the Essentials exam to test the knowledge of a technician with only 500 hours experience (about three months) and the Practical Application exam to test the knowledge of a technician with only 1000 hours experience (about six months)—so keep it simple! The exams aren't interested in your ability to overclock DDR3 CAS timings in CMOS or whether you can explain the exact difference between the Intel ICH10 and the AMD 790 southbridges. Don't bother with a lot of theory—think in terms of practical knowledge and standards. Read the book, do whatever works for you to memorize the key concepts and procedures, take the practice exams on the CD in the back of the book, review any topics you miss, and you should pass with no problem.

> Those of you who just want more knowledge in managing and troubleshooting PCs can follow the same strategy as certification-seekers. Think in practical terms and work with the PC as you go through each chapter.

Some of you may be in or just out of school, so studying for exams is nothing novel. But if you haven't had to study for and take an exam in a while, or if you think maybe you could use some tips, you may find the next section valuable. It lays out a proven strategy for preparing to take and pass the CompTIA A+ exams. Try it. It works.

Obligate Yourself

The very first step you should take is to schedule yourself for the exams. Have you ever heard the old adage, "Heat and pressure make diamonds"? Well, if you don't give yourself a little "heat," you'll end up procrastinating and delay taking the exams, possibly forever. Do yourself a favor. Using the following information, determine how much time you'll need to study for the exams, and then call Prometric or Pearson VUE and schedule them accordingly. Knowing the exams are coming up makes it much easier to turn off the television and crack open the book. You can schedule an exam as little as a few weeks in advance, but if you schedule an exam and can't take it at the scheduled time, you must reschedule at least a day in advance or you'll lose your money.

Set Aside the Right Amount of Study Time

After helping thousands of techs get their CompTIA A+ certification, we at Total Seminars have developed a pretty good feel for the amount of study time needed to pass the CompTIA A+ certification exams. The following table provides an estimate to help you plan how much study time you must commit to the CompTIA A+ certification exams. Keep in mind that these are averages. If you're not a great student or if you're a little on the nervous side,

		Amount of Experience		

Table 1.3   **Analyzing Skill Levels**

Tech Task	None	Once or Twice	Every Now and Then	Quite a Bit
Installing an adapter card	12	10	8	4
Installing and configuring hard drives	12	10	8	2
Installing modems and NICs	8	6	6	3
Connecting a computer to the Internet	8	6	4	2
Installing printers and scanners	4	3	2	1
Installing RAM	8	6	4	2
Installing CPUs	8	7	5	3
Fixing printers	6	5	4	3
Fixing boot problems	8	7	7	5
Fixing portable computers	8	6	4	2
Building complete systems	12	10	8	6
Using the command line	8	8	6	4
Installing/optimizing Windows	10	8	6	4
Using Windows 2000/XP	6	6	4	2
Using Windows Vista	10	8	4	2
Configuring NTFS permissions	6	4	3	2
Configuring a wireless network	6	5	3	2
Configuring a software firewall	6	4	2	1
Installing a sound card	2	2	1	0
Removing malware	4	3	2	0
Using OS diagnostic tools	8	8	6	4
Using a volt-ohm meter	4	3	2	1

add 10 percent; if you're a fast learner or have a good bit of computer experience, you may want to reduce the figures.

To use Table 1.3, just circle the values that are most accurate for you and add them up to get your estimated total hours of study time.

To that value, add hours based on the number of months of direct, professional experience you have had supporting PCs, as shown in Table 1.4.

A total neophyte usually needs a little over 200 hours of study time. An experienced tech shouldn't need more than 60 hours.

Total hours for you to study: _____.

Table 1.4   **Adding Up Your Study Time**

Months of Direct, Professional Experience...	To Your Study Time...
0	Add 50
Up to 6	Add 30
6 to 12	Add 10
Over 12	Add 0

A Strategy for Study

Now that you have a feel for how long it's going to take, you're ready to develop a study strategy. I'd like to suggest a strategy that has worked for others who've come before you, whether they were experienced techs or total newbies. This book is designed to accommodate the different study agendas of these two groups of students. The first group is experienced techs who already have strong PC experience but need to be sure they're ready to be tested on the specific subjects covered by the CompTIA A+ Essentials exam. The second group is those with little or no background in the computer field. These techs can benefit from a more detailed understanding of the history and concepts that underlie modern PC technology, to help them remember the specific subject matter information they must know for the exams. I'll use the shorthand terms Old Techs and New Techs for these two groups. If you're not sure which group you fall into, pick a few chapters and go through some end-of-chapter questions. If you score less than 70%, go the New Tech route.

I have broken most of the chapters into three distinct parts:

- **Historical/Conceptual**   Topics that are not on the CompTIA A+ exams but will help you understand more clearly what is on the CompTIA A+ exams.

- **Essentials**   Topics that clearly fit under the CompTIA A+ Essentials exam domains.

- **Beyond A+**   More advanced issues that probably will not be on the CompTIA A+ exams—yet.

 Not all chapters will have all three sections.

The beginning of each of these areas is clearly marked with a large banner that looks like this:

Historical/Conceptual

Those of you who fall into the Old Tech group may want to skip the Historical/Conceptual sections, since they cover information that you may already know. After reading the other sections, jump immediately to the questions at the end of the chapter. The end-of-chapter questions concentrate on information in the non-Historical/Conceptual sections. If you run into problems, review the Historical/Conceptual sections in that chapter. Note that you may need to skip back to previous chapters to get the Historical/Conceptual information you need for later chapters.

After going through every chapter as described, Old Techs can move directly to testing their knowledge by using the free practice exams on the CD-ROM that accompanies the book. Once you start scoring above 90%, you're ready to take the exams. If you're a New Tech—or if you're an Old Tech who wants the full learning experience this book can offer—start by reading the book, *the whole book,* as though you were reading a novel, from page one to the end without skipping around. Because so many computer terms and concepts build on each other, skipping around greatly increases the odds that you will become confused and end up closing the book and firing up your favorite PC game. Not that I have anything against PC games, but unfortunately that skill is *not* useful for the CompTIA A+ exams!

Your goal on this first read is to understand concepts, the *whys* behind the *hows*. Having a PC nearby as you read is helpful so you can stop and inspect the PC to see a piece of hardware or how a particular concept manifests in the real world. As you read about floppy drives, for example, inspect the cables. Do they look like the ones in the book? Is there a variation? Why? It is imperative that you understand why you are doing something, not just how to do it on one particular system under one specific set of conditions. Neither the exams nor real life as a PC tech works that way.

If you're reading this book as part of a managing and troubleshooting PCs class rather than a certification-prep course, I highly recommend going the New Tech route, even if you have a decent amount of experience. The book contains a lot of details that can trip you up if you focus only on the test-specific sections of the chapters. Plus, your program might stress historical and conceptual knowledge as well as practical, hands-on skills.

The CompTIA A+ certification exams assume that you have basic user skills. The exams really try to trick you with questions on processes that you may do every day and not think much about. Here's a classic: "To move a file from the C:\DATA folder to the D:\ drive using Windows Explorer, what key must you hold down while dragging the file?" If you can answer that without going to your keyboard and trying a few likely keys, you're better than most techs! In the real world, you can try a few wrong answers before you hit on the right one, but for the exams, you have to *know* it. Whether Old Tech or New Tech, make sure you are proficient at user-level Windows skills, including the following:

- Recognizing all the components of the standard Windows desktop (Start menu, notification area, etc.)
- Manipulating windows—resizing, moving, and so on
- Creating, deleting, renaming, moving, and copying files and folders within Windows
- Understanding file extensions and their relationship with program associations
- Using common keyboard shortcuts/hotkeys
- Installing, running, and closing a Windows application

Any PC technician who has been around a while will tell you that one of the great secrets in the computer business is that there's almost never anything completely new in the world of computer technology. Faster, cleverer, smaller, wider—absolutely—but the underlying technology, the core of what makes your PC and its various peripheral devices operate, has changed remarkably little since PCs came into widespread use a few decades ago. When you do your initial read-through, you may be tempted to skip the Historical/Conceptual sections—don't! Understanding the history and technological developments behind today's PCs helps you understand why they work—or don't work—the way they do. Basically, I'm passing on to you the kind of knowledge you might get by apprenticing yourself to an older, experienced PC tech.

After you've completed the first read-through, go through the book again, this time in textbook mode. If you're an Old Tech, start your studying here. Try to cover one chapter at a sitting. Don't focus too much on the Historical/

Conceptual sections. Get a highlighter and mark the phrases and sentences that bring out major points. Be sure you understand how the pictures and illustrations relate to the concepts being discussed.

Once you feel you have a good grasp of the material in the book, you can check your knowledge by using the practice exams included on the CD-ROM in the back of the book. You can take these in Practice mode or Final mode. In Practice mode, you can use the Assistance window to get a helpful hint for the current questions, use the Reference feature to find the chapter that covers the question, check your answer for the question, and see an explanation of the correct answer. In Final mode, you answer all the questions and receive an exam score at the end, just like the real thing.

Both modes show you an overall grade, expressed as a percentage, as well as a breakdown of how well you did on each exam domain. The Review Questions feature lets you see what questions you missed and what the correct answers are. Use these results to guide further studying. Continue reviewing the topics you miss and taking additional exams until you are consistently scoring in the 90% range. When you get there, you are ready to pass the CompTIA A+ Essentials exam.

Study Tactics

Perhaps it's been a while since you had to study for a test. Or perhaps it hasn't, but you've done your best since then to block the whole experience from your mind. Either way, savvy test-takers know that certain techniques make studying for tests more efficient and effective.

Here's a trick used by students in law and medical schools who have to memorize reams of information: write it down. The act of writing something down (not typing, *writing*) in and of itself helps you to remember it, even if you never look at what you wrote again. Try taking separate notes on the material and re-creating diagrams by hand to help solidify the information in your mind.

Another oldie but goodie: Make yourself flash cards with questions and answers on topics you find difficult. A third trick: Take your notes to bed and read them just before you go to sleep. Many people find they really do learn while they sleep!

Contact

If you have any problems, any questions, or if you just want to argue about something, feel free to send an e-mail to the author—michaelm@totalsem.com— or to the editor—scottj@totalsem.com.

For any other information you might need, contact CompTIA directly at their Web site: www.comptia.org.

Chapter 1 Review

■ Chapter Summary

After reading this chapter and completing the exercises, you should understand the following about the path of the PC tech.

Explain the importance of gaining skill in managing and troubleshooting PCs

■ The IT workforce designs, builds, and maintains computers, computer programs, and networks. PC techs take care of personal computers, thus representing an essential component in that workforce. As PCs become more complex, the IT workforce needs specialized PC techs.

■ Certifications prove to employers that you have the necessary skills. If you want a job fixing automobiles, for example, you get the *Automotive Service Excellence* (*ASE*) certification. To be certified, you take and successfully pass exams. Then the organization that administers those exams grants you certification. This is particularly important for IT workers.

Explain the importance of CompTIA A+ certification

■ In the early days of the personal computer, you could get vendor-specific certifications, such as IBM Technician, but nothing general for PC techs. Worse, you often had to have a job at that company to get the vendor-specific certification. The software and networking side of IT doesn't have that issue. To prove skill in working with Windows, for example, you could become a Microsoft Certified Technology Specialist (MCTS).

■ CompTIA A+ certification is an industry-wide, vendor-neutral certification program that shows that you have a basic competence in supporting microcomputers. You achieve this certification by taking two computer-based, multiple-choice examinations. The tests cover what technicians should know after nine months of full-time PC support experience. CompTIA A+ certification enjoys wide recognition throughout the computer industry.

■ CompTIA is a nonprofit, industry trade association based in Oakbrook Terrace, Illinois. It consists of over 20,000 members in 102 countries. CompTIA provides a forum for people in these industries to network, represents the interests of its members to the government, and provides certifications for many aspects of the computer industry. CompTIA sponsors A+, Network+, Security+, and other certifications.

■ The CompTIA A+ certification is the de facto entry point to IT. From CompTIA A+, you have a number of certification options, depending on whether you want to focus more on hardware and operating systems or move into network administration. You can get CompTIA Network+ certification, for example, or go on to get Microsoft or Cisco certified. CompTIA Network+ certification is the most obvious certification to get after becoming CompTIA A+ certified.

Describe how to become a CompTIA A+ Certified Technician

■ You become CompTIA A+ certified, in the simplest sense, by taking and passing two computer-based, multiple-choice exams. No prerequisites are required for taking the CompTIA A+ certification exams. There is no required training course and no training materials to buy. You *do* have to pay a testing fee for each of the two exams.

■ The CompTIA exams introduced in 2009 are *220-701* (*Essentials*) and *220-702* (*Practical Application*). It's common to refer to these two exams as the 2009 exams to differentiate them from older CompTIA exams. Although you may take either of the two exams first, I recommend taking the Essentials, followed by the Practical Application.

■ Both of the exams are extremely practical, with little or no interest in theory. All questions are multiple choice or "click on the right part of the picture" questions. CompTIA may add new questions to the exams at any time to keep the content fresh, although the subject matter covered by the exams won't change.

■ Two companies, Prometric and Pearson VUE, administer the actual CompTIA A+ testing. You can schedule exam time and location via the Web site for either company, www.prometric.com or www.vue.com. Check CompTIA's Web site for international links.

- To achieve success with the CompTIA A+ certification exams, think in terms of practical knowledge. Read the book. Work through the problems. Work with computers. Take the practice exams. You should obligate yourself by scheduling your exams. This keeps you focused on study.

- Read the book all the way through once. Experienced techs should then concentrate on the test-specific sections to prepare for the exams. Less experienced techs should read the book all the way through again until everything makes sense.

- If you're reading this book as part of a managing and troubleshooting PCs class rather than a certification-prep course, I highly recommend going the New Tech route, even if you have a decent amount of experience. The book contains a lot of details that can trip you up if you focus only on the test-specific sections of the chapters.

■ Key Terms

certification *(1)*
Certified Cisco Network Associate (CCNA) *(4)*
CompTIA A+ 220-701 (Essentials) *(4)*
CompTIA A+ 220-702 (Practical Application) *(4)*
CompTIA A+ certification *(2)*
CompTIA Network+ certification *(3)*
Computing Technology Industry Association (CompTIA) *(2)*

Information Technology (IT) *(1)*
Microsoft Certified Professional (MCP) *(3)*
network *(1)*
PC tech *(1)*
Pearson VUE *(8)*
Prometric *(8)*
voucher *(9)*
www.comptia.org *(2)*

■ Key Term Quiz

Use the Key Terms list to complete the sentences that follow. Not all terms will be used.

1. You can lump together all the folks who design, build, program, and fix computers into the _____ workforce.

2. You can become CompTIA A+ certified by passing the _____ and CompTIA A+ 220-702 (Practical Application) exams.

3. A _____ gives clients and employers a level of confidence that you can do what you say you can do.

4. A casual term for a person who builds and maintains computers is _____.

5. Prometric and _____ administer the CompTIA A+ certification exams.

6. You can use a _____ when you schedule your exam to save some money.

7. Persons desiring to work in Windows-based networking should pursue _____ certification after completing their CompTIA certifications.

8. You can find the latest information about the CompTIA A+ certification exams here: _____.

9. Typically, techs who attain CompTIA A+ certification then pursue _____ to add to their computer credentials.

10. A grouping of computers that enables people to share resources is called a _____.

Multiple-Choice Quiz

1. Which of the following is a vendor-specific certification? (Select all that apply.)
   A. Certified Cisco Network Associate
   B. CompTIA A+
   C. CompTIA Network+
   D. Microsoft Certified Systems Engineer

2. Which of the following certifications is the de facto requirement for entrance into the PC industry?
   A. Certified Cisco Network Associate
   B. CompTIA A+
   C. CompTIA Network+
   D. Microsoft Certified Systems Engineer

3. John loves the Internet and wants a career working on the machines that make the Internet work. He has completed both CompTIA A+ and Network+ certifications. Which of the following certifications would make a good next step?
   A. Certified Cisco Network Associate
   B. Certified Cisco Network Professional
   C. CompTIA Security+
   D. Microsoft Certified Systems Engineer

4. Which of the following exams focuses on installing, configuring, and maintaining all the standard technology involved in a personal computer?
   A. Certified Cisco Network Associate
   B. CompTIA A+ 220-701 (Essentials)
   C. CompTIA A+ 220-702 (Practical Application)
   D. Microsoft Certified Systems Engineer

5. At which of the following Web sites can you register to take the CompTIA A+ certification exams?
   A. www.comptia.org
   B. www.microsoft.com
   C. www.totalsem.com
   D. www.vue.com

6. How many exams must you pass to become CompTIA A+ certified?
   A. One
   B. Two

C. Three
D. Four

7. How much practical IT experience do you need to become CompTIA A+ certified?
   A. Six months
   B. One year
   C. Two years
   D. None

8. How many questions should you expect on the 220-702 Practical Application exam?
   A. 25
   B. 50
   C. 100
   D. The number of questions varies because the exams are adaptive.

9. The CompTIA A+ certification covers which of the following operating systems? (Select two.)
   A. Linux
   B. OS X
   C. Windows XP Media Center
   D. Windows Vista

10. What percentage of questions should you expect on operating systems in the 220-701 Essentials exam?
    A. 10%
    B. 15%
    C. 20%
    D. 25%

11. What percentage of questions should you expect on operating systems in the 220-702 Practical Application exam?
    A. 10%
    B. 13%
    C. 20%
    D. 34%

12. How much does it cost to take each exam (at the time of this book's publication)?
    A. $100 each
    B. $138 each
    C. $168 each
    D. $150 each

13. What percentage of questions should you expect on Windows 7 in the 220-702 Practical Application exam?

    A. 10%

    B. 13%

    C. 20%

    D. None

14. The 220-701 Essentials exam will *not* test you on which of the following computer components?

    A. Biometric devices

    B. Keyboards

    C. Printers

    D. Zip drives

15. What is CompTIA?

    A. A vendor-specific certification association

    B. A testing administration company

    C. A for-profit, industry trade corporation

    D. A nonprofit, industry trade association

■ Essay Quiz

1. Write a short essay on the benefits of certification in the field of computers. Include discussion on how the CompTIA certifications function within the broader category of computer certification. Why do you suppose people get certifications rather than (or in addition to) two- and four-year college degrees in IT?

Lab Project

• Lab Project 1.1

If you have access to the Internet, do some searching on computer certifications. Make a personal certification tree or pathway that maps out a series of certifications to pursue that might interest you. What certifications would be useful if you want to be a graphics designer, for example? What if you want to create computer games?

Operational Procedures

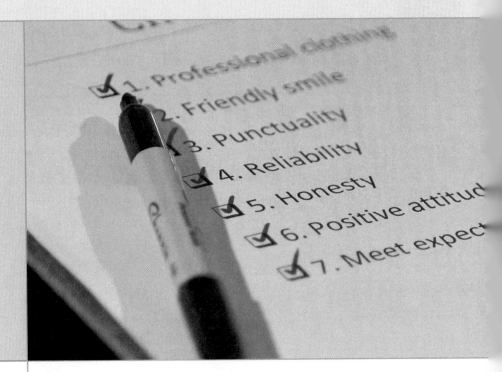

1. Professional clothing
2. Friendly smile
3. Punctuality
4. Reliability
5. Honesty
6. Positive attitud
7. Meet expect

"Just keep it clean. (You know, the new language policy and all.)"

—JON PHILLIPS, MAXIMUM PC

In this chapter, you will learn how to

- **Present yourself with a proper appearance and professional manner**
- **Talk to customers in a professional, productive manner**
- **Work with PCs safely using the proper tools**

One of the interesting parts of teaching new techs is keeping up with the skills that get a tech a job and the issues that cause them to lose the jobs they get. To me, the number one reason techs fail to get or hold onto a job isn't lack of technical skill; it's lack of what CompTIA calls "operational procedures." Personally, I think a better name might be "life skills and basic safety," but it boils down to the same thing: nontechnical skills that technicians are famous for lacking.

I like to describe myself as a "nerd" and I consider it a compliment if you call me one. Nerds are smart and like to work with technology—these are the good aspects of nerd-dom. On the other hand, most people would think of the term nerd as an insult. Nerds are rarely portrayed in a positive manner in the media, and I think I know why. Nerds generally suffer from some pretty serious social weaknesses. These weaknesses are classics: bad clothing, shyness, and poor communication skills. This chapter covers some basic life skills to enable you to enjoy your nerdiness and yet function out in the real world. You'll learn how to dress, how to act, and how to communicate. After you're well on your way to the beginnings of social graces, we'll discuss some of the hazards (such as static electricity) you may run into in your job and the tools you can use to prevent problems. After all, nerds who cannot stay organized—or who break equipment or themselves—need to learn some tricks to keep everything organized and safe.

■ The Professional Tech

A professional tech displays professionalism, which might seem a little trite if it weren't absolutely true. The tech presents a professional appearance and follows a proper ethical code. I call the latter the Traits of a Tech. Let's take a look at these two areas in more detail.

Appearance

Americans live in a casual society, and I think that's great, because I prefer dressing casually. The problem with casual is that perhaps our society is becoming *too* casual. New techs sometimes fail to appreciate that customers equate casual clothing with a casual attitude. You might think you're just fixing somebody's computer, but you're doing much more than that. You are saving precious family photos. You are keeping a small business in operation. This is serious stuff, and nobody wants an unclean, slovenly person doing these important jobs. Take a look at Figure 2.1. This is our resident illustrator (among other job descriptions), Ford Pierson, casually dressed to hang with his buddies.

● **Figure 2.1** Casual Ford

I have a question for you. If you ran a small business and your primary file server died, leaving 15 employees with nothing to do, how would you feel about Ford as a tech coming into your office looking like this? I hope your answer would be "not too confident." Every company has some form of dress code for techs. Figure 2.2 shows Ford dressed in a fairly typical example, with a company polo shirt, khaki pants, and dark shoes (trust me on that score). Please also note that both his shirt and his pants are wrinkle free. All techs either know how to iron or know the location of the nearest cleaners.

While we are looking at this model of a man, do you appreciate that his hair is combed and his face is cleanly shaven? It's too bad I can't use scratch-and-sniffs, but if I did, you'd also notice that Professional Ford took a shower, used some deodorant, and brushed his teeth.

I hope that most of the people who read this smile quietly to themselves and say, "Well, of course." The sad truth tells me otherwise. Next time you look at a tech, ask yourself how many of these simple appearance and hygiene issues were missed. Then make a point not to be one of the unkempt techs.

The Traits of a Tech

When I was a Boy Scout in the United States, we learned something called The Boy Scout Creed, a list of traits that define the ethics of a Boy Scout. Even thought I haven't been a Boy Scout for a long time, I still have them memorized. "A Scout is trustworthy, loyal, helpful, friendly, courteous, kind, obedient, cheerful, thrifty, brave, clean, and reverent."

● **Figure 2.2** Professional Ford

My goal here isn't a sales pitch for scouting in any form, but rather to give you an idea of what we are trying to achieve: a list of ethics that will help you be a better technician. The list you are about to see is my own creation, but it does a great job of covering the CompTIA A+ objectives. Let's dive into the traits of a tech: honesty/integrity, dependability/reliability, adaptability/versatility, and sensitivity.

Honesty/Integrity

Honesty and integrity are not the same thing, but for a tech, they are so closely related that it is best to think of them as one big ethic. **Honesty** means to tell the truth, and **integrity** means doing the right thing.

It's simple to say you have to be honest, but be warned that our industry often makes it difficult. IT technicians get a lot of leeway compared to most starting jobs, making dishonesty tempting. One of the biggest temptations is lying to your boss. A new tech driving around in a van all day may find it convenient to stretch the truth on how long he took for lunch or how far along he is on the next job. Being up front and honest with your boss is pretty obvious and easy to understand.

Being honest with your customers is a lot harder. Don't sell people goods and services they don't need, even if you get a cut of what you sell. Don't lie to your customers about a problem. If you can't explain the problem to them in plain English, don't create techno-babble (see note) and don't be afraid to say, "I don't know." Too many techs seem to think that not knowing exactly what a problem might be is a reflection of their skill. In your humble author's opinion, there is no greater proof of a quality technician than the ability to say "I don't know, but I know how to figure it out, and I will get you the right answer."

A computer tech must bring *integrity* to the job, just like any other service professional. Anything said to you and anything you see, you should treat as a personal confidence, not to be repeated to customers, coworkers, or bosses. Here's Mike's Rule of Confidentiality: "Unless it's a felony or an imminent physical danger, you didn't see nothin'."

There is an exception to this rule. Sometimes you need to separate paying customers from in-house users. A paying customer is someone who doesn't work for your company, who is paying for your services. An in-house user is someone who works for the same company you do and is not directly paying for your services. It's often your job (but not always) to police in-house IT policies. Here's a great example. If you are at a customer's site and you see a post-it note with a password on a user's monitor, you say nothing. If you are in-house and you see the same thing, you probably need to speak to the user about the dangers of exposing passwords.

You have a lot of power when you sit in front of someone's computer. You can readily read private e-mail, discover Web sites surfed, and more. With a click of the Start button, you can know the last five programs the user ran, including Word and Solitaire, and the last few documents the user worked on. Don't do this; you really don't want to know. Plus, if you are caught violating a customer's privacy, not only will you lose credibility and respect, you could also lose your job.

Passwords are a big issue for techs. We have to reboot computers and access shares and other jobs that require passwords. The rule here is to *avoid learning other folks' passwords at all costs* (Figure 2.3). If you know a password

> Techno-babble is the use of (often nonsensical) jargon and technical terms to intimidate and silence a challenge to a technical issue.

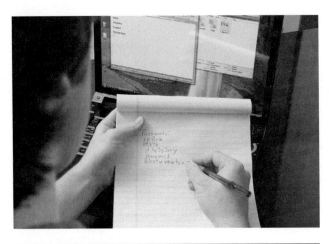

• Figure 2.3 Don't do this!

to access a mission-critical machine and that machine ends up compromised or with data missing, who might be blamed? You, that's who, so avoid learning passwords! If you only need a password once, let the user type it in for you. If you anticipate accessing something multiple times (the more usual situation), ask the user to change the password temporarily.

It's funny, but people assume ownership of things they use at work. John in accounting doesn't call the computer he uses anything but "my PC." The phone on Susie's desk isn't the company phone, it's "Susie's phone." Regardless of the logic or illogic involved with this sense of ownership, a tech needs to respect that feeling. You'll never go wrong if you follow the **Ethic of Reciprocity**, also known as the *Golden Rule:* "Do unto others as you would have them do unto you." In a tech's life, this can translate as "treat people's things as you would have other people treat yours." Don't use or touch anything—keyboard, printer, laptop, monitor, mouse, phone, pen, paper, or cube toy—without first asking permission. Follow this rule at all times, even when the customer isn't looking.

Dependability/Responsibility

Dependability and responsibility are another pair of traits that, while they don't mean the same thing, often go together. A responsible person is answerable for the acts she does. A dependable person can be counted on to perform those acts. Again, the freedom of the typical IT person's job makes dependability and responsibility utterly critical.

The single biggest dependability issue for an IT technician is to show up for job appointments and to show up on time. It seems to me we now live in a society where not showing up and not letting anyone know is normal. I call it the "Age of the Blow-off." We've all had an experience where we counted on someone to show up to get work done, and we can all share experiences when they simply did not show up. Failure to show up for an appointment is not only inconvenient, but it can also cost your customer a lot of money in lost time and productivity.

If you or your company makes an appointment for you, show up. Be there. Don't let simple problems (such as bad traffic) prevent you from showing up on time. Take some time to prepare. Figure out traffic times. Figure out if preceding appointments will cause a problem, and check for traffic. There is a popular old saying in the United States, "Five minutes early is on time, and on time is late." Sometimes events take place that prevent you from being on time. When that happens, call the customer as soon as you know and give them your best estimate of when you can be there. A simple apology wouldn't hurt, either.

Responsibility is a tricky subject for IT folks. Certainly you should be responsible for your actions, but the stakes are high when critical data and expensive equipment are at risk. Before you work on a computer, always ask if there are backups. If there aren't, offer to make backups for the customer, even if this incurs an extra charge for the customer. If they choose not to make a backup, make sure the customer understands, very clearly, the risk to the data on the system you are about to repair.

Adaptability/Versatility

Adaptability defines how someone adjusts to changes. Versatility, at least within the scope of an IT technician, is bringing a broad set of skills to the PC

Tech Tip

Paperwork
Most PC repair companies require a signed Authorization of Work or Work Authorization form to document the company name, billing information, date, scope of work, and that sort of thing. Even if you do your own repairs, these forms can save you from angst and from litigation. You can create your own or do an Internet search for examples.

repair process. Every PC repair is to some degree a guessing game. No one knows all the possible problems that can go wrong with a computer. There is no universal PC repair manual to which you can refer to tell you how to fix computers. Good techs must be able to adapt to any situation, both technically and in the environment. For example, good techs should be able to fix most peripherals, even if they are not experts on that particular device. As you progress through the book, you'll discover that most devices fit into one family or another and that there are certain diagnostic/repair steps that you can at least try to enact a repair.

Adaptability isn't just for technical issues. PCs find themselves broken in the strangest places and ways. An adaptable tech doesn't have a problem if a computer sits at the top of a suspension bridge or behind a desk. An adaptable tech can work around mean dogs, broken water lines, and noisy little kids. (But there are some very important rules to dealing with kids. See later in this chapter.)

A technician has to be versatile. The best example of this is what I call the User Advocate. User Advocates are technicians who take the time to learn the processes of whatever organization they work for and look to create technology solutions for problems and inefficiencies. This also means a tech should be at least competent if not expert at all the computer applications used by the organization. When you combine your IT skills with an understanding of how the business works, you become amazingly versatile, quickly finding yourself with more responsibility and (hopefully) more money.

A big part of versatility is offering different repair options in certain situations. When there is more than one way to fix things, make sure the customer knows all the options, but also give them your recommendation. Tell them why you feel your recommendation is the best course of action, but give them knowledge necessary to make their own decision.

A tech's versatility isn't limited to IT skills. Woe to the tech who doesn't understand basic electrical wiring and building codes. I've had hundreds of repair scenarios where the fix was as simple as knowing how to turn on an electrical breaker or moving a PC away from an electrical motor. No, these aren't IT skills, but a versatile tech knows these problems exist.

Sensitivity

Sensitivity is the ability to appreciate another's feeling and emotions. Sensitivity requires observing others closely, taking time to appreciate their feelings, and acting in such a way that makes them feel comfortable. I've rarely felt that technicians I've met were good at sensitivity. The vast majority of nerds I know, including myself, tend to be self-centered and unaware of what's going on around them. Let me give you a few tips I've learned along the way.

Understand that the customer is paying for your time and skills. Also understand that your presence invariably means something is wrong or broken, and few things make users more upset than broken computers. When you are "on the clock," you need to show possibly very upset customers that you are giving their problem your full attention. To do this, you need to avoid distractions. If you get a personal call, let it roll over to voicemail. If you get a work-related call, politely excuse yourself, walk away for privacy, and keep the call brief. Never talk to coworkers in a place where your customer can hear. Never speak badly of a customer; you never know where you'll run into them next.

Last, be culturally sensitive. We live in a diverse world of races, religions, etiquettes, and traditions. If a customer's religious holiday conflicts with your work schedule, the customer wins. If the customer wants you to take off your shoes, take them off. If the customer wants you to wear a hat, wear one. When in doubt, always ask the customer for guidance.

■ Communication

When you deal with users, managers, and owners who are frustrated and upset because a computer or network is down and they can't work, your job requires you to take on the roles of detective and psychologist. Talking with frazzled and confused people and getting answers to questions about how the PC got into the state it's in takes skill. Communicating clearly and effectively is important. Plus, you need to follow the rules of tech-person decorum, acting with personal integrity and respect for the customer. Finally, use assertive communication to empathize with and educate the user. Great techs spend the time needed to develop these essential skills.

Assertive Communication

In many cases, a PC problem results from user error or neglect. As a technician, you must show users the error of their ways without creating anger or conflict. You do this by using assertive communication. **Assertive communication** isn't pushy or bossy, but it's also not the language of a pushover. Assertive communication first requires you to show the other person that you understand and appreciate the importance of his feelings. Use statements such as "I know how frustrating it feels to lose data" or "I understand how infuriating it is when the network goes out and you can't get your job done." Statements like these cool off the situation and let customers know you are on their side. Avoid using the word "you," as it can sound accusatory.

The second part of assertive communication is making sure you state the problem clearly without accusing the user directly: "Not keeping up with defragmenting your hard drive slows it down," or "Help me understand how the network cable keeps getting unplugged during your lunch hour." Last, tell the user what you need to prevent this error in the future. "Please call me whenever you hear that buzzing sound," or "Please check the company's approved software list before installing anything." Always use "I" and "me," and never make judgments. "I can't promise the keyboard will work well if it's always getting dirty" is much better than "Stop eating cookies over the keyboard, you slob!"

Respectful Communication

The final key in communicating with users revolves around **respect**. You don't do the user's job, but you should respect that job and person as an essential cog in the organization. Communicate with users the way you would like them to communicate with you, were the roles reversed. Again, this follows the Ethic of Reciprocity.

Generally, IT folks are there to support the people doing a company's main business. You are there to serve their needs and, all things being equal, to do so at their convenience, not yours.

Don't assume the world stops the moment you walk in the door and that you may immediately interrupt their work to do yours. Although most customers are thrilled and motivated to help you the moment you arrive, this may not always be the case. Ask the magic question, "May I start working on the problem now?" Give customers a chance to wrap up, shut down, or do anything else necessary to finish their business and make it safe for you to do yours.

Engage the user with the standard rules of civil conversation. Take the time to listen. Don't interrupt customers as they describe a problem; just listen and take notes. You might hear something that leads to resolving the problem. Rephrase and repeat the problems back to the customer to verify you understand the issue ("So the computer is locking up three times a day?"). Use an even, nonaccusatory tone, and although it's okay to try to explain a problem if the user asks, never condescend and never argue.

Remain positive in the face of adversity. Don't get defensive if you can't figure something out quickly and the user starts hassling you. Remember that an angry customer isn't really angry with you—he's just frustrated—so don't take his anger personally. Take it in stride; smile, and assure him that computer troubleshooting sometimes takes a while.

Avoid letting outside interruptions take your focus away from the user and her computer problem. Things that break your concentration slow down the troubleshooting process immensely. Plus, customers will feel insulted if you start chatting on your cell phone with your significant other about a movie date later that night when you're supposed to be fixing their computers! You're not being paid to socialize, so turn those cell phones and pagers to vibrate. That's why the technogods created voicemail. Never take any call except one that is potentially urgent. If a call is potentially urgent, explain the urgency to the customer, step away, and deal with the call as quickly as possible.

If you discover that the user caused the problem, either through ignorance or by accident, don't minimize the importance of the problem, but don't be judgmental or insulting about the cause. We all screw up sometimes, and these kinds of mistakes are your job security. *You get paid because people make mistakes and machines break*. Chances are you'll be back at that workstation six months or a year later, fixing something else. By becoming the user's advocate and go-to person, you create a better work environment. If a mistaken action caused the problem, explain in a positive and supportive way how to do the task correctly and then have the user go through the process while you are there to reinforce what you said.

Eliciting Answers

Your job as a tech is to get the computer fixed, and the best way to start that process is to determine what the computer is doing or not doing. You must start by talking to the customer. Allow the customer to explain the problem fully while you record the information. Once the person has described the situation, you must then ask questions. This process is called **eliciting answers**.

Although each person is different, most users with a malfunctioning computer or peripheral will be afraid and often defensive about the problem. To overcome this initial attitude, you need to ask the right questions *and* listen to the customer's answers. Then ask the proper follow-up questions.

Always avoid accusatory questions, because they won't help you in the least (Figure 2.4). "What did you do?" generally gets a confused or defensive "Nothing" in reply, which doesn't get you closer to solving the problem. First, ask questions that help clarify the situation. Repeat what you think is the problem after you've listened all the way through the user's story.

Follow up with fact-seeking questions. "When did it last work?" "Has it ever worked in this way?" "Has any software changed recently?" "Any new hardware?" Ask open-ended questions to narrow the scope ("What applications are running when the computer locks up?").

By keeping your questions friendly and factual, you show users that you won't accuse them or judge their actions (Figure 2.5). You also show them that you're there to help them. After the initial tension drops away, you'll often get more information: for instance, a recitation of something the user might have tried or changed. These clues can help lead to a quick resolution of the problem.

Remember that you may know all about computer technology, but the user probably does not. This means a user will often use vague and/or incorrect terms to describe a particular computer component or function. That's just the way it works, so don't bother to correct them. Wherever possible, avoid using jargon, acronyms, or abbreviations specific to computers. They simply confuse the already upset user and can make you sound like you're talking down to them. Just ask direct, factual questions in a friendly tone, using simple, non-jargon language to zero in on what the user was trying to accomplish and what happened when things went wrong. Use visual aids when possible. Point at the machine or go to a working PC to have the user show what went wrong or what she did or tried to do.

People do usually want to get a handle on what you are doing—in a simplified way. You don't want to overwhelm them, but don't be afraid to use simple analogies or concepts to give them an idea of what is happening. If you have the time (and the skills), use drawings, equipment, and other visual aids to make technical concepts more clear. If a customer is a closet tech and is really digging for answers—to the point that it's affecting your ability to do your job—compliment her initiative and then direct her to outside training opportunities. Better yet, tell her where she can get a copy of this book!

• **Figure 2.4**   Never accuse!

• **Figure 2.5**   Keeping it friendly

Beyond basic manners, never assume that just because you are comfortable with friendly or casual behavior, the customer will be too. Even an apparently casual user will expect you to behave with professional decorum. On the flip side, don't allow a user to put you in an awkward or even potentially dangerous or illegal situation. Never do work outside the scope of your assigned duties without the prior approval of your supervisor (when possible in such cases, try to direct users to someone who *can* help them). You are not a babysitter; never volunteer to "watch the kids" while the customer leaves the job site or tolerate a potentially unsafe situation if a customer isn't properly supervising a child. Concentrate on doing your job safely and efficiently, and maintain professional integrity.

Expectations and Follow-up

Users are terrified when their PCs and networks go down so hard that they need to call in a professional. Odds are good that they've left critical, or at least important, data on the computer. Odds are equally good they need this computer to work to do their job. When they're ready to lay down money for a professional, they're expecting you to make their system exactly the way it was before it broke.

Hopefully you can do exactly that for them, but you also must deal with their expectations and let them know what to expect. Equally, you should give your customers some follow-up after the job is finished. We've already covered data backups and Authorization of Work forms (and those are very important), but you need to keep the customer's needs in mind. You also want to keep them thinking about you, should they need more help in the future. Here are a few items you should consider.

Time Frame

If you can give the customer a best guess as to how long the repair will take, you'll be a hero. Don't be afraid to hold off on your time-frame prediction until you've diagnosed the machine. If you truly don't have a feel for the time involved, tell the customer that and then tell them what you'll need to know before you can make the prediction.

Stick to the timeline. If you finish more quickly, great! People love a job that goes faster than predicted. If you're moving past the predicted time frame, contact the customer and tell them as soon as possible. Let them know what's happened, why you're going over, and give them a new time frame. The biggest secret here is to keep in communication with the customer on any change in status. People understand delays—they take place in our lives daily. People resent not knowing, especially when a precious computer is at stake.

Documentation

At the completion of work, document the problem, including the time and day you started work, the solution (again including the time and day the work ended), the hours worked, and a list of all parts replaced. If the customer owns the parts, offer them to the customer (this is especially true if you replace any storage media). This documentation may or may not include your charges.

Follow-up

I call follow-up the Lost Art: a simple follow-up, usually just a phone call, to confirm that the customer is happy with your work. This gives the customer a chance to detail any special issues that may have arisen and it also gives that final extra touch that ensures they will come to you again.

■ Safety and Tools

Effective communication with your customer enables you to *start* the troubleshooting process, getting details about the problem and clues about things that happened around the same time. To continue troubleshooting, though, you need to be adept at handling the computer. That starts with knowing how to handle computer components safely and how to use the tools of a tech. Let's begin by identifying and discussing some of the problems you may run into and how to deal with them.

Electrostatic Discharge (ESD)

If you decide to open a PC while reading this chapter, as I encourage you to do, you must take proper steps to avoid the greatest killer of PCs: **electrostatic discharge (ESD)**. ESD simply means the passage of a static electrical charge from one item to another. Have you ever rubbed a balloon against your shirt, making the balloon stick to you? That's a classic example of static electricity. When that static charge discharges, you may not notice it happening—although on a cool, dry day, I've been shocked so hard by touching a doorknob that I could see a big, blue spark! I've never heard of a human being getting anything worse than a rather nasty shock from ESD, but I can't say the same thing about computers. ESD will destroy the sensitive parts of your PC, so it is essential that you take steps to avoid ESD when working on your PC.

 All PCs are well protected against ESD on the outside. Unless you take a screwdriver and actually open up your PC, you don't need to concern yourself with ESD.

Anti-static Tools

ESD only takes place when two objects that store different amounts (the hip electrical term to use is **potential**) of static electricity come in contact. The secret to avoiding ESD is to keep you and the parts of the PC you touch at the same electrical potential. You can accomplish this by connecting yourself to the PC via a handy little device called an **anti-static wrist strap**. This simple device consists of a wire that connects on one end to an alligator clip and on the other end to a small metal plate that secures to your wrist with an elastic

Static electricity, and therefore the risk of ESD, is much more prevalent in dry, cool environments.

● **Figure 2.6**   Anti-static wrist strap in use

strap. You snap the alligator clip onto any handy metal part of the PC and place the wrist strap on either wrist. Figure 2.6 shows a typical anti-static wrist strap in use.

Anti-static wrist straps are standard equipment for anyone working on a PC, but other tools might also come in handy. One of the big issues when working with a PC occurs if you find yourself pulling out parts from the PC and setting them aside. The moment you take a piece out of the PC, it no longer has contact with the systems and may pick up static from other sources. Techs use anti-static mats to eliminate this risk. An **anti-static mat** acts as a point of common potential; it's typical to purchase a combination anti-static wrist strap and mat that all connect to keep you, the PC, and any loose components at the same electrical potential (Figure 2.7).

● **Figure 2.7**   Anti-static wrist strap and mat combination

Anti-static wrist straps and mats use tiny **resistors**—devices that stop or *resist* the flow of electricity—to prevent anti-static charge from racing through the device. These resistors can fail over time, so it's always a good idea to read the documentation that comes with your anti-static tools to see how to test those small resistors properly.

Any electrical component not in a PC needs to be stored in an **anti-static bag,** a specially designed bag that sheds whatever static electricity you have when you touch it, thus preventing any damage to components stored within (Figure 2.8). Almost all PC components come in an anti-static bag when purchased. Experienced techs never throw these bags away, as you never know when you'll want to pull a part out and place it on a shelf for a while.

Always put components *in* an anti-static bag, not *on* the bag.

Although having an anti-static wrist strap with you at all times would be ideal, the reality is that from time to time you'll find yourself in a situation where you lack the proper anti-static tools. This shouldn't keep you from working on the PC—if you're careful! Before working on a PC in such a situation, take a moment to touch the power supply every once in a while as you work—I'll show you where it is in Chapter 3, "The Visible PC"—to keep

Try This!

Anti-static Protection Devices

In some circumstances, an anti-static wrist strap could get in the way. Manufacturers have developed some alternatives to the wrist strap, so try this:

1. Take a field trip to a local computer or electronics store.

2. Check out their selection of anti-static devices. Can you find anything other than wrist straps or mats?

3. Do a Web search for "static control products." Can you find anything other than wrist straps or mats?

4. Report what options you can find for protecting your equipment from ESD. Weigh the pros and cons and decide what you would use in various situations.

● **Figure 2.8**   Anti-static bag

yourself at the same electrical potential as the PC. Although this isn't as good as a wrist strap, it's better than nothing at all.

The last issue when it comes to preventing ESD is that never-ending question—should you work with the PC plugged in or unplugged? The answer is simple: Do you really want to be physically connected to a PC that is plugged into an electrical outlet? Granted, the chances of electrocution are slim, but why take the risk?

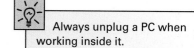

Always unplug a PC when working inside it.

Electromagnetic Interference (EMI)

A magnetic field interfering with electronics is **electromagnetic interference (EMI)**. EMI isn't nearly as dangerous as ESD, but it can cause permanent damage to some components and erase data on some storage devices. You can prevent EMI by keeping magnets away from computer equipment. Certain components are particularly susceptible to EMI. Never get a magnet close to

- Floppy disks
- Hard drives
- Flash drives
- CRT (tube) monitors

The biggest problem with EMI is that we often use magnets without even knowing we are doing so. Any device with an electrical motor has a magnet. Many telephones have magnets. Power bricks for laptops and speakers also have magnets. Keep them away!

Radio Frequency Interference (RFI)

Do you ever hear strange noises on your speakers even though you aren't playing any sounds? Do you ever get strange noises on your cell phone? If

Protective Bag Types

Computer gear manufacturers package their product in a variety of ways to shield against accidental damage, whether that's physical damage, ESD, EMI, or RFI. The typical pink translucent computer bag is coated with a film that prevents the bag from producing static electricity and mildly protects the contents against physical contact (and thus damage). The two types of metal bags offer shielding against EMI and RFI as well as ESD. These are the silvery bags (such as in Figure 2.8) you'll see hard drives packed in, for example, and the black and silver woven bags you'll sometimes see.

A word of caution is in order here. The metal bags provide proper protection only when sealed, so fold the open end over and slap a piece of tape on it when storing a component.

so, you've probably run into **radio frequency interference (RFI)**. Many devices emit radio waves:

- Cell phones
- Wireless network cards
- Cordless phones
- Baby monitors
- Microwave ovens

In general, the radio waves that these devices emit are very weak, and almost all electronic devices are shielded to prevent RFI. A few devices, speakers in particular, are susceptible to RFI. RFI will never cause any damage, but it can be incredibly irritating. The best way to prevent RFI is to keep radio-emitting devices as far away as possible from other electronics.

RFI becomes a big problem when two devices share the same frequencies. Cordless phones, baby monitors, and wireless networks share the same range of frequencies. They sometimes interfere with each other, causing poor signals or even blocking signals completely. These devices need to be tuned to avoid stomping on each other's frequencies. In Chapter 17, "Learning Wireless," you'll see how to tune a wireless network to prevent RFI.

Physical Safety

IT techs live in a dangerous world. We're in constant danger of tripping, hurting our backs, and getting burned by hot components. Let's take a moment to discuss these three physical safety issues and what to do about them.

If you don't keep organized, hardware technology will take over your life. Figure 2.9 shows a corner of my office, a painful example of a cable "kludge."

Cable messes such as these are dangerous tripping hazards. While I may allow a mess like this in my home office, all cables in a business environment are carefully tucked away behind computer cases, run into walls, or placed under cable runners. If you see a cable that is an obvious tripping hazard, contact the person in charge of the building (CompTIA calls these folks

• **Figure 2.9** Mike's cable kludge

● Figure 2.10   What a strange, bad trip it's been.

"building services") to take care of it immediately. The results of ignoring such hazards can be catastrophic (Figure 2.10).

Another physical safety issue is heavy boxes. Computers, printers, monitors—everything we use—all seem to come to us in heavy boxes. Remember never to lift with your back; lift with your legs, and always use a hand truck if available. You are never paid enough to risk your own health.

The last physical safety issue to discuss is burns. The computing world is filled with hot components. It's hard to burn yourself unless you actually open up a computer, printer, or monitor. First, watch for anything with a cooling fin like the one shown in Figure 2.11. If you see a cooling fin, odds are good that something is hot enough to burn you. Also look for labels/stickers warning about hot components. Last, when in doubt, move your hand over components as if you were checking the heat on a stove.

● Figure 2.11   Checking for hot cooling fins

Tools of the Trade

The basic **tech toolkit** consists of a **Phillips-head screwdriver** and not much else—seriously—but a half-dozen tools round out a fully functional toolkit. Most kits have a star-headed Torx wrench, a nut driver or two, a pair of plastic tweezers, a little grabber tool (the technical term is *parts retriever*), and a hemostat to go along with Phillips-head and flat-head screwdrivers (Figure 2.12).

A lot of techs throw in an extension magnet to grab hard-to-reach bits that drop into cases. Many also add a magnifying glass and a flashlight for those hard-to-read numbers and text on the printed circuit boards (PCBs) that make up a large percentage of devices inside the system unit. Contrary to what you might think, techs rarely need a hammer.

• **Figure 2.12**   Typical technician toolkit

Chapter 2 Review

■ Chapter Summary

After reading this chapter and completing the exercises, you should understand the following about operational procedures.

Present yourself with a proper appearance and professional manner

- Professional techs dress appropriately. This means decent, clean clothes that are wrinkle-free, such as khaki trousers and a polo or button-down shirt. Professional techs bathe. Regularly.

- Professional techs cultivate proper traits, such as honesty/integrity, dependability/reliability, adaptability/versatility, and sensitivity.

Talk to customers in a professional, productive manner

- Techs should use effective communication techniques such as assertive communication to interact with customers. Assertive communication means showing empathy for the customer's plight and clearly stating the perceived problem without directly accusing the customer. Assertive communication also means telling the user what needs to happen to avoid the problem in the future.

- A good tech respects the customer, following the Ethic of Reciprocity. Do not interrupt the customer. Engage in conversation, using proper manners, and actively listening. Remain positive, even when the customer gets upset. Avoid letting outside interruptions take your focus away from the user and the user's computer problem.

- When eliciting answers, ask questions to help clarify the situation. Follow up with fact-seeking questions. Always explain what you're doing, but avoid excessive jargon.

- Never do work outside the scope of your assigned duties without the prior approval of your supervisor. Don't babysit the kids while the customer wanders off.

- Manage your customer's expectations by explaining how much time you expect to take and the price. Document everything you do to solve the problem, including the time you spend. Follow up with the customer after solving the problem—a quick phone call will do—to make certain nothing has gone wrong and that he is satisfied with your work.

Work with PCs safely using the proper tools

- Take precautionary measures when working on computers. Use best practices for avoiding electrostatic discharge. Put unused components in anti-static bags. Protect sensitive equipment from electromagnetic interference.

- Use the right tools to get the job done, especially your Phillips-head screwdriver!

■ Key Terms

anti-static bag *(28)*
anti-static mat *(28)*
anti-static wrist strap *(27)*
assertive communication *(23)*
electromagnetic interference (EMI) *(29)*
electrostatic discharge (ESD) *(27)*
eliciting answers *(25)*
Ethic of Reciprocity *(21)*
honesty *(20)*

integrity *(20)*
passwords *(20)*
Phillips-head screwdriver *(32)*
potential *(27)*
radio frequency interference (RFI) *(30)*
resistor *(28)*
respect *(23)*
tech toolkit *(32)*

Key Term Quiz

Use the Key Terms list to complete the sentences that follow. Not all terms will be used.

1. Always place an expansion card or other computer part into a(n) _____ when it's not in use to protect against electrostatic discharge.

2. A few screwdrivers and an anti-static wrist strap should be in your _____.

3. An effective use of _____ means clearly stating a problem without accusing the user of creating that problem.

4. Accomplished computer techs should treat anything said to them as a personal confidence, not to be repeated to coworkers or bosses. A tech brings _____ to the job.

5. You should avoid learning _____ to other folks' computers so you don't get blamed if something happens to those computers.

6. Treating other people the way you want to be treated is an example of the _____.

7. A magnetic field interfering with electronics is _____.

8. A(n) _____ is a device that stops the flow of electricity.

9. To begin troubleshooting a computer problem, start by talking to the customer and allowing the customer to explain the problem fully, and then ask follow-up questions. This process is called _____.

10. A customer complains that he can hear music coming from his computer speakers, even though the computer's not playing any music. This is most likely caused by _____.

Multiple-Choice Quiz

1. While troubleshooting a fairly routine printing problem, the customer explains in great detail precisely what he was trying to do, what happened when he tried to print, and what he had attempted as a fix for the problem. At what point should you interrupt him?

   A. After he describes the first problem

   B. As soon as you understand the problem

   C. As soon as you have a solution

   D. Never

2. While manning the help desk, you get a call from a distraught user who says she has a blank screen. What would be a useful follow-up question? (Select two.)

   A. Is the computer turned on?

   B. Is the monitor turned on?

   C. Did you reboot?

   D. What did you do?

3. While manning the help desk, you get a call from Sharon in accounting. She's lost a file that she knows she saved to her hard drive. Which of the following statements would direct Sharon to open her My Documents folder in the most efficient and professional manner?

   A. Sharon, check My Documents.

   B. Sharon, a lot of programs save files to a default folder, often to a folder called My Documents. Let's look there first. Click on the Start button and move the mouse until the cursor hovers over My Documents. Then press the left mouse button and tell me what you see when My Documents opens.

   C. It probably just defaulted to My Docs. Why don't you open Excel or whatever program you used to make the file, and then open a document and point it to My Documents?

   D. Look, Sharon, I know you're a clueless noob when it comes to computers, but how could somebody lose a file? Just open up My Documents and look there for the file.

4. Al in marketing calls in for tech support, complaining that he has a dead PC. What is a good first question or questions to begin troubleshooting the problem?

   A. Did the computer ever work?

   B. When did the computer last work?

   C. When you say "dead," what do you mean? What happens when you press the power button?

   D. What did you do?

5. While manning the help desk, you get a call from Bryce in sales complaining that he can't print and every time he clicks on the network shared drive, his computer stops and freezes. He says he thinks it's his hard driver. What would be a good follow-up question or statement?

   A. Bryce, you're an idiot. Don't touch anything. I'll be there in five minutes.

   B. Okay, let's take this one step at a time. You seem to have two problems, one with printing and the second with the network shared drive, right?

   C. First, it's not a hard *driver*; it's a hard *drive*. It doesn't have anything to do with the network share or printing, so that's just not right.

   D. When could you last print?

6. When troubleshooting a software problem on Phoebe's computer and listening to her describe the problem, your beeper goes off. It's your boss. What would be an acceptable action for you to make?

   A. Excuse yourself, walk out of the cube, and use a cell phone to call your boss.

   B. Pick up Phoebe's phone and dial your boss's number.

   C. Wait until Phoebe finishes her description and then ask to use her phone to call your boss.

   D. Wait until Phoebe finishes her description, run through any simple fixes, and then explain that you need to call your boss on your cell phone.

7. While fixing a printing problem on Paul's computer, you check his e-mail out of curiosity to see if there are any interesting messages there. You notice several personal e-mails he has sent sitting in his Sent Items mail folder. Using the company computer for personal e-mail is against regulations, so what should you do?

   A. Leave the e-mail on the computer and notify your boss.

   B. Delete the e-mails from the computer and notify your boss.

   C. Delete the e-mails from the computer and remind Paul of the workplace regulations.

   D. You shouldn't be looking in his e-mail folders at all as it compromises your integrity.

8. Upon responding to a coworker's request for help, you find her away from her desk and Microsoft Excel on the screen with a spreadsheet open. How do you proceed?

   A. Go find the coworker and ask her to exit her applications before touching her computer.

   B. Exit Excel and save changes to the document and begin troubleshooting the computer.

   C. Exit Excel without saving changes to the document and begin troubleshooting the computer.

   D. Use the Save As command to save the file with a new name, exit Excel, and begin troubleshooting the computer.

9. You are solving a problem on Kate's computer that requires you to reboot several times. Upon each reboot, the logon screen appears and prompts you for a username and password before you can continue working. Kate has gone to another office to continue her work on another computer. How do you proceed?

   A. Call Kate, ask her for her password, type it in, and continue working on the problem.

   B. Insist that Kate stay with you and have her type the password each time it is needed.

   C. Call Kate and have her come in to type the password each time it is needed.

   D. Have Kate temporarily change her password for you to use as you work; then have her change it back when you are through.

10. You are working in a customer's home and his five-year-old child continues to scream and kick the back of your chair. What do you do?

    A. Ignore the child and finish your work as quickly as you can.

    B. Discipline the child as you see fit.

    C. Politely ask your client to remove the child from your work area.

    D. Tell your client you refuse to work under such conditions and leave the premises with the job half done.

11. After replacing a keyboard a user has spilled coffee on for the fifth time, what should you say to the user?

    A. I can't guarantee the new keyboard will work if it gets dirty.

    B. I can't guarantee the new keyboard will work if you continue to spill coffee on it.

    C. These keyboards are expensive. Next time we replace one because you spilled coffee, it's coming out of your paycheck.

    D. You need to be more careful with your coffee.

12. When is it appropriate to yell at a user?

    A. When he screws up the second time.

    B. When he interrupts your troubleshooting.

    C. When he screws up the fifth time.

    D. Never.

13. What's the best practice when working inside a system unit and installing and removing components?

    A. Wear an anti-static wrist strap.

    B. Touch a doorknob to ground yourself before going into the case.

    C. Place components on the motherboard to keep them grounded.

    D. Use plastic tools.

14. Which of the following tools would you find in a typical PC tech's toolkit? (Select two.)

    A. Phillips-head screwdriver

    B. Torx wrench

    C. Hammer

    D. File

15. What term describes the flow of a static electrical charge from a person to the inside of the PC?

    A. EMI

    B. ESD

    C. HDMI

    D. TTFN

■ Essay Quiz

1. Your worksite currently has no ESD protection. In fact, your supervisor doesn't feel that such protection is necessary. Write a proposal to purchase ESD protection equipment for the computer assembly/repair facility that will convince your supervisor that ESD protection is necessary and cost-effective in the long run. What kinds of protection will you recommend?

2. A friend is considering turning his computer hobby into a career and has asked your advice on outfitting himself as a freelance computer technician. What tools can you recommend to your friend?

3. A user phones you at your desk and reports that after pressing the power button on his computer and hearing the hard drive spin up, his screen remains blank. What questions can you ask to determine the problem?

Lab Projects

• Lab Project 2.1

Visit your local computer store or hardware store and purchase the items for a hardware tech toolkit.

You may want to include a variety of screwdrivers, anti-static wrist strap, tweezers, or other items.

• Lab Project 2.2

Visit your local computer store to observe how techs interact with people and how professionally they dress and appear. I suggest this not to judge the store's techs, but simply to watch and learn. How do the techs talk to customers? How do the customers react? How would you handle the same situation if you followed the guidelines in this chapter?

The Visible PC

In this chapter, you will learn how to

- **Describe how the PC works**
- **Identify all the connectors and devices on a typical PC system unit**
- **Discuss the major internal components of a PC**

Mastering the craft of a PC technician requires you to learn a lot of details about the many pieces of hardware in the typical PC. Even the most basic PC contains hundreds of discrete hardware components, each with its own set of characteristics, shapes, sizes, colors, connections, and so on. By the end of this book, you will be able to discuss all of these components in detail. This chapter takes you on a tour of a typical PC, starting with an overview of how computers work, and then examining both external connectors and internal components.

Remember the children's song that goes, "Oh, the leg bone connects to the thigh bone…"? Well, think of the rest of the chapter in that manner, showing you what the parts look like and giving you a rough idea about how they work and connect. In later chapters, you'll dissect all of these PC "leg bones" and "thigh bones" and get to the level of detail you need to install, configure, maintain, and fix computers. Even if you are an expert, do not skip this chapter! It introduces a large number of terms used throughout the rest of the book. Many of these terms you will know, but some you will not, so take some time and read it.

It is handy, although certainly not required, to have a PC that you can take the lid off of and inspect as you progress. Almost any old PC will help—it doesn't even need to work. So get thee a screwdriver, grab your PC, and see if you can recognize the various components as you read about them.

Historical/Conceptual

How the PC Works

You've undoubtedly seen a PC in action: a nice, glossy monitor displaying a picture that changes according to the actions of the person sitting in front of it, typing away on a keyboard and clicking on a mouse. Sound pours out of tiny speakers that flank the screen, and a box whirs happily beneath the table. The PC is a computer: a machine that enables you to do work, produce documents, play games, balance your checkbook, and look up the latest sports scores on the Internet.

Although the computer is certainly a machine, it's also **programming**: the commands that tell the computer what to do to get work done. These commands are just ones and zeros that the computer's hardware understands, enabling it to do amazing actions, such as perform powerful mathematic functions, move data (also ones and zeros), realize the mouse has moved, and put pretty icons on the screen. So a computer is a complex interaction between hardware and computer programming, created by your fellow humans.

Ever heard of Morse code? Morse code is nothing more than dots and dashes to those who do not understand it, but if you send dots and dashes (in the right order) to someone who understands Morse code, you can tell the recipient a joke. Think of programming as Morse code for the computer (Figure 3.1). You may not understand those ones and zeros, but your computer certainly does!

There's more to the ones and zeros than just programming. All of the data on the computer—the Web pages, your documents, your e-mail—is also stored as ones and zeros. Programs know how to translate these ones and zeros into a form humans understand.

Programming comes in two forms. First are the applications: the programs that get work done. Word processing programs, Web browsers, and e-mail programs are all considered applications. But applications need a main program to support them. They need a program that enables you to start and stop applications, copy/ move/delete data, talk to the hardware, and perform lots of other jobs. This program is called the operating system (OS). Microsoft Windows is the most popular OS today, but there are other computer operating systems, such as Apple Macintosh OS X and the popular (and free) Linux (Figure 3.2). Computer people lump operating systems and applications into the term **software** to differentiate them from the hardware of the computer.

Understanding the computer at this broad conceptual level—in terms of hardware, OS, and programs—can help you explain things

I know this. This is binary! It all makes sense now.

• **Figure 3.1**   Computer musing that a string of ones and zeros makes perfect sense.

● **Figure 3.2**   Typical OS X, Linux, and Windows interfaces

to customers, but good techs have a much more fundamental appreciation and understanding of the complex interplay of all of the software and the individual pieces of hardware. In short, techs need to know the processes going on behind the scenes.

From the CompTIA A+ tech's perspective, the computer functions through four stages: input, processing, output, and storage. Knowing which parts participate in a particular stage of the computing process enables you to troubleshoot on a fundamental and decisive level.

Input

To illustrate this four-step process, let's walk through the steps involved in a fairly common computer task: preparing your taxes. [Insert collective groan here.] February has rolled around and, at least in the United States, millions of people install their favorite tax software, TurboTax from Intuit, onto their computers to help them prepare their taxes. After starting TurboTax, your first job is to provide the computer with data: essential information, such as your name, where you live, how much you earned, and how many dollars you gave to federal and state governments.

Various pieces of hardware enable you to input data, the most common of which are the keyboard and mouse. Most computers won't react when you say, "Hey you!"—at least not anywhere outside of a *Star Trek* episode. Although that day will come, for now you must use something decidedly more mechanical: a keyboard to type in your data. The OS provides a fundamental service in this process as well. You can bang on a keyboard all day and accomplish nothing unless the OS translates your keystrokes into code that the rest of your computer's hardware understands.

Tech Tip

Voice Recognition

Some might argue that voice recognition, the ability for a computer to understand your voice, has been around for a long time. In my opinion, it doesn't work well enough to replace my keyboard—yet.

Processing

Next, the computer processes your data. After you place information in various appropriate "boxes" in TurboTax, the computer does the math for you. Processing takes place inside the system unit—the box under your desk (see Figure 3.3)—and happens almost completely at a hardware level, although that hardware functions according to rules laid out in the OS. Thus again you have a complex interaction between hardware and software.

The processing portion is the magical part—you can't see it happen. The first half of this book demystifies this stage, because good techs understand all of the pieces of the process. I won't go through the specific hardware involved in the processing stage here, because the pieces change according to the type of process.

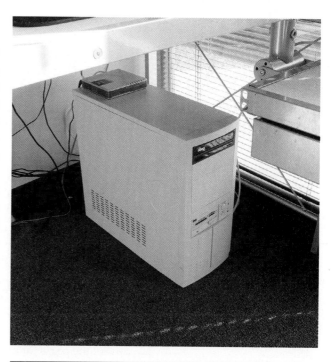

• **Figure 3.3**   Processing takes place somewhere in here!

Output

Simply adding up your total tax for the year is useless unless the computer shows you the result. That's where the third step—output—comes into play (Figure 3.4). Once the computer finishes processing data, it must put the information somewhere for you to inspect it. Often it places data on the monitor so you can see what you've just typed. It might send the data over to the printer if you tell it, so you can print out copies of your tax return to mail to the Internal Revenue Service (or whatever the Tax Man is called where you live). A hardware device does the actual printing, but the OS controls the printing process. Again, it's a fundamental interaction of hardware and software.

• **Figure 3.4**   Output devices

Storage

Once you've sent in your tax return, you most likely do not want all that work simply to disappear. What happens if the IRS comes back a couple of months later with a question about your return? Yikes! You need to keep permanent records and you need to keep a copy of the tax program. The fourth stage in the computing process is storage. A lot of devices are used in the storage process, the most visible of which are the external storage parts, such as a thumb drive or recordable CD discs (Figure 3.5).

The Art of the PC Technician

Using the four stages of the computing process—input, processing, output, and storage—to master how the PC works and, in turn, become a great technician requires that you understand all of the pieces of hardware and software involved *and* the interactions between them that make up the various stages. You have to know what the parts do,

• **Figure 3.5**   Typical storage (CD-R discs)

in other words, and how they work together. The best place to start is with a real computer. Let's go through the process of inspecting a typical, complete PC, including opening up a few important pieces to see the components inside. Hopefully, you have a real computer in front of you right now that you may dismantle a bit. No two computers are exactly the same, so you'll see differences between your PC and the one in this chapter—and that's okay. You'll come to appreciate that all computers have the same main parts that do the same jobs even though they differ in size, shape, and color.

By the time you reach the end of this book, you'll have a deeper, more nuanced understanding of the interaction of hardware and software in the four-stage computing process. Just as great artists have mastered fundamental skills of their trade before creating a masterpiece, you'll have the fundamentals of the art of the computer technician and be on your road to mastery.

■ The Complete PC

Sometimes I hate the term "personal computer." That term implies a single device, like a toaster. A typical PC is more than one device, and you need all of the parts (or at least most) to make the PC work. The most important part of the PC is the box that usually sits under your desk: the one that all of the other parts connect to, called the **system unit**. All of the processing and storage takes place in the system unit. All of the other parts of the PC—the printer, the keyboard, the monitor—connect to the system unit and are known collectively as **peripherals**. Figure 3.6 shows a typical desktop PC, with the system unit and peripherals as separate pieces.

Most computers have a standard set of peripherals to provide input and output. You'll see some variation in color, bells, and whistles, but here's the standard set.

- **Monitor** The big television thing that provides a visual output for the computer.

- **Keyboard** Keypad for providing keyed input. Based on a typewriter.

- **Mouse** Pointing device used to control a graphical pointer on the monitor for input.

- **Speakers/headphones** Speakers provide sound output.

- **Printer** Provides printed paper output.

A typical PC has all of these peripherals, but no law requires a PC to have them. Plenty of PCs may not have a printer. Some PCs don't have speakers. Some computers don't even have a keyboard, mouse, or monitor—but they tend to hide in unlikely places, such as the inside of a jet fighter or next to the engine in an automobile. Other PCs may have many more peripherals. Installing four or five printers on a single PC is easy, if you so

System unit   Peripherals

● **Figure 3.6**   Typical desktop computer with peripherals

desire. You'll also find hundreds of other types of peripherals, such as Web cameras and microphones, on many PCs. You add or remove peripherals depending on what you need from the system. The only limit is the number of connections for peripherals available on the system unit.

External Connections

Every peripheral connects to the system unit through one of the many types of ports. The back of a typical system unit (Figure 3.7) has many cables running from the system unit to the various peripherals. You may even have a few connectors in the front. All of these connectors and ports have their own naming conventions, and a good tech knows all of them. It's not acceptable to go around saying such things as "That's a printer port" or "That's a little-type keyboard connector." You need to be comfortable with the more commonly used naming conventions so you can say "That's a female DB-25" or "That's a USB connector."

Plugs, Ports, Jacks, and Connectors

Although PCs use close to 50 different types of connections, almost all fit into one of six major types: DIN, USB, FireWire, DB, RJ, and audio. Read the next paragraphs to get your terminology straight and then you can jump into the various connectors with gusto.

No one seems to use the terms *plug*, *port*, *jack*, or *connector* correctly, so let's get this right from the start. To connect one device to another, you need a cable containing the wires that make the connection. On each device, as well as on each end of the connecting cable, you need standardized parts to make that connection. Because these are usually electrical connections, one part needs to fit inside another to make a snug, safe connection.

A **plug** is a part with some type of projection that goes into a *port*. A **port** is a part that has some type of matching hole or slot that accepts the plug. You never put a port into a plug; it's always the other way around. The term **jack** is used as an alternative to port, so you may also put a plug into a jack. The term **connector** describes either a port or a plug. As you progress though this chapter and see the various plugs and ports, this will become clearer (Figure 3.8).

• Figure 3.7   Connections in the back of a PC

• Figure 3.8   Plug, port, and jack

● **Figure 3.9** DIN (top) and mini-DIN (bottom) connectors

Tech Tip

Downstream and Upstream

You'll sometimes hear USB ports and plugs described as upstream *or* downstream, *terms that create rather amusing conversation and confusion. It's all about whether you refer to the plug or the port, so here's the scoop. The USB A plugs go upstream to USB A ports on the host or hub. USB A ports provide downstream output from the host or hub. So the plug is upstream and the port is downstream.*

Just to add more fun to the mix, USB B plugs go downstream to devices. USB B ports provide upstream output from the device to the host or hub. My advice? Stick with A or B and nobody will get confused.

Mini-DIN Connectors

Most PCs sport the European-designed **mini-DIN connectors**. The original DIN connector was replaced by mini-DIN a long time ago, so you'll only see mini-DIN connectors on your PC (see Figure 3.9 bottom). Older-style keyboards and mice plugged into DIN ports (Figure 3.9 top).

USB Connectors

Universal serial bus (USB) provides the most common general-purpose connection for PCs. You'll find USB versions of many devices, such as mice, keyboards, scanners, cameras, and printers. USB connections come in three sizes: A, B, and mini-B. The USB A connector's distinctive rectangular shape makes it easily recognizable (Figure 3.10).

You never see a USB B connector on your computer. USB B connectors are for the other end of the USB cable, where it attaches to the USB device (Figure 3.11).

The USB B connector's relatively large size makes it less than optimal for small devices such as cameras, so the USB folks also make the smaller mini-B–style connector shown in Figure 3.12.

USB has a number of features that make it particularly popular on PCs. First, USB devices are **hot-swappable**, which means you can insert or remove them without restarting your PC. Almost every other type of connector requires you to turn the system off, insert or remove the connector, and then turn the system back on. Hot-swapping completely eliminates this process.

Second, many USB devices get their electrical power through the USB connection, so they don't need batteries or a plug for an electrical outlet. You can even recharge some devices, such as cellular phones, by plugging them into a USB port (Figure 3.13).

FireWire Connectors

FireWire, also known as **IEEE 1394**, moves data at incredibly high speeds, making it the perfect connection for highly specialized applications such as

● **Figure 3.10** USB A connector and port

● **Figure 3.11** USB B connector

● **Figure 3.12**   USB mini-B connector

streaming video from a digital video camera onto a hard drive. FireWire consists of a special 6-wire connector, as shown in Figure 3.14, or a 9-wire connector for devices that need more speed and power. A smaller, 4-pin version is usually seen on peripherals. Like USB, FireWire devices are hot-swappable.

DB Connectors

Over the years, **DB connectors** have been used for almost any type of peripheral you can think of, with the exception of keyboards. They have a slight *D* shape, which allows only one proper way to insert a plug into the socket and makes it easier to remember what they're called. Technically, they're known as D-sub or **D-subminiature** connectors, but most techs call them DBs.

Each male DB plug has a group of small pins that connect to DB ports. Female DB plugs connect to male DB ports on the system unit. DB connectors in the PC world can have from 9 to 37 pins or sockets, although you rarely see a DB connector with more than 25 pins or sockets. Figure 3.15 shows an example. DB-type connectors are some of the oldest and most common connectors used in the back of PCs.

It wasn't that long ago that a typical PC used at least three or more different DB connectors. Over the past few years, the PC world has moved away from DB connectors. A typical modern system has only one or two, usually for video.

● **Figure 3.13**   Cell phone charging via a USB connection

> **Tech Tip**
>
> **D-Subminiature Naming Scheme**
> *Each size D-sub connector— called the* shell size*—has a specific name in the D-sub manufacturing world. A two-row, 9-pin connector, for example, is officially a DE-9 connector rather than a DB-9. The E refers to the 9-pin shell size. Why all of the DA, DB, DC, DD, and DE connectors became DB-x in the world of personal computers is a mystery, but most techs simply call them DB connectors.*

● **Figure 3.14**   FireWire connector and port

● **Figure 3.15**   DB-25 connector and port

RJ Connectors

You have more than likely seen an **RJ connector**, whether or not you knew it by that name. The little plastic plug used to connect your telephone cord to the jack (techs don't use the word "port" to describe RJ connectors) is a classic example of an RJ plug. Modern PCs use only two types of RJ jacks: the RJ-11 and the RJ-45. The phone jack is an RJ-11. It is used almost exclusively for modems. The slightly wider RJ-45 jack is used for your network connection. Figure 3.16 shows an RJ-11 jack (top) and an RJ-45 jack (bottom).

• **Figure 3.16**   RJ-11 (top) and RJ-45 (bottom)

• **Figure 3.17**   Mini-audio jacks and plug

Audio Connectors

Speakers and microphones connect to audio jacks on the system unit. The most common type of sound connector in popular use is the *1/8-inch* connector, also called a **mini-audio connector**. These small connectors have been around for years; they're just like the plug you use to insert headphones into a radio, music player, or similar device (Figure 3.17). Traditionally, you'd find the audio jacks on the back of the PC, but many newer models sport front audio connections as well.

Devices and Their Connectors

Now that you have a sense of the connectors, let's turn to the devices common to almost every PC to learn which connectors go with which device.

Cards Versus Onboard

All of the connectors on the back of the PC are just that: connectors. Behind those connectors are the actual devices that support whatever peripherals plug into those connectors. These devices might be built into the computer, such as a keyboard port. Others might be add-on expansion cards that a tech installed into the PC.

Most PCs have special **expansion slots** inside the system unit that enable you to add more devices on expansion cards. Figure 3.18 shows a typical card. If you want some new device and your system unit doesn't have that device built into the PC, you just go to the store, buy a card version of that

Keep in mind that the variety of connectors is virtually endless. The preceding types of connectors cover the vast majority, but many others exist in the PC world. No law or standard requires device makers to use a particular connector, especially if they have no interest in making that device interchangeable with similar devices from other manufacturers.

Almost all connectors are now color-coordinated to help users plug the right device into the right port. These color codes are not required, and not all PCs and devices use them.

> **Try This!**
>
> **Feeling Your Way Around Connectors**
> Given that most PCs tend to sit on the floor under desks, a good PC tech learns to recognize most every PC connector by touch. This is a great exercise to do with a partner.
>
> 1. Look at all of the connectors on the back of any PC's system unit.
> 2. Turn the system unit around so you can no longer see the connections.
> 3. Try to identify the connectors by feel.

device, and snap it in. Later chapters of the book go into great detail on how to do this, but for now just appreciate that a device might be built in or it might come on a card.

Be careful handling cards. Touch the metal plate with the 90-degree bend and try to avoid touching any of the electronics. As mentioned in Chapter 2, "Operational Procedures," always put cards into an anti-static bag when moving them to prevent ESD.

Keyboard

Today's keyboards come in many shapes and sizes, but they always connect to your computer by either a mini-DIN port or a USB port. Many keyboards ship with an adapter so you can use either port. Most keyboard plugs and mini-DIN keyboard ports are colored purple (see Figure 3.19).

Monitor

A monitor connects to the video connector on the system unit. You'll usually see one of two types of video connectors: the older 15-pin female DB **Video Electronics Standards Association (VESA)** connector or the unique **digital video interface (DVI)** connector. VESA connectors are colored blue, whereas DVI connectors are white. Many video cards have both types of connectors (see Figure 3.20) or two VESA or two DVI connectors. Video cards with two connectors support two monitors, a very cool thing to do!

The newest video connector is called **Hi-Definition Multimedia Interface (HDMI)**, shown in Figure 3.21. HDMI is still very new to the video scene and brings a number of enhancements, such as the ability to carry both video and sound on the same cable. Primarily designed for home theater, computers with HDMI connectors grow more common every year.

Sound

The sound device in a computer performs two functions. First, it takes digital information and turns it into sound, outputting the sound through speakers. Second, it takes sound that is input through a microphone or some other audio source and turns it into digital data.

To play and record sounds, your sound device needs to connect to a set of speakers and a microphone or more. All PCs have at least two miniature audio jacks:

• **Figure 3.18**   Typical expansion card

• **Figure 3.19**   Keyboard plug and port

• **Figure 3.21**   HDMI connector

• **Figure 3.20**   Video card with (from left to right) S-Video, DVI, and VESA ports

• **Figure 3.22** Typical bank of 1/8-inch audio jacks

• **Figure 3.23** Legacy joystick/MIDI port

Modern PCs have built-in network connections, but this is a fairly recent development. For many years, network devices only came on an expansion card, called a **network interface card (NIC)**. The term is so common that even built-in network connections—which most certainly are not cards—are still called NICs.

one for a microphone and another for stereo speakers. Better cards provide extra miniature audio jacks for surround sound. Figure 3.22 is a typical onboard soundcard showing six different 1/8-inch jacks. Four of these are for speakers and two are for input (such as microphones). The color scheme for sound connections is complex, but for now remember one color—green. That's the one you need to connect a standard pair of stereo speakers.

An older sound card may still provide a female 15-pin DB port that enables you to attach an electronic musical instrument interface or add a joystick to your PC (see Figure 3.23). These multi-function joystick/MIDI ports are rare today.

Adding more and more audio jacks to sound cards made the back of a typical sound card a busy place. In an effort to consolidate the various sound signals, the industry invented the **Sony/Philips Digital Interface Format (S/PDIF)** connection. S/PDIF comes in coaxial and optical versions. Figure 3.24 shows a motherboard with both (the coaxial connection is on the left). One S/PDIF connection replaces all of the mini-audio connections, assuming your surround speaker system also comes with an S/PDIF connection.

Network

Networks are groups of connected PCs that share information. The PCs most commonly connect via some type of cabling that usually looks like an extra-thick phone cable. A modern PC uses an RJ-45 connection to connect to the network. Figure 3.25 shows a typical RJ-45 network connector. Network connectors do not have a standard color.

Mouse

Most folks are pretty comfortable with the function of a mouse—it enables you to select graphical items on a graphical screen. A PC mouse has at least two buttons (as opposed to the famous one-button mouse that came with Apple Macintosh computers

S/PDIF

• **Figure 3.24** S/PDIF connection

Mike Meyers' CompTIA A+ Guide: Essentials

• **Figure 3.25**   Typical network connection

• **Figure 3.26**   Mouse with mini-DIN connection

until recently), while a better mouse provides a scroll wheel and extra buttons. A mouse uses either a USB port or a dedicated, light-green mini-DIN connector (see Figure 3.26).

A variation of the mouse is a **trackball**. A trackball does the same job as a mouse, but instead of pushing it around like a mouse, the trackball stays in one place as you roll a ball with your fingers or thumb (Figure 3.27).

Modem

The old **modem** enables you to connect your PC to a telephone. Modems are another easily identifiable device in PCs as they have one or

• **Figure 3.27**   Trackball

Tech Tip

Serial Ports

External modems traditionally connected to a male 9-pin or 25-pin D-subminiature port on the system unit called a **serial port** *(shown in the following illustration). Although just about every external modem today connects to USB, a few computers still come with a serial port for legacy devices.*

Serial ports are one of the few connectors on modern systems that were also used in the first PCs more than 20 years ago.

• Figure 3.28   Internal modem

two RJ-11 jacks. One jack is to connect the modem to the telephone jack on the wall. If the modem has a second RJ-11 jack, it is for an optional telephone so you can use the phone line when the modem is not in use (see Figure 3.28).

Printer

For many years, printers only used a special connector called a **parallel port**. Parallel ports use a 25-pin female DB connector that's usually colored fuchsia (see Figure 3.29).

After almost 20 years of domination by parallel ports, most printers now come with USB ports, FireWire, Ethernet, and Wi-Fi 802.11 b/g/n connectivity options. Parallel ports are quickly fading away from the backs of most computers.

• Figure 3.29   Parallel port

Joystick

Joysticks weren't supposed to be used just for games (see Figure 3.30). When the folks at IBM added the 2-row, 15-pin female DB joystick connector to PCs, they envisioned joysticks as hard-working input devices, just as the mouse is today. Except in the most rare circumstances, however, the only thing a **joystick** does today is enable you to turn your PC into a rather expensive game machine. But is there a more gratifying feeling than easing that joystick over, pressing the Fire button, and watching an enemy fighter jet get blasted by a well-placed Sidewinder missile? I think not. Traditional joystick connecters are colored orange, but most joysticks today connect to USB ports.

• Figure 3.30   Joystick

eSATA

More and more PCs are showing up with eSATA ports like the one shown in Figure 3.31. The **eSATA** is a special connector for external hard drives and optical drives.

Plenty More!

Keep in mind that there are lots more devices and connectors out there. This section includes only the most common and the ones you're most likely to see. As you progress through this book, you'll see some less common connecters and where they are used.

• **Figure 3.31**   eSATA port

■ Inside the System Unit

Now that you've seen the devices that connect to the PC, it's time to open up the system unit to inspect the major internal components of a typical PC. A single PC is composed of thousands of discrete components. Although no one can name every tiny bit of electronics in a PC, a good technician should be able to name the major internal components that make up the typical PC. Let's open and inspect a system unit to see these components and gain at least a concept of what they do. In later chapters, you'll see all of these components in much more detail.

Case

The system unit's case is both the internal framework of the PC and the external skin that protects the internal components from the environment.

Cases come in an amazing variety of styles, sizes, and colors. Figure 3.32 shows the front and back of a typical PC case. The front of the case holds the buttons for turning the system on and off, lights to tell you the status of the system, and doors for accessing removable media drives such as floppy, CD-ROM, and DVD drives. This system also provides USB, FireWire, and audio connections in the front for easy access if you want to use a device that needs these connections.

The back of the case holds the vast majority of the system unit connections. You will also notice the power supply—almost always at the top of the case—distinguished by its cooling fan and power plug. Note that one area of the back, the I/O area, holds all of the onboard connections (see Figure 3.33), while another area in the back contains slots for cards. Similarly, the case uses slots to enable access to the external connectors on cards installed in the system unit.

Opening a case is always…interesting. There's no standard way to open a case, and I'm convinced that the folks making system units enjoy some sick humor inventing new and complex ways to open them. In general,

• **Figure 3.32**   Case—front and back

You'll hear the PC case called the *enclosure*, especially at the more expensive end of the spectrum. Case, enclosure, and system unit are interchangeable terms.

• **Figure 3.33**   Onboard devices

you detach the sides of a case by removing a few screws in the back of the system unit, as shown in Figure 3.34. Use common sense and you won't have too many problems. Just don't lose track of your screws or where each one was inserted!

Once you've opened the case, take a look inside. You'll see metal framework, all kinds of cables, and a number of devices. As you inspect the devices, you may gently push cables to the side to get a better view. Don't forget to wear an anti-static wrist strap (attaching it to any handy metal part of the case) or touch the metal case occasionally to prevent ESD.

CPU

The **central processing unit (CPU)**, also called the **microprocessor**, performs all of the calculations that take place inside a PC. CPUs come in a variety of shapes and sizes, as shown in Figure 3.35.

• **Figure 3.34**   Opening a system unit

• **Figure 3.35**   Typical CPUs still in protective packaging

Modern CPUs generate a lot of heat and thus require a cooling fan and heat sink assembly to avoid overheating (see Figure 3.36). A heat sink is a big slab of copper or aluminum that helps draw heat away from the processor. The fan then blows the heat out into the case. You can usually remove this cooling device if you need to replace it, although some CPU manufacturers have sold CPUs with a fan permanently attached.

CPUs have a make and model, just like automobiles do. When talking about a particular car, for example, most people speak in terms of a Ford Taurus or a Toyota Camry. When they talk about CPUs, people say Intel Core i7 or AMD Phenom. Over the years, there have been only a few major CPU manufacturers, just as there are only a few major auto manufacturers. The two most common makes of CPUs used in PCs are AMD and Intel.

Although only a few manufacturers of CPUs have existed, those manufacturers have made hundreds of models of CPUs. Some of the more common models made over the past few years have names such as Core 2, Core i7, Celeron, Athlon, and Phenom.

Finally, CPUs come in a variety of packages. The package defines how the CPU looks physically and how it connects to the computer. Intel CPUs currently use a package type called *land grid array* (*LGA*), and AMD likes *pin grid array* (*PGA*). Every CPU package type has a number of versions and each type is designed to fit into a particular connection called a socket. Sockets have such names as Socket AM3 or Socket B. Figure 3.37 shows a CPU with its matching socket.

Chapter 5, "Learning CPUs," goes into great detail on CPUs, but for now remember that every CPU has a make, a model, and a package type.

• **Figure 3.36**   CPU with fan

• **Figure 3.37**   CPU and matching socket

RAM

Random access memory (RAM) stores programs and data currently being used by the CPU. The maximum amount of programs and data that a piece of RAM can store is measured in units called *bytes*. Modern PCs have many millions, even billions, of bytes of RAM, so RAM is measured in units called *megabytes* (*MB*) or *gigabytes* (*GB*). An average PC will have from 1 to 4 GB of RAM, although PCs may have more or less RAM. Each piece of RAM is called a *stick*. One common type of stick found in today's PC is called a *dual inline memory module* (*DIMM*). Figure 3.38 shows two examples of DIMMs used in PCs.

Your PC takes only one type of DIMM, and you must know the type so you can add or replace RAM when needed. Chapter 6, "Learning RAM," covers everything you need to know to work comfortably with RAM.

> ⚠ Some parts of your PC are much more sensitive to ESD than others. Your CPU and RAM are very sensitive to ESD. If you touch the metal parts of your CPU or RAM and you have even the tiniest amount of charge, you can destroy them.

• Figure 3.38   Two DIMMs

• Figure 3.39   Typical motherboard

Motherboard

You can compare a motherboard to the chassis of an automobile. In a car, everything connects to the chassis either directly or indirectly. In a PC, everything connects to the motherboard either directly or indirectly. A **motherboard** is a thin, flat piece of circuit board, usually green or gold, and often slightly larger than a typical piece of notebook paper (see Figure 3.39).

A motherboard contains a number of special sockets that accept various PC components. The CPU and RAM, for example, plug directly into the motherboard. Other devices, such as floppy drives, hard drives, CD and DVD drives, connect to the motherboard sockets through short cables. Motherboards also provide onboard connectors for external devices such as mice, printers, joysticks, and keyboards.

All motherboards use multipurpose expansion slots in which you can add adapter cards. Different types of expansion slots exist for different types of cards (see Figure 3.40).

Power Supply

The **power supply**, as its name implies, provides the necessary electrical power to make the PC operate. The power supply takes standard electrical power and converts it into power your PC can use. Most power supplies are about the size of a shoebox cut in half and are usually a gray or metallic color (see Figure 3.41).

A number of connectors lead out of the power supply. Every power supply provides special connectors to power the motherboard and a number of other general-use connectors that provide power to any device that needs electricity. Check out Chapter 8, "Learning PC Power," for more information.

• Figure 3.40   Placing a card into an expansion slot

• Figure 3.41   Power supply

Floppy Drive

The **floppy drive** enables you to access removable floppy disks (diskettes). The floppy drive used in PCs today is a 3.5-inch floppy drive. Floppy drives only store a tiny amount of data and have all but disappeared from PCs.

The floppy drive's data connection to the computer is via a ribbon cable, which in turn connects to the motherboard. The connection to the motherboard is known as the *floppy drive controller* (Figure 3.42).

• **Figure 3.42** Floppy drive connected to motherboard

Hard Drive

A **hard drive** stores programs and data that are not currently being used by the CPU. Although RAM storage is measured in megabytes and gigabytes, a PC's hard drive stores much more data than a typical PC's RAM—hundreds of gigabytes to *terabytes*. A terabyte is 1000 gigabytes.

An average PC has one hard drive, although most PCs accept more. Special PCs that need to store large amounts of data, such as a large corporation's main file-storage computer, can contain many hard drives—8 to 16 drives in some cases.

The two most common types of hard drives seen in today's PCs are the older *Parallel Advanced Technology Attachment* (*PATA*) and the more modern *Serial Advanced Technology Attachment* (*SATA*). PATA drives use a ribbon cable very similar to the one used by floppy drives, whereas SATA drives use a very narrow cable. Figure 3.43 shows a SATA drive (left) next to a PATA drive (right). Most motherboards come with connections for both types of drives.

Optical drives use the same PATA or SATA connections used with hard drives. Figure 3.44 shows a DVD drive sharing a single ribbon cable with a PATA hard drive—a common sight inside a PC.

Tech Tip

SCSI

A very few PCs use small computer system interface (SCSI) *drives. SCSI drives are generally faster and more expensive, so they usually show up only in high-end PCs such as network servers or graphics workstations.*

Optical Drives

Optical drives enable a computer to read one or more types of optical discs, such as CD, DVD, or Blu-ray Disc (Figure 3.45). CDs store around 700 MB

• **Figure 3.43** SATA and PATA drives showing data connectors

• **Figure 3.44** Hard drive and DVD drive

• Figure 3.45   Assorted optical discs

Chapter 10, "Removable Media," goes into great detail on the assorted discs and drive types.

and come in three varieties: CD-ROM (*read only memory*: you can't change the data on them), CD-R (*recordable*: you can change the data once), and CD-RW (*rewritable*: you can change the data on them over and over). DVDs store much more data—the smallest capacity DVDs store around 4 GB, enough for a Hollywood movie—and come in even more varieties: DVD-ROM, DVD+R, DVD-R, DVD+RW, and DVD-RW, just to name the more famous ones. Blu-ray Discs are popular for high-definition movies, but there are also Blu-ray Discs for storing data with capacities starting at 25 GB.

All of these optical discs require an optical drive that knows how to read them. If you want to do anything with a CD-RW disc, for example, you need a CD-RW drive. If you want to use a DVD+R disc, you need a DVD+R drive. Luckily, most optical drives support many different types of discs, and some support every common type of optical disc available. Figure 3.46 shows typical optical drives. Note that some of them advertise what disc types they use. Others give no clue whatsoever.

Know Your Parts

The goal of this chapter was to get you to appreciate the names and functions of the various parts of the PC: peripherals, connectors, and components. By starting with the Big Picture view, you may now begin breaking down the individual components on a chapter-by-chapter basis and truly understand at great depth how each component works and how it interconnects with the PC system as a whole.

• Figure 3.46   Optical drives

Chapter 3 Review

■ Chapter Summary

After reading this chapter and completing the exercises, you should understand the following about the visible PC.

Describe how the PC works

- The two parts of the PC—hardware and software—work intimately together to enable you to do work.

- The computer tech knows the four stages of computing: input, processing, output, and storage. Understanding how the various pieces of hardware and software interact in each stage enables you to master the art of the PC tech.

Identify all the connectors and devices on a typical PC system unit

- Most computers have a standard set of peripherals to provide input and output. Typical devices include the monitor, keyboard, mouse, speakers, and printer.

- PCs use many kinds of external connectors, but most fit into one of six major types: mini-DIN, USB, FireWire, DB, RJ, and mini-audio. A plug goes into a port or jack. Connectors are often identified by their shape (such as DB connectors that look like a capital D), by their gender (male or female), and by the number of pins. Most PCs have two round mini-DIN connectors, one for the keyboard and the other for the mouse.

- Universal serial bus (USB) connectors come in three sizes, A, B, and mini-B. Many devices plug into USB ports, including keyboards and cameras. USB is hot-swappable, so you may insert or remove devices without restarting the computer.

- Also known as IEEE 1394, the FireWire interface is perfect for high-speed devices such as digital video cameras. PCs rarely have built-in 4- or 6-wire FireWire connectors, so users typically purchase a FireWire adapter card.

- DB connectors come in a variety of sizes, but only one shape. You'll find only a few DB connectors on modern PCs, primarily for printers and video.

- The telephone jack is an RJ connector, called an RJ-11. Most network cards have a wider RJ-45 jack.

- Speakers and microphones connect to mini-audio jacks. You'll always find these on the back of the system unit; newer models have connectors on the front as well.

- Keyboards connect into either a dedicated mini-DIN keyboard port or a USB port. Monitors connect to VGA or DVI ports. Mice and trackballs use the mini-DIN or USB ports as well. Keeping with the same trend, printers come in one of two common varieties: those that plug into a DB-25 port and those that plug into a USB port. A joystick plugs into either a 15-pin female DB port or a USB port.

Discuss the major internal components of a PC

- Everything fits inside or connects to the case, more technically called a system unit. The system unit provides the framework for buttons, lights, drives, access doors, and so forth. Opening the case is usually a matter of unscrewing screws and pulling one side open.

- The central processing unit (CPU), also called the microprocessor or brain of the computer, has a make, a model, a speed, and a package. AMD and Intel are the two most common makers of CPUs. CPU speed is measured in megahertz (MHz) or gigahertz (GHz). The pin grid array (PGA) is the most common CPU package. A CPU cooling fan or heat sink is essential to dissipate the heat.

- Random access memory (RAM) contains the current programs and data that the CPU is using. Most PC memory is installed on sticks called dual inline memory modules (DIMMs). RAM capacity is measured in megabytes (MB) or gigabytes (GB).

- The motherboard contains soldered components, expansion slots, and sockets for the CPU, RAM, and other components. Expansion slots are connectors for expansion cards that enable optional devices to communicate with the PC.

- A floppy drive uses a ribbon cable to connect to the floppy drive controller on the motherboard. The most common type is the 3.5-inch floppy drive.

- Hard drives store programs and data that the CPU is not currently using. An average PC has one hard drive, although most PCs accept more. Most PCs use either PATA or SATA drives, both of which commonly connect to controllers built into the motherboard.

- Optical drives enable the computer to access optical discs. Some optical drives can record CDs, such as the compact disc-recordable (CD-R) or the compact disc-rewritable (CD-RW) drives. Most PCs now have digital versatile disc (DVD) drives that support capacities large enough for a full-length movie.

■ Key Terms

central processing unit (CPU) (52)
connector (43)
DB connector (45)
digital video interface (DVI) (47)
D-subminiature (45)
eSATA (51)
expansion slot (46)
FireWire (44)
floppy drive (55)
hard drive (55)
Hi-Definition Multimedia Interface (HDMI) (47)
hot-swappable (44)
IEEE 1394 (44)
jack (43)
joystick (50)
keyboard (42)
microprocessor (52)
mini-audio connector (46)
mini-DIN connector (44)
modem (49)
monitor (42)

motherboard (54)
mouse (42)
network interface card (NIC) (48)
optical drive (55)
parallel port (50)
peripherals (42)
plug (43)
port (43)
power supply (54)
printer (42)
programming (39)
random access memory (RAM) (53)
RJ connector (46)
serial port (49)
software (39)
Sony/Philips Digital Interface Format (S/PDIF) (48)
speakers (42)
system unit (42)
trackball (49)
universal serial bus (USB) (44)
Video Electronics Standards Association (VESA) (47)

■ Key Term Quiz

Use the Key Terms list to complete the sentences that follow. Not all terms will be used.

1. The monitor attaches to the video card with a 15-pin female DB connector called a(n) _____ connector.

2. If you install a DIMM stick, your computer will have more _____.

3. The _____ has a make, a model, a speed, and a package.

4. Two RJ-11 connectors identify the _____.

5. When attaching a peripheral, put the plug into the _____ or jack.

6. The _____ takes standard electrical power from a wall outlet and converts it to power your PC can use.

7. If an expansion card contains an RJ-45 jack, it is a(n) _____.

8. A 25-pin female DB connector with a printer attached to it is a(n) _____.

9. An internal storage device that typically holds 200 GB or more is a(n) _____.

10. The box that all the other components plug into is called the _____.

■ Multiple-Choice Quiz

1. Which of the following connections can replace all of the mini-audio jacks on a system unit?
   A. FireWire
   B. HDMI
   C. S/PDIF
   D. VESA

2. A modern keyboard generally connects to which of the following ports? (Select two.)
   A. FireWire
   B. Mini-DIN
   C. USB
   D. VESA

3. USB connectors come in which of the following sizes? (Select three.)
   A. A
   B. B
   C. Mini-A
   D. Mini-B

4. Which of the following devices attaches with a ribbon cable?
   A. CPU
   B. CD-ROM drive
   C. RAM
   D. Sound card

5. Which of the following devices measure(s) storage capacity in megabytes or gigabytes?
   A. Floppy disk and hard drive
   B. NIC
   C. CPU
   D. Modem

6. Which of the following devices has enough storage capacity to hold a movie?
   A. CD-ROM
   B. CD-R
   C. CD-RW
   D. DVD

7. Which of the following connector types enable you to plug a device into them and have the device function without your restarting the computer? (Select two.)
   A. FireWire
   B. Mini-DIN
   C. Serial
   D. USB

8. Which of the following ports would you most likely find built into a motherboard?
   A. A keyboard port
   B. A DVI port
   C. An HDMI port
   D. An RDA port

9. Which of the following connectors is used mostly for external hard drives?
   A. PATA
   B. eSATA
   C. HDMI
   D. PS/2

10. Which of the following ports can handle a connection from a monitor?
    A. DVI
    B. FireWire
    C. Mini-DIN
    D. USB

11. Which of the following ports enables a modern PC to connect to a network?

    A. Mini-audio

    B. Mini-DIN

    C. RJ-13

    D. RJ-45

12. Which of the following connectors is used for hard drives?

    A. Parallel

    B. SATA

    C. HDMI

    D. TTFN

13. Of the following, what do USB and FireWire connections have in common?

    A. Both are used for connecting keyboards

    B. Both support dual monitors

    C. Both support hot-swapping devices

    D. Both use D-subminiature connectors

14. Which devices enable you to select graphical items on a graphical screen? (Select two.)

    A. Modem

    B. Mouse

    C. Touchball

    D. Trackball

15. Which device traditionally used a 2-row, 15-pin DB connector (though current models connect through USB)?

    A. Joystick

    B. Keyboard

    C. Mouse

    D. Printer

■ Essay Quiz

1. Although serial and parallel ports have been around forever, newer and faster ports such as USB and FireWire are now available. At the same time, new computers have faster CPUs, more RAM, and larger-capacity hard drives. What factors do you think are driving the PC market for these improvements? Do you feel that you need to have the newest and the greatest PC? Why or why not?

2. Jason, one of your coworkers who knows nothing about computer hardware, needs to move his computer and will be responsible for reassembling it himself in his new office across town. What advice can you give him about disassembly steps that will help him reassemble the computer successfully? List at least five things Jason should do as he disassembles the computer, transports it, and reassembles it. Do shapes and colors help him?

3. A floppy drive was a standard component for personal computers from their beginning. Today, most manufacturers build PCs without a floppy drive. Would you want to purchase a PC without a floppy drive? Why or why not? If so, what kinds of alternative devices would you want your computer to have?

4. Hearing that you are taking a computer hardware course, Aunt Sally approaches you about helping her select a new computer. She wants to use the computer primarily for office applications, to track her budget, to receive and send e-mail, and to surf the Internet. What are you going to tell her about the kind of PC to buy? What peripherals should she purchase? Why?

Lab Projects

• Lab Project 3.1

Many personal computers do not normally include the relatively new eSATA port. Check the following three Web sites: www.dell.com, www.hp.com, and www.lenovo.com. Is an eSATA port standard built-in equipment on their new computers? If so, how many eSATA ports are included? If not, do the sites offer eSATA as an optional add-on?

• Lab Project 3.2

Find an advertisement for a new personal computer in a current newspaper or magazine and examine it to determine the following:

- What make, model, and speed of CPU does it have?
- How much RAM does it have?

- What is the storage capacity of the hard drive?
- Does it include a Blu-ray Disc, CD-RW, or DVD drive?
- Does it come with a network interface card?
- Is a monitor included? If so, what kind and size?

chapter 4

Understanding Windows

"Hard-working, Easy-going Software Everyone Will Use"

—Tagline for Microsoft Bob, an operating system interface

In this chapter, you will learn how to

- Relate the history of Microsoft Windows
- Explain the Windows interface
- Explain some advanced Windows features
- Maintain Windows
- Optimize Windows

As a tech, you need to understand Windows at a level beyond that of regular users. This chapter introduces you to some of the more powerful aspects of Windows, such as NTFS and the Registry. Not only must techs run through the standard Windows features that everyone uses every day (Start button, Recycle Bin, and so on), they must also be comfortable drilling down underneath that user-friendly surface to get their hands a little dirty.

This chapter begins by introducing and organizing the many variations of Windows on the market today and helping you appreciate the difference between, for example, Windows XP Home and Windows Vista Ultimate. The chapter then takes you through the Windows interface in detail. The third section looks more closely at the techie aspects of Windows, including some of the powerful, built-in tools that enable you to modify and tweak your operating system to your heart's content. The fourth section provides an overview of a few more tools used to maintain a functional Windows install. The chapter closes with a section on optimizing Windows for maximum performance. Let's get started!

■ A Brief History of Microsoft Windows

Many users think of Windows as a monolithic thing, as *the* operating system (OS) for the PC (as opposed to the Macintosh), but as a tech you need to understand that Microsoft produces many varieties of the OS, each with specific tools, utilities, file structures, and interfaces. And you need to be able to navigate through any modern version of Windows fluidly.

Microsoft currently supports seven families of Windows, of which three concern the CompTIA A+ certified technician: Windows 2000, Windows XP, and Windows Vista. Within each of these families—my word, not Microsoft's—Windows comes in multiple versions. Table 4.1 presents the list for the top three.

Table 4.1	Versions of Windows on the CompTIA A+ Essentials Exam	
Windows Family	**Versions (32-bit)**	**Versions (64-bit)**
Windows 2000	■ Windows 2000 Professional ■ Windows 2000 Server	Nothing widely available
Windows XP	■ Windows XP Home ■ Windows XP Professional ■ Windows Media Center ■ Windows XP Tablet PC Edition[1]	■ Windows XP 64-bit version ■ Windows XP Professional x64 Edition
Windows Vista[2]	■ Windows Vista Home Basic ■ Windows Vista Home Premium ■ Windows Vista Business ■ Windows Vista Ultimate	■ Windows Vista Home Basic ■ Windows Vista Home Premium ■ Windows Vista Business ■ Windows Vista Ultimate

1   Windows XP Tablet PC Edition is not covered on the CompTIA A+ Essentials exam but is included here for completeness.
2   Microsoft has released two other versions of Windows Vista: Starter Edition and Enterprise. Vista Starter Edition is a simplified version of the operating system designed for the developing world and is not sold in developed countries. Vista Enterprise is a version of Vista Business designed for large-volume customers and is only sold to Microsoft's enterprise-level customers.

The problem of variety is compounded the minute you start working with older computers or talking with users or techs who've been in computers for a few years. You'll hear about Windows 95, for example, or Windows Me, or even Windows 3.*x*. Huh? What are these versions (Figure 4.1)? How do they fit in the picture?

This section outlines the history of Microsoft Windows and then takes an in-depth look at the differences among the many versions of Microsoft's flagship operating system. That way you can sort out the essentials for today's techs from the many varieties you'll hear about.

Microsoft entered the operating system game in the early 1980s with a command-line OS called Microsoft Disk Operating System, or MS-DOS. With a command-line OS, you interacted with the computer to run programs and save files and all the other computing functions by typing and then pressing the ENTER key on your keyboard. This whole typing thing worked for people who could memorize commands and such, but alternative operating systems, such as the Apple Macintosh, offered a visual interface, where you could interact with the computer by clicking on pictures.

● **Figure 4.1**   Lots of Windows!

The time came for Microsoft to step up its game and produce a graphical user interface (GUI) where users could use a mouse to point and click.

Microsoft released several versions of Windows 3.1, with minor differences in name. Techs call the versions collectively Windows 3.*x*.

Early Windows

The earliest version of Windows, Microsoft Windows 1.0, dates from 1985 and was little more than a graphical overlay of the DOS command-line operating system. This overlay version of Windows went through a number of updates, ending with the first truly popular version of Windows, Windows for Workgroups version 3.1 (Figure 4.2).

In 1989, Microsoft offered a completely separate version of Windows called Windows NT. Windows NT was a true graphical operating system and was dramatically more powerful than the Windows overlay versions. Windows NT also cost more than other versions of Windows, however, and saw little adoption outside of servers and systems where users needed a lot of power. Windows NT went through a number of versions, culminating with Windows NT 4.0 in 1996 (Figure 4.3).

Comparing Windows NT to the old overlay versions of Windows is akin to comparing the first computer game you ever played to the games you play today: technically the same thing (a game), but that's about it. Windows NT

● **Figure 4.2**   Windows for Workgroups

had so many features that showing them all could take days, but one is important. NT came with a new way to organize hard drives and files, called the NT File System (NTFS). Before NTFS, all versions of Windows used an ancient file system called the file allocation table (FAT). FAT was great when first invented in the late 1970s, but by the mid-80s it was showing its age. NTFS took care of a number of problems, the biggest of which was security. FAT had no security. There was no way to control what people did with your files. NTFS was built from the ground up with security in mind. We'll cover both FAT and NTFS later in the book, but for now appreciate that only Windows NT had NTFS.

• **Figure 4.3** Windows NT 4.0

It wasn't until 1995 that Microsoft dumped the overlay concept and introduced Windows 95, the first version of Windows for the standard user that was also a full-blown operating system (Figure 4.4). Windows 95 offered many improvements over Windows 3.x, and eventually Microsoft released several upgraded versions as well, such as Windows 98, Windows 98 SE, and Windows Me. The upgraded versions continued to use the FAT file system. Over the years, Windows has gone through massive changes and a large number of improved versions. The later versions have nothing in common with earlier versions other than the name "Windows."

When we describe Windows 95, 98, 98 SE, and Me from a historical standpoint, we lump them all together, using the term "Windows 9x."

Modern Windows

The vast majority of computers in the field today run one of the three modern families of Windows, so the CompTIA A+ certification focuses on those as well: Windows 2000, Windows XP, and Windows Vista. But as you know from Table 4.1 at the beginning of this chapter, just saying the name of a Windows family doesn't do the varieties within that family justice. The trick is to organize these versions in such a way to discover their similarities and differences. In this section, we'll look at versions of Windows 2000, XP, and Vista, as well as a few other versions of Windows, and see the differences in detail.

A great place to start is with the arrival of Windows 2000 in 2001. Throughout most of the 1990s, before Windows 2000 came along (followed very quickly by Windows XP), Windows was in a bit of a mess. Microsoft

● **Figure 4.4** Windows 95—The Windows of your forefathers

had two totally different operating systems—each called Windows—that it sold for two different markets. Microsoft sold the Windows 9x series for the home user and small office, and the much more powerful Windows NT series for corporate environments.

Windows 2000

Windows 2000 was the first step toward changing this mess. It was based on the old Windows NT (including support for NTFS), but for the first time it included a great interface, provided support for dang near any program, and was substantially easier to use than the old Windows NT. Microsoft originally presented Windows 2000 as a replacement for Windows NT, but its stability and ease of use motivated many knowledgeable Windows 9x users to upgrade to Windows 2000. Windows 2000 started to appear as "the single Windows to replace all the other versions."

Windows 2000 came in two versions: Professional and Server. The CompTIA A+ Essentials exam does not cover Windows Server versions, but a good tech should at least know that these server versions exist. If you were to look at the Windows 2000 Server desktop, you'd be hard pressed to see any obvious differences from the Windows 2000 Professional version. Don't let Windows 2000 Server fool you (Figure 4.5). Windows Server is a heavy-duty version, loaded with extra software and features that make it superb for running an office server. Windows Server versions are also extremely expensive, costing on average of around $200 per computer that accesses the server.

Windows 2000 was the last version of Windows to come in both Server and Professional versions. After the release of Windows XP, Microsoft introduced the next version of Windows Server as Server 2003. Windows Server 2008 is the latest version of Windows Server.

● **Figure 4.5** Windows 2000 Server

Windows XP

Windows XP came hot on the heels of Windows 2000. Under the hood, XP was basically the same as Windows 2000 but added a dramatically improved interface and a number of new features, such as a built-in CD writer. Microsoft also broke with the beauty of 2000's "one OS for everyone" idea. Microsoft visualized three types of users—professionals, home users, and media junkies—so Windows XP came in several versions, such as Windows XP Professional, Windows XP Home, and Windows XP Media Center.

Windows XP Professional   Microsoft Windows XP Professional is, in many people's opinions, the most versatile and therefore the most mainstream version of Windows XP. Microsoft tuned Windows XP Professional for office environments with many users sharing lots of data and multiple users sharing single computers. Windows XP Professional provides full-blown data security, and it is the only version of Windows XP with the capability of logging on to a special Windows Server–controlled network called a *domain*.

A Windows domain is a group of networked computers all under the control of a single computer running some version of Windows Server. Users on a domain can make a single login to their computer that defines everything they can do on every other computer on the domain. (See Chapter 16, "Learning Local Area Networking," for all the details of the amazing Windows domain.) Figure 4.6 shows a typical Windows XP Professional desktop.

● **Figure 4.6**   Windows XP Professional

Windows XP Home   As its name implies, Windows XP Home is designed for the home and small-office user. Windows XP Home is a stripped-down version of XP Professional. The best way to describe Windows XP Home is to list the Windows XP Professional features that Windows XP Home lacks. Windows XP Home does *not* have

- **The ability to log on to a Windows domain**   A Windows Home PC may log in to any single Windows server, but you must have a user name and password on every single server. With a domain, you can have one user name and password that works on all computers that are members of the domain.

- **Encrypting file system**   With Windows XP Professional, you can encrypt a file or a folder so that only you can read it. Windows XP Home lacks this feature.

- **Support for multiple processors**   Windows XP Home does not support more than one physical CPU. Windows XP Professional supports two separate CPUs.

- **Support for Remote Desktop**   A Windows XP Professional PC may be remotely accessed from another computer by using Remote Desktop (Figure 4.7). You cannot access a Windows XP Home system in this fashion.

- **Support for NTFS Access Control**   The NTFS file system is capable of powerful controls on what users may do to a file or folder. Windows XP Home doesn't give you the ability to control these NTFS permissions individually. When you look at the properties of

CPU support is based on physical CPUs, not the number of cores in a single CPU. See Chapter 5, "Learning CPUs," for details on multicore CPUs.

● **Figure 4.7**   Remote Desktop

a file or folder in Windows XP Home, you'll notice that there is no Security tab. Instead, Windows XP Home's Sharing tab (Figure 4.8) shows that only one folder, the Shared Documents folder, is open for sharing—very different from XP Professional.

- ■ **Support for group policies**   Do you need to keep users from using a certain program? Do you want to prevent them from changing the screensaver? What do you want to do if they try to log in three times unsuccessfully? That's the job of group polices. Well, if you want this level of control on your system, get Windows XP Professional, because XP Home doesn't support them. Group policies are discussed in Chapter 19, "Learning Computer Security."

A few more differences exist between Windows XP Professional and XP Home, but these are the ones you're most likely to run into. Basically, if you want serious control of the folders, files, users, and network, you need XP Professional.

Windows XP Media Center   Microsoft Media Center is a specialized XP version that includes the very handy Windows Media Center program (Figure 4.9). Media Center is a Personal Video Recorder (PVR) program that enables you to watch and record television (you'll need a TV tuner card) and organize all of your media, from photos to music.

On the Microsoft Media Center Web site, Microsoft declares that the Windows XP Microsoft Media Center edition is based on Windows

● **Figure 4.8**   Windows XP Home Sharing tab

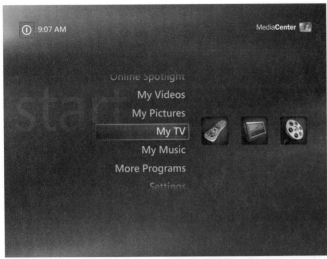

XP Professional; however, other than the Media Center program, Windows XP Media Center's capabilities are identical to those of Windows XP Home.

Windows Vista

Even though Windows 7 is available, Windows Vista is the latest version of Windows covered on the current CompTIA A+ Essentials exam. It's important to recognize Vista and know what choices you have when deciding which version of Vista you need for a particular PC. Windows has a number of versions of Vista, each geared toward a particular market segment. Let's look at the most common versions of Vista.

Windows Vista Home Basic   Windows Vista Home Basic is roughly equivalent to Windows XP Home. Microsoft gears it to home users not needing more advanced multimedia support.

Windows Vista Home Premium   Windows Vista Home Premium is the same as Windows Vista Home Basic, but it adds an upgraded Windows Media Center PVR application, similar to the one found in Windows XP Media Center (Figure 4.10).

Windows Vista Business   Windows Vista Business is the basic business version and has all the security, file-sharing, and access controls seen in Windows XP Professional.

Windows Vista Ultimate   Windows Vista Ultimate combines all of the features of every other Vista version and includes some other features, such as a game performance tweaker and DVD ripping capability (Figure 4.11).

● **Figure 4.9**   Microsoft Media Center

● **Figure 4.10**   Vista Home Premium Media Center

 You can determine your Windows version by right-clicking My Computer in Windows 2000 or XP, or Computer in Vista and Windows 7, and selecting Properties.

CPUs and 32- and 64-bit processing are covered in much greater detail in Chapter 5, "Learning CPUs."

Enter 64-bit Windows

From roughly 1986 to around 2001, all CPUs were 32-bit. While we will save the big discussion of what 32-bit means for Chapter 5, "Learning CPUs," for now let's keep it simple: a 32-bit CPU can only use a maximum of 4 gigabytes of RAM (2^{32} = 4,294,967,296). Starting in 2001 we began to see 64-bit CPUs that could accept more than 4 gigabytes. 64-bit CPUs are now extremely common.

The leap from 32-bit to 64-bit processing has a number of advantages. The really big compelling reason to go from 32-bit to 64-bit is that 64-bit CPUs support more than 4 gigabytes of RAM. The more RAM you have, the more programs—and the bigger the programs—your system will run. Until fairly recently, not too many of us cared to go above 4 gigabytes of RAM.

• **Figure 4.11**   Vista Ultimate

We didn't need the RAM and we didn't have a CPU that could run at 64 bits. My, how things have changed over the past few years!

The 64-bit CPUs first showed up with the Intel Itanium back in 2001. At that time the only folks interested in 64-bit processing were large data centers and a few organizations that needed to crunch big numbers. To run a computer with an Itanium, you needed an operating system that worked with a 64-bit processor. Up to this point, every version of Windows only ran at 32 bits. Microsoft answered the call by creating special 64-bit versions of Windows 2000 and XP, but these 64-bit versions of Windows 2000 were very rare.

In 2003, Advanced Micro Devices (AMD) started to ship the popular Athlon 64 CPU. This CPU could run in either 32-bit or 64-bit mode, making 64-bit a realistic option for most of us. Intel followed AMD around 2004 with Pentium 4 CPUs also capable of 32-bit or 64-bit processing. Since then, almost every CPU sold by Intel or AMD has the ability to run in either 32-bit or 64-bit mode. Moving from the 32-bit to the 64-bit world is easy, but only if you have a version of Windows to support 64-bit. Microsoft has multiple versions of Windows designed to support 64-bit CPUs.

Windows XP 64-bit Versions

The 64-bit-only version of Windows XP was called Windows XP 64-bit Edition (apparently Microsoft decided not to get cute when naming that one). Given that it only worked on Intel Itanium processors, the chance of your seeing this operating system is pretty small unless you decide to work in a place with powerful server needs. The Windows XP Professional x64

> Remember for the exam that 32-bit CPUs can support up to 4 GB of RAM. In concept, 64-bit CPUs can support up to 16 *exabytes* of memory, although you certainly won't find that much memory in the typical PC.

Tech Tip

Four-Gigabyte Limit

All 32-bit versions of Windows support a maximum of 4 gigabytes of RAM. If your PC has more than 4 gigabytes and you're not running 64-bit Windows, you might as well remove any RAM above 4 gigabytes. You're wasting it!

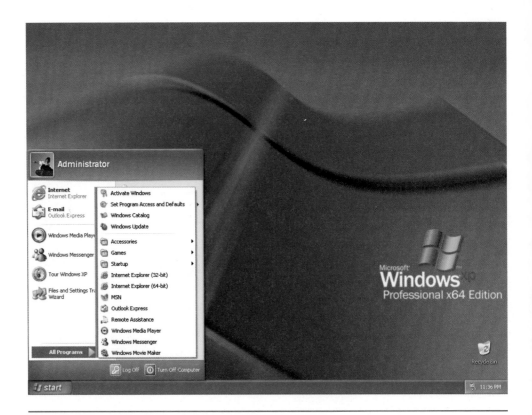

• **Figure 4.12**   Windows XP Professional x64 Edition

Edition is much more common, as it runs on any AMD or Intel processor that supports both 32 and 64 bits (Figure 4.12).

Windows XP 64-bit versions have had some impact, as they were the first stable Windows versions that truly supported 64-bit processing, but it was the introduction of Microsoft Vista that really started the move into the 64-bit world.

Windows Vista 64-bit Versions

Every one of the earlier listed Vista versions comes in both 32-bit and 64-bit versions. As we move into PCs with more than 4 gigabytes of RAM, it's important to make sure your version of Windows is a 64-bit version (Figure 4.13).

Transitioning to 64-bit Windows

Techs use the x# terminology to describe a particular computer architecture, implying that there is some compatibility within that architecture. This matters because people need some comfort that the software they purchase will work properly with the computer they have. The transition from 32-bit versions of Windows to 64-bit versions of Windows requires a certain update in terminology.

x86 versus x64   Intel originally used numbers to name its CPUs, such as 8086, 80286, 80386, and so on. To talk about them collectively, the industry replaced the leading numbers with an *x* and kept the numbers that stayed consistent for all the processors, thus **x86** describes the Intel CPU architecture for PCs. All the 32-bit versions of Windows were designed to run on x86 architecture.

Windows 7 is not covered on the CompTIA A+ Essentials exam, but you should still know it. Every version of Windows 7 comes in 32-bit and 64-bit on the same installation disc.

The move to 64-bit CPUs and, equally important, to 64-bit versions of Windows required some sort of change in terminology. Microsoft and others picked up the x# terminology and changed it to market 64-bit-only versions of their software, branding the 64-bit software as **x64**. A consumer, therefore, could look at a product such as Windows XP Professional x64 Edition and very quickly know that the software was designed for 64-bit CPUs rather than 32-bit CPUs.

The two x# uses—x86 and x64—don't really compare, but that's okay. Computer people love the letter *X* almost as much as car manufacturers do.

Software Compatibility

Transitions to updated architecture, such as the change from x86 to x64,

• **Figure 4.13**   64-bit Vista

create concern among users, because they fear that their old programs won't run or will run poorly, or that they'll have problems with compatibility down the road. Techs need to allay those fears by educating users properly. Here's the scoop in a nutshell.

Most of the 64-bit processors run either 32-bit or 64-bit versions of Windows without missing a beat. The 64-bit versions of Windows require a 64-bit CPU; they snicker at 32-bit (or x86) processors and refuse to play. Many companies have produced 64-bit versions of application software that only work with 64-bit Windows running with a 64-bit CPU. Great, right? But what about all those 32-bit applications out there working for a living? It gets interesting.

Windows Vista 64-bit versions support most 32-bit applications, sometimes without any user intervention and sometimes through explicit use of the Windows **compatibility mode** options. (Just for the record, you sometimes need to use Windows compatibility mode options to run older programs on Windows Vista 32-bit versions, so it's not just a function of 64-bit support for 32-bit apps.) Windows can try to emulate previous versions of Windows if an application balks at loading.

To run a program in an emulated version of Windows, you need to access the primary executable file that, when double-clicked, makes the program run. You may find these files in any one of a countless number of

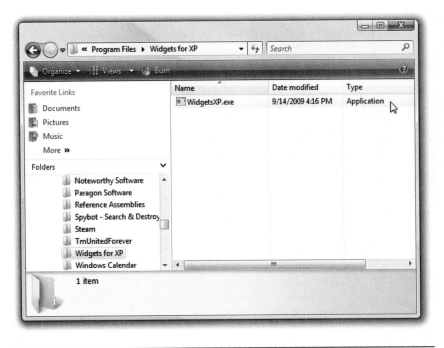

different places throughout your computer, but a quick example should suffice here. A user has a custom program—called "Widgets for XP"—designed to take advantage of particular features in Windows XP Professional with Service Pack 2 installed, but the program doesn't work in Windows Vista. Open Computer and go to C:\ Program Files\Widgets for XP and look for a file with the type listed as Application, such as WidgetsXP.exe (Figure 4.14). Right-click and select Properties.

On the Compatibility tab, select the checkbox next to *Run this program in compatibility mode for:* and select the OS of choice (Figure 4.15). In this case, you would select Windows XP (Service Pack 2) to provide optimal compatibility for the application. Windows saves the configuration change and tries to open the program in compatibility mode each time the program loads.

• **Figure 4.14**   Finding an executable file

• **Figure 4.15**   Compatibility mode options

■ The Windows Interface

All versions of Windows share certain characteristics, configuration files, and general look and feel. Here's some good news: You'll find the same, or nearly the same, utilities in almost all versions of Windows, and once you master one version—both GUI and command-line interface—you'll pretty much have them all covered. This section covers the essentials: where to find things, how to maneuver, and what common utilities are available. Where versions of Windows differ in concept or detail, I'll point that out along the way. For now, let's look at the common user interface.

User Interface

Windows offers a set of utilities, or **interfaces**, that every user should know about—both how and why to access them. And since every user should know about them, certainly every CompTIA A+ certified tech should as well! Let's take a quick tour of the typical Windows GUI.

Tech Tip

Knowledge Is Power
Odds are pretty good you already know the Windows interface— but do you know what the CompTIA A+ calls all these parts? Don't skip this section!

Login

Logging in to a Windows computer is something that we all do but few of us take time to appreciate. Your user name and password define what you can do on your computer. Every version of Windows supports multiple users on a single machine, so the starting point for any tour of the Windows user interface starts with the **login screen**. Figure 4.16 shows the old, ugly, but very functional Windows 2000 login screen.

Microsoft improved the login screen in Windows XP, creating a new type of login called the **Welcome screen** (Figure 4.17). If you're using Windows XP Home or Media Center, this is the only login screen you will see. Windows XP Professional also has the Welcome screen. If you're running a Windows XP Professional system that connects to a Windows domain, however, you go right back to the classic login screen (Figure 4.18).

● **Figure 4.16**   Windows 2000 login screen

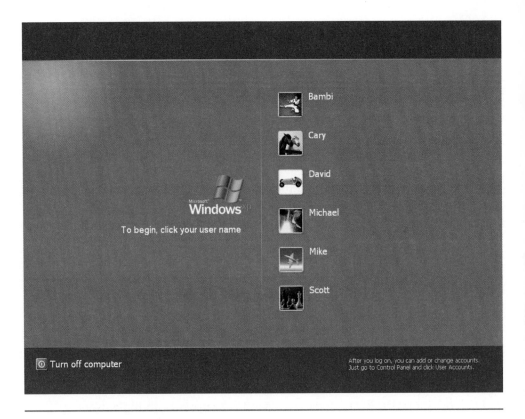

● **Figure 4.17**   Windows XP Welcome screen

Windows Vista dumped the old login screen entirely. All versions of Windows Vista use an improved version of XP's Welcome screen (Figure 4.19).

Desktop

The Windows **desktop** is your primary interface to the computer. The desktop is always there, underneath whatever applications you have open. The desktop analogy appeals to most people—we're used to sitting down at a desk to get work done. Figure 4.20 shows a nice, clean Windows XP desktop; note the

● **Figure 4.18**   Windows XP domain login screen

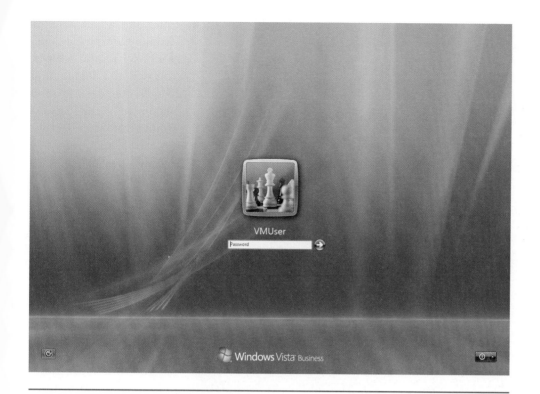

● **Figure 4.19**   Windows Vista Welcome screen

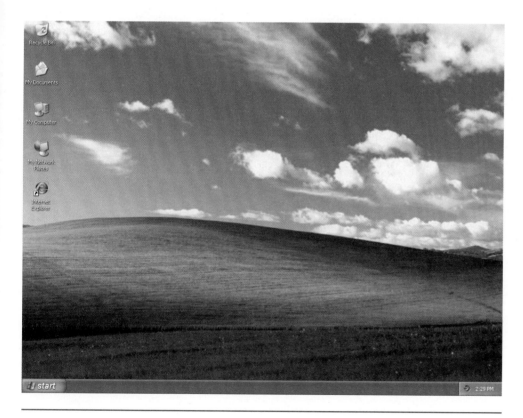

● **Figure 4.20**   Windows XP desktop

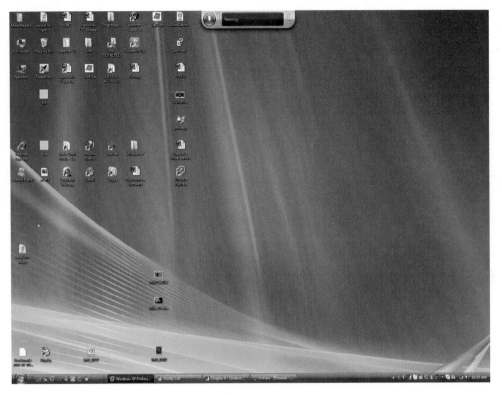

icons on the left and the various graphical elements across the bottom. You can add folders and files to the desktop and customize the background to change its color or add a picture. Most people like to do so—certainly, I do! As an example, Figure 4.21 shows the desktop from my home system—a Windows Vista Ultimate PC.

Clearly the Vista desktop differs a lot compared to the Windows XP desktop. What you're seeing is something called the Aero desktop. The **Aero** desktop adds a number of impressive aesthetic features to your desktop that Microsoft claims make the user experience more enjoyable and productive.

• **Figure 4.21**   Mike's messy desktop

Tech Tip

Your Desktop Is a Folder

Your desktop is actually a folder in your computer. Whatever is in that folder shows up on your desktop.

Vista Home Basic does not support the Aero desktop.

I'm not going to get into an argument on the value of the Aero desktop, but it is an important part of the Windows Vista (and Windows 7) interface. Most of the Aero features are overly technical—even for the CompTIA A+ exams—but the end result is a faster, smoother desktop with two interesting features: transparency and Flip 3D. **Transparency**, as the name implies, gives an adjustable amount of transparency to the edges of your windowed programs, as you can see in Figure 4.22.

Flip 3D enables you to view and select all of your open Windows in a 3-D format, as shown in Figure 4.23. It's actually very handy once you start using it.

• **Figure 4.22**   Transparency

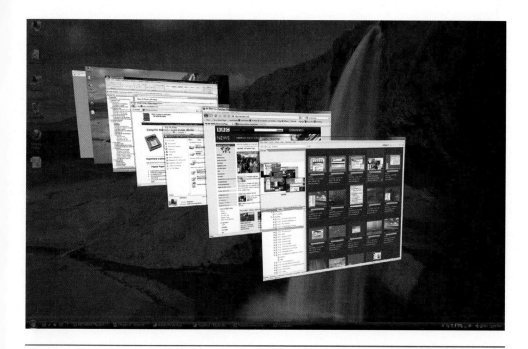

• **Figure 4.23**   Flip 3D

Flip 3D is fun to use. Press the WINDOWS KEY-TAB key combination to start it. Keep pressing the key combination to cycle through the windows. When the window you want is in the forefront, release the keys, and that window will be the active window on your screen. Try WINDOWS KEY-TAB-SHIFT to scroll through your windows in the opposite direction.

To use the Aero desktop, you must have a video card that supports Aero. We'll save the in-depth discussion for Chapter 13, "Learning Video and Multimedia," but for now here's what Microsoft says your video needs:

■ DirectX 9 capability or better

■ At least 128 megabytes of video RAM

■ Windows Display Driver Model (WDDM) driver

■ Pixel Shader version 2.0

Now that you know what you need (again, these will be covered in detail in Chapter 13), here's the easy way. When you install Vista, the installer checks your video to determine if it can support Aero. If your video card is capable, Aero is turned on automatically.

On an installed system, press the WINDOWS KEY-TAB combination. If Flip 3D appears, you have Aero. If it doesn't, Aero is not active.

To turn on Aero, right-click on your desktop and select the Personalize menu option. Next, select Window Color and Appearance. If you see a screen that looks like Figure 4.24, you already have Aero running. If you see a screen that looks like Figure 4.25, select the Windows Aero color scheme to activate the Aero desktop.

If you're running Aero, note that the Window Color and Appearance screen shown in Figure 4.24 has a slider to adjust the transparency settings and a checkbox to turn transparency off completely.

Tech Tip

Upgrade Time!

If you can't run on the Aero desktop, you need to upgrade your system to meet the minimum requirements. This usually means a new video card or updated video card drivers. See Chapter 13, "Learning Video and Multimedia," for details.

• **Figure 4.24**   You've got Aero!

There are a number of other features that, although not on the CompTIA A+ Essentials exam, you really should try. The WINDOWS KEY-T combination gives a preview of all minimized windows. ALT-TAB gives a preview of all running windows. Try Aero. It may not be the productivity tool Microsoft promises it to be, but it sure is fun.

Taskbar and Start Menu

The **taskbar** runs along the bottom of all Windows desktops and includes up to four sections (depending on the version of Windows and your configuration). Starting at the left side, these are the Start button, the Quick Launch toolbar,

• **Figure 4.25**   The lack of transparency and the flat window with no drop shadow show that Aero is not activated.

the running programs area, and the notification area. Although the taskbar by default sits at the bottom of the desktop, you can move it to either side or to the top of the screen.

One of the main jobs of the taskbar is to show the **Start button**, probably the most clicked button on all Windows systems. You can find the Start button on the far left end of the taskbar. Figure 4.26 shows the Start buttons for Windows 2000, Windows XP, and Windows Vista (in order). Click the Start button to bring up the Start menu, where you can see the applications installed on the system and start them. Now, move your mouse cursor onto the All Programs (Windows XP) or Programs (all other versions) menu item. When the All Programs/Programs menu appears, move the cursor to the Accessories menu. Locate the Notepad program and click it. By default, Windows hides lesser-used menu options, so if you don't see Notepad, click the double down arrows at the bottom of the Accessories menu to make Notepad appear.

Great! If you opened Notepad properly, you should see something like Figure 4.27, with Notepad displaying an untitled text page. Notice how Notepad shows up on the taskbar at the bottom of your screen. Most running programs appear on the taskbar in this way. Close the Notepad program by clicking on the button with the X in the upper-right corner of the Notepad window. Look again at the taskbar to see that Notepad no longer appears there.

Now look all the way to the right end of the taskbar. This part of the taskbar is known officially as the **notification area**, though many techs and the CompTIA A+ Essentials exam call it the **system tray**. You will at a minimum see the current time displayed in the system tray, and on most Windows systems you'll also see a number of small icons there. Figure 4.28 shows the system tray on my PC.

These icons show programs running in the background. Most programs run in a window. Background programs function like any other program except they do not use a window, simply because the nature of their particular jobs makes a window unnecessary. Thousands of programs like to run in the system tray: network status, volume controls, battery state (on laptops), and removable device status are just a few examples. What shows up on yours

● **Figure 4.26** Three different Windows Start buttons

You have a lot of clicking to do in this chapter, so take a moment to reflect on what I call the General Rules of Clicking. With a few exceptions, these rules always apply, and they really help in manipulating the Windows interface to do whatever you need done:

■ Click menu items once to use them.
■ Click icons once to select them.
■ Click icons twice to use them.
■ Right-click anything and select Properties to see its properties.

Microsoft calls the area at the far right of the taskbar the *notification area*, but you might see it referred to on the CompTIA A+ Essentials exam as the *system tray*.

● **Figure 4.27** Notepad application (note the buttons in the upper-right corner)

● **Figure 4.28** System tray showing several icons and the time

depends on your version of Windows, what hardware you use, and what background programs you have installed. Some of the icons in Figure 4.28, for example, include my antivirus program, a handy notification program for incoming Facebook and Twitter messages, and my UPS program.

Near the left end of the taskbar, next to the Start button, you will find the **Quick Launch toolbar** (Figure 4.29), a handy extra where you can select often-used programs with a single click. On Windows XP systems, the Quick Launch toolbar is not displayed on the taskbar by default, so before you can use this convenient feature, you must right-click the taskbar, select Properties, and check Show Quick Launch. To change the contents of the Quick Launch toolbar, simply drag icons onto or off of it.

• **Figure 4.29**   Quick Launch toolbar

The Many Faces of Windows Explorer

Windows Explorer enables you to manipulate files and folders stored on all the drives in or connected to your computer. Microsoft presents the tool in a variety of ways to help you focus quickly on what you want to accomplish. If you want to see the contents of an optical disc, for example, you can open **My Computer** (Windows 2000/XP) or **Computer** (Windows Vista/7) by double-clicking the icon on the desktop or selecting the icon from the Start menu to have Windows Explorer open with the drives displayed (Figure 4.30). To display the contents of a drive or folder, double-click it.

Windows Explorer in Windows 2000 has a fairly Spartan interface, whereas Windows XP offers a series of common tasks in a bar along the left side of the screen, as you can see in Figure 4.30. Windows Vista also offers tasks, but the options display in a bar below the location bar, near the top of the window (Figure 4.31).

When you access My Documents (Windows 2000/XP) or Documents (Windows Vista/7) by double-clicking the icon on the desktop or selecting from the Start menu, Windows opens Windows Explorer with your user folders displayed. Because your My Documents/Documents folder is stored (by default) on the C: hard drive, Windows Explorer shows the contents of that drive, drilled down specifically to your folders.

The fact that one way to open Windows Explorer is to double-click My Computer or Computer, and another way to open Windows Explorer is to double-click My Documents or Documents—and the two methods show different contents initially—leads many users to assume that they have two distinct tools. That's simply not the case. Windows Explorer

• **Figure 4.30**   Windows Explorer in Windows XP displaying the drives installed, as well as common tasks on the left

Mike Meyers' CompTIA A+ Guide: Essentials

● **Figure 4.31**   Windows Explorer in Windows Vista displaying the drives installed and showing tasks

changes what's displayed to suit specific tasks preset by Microsoft, but it's a single tool that can point to different locations on your computer.

Even better, you can change the look of Windows Explorer by clicking a button. The Folders button in Windows 2000 and Windows XP toggles the **Folders list** on or off on the left (Figure 4.32). The Folders list is a tree menu that enables you to move the focus of Windows Explorer to different folders or drives. The Folders list replaces the common tasks bar in Windows XP. Note that the Folders list is enabled by default in Windows Vista no matter whether you open the tool through Computer or Documents.

In Windows Vista, you can alter the view of Windows Explorer in several ways. On the taskbar, you can click the down arrow next to Views to change the size of the icons, the details displayed, and more. You can turn off the Folders list if desired by clicking the down arrow next to Organize and then selecting Layout from the menu options.

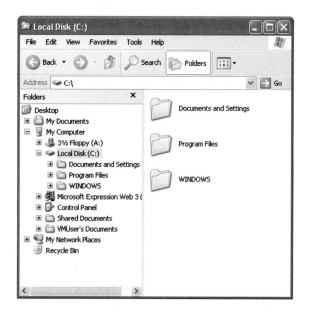

● **Figure 4.32**   Windows Explorer in Windows XP with the Folders list toggled on

You can easily create new folders in Windows Explorer by right-clicking inside a folder and selecting New | Folder from the context menu. Creating folders is a great way to keep your files organized!

The Folders list view makes copying and moving files and folders from one location to another very easy. The steps differ slightly when you copy to a folder on the same drive versus when you copy to a folder on a different drive, although the first step is the same: select a folder in the Folders list, and the contents of that folder appear in the main pane on the right.

To move or copy a file from one folder to another folder on the same drive, click and hold a file or folder in the main pane and then drag the cursor over to any folder in the Folders list. A → symbol will appear in Windows Vista and 7, although not in Windows 2000 or XP. Release the mouse button, and you move that file or folder to the new folder. If you want to copy a file or folder rather than move it, press the CTRL key on your keyboard and then click and drag into the desired folder. The → symbol (if any) changes to a +; release the mouse button to copy the file or folder.

To copy or move a file from one folder to another folder on a different drive, click and hold a file or folder in the main pane and then drag the cursor over to any folder in the Folders list, and a + symbol will appear. Release the mouse button, and you'll make a copy of that file or folder in the new folder. If you want to move a file or folder rather than just copy it, press the SHIFT key on your keyboard and then click and drag into the desired folder. The + symbol changes to a ? in Windows Vista/7 or just goes away in Windows 2000/XP; release the mouse button to move the file or folder.

Notice the differences in the icons displayed in Windows Explorer? Windows assigns different icons to different types of files, based on their **extensions**, the set of characters at the end of a filename, such as .EXE, .TXT, or .JPG. The oldest extensions, starting from back in the DOS era, are usually three characters, but current programs may use two-character extensions, such as .JS (JavaScript) or .AU (audio), or even four-character extensions, such as the

Try This!

Practice Moving and Copying

If the Folders list option is new to you and you haven't done a lot of moving or copying files or folders, Try This!

1. Open My Computer or Computer and double-click on the C: drive.

2. Right-click in a blank spot and select New | Folder from the context menu. This will create a new folder named New Folder by default. The name of the New Folder is highlighted for changing when you first create it. If you click elsewhere, the folder gets the default New Folder name.

3. Select the folder and press F2 or right-click and select Rename from the options. Change the name to something other than New Folder, such as temp, tmp, practice, etc. The rest of this exercise assumes you named the new folder "temp."

4. Click the Folders button if necessary to display the Folders list on the left part of the Windows Explorer screen.

5. In the Folders list, select the temp folder. The contents of that folder should be blank in the main pane.

6. Select any other folder in the Folders list to change the focus of the main pane.

7. Hold down the CTRL key and then click and drag a file or folder from that new folder so that the cursor hovers over the temp folder and you see the + symbol. Release the mouse button and then select the temp folder to see the file or folder you just copied. Note that if you don't hold the CTRL key down, you'll move rather than copy the file.

8. Try this a few more times to increase your comfort level with copying.

9. Move a file or folder from one folder to the temp folder and then back, verifying that you moved rather than just copied the file. Do *not* do this with any files or folders in the C:\Windows folder! When you move a file in Vista, you'll see the → appear before you release the mouse button. In Windows 2000/XP you won't see any symbol at all.

ubiquitous .HTML for Web pages. In rare cases, a filename might actually have no extension.

As you look at these icons on your own screen, some of you might say, "But I don't see any extensions!" That's because Windows hides them by default. To see the extensions in 2000/XP, select Tools | Folder Options to open the Folder Options dialog box (Figure 4.33). Click the View tab and uncheck *Hide extensions for known file types*. In Vista, click on Organize | Folder and Search Options | View tab to see the same dialog box.

There are two other very handy settings under the View tab, but to see the results well, you need to be in the C: drive of My Computer, as shown in Figure 4.34.

Go back into the View tab under Folder Options, click the *Show hidden files and folders* radio button, and then uncheck *Hide protected operating system files*. Click the *Apply to Folders* button in Windows Vista, the *Apply to All Folders* button in Windows XP, or the Apply button in Windows 2000. Your C: drive should look like Figure 4.35 (it shows the Windows XP version) when you are finished. As before, when you return to examining the folder contents, you will see the file extensions, and possibly some previously hidden files.

Now that those files are visible, you have the awesome responsibility of keeping them safe. In general, the less you handle your vital system files, the better. You'll learn some ways to do useful things with files that were previously hidden, but unless you really know what you're doing, it's best to leave them alone. Before you turn a PC over to someone who isn't a trained PC tech, you'll probably want to hide those system files again.

Microsoft has tried to help users organize their files and folders through various user folders and subfolders that you access through Windows Explorer. The different operating systems offer different choices, so let's look at My Documents and the User's Files.

My Documents, My [*Whatever*]   All versions of Windows provide a special folder structure for each user account so users have their own places to store

• **Figure 4.33**   Folder Options dialog box

• **Figure 4.34**   Default My Computer view where many things are hidden

• **Figure 4.35**   My Computer displaying hidden files and folders

• **Figure 4.36** XP Desktop Items dialog box

As with most tools in Windows, Microsoft gives you more than one way to accomplish tasks. In XP and Vista, try right-clicking the Start menu icon, selecting Properties, and choosing the Classic Start Menu radio button.

personal data. This folder grouping is called **My Documents** in Windows 2000 and XP. Many Windows programs take advantage of My Documents and by default store their files in the folder or in a subfolder.

Windows XP installations do not show My Documents on the desktop by default. On Windows XP, you can access it readily through the Start menu, or you can add it to your desktop. Right-click the desktop and select Properties to open the Display Properties dialog box. Select the Desktop tab, and then click on the Customize Desktop button to open the Desktop Items dialog box (Figure 4.36). On the General tab, select the checkbox next to My Documents, My Computer, or both, and then click OK to close the dialog box and make any selected icons appear on the desktop.

Windows XP adds a number of subfolders to My Documents: My Pictures (which offers filmstrip and thumbnail views of pictures you store there), My Music (which will fire up Media Player to play any file), My Videos (which, again, starts Media Player), and more. Figure 4.37 shows My Pictures, using the thumbnail view. Many applications have since jumped on the bandwagon and added their own My [*Whatever*] folders in My Documents. Before I retired my Windows XP machine, for example, I had My eBooks, My Web Sites, My Received Files, My Virtual Machines...My Goodness!

User's Files Windows Vista takes the equivalent of My Documents to a whole new level with the **User's Files** option. (Although a Documents folder is available, it's designed literally for documents, such as text files.) Click on

• **Figure 4.37** My Pictures subfolder in My Documents

the Start menu and you'll see a folder option with the user name of the account that's currently logged in to the computer. With that option, not only do you get all of the folders you get in Windows 2000/XP, but Vista also adds a number of other folders as well as interesting but important data such as your Internet Explorer favorites and copies of recent searches.

Just as with Windows XP, the user's folder does not show on the desktop by default. To see this folder, right-click on the desktop, select Personalize, and then click *Change desktop icons* on the left of the Personalization window. You'll see a Desktop Icon Settings dialog box where you can select the User's Files option to display the personal files of the logged-in user account. Figure 4.38 shows the User's Files folder for my editor, with the Desktop Icon Settings dialog box in the background.

No matter what your version of Windows decides to call it, My Documents/ User's Files is an incredibly critical part of your computer's directory structure. Not only does this store your most personal (and important) documents, it also stores most of the personalization settings for each user.

• **Figure 4.38** Typical user accounts folder in Windows Vista

Cross Check

The Computing Process

While you're reading about the various interface features of Windows, now would be a good time to review the section "How the PC Works" in Chapter 3, "The Visible PC," and put things in context. What are the four functions of computing? With which function does the operating system interact? Why is that a trick question?

The Command Line

Lest you get too comfortable with your nice, shiny GUI, remember that operating systems existed long before PCs were invented. Ancient, massive computers called *mainframes* and *minicomputers* employed sophisticated operating systems. It wasn't until the late 1970s that IBM went looking for an OS for a new *microcomputer*—the official name for the PC—the company was developing, called the IBM Personal Computer, better known as the PC. After being rebuffed by a company called Digital Research, IBM went to a tiny company that had written a popular new version of the programming language called BASIC. They asked the company president if he could create an OS for the IBM PC. Although his company had never actually written an OS, he brazenly said "Sure!" That man was Bill Gates, and the tiny company was Microsoft.

After shaking hands with IBM representatives, Bill Gates hurriedly began to search for an OS based on the Intel 8086 processor. He found a primitive OS called *Quick-and-Dirty Operating System* (*QDOS*), which was written by a one-man shop, and he purchased it for a few thousand dollars. After several minor changes, Microsoft released it as MS-DOS (Microsoft Disk Operating System) version 1.1. Although primitive by today's standards, MS-DOS 1.1 could provide all of the functions an OS needed. Over the years, MS-DOS went through version after version until the last Microsoft version, MS-DOS 6.22, was released in 1994. Microsoft licensed MS-DOS to PC makers so they could add their own changes and then rename the program. IBM called its version PC-DOS.

DOS used a command-line interface. You typed a command at a prompt, and DOS responded to that command. When Microsoft introduced Windows 95 and Windows NT, many computer users and techs thought that the command-line interface would go away, but techs not only continued to use the command line, they also *needed it* to troubleshoot and fix problems. With Windows 2000, it seemed once again that the command line would die, but again, that just didn't turn out to be the case.

Finally recognizing the importance of the command-line interface, Microsoft beefed it up in Windows XP and then again in Windows Vista. The command line in Windows XP and in Vista offers commands and options for those commands that go well beyond anything seen in previous Microsoft operating systems.

You can access the command line in Windows 2000 and XP by going to Start | Run, typing **cmd**, and pressing ENTER. In Windows Vista/7, you can simply type **cmd** in the Start menu Search box and press ENTER.

Recycle Bin

In Windows, a file is not erased when you delete it. Windows adds a level of protection in the form of a special folder called the **Recycle Bin**. When you delete a file in Windows, the file moves into the Recycle Bin. It stays there until you empty the Recycle Bin or restore the file, or until the Recycle Bin reaches a preset size and starts erasing its oldest contents.

To access the Recycle Bin's properties, right-click the icon and select Properties. The Recycle Bin's properties look different in different versions of Windows, but they all work basically the same. Figure 4.39 shows the properties of a typical Windows XP Recycle Bin. Note that you set the amount of drive space to use for the Recycle Bin, 10 percent being the default amount. If a hard drive starts to run low on space, this is one of the first places to check.

My Network Places/Network

Systems tied to a network, either via a network cable or by a modem, have a folder called **My Network Places** in XP or simply **Network** in Vista (Figure 4.40). This shows all the current network connections available to you. You'll learn about My Network Places in Chapter 16, "Learning Local Area Networking."

• **Figure 4.39**   Windows XP Recycle Bin Properties

● **Figure 4.40**   Network in Windows Vista

Control Panel

Accessed via the Start menu, the **Control Panel** (Figure 4.41) serves as a home for all manner of handy Windows applications, called **applets**, that enable you to modify Windows settings, create new user accounts, and even change your mouse cursor! Every tech worth their salt is intimately familiar with the Control Panel, so you'll be seeing a lot of it over the course of your CompTIA A+ Essentials exam preparation. If that sounds intimidating, don't worry. While there are quite a few applets in the Control Panel by default, you only really need to know about a handful of them, so the job is not quite as herculean as you might at first fear. In addition to all the default applets, some software applications that you install on your computer will add even more applets to the Control Panel, and the CompTIA A+ Essentials exam definitely doesn't cover those.

Windows Sidebar

Windows Vista comes with a GUI feature called the **Windows Sidebar**, a tool that sits on the desktop and enables small

● **Figure 4.41**   The Windows XP Control Panel in two views: Category (left) and Classic (right)

helper applications—called Microsoft Gadgets—to run. You can display a clock, for example, or a dynamic weather update. Vista comes with a handful of Gadgets, but developers have gone crazy with them, enabling you to add all sorts of useful tools, such as the Twitter feed and World of Warcraft search and realm status Gadgets in Figure 4.42.

Hot Keys

In Windows, you can use key combinations to go directly to various programs and places. Here's a fairly extensive list of general-purpose commands for Windows. Be aware that some applications may change the use of these commands.

Function Keys

- **F1**   Help
- **F2**   Rename
- **F3**   Search menu
- **F5**   Refresh the current window
- **F6**   Move among selections in current windows

Popular Hot Keys

- **CTRL-ESC**   Open Start menu
- **ALT-TAB**   Switch between open programs
- **ALT-F4**   Quit program
- **CTRL-Z**   Undo the last command
- **CTRL-A**   Select all the items in the current window
- **SHIFT-DELETE**   Delete item permanently
- **SHIFT-F10**   Open a shortcut menu for the selected item (this is the same as right-clicking an object)
- **SHIFT**   Bypass the automatic-run feature for optical media (by pressing and holding down the SHIFT key while you insert optical media)
- **ALT-SPACE**   Display the main window's System menu (from this menu you can restore, move, resize, minimize, maximize, or close the window)
- **ALT-ENTER**   Open the properties for the selected object

Working with Text

- **CTRL-C**   Copy
- **CTRL-X**   Cut
- **CTRL-V**   Paste
- **CTRL-Z**   Undo

• **Figure 4.42**   Windows Sidebar in action

Windows Key Shortcuts

These shortcuts use the special Windows key:

- **WINDOWS KEY**   Start menu
- **WINDOWS KEY-D**   Show desktop
- **WINDOWS KEY-E**   Windows Explorer
- **WINDOWS KEY-L**   Locks the computer
- **WINDOWS KEY-TAB**   Cycle through taskbar buttons (or Flip 3D with Windows Aero in Vista)
- **WINDOWS KEY-BREAK**   Open the System Properties dialog box

I've covered only the most basic parts of the Windows desktop in this chapter. The typical Windows desktop includes many other parts, but for techs and for the CompTIA A+ Essentials exam, what you've learned here about the desktop is more than enough.

Advanced Windows Features

In addition to the basics of the user interface, the CompTIA A+ Essentials exam expects you to know a few of Windows' more advanced features. After all, while you definitely need to know how to identify and navigate the various parts of the Windows interface, that information is only a tiny fraction of what you need to know to use the Windows operating system effectively. This section will familiarize you with a few powerful Windows features that you'll need to know about as a tech. Most of the information in this section applies to every version of Windows covered by the CompTIA A+ Essentials exam, but I'll point out differences wherever they arise.

Registry

The **Registry** is a huge database that stores everything about your PC, including information on all of the hardware in the PC, network information, user preferences, file types, and virtually anything else you might run into with Windows. Almost any form of configuration you do to a Windows system involves editing the Registry. Every version of Windows stores the numerous Registry files (called *hives*) in the \%SystemRoot%\System32\config folder. Fortunately, you rarely have to access these massive files directly. Instead, you can use a set of relatively tech-friendly applications to edit the Registry.

The CompTIA A+ Essentials exam does not expect you to memorize every aspect of the Windows Registry. You should, however, understand the basic components of the Registry, know how to edit the Registry manually, and know the best way to locate a particular setting.

Accessing the Registry

Before you look in the Registry, let's look at how you access the Registry directly by using a Registry editor. Once you know that, you can open the Registry on your machine and compare what you see to the examples in this chapter.

Windows 2000 comes with two Registry editors: REGEDT32.EXE, shown in Figure 4.43, and the much older REGEDIT.EXE, shown in Figure 4.44. You start either of these programs by going to a command prompt and typing its filename.

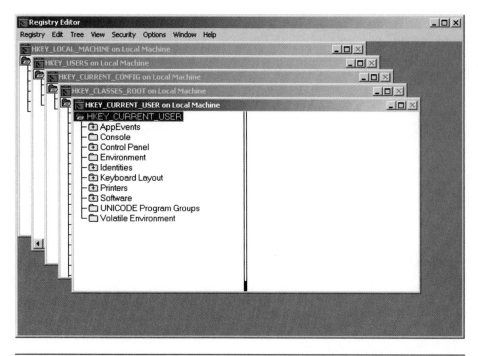

The reason for having two different Registry editors is long and boring, and explaining it would require a very dull 15-minute monologue (preferably with an angelic chorus singing in the background) about how the Registry worked in Windows 9*x* and Windows NT. Suffice it to say that in Windows 2000, only REGEDT32 is safe to use for actual editing, but you can use the older REGEDIT to perform searches, because REGEDT32's search capabilities are not very good.

Starting with Windows XP, Microsoft eliminated the entire two-Registry-editor nonsense by creating a new REGEDT32 that includes strong search functions. No longer are there two separate programs, but interestingly, entering either REGEDIT or REGEDT32 at a command prompt brings up the same program, so feel free to use either program name. We can also dispense with calling the Registry Editor by its filename and use its proper title.

• **Figure 4.43** REGEDT32 in Windows 2000

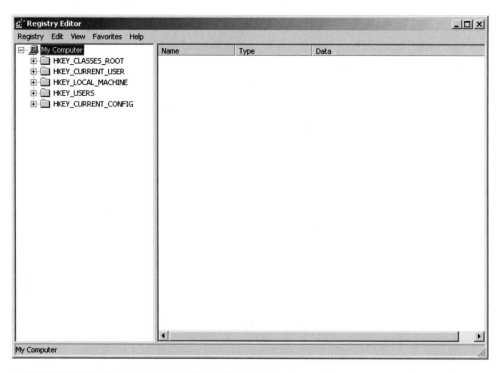

• **Figure 4.44** REGEDIT in Windows 2000

Registry Components

The Registry is organized in a tree structure similar to the folders in the PC. Once you open the Registry Editor in Windows, you will see five main subgroups, or **root keys**:

- HKEY_CLASSES_ROOT
- HKEY_CURRENT_USER
- HKEY_USERS
- HKEY_LOCAL_MACHINE
- HKEY_CURRENT_CONFIG

Try opening one of these root keys by clicking on the plus sign to its left;

note that more subkeys are listed underneath. A subkey also has other subkeys, or *values*. Figure 4.45 shows an example of a subkey with some values. Notice that the Registry Editor shows keys on the left and values on the right, just as Windows Explorer shows directories on the left and files on the right.

The secret to understanding the Registry is to understand the function of the five root keys first. Each of these root keys has a specific function, so let's take a look at them individually.

● **Figure 4.45** Typical Registry keys and values

HKEY_CLASSES_ROOT

This root key defines the standard *class objects* used by Windows. A class object is a named group of functions that define what you can do with the object it represents. Pretty much everything that has to do with files on the system is defined by a class object. For example, the Registry uses two class objects to define the popular MP3 sound file. If you search the Registry for the .MP3 file extension, you will find the first class object, which associates the .MP3 file extension with the name "Winamp.File" on this computer (Figure 4.46).

When writing about keys and values, I'll use the expression *key = value*.

● **Figure 4.46** Association of .MP3 with Winamp

Ah, but what are the properties of Winamp.File? That's what the HKEY_CLASSES_ROOT root key is designed to handle. Search this section again for "Winamp.File" (or whatever it said in the value for your MP3 file) and look for a subkey called "open." This variable determines the **file association** (Figure 4.47), which is the Windows term for what program to use to open a particular type of file.

This subkey tells the system everything it needs to know about a particular software item, from which program to use to open a file, to the type of icon used to show the file, to what to show when you right-click on that file type. Although it is possible to change most of these settings in the Registry Editor, the normal way is to choose more user-friendly methods. In Windows XP, for example, you can right-click on a file and select Properties, and then click the Change button on the General tab to open the Open With dialog box (Figure 4.48). From there you can browse to select the program you want to use.

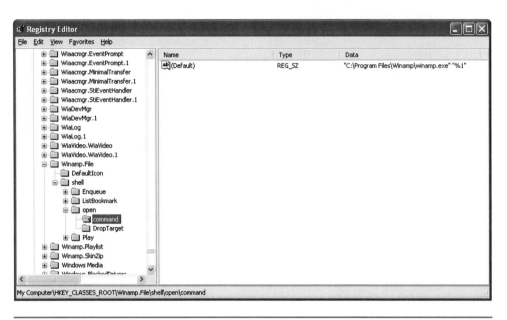

• **Figure 4.47**   Winamp file settings

• **Figure 4.48**   Changing the file association the easy way

HKEY_CURRENT_USER and HKEY_USERS

Windows is designed to support more than one user on the same PC, storing personalized information such as desktop colors, screensavers, and the contents of the desktop for every user that has an account on the system. HKEY_CURRENT_USER stores the current user settings, and HKEY_USERS stores all of the personalized information for all users on a PC. While you certainly can change items such as the screensaver here, the better way is to right-click on the desktop and select Properties.

HKEY_LOCAL_MACHINE

This root key contains all the data for a system's non-user-specific configurations. This encompasses every device and every program in your PC. For example, Figure 4.49 shows the description of a DVD drive.

HKEY_CURRENT_CONFIG

If the values in HKEY_LOCAL_MACHINE have more than one option, such as two different monitors, this root key defines which one is currently being used. Because most people have only one type of monitor and similar equipment, this area is almost never touched.

• **Figure 4.49** Registry information for a DVD drive

Microsoft Management Console

One of the biggest complaints about earlier versions of Windows was the wide dispersal of the many utilities needed for administration and trouble-shooting. Despite years of research, Microsoft could never find a place for all the utilities that would please even a small minority of support people. In a moment of sheer genius, Microsoft determined that the ultimate utility was one that the support people made for themselves! This brought on the creation of the amazing Microsoft Management Console.

The **Microsoft Management Console (MMC)** is simply a shell program in Windows that holds individual utilities called *snap-ins*. You can start the MMC by selecting Start | Run, typing **mmc**, and pressing ENTER to get a blank MMC. Blank MMCs aren't much to look at (Figure 4.50).

• **Figure 4.50** Blank MMC

You make a blank MMC useful by adding snap-ins, which include most of the utilities you use in Windows. Even the good old Device Manager is a snap-in. You can add as many snap-ins as you like, and you have many to choose from. Many companies sell third-party utilities as MMC snap-ins.

For example, to add the Device Manager snap-in, open the blank MMC, select File | Add/Remove Snap-in (Console | Add/Remove Snap-in in Windows 2000), and then click the Add button to open the Add Standalone Snap-in dialog box (in Vista, the Add or Remove Snap-ins dialog box). Here you will see a list of available snap-ins (Figure 4.51). Select Device Manager, and click the Add button to open a dialog box that prompts you to choose the local or a remote PC for the snap-in to work with. Choose Local Computer for this exercise, and click the Finish button. Click the Close button to close the Add Standalone Snap-in dialog box, and then click OK to close the Add/Remove Snap-in dialog box.

You should see Device Manager listed in the console. Click it. Hey, that looks kind of familiar, doesn't it (Figure 4.52)?

• **Figure 4.51**   Available snap-ins

• **Figure 4.52**   Device Manager as a snap-in

Once you've added the snap-ins you want, just save the console under any name, anywhere you want. I'll save this console as Device Manager, for example, and drop it on my desktop (Figure 4.53). I'm now just a double-click away from the Device Manager.

Administrative Tools

Windows combines the most popular snap-ins into an applet in the Control Panel called **Administrative Tools**. Open the Control Panel and open Administrative Tools (Figure 4.54).

Administrative Tools is really just a folder that stores a number of pre-made consoles. As you poke through these, notice that many of the consoles share some of the same snap-ins—nothing wrong with that. Of the consoles in a standard Administrative Tools collection, the ones you'll spend the most time with are Computer Management, Event Viewer, Reliability and Performance (or just Performance in Windows 2000/XP), and Services.

• **Figure 4.53**   The Device Manager shortcut on the desktop

The CompTIA A+ Essentials exam has little interest in some of these snap-ins, so this book won't cover them all. If I don't mention it, it's almost certainly not on the exam!

Page File

Windows uses a portion of the hard drive as an extension of system RAM, through what's called a *RAM cache*. A RAM cache is a block of cylinders on a hard drive set aside as what's called a **page file**, *swap file*, or *virtual memory*. When the PC starts running out of real RAM because you've loaded too many programs, the system swaps programs from RAM to the page file, opening more space for programs currently active. All versions of Windows use a page file, so here's how one works.

The default and recommended page file size is 1.5 times the amount of installed RAM on your computer.

• **Figure 4.54**   Administrative Tools

0 MB   4 GB

A   B   C

• **Figure 4.55**   A RAM thermometer showing that more programs take more RAM

Not enough RAM

0 MB   4 GB

A   B   C   D

• **Figure 4.56**   Not enough RAM to load program D

Virtual memory is a fully automated process and does not require any user intervention. Tech intervention is another story!

Let's assume you have a PC with 4 GB of RAM. Figure 4.55 shows the system RAM as a thermometer with gradients from 0 to 4 GB. As programs load, they take up RAM, and as more and more programs are loaded (labeled A, B, and C in the figure), more RAM is used.

At a certain point, you won't have enough RAM to run any more programs (Figure 4.56). Sure, you could close one or more programs to make room for yet another one, but you can't keep all of the programs running simultaneously. This is where virtual memory comes into play.

Windows' virtual memory starts by creating a page file that resides somewhere on your hard drive. The page file works like a temporary storage box. Windows removes running programs temporarily from RAM into the page file so other programs can load and run. If you have enough RAM to run all your programs, Windows does not need to use the page file—Windows brings the page file into play only when insufficient RAM is available to run all open programs.

To load, Program D needs a certain amount of free RAM. Clearly, this requires unloading some other program (or programs) from RAM without actually closing any programs. Windows looks at all running programs—in this case A, B, and C—and decides which program is the least used. That program is then cut out of or swapped from RAM and copied into the page file. In this case, Windows has chosen Program B (Figure 4.57). Unloading Program B from RAM provides enough RAM to load Program D (Figure 4.58).

0 MB   4 GB

A   C

B
Page file

D

• **Figure 4.57**   Program B being unloaded from memory

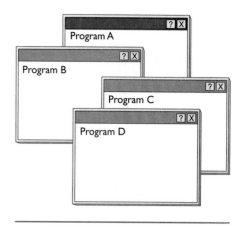

• Figure 4.59 You can't tell whether a program is swapped or not.

• Figure 4.58 Program B stored in the page file—room is made for Program D

It is important to understand that none of this activity is visible on the screen. Program B's window is still visible, along with those of all the other running programs. Nothing tells the user that Program B is no longer in RAM (Figure 4.59).

So what happens if you click on Program B's window to bring it to the front? The program can't actually run from the page file; it must be loaded back into RAM. First, Windows decides which program must be removed from RAM, and this time Windows chooses Program C (Figure 4.60). Then it loads Program B into RAM (Figure 4.61).

Swapping programs to and from the page file and RAM takes time. Although no visual clues suggest that a swap is taking place, the machine slows down quite noticeably as Windows performs the swaps. The alternative (Figure 4.62) is far less acceptable. Page files are a crucial aspect of Windows operation.

If you have a second hard drive installed in your PC, you can often get a nice performance boost by moving your page file from the C: drive (the default) to the second drive. To move your page file in all versions of Windows, go to the Control Panel | System applet and select the Advanced tab in 2000/XP or the Advanced system settings menu in Vista/7. This opens the System Properties dialog box with the Advanced tab selected. In the Performance section, click the Settings button to open the Performance Options dialog box. Select the Advanced tab, and then click the Change button in the Virtual Memory section. Select a drive from the list and give it a size or range, and you're ready to go.

Just don't turn virtual memory off completely. Although Windows can run without virtual memory, you will definitely take a performance hit.

• Figure 4.60 Program C is swapped to the page file.

0 MB   4 GB

A   B   D

C

Page file

• **Figure 4.61**   Program B is swapped back into RAM.

Application Execution Error

Insufficient memory to run this application. Quit one or more Windows applications and then try again.

OK

• **Figure 4.62**   The alternative to page files

Windows handles page files automatically, but occasionally you'll run into problems and need to change the size of the page file or delete it and let Windows re-create it automatically. The page file is PAGEFILE.SYS. You can often find it in the root directory of the C: drive, but again, that can be changed. Wherever it is, the page file is a hidden system file, which means in practice that you'll have to play with your folder-viewing options to see it.

■ Maintaining Windows

Every computer running a Windows operating system requires ongoing maintenance to make sure nothing goes wrong and that the system keeps running smoothly. Not that long ago, Windows had a bad rap as being difficult to maintain and challenging when troubleshooting problems. That's no longer true. Microsoft used its decades of experience with operating systems to search for ways to make the tasks of maintaining and troubleshooting less onerous. They've done such a good job with the latest versions of Windows that, out of the box, they are easy to optimize and maintain, although troubleshooting—and all operating systems share this—is still a bit of a challenge.

This section starts with maintenance and optimization, so let's make sure you know what these two terms mean. *Maintenance* means jobs you do from time to time to keep Windows running well, such as running hard drive utilities. CompTIA sees *optimization* as jobs you do to your Windows system to make it better—a good example is adding RAM. This section covers the standard maintenance and optimization activities performed on Windows and the tools techs use to perform them.

Maintaining Windows can be compared to maintaining a new automobile. Of course, a new automobile comes with a warranty, so most of us just take it to the dealer to get work done. In this case, *you* are the mechanic, so you need to think as an auto mechanic would think. First, an auto mechanic needs to apply recalls when the automaker finds a serious problem. For a PC tech, that means keeping the system patches announced by Microsoft up to date. You also need to check on the parts that wear down over time. On a car that might mean changing the oil or rotating the tires. In a Windows system that includes keeping the hard drive and Registry organized and uncluttered.

Patches, Updates, and Service Packs

Updating Windows has been an important, but often neglected, task for computer users. Typically, Microsoft finds and corrects problems with its software and releases patches on the second Tuesday of every month. Sadly, because earlier versions of Windows let users decide when, if ever, to update their computers, the net result could be disastrous. The Blaster worm hammered computers all over the world in the summer of 2003, causing thousands of computers to start rebooting spontaneously—no small feat for a tiny piece of programming! Blaster exploited a flaw in Windows 2000/XP and spread like wildfire, but Microsoft had *already corrected* the flaw with a security update weeks earlier. If users had simply updated their computers, the virus would not have caused such widespread damage.

The Internet has enabled Microsoft to make updates available, and **Windows Update** can grab those updates and patch user systems easily and automatically. Even if you don't want to allow Windows Update to patch your computer automatically, it'll nag you about updates until you patch your system. Microsoft provides the Windows Update service for all versions of Windows.

Once Microsoft released Service Pack 2 for Windows XP, it began pushing for wholesale acceptance of automatic updates from Windows Update. You can also start Windows Update manually. When your computer is connected to the Internet, start the utility in Windows 2000 by selecting Start | Windows Update. In Windows XP/Vista/7 you will find it at Start | All Programs | Windows Update. When you run Windows Update manually, the software connects to the Microsoft Web site and scans your computer to determine what updates you may need. Within a few seconds or minutes, depending on your connection speed, you'll get a straightforward screen like the one shown in Figure 4.63.

You have several choices here, although two are most obvious. If you click the

> You might be asked about installing service packs and patches on the CompTIA A+ Essentials exam. Pay attention to the steps listed here.

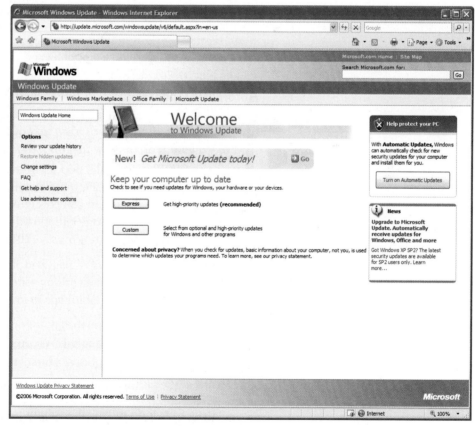

• **Figure 4.63**   Microsoft Windows Update page

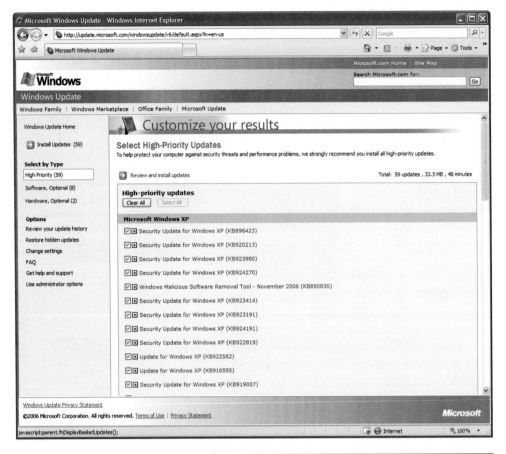

Express button, Windows Update will grab any high-priority updates—these are security patches—and install them on your computer. If you click the Custom button, you can select from a list of optional updates.

Figure 4.64 shows the updater with a list of patches and security updates. You can scroll through the list and review the description of each update. You can deselect the checkbox next to a patch or update, and Windows Update will not download or install it. If you click the Clear All button, as you might suspect, all the updates will be removed from the list. When you click Install Updates, all the updates remaining in the list will be installed.

• **Figure 4.64**   Choose updates to be installed.

Automatic Updates

Updates are so important that Microsoft gives you the option to update Windows automatically through the **Automatic Updates** feature. Actually, it nags you about it! Soon after installing Windows (a day or two, in my experience), a message balloon will pop up from the taskbar suggesting that you automate updates. If you click this balloon, the Automatic Updates Setup Wizard runs, with which you can configure the update program. You say you've never seen this message balloon but would like to automate the update process? No problem. In Windows 2000 and XP, simply right-click My Computer (on the Start menu), select Properties, click the Automatic Updates tab, and select Automatic Update options. Or, open the Control Panel and double-click the Automatic Updates icon. In Windows Vista, go to Start | Windows Update to open the Windows Update dialog box. Click the Change settings menu item on the left for options. Whenever your computer connects to the Web, it checks the Windows Update page. What happens next depends on the setting you choose. You have four choices:

- **Automatic (recommended)** or **Install updates automatically (recommended)**   Windows Update will simply keep your computer patched up and ready to go. This is the best option for most users, although not necessarily good for users of portable computers. Nobody wants to log in to a slow hotel dial-up connection and have most of your bandwidth sucked away by Automatic Updates downloading hot fixes!

- **Download updates…** Windows Update downloads all patches in the background and then, when complete, tells you about them. You have the option at that point to install or not install.

- **Notify me…** or **Check for updates…** Windows Update simply flashes a dialog box that tells you updates are available but does not download anything until you say go. This is the best option for users of portable computers. You can download files when it's convenient for you, such as when you're home rather than traveling on business.

- **Turn off Automatic Updates** or **Never check for updates (not recommended)** This does precisely what is advertised. You get neither automatic patches nor notification that patches are available. Only use this option on a system that does not or cannot connect to the Internet. If you're online, your computer needs to be patched!

When Windows Update works the way Microsoft wants it to work, it scans the Microsoft Web site periodically, downloads important patches as they appear, and then installs them on your computer. If you opted for the download-but-don't-install option, Windows Update simply notifies you when updates are downloaded and ready to install (Figure 4.65).

Windows Vista gives you the option—enabled by default—to have Windows Update include recommended updates along with important updates when it downloads or notifies you about their availability. If you've got a decent Internet connection, this can be a useful tool for keeping your drivers and such updated.

Temporary File Management with Disk Cleanup

You should run the **Disk Cleanup** utility regularly to make sure you've cleared out the junk files that accumulate from daily use. All that late-night Web surfing doesn't just use up time; it also uses up disk space, leaving behind hundreds of temporary Internet files. Those, and other bits and pieces (such as those "deleted" files still hanging around in your Recycle Bin), can add up to a lot of wasted disk space if you don't periodically clean them out.

You can reach this tool through the Start menu (Start | All Programs | Accessories | System Tools), or you can open My Computer or Computer, right-click the drive you want to clean up, and select Properties. Right there in the middle of the General tab, you'll find the Disk Cleanup button.

When you click the Disk Cleanup button, the application firsts calculates the space you can free up and then displays the Disk Cleanup dialog box, which tells you how much disk space it can free up—the total amount possible as well as the amount you'll get from each category of files it checks. Vista adds an extra feature when you click the Disk Cleanup button, asking if you wish to clean up all the files on the computer or just your files. In Figure 4.66, the list of files to delete only has a few categories checked, and the actual amount of disk space to be gained by allowing Disk Cleanup to delete these files is much smaller than the estimate. As you select and deselect choices, watch this value change.

• **Figure 4.65** Windows Update balloon message

Microsoft offers the Microsoft Update tool (Windows XP) and the System Update Readiness Tool (Vista, 7) to help you determine if your system is ready to update to a newer version of Windows. You can obtain this tool from the Microsoft Web site.

If you scroll down through the list, you will see a choice to compress old files. What do you know, Disk Cleanup does more than just delete files? In fact, this file compression trick is where Disk Cleanup really, uh, cleans up. This is one of the few choices where you will gain the most space. The other big heavyweight category is Temporary Internet Files, which Disk Cleanup will delete. Try Disk Cleanup on a computer that gets hours of Internet use every day and you'll be pleased with the results.

• **Figure 4.66**   Disk Cleanup dialog box

CCleaner also helps clean all of the most common Web browsers and a number of popular applications.

Registry Maintenance

Your Registry is a huge database that Windows updates every time you add a new application or hardware or make changes to existing applications or hardware. As a result, the Registry tends to be clogged with entries that are no longer valid. These usually don't cause any problems directly, but they can slow down your system. Interestingly, Microsoft does not provide a utility to clean up the Registry. To clean your Registry, you need to turn to a third-party utility. Quite a few Registry cleaner programs are out there, but my favorite is the freeware CCleaner by Piriform. You can download the latest copy at www.ccleaner.com.

Before you start cleaning your Registry with wild abandon, keep in mind that all Registry cleaners are risky in that they may delete something you want in the Registry. Because Microsoft makes changes to the Registry for every version of Windows, make sure your utility supports the Windows version you're running. This is especially true for any 64-bit version of Windows! I've used CCleaner for a while and it has worked well for me—your experience may differ.

Security: Spyware/Antivirus/Firewall

You simply cannot run a computer today without a large number of security programs to protect you from malicious attacks from spyware, malware, viruses, and hacking. In fact, the installation, monitoring, and updating of these programs (and possibly even hardware) is so important that they get their own chapter. Head to Chapter 19, "Learning Computer Security," for a complete discussion of how to keep your computer safe!

Error-Checking and Disk Defragmentation

Keeping drives healthy and happy is a key task for every tech. Error-checking and Disk Defragmenter are the key Windows maintenance tools used to accomplish this task.

When you can't find a software reason (and there are many possible ones) for a problem such as a system freezing on shutdown, the problem might be the actual physical hard drive. The tool to investigate that is Error-checking. You can perform Error-checking by using the CHKDSK command from a command line, from the Start | Run dialog box, or by using Start | Start Search. You can also access the tool through the GUI by opening My Computer or Computer, right-clicking on the drive you want to check, selecting Properties, and then clicking the Tools tab. Click Check Now to have Error-checking scan the drive for bad sectors, lost clusters, and similar problems, and repair them if possible.

Run the Disk Defragmenter (Figure 4.67) on a regular basis to keep your system from slowing down due to files being scattered in pieces on your hard drive. Before you click the Defragment button, click the Analyze button to have Windows analyze the disk and determine if defragmentation is actually necessary. If you use Vista/7, your system is defragged automatically.

• **Figure 4.67**   Vista Disk Defragmenter

Error-checking and Disk Defragmenter are such critical maintenance features that you really should have them run automatically. Take a moment to see how to schedule these and other critical jobs.

Scheduling Maintenance

Maintenance only works properly when you do it at regular intervals. Depending on the version of Windows installed, you can schedule maintenance jobs to run automatically. The CompTIA Essentials objectives define three areas to consider for scheduled maintenance: Defragmentation, Scandisk/Check Disk, and Startup programs. For the most part, we use the Task Scheduler, although this depends on the task and the version of Windows.

Task Scheduler/Scheduled Tasks

Two versions of Task Scheduler are available: Windows 2000 and XP run Version 1.0, and Vista/7 run Version 2.0. Microsoft called it Scheduled Tasks in Windows 2000/XP, but reverted to Task Scheduler in Windows

Vista. In both versions you can choose an executable program and define when you want that program to run. Figures 4.68 and 4.69 show Scheduled Tasks running a backup at a certain time of day.

Version 2.0 is much more powerful and flexible, dividing tasks into triggers, actions, and conditions. *Triggers* are actions or schedules that start a program. *Actions* are steps that define

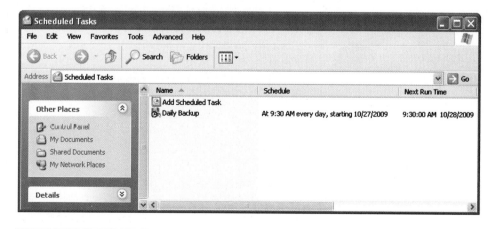

• **Figure 4.68**   Windows XP Scheduled Tasks (Version 1.0)

● **Figure 4.69**   Daily Backup Schedule tab in Windows XP

both the program to run and how it is to run. *Conditions* are extra criteria that must be met for the program to run. (Is the system idle? Is it connected to the Internet?) Figure 4.70 shows the Conditions tab for a sample task.

To open Task Scheduler, go to Start I All Programs or Programs I Accessories I System Tools I Task Scheduler or Scheduled Tasks. Note the variation in the name of the utility in the Start menu options.

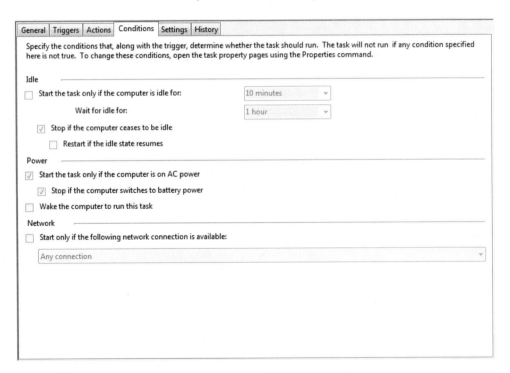

● **Figure 4.70**   Conditions tab in the Windows Vista Task Scheduler (Version 2.0)

The key to running scheduled maintenance is to know the names of the executable programs and any special switches you may need to enter. As we go through each of these I'll show you the names.

Defragmentation

To defragment, you need to run Disk Defragmenter (as you know), so you'll look for the executable file called DEFRAG.EXE. In Windows 2000 and XP, open Scheduled Tasks, browse for DEFRAG.EXE, and then add the drive you want to defragment, as shown in Figure 4.71.

If you use Windows Vista/7 and want to change when Disk Defragmenter runs (or turn it off completely), open the Start menu, type **defrag**, and press ENTER. You can start defragging right away or modify/disable the task in the Disk Defragmenter: Modify Schedule dialog box (Figure 4.72).

It's best to run Disk Defragmenter every evening if possible. If you're using Vista, take advantage of the "only run when idle" condition to keep Disk Defragmenter from interrupting possibly more important tasks.

• **Figure 4.71**   Scheduling a disk defragmentation in Windows XP

Error-checking (Scandisk and Check Disk)

The tool you know and love as Error-checking appears on the CompTIA A+ objectives as *Scandisk* and *Check Disk*. (Neither tool exists on modern versions of Windows.) Regardless of what you call Error-checking, setting up Task Scheduler to run it automatically is a good thing.

Using the technique you just learned to set up a scheduled task with Disk Defragmenter, create another scheduled task to run Error-checking. Its executable is called CHKDSK.EXE (Figure 4.73). There are two switches you should use: /F to repair sectors and /R to tell Error-checking to attempt to recover data on known bad sectors.

The CompTIA A+ Essentials exam may use either name for the utility for scheduling maintenance in Windows. Remember that Windows 2000 and Windows XP label the tool *Scheduled Tasks*; Windows Vista (and Windows 7) label it *Task Scheduler*.

The CompTIA A+ Essentials exam calls the Disk Defragmenter program "Defrag," the common tech slang term for it.

No versions of Windows run Error-checking automatically, so you'll need to set up a task on the computer if you wish to do so.

• **Figure 4.72**   Vista's Disk Defragmenter schedule

• Figure 4.73 Scheduling Error-checking in Windows XP

You should remember that you can configure the System Configuration utility with startup selections for troubleshooting. After using the System Configuration utility to change your startup programs, you can choose Normal startup to load all drivers and services. A Diagnostic startup loads basic services only, and a Selective startup enables you to select which system services and startup items to load on startup.

Opinions vary on how often you should run Error-checking as a scheduled task. For the CompTIA Essentials exam, a monthly check is considered a good idea. For the real world, you should run Error-checking when you suspect a problem with your drives.

Startup Programs

Techs use the **System Configuration utility (MSCONFIG.EXE)** to edit and troubleshoot operating system and program startup processes and services. It has been available in all Windows operating systems except Windows 95 and Windows 2000. Prior to Windows Vista, the System Configuration utility offered quick access to troubleshoot and edit the BOOT.INI file. It still offers some of these features in Vista, such as the capability to disable or enable troublesome or unwanted services and startup items. The BCD data store is used in place of the BOOT.INI file in Windows Vista, however, so you obviously cannot use the System Configuration utility to edit the BOOT.INI file in Vista.

To start the System Configuration utility, go to Start | Run or Start | Start Search, enter **msconfig**, and click OK or press EN-TER (Figure 4.74). The program will run automatically in Windows XP; in Vista you may need to provide the necessary credentials or response, depending on the User Account Control (UAC) setup.

• Figure 4.74   The Windows Vista System Configuration utility

Optimizing Windows

Maintenance is about keeping Windows' performance from degrading with time and use. Of course, you don't just want to keep trouble at bay—you want to make your systems better, stronger, faster! Anything you do that makes Windows better than it was before, such as adding a piece of software or hardware to make something run better, is an optimization.

Installing and Removing Software

Probably the most common optimization performed on any PC is adding and removing applications. Installing and removing software is part of the normal life of any PC. Each time you add or remove software, you are making changes and decisions that can affect the system beyond whatever the program does, so it pays to know how to do it right.

System Information

Windows comes with a handy built-in utility known as the **System Information tool** (Figure 4.75) that collects information about hardware resources, components, and the software environment. When it finishes doing that, it provides a nice and tidy little report, enabling you to troubleshoot and diagnose any issues and conflicts. As with many other tools you can access from the Start | Run or Start | Start Search dialog box, the CompTIA A+ Essentials exam refers to System Information by its executable, **MSINFO32.EXE**.

• **Figure 4.75**   System Information

You can start System Information in one of the following ways:

- Choose Start | Programs or All Programs | Accessories | System Tools | System Information.

- In Windows XP, click Start, click Run, and then type **msinfo32** and click OK. In Windows Vista, open the Start Search box, type **msinfo32**, and press ENTER.

It is also important to note that you can use System Information to gather information about remote computers by selecting View | Remote Computer and then entering the remote computer's network machine name. Under Tools, you even get quick access to System Restore and the DirectX Diagnostic Tool, a tool for checking your video card.

Installing Software

Most application programs are distributed on optical discs (although this is slowly changing). Windows supports **Autorun**, a feature that enables the operating system to look for and read a special file called—wait for it— AUTORUN.INF. Immediately after a removable media device (optical disc or thumb drive) is inserted into your computer, whatever program is listed in AUTORUN.INF runs automatically. Most application programs distributed on removable media have an autorun file that calls up the installation program.

Sometimes, however, you need to institute the installation sequence yourself. Perhaps the installation disc lacks an Autorun installation program, or perhaps Windows is configured so that you must start programs on optical discs manually. In some cases, a disc may contain more than one program, and you must choose which of them to install. Regardless of the reason, beginning the installation manually is a simple and straightforward process of using the **Add or Remove Programs** applet in the Control Panel in Windows XP. Windows 2000 calls the applet Add/Remove Programs. Click the Add New Programs button (Figure 4.76), follow the prompts, and provide the media or location of the files. In Windows Vista and 7, Microsoft has replaced the Add or Remove Programs applet with **Programs and Features**, which does not have the Add New Programs feature.

• **Figure 4.76**   Add New Programs

If you have sufficient permissions to install an application—your account is a member of the Administrators group in Windows 2000, for example, or is an Administrator account in Windows XP and up—the application will begin its installation routine. If you don't have sufficient permissions to install an application, Windows will stop the installation.

With Windows Vista/7, UAC complicates the installation process a bit. You will most likely be prompted by UAC when installing an application to give you time to review what is happening to your system in case you did not approve of the program being installed. If you are using an Administrator account, you can simply click Continue and finish the installation. Should you be logged in with a less privileged account, you will need to enter a user name and password of an account with administrative privileges. Some installers have trouble letting UAC know that they need more privileges and simply fail no matter what account you are logged in with. In those cases it is best to right-click the installer icon and select Run as Administrator to give the installer the access it expects from the start.

Assuming all is well, you typically first must accept the terms of a software license before you can install an application. These steps are not optional; the installation simply won't proceed until you accept all terms the software manufacturer requires and, in many cases, enter a correct code. You may also be asked to make several decisions during the installation process. For example, you may be asked where you would like to install the program and if you would like certain optional components installed. Generally speaking, it is best to accept the suggested settings unless you have a very specific reason for changing the defaults.

Removing Software

Each installed application program takes up space on your computer's hard drive, and programs that you no longer need simply waste space that could be used for other purposes. Removing unnecessary programs can be an important piece of optimization.

You remove a program from a Windows PC in much the same manner as you install it. That is, you use the application's own uninstall program, when possible. You normally find the uninstall program listed under the application's icon on the Start menu, as shown in Figure 4.77.

If an uninstall program is not available, use the appropriate Windows Control Panel applet to remove the software. Figure 4.78 shows this applet in Windows Vista. You select the program you want to remove and click the Uninstall/Change button or Change/Remove button. Windows displays a message warning you that the program will be permanently removed from your PC. If you're certain you want to continue, click Yes.

• **Figure 4.77**   Uninstall me!

You may then see a message telling you that a shared file that appears to no longer be in use is about to be deleted, and asking your approval. Generally speaking, it's safe to delete such files. If you do not delete them, they will likely be orphaned and remain unused on your hard disk forever. In some cases, clicking the Uninstall/Change or Change/Remove button starts the application's install program (the one you couldn't find before) so you can modify the installed features. This is a function of the program you're attempting to remove. The end result should be the removal of the application and all of its pieces and parts, including files and Registry entries.

Adding or Removing Windows Components/Features

When you installed Windows, it tried to guess which optional Windows components you would need. It installed Notepad, modem support, and games on your computer. You can remove these Windows components from your system if you

• Figure 4.78   Programs and Features applet

like, and add other components as well. If you're adding components, you'll need a copy of your Windows CD/DVD, or another location where the Windows source files are stored. This task really hasn't changed from previous versions of Windows.

To add or remove a Windows component in Windows 2000/XP, open the Add/Remove Programs or Add or Remove Programs applet in the Control Panel. From here, select Add/Remove Windows Components, which opens the Windows Components Wizard (Figure 4.79). You can select an installed program here. You can see how frequently it is used, how much disk space it uses, and (sometimes) the last time it was used.

In Windows Vista/7, open the Programs and Features applet in the Control Panel, and then click the *Turn Windows features on or off* option on the Tasks list. Click Continue if prompted by UAC and you will be presented with the Windows Features dialog box (Figure 4.80). To toggle a feature on or off, simply click its checkbox. Unlike previous versions of Windows, you no longer need to have the installation disc to turn on features.

• Figure 4.79   Windows Components Wizard

• **Figure 4.80**   Windows Features dialog in Vista

Installing/Optimizing a Device

The processes for optimizing hardware in Windows are absolutely identical, even down to the troubleshooting utilities, and are very similar to the steps for installing a new device. The installation process is covered in every chapter of this book that deals with one type of device or another, so this section concentrates on the issues that fit best under optimization.

The CompTIA A+ Essentials exam tests you on installing and optimizing devices.

Driver Updates

Device manufacturers occasionally update their drivers. Most of these updates take place to fix problems, but many updates incorporate new features. Whatever the case, when one of your devices gets an updated driver, it's your job to install it. Windows/Microsoft Update provides an easy method to update drivers from manufacturers that take advantage of the service. If you are using Windows 2000 or XP, you usually need to select the Custom option to see these updates because the Express option only installs high-priority updates. When you click on the Custom option, look under Hardware, Optional (on the left) to see if Windows has any driver updates (Figure 4.81).

If you are using Vista/7, you will need to click *View available updates* to see if any drivers are available for your system. No matter what version of Windows you have, take some time to read what these updates do—sometimes you may choose not to install a driver update because it's not necessary or useful to your system.

If Windows does not put a driver update in the Windows Update tool, how do you know a device needs updating? The trick is to know your devices. Video card manufacturers update drivers quite often. Get in the habit of registering your video card with the manufacturer to stay up to date. Any very new device is also a good candidate for an update. When you buy that new cool toy for your system, make a point to head over to the

● **Figure 4.81**   Optional Hardware updates

● **Figure 4.82**   A digitally signed driver

manufacturer's Web site and see if any updates have come out since it was packaged for sale. That happens more often than you might think!

Driver Signing

Device drivers become part of the operating system and thus have the potential to cause lots of problems if they're written poorly. To protect Windows systems from bad device drivers, Microsoft uses **driver signing**, which means that each driver has a digital signature. Any drivers included on the Windows installation media or at the Windows Update Web site are digitally signed. Once you have installed a driver, you can look at its Properties to confirm that it was digitally signed. Figure 4.82 shows a digitally signed network card driver.

When an unsigned driver is detected during hardware installation, you'll see the message shown in Figure 4.83 offering you the choice to stop or continue the installation. Signed drivers are more or less a sure thing, but that doesn't mean unsigned ones are a problem—just consider the source of the driver and ensure that your device works properly after installation.

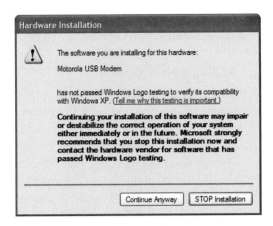

● **Figure 4.83**   Stop or continue installation of an unsigned driver

You can control how Windows behaves when drivers are being installed. Click the Driver Signing button on the Hardware tab of the System Properties dialog box to display the Driver Signing Options dialog box, shown in Figure 4.84. If you select Ignore, Windows will install an unsigned driver without warning you. If you select Warn, you will be prompted when Windows detects an unsigned driver during driver installation, and you will be given the opportunity to either stop or continue the installation. Choosing Block will prevent the installation of unsigned drivers.

The default Driver Signing setting is Warn. This also is the default setting during installation, so you will always be warned when Windows detects an unsigned driver during Windows installation. This is no problem for a standard installation, when you are sitting at the computer, responding to all prompts—but it is a problem for automated, unattended installations. This is a good reason to check out all your device drivers before installing Windows. In 64-bit versions of Windows, all drivers must be signed. No exceptions. Microsoft wants to keep tight controls on the drivers to improve stability.

● **Figure 4.84**   Driver Signing Options dialog box

Device Manager

You've worked a bit with **Device Manager** earlier in this chapter when configuring snap-ins; it's also the tool to use when optimizing device drivers. Right-click on a device in Device Manager to display the context menu. From here you can update or uninstall the driver, disable the device, scan for hardware changes, or display the Properties dialog box. When you open the Properties dialog box, you'll see several tabs that vary according to the specific device. Most devices have General, Driver, Details, and Resources tabs. The tab that matters most for optimization is the Driver tab.

The Driver tab has buttons labeled Driver Details, Update Driver, Roll Back Driver, and Uninstall. Driver Details lists the driver files and their locations on disk. Update Driver opens the Hardware Update Wizard—not very useful given that the installation programs for almost all drivers do this automatically. The Roll Back Driver option is a different story. It enables you to remove an updated driver, thus rolling back to the previous driver version. Roll Back Driver (Figure 4.85) is a lifesaver when you install a new driver

● **Figure 4.85**   Rolling back to the previous driver

• **Figure 4.86**   Add Hardware Wizard

• **Figure 4.87**   List of installed hardware

and suddenly discover it's worse than the driver it replaced! Uninstall removes the driver.

Adding a New Device

Windows should automatically detect any new device you install in your system. If Windows does not detect a newly connected device, use the Add Hardware Wizard or Add Hardware to get the device recognized and drivers installed (Figure 4.86). You'll find it on the Hardware tab of the System Properties dialog box.

Click Next on the Welcome screen, and the wizard searches for hardware that has been connected but does not yet have a driver installed. If it detects the device, select it, and the wizard installs the driver. You may have to point to the source location for the driver files. If the wizard does not detect the device, which is very likely, it will ask you if the hardware is connected. When you answer yes and click Next, it gives you a list of installed hardware, similar to Figure 4.87.

If the device is in the list, select it and click Next. If not, scroll to the bottom and select *Add a new hardware device*, and then click Next. If the device is a printer, network card, or modem, select *Search for and install the hardware automatically* and click Next. In that case, once the wizard detects the device and installs the driver, you're finished. If you do see your device on the list, your best hope is to select *Install the hardware that I manually select from a list*. In the subsequent screens, select the appropriate device category, select the device manufacturer and the correct model, and respond to the prompts from the Add Hardware Wizard to complete the installation.

Performance Options

One optimization you can perform on all Windows versions is setting Performance Options. **Performance Options** are used to configure CPU, RAM, and virtual memory (page file) settings. To access these options in Windows 2000/XP, right-click My Computer and select Properties, click the Advanced tab, and click the Options button (Windows 2000) or Settings button (Windows XP) in the Performance section of that tab. In Windows Vista/7, right-click Computer and select Properties; then click the *Advanced system settings* option in the Tasks list. If you are prompted for an administrator password or confirmation, type the password or confirmation. Click the Settings button in the Performance section of the Advanced tab. Once you get to the Performance Options dialog box, its behavior differs between Windows 2000 and Windows XP/Vista (one of the few places where Vista acts the same as XP!).

In Windows 2000, the Performance Options dialog box shows a pair of radio buttons called Applications and Background Services. These radio buttons set how processor time is divided between the foreground application and all other background tasks. Set this to Applications if you run applications that need more processor time. Set it to Background Services to give all running programs the same processor usage. You can also adjust the size of the page file in this dialog box, but in most cases I don't mess with these settings and instead leave control of the page file to Windows.

The Windows XP/Vista Performance Options dialog box has three tabs: Visual Effects, Advanced, and Data Execution Prevention (Figure 4.88). The Visual Effects tab enables you to adjust visual effects that impact performance. Try clicking the top three choices in turn and watch the list of settings. Notice the tiny difference between the first two choices. The third choice, *Adjust for best performance*, turns off all visual effects, and the fourth option is an invitation to make your own adjustments. If you're on a computer that barely supports Windows XP, turning off visual effects can make a huge difference in the responsiveness of the computer. For the most part, though, just leave these settings alone.

The Advanced tab in Windows XP, shown in Figure 4.89, has three sections: Processor scheduling, Memory usage, and Virtual memory. Under the Processor scheduling section, you can choose to adjust for best performance of either Programs or Background services. The Memory usage settings enable you to allocate a greater share of memory to programs or to the system cache. The Virtual memory section enables you to modify the size and location of the page file. Microsoft dropped the Memory usage settings option in Windows Vista.

Microsoft introduced *Data Execution Prevention* (*DEP*) with Windows XP Service Pack 2. DEP works in the background to stop viruses and other malware from taking over programs loaded in system memory. It doesn't prevent viruses from being installed on your computer, but makes them less effective. By default, DEP monitors only critical operating system files in RAM, but the Data Execution Prevention tab enables you to have DEP monitor all running programs. It works, but you'll take a performance hit. Like other options in the Performance Options dialog box, leaving the DEP settings as default is the best option most of the time.

Resource Tracking

One big issue with optimization is knowing when something needs optimization. Let's say your Windows computer seems to be running more slowly. Resource tracking is very important for identifying the performance problem. Task Manager and the Performance console are tools you can use to figure out what (if anything) has become a bottleneck.

Task Manager

The **Task Manager** has many uses. Most users are only aware of the Applications tab, used to shut down a troublesome program. For optimization purposes, Task Manager is a great tool for investigating how hard your RAM and CPU are working at any given moment and why.

• **Figure 4.88**   Windows XP Performance Options dialog box

• **Figure 4.89**   Advanced tab of Performance Options dialog box

• **Figure 4.90** Task Manager

> Every program that runs on your system is composed of one or more processes.

The quick way to open the Task Manager is to press CTRL-SHIFT-ESC. Click the Performance tab to reveal a handy screen with the most commonly used information: CPU usage, available physical memory, size of the disk cache, commit charge (memory for programs), and kernel memory (memory used by Windows). Figure 4.90 shows a system with a dual-core processor, which is why you see two screens under CPU Usage History. A system with a single-core processor would have a single screen.

Not only does Task Manager tell you how much CPU and RAM usage is taking place, it also tells you what program is using those resources. Let's say your system is running slowly. You open up Task Manager and see that your CPU usage is at 100 percent. You then click on the Processes tab to see all the processes running on your system. Click on the CPU column heading to sort all processes by CPU usage to see who's hogging the CPU (Figure 4.91)! To shut off a process, just right-click the process and select End Process. Many times a single process opens many other processes. If you want to be thorough, click End Process Tree to turn off not only the one process but also any other processes it started.

Task Manager is also a great tool for turning off processes that are hogging memory. Let's say you're experiencing a slowdown, but this time you also notice your hard drive light is flickering nonstop—a clear sign that you've run out of memory and the page file is now in use. You go into Task Manager and see no available system memory—now you *know* the page file is in use! To make the PC run faster, you have to start unloading programs—but which ones? By going into the Processes tab in Task Manager, you can see exactly which processes are using the most memory. Just be careful not to shut down processes you don't recognize; they might be something the computer needs.

Performance Console

Task Manager is good for identifying current problems, but what about problems that happen when you're not around? What if your system is always running at a CPU utilization of 20 percent—is that good or bad? Windows 2000 and XP provide a tool called the **Performance console** that logs resource usage so you can track items such as CPU and RAM usage over time. Performance is an MMC console file, PERFMON.MSC, so you call it from Start | Run or through the Performance icon in Administrative Tools. Use either method to open the Performance console (Figure 4.92). As you can see, there are two nodes, System Monitor and Performance Logs and Alerts.

Objects and Counters   To begin working with the Performance console, you need to understand two terms: object and counter. An **object** is a system component that is given a set of characteristics and can be managed by the operating system as a single entity. A **counter** tracks specific information about an object. For example, the Processor object has a counter, %Processor Time, that tracks the percentage of elapsed time the processor uses to execute a non-idle thread. Many counters can be associated with an object.

• **Figure 4.91** CPU usage

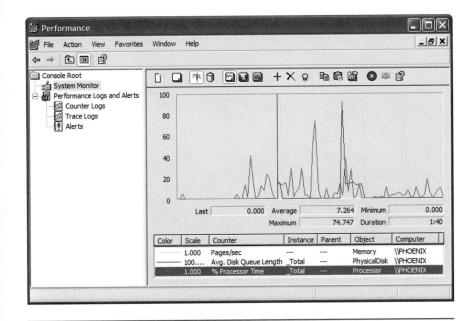

● **Figure 4.92**   Performance console

System Monitor   **System Monitor** gathers real-time data on objects such as memory, physical disk, processor, and network, and displays this data as a graph (line graph), histogram (bar graph), or simple report. Think of System Monitor as a more detailed, customizable Task Manager. When you first open the Performance console, the System Monitor shows data in graph form. The data displayed is from the set of three counters listed below the chart. If you want to add counters, click the Add button (the one that looks like a plus sign) or press CTRL-I to open the Add Counters dialog box. Click the Performance object drop-down list and select one of the many different objects you can monitor. The Add Counters dialog box includes a helpful feature: you can select a counter and click the Explain button to learn about the counter, as shown in Figure 4.93.

Even with just three counters selected, the graph can get a little busy. That's where one of my favorite System Monitor features shines. If you want the line of charted data from just one counter to stand out, select the counter in the list below the graph and then press CTRL-H. See how this trick makes the %Processor Time line stand out in Figure 4.94? Imagine how useful that is when you are monitoring a dozen counters.

Performance Logs and Alerts   The **Performance Logs and Alerts** snap-in enables Windows to create a written record of just about anything that happens on your system. Do you want to know if someone is trying to log on to your system when you're not around? The following procedure is specific to Windows XP, but the steps are nearly identical in Windows 2000.

To create the new event log, right-click Counter Logs and select New Log Settings. Give the new log a name—in this example, "Unauthorized Accesses." Click OK, and a properties dialog box for the new log appears, similar to that shown in Figure 4.95.

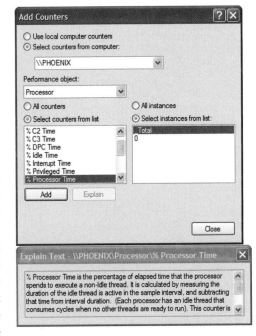

● **Figure 4.93**   Add Counters dialog box

- **Figure 4.94** CTRL-H makes one set of data stand out.

- **Figure 4.95** Creating a new performance log

To select counters for the log, click Add Counters and then select the *Use local computer counters* radio button. Select Server from the Performance object pull-down menu and then select Errors Logon from the list of counters; click Add and then click Close.

Back in the properties dialog box for your new log, click the Schedule tab and set up when you want this thing to start running—probably at the end of the workday today. Then select when it should stop logging—probably tomorrow morning when you start work. Click the Log Files tab to see where the log file will be saved—probably C:\PerfLogs—and make a note of the filename. The filename will consist of the name you gave the log and a number. In this example I named the new performance log "Unauthorized Accesses," so the filename is Unauthorized Accesses_000001.blg.

When you come back in the morning, open the Performance console, select Performance Logs and Alerts, and then select Counter Logs. Your log should be listed on the right. The icon by the log name will be green if the log is still running or red if it has stopped. If it has not stopped, select it and click the Stop button (the one with the black square, circled in Figure 4.96).

To view the log, open the Performance console, select System Monitor, change to Report view, and load the file as a new source by using the properties dialog box.

- **Figure 4.96** Stopping the performance log

Reliability and Performance Monitor

Windows Vista improves on the old Performance console dramatically with the **Reliability and Performance Monitor**. The Reliability and Performance Monitor still has a complete Performance console with all the objects and counters you see in Windows 2000 and XP, but it adds an excellent Resource Overview, a Reliability Monitor, and a much more flexible way to use counters with Data Collector Sets and Reports.

You can open the Reliability and Performance Monitor in Windows Vista by starting the Performance Information and Tools in the Administrative Tools Control Panel applet to get the Resource Overview dialog box (Figure 4.97). You can also open the tool by going to Start | Start Searching, typing **perfmon.msc**, and pressing ENTER.

Think of the Resource Overview as an advanced Task Manager, giving details on CPU, hard drive, network, and memory usage. When you click on one of the four bars, you get details on exactly which processes are using those resources—a powerful tool when you suspect a program might be hogging something! Figure 4.98 shows the Network bar opened to reveal the processes using the network and how much data each is sending.

The Reliability and Performance Monitor option you can select under the Monitoring Tools is simply a re-creation of the Performance console and works as described earlier for Windows 2000 and XP (Figure 4.99). This is a great tool for quick checks on specific counters.

Microsoft included Data Collector Sets in the Reliability and Performance Monitor, groupings of counters you can use to make reports. You can make you own Data Collector Sets (User Defined) or you can just grab one of the predefined system sets. Once you start a Data Collector

A complete discussion of the Reliability and Performance Monitor is outside the scope of the CompTIA A+ objectives, but it's an amazing tool!

• **Figure 4.97**   Resource Overview in Vista

The CompTIA A+ Essentials exam isn't going to ask too many detailed questions on either the Performance console or Reliability and Performance Monitor. That doesn't mean you can ignore these amazing tools! Make sure you understand that these tools give you the power to inspect anything happening on your system to help you diagnose problems.

• **Figure 4.98**   Network bar in the Reliability and Performance Monitor

• **Figure 4.99**   Reliability and Performance Monitor

Set, you can use the Reports option to see the results (Figure 4.100). Data Collector Sets not only enable you to choose counter objects to track, but they also enable you to schedule when you want them to run.

Preparing for Problems

As part of optimizing Windows, techs need to prepare for problems. You must have critical system files and data backed up and tools in place for the inevitable glitches. Different versions of Windows enable you to prepare for problems differently. Microsoft seems to break backups into certain areas: backing up personal data, backing up local copies of critical system state information, backing up a small amount of very critical system information on some form of removable media, and providing some way to use backups if your system won't boot. Let's see all of these.

• **Figure 4.100**   Sample report

Back Up Personal Data

The most important data on your computer is the personal data: your documents, e-mail messages and contacts, Web favorites, photographs, and other files. To handle backing up personal data, every version of Windows comes with some form of backup utility. There are big differences between the backup utility that comes with Windows 2000 and XP compared to the one that comes with Vista (and the one that comes with Windows 7 is different still), so let's break up the idea of backing up personal data between Windows 2000/XP and Vista.

Backup Utility for Windows 2000 and XP (NTBackup)

Windows 2000 Backup/Windows XP **Backup Utility** (different names, but the same program under the hood, **NTBackup**) provides almost all the tools you need to back up files and folders. It has come a long way from its origins in Windows NT. NTBackup supports a greater variety of devices, enabling you to back up to network drives, logical drives, tape, and removable disks (but not optical discs). Most folks, however, still turn to third-party utilities to create system, e-mail, browser, and personal data backups.

You can start NTBackup by navigating the Start menu to Accessories | System Tools, or by clicking the Backup Now button on the Tools tab of the Local Disk Properties dialog box. I prefer to start it from Start | Run with the command **ntbackup**. Click the Backup Wizard button to run the Backup Wizard. This technique works in both Windows 2000 and Windows XP. To use the Windows XP version in Advanced Mode, click Advanced Mode on the opening screen (Figure 4.101). To have it always open in Advanced Mode, deselect the *Always start in wizard mode* checkbox. If the program is in Advanced Mode and you want to run it as a wizard, click the Wizard Mode link to open the Backup or Restore Wizard.

To create a backup, start the Backup Utility, click Advanced Mode, and choose the Backup tab. Check the boxes next to the drives and files you want to include in the backup. To include your system state information, such as Registry and boot files (which you should do), click the System State checkbox. To specify where to put the backup file you're creating, either type the path and file name in the *Backup media or file name* box or click Browse, select a location, type the file name, and click Save. Click Start Backup. Choose whether you want to append this backup to a previous one or overwrite it. Click Advanced to open the Advanced Backup Options dialog box, select *Verify data after backup*, and click OK. Click Start Backup again. A dialog box shows you the utility's progress. When it finishes, click Close and then close the Backup Utility.

Both versions of NTBackup give you three choices after you click Advanced Mode: Backup Wizard (Advanced), Restore Wizard (Advanced), and a third choice that is very important. The third option in Windows 2000 is the Emergency Repair Disk. As you can see in Figure 4.102, the third option in Windows XP is Automated System Recovery Wizard.

Windows 2000 Emergency Repair Disk (ERD) The Windows 2000 **Emergency Repair Disk (ERD)** saves critical boot files and partition information

The Backup Utility is not included in the default installation of Windows XP Home. You must install it manually from the Windows CD-ROM.

Microsoft has been dreadfully inconsistent on the naming of the backup programs that bundle with Windows. Here's the scoop in a nutshell. In Windows 2000, the official name of the backup program is *Microsoft Windows Backup*, but the dialog box that opens is simply called *Backup*. The wizard interface is called the *Backup Wizard*. The quick command-line command you run to get to the utility is *NTBACKUP*. Are you with me?

The backup program in Windows XP has a similar slew of names. The official name of the program is *Backup Utility for Windows*. The Advanced Mode dialog box is called *Backup Utility*, but the wizard interface differs depending on whether you run the utility in Wizard Mode or click the Backup Wizard button in the Advanced Mode dialog box. The former runs the *Backup or Restore Wizard*; the latter runs the *Backup Wizard*. These wizards offer different options, with the Backup or Restore Wizard providing the simpler, consumer-oriented interface. Both wizards are only different faces for the Backup Utility. Got it? Oh, and NTBACKUP is the command-line command to run the program in Windows XP, so Microsoft provides at least a nod at naming consistency.

Most seasoned techs call the backup programs in Windows 2000 and Windows XP *Backup* or *NTBackup*. You need to know the variety of names, though, to provide proper customer support. This is especially true in a help desk environment.

• **Figure 4.101** Choosing to run the Backup Wizard in Advanced Mode

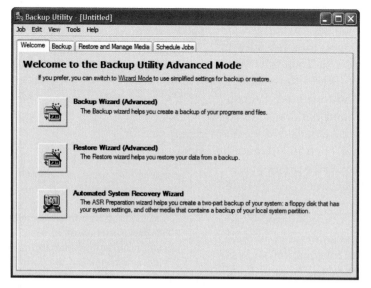

• Figure 4.102   Windows XP Backup Utility options

and is your main tool for fixing boot problems in Windows 2000. It is not a bootable disk, nor does it store very much information; the ERD does not replace a good system backup! It works with a special folder called \WINNT\REPAIR to store a copy of your Registry. It's not perfect, but it gets you out of most startup problems. Making a new ERD before you install a new device or program is good practice. Then the ERD is ready if you need it.

So you have this great Emergency Repair Disk that'll take care of all of your system repair problems. You just pop it in the floppy drive and go, right?

Not just yet. As I mentioned, the ERD itself is not a bootable disk. To use the ERD, you must first boot the system by using the Windows installation CD-ROM. Follow these steps to repair a system by using the ERD:

1. Boot the system, using either your set of boot diskettes or the installation CD-ROM.

2. In the Welcome to Setup dialog box, press the R key to select the option to repair a Windows 2000 installation.

3. The Windows 2000 Repair Options menu appears. You have the option of either entering the Recovery Console or using the Emergency Repair Disk.

4. Press the R key to select the option to repair Windows 2000 by using the emergency repair process.

5. The next screen offers the choice of Manual or Fast repair.

   ▪ Manual repair lets you select the following repair options: inspect the startup environment, verify the system files, and inspect the boot sector.

   ▪ Fast repair doesn't ask for any further input.

6. Follow the onscreen instructions and insert the ERD when prompted.

7. Your system will be inspected and, if possible, restored. When the process finishes, the system restarts.

Windows XP Automated System Recovery (ASR)   The Windows XP **Automated System Recovery (ASR)** looks and acts very similar to the Windows 2000 ERD. The ASR Preparation Wizard lets you create a backup of your system. This backup includes a floppy disk and backup media (tape or CD-R) containing the system partition and disks containing operating system components (Figure 4.103).

The restore side of ASR involves a complete reinstallation of the operating system, preferably on a new partition. This is something you do when all is lost. Run Setup and press F2 when prompted during the text-mode portion of Setup. Follow the prompts on the screen, which will first ask for the floppy disk and then for the backup media.

Backup Wizard Data files are not backed up by the ERD or by the ASR. Therefore, you have to back up data files. If you run the Backup Wizard and click the Next button on the Welcome screen, you'll open the dialog box shown in Figure 4.104. You have three options here. The first two are fairly self-explanatory: you can back up everything or just selected drives and files.

The third option needs some explanation. The *Only back up the System State data* radio button enables you to save "other" system-critical files, but with Windows 2000/XP, it's not much more than making an ERD with the Registry backup. This option really makes sense for Windows 2000 Server and Windows Server 2003 systems because it saves Active Directory information (which your Windows 2000/XP systems do not store) as well as other critical, server-specific functions. (I cover more on these topics in Chapter 16, "Learning Local Area Networking.") But the CompTIA A+ Essentials exam may still expect you to know about it!

Tape Backup The odd fact that Microsoft has not updated the Backup or Restore Wizard to enable you to back up to optical discs of any sort has kept alive the practice of tape backups. Tape drives connect to the ATA or SCSI bus, just like optical drives, but rather than using a shiny CD-R or DVD+R disc, you have to back up to magnetic tape (Figure 4.105).

Tape drive manufacturers have done pretty much everything they can do to make tape backups as fast as possible, but the technology suffers from two huge drawbacks. First, it's tape, which means all data must be stored and restored in sequential access. The drive has to go through Files 1 and 2 before reaching File 3, in other words. Second, tape is painfully slow in comparison to hard drives, optical drives, or Flash drives.

The only great benefit to tape is that it's relatively cheap to buy multiple tapes with a lot of storage capacity. With hard drive and recordable DVD prices at rock bottom today, though, tape's days are numbered.

Backup Options The goal of backing up data is to ensure that when a system dies, there will be an available, recent copy you can use to restore the system. You could simply back up the complete system at the end of each day—or whatever interval you feel is prudent to keep the backups fresh—but complete backups can be a tremendous waste of time and materials. Instead of backing up the entire system, take advantage of the fact that all the files won't be changed in any given period; much of the time you only

• **Figure 4.103** Creating an ASR backup

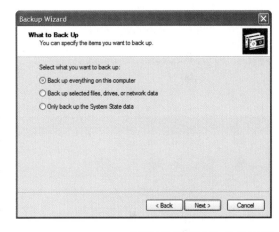

• **Figure 4.104** Backup Wizard options

• **Figure 4.105** Backup tapes

need to back up what's changed since your last backup. Recognizing this, most backup software solutions have a series of options available beyond the complete backup.

The key to understanding backups other than the full backup is *attributes*, 1-bit storage areas that all files have. The most common attributes are Hidden (don't show the file in Computer or when `dir` is typed at the command line), System (it's a critical file for the system), Read-Only (can't erase it), and Archive. These attributes were first used in FAT-formatted drives in the DOS era, but they are still completely supported by all file formats. The archive bit works basically like this: Whenever a file is saved, the archive bit is turned on. Simply opening a file affects the current state of the archive bit. Backup programs usually turn off a file's archive bit when the file is backed up. In theory, if a file's archive bit is turned off, there's a good backup of that file on some tape. If the archive bit is turned on, it means that the file has been changed since it was last backed up (Figure 4.106).

Archive bits are used to perform backups that are not full backups. The following backup types are most often supported:

- A *normal backup* is a full backup. Every file selected is backed up, and the archive bit is turned off for every file backed up. This is the standard "back it all up" option.

- A *copy backup* is identical to a normal backup, with the important distinction being that the archive bits are *not* changed. This is used (although not often) for making extra copies of a previously completed backup.

- An *incremental backup* includes only files with the archive bit turned on. In other words, it copies only the files that have been changed since the last backup. This backup turns off the archive bits.

- A *differential backup* is identical to an incremental backup, except that it doesn't turn off the archive bits.

- A *daily backup*, also known as a *daily copy backup*, makes copies of all the files that have been changed that day. It does not change the archive bits.

• **Figure 4.106**   The archive bit on these files is on.

The motivation for having both the incremental and differential backups may not be clear at first glance—they seem so similar as to be basically the same. Incremental seems the better option at first. If a file is backed up, you would want to turn off the archive bit, right? Well, maybe. But there is one scenario where that might not be too attractive. Most backups do a big weekly normal backup, followed by daily incremental or differential backups at the end of every business day. Figure 4.107 shows the difference between incremental and differential backups.

Notice that a differential backup is a cumulative backup. Because the archive bits are not set, it keeps backing up all changes since the last normal backup. This means the backup files will get progressively larger throughout the week (assuming a standard weekly normal backup). The incremental

Mike Meyers' CompTIA A+ Guide: Essentials

backup, by contrast, only backs up files changed since the last backup. Each incremental backup file will be relatively small and also totally different from the previous backup file.

Let's assume that the system is wiped out on a Thursday morning. How can you restore the system to a useful state?

If you're using an incremental backup, you first have to restore the last weekly backup you ran on Monday, then the Tuesday backup, and then the Wednesday backup before the system is restored to its Thursday morning state. The longer the time between normal backups, the more incremental backups you must restore.

Using the same scenario but assuming you're doing differential instead of incremental backups, you only need the weekly backup and then the Wednesday backup to restore your system. A differential backup always requires only two backups to restore a system. Suddenly, the differential backup looks better than the incremental! On the other hand, one big benefit of incremental over differential is backup file size. Differential backup files are massive compared to incremental ones.

Incremental

MON	TUE	WED	THU	FRI
Full backup	All Tuesday changes	All Wednesday changes	All Thursday changes	All Friday changes

Differential

MON	TUE	WED	THU	FRI
Full backup	All changes through Tuesday	All changes through Wednesday	All changes through Thursday	All changes through Friday

• **Figure 4.107**   Incremental versus differential

Backup and Restore Center for Vista

One of the many changes between XP and Vista was the elimination of NTBackup, replaced with the Windows Backup and Restore Center. If you open this program, you'll notice that you only have two options: back up everything or restore from a backup (Figure 4.108).

If you choose to back up your computer, you have another two choices: back up files or back up the entire computer. *Back up files* gives you a choice of the file types you wish to back up (Figure 4.109). *Back up computer* backs up the entire computer: every single file and folder. Vista no longer supports tape backups nor can you choose between differential or incremental

• **Figure 4.108**   Backup and Restore Center

Back Up Files

Which file types do you want to back up?

All files on this computer of the type that you select will be backed up, including files that belong to other users of this computer. We recommend that you back up all of the file types selected below.

☑ Pictures
☑ Music
☑ Videos
☑ E-mail
☑ Documents
☑ TV shows
☑ Compressed files
☑ Additional files

Category details

Move the mouse pointer over a category on the left or select it with the keyboard to see what types of files will be backed up.

Only files on NTFS disks can be backed up. System files, executable files, and temporary files will not be backed up. What other file types are not included in the backup?

Next   Cancel

• **Figure 4.109**   Back Up Files option

backups. If you want these options, you need to buy a third-party backup tool.

The Vista tool comes with a handy wizard that automatically configures when you want to back up. So although you lose some of the options from NTBackup, you'll find this to be a powerful tool that works for most of your backup needs.

System Restore

Every technician has war stories about the user who likes to add the latest gadget and cool software to his computer. Then the user is amazed when things go very, very wrong: the system locks up, refuses to boot, or simply acts weird. This guy also can't remember what he added or when. All he knows is that you should be able to fix it—fast.

This is not news to the folks at Microsoft, and they have a solution to this problem. It's called **System Restore**, and they first introduced it in Windows Me, with further refinements in Windows XP. The System Restore tool enables you to create a **restore point**, a copy of your computer's configuration at a specific point in time. If you later crash or have a corrupted OS, you can restore the system to its previous state.

To create a restore point, go to Start | All Programs | Accessories | System Tools | System Restore. When the tool opens, select *Create a restore point* and then click Next (Figure 4.110). Type in a description on the next screen. There's no need to include the date and time because the System Restore adds them automatically. Click Create and you're finished.

System Restore in Windows Vista is much more automatic, with the operating system making a number of restore points automatically. To make your own restore point, go to System Properties, select System Protection, and then click the Create button as shown in Figure 4.111.

If you click the System Restore button, you might be surprised at how many system restore points are already made for you (Figure 4.112). In most cases, one of these is all you'll need to return your system to an earlier point.

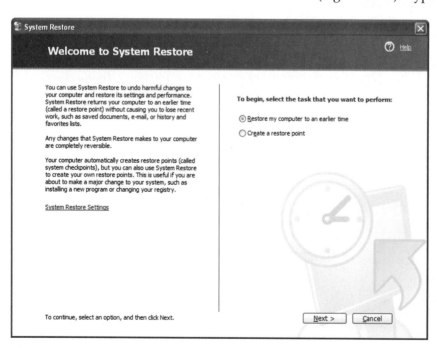

System Restore

Welcome to System Restore   ? Help

You can use System Restore to undo harmful changes to your computer and restore its settings and performance. System Restore returns your computer to an earlier time (called a restore point) without causing you to lose recent work, such as saved documents, e-mail, or history and favorites lists.

Any changes that System Restore makes to your computer are completely reversible.

Your computer automatically creates restore points (called system checkpoints), but you can also use System Restore to create your own restore points. This is useful if you are about to make a major change to your system, such as installing a new program or changing your registry.

System Restore Settings

To begin, select the task that you want to perform:

⦿ Restore my computer to an earlier time
◯ Create a restore point

To continue, select an option, and then click Next.

Next >   Cancel

• **Figure 4.110**   Create a restore point

● Figure 4.111   Creating a manual System Restore
in Vista

● Figure 4.112   Restore points in Vista

The System Restore tool creates some of the restore points in time automatically. For instance, by default, every time you install new software, XP creates a restore point. Thus, if installation of a program causes your computer to malfunction, simply restore the system to a time point prior to that installation, and the computer should work again.

During the restore process, only settings and programs are changed. No data is lost. Your computer includes all programs and settings as of the restore date. This feature is absolutely invaluable for overworked techs. A simple restore fixes many user-generated problems.

To restore to a previous time point, start the System Restore Wizard by choosing Start | All Programs | Accessories | System Tools | System Restore. Then select the first radio button, *Restore my computer to an earlier time*, and click Next. Figure 4.113 shows a calendar with restore points. Any day with a boldface date has at least one restore point. These points are created after you add or remove software or install Windows updates and during the normal shutdown of your computer. Select a date on the calendar; then select a restore point from the list on the right and click Next.

The last screen before the system is restored shows a warning. It advises you to close all open programs and reminds you that Windows will shut down during the restore process. It also states that the restore operation is completely reversible. Thus, if you go too far back in time, you can restore to a more recent date.

● Figure 4.113   Calendar of restore points

You don't have to count on the automatic creation of restore points. You can open System Restore at any time and simply select *Create a restore point*. Consider doing this before making changes that might not trigger an automatic restore point, such as directly editing the Registry.

System Restore is turned on by default and uses some of your disk space to save information on restore points. To turn System Restore off or change the disk space usage, open the System Properties applet in Control Panel and select the System Restore tab (Figure 4.114).

Installing Recovery Console

When things get really bad on a Windows system, you need to turn to the Recovery Console. The **Recovery Console** is a text-based startup of Windows that gets you to a command prompt similar to the Windows command prompt.

If you have the Windows 2000/XP CD-ROM, you can start the Recovery Console by running Setup, selecting Repair, and then selecting Recovery Console. If you like to be proactive, however, you can install the Recovery Console on your hard drive so that it is one of your startup options and does not require the Windows 2000 or XP CD-ROM to run. The steps to do this in Windows 2000 and Windows XP are very nearly identical.

First, you need to log in to the system with the Administrator account. Grab your Windows 2000 or XP installation CD-ROM and drop it in your system. If the Autorun function kicks in, just click the No button. To install the Recovery Console and make it a part of your startup options, click the Start button, select Run, and type the following:

```
d:\i386\winnt32 /cmdcons
```

If your CD-ROM drive uses a different drive letter, substitute it for the D: drive. Then just follow the instructions on the screen. If you are connected to the Internet, allow the Setup program to download updated files. From now on, every time the system boots, the OS selection menu will show your Windows OS (Windows 2000 Professional or Windows XP) and the Microsoft Windows Recovery Console. It may also show other choices if yours is a multiboot computer.

System Recovery Options

Windows Vista and Windows 7 have dropped the Recovery Console, replacing it with the graphical System Recovery Options. System Recovery Options is on the Vista/7 installation media, and you run it by booting to the media as though you were installing Windows. When you boot from the installation media, choose your language settings, click Next, select *Repair your computer*, and then click Next a second time to see the System Recovery Options menu, as shown in Figure 4.115. The System Recovery Options menu has a number of items, each designed to help in a particular situation.

• **Figure 4.114** System Restore tab in System Properties applet

Startup Repair Startup Repair should be your first choice when running System Recovery. This option tells Windows to attempt to repair your system automatically. Startup Repair rebuilds all of your most important system files, which in most cases will at least enable you to get Windows to boot. If Startup Repair doesn't work, hope you made some system restore points!

System Restore The System Restore option searches your computer for restore points, enabling you to choose one. Hopefully, this will fix whatever is preventing your system from booting. If not, you may want to consider the Windows Complete PC Restore option.

Windows Complete PC Restore Assuming you made a backup while the system was running properly, you can select this option to restore your PC.

• **Figure 4.115** System Recovery Options in Windows Vista

Windows Memory Diagnostic Tool Bad RAM is an all-too-common problem for any computer and often shows itself during startup. Recognizing this, Microsoft added this tool to test your RAM for errors. This is an incredibly powerful tool for the job. If your RAM is bad, the Memory Diagnostic Tool will locate and report the error to you. You replace your RAM and the problem is solved.

Command Prompt The Command Prompt option is just as it is named: a full-blown command prompt, not to be confused with the Windows 2000/XP Recovery Console. You can run any command-prompt program from here.

Safe Mode (All Versions)

If you're experiencing problems with Windows—or even if you're expecting to—then you might want to try booting your computer into Safe Mode. Safe Mode starts up Windows but loads only very basic, non–vendor-specific drivers for mouse, VGA monitor (not in Vista), keyboard, mass storage, and system services. You get to Safe Mode by holding the F8 key during system boot, before Windows begins to load. You'll be presented with a menu containing several different boot options, but the only one you need to know about for the Essentials exam is Safe Mode.

Once in Safe Mode, you can use tools such as Device Manager to locate and correct the source of the problem. When you use Device Manager in Safe Mode, you can access the properties for all the devices, even those that are not working in Safe Mode. The status displayed for the device is the status for a normal startup. Even the network card will show as enabled. You can disable any suspect device or perform other tasks, such as removing or updating drivers. If a problem with a device driver is preventing the operating system from starting normally, check the Device Manager for warning icons that indicate an unknown device.

Chapter 4 Review

■ Chapter Summary

After reading this chapter and completing the exercises, you should understand the following about Microsoft Windows.

Relate the history of Microsoft Windows

■ Microsoft entered the operating system game in the early 1980s with a command-line OS called Microsoft Disk Operating System, or MS-DOS. With a command-line OS, you interacted with the computer to run programs and save files and all the other computing functions by typing and pressing the ENTER key on your keyboard.

■ The earliest versions of Windows were little more than a graphical overlay of the DOS command-line operating system. This overlay version of Windows went through a number of updates, ending with the first truly popular version of Windows, Windows for Workgroups version 3.1. The last versions are collectively referred to as Windows 3.x.

■ In 1989, Microsoft offered a completely separate version of Windows called Windows NT, a true graphical operating system that was dramatically more powerful than the Windows overlay versions. It cost a lot more, unfortunately, so it did not see widespread adoption by regular users, only by business users. What set NT apart from other versions of Windows (including later consumer-oriented products) was its very secure file system, NTFS.

■ From 1995 through 2000, Microsoft offered consumers an alternative version of Windows that went through several updates, such as Windows 95 and Windows 98. Collectively these versions of Windows are called Windows 9x. All of these versions of Windows used forms of FAT for file systems, not the more secure NTFS.

■ Microsoft currently supports seven families of Windows, of which three concern the CompTIA A+ certified technician: Windows 2000, Windows XP, and Windows Vista. All can use the NTFS file system.

■ Windows 2000 came in two versions: Professional and Server. The CompTIA A+ Essentials exam does not cover Windows Server versions, but a good tech should at least know these server versions exist. If you were to look at the Windows 2000 Server desktop, you'd be hard pressed to see any obvious differences from the Windows 2000 Professional version.

■ Microsoft released several versions of the successor to Windows 2000, such as Windows XP Professional and Windows XP Home. Windows XP Professional provides full-blown data security, and it is the only version of Windows XP with the capability of logging on to a special Windows Server–controlled domain. Windows XP Home is a stripped-down version of XP Professional, without some of the important security features, such as no access to the Encrypting File System. Windows XP Media Center offers features for the media junkie, such as a personal video recorder to capture television shows for later viewing.

■ Windows Vista comes in many flavors, such as Windows Vista Home Premium and Windows Vista Business. Windows Vista Ultimate combines all of the features of every other Vista version and includes some other features, such as a game performance tweaker and DVD ripping capability.

■ Windows XP and Windows Vista come in 64-bit versions to take advantage of the extra computing power and memory capacity available with modern 64-bit processors. A 32-bit operating system is limited to a mere 4 GB of RAM, whereas a 64-bit OS can have gobs more. The 64-bit versions of Windows XP saw some use, but the 64-bit versions of Vista took the 64-bit OS into the mainstream.

Explain the Windows interface

■ Every version of Windows supports multiple users on a single machine, so the starting point for any tour of the Windows user interface starts with the login screen. Windows 2000 has a straightforward login screen where you enter a user name and password. Windows XP offers the Welcome screen in addition to the standard login, where users can click an icon next to their user name to log in, although this feature is disabled in a domain environment. Windows Vista has a beefed-up

Welcome screen that works in both a workgroup and a domain.

- The Windows desktop is the primary interface to the computer in every version of Windows. Windows Vista differs from previous versions of Windows with the use of transparencies and other nice features of the Windows Aero interface. Flip 3D enables users to quickly and visually cycle through open programs.

- Some of the important items on the desktop are the taskbar, Start button, Quick Launch toolbar, and notification area, or system tray. The taskbar shows running programs. The Start button gives you access to the Start menu where you can run installed applications. The Quick Launch toolbar enables you to select often-used programs with a single click, though it's not displayed by default in Windows XP. The notification area shows icons for applications running in the background, such as your antivirus software.

- My Computer in Windows 2000 and Windows XP and Computer in Windows Vista offer access to the files and folders on mass storage drives on the computer. To view the contents of any device, double-click its icon in My Computer/Computer. You can tell by a file's icon or extension—if you alter the default folder view to show file extensions—what type of file it is, such as a .JPG picture file.

- Windows Explorer is the main tool for observing and manipulating files on a system. The tool differs in some ways among the versions tested on the CompTIA A+ Essentials exam. Windows Explorer and My Computer/Computer are two facets of the same application in Windows XP and Windows Vista but two distinct applications in Windows 2000.

- When you delete a file in Windows, it moves into the Recycle Bin. It stays there until you empty the Recycle Bin or restore the file, or until the Recycle Bin reaches a preset size and starts erasing its oldest contents.

- Windows offers many useful keyboard key combinations for accomplishing common tasks. Some combinations work specifically with the operating system utilities, such as pressing the WINDOWS KEY and the PAUSE key to open the System applet. Other combinations work throughout most applications, such as CTRL-C to copy something and CTRL-V to paste whatever was copied.

Explain some advanced Windows features

- The Registry is a database that stores everything about your PC, including information on all of the hardware in the PC, network information, user preferences, file types, and virtually anything else you might run into with Windows. The Registry is composed of several hives.

- You can access the Registry Editor by typing **regedt32** or **regedit** at the Start | Run menu or at the Start | Start Search dialog box, depending on the version of Windows.

- The Registry has five root keys that define various elements of Windows. HKEY_CLASSES_ROOT, for example, defines the standard class objects used by Windows. A class object is a named group of functions that define what you can do with the object it represents. A .JPG file is defined here, for example, as a type of image file associated with a specific program.

- The Microsoft Management Console (MMC) is simply a shell program in Windows that holds individual utilities called snap-ins. These snap-ins enable you to accomplish varying tech tasks. You can create custom MMCs or use ones preconfigured by Microsoft.

- The Administrative Tools in the Control Panel are preconfigured MMCs, such as Computer Management and Event Viewer. Users rarely need to access these MMCs, but techs know their Administrative Tools.

- Windows uses a portion of the hard drive as an extension of system RAM, through what's called a page file. A page file is a block of cylinders on a hard drive set aside as what's called a RAM cache, swap file, or virtual memory. When the PC starts running out of real RAM because you've loaded too many programs, the system swaps programs from RAM to the page file, opening more space for programs currently active.

Maintain Windows

- The Internet has enabled Microsoft to make updates available, and Windows Update can grab those updates and patch user systems easily and automatically. Keeping your system updated prevents viruses and malicious software from exploiting vulnerabilities in your operating system. With the release of Windows XP Service Pack 2, Microsoft began pushing for wholesale acceptance of automatic updates from Windows Update. However, you can customize automatic updates to allow various levels of automation.

■ You have two choices when updating your system with Windows Update: Express installation or Custom installation. An Express installation installs only the essential security fixes and patches; a Custom installation enables you to select from a wide range of software and driver updates.

■ Disk Cleanup clears out the junk files that accumulate from daily use. You can reach this tool through the Start menu (Start | All Programs | Accessories | System Tools), or you can open My Computer or Computer, right-click the drive you want to clean up, select Properties, and click the Disk Cleanup button.

■ Keeping your Registry clean ensures that your system continues to run efficiently and without errors. Unfortunately, Microsoft doesn't offer any built-in Registry cleaner tools, so you have to use third-party tools such as CCleaner to perform this task.

■ If your computer is going to be connected to the Internet, it's critical that you run some sort of antispyware or antivirus software on your system.

■ When you can't find a software reason for a problem such as a system freezing on shutdown, the problem might be the actual physical hard drive. The tool to investigate that is Error-checking. You can perform Error-checking from a command line or the Start | Run dialog box, using the CHKDSK command.

■ Run the Disk Defragmenter on a regular basis to keep your system from slowing down because of files scattered in pieces on your hard drive.

■ Maintenance only works properly when it's done at regular intervals. You can use Task Scheduler to schedule regular maintenance on your computer.

■ The System Configuration utility enables techs to edit and troubleshoot operating system and program startup processes and services. Prior to Windows Vista, the System Configuration utility also offered quick access to troubleshoot and edit the BOOT.INI file.

Optimize Windows

■ Windows comes with the System Information tool, which collects information about hardware resources, components, and the software environment. When it finishes doing that, it provides a nice and tidy little report, allowing you to troubleshoot and diagnose any issues and conflicts. You can also use System Information to gather information about remote computers by simply selecting View | Remote Computer and then entering the remote computer's network machine name.

■ Windows supports Autorun, a feature that enables it to look for and read a special file called Autorun immediately after a removable media device (optical disc or thumb drive) is inserted and then run whatever program is listed in AUTORUN.INF. If you need to install a program manually, however, you can use the Add or Remove Programs applet in the Control Panel. With Windows Vista/7, you most likely will be prompted by UAC when installing an application. This is to give you time to review what is happening to your system in case you did not approve of the program being installed.

■ Each installed application program takes up space on your computer's hard drive, and programs that you no longer need simply waste space that could be used for other purposes. Removing unnecessary programs can be an important piece of optimization. You remove programs by using the Add or Remove Programs applet in the Control Panel by selecting the desired program from the list of installed programs and then clicking Uninstall.

■ The third function of the Add or Remove Programs applet is to add or remove Windows components and features. This is done by selecting Add/Remove Windows Components, which opens the Windows Components Wizard. In Windows Vista/7, Windows Components have been renamed to Windows Features.

■ Windows/Microsoft Update provides an easy method to update drivers from manufacturers that take advantage of the service. If you are using 2000/XP, the only trick to this is that you usually need to select the Custom option to see these updates because Windows only installs high-priority updates when using the Express option.

When you click on the Custom option, look under Hardware, Optional (on the left) to see if Windows has any driver updates. If you are using Vista/7, you will need to click *View available updates* to see if any drivers are available for your system.

- Device drivers become part of the operating system and thus have the potential to cause lots of problems if they're written poorly. To protect Windows systems from bad device drivers, Microsoft uses driver signing, which means that each driver has a digital signature. When an unsigned driver is detected during hardware installation, you'll see a message offering you the choice to stop or continue the installation. Signed drivers are more or less a sure thing, but that doesn't mean unsigned ones are a problem—just consider the source of the driver when installing it. You can control how Windows behaves when drivers are being installed by clicking the Driver Signing button on the Hardware tab of the System Properties dialog box. This displays the Driver Signing Options dialog box. If you select Ignore, Windows will install an unsigned driver without warning you.

- Right-clicking on a device in Device Manager displays the context menu. From here you can update or uninstall the driver, disable the device, scan for hardware changes, or display the Properties dialog box. The Driver tab has buttons labeled Driver Details, Update Driver, Roll Back Driver, and Uninstall. The Roll Back Driver option enables you to remove an updated driver, thus rolling back to the previous driver version.

- Windows should automatically detect any new device you install in your system. If not, use the Add Hardware Wizard (or simply Add Hardware if using Vista) to get the device recognized and drivers installed. You'll find it on the Hardware tab of the System Properties dialog box.

- One optimization you can perform on all Windows versions is setting Performance Options. Performance Options are used to configure CPU, RAM, and virtual memory (page file) settings. In Windows 2000, the Performance Options dialog box shows a pair of radio buttons called Applications and Background Services that set how processor time is divided between the foreground application and all other background tasks. In Windows XP, Vista, and 7, the Performance Options dialog box has

three tabs: Visual Effects, Advanced, and Data Execution Prevention. The Visual Effects tab enables you to adjust visual effects that impact performance. The Advanced tab has three sections: Processor scheduling, Memory usage (not in Vista), and Virtual memory.

- Microsoft introduced Data Execution Prevention (DEP) with Windows XP Service Pack 2. DEP works in the background to stop viruses and other malware from taking over programs loaded in system memory. It doesn't prevent viruses from being installed on your computer, but makes them less effective.

- Task Manager is a great tool for investigating how hard your RAM and CPU are working at any given moment and why. The Performance tab reveals a handy screen with the most commonly used information: CPU usage, available physical memory, the size of the disk cache, commit charge (memory for programs), and kernel memory (memory used by Windows). Task Manager also tells you which program is using your system resources.

- The Performance console is used to log resource usage so you can track items such as CPU and RAM usage over time.

- System Monitor gathers real-time data on objects such as memory, physical disk, processor, and network, and displays this data as a graph (line graph), histogram (bar graph), or simple report.

- The Performance Logs and Alerts snap-in enables Windows to create a written record of just about anything that happens on your system.

- The most important data on your computer is the personal data: your documents, e-mail messages and contacts, Web favorites, photographs, and other files. To handle backing up personal data, every version of Windows comes with some form of backup utility.

- Windows 2000 Backup and Windows XP Backup Utility (NTBackup) provides almost all the tools you need to back up files and folders. It has come a long way from its origins in Windows NT. NTBackup supports a greater variety of devices, enabling you to back up to network drives, logical drives, tape, and removable disks (but not optical discs).

- The Windows 2000 Emergency Repair Disk (ERD) saves critical boot files and partition information and is your main tool for fixing boot problems in Windows 2000.

- The Windows XP Automated System Recovery (ASR) enables you to create a backup of your system. This backup includes a floppy disk and backup media (tape or CD-R) containing the system partition and disks containing operating system components.

- The archive bit works basically like this: Whenever a file is saved, the archive bit is turned on. Simply opening a file affects the current state of the archive bit. Backup programs usually turn off a file's archive bit when the file is backed up. If the archive bit is turned on, it means that the file has been changed since it was last backed up.

- A normal backup is a full backup. Every file selected is backed up, and the archive bit is turned off for every file backed up.

- A copy backup is identical to a normal backup, except that the archive bits are *not* changed. This is used (although not often) for making extra copies of a previously completed backup.

- An incremental backup includes only files with the archive bit turned on. In other words, it copies only the files that have been changed since the last backup. This backup turns off the archive bits.

- A differential backup is identical to an incremental backup, except that it doesn't turn off the archive bits.

- A daily backup, also known as a daily copy backup, makes copies of all the files that have been changed that day. It does not change the archive bits.

- In Windows Vista/7, NTBackup has been replaced with the Windows Backup and Restore Center, which has only two options: back up everything or restore from a previous backup. Vista no longer supports tape backups, nor does it let you choose between differential and incremental backups.

- You can use the System Restore tool to create a restore point, a copy of your computer's configuration at a specific point in time. If you later crash or have a corrupted OS, you can restore the system to its previous state. During the restore process, only settings and programs are changed. No data is lost. Your computer will include all programs and settings as of the restore date. System Restore is turned on by default and uses some of your disk space to save information on restore points. To turn System Restore off or change the disk space usage, open the System Properties applet in Control Panel and select the System Restore tab.

- The Recovery Console is a text-based startup of Windows that gets you to a command prompt similar to the Windows command prompt. If you have the Windows 2000/XP CD-ROM, you can start the Recovery Console by running Setup, selecting Repair, and then selecting Recovery Console.

- Windows Vista and Windows 7 have dropped the Recovery Console, replacing it with the graphical System Recovery Options. Startup Repair tells Windows to automatically attempt to repair your system. You can also perform a system restore from the System Recovery Options. The Memory Diagnostic Tool locates and reports RAM errors to you. The command prompt is also accessible from the System Recovery Options.

■ Key Terms

Add or Remove Programs *(110)*
Administrative Tools *(97)*
Aero *(78)*
applet *(89)*
Automated System Recovery (ASR) *(124)*
Automatic Updates *(102)*
Autorun *(110)*

Backup Utility *(122)*
compatibility mode *(73)*
counter *(118)*
Computer *(82)*
Control Panel *(89)*
desktop *(76)*
Device Manager *(115)*

■ Key Term Quiz

Use the Key Terms list to complete the sentences that follow. Not all terms will be used.

1. You can readily see programs running in the background by looking at the _____.

2. The _____ stores information about all the hardware, drivers, and applications on a Windows system.

3. Most tech tools in Windows can be found in _____.

4. The _____ in Windows offers a great spot for accessing favorite programs without resorting to the Start menu.

5. Jill accidentally deleted a critical file. Winona the tech assures her that the file is no doubt in the _____ and not lost forever.

6. Windows uses the _____ or swap file for virtual memory.

7. Windows Vista desktop uses _____ to enable transparency and Flip 3D.

8. You can use the login screen to log in to a Windows 2000 computer, but Windows XP and Windows Vista offer the option of using the _____ to log in.

9. A file association is defined by its _____.

10. Although not bootable, the _____ works with the \WINNT\REPAIR folder to store a copy of the Windows 2000 Registry.

1. What is the best way to access the Registry Editor in Windows XP?

   A. Start | Programs | DOS prompt icon. Type **edit**.

   B. Start | Programs | Registry Editor.

   C. Start | Run. Type **regedit32** and click OK.

   D. Start | Run. Type **regedt32** and click OK.

2. Windows XP provides a number of ready-made MMC snap-ins stored in the _____ applet in the Control Panel.

   A. System

   B. Network

   C. Administrative Tools

   D. MMC

3. Which of the following are part of the Windows desktop?

   A. Services, command line, applications

   B. Right-click, drag and drop, point and click

   C. Quick Launch toolbar, system tray, taskbar

   D. CPU, RAM, hard drive

4. The Microsoft Management Console holds individual utilities called what?

   A. Built-ins

   B. Snap-ins

   C. Applets

   D. MMCs

5. What is the name of the virtual memory file in Windows 2000/XP?

   A. SWAP.SYS

   B. CACHE.VM

   C. SYSTEM.RAM

   D. PAGEFILE.SYS

6. How do you access a command prompt in Windows Vista?

   A. Start | Run, type **cmd**, and press ENTER.

   B. Start | Run, type **dos**, and press ENTER.

   C. Start | Start Search, type **cmd**, and press ENTER.

   D. Start | Start Search, type **dos**, and press ENTER.

7. What copy protection scheme is used in Windows Vista?

   A. Activation

   B. BitLocker

   C. Event Viewer

   D. Services

8. Which key combination enables you to switch between loaded programs?

   A. ALT-ESC

   B. ALT-TAB

   C. CTRL-C

   D. CTRL-X

9. What is the benefit of 64-bit Windows over 32-bit Windows?

   A. Supports more hard drives

   B. Fewer lockups

   C. Supports more memory

   D. Supports more monitors

10. Which version of Windows provides multimedia support, such as a personal video recorder?

    A. Windows 2000 Professional

    B. Windows XP Home

    C. Windows XP Media Center

    D. Windows Vista Home Basic

11. What is the primary tool you use to observe and manipulate files on a computer?

    A. Registry

    B. Windows Aero

    C. Windows desktop

    D. Windows Explorer

12. Which of the following should be your first choice to remove an application that you no longer need?

    A. Delete the program files

    B. Use the uninstall program that came with the application

    C. Use the Add or Remove Programs applet

    D. Use the Registry Editor to remove references to the application

■ Essay Quiz

1. Your department just added four new interns who will share two PCs running Windows XP. Your boss has decided that you're the person who should take the newbies under your wing and teach them about Windows. Write a brief essay on some essential Windows folders and interfaces that every *user* should know.

2. Your boss just got off the phone with the corporate headquarters and is in somewhat of a panic. She doesn't know the first thing about the Microsoft Management Console, but now every tech is going to be issued a custom MMC. Write a brief essay explaining the function of the MMC to help allay her worries.

3. A colleague has approached you with a serious problem. He was on tech support for his home PC, and the support person told him the only way to fix the problem he was having on his Windows XP Home PC was to edit the Registry manually. Then the tech scared him, saying that if he messed up, he could destroy his PC forever. Write a short essay discussing the Registry and the tools for editing it.

Lab Project

• Lab Project 4.1

In a couple of places in the chapter, you got a taste of working with some of the more complex tools in Windows, such as the Task Manager and Performance console. Go back through the text and reread those sections, and then do an Internet search for a how-to article. Then work with the tools.

Learning CPUs

chapter
5

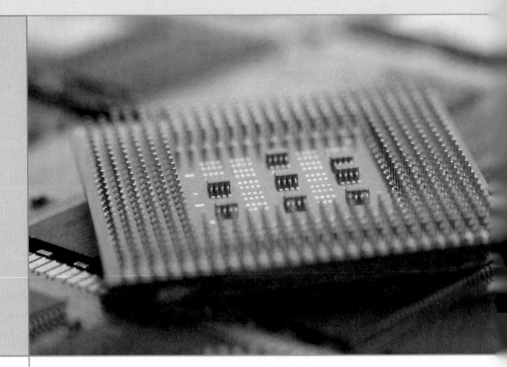

> "MEGAHERTZ: This is a
> really, really big hertz."
> —DAVE BARRY

**In this chapter, you will learn
how to**

- Identify the core components of
  a CPU
- Describe the relationship of CPUs
  and memory
- Explain the varieties of modern
  CPUs

For all practical purposes, the terms **microprocessor** and **central processing unit (CPU)** mean the same thing: it's that big chip inside your computer that many people often describe as the brain of the system. CPU makers name their microprocessors in a fashion similar to the automobile industry: CPU names get a make and a model, such as Intel Core i7 or AMD Phenom II X4. But what's happening inside the CPU to make it able to do the amazing things asked of it every time you step up to the keyboard?

CPU Core Components

Although the computer might seem to act quite intelligently, comparing the CPU to a human brain hugely overstates its capabilities. A CPU functions more like a very powerful calculator than like a brain—but, oh, what a calculator! Today's CPUs add, subtract, multiply, divide, and move billions of numbers per second. Processing that much information so quickly makes any CPU look intelligent. It's simply the speed of the CPU, rather than actual intelligence, that enables computers to perform feats such as accessing the Internet, playing visually stunning games, or creating graphics.

A good PC technician needs to understand some basic CPU functions to support PCs, so let's start with an analysis of how the CPU works. If you wanted to teach someone how an automobile engine works, you would use a relatively simple example engine, right? The same principle applies here. Let's begin our study of the CPU with the granddaddy of all PC CPUs: the famous Intel 8088, invented in the late 1970s. Although this CPU first appeared over 25 years ago, it defined the idea of the modern microprocessor and contains the same basic parts used in even the most advanced CPUs today. Stick with me, my friend. Prepare to enter that little bit of magic called the CPU.

The Man in the Box

Let's begin by visualizing the CPU as a man in a box (Figure 5.1). This is one clever guy in this box. He can perform virtually any mathematical function, manipulate data, and give answers *very quickly*.

This guy is potentially very useful to us, but there's a catch—he lives closed up in a tiny box. Before he can work with us, we must come up with a way to exchange information with him (Figure 5.2).

Imagine that we install a set of 16 light bulbs, 8 inside his box and 8 outside his box. Each of the 8 light bulbs inside the box connects to one of the 8 bulbs outside the box to form a pair. Each pair of light bulbs is always either on or off. You can control the 8 pairs of bulbs by using a set of 8 switches outside the box, and the Man in the Box can also control them by using an identical set of 8 switches inside the box. This light-bulb communication device is called the **external data bus (EDB)**.

Figure 5.3 shows a cutaway view of the external data bus. When either you or the Man in the Box flips a switch on, *both* light bulbs go on, and the switch on the other side is also flipped to the on position. If you

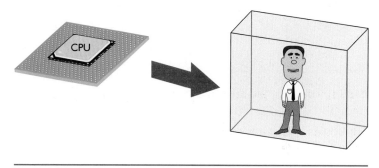

Figure 5.1   Imagine the CPU as a man in a box.

Figure 5.2   How do we talk to the Man in the Box?

Figure 5.3 Cutaway of the external data bus—note that one light bulb pair is on

Figure 5.4   Close-up of the underside of a CPU

or the Man in the Box turns a switch off, the light bulbs on both sides are turned off, along with the other switch for that pair.

Can you see how this works? By creating on/off patterns with the light bulbs that represent different pieces of data or commands, you can send that information to the Man in the Box, and he can send information back in the same way—*assuming that you agree ahead of time on what the different patterns of lights mean*. To accomplish this, you need some sort of codebook that assigns meanings to the many patterns of lights that the external data bus might display. Keep this thought in mind while we push the analogy a bit more.

Before going any further, make sure you're clear on the fact that this is an analogy, not reality. There really is an external data bus, but you won't see any light bulbs or switches on the CPU. You can, however, see little wires sticking out of the CPU (Figure 5.4). If you apply voltage to one of these wires, you in essence flip the switch. Get the idea? So if that wire had voltage, and if a tiny light bulb were attached to the wire, that light bulb would glow, would it not? By the same token, if the wire had no power, the light bulb would not glow. That is why the switch-and-light-bulb analogy may help you picture these little wires constantly flashing on and off.

Now that the external data bus enables you to communicate with the Man in the Box, you need to see how it works by placing voltages on the wires. This brings up a naming problem. It's a hassle to say something like "on-off-on-off-on-on-off-off" when talking about which wires have voltage. Rather than saying that one of the external data bus wires is on or off, use the number 1 to represent on and the number 0 to represent off (Figure 5.5). That way, instead of describing the state of the lights as "on-off-on-off-on-on-off-off," I can instead describe them by writing "10101100."

In the world of computers, we constantly turn wires on and off. As a result, we can use this "1 and 0" or **binary** system to describe the state of these wires at any given moment. (See, and you just thought computer geeks spoke in binary to confuse normal people. Ha!) There's much more to binary numbering in the world of computing, but this is a great place to start. We will revisit the binary numbering system in greater detail in Chapter 7, "Learning Motherboards."

Figure 5.5   Here "1" means on, "0" means off.

Registers

The Man in the Box provides good insight into the workspace inside a CPU. The EDB gives you a way to communicate with the Man in the Box so you can give him work to do. But to do this work, he needs a worktable; in fact, he needs at least four worktables. Each of these four worktables has 16 light bulbs. These light bulbs are not in pairs; they're just 16 light bulbs lined up straight across the table. Each light bulb is controlled by a single switch, operated only by the Man in the Box. By creating on/off patterns like the ones on the EDB, the Man in the Box can use these four sets of light bulbs to work math problems. In a real computer, these worktables are called **registers** (Figure 5.6).

Registers provide the Man in the Box with a workplace for the problems you give him. All CPUs contain a large number of registers, but for the moment let's concentrate on the four most common ones: the *general-purpose registers*. Intel named them AX, BX, CX, and DX.

Great! We're just about ready to put the Man in the Box to work, but before you close the lid on the box, you must give the Man one more tool. Remember the codebook we mentioned earlier? Let's make one to enable us to communicate with him. Figure 5.7 shows the codebook we'll use. We'll give one copy to him and make a second for us.

In this codebook, for example, 10000111 means *Move the number 7 into the AX register*. These commands are called the microprocessor's **machine language**. The commands listed in the figure are not actual commands; as you've probably guessed, I've simplified dramatically. The Intel 8088 CPU, invented in the late 1970s, actually used commands very similar to these, plus a few hundred others.

Here are some examples of real machine language for the Intel 8088:

• **Figure 5.6**   The four general-purpose registers

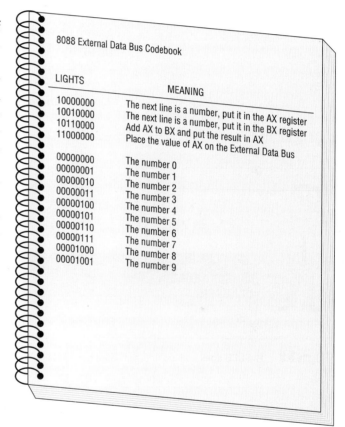

• **Figure 5.7**   CPU codebook

10111010	The next line of code is a number. Put that number into the DX register.
01000001	Add 1 to the number already in the CX register.
00111100	Compare the value in the AX register with the next line of code.

By placing machine language commands—called *lines of code*—onto the external data bus one at a time, you can instruct the Man in the Box to do

• Figure 5.8   The CPU so far

specific tasks. All of the machine language commands that the CPU understands make up the CPU's **instruction set**.

So here is the CPU so far: the Man in the Box can communicate with the outside world via the external data bus; he has four registers he can use to work on the problems you give him; and he has a codebook—the instruction set—so he can understand the different patterns (machine language commands) on the external data bus (Figure 5.8).

Clock

Okay, so you're ready to put the Man in the Box to work. You can send the first command by lighting up wires on the EDB. How does he know when you've finished setting up the wires and it's time to act?

Have you ever seen one of those old-time manual calculators with the big crank on one side? To add two numbers, you pressed a number key, the + key, and another number key, but then to make the calculator do the calculation and give you the answer, you had to pull down the crank. That was the signal that you had finished entering data and instructions and were ready for the calculator to give you an answer.

• Figure 5.9   The CPU does nothing until activated by the clock.

Well, a CPU also has a type of crank. To return to the Man in the Box, imagine there's a bell inside the box activated by a button on the outside of the box. Each time you press the button to sound the bell, the Man in the Box reads the next set of lights on the external data bus. Of course, a real computer doesn't use a bell. The bell on a real CPU is a special wire called the **clock wire** (most diagrams label the clock wire CLK). A charge on the CLK wire tells the CPU that another piece of information is waiting to be processed (Figure 5.9).

For the CPU to process a command placed on the external data bus, a certain minimum voltage must be applied to the CLK wire. A single charge to the CLK wire is called a **clock cycle**. Actually, the CPU requires at least two clock cycles to act on a command, and usually more. Using the manual calculator analogy, you need to pull the crank at least twice before anything happens. In fact, a CPU may require hundreds of clock cycles to process some commands (Figure 5.10).

The maximum number of clock cycles that a CPU can handle in a given period of time is referred to as its **clock speed**. The clock speed is the

• Figure 5.10   The CPU often needs more than one clock cycle to get a result.

fastest speed at which a CPU can operate, determined by the CPU manufacturer. The Intel 8088 processor had a clock speed of 4.77 MHz (4.77 million cycles per second), extremely slow by modern standards, but still a pretty big number compared to using a pencil and paper. CPUs today run at speeds in excess of 3 GHz (3 billion cycles per second).

1 hertz (1 Hz) = 1 cycle per second

1 megahertz (1 MHz) = 1 million cycles per second

1 gigahertz (1 GHz) = 1 billion cycles per second

Understand that a CPU's clock speed is its *maximum* speed, not the speed at which it *must* run. A CPU can run at any speed, as long as that speed does not exceed its clock speed. Manufacturers used to print the CPU's clock speed directly onto the CPU, but for the past few years they've used cryptic codes (Figure 5.11). As the chapter progresses you'll see why they do this.

The **system crystal** determines the speed at which a CPU and the rest of the PC operate. The system crystal is usually a quartz oscillator, very similar to the one in a wristwatch, soldered to the motherboard (Figure 5.12). The quartz oscillator sends out an electric pulse at a certain speed, many millions of times per second. This signal goes first to a clock chip that adjusts the pulse, usually increasing the pulse sent by the crystal by some large multiple. (The folks who make motherboards could connect the crystal directly to the CPU's clock wire, but then if you wanted to replace your CPU with a CPU with a different clock speed, you'd need to replace the crystal too.) As long as the PC is turned on, the quartz oscillator, through the clock chip, fires a charge on the CLK wire, in essence pushing the system along.

Visualize the system crystal as a metronome for the CPU. The quartz oscillator repeatedly fires a charge on the CLK wire, setting the beat, if you will, for the CPU's activities. If the system crystal sets a beat slower than the CPU's clock speed, the CPU will work just fine, though at the slower speed of the system crystal. If the system crystal forces the CPU to run faster than its clock speed, it can overheat and stop working.

 CPU makers sell the exact make and model of CPU at a number of different speeds. All of these CPUs come off of the same assembly lines, so why different speeds? Every CPU comes with subtle differences— flaws, really—in the silicon that makes one CPU run faster than another. The speed difference comes from testing each CPU to see what speed it can handle.

AMD Phenom™ II
HDX810WFK4FGI
CACZC AC 0904GPMW
9069529A90617

• **Figure 5.11**   Where is the clock speed?

 Aggressive users sometimes intentionally **overclock** CPUs by telling the clock chip to multiply the pulse faster than the CPU's designed speed. They do this to make slower (cheaper) CPUs run faster. This is a risky business that can destroy your CPU, but those willing to take that risk often do it.

• **Figure 5.12**   One of many types of system crystals

Some motherboards enable you to override the default or automatic settings by changing a jumper or making a change in CMOS. A few enthusiasts' motherboards even enable you to make software changes to alter the speed of your CPU.

Before you install a CPU into a system, you must make sure that the crystal and clock chip send out the correct clock pulse for that particular CPU. In the not-so-old days, this required very careful adjustments. With today's systems, the motherboard talks to the CPU (at a very slow speed), the CPU tells the motherboard the clock speed it needs, and the clock chip automatically adjusts for the CPU, making this process now invisible.

Back to the External Data Bus

One more reality check. We've been talking about tables with racks of light bulbs, but of course real CPU registers don't use light bulbs to represent on/1 and off/0. Registers are tiny storage areas on the CPU, microscopic semiconductor circuits. When one of these circuits holds a charge, you can think of the light bulb as on; no charge, the light bulb is off.

Figure 5.13 is a diagram of a real 8088 CPU, showing the wires that comprise the external data bus and the single clock wire. Because the registers are inside the CPU, you can't see them in this figure.

Now that you have learned what components are involved in the process, try the following simple exercise to see how the process works. In this example, you tell the CPU to add 2 + 3. To do this, you must send a series of commands to the CPU; the CPU will act on each command, eventually giving you an answer. Refer to the codebook in Figure 5.7 to translate the instructions you're giving the Man in the Box into binary commands.

Did you try it? Here's how it works:

1. Place 10000000 on the external data bus (EDB).
2. Place 00000010 on the EDB.
3. Place 10010000 on the EDB.
4. Place 00000011 on the EDB.
5. Place 10110000 on the EDB.
6. Place 11000000 on the EDB.

When you finish step 6, the value on the EDB will be 00000101, the decimal number 5 written in binary.

Congrats! You just added 2 + 3 by using individual commands from the codebook. This set of commands is known as a **program**, which is a series of commands sent to a CPU in a specific order for the CPU to perform work. Each discrete setting of the external data bus is a line of code. This program, therefore, has six lines of code.

• **Figure 5.13** Diagram of an Intel 8088 showing the external data bus and clock wires

■ Memory

Now that you've seen how the CPU executes program code, let's work backward in the process for a moment and think about how the program code gets to the external data bus. The program itself is stored on the hard drive. In theory, you could build a computer that sends data from the hard drive directly to the CPU, but there's a problem—the hard drive is too slow. Even the ancient 8088, with its clock speed of 4.77 MHz, could conceivably process several million lines of code every second. Modern CPUs crank out billions of lines every second. Hard drives simply can't give the data to the CPU at a fast enough speed.

Computers need some other device that takes copies of programs from the hard drive and then sends them, one line at a time, to the CPU quickly enough to keep up with its demands. Because each line of code is nothing more than a pattern of eight ones and zeros, any device that can store ones and zeros eight-across will do. Devices that in any way hold ones and zeros that the CPU accesses are known generically as **memory**.

Many types of devices store ones and zeros perfectly well—technically even a piece of paper counts as memory—but computers need memory that does more than just store groups of eight ones and zeros. Consider this pretend program:

1. Put 2 in the AX register.
2. Put 5 in the BX register.
3. If AX is greater than BX, run line 4; otherwise, go to line 6.
4. Add 1 to the value in AX.
5. Go back to line 1.
6. Put the value of AX on the EDB.

This program has an IF statement, also called a *branch* by CPU makers. The CPU needs a way to address each line of this memory—a way for the CPU to say to the memory, "Give me the next line of code" or "Give me line 6." Addressing memory takes care of another problem: the memory must not only store programs but also store the result of the programs. If the CPU adds 2 + 3 and gets 5, the memory needs to store that 5 in such a way that other programs may later read that 5, or possibly even store that 5 on a hard drive. By addressing each line of memory, other programs will know where to find the data.

Memory and RAM

Memory must store not only programs but also data. The CPU needs to be able to read and write to this storage medium. Additionally, this system must enable the CPU to jump to *any* line of stored code as easily as to any other line of code. All of this must be done at or at least near the clock speed of the CPU. Fortunately, this magical device has existed for many years: **random access memory (RAM)**.

In Chapter 6, "Learning RAM," the concept of RAM is developed in detail, so for now let's look at RAM as an electronic spreadsheet, like one you can generate in Microsoft Excel (Figure 5.14). Each cell in this spreadsheet can store only a one or a zero. Each cell is called a **bit**. Each row in the spreadsheet is eight bits across to match the external data bus of the 8088. Each row of eight bits is called a **byte**. In the PC world, RAM transfers and stores data to and from the CPU in byte-sized chunks.

1	0	0	0	0	0	1	1
0	1	0	0	0	0	0	0
0	0	0	0	1	1	0	1
0	1	0	1	0	0	0	0
0	0	0	0	0	0	0	1
0	1	0	1	1	0	1	0
0	0	1	1	1	1	0	0
0	0	0	0	1	0	0	1
1	1	1	0	0	0	0	0
0	0	1	0	1	1	1	0
1	0	0	0	0	0	0	0
1	0	1	0	1	0	1	0

● **Figure 5.14**   RAM as a spreadsheet

RAM is therefore arranged in byte-sized rows. Here are the terms used to talk about quantities of bits:

- Any individual 1 or 0 = a bit
- 4 bits = a nibble
- 8 bits = a byte
- 16 bits = a word
- 32 bits = a double word
- 64 bits = a paragraph or quad word

● **Figure 5.15**   Typical RAM

The number of bytes of RAM varies from PC to PC. In earlier PCs, from around 1980 to 1990, the typical system would have only a few hundred thousand bytes of RAM. Today's systems often have billions of bytes of RAM.

Let's stop here for a quick reality check. Electronically, RAM looks like a spreadsheet, but real RAM is made of groups of semiconductor chips soldered onto small cards that snap into your computer (Figure 5.15). In Chapter 6, "Learning RAM," you'll see how these groups of chips actually make themselves look like a spreadsheet. For now, don't worry about real RAM and just stick with the spreadsheet idea.

The CPU accesses any one row of RAM as easily and as fast as any other row, which explains the "random access" part of RAM. Not only is RAM randomly accessible, it's also fast. By storing programs on RAM, the CPU can access and run them very quickly. RAM also stores any data that the CPU actively uses.

Computers use **dynamic RAM (DRAM)** for the main system memory. DRAM needs both a constant electrical charge and a periodic refresh of the circuits; otherwise, it loses data—that's what makes it dynamic rather than static in content. The refresh can cause some delays, because the CPU has to wait for the refresh to happen, but modern CPU manufacturers have clever ways to get by this issue, as you'll see when you read about the generations of processors later in this chapter.

Don't confuse RAM with mass storage devices such as hard drives and flash drives. You use hard drives and flash drives to store programs and data permanently. Chapter 9, "Hard Drive Technologies," and Chapter 10, "Removable Media," discuss permanent storage in intimate detail.

Address Bus

● **Figure 5.16**   Extending the EDB

So far, the entire PC consists of only a CPU and RAM. But the CPU and the RAM need some connection so they can talk to each other. To do so, extend the external data bus from the CPU so it can talk to the RAM (Figure 5.16).

Wait a minute. This is not a matter of just plugging the RAM into the external data bus wires! RAM is a spreadsheet with thousands and thousands of discrete rows, and you only need to look at the contents of one row of the spreadsheet at a time, right? So how do you connect the RAM to the external data bus in such a way that the CPU can see any one given row but still give the CPU the capability to look at *any* row in RAM? We need some type of chip between the RAM and the CPU to make the connection. The CPU needs to be able to say which row of RAM it wants, and the chip should handle the mechanics of retrieving that row of data from the RAM and putting it on the external data bus. Wouldn't you know I just happen to have such a chip? This chip comes with many names, but for right now just call it the **memory controller chip (MCC)**.

The MCC contains special circuitry so it can grab the contents of any single line of RAM and place that data or command on the external data bus. This in turn enables the CPU to act on that code (Figure 5.17).

Once the MCC is in place to grab any discrete byte of RAM, the CPU needs to be able to tell the MCC which line of code it needs. The CPU therefore gains a second set of wires, called the **address bus**, with which it can communicate with the MCC. Different CPUs have different numbers of wires (which, you will soon see, is very significant). The 8088 had 20 wires in its address bus (Figure 5.18).

By turning the address bus wires on and off in different patterns, the CPU tells the MCC which line of RAM it wants at any given moment. Every different pattern of ones and zeros on these 20 wires points to one byte of RAM. There are two big questions here. First, how many different patterns of on-and-off wires can exist with 20 wires? And second, which pattern goes to which row of RAM?

● **Figure 5.17**   The MCC grabs a byte of RAM.

● **Figure 5.18**   Address bus

How Many Patterns?

Mathematics can answer the first question. Each wire in the address bus exists in only one of two states: on or off. If the address bus consisted of only one wire, that wire would at any given moment be either on or off. Mathematically, that gives you (pull out your old pre-algebra books) $2^1 = 2$ different combinations. If you have two address bus wires, the address bus wires create $2^2 = 4$ different combinations. If you have 20 wires, you would have 2^{20} (or 1,048,576) combinations. Because each pattern points to one line of code and each line of RAM is one byte, if you know the number of wires in the CPU's address bus, you know the maximum amount of RAM that a particular CPU can handle.

Because the 8088 had a 20-wire address bus, the most RAM it could handle was 2^{20} or 1,048,576 bytes. The 8088, therefore, had an *address space* of 1,048,576 bytes. This is not to say that every computer with an 8088 CPU had 1,048,576 bytes of RAM. Far from it! The original IBM PC only had a measly 64 kilobytes—but that was considered plenty back in the Dark Ages of Computing in the early 1980s.

Okay, so you know that the 8088 had 20 address wires and a total address space of 1,048,576 bytes. Although this is accurate, no one uses such an exact term to discuss the address space of the 8088. Instead you say that the 8088 had one *megabyte* (1 MB) of address space.

What's a "mega"? Well, let's get some terminology down. Dealing with computers means constantly dealing with the number of patterns a set of wires can handle. Certain powers of 2 have names used a lot in the computing world. The following list explains.

1 kilo = 2^{10} = 1024 (abbreviated as "K")

1 kilobyte = 1024 bytes (abbreviated as "KB")

1 mega = 2^{20} = 1,048,576 (abbreviated as "M")

1 megabyte = 1,048,576 bytes (abbreviated as "MB")

1 giga = 2^{30} = 1,073,741,824 (abbreviated as "G")

1 gigabyte = 1,073,741,824 bytes (abbreviated as "GB")

1 tera = 2^{40} = 1,099,511,627,776 (abbreviated as "T")

1 terabyte = 1,099,511,627,776 bytes (abbreviated as "TB")

1 kilo is *not* equal to 1000 (one thousand)

1 mega is *not* equal to 1,000,000 (one million)

1 giga is *not* equal to 1,000,000,000 (one billion)

1 tera is *not* equal to 1,000,000,000,000 (one trillion)

(But they are pretty close!)

Of course, 1 kilo is equal to 1000 when you talk in terms of the metric system. It also means 1000 when you talk about the clock speed of a chip, so 1 KHz is equal to 1000 Hz. When you talk storage capacity, though, the binary numbers kick in, making 1 KB = 1024 bytes. Got it? This same bizarre dual meaning applies all the way up the food chain, so 1 MHz is 1,000,000 Hz, but 1 MB is 1,048,576 bytes; 1 GHz is 1 billion Hz, but 1 GB is 1,073,741,824 bytes; and so on.

> Bits and bytes are abbreviated differently. Bytes get a capital *B* whereas bits get a lowercase *b*. So for example, 4 KB is four kilobytes, but 4 Kb is four kilobits.

Which Pattern Goes to Which Row?

The second question is a little harder: "Which pattern goes to which row of RAM?" To understand this, let's take a moment to discuss binary counting. In binary, only two numbers exist, 0 and 1, which makes binary a handy way to work with wires that turn on and off. Let's try to count in binary: 0, 1…what's next? It's not 2—you can only use zeros and ones. The next number after 1 is 10! Now let's count in binary to 1000: 0, 1, 10, 11, 100, 101, 110, 111, 1000. Try counting to 10000. Don't worry; it hardly takes any time at all.

Super; you now count in binary as well as any math professor. Let's add to the concept. Stop thinking about binary for just a moment and think about good old base 10 (regular numbers). If you have the number 365, can you put zeros in front of the 365, like this: 000365? Sure you can—it doesn't change the value at all. The same thing is true in binary. Putting zeros in front of a value doesn't change a thing! Let's count again to 1000 in binary. In this case, add enough zeros to make 20 places:

00000000000000000000

00000000000000000001

00000000000000000010

00000000000000000011

00000000000000000100

00000000000000000101

00000000000000000110

00000000000000000111

00000000000000001000

Hey! This would be a great way to represent each line of RAM on the address bus, wouldn't it? The CPU identifies the first byte of RAM on the address bus with 00000000000000000000. The CPU identifies the last RAM row with 11111111111111111111. When the CPU turns off all of the address bus wires, it wants the first line of RAM; when it turns on all of the wires, it wants the 1,048,576th line of RAM. Obviously, the address bus also addresses all of the rows of RAM in between. So, by lighting up different patterns of ones and zeros on the address bus, the CPU can access any row of RAM it needs.

■ Modern CPUs

Modern CPUs retain the core structures of the Intel 8088, such as registers, instruction sets, and, of course, the **arithmetic logic unit (ALU)**—our friend, the Man in the Box. But in the decades of the personal computer, many manufacturers have risen to challenge Intel's dominance—some have even survived—and all processor makers have experimented with various processor shapes, connectors, and more. The amazing variety of modern CPUs presents unique challenges to a new tech. Which processors go on which motherboards? Can a motherboard use processors from two or more manufacturers? Aren't processors all designed for PCs and thus interchangeable?

This section maps out the modern processor scene. It starts with a brief look at the manufacturers so you know who the players are. Once you know who's making the CPUs, we'll go through the generations of CPUs in wide use today, starting with the Intel Pentium. All modern processors share fundamental technology first introduced by Intel in the Pentium CPU. I use the Pentium, therefore, to discuss the details of the shared technology, and then add specific bonus features when discussing subsequent processors.

Manufacturers

When IBM awarded Intel the contract to provide the CPUs for its new IBM PC back in 1980, it established for Intel a virtual monopoly on all PC CPUs. The other home-computer CPU makers of the time faded away: MOS Technology, Zilog, Motorola—no one could compete directly with Intel. Over time, other competitors have risen to challenge Intel's market-segment share dominance. In particular, a company called Advanced Micro Devices (AMD) began to make clones of Intel CPUs, creating an interesting and rather cutthroat competition with Intel that lasts to this day.

Intel

Intel Corporation thoroughly dominated the personal computer market with its CPUs and motherboard support chips. At nearly every step in the evolution of the PC, Intel has led the way with technological advances and surprising flexibility for such a huge corporation. Intel CPUs—and more specifically, their instruction sets—define the personal computer. Intel currently produces a dozen or so models of CPU for both desktop and portable computers. Most of Intel's desktop processors are sold under the Celeron, Pentium, and Core brands. Their very low-power portable/smart phone chips are branded Atom; their high-end workstation/server ones are called Xeon.

AMD

You can't really talk about CPUs without mentioning Advanced Micro Devices—the Cogswell Cogs to Intel's Spacely Sprockets. AMD makes superb CPUs for the PC market and provides competition that keeps Intel on it toes. Like Intel, AMD doesn't just make CPUs, but their CPU business is certainly the part that the public notices. AMD has made CPUs that clone the function of Intel CPUs. If Intel invented the CPU used in the original IBM PC, how could AMD make clone CPUs without getting sued? Well, chipmakers have a habit of exchanging technologies through cross-license agreements. Way back in 1976, AMD and Intel signed just such an agreement, giving AMD the right to copy certain types of CPUs.

The trouble started with the Intel 8088. Intel needed AMD to produce CPUs. The PC business was young back then, and providing multiple suppliers gave IBM confidence in their choice of CPUs. Life was good. But after a few years, Intel had grown tremendously and no longer wanted AMD to make CPUs. AMD said, "Too bad. See this agreement you signed?" Throughout the 1980s and into the 1990s, AMD made pin-for-pin identical CPUs that matched the Intel lines of CPUs (Figure 5.19). You could yank an Intel CPU out of a system and snap in an AMD CPU—no problem!

• **Figure 5.19**   Identical Intel and AMD 486 CPUs from the early 1990s

In January 1995, after many years of legal wrangling, Intel and AMD settled and decided to end the licensing agreements. As a result of this settlement, AMD chips are no longer compatible with sockets or motherboards made for Intel CPUs—even though in some cases the chips look similar. Today, if you want to use an AMD CPU, you must purchase a motherboard designed for AMD CPUs. If you want to use an Intel CPU, you must purchase a motherboard designed for Intel CPUs. So you now have a choice: Intel or AMD. You'll look at both brands as you learn more about modern processors in this chapter.

CPU Packages

One of the many features that make PCs attractive is the ability for users (okay, maybe advanced users) to replace one CPU with another. If you want a removable CPU, you need your CPUs to use a standardized package with a matching standardized socket on the motherboard. CPUs have gone

• **Figure 5.20**   The dual inline pin package of the Intel 8088

through many packages, with manufacturers changing designs like snakes shedding skins. The fragile little DIP package of the 8088 (Figure 5.20) gave way to rugged slotted processors in the late 1990s (Figure 5.21), which have in turn given way to CPUs using the now prevalent grid array packaging.

The grid array package has been popular since the mid-1980s. The most common form of grid array is the pin grid array (PGA). PGA CPUs are distinguished by their square shape with many—usually hundreds—of tiny pins (Figure 5.22).

Collectively, Intel and AMD have used close to 100 variations of the PGA package over the years for hundreds of CPU models with such names as staggered-PGA, micro-PGA, ball grid array (which uses tiny balls instead of pins), and land grid array (which uses flat pads instead of pins). Other varieties of PGA CPUs are based on the number of pins sticking out of the CPU. The CPUs snap into special sockets on the motherboard, with each socket designed to match the pins (or balls or pads) on the CPU. To make CPU insertion and removal easier, these sockets—officially called **zero insertion force (ZIF) sockets**—use a small arm on the side of the socket (Figure 5.23) or a cage that fits over the socket (Figure 5.24) to hold the CPU in place. ZIF sockets are universal and easily identified by their squarish shape.

The first generations of sockets used a numbering system that started with Socket 1 and went through Socket 8. Because of the hassle of trying to remember how many pins went with each type of socket, CPU makers started giving all sockets a name based on the number of pins. Most sockets today have names like Socket 1366 and Socket 775 to reflect the number of pins.

• **Figure 5.21**   An AMD Athlon Slot A processor

   Never, ever touch or bend the pins on the bottom of a CPU. Also, always check for bent pins before installing a new CPU!

   Although there are many types of PGA packages, most techs just call them all "PGA."

Although there are many types of PGA packages, most techs just call them all "PGA."

AMD CPUs and sockets have totally different numbering systems than Intel CPUs and sockets, so techs often use the name of the socket instead of AMD or Intel. For example: "Hey, did you see that Socket 1366 motherboard?"

• **Figure 5.22**   Samples of PGA packages

● **Figure 5.23** ZIF socket with arm on side

● **Figure 5.24** ZIF socket with cage over the top

Many of the CPU features attributed here to the Pentium actually appeared earlier, but the Pentium was the first CPU to have *all* of these features.

It's very important to know the more common CPU/socket types. As you go through each type of CPU in this chapter, pay attention to the socket types used by those particular CPUs.

The Pentium CPU: The Early Years

Since the advent of the 8088 way back in the late 1970s, CPU makers have made many improvements. As technology has progressed from the 8088 to the most current CPUs, the sizes of the external data bus, address bus, and registers have grown dramatically. The clock speeds at which CPUs run have kept pace, getting faster and faster with each successive generation of processor. The 1980s were an exciting time for CPU technology. The 8088 CPU was supplanted by a series of improved processors with names such as 80286, 80386, and 80486 (Figure 5.25). These CPU families incorporated wider buses, increasingly higher clock speeds, and other improvements.

In the early 1990s, Intel unveiled the Pentium CPU. Although no longer manufactured, the original Pentium CPU was the first Intel CPU to contain all of the core functions that define today's modern CPUs.

The Pentium retained the core features of the 8088 and subsequent processors, although the clock was much faster, the address bus and external data bus were wider, and the registers had more bits. You'll also see a number of other improvements that simply didn't exist on the original 8088.

The Rise of 32-bit Processing

The old 8088 had 16-bit registers, an 8-bit EDB, and a 20-bit address bus. Old operating systems (such as DOS and early versions of Windows) were written to work on the 8088. Over the years, later CPUs gradually increased their address buses and general-purpose register sizes to 32 bits, allowing much more powerful operating systems (such as Linux, Windows XP, and Windows Vista) to work with the Pentium to process larger numbers at a single time and to address up to $2^{32} = 4,294,967,296 = 4$ gigabytes of RAM (Figure 5.26). Running 32-bit operating systems on 32-bit hardware is called *32-bit processing*.

Both AMD and Intel now make 64-bit processors that address up to $2^{64} = 18,446,744,073,709,551,616$ bytes of RAM. To take advantage of this larger address bus, a 64-bit version of the operating system must be used. You'll learn more about 64-bit processors later in this chapter.

● **Figure 5.25**   Old CPUs

● **Figure 5.26**   A 32-bit register

Pipelining

Remember earlier when we talked about pulling the crank multiple times to get an answer out of the CPU? This is because to get a command from the EDB, do the calculation, and then get the answer back out on the EDB, the CPU takes at least four steps (each of these steps is called a *stage*):

1. **Fetch**   Get the data from the EDB.
2. **Decode**   Figure out what type of command needs to be done.
3. **Execute**   Perform the calculation.
4. **Write**   Send the data back onto the EDB.

Smart, discrete circuits inside your CPU handle each of these stages. In early CPUs, when a command was placed on the EDB, each stage did its job and the CPU handed back the answer before starting the next command, requiring at least four clock cycles to process a command. In every clock cycle, three of the four circuits sat idle. Today, the circuits are organized in a conveyer-belt fashion called a **pipeline**. With pipelining, each stage does its job with each clock-cycle pulse, creating a much more efficient process. The CPU has multiple circuits doing multiple jobs, so let's add pipelining to the Man in the Box analogy. Now, it's *Men* in the Box (Figure 5.27)!

Pipelines keep every stage of the processor busy on every click of the clock, making a CPU run more efficiently without

● **Figure 5.27**   Simple pipeline

• **Figure 5.28**   Bored integer unit

increasing the clock speed. Note that at this point, the CPU has four stages: fetch, decode, execute, and write—a four-stage pipeline. No CPU ever made has fewer than four stages, but advancements in caching have increased the number of stages over the years. Current CPU pipelines contain many more stages, up to 20 in some cases.

Pipelining isn't perfect. Sometimes a stage hits a complex command that requires more than one clock cycle, forcing the pipeline to stop. Your CPU tries to avoid these stops, called *pipeline stalls*. The decode stage tends to cause the most pipeline stalls; certain commands are complex and therefore harder to decode than other commands. The Pentium used two decode stages to reduce the chance of pipeline stalls due to complex decoding.

Pipelining certainly helped the Pentium run more efficiently, but there's another issue: the execute stage. The inside of the CPU is composed of multiple chunks of circuitry to handle the many types of calculations your PC needs to do. For example, one part, the *integer unit*, handles integer math: basic math for numbers with no decimal point. A perfect example of integer math is $2 + 3 = 5$. The typical CPU spends more than 90 percent of its work doing integer math. But the Pentium also had special circuitry to handle complex numbers, called the **floating point unit (FPU)**. With a single pipeline, only the integer unit or the FPU worked at any execution stage. Worse yet, floating point calculation often took many, many clock cycles to execute, forcing the CPU to stall the pipeline until the floating point unit finished executing the complex command (Figure 5.28).

To keep things moving, the folks at Intel gave the Pentium two pipelines: one main, do-everything pipeline and one that only handled integer math. Although this didn't *stop* pipeline stalls, a second pipeline kept running when the main one stalled (Figure 5.29).

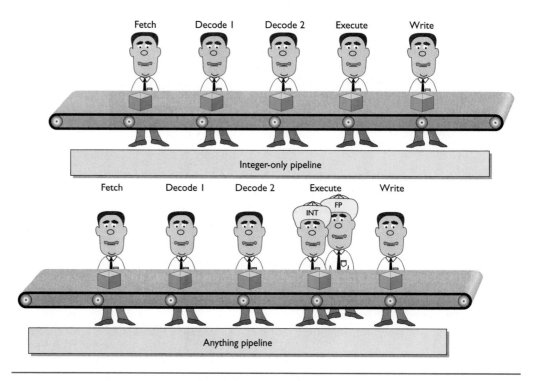

• **Figure 5.29**   The Pentium dual pipeline

The two pipelines on the old Pentium were so successful that Intel and AMD added more and more pipelines to subsequent CPUs. Most CPUs today have around eight pipelines, although there's tremendous variance from CPU to CPU.

CPU Cache

When you send a program to the CPU, you actually run lots of little programs all at the same time. Okay, let's be fair here: *you* didn't send all of these little programs—you just started your Web browser or some other program. The moment you double-clicked that icon, Windows started sending lots of programs to the CPU. Each of these programs breaks down into some number of little pieces, called *threads*, and data. Each thread is a series of instructions designed to do a particular job with the data.

Take a look at Figure 5.30. It shows four programs in RAM: a Web browser, Solitaire, an image-editing program, and an e-mail program. Note they are not the same size. Some programs need more RAM than others.

Modern CPUs don't execute instructions sequentially, first doing step 1, then step 2, and so on; but rather process all kinds of instructions. Most applications have certain instructions and data that get reused, sometimes many times.

One of the biggest differences between equivalent AMD and Intel processors is the pipelines. AMD tends to go for lots of short pipelines, whereas Intel tends to go with just a few long pipelines.

• **Figure 5.30**   Four programs in RAM

Pipelining CPUs work fantastically well as long as the pipelines stay filled with instructions. Because the CPU runs faster than the RAM can supply it with code, you'll always get pipeline stalls—called **wait states**—because the RAM can't keep up with the CPU. To reduce wait states, the Pentium came with built-in, very high-speed RAM called **static RAM (SRAM)**. This SRAM would preload as many instructions as possible and would also keep copies of already run instructions and data in the hope that the CPU would need to work on them again (Figure 5.31). SRAM used in this fashion is called a **cache**.

The SRAM cache inside the CPU was tiny, only about 16 KB, but it improved performance tremendously. In fact, it helped so much that many motherboard makers began adding a cache directly to the Pentium motherboards. These caches were much larger, usually around 128 to 512 KB. When the CPU looked for a line of code, it first went to the built-in cache; if the code wasn't there, the CPU went to the cache on the motherboard. The cache on the CPU was called the *L1 cache* because it was the one the CPU first tried to use. The cache on the motherboard was called the *L2 cache*, not because it was on the motherboard but because it was the second cache the CPU checked. Later, engineers took this cache concept even further and

You'll hear caches referred to as Level 1, Level 2, and Level 3 for L1, L2, and L3 cache, respectively. Any of the terms are acceptable.

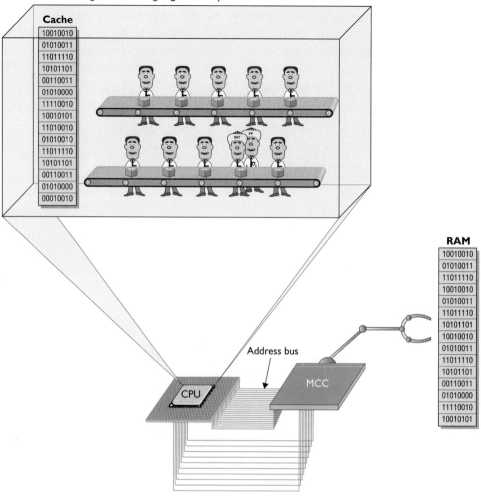

We're ready for the next line of code... oh look, it's right here in our cache! Good thing, too, because going all the way out to RAM would take forever!

• **Figure 5.31**   RAM cache

It's tempting to ask why processor manufacturers didn't just include bigger L1 caches instead of making onboard L1 and L2 caches. The answer is that a very small L1 and a larger L2 are much more efficient than a single fast L1.

added the L2 cache onboard the CPU. Some CPUs even include three caches: an L1, an L2, and an L3 cache.

The Pentium was capable of *branch prediction*, a process whereby the CPU attempted to anticipate program branches before they got to the CPU itself. An IF statement provides a nice example of this: "If the value in the AX register = 5, stop running this code and jump to another memory location." Such a jump would make all of the data in the cache useless. The Pentium could recognize a branch statement. Using a counter that kept a record about the direction of the previous branch, the CPU would guess which way the branch was going to go and make sure that side of the branch was in its cache. The counter wasn't perfect, but it was right more often than it was wrong.

Clock Speed and Multipliers

In the earliest motherboards, the clock chip pushed every chip on the motherboard, not just the CPU. This setup worked great for a while until it became obvious that CPU makers (really Intel) could make CPUs with a much higher clock speed than the rest of the chips on the motherboard. So Intel had a choice: either stop making faster CPUs or come up with some way to make CPUs run faster than the rest of the computer.

To overcome this problem, Intel developed clock-multiplying CPUs. A **clock-multiplying CPU** takes the incoming clock signal and multiplies it inside the CPU to let the internal circuitry of the CPU run faster. The secret to making clock multiplying work is caching. CPUs with caches spend the majority of their clock cycles performing calculations and moving data back and forth within the caches, not sending any data on the external buses.

All modern CPUs are clock multipliers. So in reality, every CPU now has two clock speeds: the speed that it runs internally and the speed that it runs when talking on the address bus and the external data bus. Multipliers run from 2× up to almost 30×! Multipliers do not have to be whole numbers. You can find a CPU with a multiplier of 6.5× just as easily as you would find one with a multiplier of 7×. A late-generation Pentium would have an external speed of 66 MHz multiplied by 4.5× for an internal speed of 300 MHz. The Intel Pentium 4 3.06-GHz CPU runs at an external speed of 133 MHz with a 23× multiplier to make—yes, you've got it—3.06 GHz. Without the invention of multiplying, modern CPUs would be nowhere near their current blazing speeds.

The clock speed and the multiplier on Pentium CPU systems had to be manually configured via jumpers or DIP switches on the motherboard (Figure 5.32). Today's CPUs actually report to the motherboard through a function called CPUID (CPU identifier), and the speed and multiplier are set automatically.

For years, users pushed for faster and faster CPU clock speeds, because clock speed was considered the most important way to differentiate one CPU from another. By 2003, advancements in caching, pipelining, and many other internal aspects of the CPU made clock speed an inaccurate way to compare one CPU to another. CPU makers give their processors model numbers—nothing more than marketing names—to tell one processor from another. The Intel Core Duo T2300, for example, actually runs 1.66 GHz (166 MHz external speed with a 10× multiplier). If you want to know the speed of a particular processor, you must go to the CPU maker's Web site or other source.

Clock multiplying first surfaced during the reign of the Intel 80486 CPUs. The first clock multipliers exactly doubled the clock speed, resulting in the term *clock doubling*. This term is used interchangeably with *clock multiplying*, even though modern CPUs multiply far more than just times two.

• **Figure 5.32**   DIP switch on an old motherboard

CPU Voltages

In the simplest sense, a CPU is a collection of *transistors*, tiny electrical switches that enable the CPU to handle the binary code that makes up programs. Transistors, like other electrical devices, require a set voltage to run properly. Give a transistor too much and you fry it, too little and it doesn't work. For the first ten years of the personal computer, CPUs ran on 5 volts of electricity, just like every other circuit on the motherboard. To increase the complexity and capability with new generations of CPUs, microprocessor developers simply increased the number of transistors. But eventually they altered this strategy to increase the efficiency of the CPUs and keep the size down to something reasonable.

Intel and AMD discovered that by reducing the amount of voltage used, they could reduce the size of the transistors and cram more of them into the same space. Intel released the Pentium, for example, that required only

3.3 volts. AMD responded with its versions of the Pentium-class CPUs with even lower voltages.

Motherboard manufacturers had to scramble to adapt to the changing CPU landscape by creating motherboards that could handle multiple voltages of CPUs. All of the logic circuits still ran at 5 volts, so manufacturers started installing a **voltage regulator module (VRM)** that damped down voltages specifically for the CPUs.

• **Figure 5.33**   Voltage regulator module

Because the new and improved motherboards handled many CPU voltages, initially techs had to install a VRM specific to the CPU. As manufacturers got better at the game and built VRMs into the motherboards, techs just had to change jumpers or flip switches rather than install a VRM (Figure 5.33).

Getting the voltage right on today's CPUs is no longer a concern. Just as for clock speed and multipliers, today's CPUs tell the motherboard the voltage they need automatically. The integrated VRMs take care of the rest (Figure 5.34).

The feature set of the early Pentium CPUs beats at the heart of every subsequent processor. Newer processors have a 64-bit data bus, 32-bit or larger address bus, 32-bit or larger registers, multiple pipelines, and two or three levels of cache. All run at some multiple of the system clock. So, now that you have the scoop on the Pentium, you're ready to check out subsequent CPU models.

Original Pentium

The Pentium is not a new chip; it's been around since 1990, and the last versions of the Pentium chip were discontinued in 1995. The original Pentium was the springboard for the Pentium Pro, probably the most important CPU ever made, and thus it makes sense to start there. The rest of this chapter looks at all of the popular CPUs developed since the Pentium and describes how they've built on this legacy CPU (Figure 5.35).

• **Figure 5.34**   Typical motherboard voltage regulators

• **Figure 5.35**   An early Pentium

AMD made a competitor to the Pentium called the AMD K5. The AMD K5 was pin-compatible with the Pentium, but to keep Intel from suing them, AMD made the K5 very different on the inside, using a totally new (at least for Intel) method of processing. The AMD K5 had some success but was rather quickly upstaged by better AMD CPUs.

Pentium Pro

In 1995, Intel released the next generation of CPU, the Pentium Pro, often called the P6. The Pentium Pro was a huge CPU with a distinctive, rectangular PGA package (Figure 5.36). The P6 had the same bus and register sizes as the Pentium, but three new items made the P6 more powerful than its predecessor: quad pipelining, dynamic processing, and an on-chip L2 cache. These features carried on into every CPU version that followed, so many people consider the Pentium Pro to be the true "Father of the Modern CPU."

● **Figure 5.36**   Pentium Pro

Superscalar Execution

The P6 had four pipelines, twice as many as the Pentium. These pipelines were deeper and faster. With this many pipelines, the P6 was guaranteed to always, no matter what, run at least two instructions at the same time. The ability to execute more than one instruction in any one clock cycle is called *superscalar execution*.

Out-of-Order Processing/Speculative Execution

From time to time, a CPU must go to system memory to access code, no matter how good its cache. When a RAM access takes place, the CPU must wait a few clock cycles before processing. Sometimes the wait can be 10 or 20 clock cycles. System memory is dynamic RAM and needs to be refreshed (charged up) periodically, causing further delays. When the P6 was forced into wait states, it took advantage of the wait to look at the code in the pipeline to see if it could run any commands while the wait states were active. If it found commands it could process that were not dependent on the data being fetched from DRAM, it ran these commands out of order, a feature called *out-of-order processing*. After the DRAM returned with the code, it rearranged the commands and continued processing.

The P6 improved on the Pentium's branch prediction by adding a far more complex counter that would predict branches with a better than 90-percent success rate. With the combination of out-of-order processing and the chance of a branch prediction so high, the CPU could grab the predicted side of the branch out of the cache and run it out of order in one pipeline, even before running the branch itself. This was called *speculative execution*.

On-Chip L2 Cache

The P6 had both an L1 and an L2 cache on the CPU. Because the L2 cache was on the chip, it ran almost as fast as the L1 cache (Figure 5.37). Be careful with the term "on-chip." Just because the L2 cache was on the chip, that doesn't mean it was built into the CPU. The CPU and the L2 cache shared the same package, but physically they were separate.

● **Figure 5.37**   A P6 opened to show separate CPU and L2 cache (*photo courtesy of Intel*)

Backside bus

CPU

Cache

MCC

RAM

Frontside bus

● **Figure 5.38** Frontside and backside buses

The inclusion of the L2 cache on the chip gave rise to some new terms to describe the connections between the CPU, MCC, RAM, and L2 cache. The address bus and external data bus (connecting the CPU, MCC, and RAM) were lumped into a single term called the **frontside bus**, and the connection between the CPU and the L2 cache became known as the **backside bus**.

Figure 5.38 shows a more modern configuration, labeling the important buses. Note that the external data bus and address bus are there, but the chipset provides separate address buses and external data buses—one set just for the CPU and another set for the rest of the devices in the PC. No official name has been given to the interface between the RAM and the chipset. On the rare occasions when they discuss it, most techs simply call it the *RAM interface*.

The Pentium Pro had a unique PGA case that fit into a special socket, called Socket 8. No other CPU used this type of socket. The Pentium Pro made strong inroads in the high-end server market, but its high cost made it unacceptable for most people's desktop computers.

Although the Pentium Pro never saw a large volume of sales compared with the Pentium, many people in the industry consider it the most important chip ever created by Intel. Its feature set was the prototype for all CPUs designed ever since.

Later Pentium-Class CPUs

Intel's usual game plan in the rough-and-tumble business of chip making is to introduce a new CPU and simultaneously declare all previous CPUs obsolete. That did not happen with the Pentium Pro, however, because Intel never really developed the P6 for most users. It was to be the CPU for powerful, higher-end systems. This kept the Pentium as the CPU of choice for all but the most power-hungry systems.

While the Pentium Pro languished on the high end for several years, Intel and AMD developed new Pentium-class CPUs that incorporated a series of powerful improvements, some of which were taken from the Pentium Pro. These improvements required that they be regarded as a new family of CPUs, which I call the "later Pentium-class CPUs" (Figure 5.39). Although certainly some profound differences exist between these CPUs, they all have three groups of similar improvements: multimedia extensions (MMX), increased multipliers/clocks, and improved processing.

● **Figure 5.39** Later-generation Pentium

Later-generation Pentiums were pin-compatible with earlier Pentiums, but included a large number of improvements. The most important improvement was increases in multipliers, and therefore clock speeds, but other improvements also took place—some borrowed from the P6 and some developed just for this new breed of Pentium.

MMX

In 1996, Intel added a new enhancement to its Pentium CPU, called **multimedia extensions (MMX)**, in response to the large number of programs with heavy graphics needs coming out at this time. MMX was designed to work with large graphics by calculating on large chunks of data and performing vector math (vector math is needed to handle graphical issues such as spinning a 3D object). MMX was not heavily supported by the folks who wrote graphics programs, but MMX did start the idea that CPUs should have special circuitry just for such programs. Over time, the graphics community began to work with Intel to improve MMX, eventually replacing it with better solutions.

Increased Clocks and Multipliers

Later Pentiums all have vastly increased multipliers, resulting in higher speeds. Most early Pentiums used 2.5× multipliers at best, but later Pentium-class processors had up to 4.5× multipliers.

Pentium II

Intel's next major CPU was the Pentium II. Although highly touted as the next generation of CPUs, the Pentium II was little more than a faster Pentium Pro with MMX and a refined instruction set. The Pentium II came in a distinctive **single-edge cartridge (SEC)** that gave more space for the L2 cache and made CPU cooling easier while freeing up more room on the motherboard (Figure 5.40). Aggressive advertising and pricing made the Pentium II extremely popular.

The Pentium II initially achieved the higher clock speeds by using high multiples of a 66-MHz external speed. During this time, however, AMD began to sell CPUs designed to run on 100-MHz motherboards. Although the final Pentium II models also ran on 100-MHz motherboards, Intel's slow adoption of 100-MHz external-speed CPUs lost market share for Intel.

• **Figure 5.40**   Pentium II

The SEC cartridge also created another problem: it was not free to copy. This prevented other CPU manufacturers from making CPUs that fit in the SEC's special Slot 1 connection and forced AMD to create its own SEC packages that were incompatible with Intel's. From the Pentium II to today, AMD and Intel CPUs are no longer interchangeable. We live in a world where AMD CPUs have motherboards designed for AMD, while Intel CPUs must have motherboards designed for Intel.

AMD K6 Series

From 1997 to 2000, AMD produced a series of processors called the K6 that matched—and in many people's view, surpassed—the Pentium II, propelling AMD into serious competition with Intel (Figure 5.41). Four models were included in the K6 series: the K6, K6-2, K6-2+, and K6-III, each incorporating more advanced features than the previous model. The K6 processors incorporated a number of improvements, including a 64-KB L1 cache, extremely advanced pipelining, and support for motherboard speeds of up to 100 MHz (on later models). The K6-2 added AMD's proprietary 3DNow! instruction set—a direct

• **Figure 5.41**   AMD K6 (*photo courtesy of AMD*)

competitor to Intel's MMX and a significant advancement in graphics-handling capabilities—and increased clock speeds. The K6-III included even more advancements in pipelining and added a 256-KB L2 cache, all on a standard Socket 7 PGA package.

Pentium III

The Pentium III improved on the Pentium II by incorporating *Streaming SIMD Extensions* (*SSE*), Intel's direct competitor to AMD's 3DNow!; a number of internal processing/pipelining improvements; full support for 100-MHz and 133-MHz motherboard speeds; and a high-speed L2 cache. The Pentium III was first produced by using an SEC package (Figure 5.42), but improvements in die technology enabled Intel to produce PGA versions later, ending the short reign of the SEC-package CPUs.

AMD Athlon

Athlon is the brand name for a series of CPUs released by AMD. A number of different CPUs have been launched under this brand to compete head to head against the latest Intel chips. The original Athlon, now referred to as *Athlon Classic*, was the first AMD CPU to drop any attempt at pin compatibility with Intel chips. Instead, AMD decided to make its own AMD-only slots and sockets. The first of these sockets used an SEC package and was called Slot A (Figure 5.43).

AMD then shifted back to a PGA package with the release of an Athlon CPU codenamed Thunderbird (Figure 5.44). This CPU, along with several Athlon CPUs to come, used a proprietary 462-pin socket called Socket A. Thunderbird (like its predecessor) had an interesting double-pumped frontside bus that doubled the data rate without increasing the clock speed. The Athlon Thunderbird CPUs have a smaller but far more powerful L2 cache, as well as a number of other minor improvements when compared to the Athlon Classic.

Tech tip

CPU Codenames

Intel and AMD fight to bring out new CPUs with an almost alarming frequency, making the job of documenting all of these CPUs challenging. Luckily for us, the CPU makers use special CPU codenames for new CPUs, such as Bloomfield and Deneb to describe the first version of the Core i7 and the Phenom II X4, respectively. These codenames are in common use, and a good tech should recognize these names— plus they make a dandy way to learn about what's taking place in the CPU business.

• **Figure 5.42**   Intel Pentium III

• **Figure 5.43**   Early Athlon CPU

Next, AMD launched the Athlon XP, first under the codename Palomino. AMD incorporated a number of performance enhancements to the Athlon core, including support for Intel's SSE instructions. AMD released an update to Palomino, codenamed Thoroughbred, which featured increased external bus speeds and was manufactured by using a 130-nm process that reduced the required CPU wattage. The last 32-bit CPUs to wear the Athlon badge were codenamed Barton and Thorton. Barton featured double the L2 cache of Thoroughbred and had an even faster external bus. Thorton was a cheaper version that did not increase the size of the cache.

One interesting aspect of the Athlon XP was AMD's attempt to ignore clock speeds and instead market the CPUs by using a performance rating (PR) number that matched the equivalent power of an Intel Pentium 4 processor. For example, the Athlon XP 1800+ actually ran at 1.6 GHz, but AMD claimed it processed as fast as or faster than a Pentium 4 1.8 GHz—ergo "1800+."

• **Figure 5.44**   Athlon Thunderbird (*photo courtesy of AMD*)

AMD Duron

Duron is the generic name given to lower-end CPUs based on the Athlon processor. A Duron is basically an Athlon with a smaller cache. Because the Duron supported the same frontside bus as the Athlon, it had a slight performance edge over its low-end rival from Intel at the time. The Duron connected to the same 462-pin Socket A as the later Athlon CPUs (Figure 5.45). AMD discontinued the Duron brand in 2004 and replaced it with the Sempron brand, discussed later in this chapter.

Intel Pentium 4

• **Figure 5.45**   AMD Duron (*photo courtesy of AMD*)

Although the Pentium II and III were little more than improvements on the Intel Pentium Pro, the Pentium 4 introduced a completely redesigned core, called NetBurst. NetBurst centered on a totally new 20-stage pipeline combined with features to support this huge pipeline. Each stage of the pipeline performed fewer operations than typical pipeline stages in earlier processors, allowing Intel to crank up the clock speed for the Pentium 4 CPUs. The first Pentium 4s, codenamed Willamette, included a new version of SSE called SSE2, and later versions introduced SSE3.

The Pentium 4 featured a *quad-pumped frontside bus* where the external data bus was sampled four times per clock cycle. In the early going, there were two packages for the Pentium 4 CPUs. The first Pentium 4 CPUs came in a 423-pin PGA package. This was followed with a 478-pin PGA package (Figure 5.46). Even though the new package has more pins, it is considerably smaller than the earlier package.

Intel switched to the Land Grid Array (LGA) 775 package with the release of a Pentium 4 CPU codenamed Prescott (Figure 5.47). Again, even though the

• **Figure 5.46**   Pentium 4 (423- and 478-pin)

• **Figure 5.47**   Pentium 4 LGA

P4 Prescotts and Northwoods came in hyperthreaded and non-hyperthreaded versions.

Tech Tip

Deciphering the Numbers

Give it up. Intel must have some scheme for their CPU numbering, but it doesn't match the processor speed. They call a 2.66-GHz CPU a 506, for example, which might lead you to believe that the "6" reflects the "66" in the speed. But the 2.8-GHz CPU that followed was named the 511. Go figure!

Here's what Intel says on www.intel.com/products/processor_number/: "Intel processor numbers are based on a variety of features that may include the processor's underlying architecture, cache, Front Side Bus, clock speed, power and other Intel technologies. A processor number represents a broad set of features that can influence overall computing experience but is not a measurement of performance."

LGA 775 package has more pins than a Socket 478 package, it is smaller. With the Pentium 4 CPUs codenamed Northwood and Prescott, Intel unveiled an interesting advancement in superscalar architecture called hyperthreading.

With *hyperthreading*, each individual pipeline can run more than one thread at a time—a tricky act to achieve. A single Intel P4 with hyperthreading looks like two CPUs to the operating system. Figure 5.48 shows the Task Manager in Windows XP on a system running a hyperthreaded Pentium 4. Note how the CPU box is broken into two groups—Windows thinks this one CPU is two CPUs.

• **Figure 5.48**   Windows Task Manager with the Performance tab displayed for a system running a hyperthreaded Pentium 4

Hyperthreading enhances a CPU's efficiency but with a couple of limitations. First, the operating system and the application have to be designed to take advantage of the feature. Second, although the CPU simulates the actions of a second processor, it doesn't double the processing power because the main execution resources are not duplicated.

Starting with the LGA 775 Prescotts, Intel dumped the convention of naming CPUs by their clock speed and adopted a cryptic three-digit model-numbering system. All Prescott Pentium 4s received a three-digit number starting with a 5 or a 6. One of the 2.8-GHz Pentium 4 CPUs is a 521, for example, and one of the 3-GHz processors is called the 630.

A late version of the Pentium 4 CPU was released, called the Pentium 4 Extreme Edition. The Extreme Edition CPUs incorporated a large L3 cache and other architectural details borrowed from Intel's Xeon line of server CPUs. The Pentium 4 Extreme Edition also had some of the highest wattages ever recorded on any Intel desktop CPU—over 110 watts! Extreme Edition CPUs ran incredibly fast, but their high price kept them from making any significant impact on the market.

These Pentiums reached the apex of clock speeds, approaching 4 GHz. After this, Intel (and AMD) stopped the CPU clock-speed race and instead began to concentrate on parallel and 64-bit processing (both to be discussed later in this chapter).

Mobile Processors

The inside of a laptop PC is a cramped, hot environment where no self-respecting CPU should ever need to operate. Since the mid-1980s, CPU manufacturers have endeavored to make specialized versions of their processors to function in the rugged world of laptops. Over the years, a number of CPU laptop solutions have appeared. Virtually every CPU made by Intel or AMD has come in a mobile version. You can usually tell a mobile version by the word "mobile" or the letter "M" in its name. Here are a few examples:

- Mobile Intel Pentium III

- Intel Pentium M

- Mobile AMD Athlon 64

- AMD Turion 64 (All Turions are mobile processors but don't have "mobile" or "M" in their name. AMD usually adds "mobile technology" as part of the Turion description.)

- Intel Core Duo (see the "Intel Core" section later in the chapter)

A mobile processor uses less power than an equivalent desktop model. This provides two advantages. First, the battery in the laptop lasts longer. Second, the CPU runs cooler, and the cooler the CPU, the fewer cooling devices you need.

Almost every mobile processor today runs at a lower voltage than the desktop version of the same CPU. As a result, most mobile CPUs also run at lower speeds—it takes juice if you want the speed! Mobile CPUs usually top out at about 75 percent of the speed of the same CPU's desktop version.

Reducing voltage is a good first step, but making a smart CPU that can use less power in low-demand situations reduces power usage even more.

Tech Tip

Centrino

Intel uses the marketing term **Centrino** *in the laptop market to define complete mobile solutions, including a mobile processor, support chips, and wireless networking. There is no Centrino CPU, only Centrino solutions that include some type of Intel mobile CPU.*

The first manifestation of this was the classic **System Management Mode (SMM)**. Introduced back in the times of the Intel 80386 processor, SMM provided the CPU with the capability to turn off devices that use a lot of power, such as the monitor or the hard drives. Although originally designed just for laptops, SMM has been replaced with more advanced power-management functions that are now built into all AMD and Intel CPUs.

CPU makers have taken power reduction one step further with **throttling**—the capability of modern CPUs to slow themselves down during low demand times or if the CPU detects that it is getting too hot. Intel's version of throttling is called *SpeedStep*, and AMD's version is known as *PowerNow!*.

Early 64-Bit CPUs

Both AMD and Intel now produce 64-bit CPUs. A 64-bit CPU has general-purpose, floating point, and address registers that are 64 bits wide, meaning they can handle 64-bit-wide code in one pass—twice as wide as a 32-bit processor. And they can address much, much more memory.

With the 32-bit address bus of the Pentium and later CPUs, the maximum amount of memory the CPU can address is 2^{32} or 4,294,967,296 bytes. With a 64-bit address bus, CPUs can address 2^{64} bytes of memory, or more precisely, 18,446,744,073,709,551,616 bytes of memory—that's a lot of RAM! This number is so big that gigabytes and terabytes are no longer convenient, so we now go to an exabyte (2^{60}). A 64-bit address bus can address 16 exabytes of RAM.

No 64-bit CPU uses an actual 64-bit address bus. Every 64-bit processor gets its address bus clipped down to something reasonable. The Intel Itanium, for example, only has a 44-bit address bus, for a maximum address space of 2^{44} or 17,592,186,044,416 bytes. AMD's Phenom II, on the other hand, can allow for a 48-bit physical address space for 2^{48} or 281,474,976,710,656 bytes of memory.

Initially, both AMD and Intel raced ahead with competing 64-bit processors. Interestingly, they took very different paths. Let's look at the two CPUs that made the first wave of 64-bit processing: the Intel Itanium and the AMD Opteron.

• Figure 5.49   Intel Itanium (*photo courtesy of Intel*)

Intel Itanium (Original and Itanium 2)

Intel made the first strike into the 64-bit world for PCs with the Itanium CPU. The Itanium was more of a proof-of-concept product than one that was going to make Intel any money, but it paved the way for subsequent 64-bit processors. The Itanium had a unique 418-pin **pin array cartridge (PAC)** to help house its 2- or 4-MB Level 3 cache (Figure 5.49).

The Intel Itanium 2 was Intel's first serious foray into the 64-bit world. To describe the Itanium 2 in terms of bus sizes and clock speeds is unfair. The power of this processor goes far deeper. Massive pipelines, high-speed caching, and literally hundreds of other improvements make the Itanium 2 a powerful CPU for high-end PCs. The Itanium 2 uses a unique form of PGA that Intel calls *organic land grid array* (*OLGA*) (Figure 5.50).

Intel made a bold move with the Itanium and the Itanium 2 by not making them backward compatible to 32-bit programming. In other words, every OS, every application, and every driver of every device has to be rewritten to work on the Itanium and Itanium 2. In theory, developers would create excellent new applications and devices that dump all of the old stuff (and problems) and thus would be more efficient and streamlined. If a company has a lot invested in 32-bit applications and can't make the jump to 64-bit, Intel continues to offer the Pentium 4 or Pentium Xeon. If you need 64-bit, get an Itanium 2. AMD didn't agree with Intel and made 64-bit processors that also ran 32-bit when needed. Intel would eventually follow AMD in this decision.

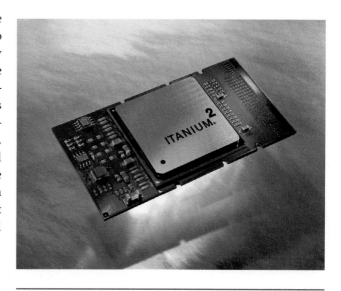

AMD Opteron

Coming in after the Itanium, AMD's Opteron doesn't try to take on the Itanium head to head. Instead, AMD presents the Opteron as the lower-end 64-bit CPU. But don't

• **Figure 5.50**   Intel Itanium 2 (*photo courtesy of Intel*)

let the moniker "lower-end" fool you. Although the Opteron borrowed heavily from the Athlon, it included an I/O data path known as HyperTransport. Think of HyperTransport as a very high-speed link, providing direct connection to other parts of the PC—and to other CPUs for multiprocessing—at a blistering speed of over 6 GB per second! The Opteron comes in a micro-PGA package, looking remarkably like a Pentium 4 (Figure 5.51).

Unlike the Itanium, the Opteron runs both 32-bit and 64-bit code. AMD gives customers the choice to move slowly into 64-bit without purchasing new equipment. This was the crucial difference between AMD and Intel in the early days of 64-bit processing.

Intel and AMD pitch the Itanium 2 and Opteron CPUs at the server market. This means that as a CompTIA A+ tech, you won't see them unless you go to work for a company that has massive computer needs. Newer CPUs from both companies fight for the desktop dollar.

Athlon 64

To place the Athlon 64 with the early generation CPUs is hardly fair. The Athlon 64 was the first for-the-desktop 64-bit processor, so in that aspect it is an early 64-bit CPU (Figure 5.52). AMD made two lines of Athlons: the "regular" Athlon 64 and the Athlon FX series. The FX series runs faster than the regular Athlon 64s, uses more wattage, and is marketed to power users who are willing to pay a premium. Underneath those two lines, AMD has almost 20 sub-lines of Athlon 64s in different codenames, making listing all of them here unwieldy.

• **Figure 5.51**   AMD Opteron (*photo courtesy of AMD*)

• **Figure 5.52**   Athlon 64

The Athlon 64s have a number of enhancements beyond moving into the 64-bit world. The most fascinating is the inclusion of a memory controller into the CPU, eliminating the need for an external MCC and for all intents also eliminating the idea of the frontside bus. The RAM directly connects to the Athlon 64. Athlon 64s support Intel's SSE and SSE2 graphics extensions (later versions support SSE3).

While regular Athlon 64s use the same AMD PR numbers to describe CPUs, Athlon 64 FXs use a two-digit model number that's just as cryptic as Intel's current three-digit numbers.

AMD Sempron CPUs

AMD produces various Sempron CPUs for the low end of the market. Semprons come in two socket sizes and have less cache than the Athlon 64, but they offer a reasonable trade-off between price and performance.

Multicore CPUs

CPU clock speeds hit a practical limit of roughly 4 GHz around 2002–2003, motivating the CPU makers to find new ways to get more processing power for CPUs. Although Intel and AMD had different opinions about 64-bit CPUs, both decided at virtually the same time to combine two CPUs into a single chip, creating a **dual-core** architecture. Dual core isn't just two CPUs on the same chip. A dual-core CPU has two execution units—two sets of pipelines—but the two sets of pipelines share caches (how they share caches differs between Intel and AMD) and RAM.

A multicore CPU can process more than one thread at a time; this is called **parallel processing**. Through parallel processing, the CPU can more readily juggle the demands of both applications and Windows, making the overall computing experience better. With multithreaded applications (programs written to take advantage of multiple CPUs or CPUs with multiple cores), this parallel processing can dramatically improve the performance of those applications.

> Putting more than two execution cores onto a single chip is called *multicore*.

Pentium D

Intel won the race for first dual-core processor with the Pentium D line of processors (Figure 5.53). The Pentium D is simply two late-generation Pentium 4s molded onto the same chip, with each CPU using its own cache—although they do share the same frontside bus. One very interesting aspect to the Pentium D is the licensing of AMD's *AMD64* extensions—the "smarts" inside AMD CPUs that enable AMD CPUs to run either 64- or 32-bit code. Intel named their version *EM64T*. There are two codenames for Pentium D processors: the Smithfield (model numbers 8*xx*), using a 90-nm process, and the Presler (model numbers 9*xx*), using a 65-nm process. Pentium Ds use the same LGA 775 package seen on the later Pentium 4s.

• **Figure 5.53**   Pentium D (*photo courtesy of Intel*)

Mike Meyers' CompTIA A+ Guide: Essentials

Athlon Dual Cores

AMD's introduction to dual core came with the Athlon 64 X2 CPUs. The X2s are truly two separate cores that share L1 caches, unlike the Intel Pentium D. Athlon 64 X2s initially came in both "regular" and FX versions packaged in the well-known AMD Socket 939. To upgrade from a regular Athlon 64 to an Athlon 64 X2, assuming you have a Socket 939 motherboard, is often as easy as simply doing a minor motherboard update, called *flashing the BIOS*. Chapter 7, "Learning Motherboards," goes through this process in detail, or you can simply check your motherboard manufacturer's Web site for the information on the process. In 2006, AMD announced the *Socket AM2*, designed to replace the Socket 939 across the Athlon line.

Intel Core

Intel introduced the *Intel Core* CPUs in 2006. Intel then followed up with the Core 2 processors, the first generation of CPUs to use the Intel Core architecture. Are you confused yet? Let's look a little closer at the Core and Core 2 CPUs.

Intel Core

Intel based the first generation of core processors, simply called Core, on the 32-bit-only Pentium M platform. Like the Pentium M, Core processors don't use the NetBurst architecture, instead falling back to a more Pentium Pro–style architecture (codenamed Yonah) with a 12-stage pipeline. Core CPUs come in single- (Solo) and dual-core (Duo) versions, but they all use the same 478-pin FCPGA package. Core also dispenses with the three-digit Pentium numbering system, using instead a letter followed by four numbers, such as T2300.

Intel Core 2

With the Core 2 line of processors (Figure 5.54), Intel released a radically revised processor architecture called Core. Redesigned to maximize efficiency, the Core 2 processors offer up to 40 percent in energy savings at the same performance level compared to the Pentium D processors. To achieve the efficiency, Intel cranked up the cache size (to 2 or 4 MB) and went with a wide, short pipeline. The CPU can perform multiple actions in a single clock cycle and, in the process, run circles around the competition.

Intel released three Core 2 versions for the desktop: the Core 2 Solo, Core 2 Duo, and Core 2 Quad. Intel has also released an enthusiast version named the Core 2 Extreme that comes in both Duo and Quad configurations. The Core 2 line also includes mobile versions. All versions incorporate AMD's 64-bit technology, rebranding it as Intel 64, so they can run 64-bit versions of Windows natively.

AMD Phenom

To achieve a quad-core processor, AMD took a different approach than Intel. Intel's Core 2 Quad series of processors combine two dual-core processors, each with their own caches, on the same physical die. These two on-die chips share a frontside bus to communicate with each other and memory.

Intel's naming conventions can leave a lot to be desired. Note that the Core Solo and Core Duo processors were based on the Pentium M architecture. The Core 2 processors are based on the Core architecture.

• **Figure 5.54**   Intel Core 2 CPU

For AMD's first quad-core desktop processor, called the Phenom, AMD decided to have each CPU core possess its own L1 and L2 caches but have all four cores share an L3 cache to facilitate communication between cores. This is why AMD refers to the Phenom as a native quad-core processor. The Phenom series of processors are all 64-bit CPUs that feature the AMD64 technology also found in the Athlon 64 CPUs.

The Phenom series processors have an integrated memory controller that supports two channels of DDR2 memory. With the inclusion of an integrated memory controller, the Phenom processors do not possess a traditional frontside bus. Instead, they use the same HyperTransport bus that the Athlon 64/Opteron series of processors have. Phenom processors are supported by AMD's Socket AM2+ or Socket AM3. The CPU may also use Socket AM2, but this may incur a performance penalty.

AMD refers to a Phenom processor with four cores as a Phenom X4. A Phenom X3 also exists and, as the name suggests, it possesses only three cores. In reality, the Phenom X3 is a quad-core processor with one of the cores shut off due to a defect. As such, AMD sells the Phenom X3 processors at a discount compared to the Phenom X4.

Similar to Intel's Extreme Edition CPUs for enthusiasts, AMD offers versions of the Phenom dubbed Black Edition. Not only are the Black Edition CPUs in the higher-end of their CPU range, but they also feature an unlocked clock multiplier allowing for fine-tuned overclocking.

• **Figure 5.55**   AMD Phenom II

AMD Phenom II

The Phenom II is a revision of the Phenom with a few improvements (Figure 5.55). It includes triple the amount of L3 cache as the original Phenom, support for Intel's SSE4a instructions, increased HyperTransport bus speeds, and an enhanced memory controller that can support two channels of DDR2 or DDR3 memory.

The Phenom II is built using a 45-nm process instead of the 65-nm process used with the original Phenom. The Phenom II is supported by Socket AM3 and AM2+; however, the CPU only supports DDR3 memory when using Socket AM3.

Like the Phenom before it, the Phenom II is available in both an X4 quad-core version and an X3 triple-core version. But unlike the Phenom, the Phenom II is also available in an X2 dual-core version. Enthusiast Black Editions of all Phenom II configurations are also available.

Intel Core i7

Intel's Core i7 family of processors is based off of a new microarchitecture called Nehalem, which succeeds Intel's Core microarchitecture. Like AMD's Phenom series of processors, the Core i7 is a native quad-core processor and all four cores share an L3 cache. This processor is Intel's first to feature an integrated memory controller. The memory controller supports up to three channels of DDR3 memory.

The Core i7 also marks the return of hyperthreading to Intel's CPUs (Figure 5.56). With hyperthreading, each individual core can support two simultaneous threads, which, in aggregate, allows a single Core i7 to support up to eight simultaneous threads.

The processor features a large 8-MB L3 cache and was first manufactured using a 45-nm process. Intel designed a new 1366-pin socket for the Core i7 family of processors, called LGA 1366. Like the Core 2 Quad before it, the Core i7 is a 64-bit CPU conforming to the Intel-64 standard, meaning that it can also run 32-bit code.

With Nehalem, Intel has done away with the traditional frontside bus and replaced it with a technology they named QuickPath Interconnect (QPI). QPI is very similar to the HyperTransport bus found on the Opteron and Phenom series of processors.

Intel Celeron

Intel uses the brand Celeron for its entire family of lower-end CPUs. There are Celerons based on the Pentium II, Pentium III, Pentium 4, Pentium-M, Core, and Core 2 Duo. The first Celerons were SEC but lacked the protective covering of the Pentium II. Intel calls this the **single-edge processor (SEP)** package (Figure 5.57). The Pentium III–based Celerons were PGA and used Socket 370 (Figure 5.58).

Celeron processors based on the Pentium 4 appeared first using Socket 478, but LGA 775 versions were eventually released. Over time, these Pentium 4–based Celerons borrowed more and more advanced features from their desktop counterparts, including support for SSE3 extensions and Intel-64 addressing.

Processors designed to rival AMD's Sempron series chips were also released under the Celeron brand. At first, these chips were based on Intel's Yonah architecture, but Intel released Celerons based on the Core microarchitecture shortly thereafter. Many processors from the latest generation of Celerons are available in dual-core models.

● **Figure 5.56**   Intel Core i7

● **Figure 5.57**   Pentium II Celeron

● **Figure 5.58**   Intel Celeron

An entire line of Celerons for mobile computers also exists. Traditionally these chips went by the names Mobile Celeron or Celeron-M. However, Intel dropped that nomenclature with the latest mobile releases, simply referring to them as Celeron.

Intel Pentium Dual-Core

Intel resurrected the Pentium brand in 2006 with the release of the Pentium Dual-Core. Although similar in name, the Pentium Dual-Core is not the same processor as the Pentium D. The Pentium Dual-Core was originally a 32-bit processor based off the Yonah core, but Intel quickly followed that processor up with a 64-bit Pentium Dual-Core based off of the Core microarchitecture.

The Pentium Dual-Core line contains both mobile and desktop processors, and recently, just as with the Celeron brand, Intel has started referring to them simply as Pentium. These Pentiums constitute a middle-of-the-road series of processors for Intel, more powerful than the Celeron line but less powerful than the Core 2 line.

Intel Xeon Processors

Just as the term Celeron describes a series of lower-end processors, the term Xeon (pronounced "Zee-on") defines a series of high-end processors Intel built around the P6, NetBurst, Core, and Nehalem microarchitectures. Both the Pentium II Xeon and the Pentium III Xeon used a unique SEC package that snapped into a Xeon-only slot called Slot 2 (Figure 5.59). With the release of the Xeon based off of the Pentium 4, however, Intel moved to PGA packaging, such as the Xeon-only 603-pin package depicted in Figure 5.60.

Xeon processors add large L2 caches and, especially with more recent Xeons, L3 caches as well. Although a few Xeon processors can only work alone, most are carefully designed to work together in sets of two, four, or more. Today's Xeon processors themselves can contain two, four, and even eight CPU cores per package. Put those two elements together, and modern Xeon systems can contain 32 CPU cores, each with hyperthreading, to support 64 simultaneous threads.

• **Figure 5.59**   Intel Pentium III Xeon

• **Figure 5.60**   Intel Pentium 4–based Xeon (*photo courtesy of Intel*)

Intel and their partners are working on delivering configurations that will allow for even more CPUs, facilitating even greater processing power. Although expensive, the Xeon processors' immense power lets them enjoy broad popularity in the high-horsepower world of server systems.

The Art of Cooling

There was a time, long ago, when CPUs didn't need any type of cooling device. You just snapped in the CPU and it worked. Well, those days are gone. Long gone. If you're installing a modern CPU, you will have to cool it. Fortunately, you have choices.

- **OEM CPU coolers**   OEM heat-sink and fan assemblies are included with a retail-boxed CPU. OEM CPUs, on the other hand, don't normally come bundled with CPU coolers. Crazy, isn't it? OEM CPU coolers have one big advantage: you know absolutely they will work with your CPU.

- **Specialized CPU coolers**   Lots of companies sell third-party heat sinks and fans for a variety of CPUs. These usually exceed the OEM heat sinks in the amount of heat they dissipate. These CPU coolers invariably come with eye-catching designs to look really cool inside your system—some are even lighted (Figure 5.61).

CPU fans are designed to work with a very limited number of CPUs. Some third-party fans come with a bunch of extra bits of hardware to work with more than one type of CPU. A small amount of thermal compound, more commonly called "heat dope" by the folks who use it, is applied to the top of the CPU and forms a seal between the CPU and the heat sink to make sure there's good heat transfer. Some cooling kits come with a bit of heat dope already on the heat sink itself. Whether the thermal compound comes on the heat sink or you have to buy a tube, you must have thermal compound between the CPU and the heat sink. No exceptions!

The last choice is the most impressive of all: liquid cooling! That's right, you can put a little liquid-cooling system right inside your PC case. Liquid cooling works by running some liquid—usually water—through a metal block that sits on top of your CPU, absorbing heat. The liquid gets heated by the block, runs out of the block and into some-

• **Figure 5.61**   Cool retail heat sink

thing that cools the liquid, and is then pumped through the block again. Any liquid-cooling system consists of three main parts:

- A hollow metal block that sits on the CPU
- A pump to move the liquid around
- Some device to cool the liquid

And of course, you need plenty of hosing to hook them all together. Figure 5.62 shows a typical liquid-cooled CPU.

A number of companies sell these liquid-cooling systems. Although they look impressive and certainly cool your CPU, unless you're overclocking or want a quiet system, a good fan will more than suffice.

Whether you have a silent or noisy cooling system for your CPU, always remember to keep everything clean. Once a month or so, take a can of compressed air and clean dust off the fan or radiator. You may also want to use a small vacuum or a compressor to remove dust from your system. CPUs are very susceptible to heat; a poorly working fan can create all sorts of problems, such as system lockups, spontaneous reboots, and more.

CPUs are *thermally sensitive devices*—keep those fans clean!

• **Figure 5.62** Liquid-cooled CPU

Chapter 5 Review

■ Chapter Summary

After reading this chapter and completing the exercises, you should understand the following about microprocessors.

Identify the core components of a CPU

- The central processing unit performs calculations on binary numbers to make the magic of computers work. The CPU interfaces with the motherboard and other components through the external data bus or frontside bus.

- CPUs contain several areas of internal memory, known as registers, in which data and addresses are stored while processing. The commands a CPU knows how to perform are dictated by its instruction set.

- A quartz crystal soldered to the motherboard and known as the system crystal provides a constant pulse known as the clock. The frequency of this pulse, or clock speed, dictates the maximum speed at which a processor can run, measured in megahertz or gigahertz. The processor typically runs at some multiple of this clock pulse, known as the internal clock speed. You can set the internal clock speed by adjusting the multiplier (which multiplies the clock speed by some number) or by configuring motherboard jumpers or making a change to a CMOS setting, or it is set automatically via CPU circuitry. Setting the clock speed higher to force the CPU to run faster than its rating is known as overclocking.

Describe the relationship of CPUs and memory

- A computer uses random access memory to take copies of programs from the hard drive and send them, one line at a time, to the CPU quickly enough to keep up with its demands. The CPU accesses any one row of RAM as easily and as quickly as any other row, which explains the "random access" part of RAM. RAM is not only randomly accessible but also fast. By storing programs on RAM, the CPU can access and run them very quickly. RAM also stores any data that the CPU actively uses.

- The CPU communicates with RAM on the motherboard via the address bus. The number of wires comprising the address bus dictates the amount of memory the CPU can access.

Explain the varieties of modern CPUs

- Most CPUs in modern PCs are manufactured by Intel or AMD.

- CPUs come in two main form factors: pin grid array (PGA) and single-edge cartridge (SEC).

- PGA CPUs connect to the motherboard by way of a zero insertion force (ZIF) socket that allows the CPU to be inserted with no force. ZIF sockets work by way of a mechanical arm that locks the CPU in place.

- The original Intel Pentium was introduced in 1990 and discontinued in 1995. AMD's competing CPU was the AMD K5.

- Pipelining enables a CPU to perform calculations as an assembly line. No longer does one calculation need to be completed before the next can begin. Modern CPUs have multiple pipelines.

- Modern CPUs contain small amounts of high-speed SRAM called a cache. As CPUs advanced, the capacities of the cache increased, as did the number of cache areas. CPU caches are also known as L1, L2, or L3 caches. Data and instructions are stored in the cache while they await processing. This increases performance, because the CPU can access data in the cache more rapidly than data in motherboard RAM.

- In 1995 Intel released the Pentium Pro. It improved on the original Pentium by offering quad pipelining, dynamic processing, and on-chip L2 cache. With four pipelines, it was guaranteed to run at least two processes at the same time. The capability to run more than one process in a single clock cycle is called superscalar execution. The Pentium Pro's advanced branch prediction allowed it to run processes out of order to increase performance in a procedure called speculative execution.

- In 1996 Intel released the Pentium II. It improved on the Pentium Pro by offering multimedia extensions (MMX) and a refined instruction set. The AMD K6 (and its varieties) was the main competitor.

- The Intel Celeron is a low-end processor. The generic name of Celeron, with no identifying letters or numbers to indicate which version, made purchasing one difficult unless you asked the right questions.

- Intel's Pentium III improved on the Pentium II by offering Streaming SIMD Extensions (SSE). AMD responded with the 3DNow! instruction set.

- The AMD Athlon was the first AMD CPU to use AMD-only slots and sockets. If you wanted an AMD Athlon, you had to purchase a motherboard with the special AMD slot/socket.

- The AMD Duron is similar to the Intel Celeron in that it was marketed toward the low-end PCs. The Duron is similar to the Athlon but contains a smaller cache.

- The Intel Pentium 4 came in several varieties identified by codenames Willamette, Northwood, and Prescott.

- The Athlon XP came in several varieties: Palomino, Thoroughbred, Thorton, and Barton.

- The Intel Pentium 4 Extreme Edition was the first non-server CPU to offer an L3 cache.

- Mobile processors, or CPUs for laptops, are usually identified by the word "mobile" or the letter "M" in their names. A mobile processor uses less power than a desktop CPU, allowing for longer battery life and cooler running. A mobile processor runs on a lower voltage than a desktop CPU, which usually translates to lower speeds. The term Centrino defines a complete mobile solution consisting of a mobile processor, support chips, and wireless networking. There is no Centrino CPU.

- Intel's SpeedStep and AMD's PowerNow! technologies enable CPUs to slow themselves down during times of low demand or if the CPU senses it is getting too hot. Generically, this is called throttling.

- The Intel Xeon is a high-end processor aimed at the server or power-user market. Xeons are intended to be used in PCs with multiple processors.

- The original Intel Itanium was Intel's first 64-bit processor. The Itanium and the follow-up Itanium 2 were not backward compatible with 32-bit systems, so users had to use a 64-bit operating system, 64-bit software, and 64-bit drivers.

- The AMD Opteron, AMD's first 64-bit processor, was backward compatible with 32-bit systems.

- The AMD Athlon 64 comes in two varieties, Athlon 64 and Athlon 64 FX, with the FX being faster and more expensive. The AMD Sempron is AMD's low-end 64-bit processor.

- Dual-core CPUs combine two CPUs into a single chip. The two CPUs have different sets of pipelines but share common caches. The Intel Pentium D (codenames Smithfield and Presler) is one such processor that can run both 32- and 64-bit code. AMD's Athlon 64 X2 CPUs are dual-core.

- The AMD Phenom X4, Phenom II X4, and Intel Core i7 are all native quad-core CPUs.

- The AMD Phenom X3 is a native triple-core CPU.

■ Key Terms

address bus (149)	**clock wire** (144)
arithmetic logic unit (ALU) (151)	**dual-core** (170)
backside bus (162)	**dynamic RAM (DRAM)** (148)
binary (142)	**external data bus (EDB)** (141)
bit (147)	**floating point unit (FPU)** (156)
byte (147)	**frontside bus** (162)
cache (157)	**instruction set** (144)
central processing unit (CPU) (140)	**machine language** (143)
Centrino (167)	**memory** (147)
clock cycle (144)	**memory controller chip (MCC)** (149)
clock-multiplying CPU (159)	**microprocessor** (140)
clock speed (144)	**multimedia extensions (MMX)** (162)

overclock *(145)*
parallel processing *(170)*
pin array cartridge (PAC) *(168)*
pipeline *(155)*
program *(146)*
random access memory (RAM) *(147)*
register *(143)*
single-edge cartridge (SEC) *(163)*

single-edge processor (SEP) *(173)*
static RAM (SRAM) *(157)*
system crystal *(145)*
System Management Mode (SMM) *(168)*
throttling *(168)*
voltage regulator module (VRM) *(160)*
wait state *(157)*
zero insertion force (ZIF) socket *(153)*

■ Key Term Quiz

Use the Key Terms list to complete the sentences that follow. Not all terms will be used.

1. All of the machine language commands that the CPU understands make up the CPU's _____.

2. By lifting the arm on the _____, you can easily install a PGA CPU.

3. Computers use _____ for main system memory.

4. Computers use the _____ numbering system.

5. Areas inside the CPU where it temporarily stores internal commands and data while it is processing them are called _____.

6. Divided into L1 and L2, the _____ consists of a small amount of _____ that serves as a

holding area. This provides data to the CPU faster than getting it from regular memory or when RAM is unavailable because of refreshes.

7. A(n) _____ enables a motherboard to support CPUs that run at differing voltage requirements.

8. Laptops sporting the _____ logo indicate that they contain a mobile processor, support chips, and a wireless network interface.

9. In a process known as _____, a CPU can slow itself down in low demand times or if it gets too hot.

10. An Athlon 64 X2 is an example of a(n) _____ processor.

■ Multiple-Choice Quiz

1. What device enables a PC to retrieve a specific row of data from system memory and place it on the external data bus?

   A. Advanced micro device

   B. Arithmetic logic unit

   C. Floating point processor

   D. Memory controller chip

2. Which of the following statements is true?

   A. The address bus enables the CPU to communicate with the MCC.

   B. The external data bus enables the CPU to communicate with the MCC.

   C. The address bus enables the CPU to communicate with the hard drive.

   D. The system bus enables the CPU to communicate with the memory.

3. Which of the following CPUs was the first microprocessor to include both an L1 and an L2 cache with the CPU?

   A. Pentium

   B. Pentium Pro

   C. Pentium II

   D. Pentium III

4. What do 64-bit processors expand over their 32-bit predecessors?

   A. System bus

   B. Frontside bus

   C. Address bus

   D. Registers

5. What is the first stage in a typical four-stage CPU pipeline?

   A. Decode

   B. Execute

C. Fetch

D. Write

6. Which of the following terms are measures of CPU speed?

   A. Megahertz and gigahertz

   B. Megabytes and gigabytes

   C. Megahertz and gigahertz

   D. Frontside bus, backside bus

7. Which of the following CPUs features a QuickPath Interconnect interface?

   A. Pentium 4

   B. Phenom II X2

   C. Core i7

   D. Opteron

8. Which of the following statements is true?

   A. If you have an AMD-compatible motherboard, you can install a Celeron processor.

   B. Replacing the CPU may not be the upgrade that is most cost effective or that has the strongest impact on your system's performance.

   C. As the size of the address bus increases, the amount of RAM the CPU can use decreases.

   D. You can upgrade your CPU if you make sure that a new CPU will fit into the socket or slot on your motherboard.

9. Which processor comes in an SEC package that fits into Slot A?

   A. Pentium II

   B. Pentium III

   C. Athlon

   D. Celeron

10. What's the main difference between the Itanium and Opteron CPUs?

    A. The Itanium is a 32-bit processor; the Opteron is a 64-bit processor.

    B. The Itanium can run only 64-bit code; the Opteron can run both 32-bit and 64-bit code.

    C. The Itanium is made by AMD; the Opteron is made by Intel.

    D. The Itanium fits in Slot 1; the Opteron fits in Slot A.

11. What connects on the backside bus?

    A. CPU, MCC, RAM

    B. CPU, MCC, L1 cache

    C. CPU, L1 cache

    D. CPU, L2 cache

12. What improvement(s) have CPU manufacturers put into processors to deal with pipeline stalls?

    A. Added multiple pipelines

    B. Increased the speed of the SRAM

    C. Created new die sizes with more pins

    D. Bundled better fans with their retail CPUs

13. What steps do you need to take to install an Athlon 64 X2 CPU into an LGA 775 motherboard?

    A. Lift the ZIF socket arm; place the CPU according to the orientation markings; snap on the heat-sink and fan assembly.

    B. Lift the ZIF socket arm; place the CPU according to the orientation markings; add a dash of heat dope; snap on the heat-sink and fan assembly.

    C. Lift the ZIF socket arm; place the CPU according to the orientation markings; snap on the heat-sink and fan assembly; plug in the fan.

    D. You cannot install an Athlon CPU into an LGA 775 motherboard.

14. Which of the following CPU manufacturing processes offers a final product that most likely uses the least amount of electricity for the same number of circuits?

    A. 3 micrometer

    B. 45 nanometer

    C. 65 nanometer

    D. 90 nanometer

15. What improvement does the Athlon 64 offer over the Athlon XP?

    A. Lower wattage

    B. Larger L1 cache

    C. Larger process size

    D. 64-bit processing

■ Essay Quiz

1. Juan wants to buy a laptop computer, but he finds that laptops are more expensive than desktop computers. Moreover, he is complaining that he can't find a laptop that is as fast as the newest desktop PCs. Explain to Juan three special considerations that make a laptop more expensive and less powerful than desktop computers.

2. On the bulletin board outside your classroom, your friend Shelley notices two flyers advertising used computers. The first one is a 700-MHz Celeron with a 100-MHz system bus, 32 KB of L1 cache, 128 KB of L2 cache, and 128 MB of RAM. The other one is an 800-MHz Athlon with a 200-MHz system bus, 128 KB of L1 cache, 512 KB of L2 cache, and 256 MB of RAM. Shelley does not know much about computer hardware, so she asks you which one is the better computer and why. In simple terms that Shelley will understand, explain five differences that determine which computer is better.

3. You're forming a study group with a few of your friends to review microprocessors. Each one of you has decided to study a particular aspect of this chapter to explain to the group. Your responsibility is buses, including the system bus, address bus, backside bus, and frontside bus. Write a few sentences that will help you explain what each bus does and the differences between the buses.

4. This chapter makes the statement that "The secret to making clock multiplying work is caching." Write a paragraph in which you explain why that statement is true. Be sure to explain what caching does and the different kinds of caches found in today's computers.

Lab Projects

• Lab Project 5.1

Perhaps newer and faster CPUs have come out recently. Go to www.intel.com and to www.amd.com and investigate the newest CPUs for desktop computers from each manufacturer. Write a paragraph comparing the newest Intel CPU with the newest AMD CPU. Try to include the following information:

- What is the size of the system bus?
- What is the size of the address bus?

- What is the speed of the CPU?
- What is the speed of the frontside bus?
- What are the sizes of the L1 and L2 caches?
- Does either CPU offer an L3 cache?
- What kind of chip package houses each CPU?
- What kind of slot or socket does each use?
- What other new features does each site advertise for its newest CPU?

• Lab Project 5.2

Imagine that you are going to buy components to build your own computer. What processor will you use? Typically, the latest and greatest CPU is a lot more expensive than less recent models. Intel processors usually cost more than comparable AMD processors. Check CPU features and prices in newspapers or magazines or on the Internet at a site such as www.newegg.com. Decide what CPU you want to use for your computer. Write a paragraph explaining why you selected it and how much you will spend for the CPU.

Learning RAM

chapter
6

"The memory be green."

—WILLIAM SHAKESPEARE, *HAMLET.*
ACT I. SC. 2

In this chapter, you will learn how to

- **Identify the different types of DRAM packaging**
- **Explain the varieties of RAM**

Whenever people come up to me and start professing their computer savvy, I ask them a few questions to see how much they really know. In case you and I ever meet and you decide you want to "talk tech" with me, I'll tell you my first two questions just so you'll be ready. Both involve *random access memory (RAM)*, the working memory for the CPU.

1. "How much RAM is in your computer?"
2. "What is RAM and why is it so important that every PC has some?"

Can you answer either of these questions? Don't fret if you can't—you'll know how to answer both of them before you finish this chapter. Let's start by reviewing what you know about RAM thus far.

Cross Check

Dynamic and Random Access

You encountered DRAM back in Chapter 5, "Learning CPUs," so see if you can answer these questions: What makes DRAM dynamic? What does random access mean?

When not in use, programs and data are held in mass storage, which usually means a hard drive but could also mean a USB thumb drive, a CD-ROM, or some other device that can hold data when the computer is turned off. When you load a program by clicking an icon in Windows, the program is copied from the mass storage device to RAM and then run (Figure 6.1).

You saw in Chapter 5, "Learning CPUs," that the CPU uses dynamic random access memory (DRAM) as RAM for all PCs. Just like CPUs, DRAM has gone through a number of evolutionary changes over the years, resulting in improved DRAM technologies with names such as SDRAM, RDRAM, and DDR RAM. This chapter starts by explaining how DRAM works, and then moves into the types of DRAM used over the past few years to see how they improve on the original DRAM.

• **Figure 6.1**   Mass storage holds programs, but programs need to run in RAM.

■ Understanding DRAM

As discussed in Chapter 5, "Learning CPUs," DRAM functions like an electronic spreadsheet, with numbered rows containing cells and each cell holding a one or a zero. Now let's look at what's physically happening. Each spreadsheet cell is a special type of semiconductor that can hold a single bit—one or zero—by using microscopic capacitors and transistors. DRAM makers put these semiconductors into chips that can hold a certain number of bits. The bits inside the chips are organized in a rectangular fashion, using rows and columns.

Each chip has a limit on the number of lines of code it can contain. Think of each line of code as one of the rows on the electronic spreadsheet; one chip might be able to store a million rows of code while another chip can store over a billion lines. Each chip also has a limit on the width of the lines of code it can handle, so one chip might handle 8-bit-wide data while another might handle 16-bit-wide data. Techs describe chips by bits rather than bytes, so ×8 (pronounced "by eight") and ×16 ("by sixteen"), respectively. Just as you could describe a spreadsheet by the number of rows and columns—John's accounting spreadsheet is huge, 48 rows × 12 columns—memory makers describe RAM chips the same way. An individual DRAM chip that holds 1,048,576 rows and 8 columns, for example, would be a *1 M × 8* chip, with "M" as shorthand for "mega," just like in megabytes (2^{20} bytes). It is difficult

• Figure 6.2 What do these numbers mean?

if not impossible to tell the size of a DRAM chip just by looking at it—only the DRAM makers know the meaning of the tiny numbers on the chips (Figure 6.2), although sometimes you can make a good guess.

Organizing DRAM

Because of its low cost, high speed, and capability to contain a lot of data in a relatively small package, DRAM has been the standard RAM used in all computers—not just PCs—since the mid-1970s. DRAM can be found in just about everything, from automobiles to automatic bread makers.

The PC has very specific requirements for DRAM. The original 8088 processor had an 8-bit frontside bus. All the commands given to an 8088 processor were in discrete 8-bit chunks. You needed RAM that could store data in 8-bit (1-byte) chunks, so that each time the CPU asked for a line of code, the memory controller could put an 8-bit chunk on the data bus. This optimized the flow of data into (and out from) the CPU.

Cross Check

Riding the 8088 Bus

You first saw the Intel 8088 CPU in Chapter 5, "Learning CPUs," and now it pops up again. What components inside the 8088 handle the data once the CPU gets it from RAM? How does the CPU know when the data is complete and ready to take?

Although today's DRAM chips may have widths greater than 1 bit, back in the old days all DRAM chips were 1 bit wide. That means you only had such sizes as 64 K × 1 or 256 K × 1—always 1 bit wide. So how was 1-bit-wide DRAM turned into 8-bit-wide memory? The answer was quite simple: Just take eight 1-bit-wide chips and electronically organize them with the memory controller chip to be eight wide. First, put eight 1-bit-wide chips in a row on the motherboard and then wire up this row of DRAM chips to the memory controller chip (which has to be designed to handle this) to make byte-wide memory (Figure 6.3). You just made eight 1-bit-wide DRAM chips look like a single 8-bit-wide DRAM chip to the CPU.

The CPU requires data in byte-sized pieces.

The MCC can produce byte-sized pieces out of eight bit-sized RAM chips.

• Figure 6.3   The MCC accessing data on RAM soldered onto the motherboard

Practical DRAM

Okay, before you learn more about DRAM, I need to make a critical point extremely clear. When you first saw the 8088's machine language in Chapter 5, "Learning CPUs," all the examples in the "codebook" were exactly 1-byte commands. Figure 6.4 shows the codebook again—see how all the commands are 1 byte?

Well, the reality is slightly different. Most of the 8088 machine language commands are 1 byte, but a few more complex commands need 2 bytes. For example, the following command tells the CPU to move 163 bytes "up the RAM spreadsheet" and run whatever command is there. Cool, eh?

1110100110100011

The problem here is that the command is 2 bytes wide, not 1 byte. So how did the 8088 handle this? Simple—it just took the command 1 byte at a time. It took twice as long to handle the command because the MCC had to go to RAM twice, but it worked.

Okay, so if some of the commands are more than 1 byte wide, why didn't Intel make the 8088 with a 16-bit frontside bus? Wouldn't that have been better? Well, Intel did. Intel invented a CPU called the 8086. The 8086 actually predates the 8088 and was absolutely identical to the 8088 except for one small detail: it had a 16-bit frontside bus. IBM could have used the 8086 instead of the 8088 and used 2-byte-wide RAM instead of 1-byte-wide RAM. Of course, they would have needed to invent a memory controller chip (MCC) that handled that kind of RAM (Figure 6.5).

Why didn't Intel sell IBM the 8086 instead of the 8088? There were two reasons. First, nobody had invented an affordable MCC or RAM that handled 2 bytes at a time. Sure, chips were invented, but they were *expensive* and IBM didn't think anyone would want to pay $12,000 for a personal computer. So IBM bought the Intel 8088, not the Intel 8086, and all our RAM came in bytes. But as you might imagine, it didn't stay that way too long.

8088 External Data Bus Codebook

LIGHTS	MEANING
10000000	The next line is a number, put it in the AX register
10010000	The next line is a number, put it in the BX register
10110000	Add AX to BX and put the result in AX
11000000	Place the value of AX on the External Data Bus
00000000	The number 0
00000001	The number 1
00000010	The number 2
00000011	The number 3
00000100	The number 4
00000101	The number 5
00000110	The number 6
00000111	The number 7
00001000	The number 8
00001001	The number 9

• **Figure 6.4**   Codebook again

The Northbridge for an **8086** system could handle two rows of RAM.

• **Figure 6.5**   Pumped-up 8086 MCC at work

DRAM Sticks

As CPU data bus sizes increased, so too did the need for RAM wide enough to fill the bus. The Intel 80386 CPU, for example, had a 32-bit data bus and thus the need for 32-bit-wide DRAM. Imagine having to line up 32 one-bit-wide DRAM chips on a motherboard. Talk about a waste of space! Figure 6.6 shows motherboard RAM run amuck.

DRAM manufacturers responded by creating wider DRAM chips, such as ×4, ×8, and ×16, and putting multiples of them on a small circuit board called a **stick** or **module**. Figure 6.7 shows an early stick, called a **single inline memory module (SIMM)**, with eight DRAM chips. To add RAM to a modern machine means you need to get the right stick or sticks for the particular motherboard. Your motherboard manual tells you precisely what sort of module you need and how much RAM you can install.

Modern CPUs are a lot smarter than the old Intel 8088. Their machine languages have some commands that are up to 64 bits (8 bytes) wide. They also have at least a 64-bit frontside bus that can handle more than just 8 bits. They don't want RAM to give them a puny 8 bits at a time! To optimize the flow of data into and out of the CPU, the modern MCC provides at least 64 bits of data every time the CPU requests information from RAM.

Modern DRAM sticks come in 32-bit- and 64-bit-wide form factors with a varying number of chips. Many techs describe these memory modules by their width, so ×32 and ×64. Note that this number does *not* describe the width of the individual DRAM chips on the module. When you read or hear about *by whatever* memory, simply note that you need to know whether that person is talking about the DRAM width or the module width. When the CPU needs certain bytes of data, it requests those bytes via the address bus. The CPU does not know the physical location of the RAM that stores that data, nor the physical makeup of the RAM—such as how many DRAM chips work

• **Figure 6.6**   That's a lot of real estate used by RAM chips!

Some MCCs are 128 bits wide.

• **Figure 6.7**   A 72-pin SIMM

Mike Meyers' CompTIA A+ Guide: Essentials

Try This!

Dealing with Old RAM

Often in the PC world, old technology and ways of doing things are reimplemented with some newer technology. Learning how things worked back in the ancient days can stand a tech in good stead. Perhaps more importantly, many thousands of companies—including hospitals, auto repair places, and more—use very old, proprietary applications that keep track of medical records, inventory, and so on. If you're called to work on one of these ancient systems, you need to know how to work with old parts, so Try This!

Obtain an old computer, such as a 386 or 486. Ask your uncle, cousin, or Great Aunt Edna if they have a PC collecting dust in a closet that you can use. Failing that, go to a secondhand store or market and buy one for a few dollars.

Open up the system and check out the RAM. Remove the RAM from the motherboard and then replace it to familiarize yourself with the internals. You never know when some critical system will go down and need repair immediately—and you're the one to do it!

together to provide the 64-bit-wide memory rows. The MCC keeps track of this and just gives the CPU whichever bytes it requests (Figure 6.8).

Consumer RAM

If modern DRAM modules come in sizes much wider than a byte, why do people still use the word "byte" to describe how much DRAM they have? Convention. Habit. Rather than using a label that describes the electronic structure of RAM, common usage describes the *total capacity of RAM on a stick in bytes*. John has a single 512-MB stick of RAM on his motherboard, for

● **Figure 6.8**   The MCC knows the real location of the DRAM.

example, and Sally has two 256-MB sticks. Both systems have a total of 512 MB of system RAM. That's what your clients care about, after all, because having enough RAM makes their systems snappy and stable; not enough and the systems run poorly. As a tech, you need to know more, of course, to pick the right RAM for many different types of computers.

Types of RAM

Development of newer, wider, and faster CPUs and MCCs motivates DRAM manufacturers to invent new DRAM technologies that deliver enough data at a single pop to optimize the flow of data into and out of the CPU.

SDRAM

Most modern systems use some form of **synchronous DRAM (SDRAM)**. SDRAM is still DRAM, but it is *synchronous*—tied to the system clock, just like the CPU and MCC, so the MCC knows when data is ready to be grabbed from SDRAM. This results in little wasted time.

SDRAM made its debut in 1996 on a stick called a **dual inline memory module (DIMM)**. The early SDRAM DIMMs came in a wide variety of pin sizes. The most common pin sizes found on desktops were the 168-pin variety. Laptop DIMMs came in 68-pin, 144-pin (Figure 6.9), or 172-pin *micro-DIMM* packages; and the 72-pin, 144-pin, or 200-pin **small-outline DIMM (SO-DIMM)** form factors (Figure 6.10). With the exception of the 32-bit 72-pin SO-DIMM, all these DIMM varieties delivered 64-bit-wide data to match the 64-bit data bus of every CPU since the Pentium.

To take advantage of SDRAM, you needed a PC designed to use SDRAM. If you had a system with slots for 168-pin DIMMs, for example, your system used SDRAM. A DIMM in any one of the DIMM slots could fill the 64-bit bus, so each slot was called a **bank**. You could install one, two, or more sticks and the system would work. Note that on laptops that used the 72-pin SO-DIMM, you needed to install two sticks of RAM to make a full bank, because each stick only provided half the bus width.

> Old RAM—really old RAM— was called *fast page mode* (*FPM*) RAM. This ancient RAM used a totally different technology that was not tied to the system clock. If you ever hear of FPM RAM, it's going to be in a system that's over a decade old. Be careful! CompTIA likes to use older terms like this to throw you off!

• Figure 6.9 144-pin micro-DIMM (*photo courtesy of Micron Technology, Inc.*)

• Figure 6.10 A 168-pin DIMM above a 144-pin SO-DIMM

Mike Meyers' CompTIA A+ Guide: Essentials

SDRAM tied to the system clock, so its clock speed matched the frontside bus. Five clock speeds were commonly used on the early SDRAM systems: 66, 75, 83, 100, and 133 MHz. The RAM speed had to match or exceed the system speed or the computer would be unstable or wouldn't work at all. These speeds were prefixed with a "PC" in the front, based on a standard forwarded by Intel, so SDRAM speeds were PC66 through PC133. For a Pentium III computer with a 100-MHz frontside bus, you needed to buy SDRAM DIMMs rated to handle it, such as PC100 or PC133.

RDRAM

When Intel was developing the Pentium 4, they knew that regular SDRAM just wasn't going to be fast enough to handle the quad-pumped 400-MHz frontside bus. Intel announced plans to replace SDRAM with a very fast, new type of RAM developed by Rambus, Inc., called **Rambus DRAM**, or simply **RDRAM** (Figure 6.11). Hailed by Intel as the next great leap in DRAM technology, RDRAM could handle speeds up to 800 MHz, which gave Intel plenty of room to improve the Pentium 4.

• **Figure 6.11**   RDRAM

RDRAM was greatly anticipated by the industry for years, but industry support for RDRAM proved less than enthusiastic due to significant delays in development and a price many times that of SDRAM. Despite this grudging support, almost all major PC makers sold systems that used RDRAM—for a while. From a tech's standpoint, RDRAM shares almost all of the characteristics of SDRAM. A stick of RDRAM is called a **RIMM**. In this case, however, the letters don't actually stand for anything; they just rhyme: SIMMs, DIMMs, and now RIMMs, get it?

RDRAM RIMMs came in two sizes: a 184-pin for desktops and a 160-pin SO-RIMM for laptops. RIMMs were keyed differently from DIMMs to ensure that even though they are the same basic size, you couldn't accidentally install a RIMM in a DIMM slot or vice versa. RDRAM also had a speed rating: 600 MHz, 700 MHz, 800 MHz, or 1066 MHz. RDRAM employed an interesting **dual-channel architecture**. Each RIMM was 64 bits wide, but the Rambus MCC alternated between two sticks to increase the speed of data retrieval. You were required to install RIMMs in pairs to use this dual-channel architecture.

The 400-MHz frontside bus speed wasn't achieved by making the system clock faster—it was done by making CPUs and MCCs capable of sending 64 bits of data two or four times for every clock cycle, effectively doubling or quadrupling the system bus speed.

☑ **Cross Check**

Double-Pumped and Quad-Pumped

You've seen double-pumped and quad-pumped frontside buses in Chapter 5, "Learning CPUs," so see if you can answer these questions. What CPU—by codename—started the double-pumped bus bandwagon? What socket did it use?

• **Figure 6.12**   CRIMM

RDRAM motherboards also required that all RIMM slots be populated. Unused pairs of slots needed a passive device called a **continuity RIMM (CRIMM)** installed in each slot to enable the RDRAM system to terminate properly. Figure 6.12 shows a CRIMM.

RDRAM offered dramatic possibilities for high-speed PCs but ran into three roadblocks that Betamaxed it. First, the technology was owned wholly by Rambus; if you wanted to make it, you had to pay the licensing fees they charged. That led directly to the second problem, expense. RDRAM cost substantially more than SDRAM. Third, Rambus and Intel made a completely closed deal for the technology. RDRAM worked only on Pentium 4 systems using Intel-made MCCs. AMD was out of luck. Clearly, the rest of the industry had to look for another high-speed RAM solution.

Betamaxed is slang for "made it obsolete because no one bought it, even though it was a superior technology to the winner in the marketplace." It refers to the VHS versus Betamax wars in the old days of video cassette recorders.

DDR SDRAM

AMD and many major system and memory makers threw their support behind **double data rate SDRAM (DDR SDRAM)**. DDR SDRAM basically copied Rambus, doubling the throughput of SDRAM by making two processes for every clock cycle. This synchronized (pardon the pun) nicely with the Athlon and later AMD processors' double-pumped frontside bus. DDR SDRAM could not run as fast as RDRAM—although relatively low frontside bus speeds made that a moot point—but cost only slightly more than regular SDRAM.

DDR SDRAM for desktops comes in 184-pin DIMMs. These DIMMs match 168-pin DIMMs in physical size but not in pin compatibility (Figure 6.13). The slots for the two types of RAM appear similar as well but have different guide notches, so you can't insert either type of RAM into the other's slot. DDR SDRAM for laptops comes in either 200-pin SO-DIMMs or 172-pin micro-DIMMs (Figure 6.14).

DDR sticks use a rather interesting naming convention—actually started by the Rambus folks—based on the number of bytes per second of data throughput the RAM can handle. To determine the bytes per second, take the MHz speed and multiply by 8 bytes (the width of all DDR SDRAM sticks). So 400 MHz multiplied by 8 is 3200 megabytes per second. Put the abbreviation "PC" in the front to make the new term: PC3200. Many techs also use the naming convention used for the individual DDR chips; for

Tech Tip

RAM Slang

Most techs drop some or all of the SDRAM part of DDR SDRAM when engaged in normal geekspeak. You'll hear the memory referred to as DDR, DDR RAM, and the weird hybrid, DDRAM.

RAM makers use the term *single data rate SDRAM* (*SDR SDRAM*) for the original SDRAM to differentiate it from DDR SDRAM.

• **Figure 6.13**   DDR SDRAM

• Figure 6.14   172-pin DDR SDRAM micro-DIMM (*photo courtesy of Kingston/Joint Harvest*)

example, *DDR400* refers to a 400-MHz DDR SDRAM chip running on a 200-MHz clock.

Even though the term DDR*xxx* is really just for individual DDR chips and the term PC*xxxx* is for DDR sticks, this tradition of two names for every speed of RAM is a bit of a challenge because you'll often hear both terms used interchangeably. Table 6.1 shows all the speeds for DDR—not all of these are commonly used.

Table 6.1	DDR Speeds	
Clock Speed	**DDR Speed Rating**	**PC Speed Rating**
100 MHz	DDR200	PC1600
133 MHz	DDR266	PC2100
166 MHz	DDR333	PC2700
200 MHz	DDR400	PC3200
217 MHz	DDR433	PC3500
233 MHz	DDR466	PC3700
250 MHz	DDR500	PC4000
275 MHz	DDR550	PC4400
300 MHz	DDR600	PC4800

Try This!

DRAM Availability

The DRAM market changes fairly rapidly at the higher end, but products tend to linger at the low end, seemingly well past their usefulness. What do your class systems need? What's available in your area today? Try This!

Check out the RAM requirements for the PCs available in your class (or home or office). You can open them up for physical examination or read the motherboard books. Then go to your friendly neighborhood computer store and see what's available. Does the store offer memory that your system cannot use, such as EDO DRAM on 72-pin SIMMs or registered DDR SDRAM? What does this tell you about the PCs available to you?

Following the lead of AMD, VIA, and other manufacturers, the PC industry adopted DDR SDRAM as the standard system RAM. In the summer of 2003, Intel relented and stopped producing motherboards and memory controllers that required RDRAM.

One thing is sure about PC technologies: any good idea that can be copied will be copied. One of Rambus' best concepts was the dual-channel architecture—using two sticks of RDRAM together to increase throughput. Manufacturers have released motherboards with MCCs that support dual-channel architecture using DDR SDRAM. Dual-channel DDR motherboards use regular DDR sticks, although manufacturers often sell RAM in matched pairs, branding them as dual-channel RAM.

Dual-channel DDR works like RDRAM in that you must have two identical sticks of DDR and they must snap into two paired slots. Unlike RDRAM, dual-channel DDR doesn't have anything like CRIMMs—you don't need to put anything into unused slot pairs. Dual-channel DDR technology is very flexible but also has a few quirks that vary with each system. Some motherboards have three DDR SDRAM slots, but the dual-channel DDR works only if you install DDR SDRAM in two of the slots. Other boards have four slots and you must install matching pairs in the same colored slots to run in dual-channel mode (Figure 6.15). If you populate a third slot, the system uses the full capacity of RAM installed but turns off the dual-channel feature.

• **Figure 6.15**   A motherboard showing the four RAM slots. By populating the same color slots with identical RAM, you can run in dual-channel mode.

DDR2

The fastest versions of DDR RAM run at a blistering PC4800. That's 4.8 gigabytes per second (GBps) of data throughput! You'd think that kind of speed would satisfy most users, and to be honest, DRAM running at approximately 5 GBps really is plenty fast—for yesterday. However, the ongoing speed increases ensure that even these speeds won't be good enough in the future. Knowing this, the RAM industry came out with DDR2, the successor to DDR. *DDR2* is DDR RAM with some improvements in its electrical characteristics, enabling it to run even faster than DDR while using less power. The big speed increase from DDR2 comes by clock-doubling the input/output circuits on the chips. This does not speed up the core RAM—the part that holds the data—but speeding up the input/output and adding special buffers (sort of like a cache) makes DDR2 run much faster than regular DDR. DDR2 uses a 240-pin DIMM that's not compatible with DDR (Figure 6.16). Likewise, the DDR2 200-pin SO-DIMM is incompatible with the DDR SO-DIMM. You'll find motherboards running both single-channel and dual-channel DDR2.

> DDR2 RAM sticks will not fit into DDR sockets, nor are they electronically compatible.

• Figure 6.16   240-pin DDR2 DIMM

Table 6.2 shows some of the common DDR2 speeds.

Table 6.2	DDR2 Speeds		
Core RAM Clock Speed	DDR I/O Speed	DDR2 Speed Rating	PC Speed Rating
100 MHz	200 MHz	DDR2-400	PC2-3200
133 MHz	266 MHz	DDR2-533	PC2-4200
166 MHz	333 MHz	DDR2-667	PC2-5300
200 MHz	400 MHz	DDR2-800	PC2-6400
250 MHz	500 MHz	DDR2-1000	PC2-8000

DDR3

DDR2 has been the standard for several years, but now there's a new kid on the block. *DDR3* boasts higher speeds, more efficient architecture, and around 30 percent lower power consumption than DDR2 RAM, making it a compelling choice for system builders. Just like its predecessor, DDR3 uses a 240-pin DIMM, albeit one that is slotted differently to make it difficult for users to install the wrong RAM in their system without using a hammer (Figure 6.17). DDR3 SO-DIMMs for portable computers have 204 pins. Neither fits into a DDR2 socket.

DDR3 doubles the buffer of DDR2 from 4 bits to 8 bits, giving it a huge boost in bandwidth over older RAM. Not only that, but some DDR3

• Figure 6.17   DDR2 DIMM on top of a DDR3 DIMM

Do not confuse DDR3 with GDDR3; the latter is a type of memory used solely in video cards. See Chapter 13, "Learning Video and Multimedia," for the scoop on video-specific types of memory.

modules also include a feature called XMP, or Extreme Memory Profile, that enables power users to overclock their RAM easily, boosting their already fast memory to speeds that would make Chuck Yeager nervous. DDR3 modules also use higher-density memory chips, which means we may eventually see 16-GB DDR3 modules.

Some chipsets that support DDR3 also support a feature called *triple-channel memory*, which works a lot like dual-channel before it, but with three sticks of RAM instead of two. You'll need three of the same type of memory modules and a motherboard that supports it, but triple-channel memory can greatly increase performance for those who can afford it.

In keeping with established tradition, Table 6.3 provides a chart of common DDR3 speeds. Note how DDR3 I/O speeds are quadruple the clock speeds, whereas DDR2 I/O speeds are only double the clock. This speed increase is due to the increased buffer size, which enables DDR3 to grab twice as much data every clock cycle as DDR2 can.

Table 6.3	DDR3 Speeds		
Core RAM Clock Speed	**DDR I/O Speed**	**DDR3 Speed Rating**	**PC Speed Rating**
100 MHz	400 MHz	DDR3-800	PC3-6400
133 MHz	533 MHz	DDR3-1066	PC3-8500
166 MHz	667 MHz	DDR3-1333	PC3-10667
200 MHz	800 MHz	DDR3-1600	PC3-12800

■ RAM Variations

Within each class of RAM, you'll find variations in packaging, speed, quality, and the capability to handle data with more or fewer errors. Higher-end systems often need higher-end RAM, so knowing these variations is of crucial importance to techs.

Double-Sided DIMMs

Every type of RAM stick, starting with the old FPM SIMMs and continuing through to 240-pin DDR3 SDRAM, comes in one of two types: **single-sided** or **double-sided RAM**. As their name implies, single-sided sticks have chips on only one side of the stick. Double-sided sticks have chips on both sides (Figure 6.18). The vast majority of RAM sticks are single-sided, but plenty of double-sided sticks are out there. Double-sided sticks are basically two sticks of RAM soldered onto one board. There's nothing wrong with double-sided RAM other than the fact that some motherboards either can't use them or can only use them in certain ways—for example, only if you use a single stick and it goes into a certain slot.

Latency

If you've shopped for RAM lately, you may have noticed terms such as "CL2" or "low latency" as you tried to determine which RAM to purchase. You might find two otherwise identical RAM sticks with a 20 percent price difference and a salesperson pressuring you to buy the more expensive one because it's "faster" even though both sticks say DDR 3200 (Figure 6.19).

RAM responds to electrical signals at varying rates. When the memory controller starts to grab a line of memory, for example, a slight delay occurs;

• **Figure 6.18**   Double-sided DDR SDRAM

think of it as the RAM getting off the couch. After the RAM sends out the requested line of memory, there's another slight delay before the memory controller can ask for another line—the RAM sat back down. The delay in RAM's response time is called its **latency**. RAM with a lower latency—such as CL2—is faster than RAM with a higher latency—such as CL3—because it responds more quickly. The CL refers to clock cycle delays. The 2 means that the memory delays two clock cycles before delivering the requested data; the 3 means a three-cycle delay.

From a tech's standpoint, you need to get the proper RAM for the system you're working on. If you put a high-latency stick in a motherboard set up

Tech Tip

Latency Is Relative

Latency numbers reflect how many clicks of the system clock it takes before the RAM responds. If you speed up the system clock, say from 166 MHz to 200 MHz, the same stick of RAM might take an extra click before it can respond. When you take RAM out of an older system and put it into a newer one, you might get a seemingly dead PC, even though the RAM fits in the DIMM slot. Many motherboards enable you to adjust the RAM timings manually. If so, try raising the latency to give the slower RAM time to respond. See Chapter 7, "Learning Motherboards," to learn how to make these adjustments (and how to recover if you make a mistake).

CAS stands for column array strobe, one of the wires (along with the row array strobe) in the RAM that helps the memory controller find a particular bit of memory. Each of these wires requires electricity to charge up before it can do its job. This is one of the aspects of latency.

• **Figure 6.19**   Why is one more expensive than the other?

Some memory manufacturers call the technology *Error Checking and Correction* (*ECC*). Don't be thrown off if you see the phrase—it's the same thing, just a different marketing slant for error correction code.

Tech Tip

Counting Chips

To determine if a DRAM stick is parity or ECC, count the individual chips on the stick. If you have an odd number of chips on the stick, you have ECC or parity DRAM.

---

for a low-latency stick, you'll get an unstable or completely dead PC. Check the motherboard manual and get the quickest RAM the motherboard can handle, and you should be fine.

Parity and ECC

Given the high speeds and phenomenal amount of data moved by the typical DRAM chip, a RAM chip might occasionally give bad data to the memory controller. This doesn't necessarily mean that the RAM has gone bad. It could be a hiccup caused by some unknown event that makes a good DRAM chip say a bit is a zero when it's really a one. In most cases you won't even notice when such a rare event happens. In some environments, however, even these rare events are intolerable. A bank server handling thousands of online transactions per second, for example, can't risk even the smallest error. These important computers need a more robust, fault-resistant RAM.

The first type of error-detecting RAM was known as parity RAM (Figure 6.20). **Parity RAM** stored an extra bit of data (called the parity bit) that the MCC used to verify whether the data was correct. Parity wasn't perfect—it wouldn't always detect an error, and if the MCC did find an error, it couldn't correct the error. For years, parity was the only available way to tell if the RAM made a mistake.

Today's PCs that need to watch for RAM errors use a special type of RAM called **error correction code RAM (ECC RAM)**. ECC is a major advance in error checking on DRAM. First, ECC detects any time a single bit is incorrect. Second, ECC fixes these errors on the fly. The checking and fixing come at a price, however, as ECC RAM is always slower than non-ECC RAM.

ECC DRAM comes in every DIMM package type and can lead to some odd-sounding numbers. You can find DDR2 or DDR3 RAM sticks, for example, that come in 240-pin, 72-bit versions. Similarly, you'll see 200-pin, 72-bit SO-DIMM format. The extra 8 bits beyond the 64-bit data stream are for the ECC.

You might be tempted to say "Gee, maybe I want to try this ECC RAM." Well, don't! To take advantage of ECC RAM, you need a motherboard with an MCC designed to use ECC. Only expensive motherboards for high-end systems use ECC. The special-use-only nature of ECC makes it fairly rare. Plenty of techs out there with years of experience have never even seen ECC RAM.

Buffered/Registered DRAM

Your average PC motherboard accepts no more than four sticks of DRAM, because more than four physical slots for sticks gives motherboard

• Figure 6.20   Ancient parity RAM stick

Mike Meyers' CompTIA A+ Guide: Essentials

designers some serious electrical headaches. Yet some systems that use a lot of RAM need the capability to use more DRAM sticks on the motherboard, often six or eight. To get around the electrical hassles, special DRAM sticks add a buffering chip to the stick that acts as an intermediary between the DRAM and the MCC. These special DRAM sticks are called **buffered** or **registered DRAM** (Figure 6.21).

Like ECC, you must have a motherboard with an MCC designed to use this type of DRAM. Rest assured that such a motherboard has a large number of RAM slots. Buffered/registered RAM is rare (maybe not quite as rare as ECC RAM), and you'll never see it in the typical desktop system.

• **Figure 6.21**   Buffered DRAM

Chapter 6 Review

■ Chapter Summary

After reading this chapter and completing the exercises, you should understand the following about RAM.

Identify the different types of DRAM packaging

- The sticks of RAM snapped into your motherboard are DRAM. Think of DRAM as a spreadsheet in which each cell holds a one or a zero. Each cell represents a single bit. The number of columns and rows are finite.

- If a chip contains 1,048,576 rows and 8 columns, it can be described as a 1 M × 8 chip. A chip containing 2,097,152 rows and 16 columns can be described as a 2 M × 16 chip.

- DRAM needs to be able to fill the data bus. A 1 M × 8 DRAM chip is only 8 bits wide and would provide the CPU with only 8 bits of data. You would need eight of the 1 M × 8 chips to fill a 64-bit data bus.

- DRAM chips are soldered to a circuit board called a stick or module, and when these chips are combined, a single stick can fill the data bus. Modern DRAM sticks come in 32-bit- and 64-bit-wide varieties.

Explain the varieties of RAM

- Synchronous dynamic random access memory, or SDRAM, is tied to the system clock. The CPU, memory controller, and RAM all work in tandem with the clock pulse. This results in little wasted time when the CPU requests data from RAM.

- SDRAM comes in sticks called dual inline memory modules (DIMMs). SDRAM DIMMs come in a variety of pin sizes, with 168 pins being the most common for desktop systems. DIMMs are 64 bits wide so that they match the 64-bit data bus of modern CPUs. DIMMs snap into slots on the motherboard. Each DIMM is 64 bits, so snapping in a single DIMM fills the data bus; therefore, each slot is called a bank.

- SDRAM is advertised by capacity and speed. The speed is prefixed with "PC"; for example, PC66 runs at 66 MHz. A stick of SDRAM advertised as 256-MB PC133 has a capacity of 256 MB and runs at 133 MHz. Five clock speeds are commonly used: 66, 75, 83, 100, and 133 MHz.

- RAM speed must match or exceed that of the system. For example, PC66 RAM can only be used on a motherboard running at (or below) 66 MHz. A motherboard with a frontside bus of 100 MHz needs at least PC100 RAM.

- Rambus DRAM (RDRAM) was created by Rambus, Inc., and came in sticks called RIMMs. Due to cost, licensing issues, and compatibility, RDRAM is now obsolete.

- RIMMs were 64 bits wide and came in speeds of 600 MHz, 700 MHz, 800 MHz, and 1066 MHz. Differences in the notches prevented you from snapping a RIMM into a motherboard DIMM slot or vice versa.

- The RIMM memory controller uses a dual-channel architecture: it alternates between two banks to increase the speed of data retrieval. You need to install RIMMs in pairs to accommodate this feature.

- All RIMM slots on the motherboard must be filled with either a RIMM or a CRIMM. A CRIMM, or continuity RIMM, is simply a stick with no memory chips on it.

- Double data rate SDRAM (DDR RAM) is faster than regular SDRAM because it doubles the throughput. Desktop PCs use 184-pin DDR DIMMs, whereas laptops use either 200-pin or 172-pin small-outline DIMMs (SO-DIMMs). DDR RAM modules have notches that differ from both regular SDRAM and RDRAM, so DDR RAM only snaps into DDR slots on a motherboard.

- DDR RAM is advertised one of two ways. One way is with "DDR" followed by the speed; for example, DDR400 for a stick of RAM runs at 400 MHz.

Because DDR RAM runs at twice the clock speed, DDR400 is meant for a 200-MHz frontside bus. DDR RAM is also advertised by "PC" followed by the throughput; for example, PC3200. The number is determined by multiplying the speed by eight (as all DDR sticks are 64 bits, or 8 bytes, wide). Thus, DDR400 has a throughput of 3200 bytes per second (400 MHz × 8 bytes). DDR400 and PC3200 are equivalent.

- Dual-channel DDR improves upon DDR by using the DIMMs in pairs, much like RDRAM. For systems to use dual-channel DDR, the motherboard and memory controller must support dual-channel DDR RAM, and the DDR DIMMs must be identical. Dual-channel DDR does not require dummy modules such as CRIMMs. Dual-channel slots are identified on a motherboard by their blue color. Some motherboards offer a third slot in black, but filling that third slot to increase your total system RAM also turns off the dual-channel feature.

- DDR2 is an improvement of DDR. DDR2 runs faster than DDR and uses a 240-pin form factor that is not compatible with DDR. You need a motherboard with DDR2 slots to use DDR2 RAM. DDR2 is rated by speed or throughput. Thus DDR2-400 is the same as PC2-3200 and is meant for a 200-MHz frontside bus.

- DDR3 boasts higher speeds, more efficient architecture, and around 30 percent lower power consumption than DDR2 RAM. DDR3 doubles the buffer of DDR2 from 4 bits to 8 bits, giving it a huge boost in bandwidth over older RAM. Some chipsets that support DDR3 also support triple-channel memory, which works a lot like dual-channel but with three sticks of RAM instead of two.

- RAM modules are either single-sided or double-sided. Single-sided sticks have chips on only one side, whereas double-sided sticks have chips on both sides. Most RAM is single-sided.

- Latency refers to the time lag between when the memory controller starts to fetch data from RAM and when RAM actually sends out the requested data. Another lag occurs when the memory controller asks for the next line from RAM. The shorter this lag time, the faster the system. CL2 indicates a shorter lag time, or lower latency, than CL3, so CL2 is faster. Check your motherboard documentation and get the lowest-latency RAM your system will support.

- Error correction code (ECC) RAM improved upon parity RAM by being able to fix single-bit errors on the fly. ECC RAM is always slower than non-ECC RAM due to the overhead of the correcting code. Only high-end motherboards and memory controllers can use ECC RAM.

- Buffered or registered RAM adds a buffering chip to compensate for the electrical interference that can result from using more than four DIMMs on a single motherboard. The motherboard and memory controller must be designed specifically to support buffered or registered RAM. You are not likely to see it in a typical desktop system.

■ Key Terms

bank *(188)*
buffered/registered DRAM *(197)*
continuity RIMM (CRIMM) *(190)*
double data rate SDRAM (DDR SDRAM) *(190)*
double-sided RAM *(194)*
dual-channel architecture *(189)*
dual inline memory module (DIMM) *(188)*
dynamic random access memory (DRAM) *(183)*
error correction code RAM (ECC RAM) *(196)*
latency *(195)*

module *(186)*
parity RAM *(196)*
Rambus DRAM (RDRAM) *(189)*
RIMM *(189)*
single inline memory module (SIMM) *(186)*
single-sided RAM *(194)*
small-outline DIMM (SO-DIMM) *(188)*
stick *(186)*
synchronous DRAM (SDRAM) *(188)*

■ Key Term Quiz

Use the Key Terms list to complete the sentences that follow. Not all terms will be used.

1. If your motherboard uses RDRAM, you must fill each slot with either a(n) _____ or a(n) _____.

2. A special kind of memory stick for laptops is called a(n) _____.

3. Memory that makes two data accesses during each clock tick is called _____.

4. Unlike regular DRAM, _____ is tied to the system clock.

5. Unlike regular DRAM, _____ enables error checking and correcting.

6. The time lag between when the memory controller starts to fetch a line of data from RAM and when the RAM actually starts to deliver the data is known as _____.

7. Motherboards that support more than four sticks of RAM may require _____ to accommodate for the additional electrical hassles caused by the additional sticks.

■ Multiple-Choice Quiz

1. What is the correct throughput of DDR-SDRAM, and what is the speed of PC1600 RAM?

   A. 4 bytes per second, 133 MHz

   B. 8 bytes per second, 200 MHz

   C. 4 bits per second, 400 MHz

   D. 8 bits per second, 200 MHz

2. How many sticks of RAM do you need to fill a bank in a computer that can use 168-pin DIMMs?

   A. One

   B. Two

   C. Four

   D. Eight

3. What does the CPU use to access the system's RAM?

   A. The system bus

   B. The MMC

   C. The address bus

   D. The expansion bus

4. Which of the following statements is true about RDRAM?

   A. It uses dual-channel architecture.

   B. It offers speeds ranging from 200 MHz to 600 MHz.

   C. It is less expensive than SDRAM.

   D. It is used by AMD but not Intel processors.

5. Which of the following SDRAM speeds would not work with a 100-MHz motherboard?

   A. 66 MHz

   B. 100 MHz

   C. 133 MHz

   D. 200 MHz

6. Which of the following is a valid package size for DDR3 DIMMs?

   A. 168-pin

   B. 172-pin

   C. 184-pin

   D. 240-pin

7. What package does DDR-SDRAM use for desktop PCs?

   A. 30-pin

   B. 72-pin

   C. 168-pin

   D. 184-pin

8. What happens if you mix RAM sticks of different speeds?

   A. Your computer will work fine as long as it uses dual-channel architecture.

   B. Your computer may slow down.

   C. Your computer will work fine if all the memory sticks are slower than the speed of the motherboard.

   D. Your computer may lock up every few seconds or provide corrupted data.

9. Why is SDRAM faster than regular DRAM?

  A. It makes two processes per clock cycle.

  B. It runs synchronously with the system clock.

  C. It uses dual-channel architecture.

  D. It has fewer pins, resulting in fewer corrupt bits.

10. What is true about a double-sided DIMM?

  A. It has memory chips on the front and back.

  B. It can be installed forward or backward.

  C. It is twice as fast as a single-sided DIMM.

  D. It has half the capacity of a quad-sided DIMM.

11. If you have two sticks of DDR 3200 and one says that it is faster than the other, what is most likely the difference between them?

  A. The faster stick has a higher capacity than the slower one.

  B. The faster stick has lower latency than the slower one.

  C. The faster stick has higher latency than the slower one.

  D. The faster stick may have more connectors than the slower one.

■ Essay Quiz

1. Celia tells you she just received a new motherboard for the system she is building. She is confused about the RAM slots. The motherboard has three of them, but two are blue and one is black. What can you tell her about the RAM slots on her motherboard?

Lab Project

• Lab Project 6.1

To learn more about memory, go to the Web site www.kingston.com, select Memory Tools from the buttons at the top of the screen, and examine the "Ultimate Memory Guide." This resource contains information about all aspects of computer memory. After using this guide, answer the following questions:

  ■ Why do memory prices vary so frequently?

  ■ What are the differences in tin- and gold-edged memory sticks, and how does one know which to choose when upgrading?

  ■ Describe the notches on a 30-pin SIMM, a 72-pin SIMM, a 168-pin DIMM, and a 184-pin DIMM. What function do the notches serve?

Learning Motherboards

"Nearly right, Penfold, it's a 32 K ROM C-moss flip flop digital homing device."

—Danger Mouse, *Danger Mouse* (1983)

In this chapter, you will learn how to

- Explain the function of BIOS
- Distinguish among various CMOS setup utility options
- Describe option ROM and device drivers
- Explain the function of the power-on self test (POST)
- Identify the structure and function of the expansion bus
- Describe the modern expansion bus
- Explain classic system resources
- Explain how motherboards work
- Identify the types of motherboards
- Explain chipset varieties

In Chapter 5, "Learning CPUs," you saw how the address bus and external data bus connect RAM to the CPU via the memory controller chip (MCC) to run programs and transfer data. Assuming you apply power in the right places, you don't need anything else to make a simple computer. The only problem with such a simple computer is that it would bore you to death—there's no way to do anything with it! A PC needs devices such as keyboards and mice to provide input, and output devices such as monitors and sound cards to communicate the current state of the running programs to you. A computer also needs permanent storage devices, such as hard drives and optical drives, to store programs and data when you turn off the computer.

In this chapter, you will look at the process that your computer uses to communicate with any hardware you install in it. You'll then look at the expansion bus in detail, starting almost at the very beginning of the PC—not because the history of the PC is inherently thrilling, but rather because the way the old PCs worked affects the latest systems. Installation today remains very similar to installation in 1987 in that you must have a physical connection, communication, and drivers for the operating system. Taking the time to learn the old ways first most definitely helps you understand and implement current technology, terminology, and practices. Finally, you'll get a general overview of motherboards, which will help put all of the rest of this chapter into a proper context.

We Need to Talk

Simply placing a number of components into a computer is useless if the CPU can't communicate with them. Getting the CPU to communicate with a device starts with some kind of interconnection—a communication bus that enables the CPU to send commands to and from devices. To make this connection, let's promote the MCC, giving it extra firepower to act as not only the interconnection between the CPU and RAM, but also the interconnection between the CPU and the other devices on the PC. The MCC isn't just the memory controller anymore, so let's now call it the **Northbridge** because it acts as the primary bridge between the CPU and the rest of the computer (Figure 7.1).

• **Figure 7.1**   Meet the Northbridge

Your PC is full of devices, so the PC industry decided to delegate some of the interconnectivity work to a second chip called the **Southbridge**. The Northbridge only deals with high-speed interfaces such as the connection to your video card and RAM. The Southbridge works mainly with lower-speed devices such as the USB controller and hard drive controllers. Chip makers design matched sets of particular models of Northbridge and Southbridge to work together. You don't buy a Northbridge from one company and a Southbridge from another—they're sold as a set. We call this set of Northbridge and Southbridge the **chipset**.

The chipset extends the data bus to every device on the PC. The CPU uses the data bus to move data to and from all of the devices of the PC. Data constantly flows on the external data bus among the CPU, chipset, RAM, and other devices on the PC (Figure 7.2).

The first use for the address bus, as you know, is for the CPU to tell the chipset to send or store data in memory and to tell the chipset which section of memory to access or use. Just as with the external data bus, the chipset extends the address bus to all of the devices (Figure 7.3). That way the CPU can use the address bus to send commands to devices, just as it sends commands to the chipset. You'll see this in action a lot more later in this chapter, but for now just go with the concept.

Chipset makers rarely use the terms "Northbridge" and "Southbridge" anymore, but because most modern chipsets consist of only two or three chips with basically the same functions, techs continue to use the terms.

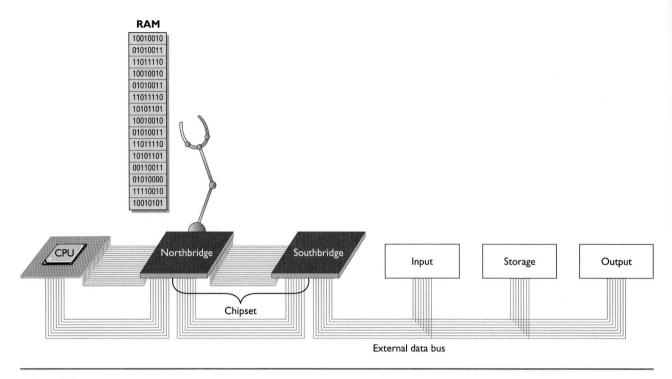

RAM

10010010
01010011
11011110
10010010
01010011
11011110
10101101
10010010
01010011
11011110
10101101
00110011
01010000
11110010
10010101

CPU Northbridge Southbridge Input Storage Output

Chipset

External data bus

● **Figure 7.2**   The chipset extending the data bus

It's not too hard to swallow the concept that the CPU uses the address bus to talk to the devices, but how does it know what to *say* to them? How does it know all of the patterns of ones and zeros to place on the address bus to tell the hard drive it needs to send a file? Let's look at the interaction between the keyboard and CPU for insight into this process.

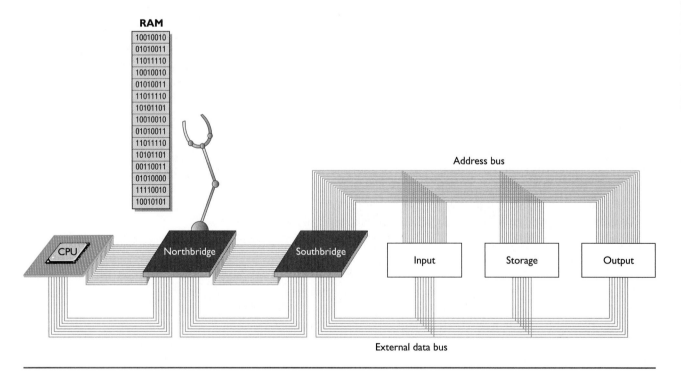

RAM

10010010
01010011
11011110
10010010
01010011
11011110
10101101
10010010
01010011
11011110
10101101
00110011
01010000
11110010
10010101

Address bus

CPU Northbridge Southbridge Input Storage Output

External data bus

● **Figure 7.3**   Every device in your computer connects to the address bus.

Talking to the Keyboard

The keyboard provides a great example of how the buses and support programming help the CPU get the job done. In early computers, the keyboard connected to the external data bus via a special chip known as the *keyboard controller*. Don't bother looking for this chip on your motherboard—the Southbridge now handles keyboard controller functions. The way the keyboard controller—or technically, the keyboard controller *circuitry*—works with the CPU, however, has changed only a small amount in the past 20+ years, making it a perfect tool to illustrate how the CPU talks to a device.

The keyboard controller was one of the last single-function chips to be absorbed into the chipset. For many years—in fact, well into the Pentium III/Early Athlon era—most motherboards had separate keyboard controller chips. Figure 7.4 shows a typical keyboard controller from those days. Electronically, it looked like Figure 7.5.

Every time you press a key on your keyboard, a scanning chip in the keyboard notices which key you pressed. Then the scanner sends a coded pattern of ones and zeros—called the scan code—to the keyboard controller. Every key on your keyboard has a unique scan code. The keyboard controller stores the scan code in its own register. Does it surprise you that the lowly keyboard controller has a register similar to a CPU? Lots of chips have registers—not just CPUs (Figure 7.6)!

Techs commonly talk about various functions of the chipset as if those functions were still handled by discrete chips. So you'll hear about memory controllers, keyboard controllers, mouse controllers, USB controllers, and so on, even though they're all just circuits on the Northbridge or Southbridge chips.

• **Figure 7.4**   A keyboard chip on a Pentium motherboard

> **Tech Tip**
>
> **The 8042**
> *Even though the model numbers changed over the years, you'll still hear techs refer to the keyboard controller as the 8042, after the original keyboard controller chip.*

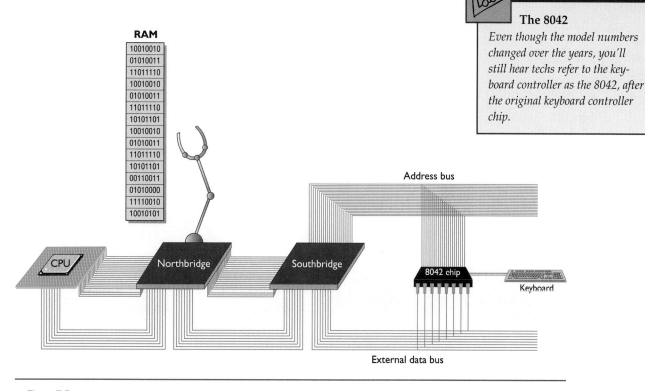

• **Figure 7.5**   Electronic view of the keyboard controller

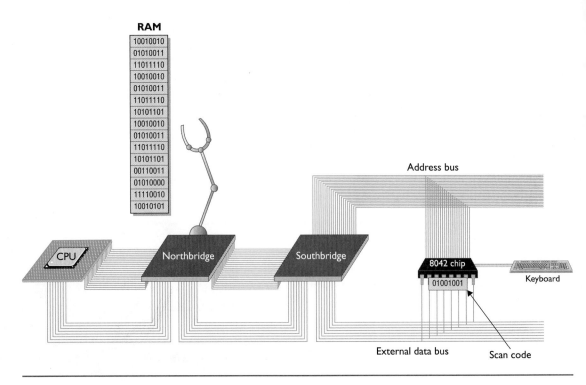

RAM
```
10010010
01010011
11011110
10010010
01010011
11011110
10101101
10010010
01010011
11011110
10101101
00110011
01010000
11110010
10010101
```

CPU

Northbridge

Southbridge

Address bus

8042 chip

01001001

Keyboard

External data bus   Scan code

● Figure 7.6   Scan code stored in keyboard controller's register

How does the CPU get the scan code out of the keyboard controller (Figure 7.7)? While we're at it, how does the CPU tell the keyboard to change the typematic buffer rate (when you hold down a key and the letter repeats) or to turn the number lock LED on and off, to mention just a few other jobs the keyboard needs to do for the system? The point is that the keyboard controller must be able to respond to multiple commands, not just one.

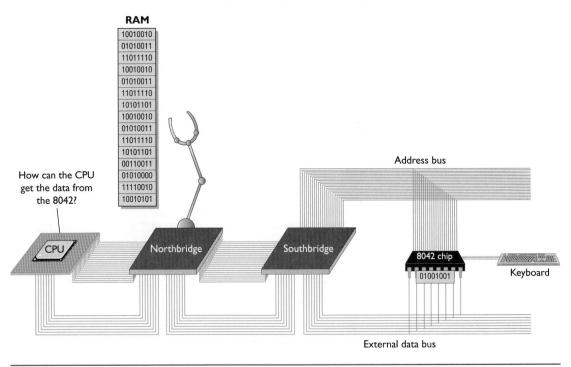

RAM
```
10010010
01010011
11011110
10010010
01010011
11011110
10101101
10010010
01010011
11011110
10101101
00110011
01010000
11110010
10010101
```

How can the CPU get the data from the 8042?

CPU

Northbridge

Southbridge

Address bus

8042 chip

01001001

Keyboard

External data bus

● Figure 7.7   The CPU ponders the age-old dilemma of how to get the 8042 to cough up its data.

The keyboard controller accepts commands exactly as you saw the CPU accept commands in Chapter 5 "Learning CPUs." Remember when you added 2 to 3 with the 8088? You had to use specific commands from the 8088's codebook to tell the CPU to do the addition and then place the answer on the external data bus. The keyboard controller has its own codebook—much simpler than any CPU's codebook, but conceptually the same. If the CPU wants to know what key was last pressed on the keyboard, the CPU needs to know the command (or series of commands) that orders the keyboard controller to put the scan code of the letter on the external data bus so the CPU can read it.

BIOS

The CPU can't magically or otherwise automatically know how to talk with any device; it needs some sort of support programming loaded into memory that teaches it about a particular device. This programming is called **basic input/output services (BIOS)**. The programs dedicated to enabling the CPU to communicate with devices are called services (or device drivers, as you'll see later in the chapter). This goes well beyond the keyboard, by the way. In fact, *every* device on the computer needs BIOS! But let's continue with the keyboard for now.

Bringing BIOS to the PC

A talented programmer could write BIOS for a keyboard if the programmer knew the keyboard's codebook; keyboards are pretty simple devices. This begs the question: where would this support programming be stored? Well, programming could be incorporated into the operating system. Storing programming to talk to the hardware of your PC in the operating system is great—all operating systems have built-in code that knows how to talk to your keyboard, your mouse, and just about every piece of hardware you may put into your PC.

That's fine once the operating system's up and running, but what about a brand new stack of parts you're about to assemble into a new PC? When a new system's being built, it has no operating system. The CPU must have access to BIOS for the most important hardware on your PC: not only the keyboard, but also the monitor, hard drives, optical drives, USB ports, and RAM. This code can't be stored on a hard drive or CD-ROM disc—these important devices need to be ready at any time the CPU calls them, even before installing a mass storage device or an operating system.

The perfect place to store the support programming is on the motherboard. That settles one issue, but another looms: What storage medium should the motherboard use? DRAM won't work, because all of the data would be erased every time the computer was turned off. You need some type of permanent program storage device that does not depend on other peripherals to work. And you need that storage device to sit on the motherboard.

ROM

Motherboards store the keyboard controller support programming, among other programs, on a special type of device called a **read-only memory (ROM)** chip. A ROM chip stores programs, called **services**, exactly like RAM:

• Figure 7.8 Typical flash ROM

Programs stored on ROM chips—flash or any other kind of ROM chip—are known collectively as *firmware*, as opposed to programs stored on erasable media that are collectively called *software*.

that is, like an 8-bit-wide spreadsheet. But ROM differs from RAM in two important ways. First, ROM chips are **nonvolatile**, meaning that the information stored on ROM isn't erased when the computer is turned off. Second, traditional ROM chips are read-only, meaning that once you store a program on one, you can't change it. Modern motherboards use a type of ROM called **flash ROM** that differs from traditional ROM in that you can update and change the contents through a very specific process called "flashing the ROM." Figure 7.8 shows a typical flash ROM chip on a motherboard. When the CPU wants to talk to the keyboard controller, it goes to the flash ROM chip to access the proper programming.

Every motherboard has a flash ROM, called the **system ROM** chip because it contains code that enables your CPU to talk to the basic hardware of your PC (Figure 7.9). As alluded to earlier, the system ROM holds BIOS for more than just the keyboard controller. It also stores programs for communicating with the floppy drives, hard drives, CD and DVD drives, video, USB ports, and other basic devices on your motherboard.

To talk to all of that hardware requires hundreds of little services (2 to 30 lines of code each). These hundreds of little programs stored on the system ROM chip on the motherboard are called, collectively, the **system BIOS** (Figure 7.10). Techs call programs stored on ROM chips of any sort **firmware**.

The system ROM chips used on modern PCs store as much as 2 MB of programs, although only 65,536 bytes are used to store the system BIOS.

• Figure 7.9   Function of the flash ROM chip

RAM

10010010
01010011
11011110
10010010
01010011
11011110
10101101
10010010
01010011
11011110
10101101
00110011
01010000
11110010
10010101

What button was pressed on the keyboard?

Hey, 8042! Put the scan code on the EDB so we can see it!

Address bus

CPU

Northbridge

Southbridge

ROM chip
10010010
01010011
11110010
10010101

8042 chip
01001001

Keyboard

External data bus

• **Figure 7.10**   CPU running BIOS service

This allows for backward compatibility with earlier systems. The rest of the ROM space is put to good use doing other jobs.

System BIOS Support

Every system BIOS has two types of hardware to support. First, the system BIOS supports all of the hardware that never changes, such as the keyboard. (You can change your keyboard, but you can't change the keyboard controller built into the Southbridge.) Another example of hardware that never changes is the PC speaker (the tiny one that beeps at you, not the ones that play music). The system ROM chip stores the BIOS for these and other devices that never change.

Second, the system BIOS supports all of the hardware that might change from time to time. This includes RAM (you can add RAM), hard drives (you can replace your hard drive with a larger drive or add a second hard drive), and floppy drives (you can add another floppy drive, although that's not common today). The system ROM chip stores the *BIOS* for these devices, but the system needs another place to store information about the specific *details* of a piece of hardware. This enables the system to differentiate between a Western Digital Caviar Black 1.5-TB hard drive and a Seagate Barracuda 60-GB drive, and yet still support both drives right out of the box.

■ CMOS

A separate memory chip, called the **complementary metal-oxide semiconductor (CMOS)** chip, stores the information that describes specific device parameters. CMOS does *not* store programs; it only stores data that is read by

● Figure 7.11   Old-style CMOS

BIOS to complete the programs needed to talk to changeable hardware. CMOS also acts as a clock to keep the current date and time.

Years ago, CMOS was a separate chip on the motherboard, as shown in Figure 7.11. Today, the CMOS is almost always built into the Southbridge.

Most CMOS chips store around 64 KB of data, but the PC usually needs only a very small amount—about 128 bytes—to store all of the necessary information on the changeable hardware. Don't let the tiny size fool you. The information stored in CMOS is absolutely necessary for the PC to function!

If the data stored on CMOS about a particular piece of hardware (or about its fancier features) is different from the specs of the actual hardware, the computer cannot access that piece of hardware (or use its fancier features). It is crucial that this information be correct. If you change any of the previously mentioned hardware, you must update CMOS to reflect those changes. You need to know, therefore, how to change the data on CMOS.

Updating CMOS: The Setup Program

The terms *CMOS setup program*, *CMOS*, and *system setup utility* are functionally interchangeable today. You'll even hear the program referred to as the *BIOS setup utility* or *CMOS setup utility*. Most techs just call it the CMOS.

Every PC ships with a program built into the system ROM called the **CMOS setup program** or the *system setup utility* that enables you to access and update CMOS data. When you fire up your computer in the morning, the first thing you likely see is the BIOS information. It might look like the example in Figure 7.12 or perhaps something like Figure 7.13.

Who or what is AMIBIOS, and who or what is Phoenix Technologies? These are brand names of BIOS companies. They write BIOS programs and sell them to computer manufacturers. In today's world, motherboard makers rarely write their own BIOS. Instead, they buy their BIOS from specialized third-party BIOS makers such as Award Software and Phoenix Technologies. Although several companies write BIOS, two big companies control 99 percent of the BIOS business: American Megatrends (AMI) and

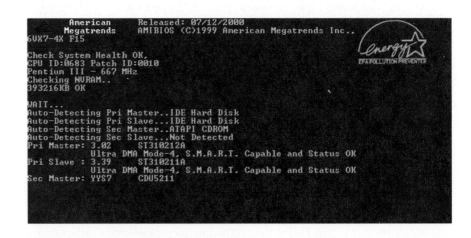

● Figure 7.12   AMI BIOS information

```
Award Modular BIOS v6.00PG, An Energy Star Ally
Copyright (C) 1984-2003 Phoenix Technologies, LTD

Main Processor : AMD Athlon(tm) 64 Processor 3200+
Memory Testing : 1048576K OK
CPU0 Memory Information: DDR 400 CL:3 ,1T Dual Channel, 128-bit

IDE Channel 1 Master : WDC WD1200JB-75CRA0 16.06V16
IDE Channel 1 Slave  : None
IDE Channel 2 Master : SONY    CD-RW  CRX175E2 S002
IDE Channel 2 Slave  : TOSHIBA CD=DVDW SDR5372V TU11

IDE Channel 3 Master : None
IDE Channel 4 Master : None

Detecting IDE drives ...




Press DEL to enter SETUP, ESC to Enter Boot Menu
07/01/2005-MF-CK804-6A61FA1DC-10
```

• **Figure 7.13**   Award/Phoenix BIOS information

Tech Tip

Term Limits

Okay, I've thrown a whole bunch of terms at you describing various pieces of hardware and software and what does what to whom. Here's the scorecard so you can sort out the various pieces of data.

1. *The system ROM chip stores the system BIOS, programs needed by the CPU to communicate with devices.*

2. *The system ROM chip also holds the program that accesses the information stored on the CMOS chip to support changeable pieces of hardware. This program is called the CMOS setup program or the system setup utility.*

3. *The CMOS holds a small amount of data that describes the changeable pieces of hardware supported by the system BIOS. The CMOS today is in the Southbridge chip of the chipset.*

Phoenix Technologies. Phoenix bought Award Software a few years ago and still sells the Award brand name as a separate product line. These three are the most common brand names in the field.

You always access a system's CMOS setup program at boot. The real question is how to access the CMOS setup at boot for your particular PC. AMI, Award, and Phoenix use different keys to access the CMOS setup program. Usually, BIOS manufacturers tell you how to access the CMOS setup right on the screen as your computer boots up. For example, at the bottom of the screen in Figure 7.13, you are instructed to "Press DEL to enter SETUP." Keep in mind that this is only one possible example. Motherboard manufacturers can change the key combinations for entering CMOS setup. You can even set up the computer so the message does not show—a smart idea if you need to keep nosy people out of your CMOS setup! If you don't see an "enter setup" message, wait until the RAM count starts and then try one of the following keys or key combinations: DEL, ESC, F1, F2, CTRL-ALT-ESC, CTRL-ALT-INS, CTRL-ALT-ENTER, or CTRL-S. It may take a few tries, but you will eventually find the right key or key combination. If not, check the motherboard book or the manufacturer's Web site for the information.

A Quick Tour Through a Typical CMOS Setup Program

Every BIOS maker's CMOS setup program looks a little different, but don't let that confuse you. They all contain basically the same settings; you just have to be comfortable poking around. To avoid doing something foolish, *do not save anything* unless you are sure you have it set correctly.

As an example, let's say your machine has Award BIOS. You boot the system and press DEL to enter CMOS setup. The screen in Figure 7.14 appears. You are now in the Main menu of the Award CMOS setup program. The setup program itself is stored on the ROM chip, but it edits only the data on the CMOS chip.

Accessing the CMOS setup utility for a system is perfectly fine, but do not make changes unless you fully understand that system!

Try This!

Accessing CMOS Setup

The key or key combination required to access CMOS setup varies, depending on your particular BIOS. It's important to know how to access CMOS setup, and how to find the BIOS information once you're in, so Try This!

1. Boot your system and turn on your monitor. Watch the information that scrolls by on the screen as your computer boots. Most BIOS makers include a line indicating what key(s) to press to access the CMOS setup program. Make a note of this useful information! You can also check your motherboard book to determine the process for accessing the CMOS setup program.

2. Reboot the system, and this time watch for information on the BIOS manufacturer. If you don't see it, and if it's okay to do so, open the system case and check the name printed on the system ROM chip. Make a note of this useful information.

3. Reboot one more time, and this time use the key or key combination you found to run the CMOS setup program. Locate and make a note of the manufacturer, date, and version number of your PC's current BIOS.

4. If you can, make a note of the exact model information for your system and visit the Web site of the company that manufactured your PC. Search their support files for the specs on your specific system and see if you can locate your BIOS information. Now take the detailed BIOS information and search the BIOS manufacturer's Web site for the same information.

If you select the Standard CMOS Features option, the Standard CMOS Features screen appears (Figure 7.15). On this screen you can change floppy drive and hard drive settings, as well as the system's date and time. You will learn how to set up the CMOS for these devices in later chapters. At this point, your only goal is to understand CMOS and know how to access the CMOS setup on your PC, so don't try to change anything yet. If you have a system that you are allowed to reboot, try accessing the CMOS setup now. Does it look anything like these examples? If not, can you find the screen that enables you to change the floppy and hard drives? Trust me, every CMOS setup has that screen somewhere! Figure 7.16 shows the same standard CMOS setup screen on a system with Phoenix BIOS. Note that this CMOS setup utility calls this screen "Main."

```
          Phoenix - Award BIOS CMOS Setup Utility

   ▶ SoftMenu Setup              ▶ PC Health Status
   ▶ Standard CMOS Features        Load Fail-Safe Defaults
   ▶ Advanced BIOS Features        Load Optimized Defaults
   ▶ Advanced Chipset Features     Set Password
   ▶ Integrated Peripherals        Save & Exit Setup
   ▶ Power Management Setup        Exit Without Saving
   ▶ PnP/PCI Configurations

   Esc : Quit                   ▲▼▶◀      : Select Item
   F10 : Save & Exit Setup      <NF-CK804-6A61FA1DC-10>

              Change CPU's Clock & Voltage
```

● **Figure 7.14** Typical CMOS main screen by Award

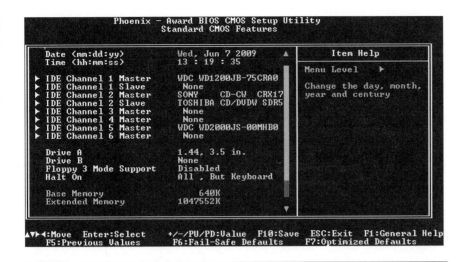

Phoenix – Award BIOS CMOS Setup Utility
Standard CMOS Features

```
Date (mm:dd:yy)              Wed, Jun 7 2009           Item Help
Time (hh:mm:ss)              13 : 19 : 35
                                                      Menu Level    ▶
▶ IDE Channel 1 Master       WDC WD1200JB-75CRA0
▶ IDE Channel 1 Slave        None                     Change the day, month,
▶ IDE Channel 2 Master       SONY    CD-CW  CRX17      year and century
▶ IDE Channel 2 Slave        TOSHIBA CD/DVDW SDR5
▶ IDE Channel 3 Master       None
▶ IDE Channel 4 Master       None
▶ IDE Channel 5 Master       WDC WD2000JS-00MHB0
▶ IDE Channel 6 Master       None

  Drive A                    1.44, 3.5 in.
  Drive B                    None
  Floppy 3 Mode Support      Disabled
  Halt On                    All , But Keyboard

  Base Memory                    640K
  Extended Memory            1047552K

▲▼◄►:Move  Enter:Select    +/-/PU/PD:Value  F10:Save  ESC:Exit  F1:General Help
   F5:Previous Values        F6:Fail-Safe Defaults    F7:Optimized Defaults
```

• **Figure 7.15** Standard CMOS Features screen

The first BIOS was nothing more than this standard CMOS setup. Today, all computers have many extra CMOS settings. They control items such as memory management, password and booting options, diagnostic and error handling, and power management. The following section takes a quick tour of an Award CMOS setup program. Remember that your CMOS setup almost certainly looks at least a little different from mine, unless you happen to have the *same* BIOS. The chances of that happening are quite slim.

Phoenix has virtually cornered the desktop PC BIOS market with its Award Modular BIOS. Motherboard makers buy a boilerplate BIOS, designed for a particular chipset, and add or remove options (Phoenix calls them *modules*) based on the needs of each motherboard. This means that seemingly identical CMOS setup utilities can be extremely different. Options that show up on one computer might be missing from another. Compare the older Award screen in Figure 7.17 with the more modern Award CMOS screen in Figure 7.14. Figure 7.17 looks different—and it should—as this much older system simply doesn't need the extra options available on the newer system.

The next section starts the walkthrough of a CMOS setup utility with the SoftMenu, followed by some of the Advanced screens. Then you'll go through other common screens, such as Integrated Peripherals, Power, and more.

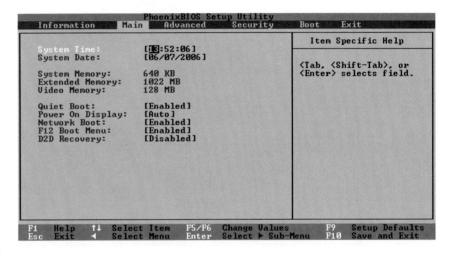

• **Figure 7.16** Phoenix BIOS CMOS setup utility Main screen

All of these screens tend to overwhelm new techs. When they first encounter the many options, some techs feel they need to understand every option on every screen to configure CMOS properly. Relax—every new motherboard comes with settings that befuddle even the most experienced techs. If I don't talk about a particular CMOS setting somewhere in this book, it's probably not important, either to the CompTIA A+ Essentials exam or to a real tech.

SoftMenu

You can use the SoftMenu to change the voltage and multiplier settings on the motherboard for the CPU from the defaults. Motherboards that cater to

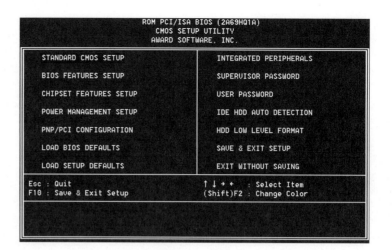

● Figure 7.17   Older Award setup screen

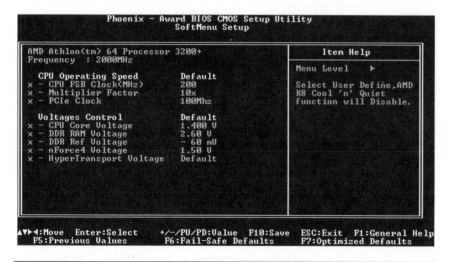

● Figure 7.18   SoftMenu

overclockers tend to have this option. Usually you just set this to Auto or Default and stay away from this screen (Figure 7.18).

Advanced BIOS Features

Advanced BIOS Features is the dumping ground for all of the settings that aren't covered in the Standard CMOS Setup menu and don't fit nicely under any other screen. This screen varies wildly from one system to the next. You most often use this screen to select the boot options (Figure 7.19).

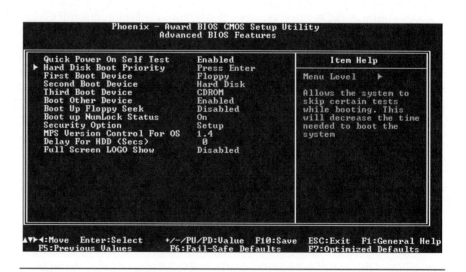

● Figure 7.19   Advanced BIOS Features

Chassis Intrusion Detection Many motherboards support the **chassis intrusion detection** feature provided by the computer case, or chassis. Compatible cases contain a switch that trips when someone opens the case. With motherboard support and a proper connection between the motherboard and the case, the CMOS logs whether the case has been opened and, if it has, posts an appropriate alert to the screen on the subsequent boot. How cool is that?

Advanced Chipset Features

The Advanced Chipset Features screen strikes fear into most everyone, because it deals with extremely low-level chipset functions. Avoid this screen unless a high-level tech (such as a motherboard maker's support tech) explicitly tells you to do something in here (Figure 7.20).

Integrated Peripherals

You will use the Integrated Peripherals screen quite often. Here you configure, enable, or disable the onboard devices, such as the integrated sound card (Figure 7.21).

Power Management Setup

As the name implies, you can use the Power Management Setup screen to set up the power management settings for the system. These settings work in concert (sometimes in conflict) with Windows' power management settings to control how and when devices turn off and back on to conserve power (Figure 7.22).

PnP/PCI Configurations

All CMOS setup utilities come with menu items that are for the most part no longer needed, but no one wants to remove them. PnP/PCI Configurations is a perfect example. Plug and play (PnP) is how devices automatically work when you snap them into your PC. PCI is a type of slot used for cards. Odds are very good you'll never deal with this screen (Figure 7.23).

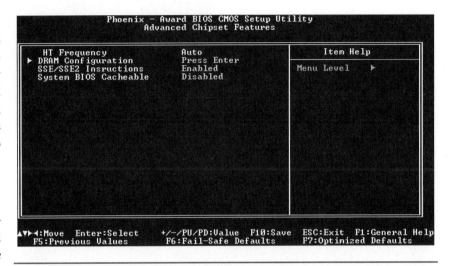

• **Figure 7.20** Advanced Chipset Features

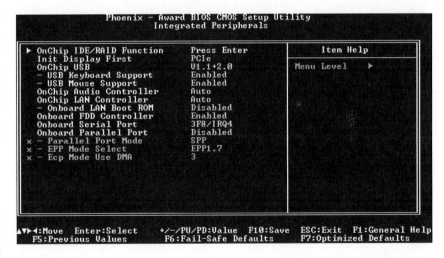

• **Figure 7.21** Integrated Peripherals

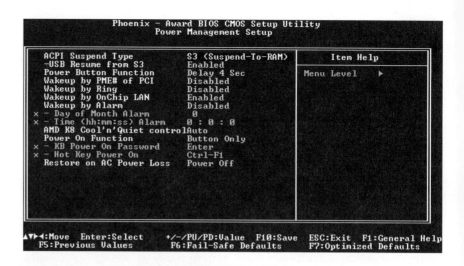

Phoenix - Award BIOS CMOS Setup Utility
Power Management Setup

• Figure 7.22   Power Management Setup

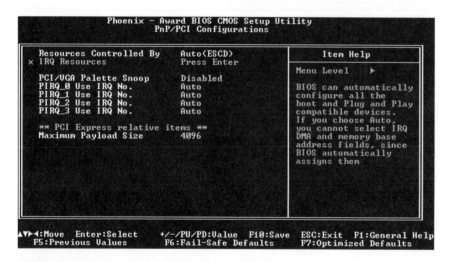

• Figure 7.23   PnP/PCI Configurations

• Figure 7.24   CMOS password prompt

And the Rest of the CMOS Settings...

The other options on the main menu of an Award CMOS do not have their own screens. Rather, these simply have small dialog boxes that pop up, usually with "Are you sure?" messages. The Load Fail-Safe/Optimized Defaults options keep you from having to memorize all of those weird settings you'll never touch. Fail-Safe sets everything to very simple settings—you might occasionally use this setting when very low-level problems such as freeze-ups occur and you've checked more obvious areas first. Optimized sets the CMOS to the best possible speed/stability for the system. You would use this option after you've tampered with the CMOS too much and you need to put it back like it was!

Many CMOS setup programs enable you to set a password in CMOS to force the user to enter a password every time the system boots. Don't confuse this with the Windows logon password. This CMOS password shows up at boot, long before Windows even starts to load. Figure 7.24 shows a typical CMOS password prompt.

Some CMOS setup utilities enable you to create two passwords: one for boot and another for accessing the CMOS setup program. This extra password just for entering CMOS setup is a godsend in, for example, schools, where non-techs tend to wreak havoc in areas (such as CMOS) that they should not access!

Drive Lock Passwords On some motherboards, the CMOS setup program enables you to control the ATA Security Mode Feature Set, also commonly referred to as drive lock or **DriveLock**. ATA Security Mode is the first line of defense for protecting hard disks from unwanted access when a system is lost or stolen. It has two passwords, a user password and a master password; and two modes, high security mode and max security mode. In high security mode, the drive can be accessed by both the master and user passwords. In addition, the master can reset the user password in CMOS setup.

In max security mode, the drive is accessible only with the user password. In this mode, the master can reset the user password, but all of the data on the drive is destroyed. Note that in either mode, if the master and user passwords are both lost, the drive is rendered unusable; these passwords are stored in the hard disk's control circuitry and cannot be reset by clearing CMOS.

Trusted Platform Module   The *Trusted Platform Module (TPM)* acts as a secure cryptoprocessor, which is to say that it is a hardware platform for the acceleration of cryptographic functions and the secure storage of associated information. The specification for the TPM is published by the Trusted Computing Group, an organization whose corporate members include Intel, Microsoft, AMD, IBM, Lenovo, Dell, Hewlett-Packard, and many others.

The TPM can be a small circuit board plugged into the motherboard, or it can be built directly into the chipset. The CMOS setup program usually contains settings that can turn the TPM on or off and enable or disable it.

TPMs can be used in a wide array of cryptographic operations, but one of the most common uses of TPMs is hard disk encryption. For example, the BitLocker Drive Encryption feature of Microsoft Windows Vista can be accelerated by a TPM, which is more secure because the encryption key is stored in the tamper-resistant TPM hardware rather than on an external flash drive. Other possible uses of TPMs include digital rights management (DRM), network access control, application execution control, and password protection.

Exiting and Saving Settings

Of course, all CMOS setups provide some method to Save and Exit or to Exit *Without* Saving. Use these as needed for your situation. Exit Without Saving is particularly nice for those folks who want to poke around the CMOS setup utility but don't want to mess anything up. Use it!

The CMOS setup utility would meet all of the needs of a modern system for BIOS if manufacturers would just stop creating new devices. That's not going to happen, of course, so let's turn now to devices that need to have BIOS loaded from elsewhere.

■ Option ROM and Device Drivers

Every piece of hardware in your computer needs some kind of programming that tells the CPU how to talk to that device. When IBM invented the PC more than a quarter century ago, they couldn't possibly have included all of the necessary BIOS routines for every conceivable piece of hardware on the system ROM chip. How could they? Most of the devices in use today didn't exist on the first PCs. When programmers wrote the first BIOS, for example, network cards, mice, and sound cards did not exist. Early PC designers at IBM understood that they could not anticipate every new type of hardware, so they gave us a few ways to add programming other than on the BIOS. I call this *BYOB—Bring Your Own BIOS*. You can BYOB in two ways: option ROM and device drivers. Let's look at both.

Option ROM

The first way to BYOB is to put the BIOS on the hardware device itself. Look at the card displayed in Figure 7.25. This is a serial ATA RAID hard drive controller—basically just a card that lets you add more hard drives to a PC. The chip in the center with the wires coming out the sides is a flash ROM storing BIOS for the card. The system BIOS does not have a clue about how to talk to this card, but that's okay, because this card brings its own BIOS on what's called an **option ROM** chip.

• **Figure 7.25** Option ROM

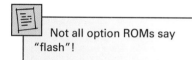

Not all option ROMs say "flash"!

Most BIOSes that come on option ROMs tell you that they exist by displaying information when you boot the system. Figure 7.26 shows a typical example of an option ROM advertising itself.

In the early days of the PC, you could find all sorts of devices with BIOSes on option ROMs. Today, option ROMs have mostly been replaced by more flexible software methods (more on device driver software in the next section), with one major exception: video cards. Every video card made today contains its own BIOS. Option ROMs work well but are hard to upgrade. For this reason, most hardware in PCs relies on software for BYOB.

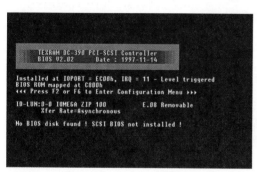

• **Figure 7.26** Option ROM at boot

Device Drivers

A **device driver** is a file stored on the PC's hard drive that contains all of the commands necessary to talk to whatever device it was written to support. All operating systems employ a method of loading these device drivers into RAM every time the system boots. They know which device drivers to install by reading a file (or files) that lists which device drivers the system needs to load at boot time. All operating systems are designed to look at this list early on in the boot process and copy the listed files into RAM, thereby giving the CPU the capability to communicate with the hardware supported by the device driver.

Device drivers come with the device when you buy it. When you buy a sound card, for example, it comes with a CD-ROM that holds all of the necessary device drivers (and usually a bunch of extra goodies). The generic name for this type of CD-ROM is **installation disc**. In most cases, you install a new device, start the computer, and wait for Windows to prompt you for the installation disc (Figure 7.27).

You might want to add or remove device drivers manually at times. Windows uses a special database called the **Registry** that stores everything you want to know about your system, including the device drivers. You shouldn't access the Registry directly to access these drivers, but instead use the venerable Device Manager utility (Figure 7.28).

• **Figure 7.27**   Windows asking for the installation disc

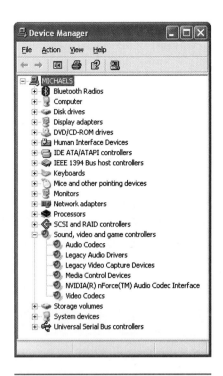

• **Figure 7.28**   Typical Device Manager

By using the **Device Manager**, you can manually change or remove the drivers for any particular device. You access the Device Manager by first opening the System applet in the Control Panel; then select the Hardware tab and click the Device Manager button. Make sure you know how to access the Device Manager. You'll see lots more of the Device Manager as you learn about different types of devices in the rest of the book.

> You can also access the Device Manager by right-clicking My Computer or Computer and selecting Manage. When the Computer Management dialog box comes up, click on Device Manager.

BIOS, BIOS, Everywhere!

As you should now understand, every piece of hardware on a system must have an accompanying program that provides the CPU with the code necessary to communicate with that particular device. This code may reside on the system ROM on the motherboard, on ROM on a card, or in a device driver file on the hard drive loaded into RAM at boot. BIOS is everywhere on your system, and you need to deal with it occasionally.

■ Power-On Self Test (POST)

BIOS isn't the only program on your system ROM. When the computer is turned on or reset, it initiates a special program, also stored on the system ROM chip, called the **power-on self test (POST)**. The POST program checks out the system every time the computer boots. To perform this check, the POST sends out a command that says to all of the devices, "Check yourselves out!" All of the standard devices in the computer then run their own internal diagnostic—the POST doesn't specify what they must check. The quality of the diagnostic is up to the people who made that particular device.

Let's consider the POST for a moment. Suppose some device—let's say it's the keyboard controller chip—runs its diagnostic and determines that it is not working properly. What can the POST do about it? Only one thing really: tell the human in front of the PC! So how does the computer tell the human? PCs convey POST information to you in two ways: beep codes and text messages.

Before and During the Video Test: The Beep Codes

The computer tests the most basic parts of the computer first, up to and including the video card. In early PCs, you'd hear a series of beeps—called **beep codes**—if anything went wrong. By using beep codes before and during the video test, the computer could communicate with you. (If a POST error occurs before the video is available, obviously the error must manifest itself as beeps, because nothing can display on the screen.) The meaning of the beep code you'd hear varied among different BIOS manufacturers. You could find the beep codes for a specific motherboard in its motherboard manual.

Most modern PCs have only a single beep code, which is for bad or missing video—one long beep followed by two or three short beeps.

You'll hear three other beep sequences on most PCs (although they're not officially beep codes). At the end of a successful POST, the PC produces one or two short beeps, simply to inform you that all is well. Most systems make a rather strange noise when the RAM is missing or very seriously damaged. Unlike traditional beep codes, this code repeats until you shut off the system. Finally, your speaker might make beeps for reasons that aren't POST or boot related. One of the more common is a series of short beeps after the system's been running for a while. That's a CPU alarm telling you the CPU is approaching its high heat limit.

You'll find lots of online documentation about beep codes, but it's usually badly outdated.

Tech Tip

Talking BIOS

Some newer motherboards can also talk to you if there is a problem during POST. To use this feature, all that is normally required is to plug a pair of speakers or headphones into the onboard sound card.

```
PhoenixBIOS 4.0 release 6.0
Copyright 1985-2000 Phoenix Technologies Ltd.
All Rights Reserved

CPU = Pentium III  500MHz
640K System RAM Passed
47M Extended RAM Passed
USB upper limit segment address:  EEFE
Mouse initialized

HDD Controller Failure
Press <F1> to resume
```

• **Figure 7.29**   POST text error messages

Text Errors

After the video has tested okay, any POST errors display on the screen as text errors. If you get a text error, the problem is usually, but not always, self-explanatory (Figure 7.29). Text errors are far more useful than beep codes, because you can simply read the screen to determine the bad device.

POST Cards

Beep codes, numeric codes, and text error codes, although helpful, can sometimes be misleading. Worse than that, an inoperative device can sometimes disrupt the POST, forcing the machine into an endless loop. This causes the PC to act dead—no beeps and nothing on the screen. In this case, you need a device, called a **POST card**, to monitor the POST and identify which piece of hardware is causing the trouble.

POST cards are simple cards that snap into expansion slots on your system. A small, two-character light-emitting diode (LED) readout on the card indicates what device the POST is currently testing (Figure 7.30). The documentation that comes with the POST card tells you what the codes mean. BIOS makers also provide this information on their Web sites. Manufacturers make POST cards for all types of desktop PCs. POST cards work with any BIOS, but you need to know the type of BIOS you have so you can interpret the readout properly.

I usually only pull out a POST card when the usual POST errors fail to appear. When a computer provides a beep or text error code that doesn't make sense, or your machine keeps locking up, some device has stalled the POST. Because the POST card tells you which device is being tested, the frozen system stays at that point in the POST, and the error stays on the POST card's readout.

Many companies sell POST cards today, with prices ranging from the affordable to the outrageous. Spend the absolute least amount of money you can. The more expensive cards add bells and whistles you do not need, such as diagnostic software and voltmeters.

Using a POST card is straightforward. Simply power down the PC, install the POST card in any unused slot, and turn the PC back on. As you watch the POST display, notice the hexadecimal readouts and refer to them

• **Figure 7.30** POST card in action

as the POST progresses. Notice how quickly they change. If you get an "FF" or "00," that means the POST is over and everything passed—time to check the operating system. If a device stalls the POST, however, the POST card displays an error code. That's the problem device! Good technicians often memorize a dozen or more POST codes because it's much faster than looking them up in a book.

So you got a beep code, a text error code, or a POST error. Now what do you do with that knowledge? Remember that a POST error does not fix the computer; it only tells you where to look. You then have to know how to deal with that bad or improperly configured component. If you use a POST card, for example, and it hangs at the "Initializing Floppy Drive" test, you'd better know how to work on a floppy drive.

Sometimes the POST card returns a bizarre or confusing error code. What device do you point at when you get a "CMOS shutdown register read/write error" beep code from an older system? First of all, read the error carefully. Let's say that on that same system you got an "8042—gate A20 failure" beep code. What will you do? Assuming you know (and you should!) that the "8042" refers to the keyboard, a quick peek at the keyboard and its connection would be a good first step. Beyond that specific example, here is a good general rule: if you don't know what the error means or the bad part isn't replaceable, replace the motherboard. Clearly, you will stumble across exceptions to this rule, but more often than not, the rule stands.

The Boot Process

All PCs need a process to begin their operations. Once you feed power to the PC, the tight interrelation of hardware, firmware, and software enables the PC to start itself, to "pull itself up by the bootstraps" or boot itself.

When you first power on the PC, the power supply circuitry tests for proper voltage and then sends a signal down a special wire called the **power good** wire to awaken the CPU. The moment the power good wire wakes it up, every Intel and clone CPU immediately sends a built-in memory address via its address bus. This special address is the same on every Intel and clone CPU, from the oldest 8086 to the most recent microprocessor. This address is the first line of the POST program on the system ROM! That's how the system starts the POST. After the POST has finished, there must be a way for the computer to find the programs on the hard drive to start the operating system. The POST passes control to the last BIOS function: the bootstrap loader. The **bootstrap loader** is little more than a few dozen lines of BIOS code tacked to the end of the POST program. Its job is to find the operating system. The bootstrap loader reads CMOS information to tell it where to look first for an operating system. Your PC's CMOS setup utility has an option that you configure to tell the bootstrap loader which devices to check for an operating system and in which order (Figure 7.31).

Almost all storage devices—floppy disks, hard disks, CDs, DVDs, and even USB thumb drives—can be configured to boot an operating system by setting aside a specific location called the *boot sector*. If the device is bootable, its boot sector contains special programming designed to tell the system where to locate the operating system. Any device with a functional operating system is called a **bootable disk** or a **system disk**. If the bootstrap loader locates a good boot sector, it passes control to the operating system and removes itself from memory. If it doesn't, it goes to the next device in the boot order you set in the CMOS setup utility. Boot order is an important tool for techs because you can set it to load in special bootable devices so you can run utilities to maintain PCs without using the primary operating system.

Now that you're familiar with CMOS and other chipset features, it's time to take an in-depth look at the expansion bus, without which the chipset would be almost useless.

```
▶ Hard Disk Boot Priority    Press Enter
  First Boot Device          Floppy
  Second Boot Device         Hard Disk
  Third Boot Device          CDROM
  Boot Other Device          Enabled
```

• **Figure 7.31**   CMOS boot order

■ Expansion Slots

Expansion slots have been part of the PC from the very beginning. Way back then, IBM created the PC with an eye to the future; the original IBM PC had slots built into the motherboard—called **expansion slots**—for adding expansion cards and thus new functions to the PC. The slots and accompanying wires and support chips on the first PC and on the latest and greatest PC are called the **expansion bus**.

The expandability enabled by an expansion bus might seem obvious today, but think about the three big hurdles a would-be expansion card developer needed to cross to make a card that would work successfully in an expansion slot. First, any expansion card needed to be built specifically for the expansion slots—that would require the creation of industry standards. Second, the card needed some way to communicate with the CPU, both to receive instructions and to relay information. And third, the operating system would need some means of enabling the user to control the new device and thus take advantage of its functions. Here's the short form of those three hurdles:

- Physical connection
- Communication
- Drivers

Structure and Function of the Expansion Bus

As you've learned, every device in the computer—whether soldered to the motherboard or snapped into a socket—connects to the external data bus and the address bus. The expansion slots are no exception. They connect to the rest of the PC through the chipset. Exactly *where* on the chipset varies depending on the system. On some systems, the expansion slots connect to the Southbridge (Figure 7.32). On other systems, the expansion slots connect to the Northbridge (Figure 7.33). Finally, many systems have more than one type of expansion bus, with slots of one type connecting to the Northbridge and slots of another type connecting to the Southbridge (Figure 7.34).

The chipset provides an extension of the address bus and data bus to the expansion slots, and thus to any expansion cards in those slots. If you plug a hard drive controller card into an expansion slot, it functions just as if it were built into the motherboard, albeit with one big difference: speed. As you'll recall from Chapter 5, "Learning CPUs," the system crystal—the clock—pushes the CPU. The system crystal provides a critical function for the entire PC, acting like a drill sergeant calling a cadence, setting the pace of activity in the computer. Every device soldered to the motherboard is designed to run at the speed of the system crystal. A 133-MHz motherboard, for example, has at least a 133-MHz Northbridge chip and a 133-MHz Southbridge chip, all timed by a 133-MHz crystal (Figure 7.35).

• **Figure 7.32**   Expansion slots connecting to Southbridge

• **Figure 7.33**   Expansion slots connecting to Northbridge

• **Figure 7.34**   Expansion slots connecting to both Northbridge and Southbridge

The system crystal sits on its own bus.

• **Figure 7.35** The system crystal sets the speed.

Clock crystals aren't just for CPUs and chipsets. Pretty much every chip in your computer has a CLK wire and needs to be pushed by a clock chip, including the chips on your expansion cards. Suppose you buy a device that did not come with your computer—say, a sound card. The chips on the sound card need to be pushed by a CLK signal from a crystal. If PCs were designed to use the system crystal to push that sound card, sound card manufacturers would need to make sound cards for every possible motherboard speed. You would have to buy a 100-MHz sound card for a 100-MHz system or a 133-MHz sound card for a 133-MHz system.

That would be ridiculous, and IBM knew it when they designed the PC. They had to make an extension to the external data bus that *ran at its own standardized speed*. You would use this part of the external data bus to snap new devices into the PC. IBM achieved this goal by adding a different crystal, called the **expansion bus crystal**, which controlled the part of the external data bus connected to the expansion slots (Figure 7.36).

The expansion slots run at a much slower speed than the frontside bus. The chipset acts as the divider between the two buses, compensating for the speed difference with wait states and special buffering (storage) areas. No matter how fast the motherboard runs, the expansion slots run at a standard speed. In the original IBM PC, that speed was about 14.318 MHz ÷ 2, or about 7.16 MHz. The latest expansion buses run much faster, but remember that old speed of roughly 7 MHz; as you learn more about expansion slots, you'll see that it's still needed on even the most modern systems.

① The system crystal pushes the CPU, RAM, and chipset. It's fast!

② The expansion crystal pushes the expansion cards at a slower, standardized speed.

• **Figure 7.36** Function of system and expansion bus crystals

PC Bus

On first-generation IBM PCs, the 8088 CPU had an 8-bit external data bus and ran at a top speed of 4.77 MHz. IBM made the expansion slots on the first PCs with an 8-bit external bus connection. IBM wanted the bus to run as fast as the CPU, and even way back then, 4.77 MHz was an easy speed to achieve. IBM settled on a standard expansion bus speed of about 7 MHz—faster than the CPU! (This was the only occurrence in the history of PCs when the expansion bus was faster than the CPU.) This expansion bus was called the **PC bus** or **XT bus**. Figure 7.37 shows these ancient 8-bit expansion slots.

IBM certainly didn't invent the idea of the expansion bus—plenty of earlier computers, including many mainframes, had expansion slots—but IBM did something no one had ever done. They allowed competitors to copy the PC bus and make their own PCs without having to pay a licensing or royalty fee. They also allowed third parties to make cards that would snap into their PC bus. Remember that IBM invented the PC bus—it was (and still is) a patented product of IBM Corporation. By allowing everyone to copy the PC expansion bus technology, however, IBM established the industry standard and fostered the emer-

• **Figure 7.37**   Eight-bit PC/XT slots

gence of the clone market. If IBM had not allowed others to copy their patented technologies for free, companies such as Compaq, Dell, and Gateway never would have existed. Equally, component makers such as Logitech, Creative, and 3Com would never be the companies they are today without the help of IBM. Who knows? If IBM had not opened the PC bus to the world, this book and the CompTIA A+ certification exams might have been based on Apple computers.

PC Bus

8 bits wide

7-MHz speed

Manual configuration

ISA Bus

When Intel invented the 286 processor, IBM wanted to create a new expansion bus that took advantage of the 286's 16-bit external data bus, yet also supported 8-bit cards. IBM achieved this by simply adding a set of connections to the end of the PC bus, creating a new 16-bit bus (Figure 7.38). Many techs called this bus the *AT bus* after the first system to use these slots, the 286-based IBM Advanced Technology (AT) computer. The AT bus ran at the same speed (approximately 7 MHz) as the earlier PC bus.

• **Figure 7.38**   Sixteen-bit ISA or AT slots

Even though IBM allowed third parties to copy the PC and AT expansion bus architecture, they never released the complete specifications for these two types of expansion buses. In the early 1980s, a number of clone makers pooled their combined knowledge of the PC/XT and AT buses to create the **Industry Standard Architecture (ISA)**.

The ISA bus enabled manufacturers to jump the first of the three hurdles for successful expansion cards, namely connectivity. If a company wanted to build a new kind of adapter card for the PC, they simply followed the specifications in the ISA standard.

ISA Bus

16 bits wide

7-MHz speed

Manual configuration

Modern Expansion Buses

The ISA expansion bus was both excellent and cutting edge for its time, and was *the* expansion bus in every PC for the first ten years of the PC's existence. Yet ISA suffered from three tremendous limitations that began to cause serious bottlenecks by the late 1980s. First, ISA was slow, running at only about 7 MHz. Second, ISA was narrow—only 16 bits wide—and therefore unable to handle the 32-bit and 64-bit external data buses of more modern processors. Finally, techs had to configure ISA cards manually, making installation a time-consuming nightmare of running proprietary configuration programs and moving tiny jumpers just to get a single card to work.

Manufacturers clearly needed to come up with a better bus that addressed the many problems associated with ISA. They needed a bus that could take advantage of the 33-MHz motherboard speed and 32-bit-wide data bus found in 386 and 486 systems. They also wanted a bus that was self-configuring, freeing techs from the drudgery of manual configuration. Finally, they had to make the new bus backward compatible, so end users wouldn't have to throw out their oftentimes substantial investment in ISA expansion cards.

False Starts

In the late 1980s, several new expansion buses designed to address these shortcomings appeared on the market. Three in particular—IBM's Micro Channel Architecture (MCA), the open standard Extended ISA (EISA), and the Video Electronics Standards Association's VESA Local Bus (VL-Bus)— all had a few years of modest popularity from the late 1980s to the mid 1990s. Although all of these alternative buses worked well, they also had shortcomings that made them less than optimal replacements for ISA: IBM charged a heavy licensing fee for MCA, EISA was expensive to make, and VL-Bus only worked in tandem with the ISA bus. By 1993, the PC world was eager for a big name to come forward with a fast, wide, easy-to-configure, and cheap new expansion bus. Intel saw the need and stepped up to the plate with the now famous PCI bus.

PCI Bus

Intel introduced the **peripheral component interconnect (PCI)** bus architecture (Figure 7.39) in the early 1990s, and the PC expansion bus was never again the same. Intel made many smart moves with PCI, not the least of which was releasing PCI to the public domain to make PCI very attractive to manufacturers. PCI provided a wider, faster, more flexible alternative than any previous expansion bus. The exceptional technology of the new bus, combined with the lack of a price tag, made manufacturers quickly drop ISA and the other alternatives and adopt PCI.

PCI really shook up the PC world with its capabilities. The original PCI bus was 32 bits wide and ran at 33 MHz, which was superb,

• **Figure 7.39**   PCI expansion bus slots

but these features were expected and not earth-shattering. The coolness of PCI came from its capability to coexist with other expansion buses. When PCI first came out, you could buy a motherboard with both PCI and ISA slots. This was important because users could keep their old ISA cards and slowly migrate to PCI. Equally impressive was that PCI devices were (and still are) self-configuring, a feature that led to the industry standard that became known as plug and play (PnP). Finally, PCI had a powerful burst-mode feature that enabled very efficient data transfers.

Before PCI, it was rare to see more than one type of expansion slot on a motherboard. Today this is not only common—it's expected!

There was a 64-bit version of the original PCI standard, but it was quite rare.

PCI Bus
32 bits wide
33-MHz speed
Self-configuring

The original PCI expansion bus has soldiered on in PCs for over ten years. Recently, more advanced forms have begun to appear. Although these new PCI expansion buses are faster than the original PCI, they're only improvements to PCI, not entirely new expansion buses. The original PCI might be fading away, but PCI in its many new forms is still "King of the Motherboard."

AGP   One of the big reasons for ISA's demise was video cards. When video started going graphical with the introduction of Windows, ISA buses were too slow and graphics looked terrible. PCI certainly improved graphics when it came out, but Intel was thinking ahead. Shortly after Intel invented

The AGP slot is almost universally brown in color, making it easy to spot.

PCI, they presented a specialized, video-only version of PCI called the **Accelerated Graphics Port (AGP)**. An AGP slot is a PCI slot, but one with a direct connection to the Northbridge. AGP slots are only for video cards—don't try to snap a sound card or modem into one. You'll learn much more about this fascinating technology in Chapter 13, "Learning Video and Multimedia." Figure 7.40 shows a typical AGP slot.

• **Figure 7.40**   AGP slot

• **Figure 7.41**   PCI-X slot

PCI-X   **PCI Extended (PCI-X)**, available in such systems as the Macintosh G5, is a huge enhancement to current PCI that is also fully backward compatible in terms of both hardware and software. PCI-X is a 64-bit-wide bus (Figure 7.41). Its slots will accept regular PCI cards. The real bonus of PCI-X is its much enhanced speed. The PCI-X 2.0 standard features four speed grades (measured in MHz): PCI-X 66, PCI-X 133, PCI-X 266, and PCI-X 533.

The obvious candidates for PCI-X are businesses using workstations and servers, because they have the "need for speed" and also the need for backward compatibility. Large vendors, especially in the high-end market, are already on board. HP, Dell, and Intel server products, for example, support PCI-X. A quick online shopping trip reveals tons of PCI-X stuff for sale: gigabit NICs, Fibre Channel cards, video adapters, and more.

Mini PCI   PCI has even made it into laptops in the specialty **Mini PCI** format (Figure 7.42). You'll find Mini PCI in just about every laptop these days. Mini PCI is designed to use low power and to lie flat—both good features for a laptop expansion slot. Mini PCI returns in Chapter 14, "Learning Portable Computing."

• **Figure 7.42**   Tiny card in Mini PCI slot. See the gold contacts at the bottom of the picture?

PCI Express   **PCI Express (PCIe)** is the latest, fastest, and most popular expansion bus in use today. As its name implies, PCI Express is still PCI, but it uses a point-to-point serial connection instead of PCI's shared parallel communication. Consider a single 32-bit chunk of data moving from a device to the CPU. In PCI parallel communication, 32 wires each carry one bit of that chunk of data. In serial communication, only one wire carries those 32 bits. You'd think that 32 are better than one, correct? Well, first of all, PCIe doesn't share the bus. A PCIe device has its own direct connection (a point-to-point connection) to the Northbridge, so it does not wait for other devices. Plus, when you start going really fast (think gigabits per second), getting all 32 bits of data to go from one device to another at the same time is difficult, because some bits get there slightly faster than others. That means you need some serious, high-speed checking of the data when it arrives to verify that it's all there and in good shape. Serial data doesn't have this problem, as all of the bits arrive one after the other in a single stream. When data is really going fast, a single point-to-point serial connection is faster than a shared 32-wire parallel connection.

And boy howdy, is PCIe ever fast! A PCIe connection uses one wire for sending and one for receiving. Each of these pairs of wires between a PCIe controller and a device is called a *lane*. Each direction of a lane runs at 2.5 Gbps, or 5 Gbps with PCIe 2.0. Better yet, each point-to-point connection can use 1, 2, 4, 8, 12, 16, or 32 lanes to achieve a maximum theoretical bandwidth of 320 Gbps. The effective data rate drops a little bit because of the *encoding scheme*—the way the data is broken down and reassembled—but full-duplex data throughput can go up to a whopping 16 Gbps on a ×16 connection.

The most common PCIe slot is the 16-lane (×16) version most commonly used for video cards, as shown in Figure 7.43. The first versions of PCIe motherboards used a combination of a single PCIe ×16 slot and a number of

• **Figure 7.43** PCIe ×16 slot (black) with PCI slots (white)

standard PCI slots. (Remember, PCI is designed to work with other expansion slots, even other types of PCI.) There is also a small form factor version of PCI Express for mobile computers called PCI Express Mini Card.

The bandwidth generated by a ×16 slot is far more than anything other than a video card would need, so most PCIe motherboards also contain slots with fewer lanes. Currently ×1 and ×4 are the most common general-purpose PCIe slots, but PCIe is still pretty new—so expect things to change as PCIe matures (Figure 7.44).

When you talk about the lanes, such as ×1 or ×8, use "by" rather than "ex" for the multiplication mark. So "by 1" and "by 8" is the correct pronunciation. You'll of course hear it spoken as both "by 8" and "8 ex" for the next few years until the technology has become a household term.

• **Figure 7.44** PCIe ×1 slots

Try This!

Shopping Trip

So, what's the latest PCIe motherboard out there? Get online or go to your local computer store and research higher-end motherboards. What combinations of PCIe slots can you find on a single motherboard? Jot them down and compare with your classmates.

■ System Resources

All devices on your computer, including your expansion cards, need to communicate with the CPU. Unfortunately, just using the word *communication* is too simplistic, because communication between the CPU and devices isn't like a human conversation. In the PC, only the CPU "talks" in the form of BIOS or driver commands—devices only react to the CPU's commands. You can divide communication into four aspects called **system resources**: I/O addresses, IRQs, DMA channels, and memory addresses.

Not all devices use all four system resources. All devices use I/O addressing and most use IRQs, but very few use DMA or memory. System resources are not new; they've been with PCs since the first IBM PC.

New devices must have their system resources configured. Configuration happens more or less automatically now through the plug-and-play process, but in the old days, configuration was handled through a painstaking manual process. (You kids don't know how good you have it. Oops! Sorry—Old Man Voice.) Even though system resources are now automated, you still might run into them in a few places on a modern PC. On those rare occasions, you'll need to understand I/O addresses, IRQs, DMAs, and memory to make changes as needed. Let's look at each system resource in detail to understand what they are and how they work.

I/O Addresses

The CPU gives a command to a device by using a pattern of ones and zeros called an **I/O address**. Every device responds to at least four I/O addresses, meaning the CPU can give at least four different commands to each device. The process of communicating through I/O addresses is called, quite logically, **I/O addressing**. Here's how it works.

The chipset extends the address bus to the expansion slots, which makes two interesting things happen. First, you can place RAM on a card, and the CPU can address it just as it can your regular RAM. Devices such as video cards come with their own RAM. The CPU draws the screen by writing directly to the RAM on the video card. Second, the CPU can use the address bus to talk to all of the devices on your computer through I/O addressing.

Normally the address bus on an expansion bus works exactly like the address bus on a frontside bus—different patterns of ones and zeros point to different memory locations. If the CPU wants to send an I/O address, however, it puts the expansion bus into what can be called I/O mode. When the bus goes into I/O mode, all devices on the bus look for patterns of ones and zeros to appear on the address bus.

Back in the old Intel 8088 days, the CPU used an extra wire, called the *input/output or memory (IO/MEM) wire*, to notify devices that it was using the address bus either to specify an address in memory or to communicate with a particular device (Figure 7.45). You won't find an IO/MEM wire on a modern CPU, as the process has changed and become more complex—but the concept hasn't changed one bit. The CPU sends commands to devices by placing patterns of ones and zeros—I/O addresses—on the address bus.

No two devices share the same I/O address because that would defeat the entire concept. To make sure no two devices share I/O addresses, all I/O addresses either are preset by standard (for example, all hard drive controllers use the same I/O addresses on every PC) or are set at boot by the operating system. You can see the I/O addresses for all of the devices on your computer by going into the Device Manager. Go to the View menu option and select *Resources by type*. Click on the plus sign directly to the left of the Input/output (IO) option to see a list of I/O addresses, as shown in Figure 7.46.

Whoa! What's with all the letters and numbers? The address bus is always 32 bits (even if you have a 64-bit processor, the Northbridge only allows the first 32 bits to pass to the expansion slots), so instead of showing you the raw ones and zeros, the Device Manager shows you the I/O address ranges in hexadecimal. Don't know hex? No worries; **hexadecimal** is just quick shorthand for representing the strings of ones and zeros—*binary*—that you *do* know. One hex character is used to represent four binary characters. Here's the key:

0000 = 0
0001 = 1
0010 = 2
0011 = 3
0100 = 4
0101 = 5
0110 = 6
0111 = 7
1000 = 8
1001 = 9
1010 = A
1011 = B
1100 = C
1101 = D
1110 = E
1111 = F

• **Figure 7.45**   Sending out an I/O address

• **Figure 7.46**   Viewing resources by type, with I/O addresses expanded

Let's pick an arbitrary string of ones and zeros:

00000000000000000000000111110000

To convert to hex, just chop them into chunks of four:

0000 0000 0000 0000 0000 0001 1111 0000

Then use the key above to convert:

0 0 0 0 0 1 F 0

Then push the hex values together:

000001F0

You now understand what those values mean in the Device Manager. Scroll down until you find the "[000001F0 – 000001F7] Primary IDE Channel" setting. Notice that two I/O addresses are listed. These show the entire range of I/O addresses for this device; the more complex the device, the more I/O addresses it uses. Address ranges are generally referred to by the first value in the range, commonly known as the **I/O base address**.

Here are the most important items to remember about I/O addresses. First, every device on your PC has an I/O address. Without it, the CPU wouldn't have a way to send a device commands. Second, I/O addresses are configured automatically: you just plug in a device and it works. Third, no two devices should share I/O addresses. The system handles configuration, so this happens automatically.

All I/O addresses only use the last 16 bits (they all start with 0000). Sixteen bits makes 2^{16} = 65,536 I/O address ranges— plenty for even the most modern PCs. Should PCs begin to need more I/O addresses in the future, the current I/O addressing system is ready.

Interrupt Requests

Between the standardized expansion bus connections and BIOS using I/O addressing, the CPU can now communicate with all of the devices inside the computer, but a third and final hurdle remains. I/O addressing enables the CPU to talk to devices, but how does a device tell the CPU it needs attention? How does the mouse tell the CPU that it has moved, for example, or how does the keyboard tell the CPU that somebody just pressed the J key? The PC needs some kind of mechanism to tell the CPU to stop doing whatever it is doing and talk to a particular device (Figure 7.47). This mechanism is called **interruption**.

Every CPU in the PC world has an INT (interrupt) wire, shown in Figure 7.48. If a device puts voltage on this wire, the CPU stops what it's doing and deals with the interrupting device. Suppose you have a PC with only one peripheral, a keyboard that directly connects to the INT wire. If the user presses the J key, the keyboard charges the INT wire. The CPU temporarily stops running the browser (or whatever program is active) and runs the necessary BIOS routine to query the keyboard.

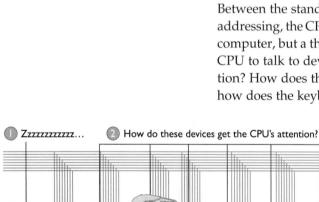

① Zzzzzzzzzzzzz... ② How do these devices get the CPU's attention?

• **Figure 7.47**   How do devices tell the CPU they need attention?

• **Figure 7.48**   The INT wire

> IOAPIC functions are usually built into the Southbridge. Many developers drop the I/O part and simply call them *APICs*.

This would be fine if the computer had only one device. As you know, however, PCs have many devices, and almost all of them need to interrupt the CPU at some point. So the PC needs some kind of traffic cop to act as an intermediary between all of the devices and the CPU's INT wire. This traffic-cop chip, called the **I/O advanced programmable interrupt controller (IOAPIC)**, uses special interrupt wires that run to all devices on the expansion bus (Figure 7.49).

If a device wants to get the CPU's attention, it lights the interrupt wires with a special pattern of ones and zeros just for that device. The IOAPIC then interrupts the CPU. The CPU queries the IOAPIC to see which device interrupted, and then it begins to communicate with the device over the address bus (Figure 7.50).

These unique patterns of ones and zeros manifest themselves as something called **interrupt requests (IRQs)**. Before IOAPICs, IRQs were actual

• **Figure 7.49**   Eight interrupt wires (IRQs) run from the expansion bus to the IOAPIC.

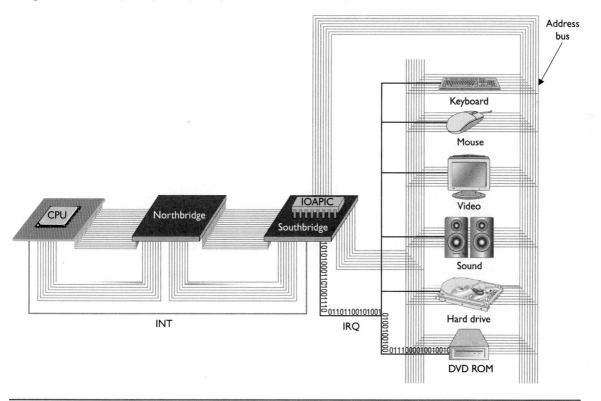

• **Figure 7.50**   IOAPIC at work

● **Figure 7.51**   IRQs in an IOAPIC system

wires leading to the previous generation of traffic cops, called PICs. It's easy to see if your system has a PIC or an IOAPIC. Go into the Device Manager and select Interrupt request (IRQ) with the view set to *Resources by type*.

Figure 7.51 shows nearly a dozen IRQs, numbered 0 through 22, making this an IOAPIC system. IRQ 9 is special—this IRQ is assigned to the controller itself and is the IOAPIC's connection to the CPU. If you look closely, you'll also notice that some IRQs aren't listed. These are unused or "open" IRQs. If you add another device to the system, the new device will take up one of these unused IRQs. Now look at the older PIC system in Figure 7.52—note that it only shows IRQs ranging from 0 through 15.

Modern systems running Windows Vista or Windows 7 can use virtual IRQs to support devices. A quick glance at the Device Manager IRQ list in Vista shows a giant list of IRQs, ranging from 0 to upwards of 190 (Figure 7.53). Some systems even display negative IRQs, such as –2 or –4. Once you get into a Windows Vista or Windows 7 machine, you can pretty much forget about IRQs. The OS handles it all automatically.

● **Figure 7.52**   IRQs in a PIC system

• **Figure 7.53** IRQs in Windows Vista

Let's look at the last serious vestige of the "bad old days" on your PC: COM and LPT ports.

COM and LPT Ports

When the PC first came out, the I/O addresses and IRQ for every device had to be manually configured. How you did this varied from device to device: you moved jumpers, turned dials, or ran weird configuration programs. It was never easy. IBM tried to make configuration easier by creating preset I/O address and IRQ combinations for the serial and parallel ports, because they were the most commonly used ports on the original PC. These preset combinations were called **COM ports** for serial connections and **LPT ports** for parallel ports. Table 7.1 lists the early preset combinations of I/O addresses and IRQs.

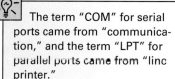

The term "COM" for serial ports came from "communication," and the term "LPT" for parallel ports came from "line printer."

Table 7.1	COM and LPT Assignments	
Port	I/O Base Address	IRQ
COM1	03F8	4
COM2	02F8	3
COM3	03E8	4
COM4	02E8	3
LPT1	0378	7
LPT2	0278	5

Notice that the four COM ports share two IRQs. In the old days, if two devices shared an IRQ, the system instantly locked up. The lack of available IRQs in early systems led IBM to double up the IRQs for the serial devices, creating one of the few exceptions to the rule that no two devices could share IRQs. You could share an IRQ between two devices, but only if one of the devices would never actually access the IRQ. You'd see this with a dedicated fax/modem card, for example, which has a single phone line connected to a single card that has two different functions. The CPU needed distinct sets of I/O addresses for fax commands and modem commands, but as there was only the one modem doing both jobs, it needed only a single IRQ.

Direct Memory Access

CPUs do a lot of work. They run the BIOS, operating system, and applications. CPUs handle interrupts and I/O addresses. CPUs also deal with one other item: data. CPUs constantly move data between devices and RAM. CPUs move files from the hard drive to RAM. They move print jobs from RAM to laser printers, and they move images from scanners to RAM, just to name a very few examples of this RAM-to-device-and-back process.

Moving all this data is obviously necessary, but it is a simple task—the CPU has better things to do with its power and time. Moreover, with all of the caches and such on today's CPUs, the system spends most of its time waiting around doing nothing while the CPU handles some internal calculation. Add these facts together and the question arises: Why not make devices that access memory directly, without involving the CPU (Figure 7.54)? The process of accessing memory without using the CPU is called **direct memory access (DMA)**.

DMA is very common and is excellent for creating background sounds in games and for moving data from floppy and hard drives into RAM (Figure 7.55).

Nice as it may sound, the concept of DMA as just described has a problem—there's only one expansion bus. What if more than one device wants to use DMA? What keeps these devices from stomping on the external data bus all at the same time? Plus, what if the CPU suddenly needs the data bus? How can

• **Figure 7.54**   Why not talk to the chipset directly?

you stop the device using DMA so the CPU, which should have priority, can access the bus? To deal with this, IBM added another traffic cop.

The **DMA controller**, which seasoned techs often call the *8237* after its old chip name, controls all DMA functions. DMA is similar to IRQ handling in that the DMA controller assigns numbers, called DMA channels, by which devices can request use of the DMA. The DMA also handles the data passing from peripherals to RAM and vice versa. This takes necessary but simple work away from the CPU so the CPU can spend time doing more productive work.

The DMA chip sends data along the external data bus when the CPU is busy with internal calculations and not using the external data bus. This is perfectly acceptable, because the CPU accesses the external data bus only about 5 percent of the time on a modern CPU.

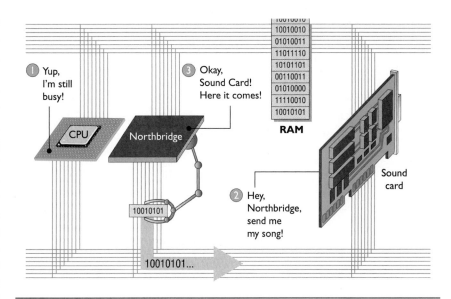

• **Figure 7.55**   DMA in action

The DMA just described is called classic DMA; it was the first and for a long time the only way to do DMA. Classic DMA is dying out because it's very slow and only supports 16-bit data transfers, a silly waste in a world of much wider buses. On most systems, only floppy drives still use classic DMA.

All systems still support classic DMA, but most devices today that use DMA do so without going through the DMA controller. These devices are known as bus masters. **Bus mastering** devices have circuitry that enables them to watch for other devices accessing the external data bus; they can detect a potential conflict and get out of the way on their own. Bus mastering has become extremely popular in hard drives. All modern hard drives take advantage of bus mastering. Hard drive bus mastering is hidden under terms such as *Ultra DMA*, and for the most part is totally automatic and invisible.

Bus mastering devices ignore the DMA controller; they don't have DMA channels.

If you want to see your DMA usage, head back to the Device Manager and change the view to *Resources by type*. Click on *Direct memory access (DMA)* and you'll see something like Figure 7.56. This system has only two DMA channels: one for the floppy drive and one for the connection to the CPU.

One interesting note to DMA is that neither PCI nor PCIe supports DMA, so you'll never find a DMA device that snaps into these expansion buses. A hard drive, floppy drive, or any other device that still wants to use DMA must do so through onboard connections. Sure, you can find hard drive and floppy drive cards, but they're not using DMA.

• **Figure 7.56**   DMA settings in the Device Manager

Memory Addresses

Some expansion cards need memory addresses, just like the system RAM. There are two reasons a card may need memory addresses. First, a card may have onboard RAM that the CPU needs to address. Second, a few cards come with an onboard ROM, the so-called adapter or option ROM you read about earlier in this chapter. In either of these situations, the RAM or ROM must steal memory addresses away from the main system RAM to enable the CPU to access the RAM or ROM. This process is called **memory addressing**. You can see memory addresses assigned to expansion cards by clicking on Memory in the Device Manager when viewing resources by type.

The key fact for techs is that, just like I/O addresses, IRQs, and DMA channels, memory addressing is fully automatic and no longer an issue.

■ Motherboards

So now you understand CMOS and BIOS, you understand the expansion bus, you understand system addressing…in short, you understand a whole host of stuff that you probably never thought you'd know. That's great and all, but have you wondered where all this stuff is actually located inside the computer? Well, wonder no more, because it's time to take a long, hard look at motherboards!

The **motherboard** provides the foundation for the personal computer. Every piece of hardware, from the CPU to the lowliest expansion card, directly or indirectly plugs into the motherboard. The motherboard contains the wires—called **traces**—that make up the buses of the system. It holds the vast majority of the ports used by the peripherals, and it distributes the power from the power supply (Figure 7.57). Without the motherboard, you literally have no PC.

Three variable and interrelated characteristics define modern motherboards: form factor, chipset, and components. The **form factor** determines the physical size of the motherboard as well as the general location of components and ports. The chipset defines the type of processor and RAM the motherboard requires and determines to a degree the built-in devices the motherboard supports, including the expansion slots. Finally, the built-in components determine the core functionality of the system.

● **Figure 7.57**   Traces visible beneath the CPU socket on a motherboard

Mike Meyers' CompTIA A+ Guide: Essentials

Any good tech should be able to make a recommendation to a client about a particular motherboard simply by perusing the specs. Because the motherboard determines function, expansion, and stability for the whole PC, it's essential that you know your motherboards!

Form Factors

Form factors are industry-standardized shapes and layouts that enable motherboards to work with cases and power supplies. A single form factor applies to all three components. All motherboards come in a basic rectangular or square shape but vary in overall size and in the layout of built-in components (Figure 7.58). You need to install a motherboard in a case designed to fit it, so the ports and slot openings on the back fit correctly.

The power supply and the motherboard need matching connectors, and different form factors define different connections. Given that the term "form factor" applies to the case, motherboard, and power supply—the three parts of the PC most responsible for moving air around inside the PC—the form factor also defines how the air moves around in the case.

To perform motherboard upgrades and provide knowledgeable recommendations to clients, techs need to know their form factors. The PC industry has adopted—and dropped—a number of form factors over the years with such names as AT, ATX, and BTX. Let's start with the granddaddy of all PC form factors, AT.

AT Form Factor

The **AT** form factor (Figure 7.59), invented by IBM in the early 1980s, was the predominant form factor for motherboards through the mid-1990s. AT is now obsolete.

• **Figure 7.58**   Typical motherboard

P8/P9 socket

All AT motherboards had a split power socket called *P8/P9*. You can see the white P8/P9 socket near the keyboard port in Figures 7.59 and 7.60.

• **Figure 7.59**   AT-style motherboard

P8/P9 socket

• **Figure 7.60**   AT motherboard (bottom) and Baby AT motherboard (top)

• **Figure 7.61**   Keyboard connector on the back of an AT motherboard

The AT motherboard had a few size variations (Figure 7.60), ranging from large to very large. The original AT motherboard was huge, around 12 inches wide by 13 inches deep. PC technology was new and needed lots of space for the various chips necessary to run the components of the PC.

The single greatest problem with AT motherboards was the lack of external ports. When PCs were first invented, the only devices plugged into the average PC were a monitor and a keyboard. That's what the AT was designed to handle—the only dedicated connector on an AT motherboard was the keyboard port (Figure 7.61).

Over the years, the number of devices plugged into the back of the PC has grown tremendously. Your average PC today has a keyboard, a mouse, a printer, some speakers, a monitor, and—if your system's like mine—four to six USB devices connected to it at any given time. These added components created a demand for a new type of form factor, one with more dedicated connectors for more devices. Many attempts were made to create a new standard form factor. Invariably, these new form factors integrated dedicated connectors for at least the mouse and printer, and many even added connectors for video, sound, and phone lines.

One variation from the AT form factor that enjoyed a degree of success was the **slimline** form factor. The first slimline form factor was known as **LPX** (defined in some sources as *low profile extended*, although there's some disagreement). It was replaced by the **NLX** form factor. (NLX apparently stands for nothing, by the way. It's just a cool grouping of letters.) The LPX and NLX form factors met the demands of the slimline market by providing a central riser slot to enable the insertion of a special **riser card** (Figure 7.62) or, as it's sometimes called, a *daughterboard*. Expansion cards then fit into the riser card horizontally. Combining built-in connections with a riser card enabled manufacturers to produce PCs shorter than 4 inches.

The main problem with form factors such as LPX and NLX was their inflexibility. Certainly, no problem occurred with dedicated connections for such devices as mice or printers, but the new form factors also added connectors for such devices as video and sound—devices that were prone to obsolescence, making the motherboard out of date the moment a new type of video or sound card came into popularity.

• Figure 7.62   Riser card on an older motherboard

ATX Form Factor

There continued to be a tremendous demand for a new form factor: a form factor that had more standard connectors and also was flexible enough for possible changes in technology. This demand led to the creation of the ATX form factor in 1995 (Figure 7.63). ATX got off to a

• Figure 7.63   Early ATX motherboard

slow start, but by around 1998, ATX overtook AT to become the most common form factor used today.

ATX is distinct from AT in the lack of an AT keyboard port, replaced with a rear panel that has all necessary ports built in. Note the mini-DIN (PS/2) keyboard and mouse ports at the left of Figure 7.64, standard features on almost all ATX boards. You recall those from Chapter 3, "The Visible PC," right?

The ATX form factor includes many improvements over AT. The position of the power supply allows better air movement. The CPU and RAM are placed to provide easier access, and the rearrangement of components prevents long expansion cards from colliding with the CPU or Northbridge. Other improvements, such as placing the RAM closer to the Northbridge and CPU than on AT boards, offer users enhanced performance as well. The shorter the wires, the easier to shield them and make them capable of handling double or quadruple the clock speed of the motherboard. Figure 7.65 shows AT and ATX motherboards—note the radical differences in placement of internal connections.

• **Figure 7.65**   AT (left) and ATX (right) motherboards for quick visual comparison

The success of ATX has spawned two form factor subtypes for specialty uses. The **microATX** motherboard (Figure 7.66) floats in at a svelte 9.6 by 9.6 inches or about 30 percent smaller than standard ATX, yet uses the standard ATX connections. A microATX motherboard fits into a standard ATX case or in the much smaller microATX cases. Note that not all microATX motherboards have the same physical size. You'll sometimes see microATX motherboards referred to with the Greek symbol for micro, as in µATX.

Tech Tip

Soft Power

*ATX motherboards use a feature called **soft power**. This means they can use software to turn the PC on and off. The physical manifestation of soft power is the power switch. Instead of the thick power cord used in AT systems, an ATX power switch is little more than a pair of small wires leading to the motherboard. We delve into this in more detail in Chapter 8, "Learning PC Power."*

Cross Check

High-Speed CPUs and RAM

Modern CPUs such as the Intel Core i7 and the AMD Phenom II incorporate the memory controller on the processor rather than locating it on the Northbridge. This move has facilitated even further increases in the speed at which the processor can fetch data from RAM. Refer to Chapters 5, "Learning CPUs," and 6, "Learning RAM," and see if you can answer these questions.

1. What different clock frequencies are supported by DDR2 and DDR3 types of memory?

2. What processors support DDR3 memory?

Many techs and Web sites use the term *mini-ATX* to refer to motherboards smaller than a full ATX board. This is technically incorrect. The specifications for these small boards use only the terms *microATX* and *FlexATX*.

● **Figure 7.66**   A microATX motherboard

In 1999, Intel created a variant of the microATX called the FlexATX. **FlexATX** motherboards have maximum dimensions of just 9 by 7.5 inches, which makes them the smallest motherboards in the ATX standard. Although FlexATX motherboards can use a standard ATX power supply, most FlexATX systems use a special FlexATX-only power supply. This diminutive power supply fits into tight FlexATX cases.

Keep in mind that each main type of form factor requires its own case. AT motherboards go into AT cases, NLX motherboards go into NLX cases, and ATX motherboards go into ATX cases. You cannot replace one form factor with another without purchasing a new case (Figure 7.67). The exception to this rule is that larger form factor ATX cases can handle any smaller-sized form factor motherboards.

● **Figure 7.67**   That's not going to fit!

BTX Form Factor

Even though ATX addressed ventilation, faster CPUs and powerful graphics cards create phenomenal amounts of heat, motivating the PC industry to create the "coolest" new form factor used today—the **Balanced Technology eXtended (BTX)** form factor (Figure 7.68). BTX defines three subtypes: standard BTX, **microBTX**, and **picoBTX**, designed to replace ATX, microATX, and FlexATX, respectively.

At first glance, BTX looks like ATX, but notice that the I/O ports and the expansion slots have switched sides. You can't put a BTX motherboard in an ATX case. BTX does not change the power connection, so there's no such thing as a BTX power supply.

Many manufacturers sell what they call BTX power supplies. These are actually marketing gimmicks. See Chapter 8, "Learning PC Power," for details.

• **Figure 7.68**   A microBTX motherboard

Everything in the BTX form factor is designed to improve cooling. BTX cases vent cool air in from the front and warm air out the back. CPUs are moved to the front of the motherboard so they get cool air coming in from the front of the case. BTX defines a special heat sink and fan assembly called the **thermal unit**. The thermal unit's fan blows the hot CPU air directly out the back of the case, as opposed to the ATX method of just blowing the air into the case.

The BTX standard is clearly a much cooler option than ATX, but the PC industry tends to take its time when making big changes such as moving to a new form factor. As a result, BTX has not yet made much of an impact in the industry, and BTX motherboards, cases, and thermal units are still fairly rare. BTX could take off to become the next big thing or disappear in a cloud of disinterest—only time will tell.

Try This!

Motherboard Varieties

Motherboards come in a wide variety of form factors. Go to your local computer store and check out what is on display. Note the different features offered by ATX, microATX, and FlexATX (if any) motherboards.

1. Does the store still stock any AT motherboards?

2. What about NLX, BTX, or proprietary motherboards?

3. Did the clerk use tech slang and call the motherboards "mobos"? (It's what most of us call them outside of formal textbooks, after all!)

Proprietary Form Factors

Several major PC makers, including Dell and Sony, make motherboards that work only with their cases. These *proprietary* motherboards enable these companies to create systems that stand out from the generic ones and, not coincidently, push you to get service and upgrades from their authorized dealers. Some of the features you'll see in proprietary systems are riser boards like you see with the NLX form factor—part of a motherboard separate from the main one but connected by a cable of some sort—and unique power connections. Proprietary motherboards drive techs crazy because replacement parts tend to cost more and are not readily available.

Chipset

Every motherboard has a chipset. The chipset determines the type of processor the motherboard accepts, the type and capacity of RAM, and the sort of internal and external devices that the motherboard supports. As you learned earlier, the chips in a PC's chipset serve as electronic interfaces through which the CPU, RAM, and input/output devices interact. Chipsets vary in features, performance, and stability, so they factor hugely in the purchase or recommendation of a particular motherboard. Good techs know their chipsets!

Because the chipset facilitates communication between the CPU and other devices in the system, its component chips are relatively centrally located on the motherboard (Figure 7.69). Most modern chipsets are composed of two primary chips: the Northbridge and the Southbridge.

The Northbridge chip on traditional Intel-based motherboards helps the CPU work with RAM, as mentioned earlier in the chapter. On newer AMD- and Intel-based motherboards, however, the Northbridge does not work directly with RAM, but instead provides the communication with the video card. The CPU has taken on the role of the memory controller. Current Northbridge chips do a lot and thus get pretty hot, so they get their own heat sink and fan assembly.

The Southbridge handles some expansion devices and mass storage drives, such as hard drives. Most Southbridge chips don't need extra cooling, leaving the chip exposed or passively cooled with only a heat sink. This makes the Southbridge a great place to see the manufacturer of the chipset, such as Intel.

Many motherboards support very old technologies such as floppy drives, infrared connections, parallel ports, and modems. Although supporting these old devices was once part of the Southbridge's job, hardly any modern chipsets still support these devices. Motherboard manufacturers add a third chip called the **Super I/O chip** to handle these chores. Figure 7.70 shows a typical Super I/O chip.

The system ROM chip provides part of the BIOS for the chipset, but only at a barebones, generic level. The chipset still needs support for the rest of the things it can do. So how do expansion devices get BIOS? From software drivers, of course, and the same holds true for modern chipsets. You have to load the proper drivers for the specific OS to support all of the features of today's chipsets. Without software drivers, you'll never create a stable, fully functional PC. All motherboards ship with a CD-ROM disc with drivers, support programs, and extra-special goodies such as antivirus software (Figure 7.71).

There are a limited number of chipset makers. The dominant chipset vendors today are Intel and NVIDIA, although several other companies continue to produce chipsets, such as AMD through its ATI brand. Motherboard manufacturers incorporate the chipsets into motherboards that match the feature set of the chipset. Chipset companies rise and fall every few years, with one company seeming to hold the hot position for a while until another company comes along to unseat them.

Chipset makers don't always use the terms Northbridge and Southbridge. Chipsets for AMD-based motherboards tend to use the terms, but Intel-based motherboards prefer to say **Memory Controller Hub (MCH)** for the Northbridge

• **Figure 7.69**   Northbridge (under the fan) and Southbridge (lower right, labeled VIA)

Super I/O chips work with chipsets but are not part of the chipset. Motherboard makers purchase them separate from chipsets.

In an average year, chipset makers collectively produce around 100 new chipset models for the PC market.

• **Figure 7.70**   Super I/O chip on ASUS motherboard

● Figure 7.71   Driver disc for ASUS motherboard

and **I/O Controller Hub (ICH)** for the Southbridge. With the launch of the X58 Express Chipset, Intel has further refined their terminology, calling the Northbridge simply the *I/O Hub* (*IOH*) since the memory controller is located on the CPU. Sometimes Intel refers to the Southbridge as the *Legacy I/O Controller Hub.* Regardless of the official name, Northbridge and Southbridge are the commonly used terms. Figure 7.72 shows a schematic with typical chipset chores for a VIA K8T900 chipset.

It would be impossible to provide an inclusive chipset chart here that wouldn't be obsolete by the time you pick this book up off the shelf at your local tech pub (doesn't everybody have one of those?), but Table 7.2 gives you an idea of what to look for as you research motherboards for recommendations and purchases.

So why do good techs need to know the hot chipsets in detail? The chipset defines almost every motherboard feature short of the CPU itself. Techs love to discuss chipsets and expect a fellow tech to know the differences between one chipset and another. You also need to be able to recommend a motherboard that suits a client's needs.

Motherboard Components

The connections and capabilities of a motherboard sometimes differ from those of the chipset the motherboard uses. This disparity happens for a couple of reasons. First, a particular chipset may support eight USB ports, but to keep costs down, the manufacturer might include only four ports. Second, a motherboard maker may choose to install extra features—ones not supported by the chipset—by adding additional chips. A common example is a motherboard that supports FireWire. Other technologies you might find are built-in sound, hard drive RAID controllers, and AMR or CNR slots for modems, network cards, and more.

USB/FireWire

Most chipsets support USB, and most motherboards come with FireWire as well, but it seems no two motherboards offer the same

● Figure 7.72   Schematic of a modern chipset (*courtesy of VIA Technologies*)

Table 7.2

Chipset Comparison Chart

Chipset	Northbridge	Southbridge	CPU	CPU Interconnect	CPU RAM Interface	Northbridge RAM Interface	Northbridge PCIe	Southbridge PCIe	SATA	RAID	USB	Integrated Video
Intel X58 Express Chipset	Intel 82X58 Express Chipset I/O Hub (IOH)	Intel 82801JIB ICH10, Intel 82801JIR ICH10R, Intel 82801JD ICH10D, or Intel 82801JDO ICH10D	LGA1366: Core i7	QuickPath Interconnect (6.4 GT/s, 4.8 GT/s)	Yes, triple-channel DDR3 (24 GB max)	No	1×16, 2×16, or 4×8	6×1	6	Yes: 0,1,5,10	12 Hi-Speed	No
Intel Q45 Express Chipset	Intel 82Q45 Graphics and Memory Controller Hub (GMCH)	Intel 82801JIB ICH10, Intel 82801JIR ICH10R, Intel 82801JD ICH10D, or Intel 82801JDO ICH10D	LGA775: Core 2 Duo, Core 2 Quad	Frontside bus (1333 MHz, 1066 MHz, 800 MHz)	No	Yes, dual-channel, DDR2 (16 GB max) or DDR3 (8 GB max)	1×16	6×1	6	Yes: 0,1,5,10	12 Hi-Speed	Yes
Intel Q965 Express Chipset	Intel 82Q965 Graphics and Memory Controller Hub (GMCH)	Intel 82801HB ICH8 or Intel 82801HR ICH8R	LGA775: Core 2 Duo, Pentium D, Pentium 4 supporting hyper-threading technology	Frontside bus (1066 MHz, 800 MHz, 533 MHz)	No	Yes, dual-channel DDR2 (8 GB max)	1×16	6×1	6	Yes: 0,1,5,10	10 Hi-Speed	Yes
NVIDIA nForce 980a SLI	NVIDIA nForce 980a SLI	N/A[1]	AM3, AM2+, AM2: Phenom X4, Phenom X3, Phenom II X4, Phenom II X3, Athlon X2, Athlon	HyperTransport 3.0 (5.2 GT/s, 2 GT/s, 1.6 GT/s)	Yes, dual-channel DDR3 (16 GB max)	No	3×16, 2×16, 1×16, 2×8, or 4×8 + 4×1	N/A[1]	6	Yes: 0, 1, 0+1, 5	12 Hi-Speed	No

Table 7.2   Chipset Comparison Chart (Continued)

Chipset	Northbridge	Southbridge	CPU	CPU Interconnect	CPU RAM Interface	Northbridge RAM Interface	Northbridge PCIe	Southbridge PCIe	SATA	RAID	USB	Integrated Video
NVIDIA GeForce 9400 mGPU	NVIDIA GeForce 9400 mGPU	N/A[1]	LGA775: Pentium D, Core 2 Quad, Core 2 Extreme, Core 2 Duo, Celeron D	Frontside bus (1333 MHz, 1066 MHz, 800 MHz)	No	Yes, dual-channel, DDR2 (16 GB max) or DDR3 (8 GB max)	1×16 + 4×1	N/A[1]	6	Yes: 0, 1, 0+1, 5	12 Hi-Speed	Yes
AMD 770 Chipset	AMD 770	AMD SB600 or AMD SB700	AM2, AM2+: Phenom X4, Phenom X3, Athlon FX, Athlon X2, Athlon, Sempron	Hyper Transport 3.0 (5.2 GT/s, 2 GT/s, 1.6 GT/s)	Yes, dual-channel DDR2 (8 GB max)	No	1×16	6×1	6	Yes: 0, 1, 10	12 Hi-Speed	No
AMD 790GX Chipset	AMD 790GX	AMD SB750	AM2+: Phenom X4, Phenom X3, Athlon FX, Athlon X2, Athlon, Sempron	Hyper Transport 3.0 (5.2 GT/s, 2 GT/s)	Yes, dual-channel DDR2 (16 GB max)	No	1×16 or 2×16	6×1	6	Yes: 0, 1, 5, 10	12 Hi-Speed	Yes

1 NVIDIA does not make a Northbridge/Southbridge distinction with their chipsets.

port arrangement. My motherboard supports eight USB ports and two FireWire ports, for example, but if you look on the back of the motherboard, you'll only see four USB ports and one FireWire port. So, where are the other ports? Well, this motherboard has special connectors for the other ports, and the motherboard comes with the dongles you need to connect them (Figure 7.73). These dongles typically use an extra slot on the back of the case.

These dongle connectors are standardized, so many cases have built-in front USB/FireWire ports that have dongles attached. This is very handy for USB or FireWire devices you might want to plug and unplug frequently, such as thumb drives or digital cameras. You can also buy add-on front USB and FireWire devices that go into a 3.5-inch drive bay (Figure 7.74).

• **Figure 7.73**   USB/FireWire dongle

Sound

Quite a few motherboards come with onboard sound chips. These sound chips are usually pretty low quality compared to even a lower-end sound card, but onboard sound is cheap and doesn't take up a slot. These connectors are identical to the ones used on sound cards, so we'll save more discussion for Chapter 13, "Learning Video and Multimedia."

• **Figure 7.74**   Front USB and FireWire drive bay device

RAID

RAID stands for *redundant array of independent* (or *inexpensive*) *disks* and is very common on motherboards. There are many types of RAID, but the RAID on motherboards usually only supports *mirroring* (the process of using two drives to hold the same data, which is good for safety, because if one drive dies, the other still has all of the data) or *striping* (making two drives act as one drive by spreading data across them, which is good for speed). RAID is a very cool but complex topic that's discussed in detail in Chapter 9, "Hard Drive Technologies."

AMR/CNR

The U.S. Federal Communications Commission (FCC) must certify any electronic device to ensure that it does not transmit unwanted electronic signals. This process is a bit expensive, so in the very late 1990s, Intel came up with a special slot called the **audio modem riser (AMR)**, shown in Figure 7.75. An AMR slot was designed to take specialized AMR devices (modems, sound cards, and network cards). An AMR device would get one FCC certification and then be used on as many motherboards as the manufacturer wanted without going through the FCC certification process again. AMR was quickly replaced with the more advanced **communications and networking riser (CNR)**. Many motherboard manufacturers used these slots in the early 2000s, but they've lost popularity because most motherboard makers simply use onboard networking and sound.

• **Figure 7.75**   AMR slot

Chapter 7 Review

■ Chapter Summary

After reading this chapter and completing the exercises, you should understand the following about BIOS and CMOS, the expansion bus, and motherboards.

Explain the function of BIOS

- The CPU must be able to communicate with all devices in a computer system. The Northbridge chip is the primary communication bridge between the CPU and the rest of the computer. The Northbridge deals with high-speed devices such as the video card, RAM, and PCI bus. A second chip, the Southbridge, works with the other devices. The Northbridge and Southbridge chips are manufactured as a set called the chipset. The chipset extends the data and address buses to every device in the PC.

- A ROM (read-only memory) chip is nonvolatile, meaning it retains the information stored on it even when the power is turned off. Usually attached to the Southbridge, the ROM chip stores hundreds of little programs that enable the CPU to communicate with basic devices such as the floppy drive, CD and DVD drives, hard drives, video card, and others. These programs, called services, are collectively referred to as the basic input/output services (BIOS). These programs are stored on a read-only medium and can't be changed by the user, so they are known as firmware, in contrast to software, which are programs stored on erasable media. The term "system ROM" refers to the ROM chip on the motherboard.

- Although the system ROM chip has room for as much as 2 MB of programs, only 65,536 bytes store the BIOS. Correspondingly, the last 65,536 addresses on the address bus are reserved for the BIOS on the ROM chip. When the CPU indicates one of these reserved addresses, the Northbridge sends the address directly to the ROM BIOS.

- The ROM BIOS includes programs that enable the CPU to talk to many basic hardware devices such as the keyboard, but other devices not supported by the ROM BIOS may have their own ROM chips.

- Each piece of hardware in the computer needs programs for everything that piece of hardware performs. The CPU must access these programs to get the hardware to do its job. IBM also devised other methods to get BIOS to the hardware of the computer. If the hardware is common, necessary, and does not change, such as the keyboard, the system ROM chip stores the BIOS. If the hardware is common and necessary but may change from time to time, such as when you install a larger hard drive or add more RAM, the BIOS for the general type of device (e.g., a hard drive) can be on the system ROM chip. The information describing specific features unique to that particular device (e.g., a Seagate Barracuda 60-GB drive), however, must be stored on a changeable storage medium such as a complementary metal-oxide semiconductor (CMOS) chip.

Distinguish among various CMOS setup utility options

- Your motherboard includes a changeable chip, capable of storing about 64 KB of data, called the complementary metal-oxide semiconductor (CMOS) chip. CMOS does not store programs. It stores the data that is read by BIOS, and that data is used by the programs residing in BIOS. Although CMOS used to be a separate chip on the motherboard, it is almost always built into the Southbridge on modern motherboards. The CMOS chip also keeps track of the date and time. To maintain its date, CMOS requires a constant trickle of electricity supplied by a small battery on the motherboard. If the data you have stored in CMOS continues to disappear or if the date/time resets itself, it may be time to change the motherboard battery.

- Within the system ROM is a CMOS setup program that lets you access and update the data on the CMOS chip. The terms CMOS setup program, CMOS, and system setup utility are functionally interchangeable today. Most techs just call it the CMOS. Two major manufacturers control 99 percent of the BIOS business: American Megatrends (AMI) and Phoenix Technology (which includes Award Software). The CMOS setup program can be started in many different ways, depending on the brand of BIOS you have on your computer. Pressing DEL when the computer boots is the most common way to access the CMOS setup program. The screen itself usually tells you how to access setup. If it doesn't, you can check the motherboard book or the Web site of your PC or BIOS manufacturer.

- All CMOS setup programs have basically the same main options. On the Standard CMOS Features screen, you can change floppy drive, hard drive, and date/time settings. Today's setup programs have extra CMOS settings that control such items as memory management, password and booting options, diagnostic and error handling, and power management. The Award Modular BIOS enables motherboard manufacturers to add or remove options from the setup program.

- Among the other things you can configure in CMOS setup are the voltage and multiplier settings for the CPU (the CPU SoftMenu), boot options (check the Advanced BIOS Features menu), power management, password protection, and ports (the Integrated Peripherals menu). All setup programs include options to *Save and Exit* or *Exit Without Saving*. You should not change CMOS settings unless you know exactly what you're doing.

- On older systems, if the information on the CMOS chip was lost or erased, the computer would not boot. The most common cause was a dead onboard battery, but other factors such as electrical surges, chip creep, or a dirty motherboard could also erase CMOS data. Lost CMOS information produces errors such as *No boot device available* or *CMOS date/time not set*. Making a backup copy of the CMOS data enabled you to restore the information and recover from this catastrophe.

- Unlike earlier ROM chips that you had to replace when you wanted to upgrade the BIOS programs, today's computers use flash ROM chips that you can reprogram without removing. If you install a CPU or other new hardware that the flash ROM chip does not support, you can run a small command-line program combined with an update file to change your BIOS. The exact process varies from one motherboard maker to another. If the flash ROM utility allows you to make a backup of your BIOS, you should always do so. Don't update your BIOS unless you have a good reason. As the old saying goes, "If it ain't broke, don't fix it!"

- Many CMOS setup programs enable you to set a boot password, a password to enter the CMOS setup program itself, or both. These passwords are stored in CMOS. If you forget your password, you simply need to clear the CMOS data. Unplug the AC power from the PC and remove the motherboard battery. This removes the trickle charge that enables CMOS to store information and clears all CMOS data, including the passwords. Reinstall the battery, plug in the power cord, boot up the computer, and re-enter your CMOS settings. Alternatively, many motherboards provide a clear CMOS jumper you can use to clear the CMOS data without removing the battery. Small padlocks on the system chassis can prevent unauthorized users from accessing the motherboard and clearing CMOS data.

Describe option ROM and device drivers

- Newer hardware devices that are not supported by the system BIOS have other ways to BYOB—bring your own BIOS. A hardware device, such as a SCSI host adapter, may contain its own BIOS chip or ROM chip known as option ROM. Every video card contains its own BIOS for internal functions. A more flexible way to BYOB is to use files called device drivers that contain instructions to support the hardware device. Device drivers load when the system boots.

- Many devices come with device driver files on installation discs. These drivers must be loaded for the PC to recognize and use the devices. In a database called the Registry, Windows keeps a list of what drivers should be loaded. Editing the Registry directly is dangerous (a mistake can prevent Windows from booting up), but you can safely install or remove drivers by using the Device Manager.

Explain the function of the power-on self test (POST)

- In addition to the BIOS routines and the CMOS setup program, the system ROM also includes a special program called the power-on self test (POST) that is executed every time the computer boots. POST first has basic devices, up to and including video, run self-diagnostics. If a device detects an error, the computer alerts you with a series of beeps. Different ROM manufacturers have used different beep codes, but your motherboard book should explain them (particularly in older systems). After the basic devices, POST tells the rest of the devices to run tests and displays a text error message on the screen if anything is wrong. Some manufacturers use numeric error codes or combine numeric and text messages.

- The computer may beep in two situations that are not related to POST beep codes. If the computer beeps constantly until you shut it off, it means RAM is missing or damaged. If the computer beeps after it is booted, it is probably warning you that the system is overheating.

- If the computer appears dead, with no beeps or screen response, you can place a POST card in an expansion slot to diagnose the problem by using the LED readout on the card. The documentation that comes with the POST card explains the LED codes for your particular BIOS.

- A beep code, text error message, or POST error may identify a problem, but it does not fix it. After you know which device is causing the problem, you should check the connection for the troublesome device and replace it if possible. If you cannot remove the bad part or if you cannot interpret the error message, you may need to replace the motherboard.

- When you first power on the PC, the power supply circuitry tests for proper voltage and then sends a signal down a special wire called the power good wire to awaken the CPU. The moment the power good wire wakes it up, the CPU sends a built-in memory address via its address bus. This address is the first line of the POST program on the system ROM, which is how the system starts the POST. After the POST has finished, it passes control to the bootstrap loader function on the system BIOS. This program looks for an operating system, checking the floppy drive, hard drives, or other bootable devices to find the boot sector that identifies the location of the OS. When the BIOS finds a bootable or system disk or device that has a functional operating system, it passes control to that disk or device.

Identify the structure and function of the expansion bus

- IBM developed the first expansion bus, the PC bus (or XT bus), as a means for users to install after-market hardware. The standardized expansion bus design addressed three main hurdles faced by expansion card manufacturers: physically

connecting expansion cards to the motherboard, facilitating communication between the expansion card and the rest of the system, and allowing the user to control the expansion card to take advantage of its features.

- Every device in the computer connects to the external data bus and the address bus. Expansion slots enable expansion cards to connect to these same buses. Depending on the system, the expansion slots may connect to the Southbridge or the Northbridge. Many systems have more than one type of expansion bus, with slots connecting to both the Southbridge and the Northbridge. It is the chipset that extends the address bus and data bus to the expansion slots.

- Expansion buses run at a standardized speed, depending on the type of expansion bus. This speed, which is much slower than the frontside bus, is dictated by the expansion bus crystal. The chipset uses wait states and buffers to compensate for the difference in speed between the expansion and frontside buses.

- The original IBM PCs ran an 8088 CPU with an 8-bit external data bus at a speed of 4.77 MHz, which was actually slower than the 7-MHz expansion bus. With the introduction of the Intel 286 CPU and its 16-bit external data bus, IBM developed what was called the AT bus and is now known as the ISA bus. The ISA expansion bus was 16 bits and ran at about 7 MHz. ISA cards required tedious manual configuration.

- The limitations of the ISA bus led to the development of other buses, including MCA, EISA, VL-Bus, and the PCI bus.

Describe the modern expansion bus

- PCI improved upon ISA in several ways. It was 32 bits, ran at 33 MHz, and was self-configuring (no more manual configuration of expansion card jumpers). Additionally, it could coexist with other expansion buses.

- As operating systems such as Windows became more graphically intense, the demand for sending video data quickly was too much for the ISA or standard PCI bus. The AGP slot is a special PCI slot for video cards, with a direct connection to the Northbridge. You can easily find the AGP slot on a motherboard: a lone slot that's brown in color.

- Enhancements to the PCI bus paved the way for a few modern variations. PCI-X is 64 bits wide, backward compatible with PCI, and available in a variety of speeds up to 533 MHz. Mini PCI is designed for laptops with an emphasis on low power consumption and a small, flat physical design. Finally, PCIe, with its point-to-point serial connection, touts speeds as high as 16 Gbps.

Explain classic system resources

- Devices in a computer system communicate via the four system resources: I/O addresses, IRQs, DMAs, and memory addresses. Not all devices use all four system resources. Earlier systems required manual configuration of each device's system resources through jumpers, DIP switches, dials, or software. Modern systems feature plug and play, which automatically configures system resources for each device. The system resources assigned to each device can be seen in the Device Manager.

- I/O addresses enable the CPU to send commands to devices. These addresses are configured automatically, and no two devices may share an I/O address. A single device may be assigned a range of I/O addresses; the first address in the range is called the I/O base address.

- IRQs enable devices to signal the CPU that they need attention. Before reaching the CPU, all interrupts pass through the I/O advanced programmable interrupt controller, which manages all of the incoming interrupts and forwards them to the CPU. In older systems, scarce IRQs and manual resource allocation meant that IRQ conflicts (and subsequent system lockups) were common. This is not a problem in modern systems, which have more IRQs and handle them automatically to avoid such conflicts.

- COM and LPT ports are simply presets of an IRQ–I/O address combination developed to make configuration of common devices easier. COM ports are for serial connections and LPT ports are for parallel connections.

- DMA enables devices to communicate with RAM without involving the CPU. The DMA controller sits between the devices and RAM and handles the DMA requests much as IRQ requests are handled. Newer systems use a type of DMA called bus mastering, which works without the need of a DMA controller.

- Memory addresses are used by devices that have either their own RAM (such as video cards) or their own ROM. When devices have their own RAM or ROM, they get memory addresses just like system RAM so the CPU can access their onboard memory.

Explain how motherboards work

- Every piece of hardware connects either directly or indirectly to the motherboard. Wires called traces make up the buses on the system, enabling hardware to communicate. Motherboards are several layers thick, with traces running across each layer, creating a veritable highway of wires.

- Motherboards are defined by their form factor, chipset, and components. The form factor defines the physical size and airflow; the chipset defines the type of CPU, the type and amount of RAM, and the components a motherboard will support.

Identify the types of motherboards

- The Advanced Technology (AT) form factor, though now obsolete, was the predominant form factor for motherboards through the mid-1990s. Its identifying features included a large keyboard plug and a split power socket called P8/P9.

- LPX and NLX were slimline form factors, meaning they were ideal for low-profile cases. They offered a central riser slot to accept a special riser card into which expansion cards fit horizontally.

- The Advanced Technology Extended (ATX) form factor replaced the AT as the form factor of choice by the late 1990s. It offered several improvements over the AT, including repositioning the power supply for better airflow, easier access to CPU and RAM slots, and better performance by moving RAM closer to the Northbridge and CPU. The microATX (μATX) and FlexATX are subtypes of the ATX and are considerably smaller.

- The Balanced Technology eXtended (BTX) form factor is newer than ATX and was designed to improve cooling. BTX cases take cool air in from the front and blow warm air out the back. As BTX motherboards place the CPU toward the front of the case, the CPU receives additional cooling from the improved airflow. Standard BTX, microBTX, and picoBTX are designed to replace ATX, microATX, and FlexATX, respectively.

- Several PC manufacturers make proprietary motherboards, meaning they do not adhere to a standard form factor such as ATX or BTX. Servicing a system like this can be frustrating, as parts may be difficult to find and are often available only from authorized dealers.

- Motherboards come with differing features or components such as USB/FireWire ports, audio, video, RAID, and AMR or CNR slots for modems and network cards. Sometimes a motherboard supports several USB/FireWire ports but does not have rear ports for all of them. In this case, the motherboard likely has connections for the additional ports to be used in conjunction with a dongle to create front-mounted ports.

Explain chipset varieties

- Every motherboard has a chipset that determines the type of CPU the motherboard supports, the type and capacity of RAM, and the devices the motherboard supports without an expansion card. Most modern chipsets are composed of two primary chips: the Northbridge and the Southbridge. As the Northbridge works with the CPU and RAM, it gets very hot and therefore needs its own heat sink and fan. The Southbridge usually does not require any extra cooling and is thus exposed, making it a great place to find the stamp of the chipset manufacturer.

- Because almost no modern chipset supports old technologies such as floppy disk drives, infrared connections, and parallel ports, motherboards contain a third chip called the Super I/O chip to support these technologies. The Super I/O chip is not part of the chipset.

- The system ROM chip provides basic support for the chipset, but to benefit from all of the features of a chipset, you need to install the operating system–specific drivers for the chipset once you've installed the operating system.

- Chipset manufacturers for AMD-based motherboards tend to use the terms Northbridge and Southbridge, whereas Intel-based boards tend to use different terminology. You might see the Northbridge referred to as the Memory Controller Hub (MCH) or I/O Hub (IOH) and the Southbridge referred to as the I/O Controller Hub (ICH) or Legacy I/O Controller Hub.

- Popular chipset manufacturers today include Intel, AMD, and NVIDIA.

■ Key Terms

Accelerated Graphics Port (AGP) (227)
AT (239)
ATX (242)
audio modem riser (AMR) (249)
Balanced Technology eXtended (BTX) (243)
basic input/output services (BIOS) (207)
beep code (220)
bootable disk (222)
bootstrap loader (222)
bus mastering (237)
chassis intrusion detection (215)
chipset (203)
CMOS setup program (210)
COM port (235)
communications and networking riser (CNR) (249)
complementary metal-oxide semiconductor (CMOS) (209)
device driver (218)
Device Manager (219)
direct memory access (DMA) (236)

DMA controller (237)
DriveLock (217)
expansion bus (222)
expansion bus crystal (224)
expansion slot (222)
firmware (208)
flash ROM (208)
FlexATX (243)
form factor (238)
hexadecimal (231)
I/O address (230)
I/O addressing (230)
I/O advanced programmable interrupt controller (IOAPIC) (233)
I/O base address (232)
I/O Controller Hub (ICH) (246)
Industry Standard Architecture (ISA) (226)
installation disc (218)
interrupt request (IRQ) (233)
interruption (232)

LPT port *(235)*
LPX *(240)*
memory addressing *(238)*
Memory Controller Hub (MCH) *(245)*
microATX *(242)*
microBTX *(243)*
Mini PCI *(228)*
motherboard *(238)*
NLX *(240)*
nonvolatile *(208)*
Northbridge *(203)*
option ROM *(218)*
picoBTX *(243)*
PC bus *(225)*
PCI Express (PCIe) *(228)*
PCI Extended (PCI-X) *(228)*
peripheral component interconnect (PCI) *(227)*
POST card *(220)*

power good *(222)*
power-on self test (POST) *(219)*
printed circuit board (PCB) *(239)*
Registry *(218)*
read-only memory (ROM) *(207)*
riser card *(241)*
service *(207)*
slimline *(240)*
soft power *(242)*
Southbridge *(203)*
Super I/O chip *(245)*
system BIOS *(208)*
system disk *(222)*
system resource *(230)*
system ROM *(208)*
thermal unit *(244)*
trace *(238)*
XT bus *(225)*

■ Key Term Quiz

Use the Key Terms list to complete the sentences that follow. Not all terms will be used.

1. The combination of a specific Northbridge and a specific _____ is collectively referred to as the _____.

2. The hundreds of programs in the system ROM chip are collectively called the _____.

3. The low-energy chip that holds configuration information and keeps track of date and time is called the _____ chip.

4. The _____ bus was designed for laptop computers.

5. A shorthand system for binary numbers is called _____.

6. The _____ is usually a brown slot used only by the video card.

7. The most common bus on today's computers, whether PC or Apple Macintosh, is the flexible _____ .

8. Everything in the _____ form factor is designed to improve cooling.

9. The _____ determines the physical size of the motherboard as well as the general location of components and ports.

■ Multiple-Choice Quiz

1. What is the correct boot sequence for a PC?

   A. CPU, POST, power good, boot loader, operating system

   B. POST, power good, CPU, boot loader, operating system

   C. Power good, boot loader, CPU, POST, operating system

   D. Power good, CPU, POST, boot loader, operating system

2. What does BIOS provide for the computer? (Select the best answer.)

   A. BIOS provides the physical interface for various devices such as USB and FireWire ports.

   B. BIOS provides the programming that enables the CPU to communicate with other hardware.

   C. BIOS provides memory space for applications to load into from the hard drive.

   D. BIOS provides memory space for applications to load into from the main system RAM.

3. Which of the following statements is true about CMOS?

   A. CMOS is a configuration program that runs from the hard drive during booting.

   B. CMOS is a low-energy chip that draws power from a battery while the computer is turned off.

   C. CMOS includes the power-on self test (POST) routines.

   D. CMOS is the Southbridge chip that controls input and output devices.

4. Which of the following enables you to add more devices to a computer? (Select the best answer.)

   A. Device bus

   B. Expansion bus

   C. Peripheral bus

   D. Yellow bus

5. What advantages did PCI have over ISA? (Select two.)

   A. Faster (33 MHz versus 7 MHz)

   B. Longer (2 m versus 1 m)

   C. Shorter (1 m versus 2 m)

   D. Wider (32 bit versus 16 bit)

6. Which of the following slots features serial data transfers?

   A. AGP

   B. PCI

   C. PCIe

   D. PCI-X

7. Which of the following are part of the ATX form factor? (Select two.)

   A. FlexATX

   B. macroATX

   C. microATX

   D. picoATX

8. Which of the following form factors dominates the PC market?

   A. AT

   B. ATX

   C. BTX

   D. NLX

9. Which chip enables an Intel Core 2 Duo processor to interact with RAM?

   A. Memorybridge

   B. Northbridge

   C. Southbridge

   D. Super I/O

▪ Essay Quiz

1. From this chapter you learned that every piece of hardware in the computer needs BIOS to make it work. Explain three ways in which these essential programs may be provided to the CPU.

2. Although today's computers use plug and play to assign system resources automatically, CompTIA still expects you to know about system resources. Why is this knowledge important?

   Briefly explain two scenarios where your knowledge of system resources may help solve computer problems.

3. Some people believe that selecting a motherboard based on the motherboard chipset is even more important than basing the decision on the kind of processor. Do you agree or disagree, and why?

Lab Projects

• Lab Project 7.1

Watch closely as your computer boots to see if it displays a message about how to reach the setup program. If it does not, consult your motherboard book to try to locate this information. Then, using the method appropriate for your system BIOS chip, access the setup program and examine the various screens. Do not change anything! Usually, your motherboard book includes default settings for the various setup screens and perhaps includes explanations of the various choices. Compare what you see on the screen with what the book says. Do you see any differences? If so, how do you account for these differences? As you examine the setup program, answer the following questions:

1 How do you navigate from one screen to the next? Are there menus across the top or do you simply jump from one page of options to the next? Are there instructions on the screen for navigating the setup program?

2 What is the boot sequence for your computer? In other words, in what order does the BIOS look for a bootable device?

3 What is the core voltage of the CPU?

4 How many SATA drives does the BIOS list?

When you have finished, choose *Exit Without Saving*.

• Lab Project 7.2

Open your computer case and determine the kind of expansion slots available on your motherboard. How many of each kind are available? What cards are installed in the slots? Now examine the back and front of the computer case to see what ports are available. What devices do you have plugged into the ports?

Learning PC Power

"This flipping circuit board, Jen. Some chump has run the data lines right through the power supply. Amateur hour! I've got tears in my eyes!"

—Moss, THE IT CROWD ("THE RED DOOR," 2006)

In this chapter, you will learn how to

- **Explain the basics of electricity**
- **Describe the details about powering the PC**

Powering the PC requires a single box—the power supply—that takes electricity from the wall socket and transforms it into electricity to run the motherboard and other internal components. Figure 8.1 shows a typical power supply inside a case. All of the wires dangling out of it connect to the motherboard and peripherals.

As simple as this appears on the surface, power supply issues are of critical importance for techs. Problems with power can create system instability, crashes, and data loss—all things most computer users would rather avoid! Good techs therefore know an awful lot about powering the PC, from understanding the basic principles of electricity to knowing the many variations of PC power supplies. Plus, you need to know how to recognize power problems and implement the proper solutions. Too many techs fall into the "just plug it in" camp and never learn how to deal with power, much to their clients' unhappiness.

● Figure 8.1   Typical power supply mounted inside the PC system unit

Some questions on the CompTIA A+ Essentials exam could refer to a power supply as a **PSU**, for **power supply unit**. A power supply also falls into the category of **field replaceable unit (FRU)**, which refers to the typical parts a tech should carry, such as RAM and a hard drive.

Historical/Conceptual

■ Understanding Electricity

Electricity is simply a flow of negatively charged particles, called electrons, through matter. All matter enables the flow of electrons to some extent. This flow of electrons is very similar to the flow of water through pipes; so similar that the best way to learn about electricity is by comparing it to how water flows though pipes. So let's talk about water for a moment.

Water comes from the ground, through wells, aquifers, rivers, and so forth. In a typical city, water comes to you through pipes from the water supply company that took it from the ground. What do you pay for when you pay your water bill each month? You pay for the water you use, certainly, but built into the price of the water you use is the surety that when you turn the spigot, water will flow at a more or less constant rate. The water sits in the pipes under pressure from the water company, waiting for you to turn the spigot.

Electricity works essentially the same way as water. Electric companies gather or generate electricity and then push it to your house under pressure through wires. Just like water, the electricity sits in the wires, waiting for you to plug something into the wall socket, at which time it'll flow at a more or less constant rate. You plug a lamp into an electrical outlet and flip the switch, electricity flows, and you have light. You pay for reliability, electrical pressure, and electricity used.

The pressure of the electrons in the wire is called *voltage* and is measured in units called **volts (V)**. The amount of electrons moving past a certain point on a wire is called the *current* or *amperage*, which is measured in units called **amperes (amps or A)**. The amount of amps and volts needed so that a particular device will function is expressed as how much **wattage (watts or W)** that device needs. The correlation between the three is very simple math: V × A = W. You'll learn more about wattage a little later in this chapter.

Wires of all sorts—whether copper, tin, gold, or platinum—have a slight **resistance** to the flow of electrons, just as water pipes have a slight amount of friction that resists the flow of water. Resistance to the flow of electrons is measured in **ohms (Ω)**.

- Pressure = voltage (V)
- Volume flowing = amperes (A)
- Work = wattage (W)
- Resistance = ohms (Ω)

A particular thickness of wire only handles so much electricity at a time. If you push too much through, the wire will overheat and break, much as an overloaded water pipe will burst. To make sure you use the right wire for the right job, all electrical wires have an amperage rating, such as 20 amps. If you try to push 30 amps through a 20-amp wire, the wire will break and electrons will seek a way to return into the ground. Not a good thing, especially if the path back to the ground is through you!

Circuit breakers and ground wires provide the basic protection from accidental overflow. A circuit breaker is a heat-sensitive electrical switch rated at a certain amperage. If you push too much amperage through the circuit breaker, the wiring inside detects the increase in heat and automatically opens, stopping the flow of electricity before the wiring overheats and breaks. You reset the circuit breaker to reestablish the circuit and electricity flows once more through the wires. A ground wire provides a path of least resistance for electrons to flow back to ground in case of an accidental overflow.

Many years ago your electrical supply used fuses instead of circuit breakers. Fuses are small devices with a tiny filament designed to break if subjected to too much current. Unfortunately, fuses had to be replaced every time they blew, making circuit breakers much more preferable. Even though you no longer see fuses in a building's electrical circuits, many electrical devices—such as a PC's power supply—often still use fuses for their own internal protection.

Electricity comes in two flavors: **direct current (DC)**, in which the electrons flow in one direction around a continuous circuit, and **alternating current (AC)**, in which the flow of electrons alternates direction back and forth in a circuit (Figure 8.2). Most electronic devices use DC power, but all power companies supply AC power because AC travels long distances much more efficiently than DC.

An electrical outlet must have a ground wire to be suitable for PC use.

Constant voltage in one direction

Voltage in both directions, constantly switching back and forth

• **Figure 8.2**   Diagrams showing DC and AC flow of electrons

■ Powering the PC

Your PC uses DC voltage, so some conversion process must take place before the PC can use AC power from the power company. The power supply in a computer converts high-voltage AC power from the wall socket to low-voltage DC. The first step in powering the PC, therefore, is to get and maintain a good supply of AC power. Second, you need a power supply to convert AC to the proper voltage and amperage of DC power for the motherboard and peripherals. Finally, you need to control the byproduct of electricity use, namely heat. Let's look at the specifics of powering the PC.

Supplying AC

Every PC power supply must have standard AC power from the power company, supplied steadily rather than in fits and spurts, and protection against accidental blurps in the supply. The power supply connects to the power cord (and thus to an electrical outlet) via a standard **IEC-320** connector. In the United States, standard AC comes in somewhere between 110 and 120 volts, often written as ~115 VAC (volts of alternating current). The rest of the world uses 220–240 VAC, so most power supplies have a little switch in the back so you can use them anywhere. These power supplies with voltage-selection switches are referred to as fixed-input. Power supplies that you do not have to manually switch for different voltages are known as auto-switching. Figure 8.3 shows the back of a power supply. Note the three components, from top to bottom: the hard on/off switch, the 115/230 switch, and the IEC-320 connector.

Before plugging anything into an AC outlet, take a moment to test the outlet first by using a multimeter or a device designed exclusively to test outlets. Failure to test AC outlets properly can result in inoperable or destroyed equipment, as well as possible electrocution. The IEC-320 plug has three holes, called hot, neutral, and ground. These names describe the function of the wires that connect to them behind the wall plate. The hot wire carries electrical voltage, much like a pipe that delivers water. The neutral wire carries no voltage, but instead acts like a water drain, completing the circuit by returning electricity to the local source, normally a breaker panel. The ground wire makes it possible for excess electricity to return safely to the ground. When testing AC power, you want to check for three things: that the hot outputs approximately 115 V (or whatever the proper voltage is for your part of

> ⚠️ Flipping the AC switch on the back of a power supply can wreak all kinds of havoc on a PC. Moving the switch to ~230 V in the United States makes for a great practical joke (as long as the PC is off when you do it)—the PC might try to boot up but probably won't get far. You don't risk damaging anything by running at half the AC the power supply is expecting. In countries that run ~230 standard, on the other hand, firing up the PC with the AC switch set to ~115 can cause the power supply to die a horrid, smoking death. Watch that switch!

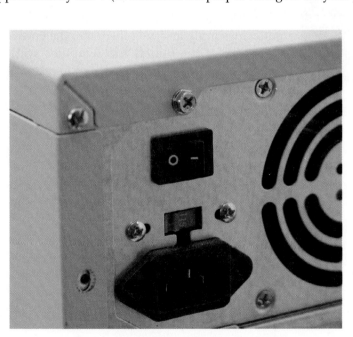

● **Figure 8.3**   Back of fixed-input power supply, showing typical switches and power connection

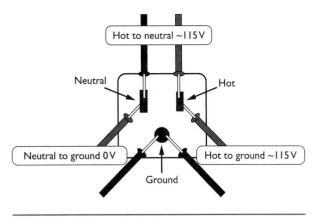

● **Figure 8.4**   Outlet voltages

● **Figure 8.5**   Digital multimeter

the world), that the neutral connects to ground (0 V output), and that the ground connects to ground (again, 0 V). Figure 8.4 shows the voltages at an outlet.

You can use a **multimeter**—often also referred to as a *volt-ohm meter* (*VOM*) or *digital multimeter* (*DMM*)—to measure a number of aspects of electrical current. A multimeter consists of two probes, an analog or digital meter, and a dial to set the type of test you want to perform. Refer to Figure 8.5 to become familiar with the components of the multimeter.

Note that some multimeters use symbols rather than letters to describe AC and DC settings. The *V* with the solid line above a dashed line, for example, in Figure 8.6, refers to direct current. The *V~* stands for alternating current.

Every multimeter offers at least four types of electrical tests: continuity, resistance, AC voltage (VAC), and DC voltage (VDC). Continuity tests whether electrons can flow from one end of a wire to the other end. If so, you have continuity; if not, you don't. You can use this setting to determine if a fuse is good or to check for breaks in wires. If your multimeter doesn't have a continuity tester (many cheaper multimeters do not), you can use the resistance tester. A broken wire or fuse will show infinite resistance, while a good wire or fuse will show no resistance. Testing AC and DC voltages is a matter of making sure the measured voltage is what it should be.

Using Special Equipment to Test AC Voltage

A number of good AC-only testing devices are available. With these devices, you can test all voltages for an AC outlet by simply inserting them into the outlet. Be sure to test all of the outlets the computer system uses: power supply, external devices, and monitor. Although convenient, these devices aren't as accurate as a multimeter. My favorite tester is made by Radio Shack,

● **Figure 8.6**   Multimeter featuring DC and AC symbols

Mike Meyers' CompTIA A+ Guide: Essentials

a simple-seeming tool (Figure 8.7). This handy device provides three light-emitting diodes (LEDs) that describe everything that can go wrong with a plug.

Protecting the PC from Spikes and Sags in AC Power

If all power companies could supply electricity in smooth, continuous flows with no dips or spikes in pressure, the next two sections of this chapter would be irrelevant. Unfortunately, no matter how clean the AC supply appears to a multimeter, the truth is that voltage from the power company tends to drop well below (sag) and shoot far above (surge or spike) the standard 115 V (in the United States). These sags and spikes usually don't affect lamps and refrigerators, but they can keep your PC from running or can even destroy a PC or peripheral device. Two essential devices handle spikes and sags in the supply of AC: surge suppressors and uninterruptible power supplies.

Surge Suppressors   Surges or spikes are far more dangerous than sags. Even a strong sag only shuts off or

Try This!

Using a Multimeter to Test AC Outlets

Every competent technician knows how to use a multimeter, so if you haven't used one in the past, get hold of one and Try This!

First you need to set up the meter for measuring AC. Follow these steps:

1. Move the selector switch to the AC V (usually red). If multiple settings are available, put it into the first scale higher than 120 V (usually 200 V). *Auto-range* meters set their own range; they don't need any selection except AC V.

2. Place the black lead in the common (–) hole. If the black lead is permanently attached, ignore this step.

3. Place the red lead in the V-Ohm-A (+) hole. If the red lead is permanently attached, ignore this step.

Once you have the meter set up for AC, go through the process of testing the various wires on an AC socket. Just don't put your fingers on the metal parts of the leads when you stick them into the socket! Follow these steps:

1. Put either lead in hot, the other in neutral. You should read 110 to 120 V AC.

2. Put either lead in hot, the other in ground. You should read 110 to 120 V AC.

3. Put either lead in neutral, the other in ground. You should read 0 V AC.

If any of these readings is different from what is described here, it's time to call an electrician.

reboots your PC; any surge can harm your computer, and a strong surge destroys components. Given the seriousness of surges, every PC should use a **surge suppressor** device that absorbs the extra voltage from a surge to protect the PC. The power supply does a good job of surge suppression and can handle many of the smaller surges that take place fairly often. But the power supply takes a lot of damage from this and will eventually fail. To protect your power supply, a dedicated surge suppressor works between the power supply and the outlet to protect the system from power surges (Figure 8.8).

The voltages supplied by most PC power supplies can safely vary by as much as ±10 percent of their stated values.

Most people tend to spend a lot of money on their PC and for some reason suddenly get cheap on the surge suppressor. Don't do that! Make sure your surge suppressor has the Underwriters Laboratories UL 1449 for 330 V rating to ensure substantial protection for your system. Underwriters Laboratories (www.ul.com) is a U.S.-based, not-for-profit, widely recognized industry testing laboratory whose testing standards are very important to the consumer electronics industry. Additionally, check the joules rating before buying a new surge suppressor. A **joule** is a unit of electrical energy. How much energy a surge suppressor can handle before it fails is described in

Tech Tip

AC Adapters

Many devices in the computing world use an AC adapter rather than an internal power supply. Even though it sits outside a device, an AC adapter converts AC current to DC, just like a power supply. Unlike power supplies, AC adapters are rarely interchangeable. Although manufacturers of different devices often use the same kind of plug on the end of the AC adapter cable, these adapters are not necessarily interchangeable. In other words, just because you can plug an AC adapter from your friend's laptop into your laptop does not mean it's going to work.

You need to make sure that three things match before you plug an AC adapter into a device: voltage, amperage, and polarity. If either the voltage or amperage output is too low, the device won't run. If the polarity is reversed, it won't work, just like putting a battery in a flashlight backward. If either the voltage or amperage—especially the latter—is too high, on the other hand, you can very quickly toast your device. Don't do it! Always check the voltage, amperage, and polarity of a replacement AC adapter before you plug it into a device.

• **Figure 8.7**   Circuit tester

joules. Most authorities agree that your surge suppressor should rate at a minimum of 800 joules—and the more joules, the better the protection. My surge suppressor rates out at 1750 joules.

While you're protecting your system, don't forget that surges also come from telephone and cable connections. If you use a modem, DSL, or cable modem, make sure to get a surge suppressor that includes support for these types of connections. Many manufacturers make surge suppressors with telephone line protection (Figure 8.9).

No surge suppressor works forever. Make sure your surge suppressor has a test/reset button so you'll know when the device has—as we say in the business—turned into an extension cord. If your system takes a hit and you have a surge suppressor, call the company! Many companies provide cash guarantees against system failure due to surges, but only if you follow their guidelines.

If you want really great surge suppression, you need to move up to **power conditioning**. Your power lines take in all kinds of strange signals that

• **Figure 8.8**   Surge suppressor

• **Figure 8.9**   Surge suppressor with telephone line protection have no business being in there, such as electromagnetic interference (EMI) and radio frequency interference (RFI). Most of the time, this line noise is so minimal it's not worth addressing, but occasionally events (such as lightning) generate enough line noise to cause weird things to happen to your PC (keyboard lockups, messed-up data). All better surge suppressors add power conditioning to filter out EMI and RFI.

UPS   An **uninterruptible power supply (UPS)** protects your computer (and, more importantly, your data) in the event of a power sag or power outage. Figure 8.10 shows a typical UPS. A UPS essentially contains a big battery that provides AC power to your computer regardless of the power coming from the AC outlet.

All uninterruptible power supplies are measured in both watts (the true amount of power they supply in the event of a power outage) and in *volt-amps* (*VA*). Volt-amps is the amount of power the UPS could supply if the devices took power from the UPS in a perfect way. Your UPS provides perfect AC power, moving current smoothly back and forth 60 times a second. Power supplies, monitors, and other devices, however, may not take all of the power the UPS has to offer at every point as the AC power moves back and forth, resulting in inefficiencies. If your devices took all of the power the UPS offered at every point as the power moved back and forth, VA would equal watts.

If the UPS makers knew ahead of time exactly what devices you planned to plug into their UPS, they could tell you the exact watts, but different devices have different efficiencies, forcing the UPS makers to go by what they can offer (VAs), not what your devices will take (watts). The watts value they give is a guess, and it's never as high as the VAs. The VA rating is always higher than the wattage rating.

Because you have no way to calculate the exact efficiency of every device you'll plug into the UPS, go with the wattage rating. You add up the total wattage of every component in your PC and buy a UPS with a higher wattage. You'll spend a lot of time and mental energy figuring precisely how much wattage your computer, monitor, drives, and so on require to get the proper UPS for your system. But you're still not finished! Remember that the UPS is a battery with a limited amount of power, so you then need to figure out how long you want the UPS to run when you lose power.

The quicker and far better method to use for determining the UPS you need is to go to any of the major surge suppressor/UPS makers' Web sites and use their handy power calculators. My personal favorite is on the

No surge suppressor in the world can handle the ultimate surge, the ESD of a lightning strike. If your electrical system takes such a hit, you can kiss your PC goodbye if it was plugged in at the time. *Always* unplug electronics during electrical storms!

Tech Tip

UPS Technologies

There are two main types of UPS: online, *where devices are constantly powered through the UPS's battery, and* standby, *where devices connected to the UPS only receive battery power when the AC sags below ~80–90 V. Another type of UPS is called* line-interactive, *which is similar to a standby UPS but has special circuitry to handle moderate AC sags and surges without the need to switch to battery power.*

• **Figure 8.10**   Uninterruptible power supply

American Power Conversion Web site: www.apc.com. APC makes great surge suppressors and UPSs, and the company's online calculator will show you the true wattage you need—and teach you about whatever new thing is happening in power at the same time.

Every UPS also has surge suppression and power conditioning, so look for the joule and UL 1449 ratings. Also look for replacement battery costs—some UPS replacement batteries are very expensive.

Last, look for a UPS with a USB or serial port connection. These handy UPSs come with monitoring and maintenance software (Figure 8.11) that tells you the status of your system and the amount of battery power available, logs power events, and provides other handy options.

Table 8.1 gives you a quick look at the low end and the very high end of UPS products (as of late 2009).

Supplying DC

After you've assured the supply of good AC electricity for the PC, the power supply unit (PSU) takes over, converting high-voltage AC into several DC voltages (notably, 5.0, 12.0, and 3.3 V) usable by the delicate interior components. Power supplies come in a large number of shapes and sizes, but the most

• **Figure 8.11** APC PowerChute software

Table 8.1		Typical UPS Devices				
Brand	**Model**	**Outlets Protected**	**Backup Time**	**Price**	**Type**
APC	BE350G	3 @ 120 V	3 min @ 200 W, 10 min @ 100 W	$49.99	Standby
APC	BP500UC	4 @ 120 V	4 min @ 315 W, 14 min @ 157 W	$129.99	Standby
CyberPower	CPS1500AVR	3 @ 120 V	18 min @ 950 W, 6 min @ 475 W	$299.99	Line-interactive
APC	SYA4K8RMP	6 @ 120, 208 V	6 min @ 3200 W, 17 min @ 1600 W	$6925.00	Double-conversion online

common size by far is the standard 150 mm × 140 mm × 86 mm desktop PSU shown in Figure 8.12.

The PC uses the 12.0-V current to power motors on devices such as hard drives and CD-ROM drives, and it uses the 5.0- and 3.3-V current for support of onboard electronics. Manufacturers may use these voltages any way they wish, however, and may deviate from these assumptions. Power supplies also come with standard connectors for the motherboard and interior devices.

Power to the Motherboard

Modern motherboards use a 20- or 24-pin **P1 power connector**. Some motherboards may require special 4-, 6-, or 8-pin connectors to supply extra power (Figure 8.13). We'll talk about each of these connectors in the form factor standards discussion later in this chapter.

• **Figure 8.12**   Desktop PSU

Power to Peripherals: Molex, Mini, and SATA

Many devices inside the PC require power. These include hard drives, floppy drives, optical drives, Zip drives (for techs who enjoy retro computing), and fans. The typical PC power supply has up to three types of connectors that plug into peripherals: Molex, mini, and SATA.

Molex Connectors   The most common type of power connection for devices that need 5 or 12 V of power is the **Molex connector** (Figure 8.14). The Molex connector has notches, called *chamfers*, that guide its installation. The

• **Figure 8.13**   Motherboard power connectors

tricky part is that Molex connectors require a firm push to plug in properly, and a strong person can defeat the chamfers, plugging a Molex in upside down. Not a good thing. *Always* check for proper orientation before you push it in!

Mini Connectors   All power supplies have a second type of connector, called a **mini connector** (Figure 8.15), that supplies 5 and 12 V to peripherals, although only floppy disk drives in modern systems use this connector. Drive manufacturers adopted the mini as the standard connector on 3.5-inch floppy disk drives. Often these mini connectors are referred to as floppy power connectors.

• **Figure 8.14**   Molex connector

Try This!

Testing DC

A common practice for techs troubleshooting a system is to test the DC voltages coming out of the power supply. Even with good AC, a bad power supply can fail to transform AC to DC at voltages needed by the motherboard and peripherals. So grab your trusty multimeter and Try This! on a powered-up PC with the side cover removed. Note that you must have P1 connected to the motherboard and the system must be running (you don't have to be in Windows, of course).

1. Switch your multimeter to DC, somewhere around 20 V DC if you need to make that choice. Make sure your leads are plugged into the multimeter properly: red to hot, black to ground. The key to testing DC is that which lead you touch to which wire matters. Red goes to hot wires of all colors; black *always* goes to ground.

2. Plug the red lead into the red wire socket of a free Molex connector and plug the black lead into one of the two black wire sockets. You should get a reading of ~5 V. What do you have?

3. Now move the red lead to the yellow socket. What voltage do you get?

4. Testing the P1 connector is a little more complicated. You push the red and black leads into the top of P1, sliding in alongside the wires until you bottom out. Leave the black lead in one of the black wire ground sockets. Move the red lead through all of the colored wire sockets. What voltages do you find?

Be extra careful when plugging in a mini connector! Whereas Molex connectors are difficult to plug in backward, you can insert a mini connector incorrectly with very little effort. As with a Molex connector, doing so will almost certainly destroy the floppy drive. Figure 8.16 depicts a correctly oriented mini connection, with the small ridge on the connector away from the body of the data socket.

SATA Power Connectors Serial ATA (SATA) hard drives need a special 15-pin **SATA power connector** (Figure 8.17). The larger pin count supports the SATA hot-swappable feature and 3.3-, 5.0-, and 12.0-V devices. SATA power connectors are *L* shaped, making it almost impossible to insert one incorrectly into a SATA drive. No other device on your computer uses the SATA power connector. For more information about SATA drives, see Chapter 9, "Hard Drive Technologies."

Splitters and Adapters You may occasionally find yourself without enough connectors to power all of the devices inside your PC. In this case, you can purchase splitters to create more connections (Figure 8.18). You might also run into the phenomenon of needing a SATA connector but having only a spare Molex. Because the voltages on the wires are the same, a simple adapter will take care of the problem nicely.

• **Figure 8.15** Mini connector

As with any power connector, plugging a mini connector into a device the wrong way will almost certainly destroy the device. Check twice before you plug one in!

• **Figure 8.16** Correct orientation of a mini connector

268

Mike Meyers' CompTIA A+ Guide: Essentials

ATX

The original ATX power supplies had two distinguishing physical features: the motherboard power connector and soft power. Motherboard power came from a single cable with a 20-pin P1 motherboard power connector. ATX power supplies also had at least two other cables, each populated with two or more Molex or mini connectors for peripheral power.

When plugged in, ATX systems have 5 V running to the motherboard. They're always "on," even when powered down. The power switch you press to power up the PC isn't a true power switch like the light switch on the wall in your bedroom. The power switch on an ATX system simply tells the computer whether it has been pressed. The BIOS or operating system takes over from there and handles the chore of turning the PC on or off. This is called **soft power**.

Using soft power instead of a physical switch has a number of important benefits. Soft power prevents a user from turning off a system before the operating system has been shut down. It enables the PC to use power-saving modes that put the system to sleep and then wake it up when you press a key, move a mouse, or receive an e-mail. (See Chapter 14, "Learning Portable Computing," for more details on sleep mode.)

All of the most important settings for ATX soft power reside in CMOS setup. Boot into CMOS and look for a Power Management section. Take a look at the Power On Function option in Figure 8.19. This determines the function of the on/off switch. You may set this switch to turn off the computer, or you may set it to the more common *4-second delay*.

ATX did a great job supplying power for more than a decade, but over time more powerful CPUs, multiple CPUs, video cards, and other components began to need more current than the original ATX provided. This motivated the industry to introduce a number of updates to the ATX power standards: ATX12V 1.3, EPS12V, multiple rails, ATX12V 2.0, other form factors, and active PFC.

ATX12V 1.3 The first widespread update to the ATX standard, ATX12V 1.3, came out in 2003. This introduced a 4-pin motherboard power connector, unofficially but commonly called the P4, that provided more 12-V power to assist the 20-pin P1 motherboard power connector. Any power supply that provides a P4 connector is called an ATX12V power supply. The term "ATX" was dropped from the ATX power standard, so if you want to get really nerdy you can say—accurately—that there's no such thing as an ATX power supply. All power supplies—assuming they have a P4 connector—are ATX12V or one of the later standards.

The ATX12V 1.3 standard also introduced a 6-pin auxiliary connector—commonly called an *AUX* connector—to supply increased 3.3- and 5.0-V current to the motherboard (Figure 8.20). This connector was based on the motherboard power connector from the precursor of ATX, called *AT*.

The introduction of these two extra power connectors caused the industry some teething problems. In particular, motherboards using AMD CPUs tended to need the AUX connector, while motherboards using Intel CPUs needed only the P4. As a result, many power supplies came with only a P4 or only an AUX connector to save money. A few motherboard makers skipped adding either connector and used a standard Molex connector so

• **Figure 8.17**   SATA power connector

• **Figure 8.18**   Molex splitter

SATA also supports a slimline connector that has a 6-pin power segment and a micro connector that has a 9-pin power segment.

It's normal and common to have unused power connectors inside your PC case.

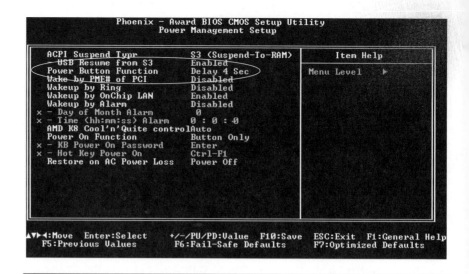

```
            Phoenix - Award BIOS CMOS Setup Utility
                      Power Management Setup

  ACPI Suspend Typr         S3 (Suspend-To-RAM)        Item Help
    USB Resume from S3       Enabled
  Power Button Function      Delay 4 Sec           Menu Level    ▶
  Wake by PME# of PCI        Disabled
  Wakeup by Ring             Disabled
  Wakeup by OnChip LAN       Enabled
  Wakeup by Alarm            Disabled
x - Day of Month Alarm       0
x - Time (hh:mm:ss) Alarm    0 : 0 : 0
  AMD K8 Cool'n'Quite controlAuto
  Power On Function          Button Only
x - KB Power On Password     Enter
x - Hot Key Power On         Ctrl-F1
  Restore on AC Power Loss   Power Off


▲▼►◄:Move  Enter:Select     +/-/PU/PD:Value  F10:Save   ESC:Exit  F1:General Help
   F5:Previous Values            F6:Fail-Safe Defaults   F7:Optimized Defaults
```

• **Figure 8.19**   Soft power setting in CMOS

Cross Check

ATX Form Factor

The power supply form factor alone does not define a system as ATX or one of the later varieties; you have to discuss the motherboard as well. Flip back to Chapter 7, "Learning Motherboards," and see if you can put the full picture of the ATX standard together. What defines a system as ATX? What improvements did ATX incorporate over AT? What ATX form factors can you purchase?

people with older power supplies wouldn't have to upgrade just because they bought a new motherboard (Figure 8.21).

The biggest problem with ATX12V was its lack of teeth—it made a lot of recommendations but few requirements, giving PSU makers too much choice (such as choosing or not choosing to add AUX and P4 connectors), which wasn't fixed until later versions.

• **Figure 8.20**   Auxiliary power connector

• **Figure 8.21**   Molex power on motherboard

EPS12V Server motherboards are thirsty for power, and sometimes ATX12V 1.3 just didn't cut it. An industry group called the Server System Infrastructure (SSI) developed a non-ATX standard motherboard and power supply called EPS12V. An EPS12V power supply came with a 24-pin main motherboard power connector that resembled a 20-pin ATX connector, but it offered more current and thus more stability for motherboards. It also came with an AUX connector, an ATX12V P4 connector, and a unique 8-pin connector. That's a lot of connectors! EPS12V power supplies were not interchangeable with ATX12V power supplies.

EPS12V may not have seen much life beyond servers, but it introduced a number of power features, some of which eventually became part of the ATX12V standard. The most important issue was something called **rails**.

Rails Generally, all of the PC's power comes from a single transformer that takes the AC current from a wall socket and converts it into DC current that is split into three primary DC voltage rails: 12.0 V, 5.0 V, and 3.3 V. Individual lines run from each of these voltage rails to the various connectors. That means the 12-V connector on a P4 draws from the same rail as the main 12-V connector feeding power to the motherboard. This works fine as long as the collective needs of the connectors sharing a rail don't exceed its capacity to feed them power. To avoid this, EPS12V divided the 12-V supply into two or three separate 12-V rails, each one providing a separate source of power.

ATX12V 2.0 The ATX12V 2.0 standard incorporated many of the good ideas of EPS12V into the ATX world, starting with the 24-pin connector. This 24-pin motherboard power connector is backward compatible with the older 20-pin connector, so users don't have to buy a new motherboard if they use an ATX12V 2.0 power supply. ATX12V 2.0 requires two 12-V rails for any power supply rated higher than 230 W. ATX12V 2.0 dropped the AUX connector and required SATA hard drive connectors.

In theory, a 20-pin motherboard power supply connector will work on a motherboard with a 24-pin socket, but doing this is risky in that the 20-pin connector may not provide enough power to your system. Try to use the right power supply for your motherboard to avoid problems. Many ATX12V 2.0 power supplies have a convertible 24-to-20-pin converter. These are handy if you want to make a nice "clean" connection, because many 20-pin connectors have capacitors that prevent plugging in a 24-pin connector. You'll also see the occasional 24-pin connector constructed in such a way that you can slide off the extra four pins. Figure 8.22 shows 20-pin and 24-pin connectors; Figure 8.23 shows a convertible connector. Although they look similar, those extra four pins won't replace the P4 connector. They are incompatible!

Many modern ATX motherboards feature an 8-pin CPU power connector like the one found in the EPS12V standard to help support high-end CPUs that demand a lot of power. This connector is referred to by several names, including EPS12V, EATX12V, and ATX12V 2x4. One half of this connector will be pin compatible with the P4 power connector and the other half may be under a protective cap. Be sure to check the motherboard installation manuals for recommendations on if and when you need to use the full 8 pins. For backward compatibility, some power supplies provide an 8-pin power connector that can split into two 4-pin sets, one of which is the P4 connector.

• **Figure 8.22** 20- and 24-pin connectors

• **Figure 8.23** Convertible motherboard power connector

• **Figure 8.24**   PCI Express 6-pin power connector

You'll commonly find niche-market power supplies bundled with computer cases (and often motherboards as well). These form factors are rarely sold alone.

The CompTIA A+ Essentials exam tests you pretty heavily on power supplies. You need to know what power supply works with a particular system or with a particular computing goal in mind.

Another notable connector is the auxiliary PCI Express (PCIe) power connector. Figure 8.24 shows the 6-pin PCIe power connector. Some motherboards add a Molex socket for PCIe, and some cards come with a Molex socket as well. Higher-end cards have a dedicated 6-pin or 8-pin PCIe power connector. The 8-pin PCIe connector should not be confused with the EPS12V connector, as they are not compatible. Some PCIe devices with the 8-pin connector will accept a 6-pin PCIe power connection instead, but this may put limits on their performance. Often you'll find that 8-pin PCIe power cables have two pins at the end that you can detach for easy compatibility with 6-pin devices.

Niche-Market Power Supply Form Factors   The demand for smaller and quieter PCs and, to a lesser extent, the emergence of the BTX form factor have led to the development of a number of niche-market power supply form factors. All use standard ATX connectors but differ in size and shape from standard ATX power supplies.

Here are some of the more common specialty power supply types:

- **TFX12V**   A small power supply form factor optimized for low-profile ATX systems

- **SFX12V**   A small power supply form factor optimized for systems using FlexATX motherboards (Figure 8.25)

- **CFX12V**   An L-shaped power supply optimized for microBTX systems

- **LFX12V**   A small power supply form factor optimized for low-profile BTX systems

Active PFC   Visualize the AC current coming from the power company as water in a pipe, smoothly moving back and forth, 60 times a second. A PC's power supply, simply due to the process of changing this AC current into DC current, is like a person sucking on a straw on the end of this pipe. It takes gulps only when the current is fully pushing or pulling at the top and

• **Figure 8.25**   SFX power supply

bottom of each cycle and creating an electrical phenomena—sort of a back pressure—that's called *harmonics* in the power industry. These harmonics create the humming sound you hear from electrical components. Over time, harmonics damage electrical equipment, causing serious problems with the power supply and other electrical devices on the circuit. Once you put a few thousand PCs with power supplies in the same local area, harmonics can even damage the electrical power supplier's equipment!

Good PC power supplies come with **active power factor correction (active PFC)**, extra circuitry that smoothes out the way the power supply takes power from the power company and eliminates harmonics. Never buy a power supply that does not have active PFC—all power supplies with active PFC proudly show you on the box (Figure 8.26).

• **Figure 8.26**   Power supply advertising active PFC

Tech Tip

Build in Aging

Don't cut the specifications too tightly for power supplies. All power supplies produce less wattage over time, simply because of wear and tear on the internal components. If you build a system that runs with only a few watts of extra power available from the power supply initially, that system will most likely start causing problems within a year or less. Do yourself or your clients a favor and get a power supply that has more wattage than you need.

Wattage Requirements

Every device in a PC requires a certain amount of wattage to function. A typical hard drive draws 15 W of power when accessed, for example, whereas some Athlon 64 X2 CPUs draw a whopping 110 W at peak usage—with average usage around 70 W. The total wattage of all devices combined is the minimum you need the power supply to provide.

If the power supply cannot produce the wattage a system needs, that PC won't work properly. Because most devices in the PC require maximum wattage when first starting, the most common result of insufficient wattage is a paperweight that looks like a PC. This can lead to some embarrassing moments. You might plug in a new hard drive for a client, push the power button on the case, and nothing happens—a dead PC! Eek! There are other ways this problem can manifest itself, however (system lock-ups, random restarts, etc.), so diagnosing an inadequate or dying power supply can be tricky.

You can quickly determine if insufficient wattage is the problem. Unplug the drive and power up the system. If the system boots up, the power supply is a likely suspect. The only fix for this problem is to replace the power supply with one that provides more wattage (or leave the new drive out—a less-than-ideal solution).

No power supply can turn 100 percent of the AC power coming from the power company into DC current, so all power supplies provide less power to the system than the wattage advertised on the box. ATX12V 2.0 standards require a power supply to be at least 70 percent efficient, but you can find power supplies with better than 80 percent efficiency. More efficiency can tell you how many watts the system puts out to the PC in actual use. Plus, the added efficiency means the power supply uses less power, saving you money.

One common argument these days is that people buy power supplies that provide far more wattage than a system needs and therefore waste power. This is untrue. A power supply provides only the amount of power your system needs. If you put a 1000-W power supply (yes, they really exist) into a system that needs only 250 W, that big power supply will put out only 250 W to the system. So buying an efficient, higher-wattage power supply gives you two benefits. First, running a power supply at less than 100 percent load lets it live longer. Second, you'll have plenty of extra power when adding new components.

As a general recommendation for a new system, use at least a 500-W power supply. This is a common wattage and gives you plenty of extra power for booting as well as for whatever other components you might add to the system in the future.

Chapter 8 Review

Chapter Summary

After reading this chapter and completing the exercises, you should understand the following about power supplies.

Explain the basics of electricity

- The power supply takes electricity from the wall outlet and transforms it into the kind of electricity that the motherboard and other internal components use. To remove the power supply, unscrew the four screws in the back of the case and lift it out. Installing it is just as simple. Be careful never to open the power supply itself, as the capacitors inside can store a dangerous electrical charge.

- Techs need to know basic principles of electricity and how to recognize power problems. Electricity is a flow of negatively charged particles or electrons through matter. Metallic wire is a good conductor, allowing electrons to move freely. The pressure of the electrons in the wire is called voltage and is measured in volts (V). Measured in units called amperes (amps or A), current or amperage is the amount of electrons flowing past a certain point on a wire. Wattage (watts or W) refers to the amount of amps and volts a particular device needs. The formula VA = W expresses the correlation among the three. Resistance to the flow of electrons is measured in ohms. Fuses and ground wires set limits for the flow of electrons. A ground wire provides a path of least resistance to allow the electrons to flow to the ground.

- Electricity may be either direct current (DC), with electrons flowing in one direction around a continuous circuit, or alternating current (AC), with electrons flowing back and forth in a circuit.

Describe the details about powering the PC

- Because power companies supply high-voltage AC, the computer's power supply converts AC to low-voltage DC that is then portioned out to the internal devices. Heat is a byproduct of electricity and must be controlled in the computer.

- The power supply connects to the electrical outlet via a standard IEC-320 connector. Although power in the United States ranges from 110 to 120 V,

the rest of the world uses 200 to 240 VAC. Most power supplies can switch between 110 and 220 V. The IEC-320 plug has three holes, called hot, neutral, and ground. The hot carries electrical voltage and should output approximately 115 V in the United States. The neutral returns electricity to the breaker panel and should have 0 V output. The ground wire returns excess electricity to the ground and should also have a 0 V output. You can use a multimeter to test voltages at the outlet.

- A multimeter, also called a volt-ohm meter (VOM), uses two probes to provide at least four measurements: AC voltage (V~), DC voltage (V with a solid line above a dashed line), continuity (whether electrons flow from one end of a wire to the other end), and resistance (whether a fuse is good or blown or whether a wire has breaks). Some AC-only testing devices are available that simply plug into the AC outlet and may display results via three light-emitting diodes (LEDs).

- A surge suppressor is an inexpensive device that protects your computer from voltage spikes. Inserted between the wall outlet and the power supply, a surge suppressor has a joule rating that measures how much electrical energy it can suppress. Be sure your surge suppressor has at least an 800 joules rating. Because telephone lines and cable connections also produce spikes, your surge suppressor should include connections for a modem, DSL, or cable modem. Make sure you purchase a surge suppressor that has the UL 1449 for 330-V rating, as this will ensure substantial protection for your system. Because surge suppressors work for only a limited time, you should check the manufacturer's recommended replacement schedules. If your surge suppressor comes with a cash guarantee, be aware that manufacturers honor it only if you follow their guidelines.

- Because the AC supply lacks consistency and actually provides power with sags and spikes, it is important that you use two devices with the computer: an uninterruptible power supply and a surge suppressor. An uninterruptible power supply (UPS) continues to supply AC power to your computer during both brownouts and blackouts via a battery that is charged from the AC current. All UPSs measure the amount of power or watts they supply, as well as listing the number of minutes the UPS will last with a certain voltage. You should cut the number of minutes in half for a truer estimate of the abilities of the UPS. The power supply converts AC into several DC voltages (5.0, 12.0, and 3.3 V). Devices such as hard drives and CD-ROM drives require 12.0 V and onboard electronics use 3.3- and 5.0-V currents.

- The power supply has several standard connectors for the motherboard and interior devices. Today's motherboards have a P1 socket that uses the P1 connector from the power supply. A standard ATX power supply has a 20-pin P1 connector, while the newer ATX12V 2.0 power supplies come with a 24-pin P1 connector. Some motherboards also need a 4-, 6-, or 8-pin connector to provide an additional 12 V of power.

- Peripherals use two or possibly three different kinds of connectors: the larger Molex connector, the smaller mini connector, and the SATA connector. Used with hard drives and CD- and DVD-media drives, the Molex has chamfers to ensure that it is connected properly. Used today only for floppy drives, the mini connector can easily be inserted incorrectly, thus destroying the floppy drive. The SATA connector is used for SATA hard drives. If you do not have enough connectors for all of the devices inside your PC, you can create more connections with a splitter. Similarly, if your power supply does not have the connector a device needs, you can purchase adapters to convert one type to another.

- The ATX power supply includes full support for power-saving functions, with the modem or network interface card able to wake up the PC when there is incoming traffic. Using the soft power feature, the ATX power supply puts a 5-V charge on the motherboard as long as there is AC from the wall socket. You can configure the ATX soft power through the Power Management section of the CMOS setup. Always unplug an ATX system before you work on it. ATX power supplies use a single P1 connector for motherboard power.

- The ATX standard has undergone several updates. ATX12V 1.3 introduced additional 4-pin (P4) and 6-pin auxiliary (AUX) connectors. ATX12V 2.0 introduced the 24-pin connector (inspired by EPS12V), dropped the AUX connector, and required SATA connectors. Additionally, ATX12V 2.0 required two 12-V rails for any power supply larger than 230 W.

- The non-ATX standard EPS12V introduced a 24-pin motherboard connector and a unique 8-pin connector. It was not swappable with ATX power supplies, and while its popularity was short-lived, it introduced several features that became part of the ATX12V standard, including rails.

- The demand for smaller and quieter PCs and the introduction of the BTX motherboard form factors led to the development of niche-market power supply form factors. TFX12V, SFX12V, CFX12V, and LFX12V have the same connectors as standard ATX power supplies but differ in size or shape.

- Active power factor correction (active PFC) helps to eliminate harmonics, which can damage electrical components. Never buy a power supply that does not have active PFC.

- Power supplies are rated in watts. If you know the amount of wattage that every device in the PC needs, you can arrive at the total wattage required for all devices, and that is the minimum wattage your power supply should provide. If the power supply does not provide sufficient wattage, the computer will not work. For a new computer system, you should select at least a 500-W power supply to have extra power for adding components in the future.

- Because converting from AC to DC may result in a significant loss of wattage, purchase a power supply that offers a high percentage of efficiency. The ATX12V 2.0 standard requires a power supply to be at least 70 percent efficient, but you can find power supplies with better then 80 percent efficiency. Be aware that power supplies produce less wattage over time, so don't cut the wattage specification too tightly. While power supplies range from 200 to 600 W, you should know that the more AC the power supply draws, the more heat it produces.

Key Terms

active power factor correction (active PFC) *(273)*
alternating current (AC) *(260)*
amperes (amps or A) *(259)*
direct current (DC) *(260)*
field replaceable unit (FRU) *(259)*
IEC-320 *(261)*
joule *(263)*
mini connector *(267)*
Molex connector *(267)*
multimeter *(262)*
ohms (Ω) *(260)*

P1 power connector *(267)*
power conditioning *(264)*
power supply unit (PSU) *(259)*
rails *(271)*
resistance *(260)*
SATA power connector *(268)*
soft power *(269)*
surge suppressor *(263)*
uninterruptible power supply (UPS) *(265)*
volts (V) *(259)*
wattage (watts or W) *(259)*

Key Term Quiz

Use the Key Terms list to complete the sentences that follow. Not all terms will be used.

1. Supply power to the floppy drive by using the _____ from the power supply.

2. The electric company provides _____ power that the power supply converts to _____ for use by the computer components.

3. The ATX form factor power supply attaches to the motherboard with a(n) _____ and supplies 5 V to the motherboard at all times.

4. Be sure your surge suppressor has a(n) _____ rating of at least 800.

5. The measurement unit for the amount of electrons flowing past a certain point on a wire is _____.

6. Be sure the _____ rating for your power supply is greater than the minimum required by all devices in the computer.

7. The ability to split voltage supplies into separate _____ ensures that no device will hog all of the available power.

8. A spare part that a tech typically carries to replace a failed component in the field is called a(n) _____.

Multiple-Choice Quiz

1. Which of the following ATX12V features was introduced as part of the EPS12V standard?

   A. The P4 motherboard power connector

   B. Voltage rails

   C. The 6-pin AUX connector

   D. Soft power

2. When you test voltage with a multimeter, you can assume the outlet or connector is functioning properly if the reading is within a certain percentage of the expected number. What is that maximum percentage by which the reading can vary?

   A. 5 percent

   B. 10 percent

   C. 20 percent

   D. 25 percent

3. What voltage does an ATX12V P4 connector provide for motherboards?

   A. 3.3 V

   B. 3.3 V, 5 V

   C. 5 V

   D. 12 V

4. When testing an AC outlet, what voltage should the multimeter show between the neutral and ground wires?

   A. 120 V

   B. 60 V

   C. 0 V

   D. –120 V

5. What sort of power connector does a hard drive typically use?

   A. Molex

   B. Mini

   C. Sub-mini

   D. Micro

6. Arthur installed a new motherboard in his case and connected the ATX power, but his system would not turn on. He sees an extra 4-wire port on the motherboard. What's he missing?

   A. He needs a power supply with a P2 connector for plugging in auxiliary components.

   B. He needs a power supply with a P3 connector for plugging in case fans.

   C. He needs a power supply with a P4 connector for plugging into Pentium IV and some Athlon XP motherboards.

   D. He needs a power supply with an Aux connector for plugging into a secondary power supply.

7. Where do you put the multimeter leads when you test a Molex connector?

   A. The red lead should always touch the red wire; the black lead should touch a black ground wire.

   B. The red lead should always touch the black ground wire; the black lead should always touch the red hot wire.

   C. The red lead should always touch the yellow hot wire; the black lead should touch the red hot wire.

   D. The red lead should touch either the red or yellow hot wire; the black lead should touch a black ground wire.

8. What is the minimum PSU required for an ATX system that requires Molex, mini, and SATA connectors?

   A. ATX

   B. ATX12V 1.3

   C. ATX12V 2.0

   D. EPS12V

9. Which of the following is not a PSU form factor?

   A. TFX12V

   B. SFX12V

   C. CFX12V

   D. LPX12V

■ Essay Quiz

1. Jack and Denise have joined your study group. Because neither has any previous experience with basic electricity and its jargon, they want you to explain voltage, amperage, and wattage. In plain language, define these terms and explain what VA = W means.

2. In the computer field, advances in one area often lead to advances in another area. Do you think improvements in the CPU and other computer devices and functions made the ATX form factor power supply necessary?

Lab Projects

• Lab Project 8.1

This chapter recommends a 500-W power supply for a new computer. Is that the wattage that manufacturers usually offer with their computers? Check the following Web sites to see what wattage comes with a new PC:

■ www.dell.com

■ www.gateway.com

■ www.hp.com

Do any of these companies mention a power supply upgrade with a higher wattage rating? If so, what are the wattages and what are the additional costs?

• Lab Project 8.2

Every technician needs a multimeter. Visit a local electronics store and look at its line of multimeters. (If a store is not nearby, you may use the Internet instead.) What features do the various multimeters offer? What kinds of measurements do they provide? Is the output from some in digital format and others in analog? Which output do you find easier to read?

Is one kind more accurate than another? What price ranges are available for multimeters? Then, select the multimeter you would like to add to your toolkit. Why did you choose that model? Now start saving your pennies so you can buy it!

Hard Drive Technologies

"Any sufficiently advanced technology is indistinguishable from magic."

—ARTHUR C. CLARKE

In this chapter, you will learn how to

- **Explain how hard drives work**
- **Identify and explain the PATA and SATA hard drive interfaces**
- **Identify and explain the SCSI hard drive interfaces**
- **Describe how to protect data with RAID**

Of all the hardware on a PC, none gets more attention—or gives more anguish—than the hard drive. There's a good reason for this: if the hard drive breaks, you lose data. As you probably know, when the data goes, you have to redo work or restore from backup—or worse. It's good to worry about the data, because the data runs the office, maintains the payrolls, and stores the e-mail. This level of concern is so strong that even the most neophyte PC users are exposed to terms such as *IDE, PATA, SATA,* and *controller*—even if they don't put the terms into practice.

This chapter focuses on how hard drives work, beginning with the internal layout and organization of hard drives. You'll look at the different types of hard drives used today (PATA, SATA, SSD, and SCSI) and how they interface with the PC. The chapter also covers how more than one drive may work with other drives to provide data safety and improve speed through a feature called RAID. Let's get started.

How Hard Drives Work

Hard drives sport one of two technologies today. The most common type has moving parts; the newer and more expensive technology has none. Let's look at both.

Platter-Based Hard Drives

A traditional **hard disk drive (HDD)** is composed of individual disks, or *platters*, with read/write heads on actuator arms controlled by a servo motor—all contained in a sealed case that prevents contamination by outside air (Figure 9.1).

The aluminum platters are coated with a magnetic medium. Two tiny read/write heads service each platter, one to read the top and the other to read the bottom of the platter (Figure 9.2).

The coating on the platters is phenomenally smooth. It has to be, as the read/write heads actually float on a cushion of air above the platters, which spin at speeds between 3500 and 10,000 rpm. The distance (flying height) between the heads and the disk surface is less than the thickness of a fingerprint. The closer the read/write heads are to the platter, the more densely the data packs onto the drive. These infinitesimal tolerances demand that the platters never be exposed to outside air. Even a tiny dust particle on a platter would act like a mountain in the way of the read/write heads and would cause catastrophic damage to the drive. To keep the air clean inside the drive, all hard drives use a tiny, heavily filtered aperture to keep the air pressure equalized between the interior and the exterior of the drive.

● **Figure 9.1** Inside the hard drive

Data Encoding

Although the hard drive stores data in binary form, visualizing a magnetized spot representing a one and a non-magnetized spot representing a zero grossly oversimplifies the process. Hard drives store data in tiny magnetic fields—think of them as tiny magnets that can be placed in either direction on the platter. Each tiny magnetic field, called a *flux*, can switch north/ south polarity back and forth through a process called *flux reversal*. When a read/write head goes over an area where a flux reversal has occurred, the head reads a small electrical current.

Today's hard drives use a complex and efficient method to interpret flux reversals. Instead of reading individual flux reversals, a modern hard drive reads groups of them called *runs*.

● **Figure 9.2** Read/write heads on actuator arms

Starting around 1991, hard drives began using a data encoding system known as *run length limited* (*RLL*). With RLL, any combination of ones and zeros can be stored in a preset combination of about 15 different runs. The hard drive looks for these runs and reads them as a group, resulting in much faster and much more densely packed data.

Current drives use an extremely advanced method of RLL called **Partial Response Maximum Likelihood (PRML)** encoding. As hard drives pack more and more fluxes on the drive, the individual fluxes start to interact with each other, making it more and more difficult for the drive to verify where one flux stops and another starts. PRML uses powerful, intelligent circuitry to analyze each flux reversal and to make a "best guess" as to what type of flux reversal it just read. As a result, the maximum run length for PRML drives reaches up to 16 to 20 fluxes, far more than the 7 or so on RLL drives. Longer run lengths enable the hard drive to use more complicated run combinations so the hard drive can store a phenomenal amount of data. For example, a run of only 12 fluxes on a hard drive might equal a string of 30 or 40 ones and zeros when handed to the system from the hard drive.

The size required by each magnetic flux on a hard drive has reduced considerably over the years, resulting in higher capacities. As fluxes become smaller, they begin to interfere with each other in weird ways. I have to say *weird* because to make sense of what's going on at this subatomic level (I told you these fluxes were small!) would require you to take a semester of quantum mechanics. Let's just say that laying fluxes flat against the platter has reached its limit. To get around this problem, hard drive makers recently began to make hard drives that store their fluxes vertically (up and down) rather than longitudinally (forward and backward), enabling them to make hard drives in the 1 terabyte (1024 gigabyte) range. Manufacturers call this vertical storage method *perpendicular recording*.

For all this discussion and detail on data encoding, the day-to-day PC technician never deals with encoding. Sometimes, however, knowing what you don't need to know helps as much as knowing what you do need to know. Fortunately, data encoding is inherent to the hard drive and completely invisible to the system. You're never going to have to deal with data encoding, but you'll sure sound smart when talking to other PC techs if you know your RLL from your PRML!

Moving the Arms

The read/write heads move across the platter on the ends of *actuator arms* or **head actuators**. In the entire history of hard drives, manufacturers have used only two technologies to move the arms: **stepper motor** and **voice coil**. Hard drives first used stepper motor technology, but today they've all moved to voice coil.

Stepper motor technology moved the arm in fixed increments or steps, but the technology had several limitations that doomed it. Because the interface between motor and actuator arm required minimal slippage to ensure precise and reproducible movements, the positioning of the arms became less precise over time. This physical deterioration caused data transfer errors. Additionally, heat deformation wreaked havoc with stepper motor drives. Just as valve clearances in automobile engines change with operating temperature, the positioning accuracy changed as the PC operated and various hard drive components got warmer. Although very small, these

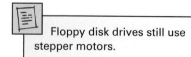
Floppy disk drives still use stepper motors.

changes caused problems. Accessing the data written on a cold hard drive, for example, became difficult after the disk warmed. In addition, the read/write heads could damage the disk surface if not parked (set in a non-data area) when not in use, requiring techs to use special parking programs before transporting a stepper motor drive.

All magnetic hard drives made today employ a linear motor to move the actuator arms. The linear motor, more popularly called a voice coil motor, uses a permanent magnet surrounding a coil on the actuator arm. When an electrical current passes, the coil generates a magnetic field that moves the actuator arm. The direction of the actuator arm's movement depends on the polarity of the electrical current through the coil. Because the voice coil and the actuator arm never touch, no degradation in positional accuracy takes place over time. Voice coil drives automatically park the heads when the drive loses power, making the old stepper motor park programs obsolete.

Lacking the discrete steps of the stepper motor drive, a voice coil drive cannot accurately predict the movement of the heads across the disk. To make sure voice coil drives land exactly in the correct area, the drive reserves one side of one platter for navigational purposes. This area essentially maps the exact location of the data on the drive. The voice coil moves the read/write head to its best guess about the correct position on the hard drive. The read/write head then uses this map to fine-tune its true position and make any necessary adjustments.

Now that you have a basic understanding of how a drive physically stores data, let's turn to how the hard drive organizes that data so we can use that drive.

Geometry

Have you ever seen a cassette tape? If you look at the actual brown Mylar (a type of plastic) tape, nothing will tell you whether sound is recorded on that tape. Assuming the tape is not blank, however, you know *something* is on the tape. Cassettes store music in distinct magnetized lines. You could say that the physical placement of those lines of magnetism is the tape's "geometry."

Geometry also determines where a hard drive stores data. As with a cassette tape, if you opened up a hard drive, you would not see the geometry. But rest assured that the drive has geometry; in fact, every model of hard drive uses a different geometry. We describe the geometry for a particular hard drive with a set of numbers representing three values: heads, cylinders, and sectors per track.

Heads   The number of **heads** for a specific hard drive describes, rather logically, the number of read/write heads used by the drive to store data. Every platter requires two heads. If a hard drive has four platters, for example, it needs eight heads (Figure 9.3).

Based on this description of heads, you would think that hard drives would always have an even number of heads, right? Wrong! Most hard drives reserve a head or two for their own use. Therefore, a hard drive can have either an even or an odd number of heads.

Cylinders   To visualize cylinders, imagine taking an empty soup can and opening both ends. Look at the shape of the can; it is a geometric shape called a cylinder. Now imagine taking that cylinder and sharpening one end

Tech Tip

Fluid Bearings

Currently, almost all hard drives (except solid state) use a motor located in the center spindle supporting the drive platters. Traditionally, tiny ball bearings support the spindle motor, and as disk technology has advanced, these ball bearings have become the limiting factor in the three critical design criteria for hard drives: rotational speed, storage capacity, and noise levels. The higher the rotational speed of a drive, the more the metal-on-metal contact creates heat and lubricant problems that impact the lifespan of the bearings. However precisely machined, ball bearings are not perfectly round. Runout, the measurement of how much the ball bearings wobble (and thus how much the drive platters wobble), is now the limiting factor on how densely you can pack information together on a disk drive.

The technological fix for this comes in the form of fluid bearings. *A fluid bearing is basically a small amount of lubricant trapped in a carefully machined housing. The use of fluid in place of metal balls means that no contact occurs between metal surfaces to generate heat and wear. The fluid also creates no mechanical vibration, so fluid bearings can support higher rotational speeds. The runout of a fluid bearing is about one-tenth that of the best ball bearing, significantly increasing potential information density. The absence of a mechanical connection between moving parts also dramatically reduces noise levels, and the fluid itself acts to dampen the sound further. Finally, liquid bearings provide better shock resistance than ball bearings.*

Four platters = eight heads

• **Figure 9.3** Two heads per platter

SOUP

All tracks of the same diameter are called a cylinder.

Track

• **Figure 9.4** Cylinder

so that it easily cuts through the hardest metal. Visualize placing the ex-soup can over the hard drive and pushing it down through the drive. The can cuts into one side and out the other of each platter. Each circle transcribed by the can is where you store data on the drive, and is called a **track.**

Each side of each platter contains tens of thousands of tracks. Interestingly enough, the individual tracks themselves are not directly part of the drive geometry. Our interest lies only in the groups of tracks of the same diameter, going all of the way through the drive. Each group of tracks of the same diameter is called a **cylinder** (Figure 9.4). There's more than one cylinder. Go get yourself about a thousand more cans, each one a different diameter, and push them through the hard drive.

Sectors per Track Now imagine cutting the hard drive like a birthday cake, slicing all of the tracks into tens of thousands of small slivers. Each sliver then has many thousands of small pieces of track. The term **sector** refers to a specific piece of track on a sliver, and each sector stores 512 bytes of data.

The sector is the universal atom of all hard drives. You can't divide data into anything smaller than a sector. Although sectors are important, the number of sectors is not a geometry value that describes a hard drive. The geometry value is called **sectors per track (sectors/track)**. The sectors/track value describes the number of sectors in each track (Figure 9.5).

The Big Three Cylinders, heads, and sectors/track combine to define the hard drive's geometry. In most cases, these three critical values are referred to as *CHS*. The three values are important because the PC's BIOS needs to know the drive's geometry to know how to talk to the drive. Back in the old days, a technician needed to enter these values into the CMOS setup program manually. Today, every hard drive stores the CHS information in the drive itself, in an electronic format that enables the BIOS to query the drive automatically to determine these values.

Two other values—write precompensation cylinder and landing zone—no longer have relevance in today's PCs; however, people still toss around these terms and a few CMOS setup utilities still support them—another classic example of a technology appendix. Let's look at these two holdouts from another era so when you access CMOS, you won't say, "What the heck are these?"

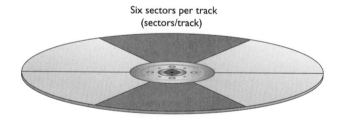
Six sectors per track (sectors/track)

• **Figure 9.5** Sectors per track

Write Precompensation Cylinder   Older hard drives had a real problem with the fact that sectors toward the inside of the drives were much smaller than sectors toward the outside. To handle this, an older drive would spread data a little farther apart once it got to a particular cylinder. This cylinder was called the write precompensation (write precomp) cylinder, and the PC had to know which cylinder began this wider data spacing. Hard drives no longer have this problem, making the write precomp setting obsolete.

Landing Zone   On older hard drives with stepper motors, the landing zone value designated an unused cylinder as a "parking place" for the read/write heads. As mentioned earlier, before moving old stepper motor hard drives, the read/write heads needed to be parked to avoid accidental damage. Today's voice coil drives park themselves whenever they're not accessing data, automatically placing the read/write heads on the landing zone. As a result, the BIOS no longer needs the landing zone geometry.

The A+ Essentials exam expects you to know how to completely remove data from a hard drive. If you simply format the drive, the information on it can still be recovered. However, if you physically destroy the platters or run a powerful magnet over the drive, the data is deleted forever. You would want to do this when disposing of or recycling an old hard drive.

Solid-State Drives

Booting up a computer takes time in part because of the time it takes for a traditional hard drive to spin up and for the read/write heads to retrieve the data off the drive to load the operating system and drivers into RAM. All of the moving metal parts of a platter-based drive use a lot of power, create a lot of heat, take up space, wear down over time, and take a lot of nanoseconds to get things done. A **solid-state drive (SSD)** addresses all of these issues nicely.

In technical terms, solid-state technology and devices are based on the combination of semiconductors, transistors, and bubble memory used to create electrical components with no moving parts. That's a mouthful! Here's the translation.

In simple terms, SSDs (Figure 9.6) use memory chips to store data instead of all those pesky metal spinning parts used in platter-based hard drives. Solid-state technology has been around for many moons. It was originally developed to transition vacuum tube–based technologies to semiconductor technologies, such as the move from cathode ray tubes (CRTs) to liquid crystal displays (LCDs) in monitors. (You'll get the scoop on monitor technologies in Chapter 13, "Learning Video and Multimedia.")

Solid-state devices use current flow and negative/positive electron charges to achieve their magic. Although Mr. Spock may find the physics of how this technology actually works "fascinating," it's more important for you to know the following points regarding solid-state drives, devices, and technology:

- Solid-state technology is commonly used in desktop and laptop hard drives, memory cards, cameras, USB thumb drives, and other handheld devices.

- SSD form factors are typically 1.8-inch, 2.5-inch, or 3.5-inch.

- SSDs can be PATA, SATA, eSATA, SCSI, or USB for desktop systems. Some portable computers have mini-PCI Express versions.

• **Figure 9.6**   A solid-state drive (*photo courtesy of Corsair*)

With solid-state drives coming into more regular use, you see the initials *HDD* used more frequently than in previous years to refer to the traditional, platter-based hard drives. Thus we have two drive technologies: SSDs and HDDs.

- SSDs that use SDRAM cache are volatile and lose data when powered off. Others that use nonvolatile flash memory such as NAND retain data when power is turned off or disconnected. (See Chapter 10, "Removable Media," for the scoop on flash memory technology.)

- SSDs are more expensive than traditional HDDs. Less expensive SSDs typically implement less reliable multi-level cell (MLC) memory technology in place of the more efficient single-level cell (SLC) technology to cut costs.

Tech Tip

IDE

The term IDE (Integrated Drive Electronics) refers to any hard drive with a built-in controller. All hard drives are technically IDE drives, although we only use the term IDE when discussing ATA drives.

Tech Tip

External Hard Drives

A quick trip to any major computer store will reveal a thriving trade in external hard drives. You used to be able to find external drives that connected to the slow parallel port, but external drives today connect to a FireWire, Hi-Speed USB 2.0, or eSATA port. All three interfaces offer high data transfer rates and hot-swap capability, making them ideal for transporting huge files such as digital video clips. Regardless of the external interface, however, inside the casing you'll find an ordinary PATA or SATA drive, just like those described in this chapter.

The ANSI subcommittee directly responsible for the ATA standard is called Technical Committee T13. If you want to know what's happening with ATA, check out the T13 Web site: www.t13.org.

Parallel and Serial ATA

Over the years, many interfaces existed for hard drives, with such names as ST-506 and ESDI. Don't worry about what these abbreviations stood for; neither the CompTIA A+ Essentials exam nor the computer world at large has an interest in these prehistoric interfaces. Starting around 1990, an interface called **Advanced Technology Attachment (ATA)** appeared that now virtually monopolizes the hard drive market. ATA hard drives are often referred to as **Integrated Drive Electronics (IDE)** drives. Only one other type of interface, the moderately popular small computer system interface (SCSI), has any relevance for hard drives.

ATA drives come in two basic flavors. The older **parallel ATA (PATA)** drives send data in parallel, on a 40- or 80-wire data cable. PATA drives dominated the industry for more than a decade but have been mostly replaced by **serial ATA (SATA)** drives that send data in serial, using only one wire for data transfers. The leap from PATA to SATA is only one of a large number of changes that have taken place with ATA. To appreciate these changes, we'll run through the many ATA standards forwarded over the years.

ATA-I

When IBM unveiled the 80286-powered IBM PC AT in the early 1980s, it introduced the first PC to include BIOS support for hard drives. This BIOS supported up to two physical drives, and each drive could be up to 504 MB—far larger than the 5-MB and 10-MB drives of the time. Although having built-in support for hard drives certainly improved the power of the PC, installing, configuring, and troubleshooting hard drives could at best be called difficult at that time.

To address these problems, Western Digital and Compaq developed a new hard drive interface and placed this specification before the *American National Standards Institute (ANSI)* committees, which in turn put out the AT Attachment (ATA) interface in March of 1989. The ATA interface specified a cable and a built-in controller on the drive itself. Most importantly, the ATA standard used the existing AT BIOS on a PC, which meant that you didn't have to replace the old system BIOS to make the drive work—a very important consideration for compatibility but one that would later haunt ATA drives. The official name for the standard, ATA, never made it into the common vernacular until recently, and then only as PATA to distinguish it from SATA drives.

Early ATA Physical Connections

The first ATA drives connected to the computer with a **40-pin ribbon cable** that plugged into the drive and into a hard drive controller. The cable has a colored stripe down one side that denotes pin 1 and should connect to the drive's pin 1 and to the controller's pin 1. Figure 9.7 shows the business end of an early ATA drive, with the connectors for the ribbon cable and the power cable.

The controller is the support circuitry that acts as the intermediary between the hard drive and the external data bus. Electronically, the setup looks like Figure 9.8.

Wait a minute! If ATA drives are IDE (see the earlier "IDE" Tech Tip), they already have a built-in controller. Why do they then have to plug into a *controller* on the motherboard? Well, this is a great example of a term that's not used properly, but everyone (including the motherboard and hard drive makers) uses it this way. What we call the ATA controller is really no more than an interface providing a connection to the rest of the PC system. When your BIOS talks to the hard drive, it actually talks to the onboard circuitry on the drive, not the connection on the motherboard. But, even though the *real* controller resides on the hard drive, the 40-pin connection on the motherboard is called the controller. We have a lot of misnomers to live with in the ATA world.

The ATA-1 standard defined that no more than two drives attach to a single IDE connector on a single ribbon cable. Because up to two drives can attach to one connector via a single cable, you need to be able to identify each drive on the cable. The ATA standard identifies the two drives as "master" and "slave." You set one drive as master and one as slave by using tiny jumpers on the drives (Figure 9.9).

The controllers are on the motherboard and manifest themselves as two 40-pin male ports, as shown in Figure 9.10.

PIO and DMA Modes

If you're making a hard drive standard, you must define both the method and the speed at which the data's going to move.

• **Figure 9.7**   Back of IDE drive showing 40-pin connector (left), jumpers (center), and power connector (right)

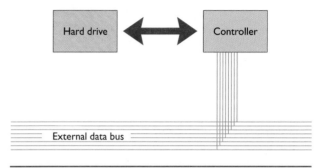

• **Figure 9.8**   Relation of drive, controller, and bus

• **Figure 9.9**   A typical hard drive with directions (top) for setting a jumper (bottom)

• **Figure 9.10**   IDE interfaces on a motherboard

ATA-1 defined two methods, the first using programmed I/O (PIO) addressing and the second using direct memory access (DMA) mode.

PIO is nothing more than the traditional I/O addressing scheme, where the CPU talks directly to the hard drive via the BIOS to send and receive data. Three different PIO speeds called **PIO modes** were initially adopted:

- PIO mode 0: 3.3 MBps (megabytes per second)
- PIO mode 1: 5.2 MBps
- PIO mode 2: 8.3 MBps

DMA modes defined a method to enable the hard drives to talk to RAM directly, using old-style DMA commands. (The ATA folks called this *single-word DMA*.) This old-style DMA was slow, and the resulting three ATA single-word DMA modes were also slow:

- Single-word DMA mode 0: 2.1 MBps
- Single-word DMA mode 1: 4.2 MBps
- Single-word DMA mode 2: 8.3 MBps

When a computer booted up, the BIOS queried the hard drive to see what modes it could use and then automatically adjusted to the fastest mode.

ATA-2

In 1990, the industry adopted a series of improvements to the ATA standard called ATA-2. Many people called these new features **Enhanced IDE (EIDE)**. EIDE was really no more than a marketing term invented by Western Digital, but it caught on in common vernacular and is still used today, although its use is fading. Regular IDE drives quickly disappeared, and by 1995, EIDE drives dominated the PC world. Figure 9.11 shows a typical EIDE drive.

ATA-2 was the most important ATA standard, as it included powerful new features such as higher capacities, support for non–hard drive storage devices, support for two more ATA devices for a maximum of four, and substantially improved throughput.

• **Figure 9.11** EIDE drive

 The terms *ATA*, *IDE*, and *EIDE* are used interchangeably.

Hard drive makers talk about hard drive capacities in millions and billions of bytes, not megabytes and gigabytes.

Higher Capacity with LBA

IBM created the AT BIOS to support hard drives many years before IDE drives were invented, and every system had that BIOS. The developers of IDE made certain that the new drives would run from the same AT BIOS command set. With this capability, you could use the same CMOS and BIOS routines to talk to a much more advanced drive. Your motherboard or hard drive controller wouldn't become instantly obsolete when you installed a new hard drive.

Unfortunately, the BIOS routines for the original AT command set allowed a hard drive size of only up to 528 million bytes (or 504 MB—remember that a mega = 1,048,576, not 1,000,000). A drive could have no more than 1024 cylinders, 16 heads, and 63 sectors/track:

1024 cylinders × 16 heads × 63 sectors/track × 512 bytes/sector = 504 MB

For years, this was not a problem. But when hard drives began to approach the 504 MB barrier, it became clear that there needed to be a way of getting past 504 MB. The ATA-2 standard defined a way to get past this limit with **logical block addressing (LBA)**. With LBA, the hard drive lies to the computer about its geometry through an advanced type of sector translation. Let's take a moment to understand sector translation, and then come back to LBA.

Sector Translation Long before hard drives approached the 504 MB limit, the limits of 1024 cylinders, 16 heads, and 63 sectors/track gave hard drive makers fits. The big problem was the heads. Remember that every two heads means another platter, another physical disk that you have to squeeze into a hard drive. If you wanted a hard drive with the maximum number of 16 heads, you would need a hard drive with eight physical platters inside the drive. Nobody wanted that many platters: it made the drives too tall, it took more power to spin up the drive, and that many parts cost too much money (Figure 9.12).

Manufacturers could readily produce a hard drive that had fewer heads and more cylinders, but the stupid 1024/16/63 limit got in the way. Plus, the traditional sector arrangement wasted a lot of useful space. Sectors toward the inside of the drive, for example, are much shorter than the sectors on the outside. The sectors on the outside don't need to be that long, but with the traditional geometry setup, hard drive makers had no choice. They could make a hard drive store a lot more information, however, if they could make hard drives with more sectors/track on the outside tracks (Figure 9.13).

The ATA specification was designed to have two geometries. The *physical geometry* defined the real layout of the CHS inside the drive. The *logical geometry* described what the drive told the CMOS. In other words, the IDE drive "lied" to the CMOS, thus side-stepping the artificial limits of the BIOS. When data was being transferred to and from the drive, the onboard circuitry of the drive translated the logical geometry into the physical geometry. This function was, and still is, called **sector translation**.

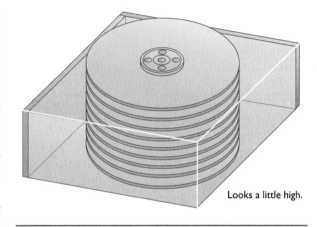

Looks a little high.

● **Figure 9.12** Too many heads

16 sectors/track

8 sectors/track

● **Figure 9.13** Multiple sectors/track

Let's look at a couple of hypothetical examples in action. First, pretend that Seagate came out with a new, cheap, fast hard drive called the ST108. To get the ST108 drive fast and cheap, however, Seagate had to use a rather strange geometry, shown in Table 9.1.

Table 9.1	Seagate's ST108 Drive Geometry		
ST108 Physical		**BIOS Limits**	
Cylinders	2048	Cylinders	1024
Heads	2	Heads	16
Sectors/track	52	Sectors/track	63
Total capacity	108 MB		

Table 9.2	Physical and Logical Geometries of the ST108 Drive		
Physical		**Logical**	
Cylinders	2048	Cylinders	512
Heads	2	Heads	8
Sectors/track	52	Sectors/track	52
Total capacity	108 MB	Total capacity	108 MB

Notice that the cylinder number is greater than 1024. To overcome this problem, the IDE drive performs a sector translation that reports a geometry to the BIOS that is totally different from the true geometry of the drive. Table 9.2 shows the actual geometry and the "logical" geometry of our mythical ST108 drive. Notice that the logical geometry is now within the acceptable parameters of the BIOS limitations. Sector translation never changes the capacity of the drive; it changes only the geometry to stay within the BIOS limits.

Back to LBA Now let's watch how the advanced sector translation of LBA provides support for hard drives greater than 504 MB. Let's use an old drive, the Western Digital WD2160, a 2.1-GB hard drive, as an example. This drive is no longer in production but its smaller CHS values make understanding LBA easier. Table 9.3 lists its physical and logical geometries.

Table 9.3	Western Digital WD2160's Physical and Logical Geometries		
Physical		**Logical**	
Cylinders	16,384	Cylinders	1024
Heads	4	Heads	64
Sectors/track	63	Sectors/track	63
Total capacity	2.1 GB	Total capacity	2.1 GB

Note that, even with sector translation, the number of heads is greater than the allowed 16. So here's where the magic of LBA comes in. The WD2160 is capable of LBA. Now assuming that the BIOS is also capable of LBA, here's what happens. When the computer boots up, the BIOS asks the drives if they can perform LBA. If they say yes, the BIOS and the drive work together to change the way they talk to each other. They can do this without conflicting with the original AT BIOS commands by taking advantage of unused commands to use up to 256 heads. LBA enables support for a maximum of $1024 \times 256 \times 63 \times 512$ bytes = 8.4-GB hard drives. Back in 1990, 8.4 GB was hundreds of time larger than the drives used at the time. Don't worry, later ATA standards will get the BIOS up to today's huge drives.

Not Just Hard Drives Anymore: ATAPI

ATA-2 added an extension to the ATA specification, called **Advanced Technology Attachment Packet Interface (ATAPI)**, that enabled non–hard drive devices such as CD-ROM drives and tape backups to connect to the PC via the ATA controllers. ATAPI drives have the same 40-pin interface and master/slave jumpers as ATA hard drives. Figure 9.14 shows an ATAPI CD-RW drive attached to a motherboard. The key difference between hard drives and every other type of drive that attaches to the ATA controller is in how the drives get BIOS support. Hard drives get it through the system BIOS, whereas non–hard drives require the operating system to load a software driver.

With the introduction of ATAPI, the ATA standards are often referred to as ATA/ATAPI instead of just ATA.

More Drives with ATA-2

ATA-2 added support for a second controller, raising the total number of supported drives from two to four. Each of the two controllers is equal in power and capability. Figure 9.15 is a close-up of a typical motherboard, showing the primary controller marked as *IDE1* and the secondary marked as *IDE2*.

Increased Speed

ATA-2 defined two new PIO modes and a new type of DMA called *multi-word DMA* that was a substantial improvement over the old DMA. Technically, multi-word DMA was still the old-style DMA, but it worked in a much more efficient manner so it was much faster.

- PIO mode 3: 11.1 MBps
- PIO mode 4: 16.6 MBps
- Multi-word DMA mode 0: 4.2 MBps
- Multi-word DMA mode 1: 13.3 MBps
- Multi-word DMA mode 2: 16.6 MBps

ATA-3

ATA-3 came on quickly after ATA-2 and added one new feature called **Self-Monitoring, Analysis, and Reporting Technology (S.M.A.R.T.)**, one of the few PC acronyms that requires the use of periods after each letter). S.M.A.R.T. helps predict when a hard drive is going to fail by monitoring the hard drive's mechanical components.

S.M.A.R.T. is a great idea and is popular in specialized server systems, but it's complex, imperfect, and hard to understand. As a result, only a few utilities can read the S.M.A.R.T. data on your hard drive. Your best sources are the hard drive manufacturers. Every hard drive maker has a free diagnostic tool (which usually works only for their drives) that will do a S.M.A.R.T. check along with other tests. Figure 9.16 shows Western Digital's

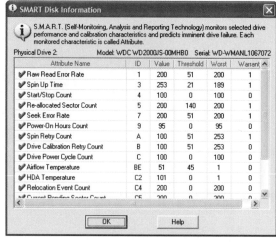

• **Figure 9.17**   S.M.A.R.T. information

• **Figure 9.16**   Data Lifeguard

Data Lifeguard Tools in action. Note that it says only whether the drive has passed or not. Figure 9.17 shows some S.M.A.R.T. information.

Although you can see the actual S.M.A.R.T. data, it's generally useless or indecipherable. Your best choice is to trust the manufacturer's opinion and run the software provided.

ATA-4

Anyone who has opened a big database file on a hard drive appreciates that a faster hard drive is better. ATA-4 introduced a new DMA mode called Ultra DMA that is now the primary way a hard drive communicates with a PC. **Ultra DMA** uses DMA bus mastering to achieve far faster speeds than were possible with PIO or old-style DMA. ATA-4 defined three Ultra DMA modes:

Ultra DMA mode 2, the most popular of the ATA-4 DMA modes, is also called ATA/33.

- Ultra DMA mode 0: 16.7 MBps
- Ultra DMA mode 1: 25.0 MBps
- Ultra DMA mode 2: 33.3 MBps

INT13 Extensions

Here's an interesting factoid for you: The original ATA-1 standard allowed for hard drives up to 137 GB. It wasn't the ATA standard that caused the 504-MB size limit; the standard used the old AT BIOS, and the BIOS, not the ATA standard, could support only 504 MB. LBA was a work-around that told the hard drive to lie to the BIOS to get it up to 8.4 GB. But eventually hard drives started edging close to the LBA limit and something had to be done. The T13 folks said, "This isn't *our* problem. It's the ancient BIOS problem. You BIOS makers need to fix the BIOS." And they did.

In 1994, Phoenix Technologies (the BIOS manufacturer) came up with a new set of BIOS commands called **Interrupt 13 (INT13) extensions**. INT13 extensions broke the 8.4-GB barrier by completely ignoring the CHS values and instead feeding the LBA a stream of addressable sectors. A system with INT13 extensions can handle drives up to 137 GB. The entire PC industry quickly adopted INT13 extensions, and every system made since 2000–2001 supports INT13 extensions.

ATA-5

Ultra DMA was such a huge hit that the ATA folks adopted two faster Ultra DMA modes with ATA-5:

- Ultra DMA mode 3: 44.4 MBps
- Ultra DMA mode 4: 66.6 MBps

Ultra DMA mode 4, the most popular of the ATA-5 DMA modes, is also called ATA/66.

Ultra DMA mode 4 ran so quickly that the ATA-5 standard defined a new type of ribbon cable that could handle the higher speeds. This **80-wire cable** still has 40 pins on the connectors, but it also includes another 40 wires in the cable that act as grounds to improve the cable's capability to handle high-speed signals. The 80-wire cable, just like the 40-pin ribbon cable, has a colored stripe down one side to give you proper orientation for pin 1 on the controller and the hard drive. Previous versions of ATA didn't define where the various drives were plugged into the ribbon cable, but ATA-5 defined exactly where the controller, master, and slave drives connected, even defining colors to identify them. Take a look at the ATA/66 cable in Figure 9.18. The connector on the left is colored blue—and you must use that connector to plug into the controller. The connector in the middle is gray—that's for the slave drive. The connector on the right is black—that's for the master drive. Any ATA/66 controller connections are colored blue to let you know it is an ATA/66 controller.

ATA/66 is backward compatible, so you may safely plug an earlier drive into an ATA/66 cable and controller. If you plug an ATA/66 drive into an older controller, it will work—just not in ATA/66 mode. The only risky action is to use an ATA/66 controller and hard drive with a non-ATA/66 cable. Doing so will almost certainly cause nasty data losses!

• **Figure 9.18**   ATA/66 cable

ATA-6

Hard drive size exploded in the early 21st century, and the seemingly impossible-to-fill 137-GB limit created by INT13 extensions became a barrier to fine computing more quickly than most people had anticipated. When drives started hitting the 120-GB mark, the T13 committee adopted an industry proposal pushed by Maxtor (a major hard drive maker) called *Big Drive* that increased the limit to more than 144 petabytes (approximately 144,000,000 GB). Thankfully, T13 also gave the new standard a less-silly name, calling it **ATA/ATAPI-6** or simply ATA-6. Big Drive was basically just a 48-bit LBA, supplanting the older 24-bit addressing of LBA and INT13 extensions. Plus, the standard defined an enhanced block mode, enabling drives to transfer up to 65,536 sectors in one chunk, up from the measly 256 sectors of lesser drive technologies.

ATA-6 also introduced Ultra DMA mode 5, kicking the data transfer rate up to 100 MBps. Ultra DMA mode 5 is more commonly referred to as ATA/100 and requires the same 80-wire cable as ATA/66.

ATA-7

ATA-7 brought two new innovations to the ATA world: one evolutionary and the other revolutionary. The evolutionary innovation came with the last of the parallel ATA Ultra DMA modes; the revolutionary was a new form of ATA called serial ATA (SATA).

ATA/133

ATA-7 introduced the fastest and probably least adopted of all of the ATA speeds, Ultra DMA mode 6 (**ATA/133**). Even though it runs at a speed of 133 MBps, the fact that it came out with SATA kept many hard drive manufacturers away. ATA/133 uses the same cables as Ultra DMA 66 and 100.

While you won't find many ATA/133 hard drives, you will find plenty of ATA/133 controllers. There's a trend in the industry to color the controller connections on the hard drive red, although this is not part of the ATA-7 standard.

Serial ATA

The real story of ATA-7 is SATA. For all its longevity as the mass storage interface of choice for the PC, parallel ATA has problems. First, the flat ribbon cables impede airflow and can be a pain to insert properly. Second, the cables have a limited length, only 18 inches. Third, you can't hot-swap PATA drives. You have to shut down completely before installing or replacing a drive. Finally, the technology has simply reached the limits of what it can do in terms of throughput.

Serial ATA addresses these issues. SATA creates a point-to-point connection between the SATA device—hard disk, CD-ROM, CD-RW, DVD-ROM, DVD-RW, BD-R, BD-RE, and so on—and the SATA controller, the **host bus adapter (HBA)**. At a glance, SATA devices look identical to standard PATA devices. Take a closer look at the cable and power connectors, however, and you'll see significant differences (Figure 9.19).

Because SATA devices send data serially instead of in parallel, the SATA interface needs far fewer physical wires—7 instead of the 80 wires typical of PATA—resulting in much thinner cabling. This might not seem significant, but the benefit is that thinner cabling means better cable control and better airflow through the PC case, resulting in better cooling.

Further, the maximum SATA-device cable length is more than twice that of an IDE cable—about 40 inches (1 meter) instead of 18 inches. Again, this might not seem like a big deal unless you've struggled to connect a PATA hard disk installed into the top bay of a full-tower case to an IDE connector located all the way at the bottom of the motherboard.

• **Figure 9.19** SATA hard disk power (left) and data (right) cables

SATA does away with the entire master/slave concept. Each drive connects to one port, so daisy-chaining drives is no longer possible. Further, there's no maximum number of drives—many motherboards are now available that support up to eight SATA drives. Want more? Snap in a SATA HBA and load 'em up!

The big news, however, is in data throughput. As the name implies, SATA devices transfer data in serial bursts instead of parallel, as PATA devices do. Typically, you might not think of serial devices as being faster than parallel, but in this case, that's exactly the case. A SATA device's single stream of data moves much faster than the multiple streams of data coming from a parallel IDE device—theoretically up to 30 times faster. SATA drives come in two common varieties, the 1.5 GB and the 3 GB, that have a maximum throughput of 150 MBps and 300 MBps, respectively.

SATA is backward compatible with current PATA standards and enables you to install a parallel ATA device, including a hard drive, optical drive, and other devices, to a serial ATA controller by using a **SATA bridge**. A SATA bridge manifests as a tiny card that you plug directly into the 40-pin connector on a PATA drive. As you can see in Figure 9.20, the controller chip on the bridge requires separate power; you plug a Molex connector into the PATA drive as normal. When you boot the system, the PATA drive shows up to the system as a SATA drive.

SATA's ease of use has made it the choice for desktop system storage, and its success is already showing in the fact that more than 90 percent of all hard drives sold today are SATA drives.

AHCI   Windows Vista and later operating systems support the *Advanced Host Controller Interface* (*AHCI*), a more efficient way to work with SATA HBAs. Using AHCI unlocks some of the advanced features of SATA, such as hot-swapping and native command queuing.

When you plug a SATA drive into a Windows computer that does not have AHCI enabled, the drive doesn't appear automatically. You need to go to the Control Panel and run the Add New Hardware Wizard to make the drive appear. AHCI makes the drive appear in Computer, just what you'd expect from a hot-swappable device.

Native command queuing (*NCQ*) is a disk-optimization feature for SATA drives. It enables faster read and write speeds.

• **Figure 9.20**   SATA bridge

Tech Tip

SATA Names

Number-savvy readers might have noticed a discrepancy between the names and throughput of the two SATA drives. After all, 1.5 GB per second throughput translates to 192 MB per second, a lot higher than the advertised speed of a "mere" 150 MBps. The same is true of the 3 GB/300 MBps drives. The encoding scheme used on SATA drives takes about 20 percent of the overhead for the drive, leaving 80 percent for pure bandwidth. The 3 GB drive created all kinds of problems, because the committee working on the specifications was called the SATA II committee, and marketers picked up on the SATA II name. As a result, you'll find many brands called SATA II rather than 3 GB. The SATA committee now goes by the name SATA-IO.

As this book went to press, a few motherboards and hard drive controller cards appeared that support the SATA 3.0 standard, with data rates up to 6 GBps. Look for the SATA 3.0 drives on the store shelves after you read this, but don't expect the technology to be on the CompTIA A+ Essentials exam this time around.

Tech Tip

Enabling AHCI After the Fact

If you want to enable AHCI but you've already installed Windows Vista, don't worry! Microsoft has developed a procedure (http://support.microsoft.com/kb/922976) that will have you enjoying all that AHCI fun in no time. Before you jump in, note that this procedure requires you to edit your Registry, so remember to always make a backup before you start editing.

• **Figure 9.21** eSATA connectors

For the scoop on PC Cards and ExpressCards—both technologies designed to add expansion options for portable computers—see Chapter 14, "Learning Portable Computing."

AHCI is implemented at the CMOS level and generally needs to be enabled before you install the operating system. Enabling it after installation will cause Vista to Blue Screen. Nice.

eSATA **External SATA (eSATA)** extends the SATA bus to external devices, as the name would imply. The eSATA drives use connectors similar to internal SATA, but they're keyed differently so you can't mistake one for the other. Figure 9.21 shows eSATA connectors on the back of a motherboard. External SATA uses shielded cable lengths up to 2 meters outside the PC and is hot pluggable. The beauty of eSATA is that it extends the SATA bus at full speed, so you're not limited to the meager 50 or 60 MBps of FireWire or USB.

If a desktop system doesn't have an eSATA external connector, or if you need more external SATA devices, you can install an eSATA HBA PCIe card or eSATA internal-to-external slot plate. You can similarly upgrade laptop systems to support external SATA devices by inserting an eSATA ExpressCard (Figure 9.22). There are also USB to eSATA adapter plugs, although you'll be limited to the much slower USB data-transfer rates. Install eSATA PCIe, PC Card, or ExpressCard adapters following the same rules and precautions for installing any expansion device.

• **Figure 9.22** eSATA ExpressCard

■ SCSI: Still Around

Many specialized server machines and enthusiasts' systems use the **small computer system interface (SCSI)** technologies for various pieces of core hardware and peripherals, from hard drives to printers to high-end tape-backup machines. SCSI (pronounced "scuzzy") is different from ATA in that SCSI devices connect together in a string of devices called a *chain*. Each device in the chain gets a SCSI ID to distinguish it from other devices on the chain. Last, the ends of a SCSI chain must be terminated. Let's dive into SCSI now, and see how SCSI chains, SCSI IDs, and termination all work.

SCSI is an old technology dating from the late 1970s, but it has been updated continually. SCSI is faster than ATA (though the gap is closing fast), and until SATA arrived, SCSI was the only good choice for anyone using RAID (see the "RAID" section a little later). SCSI is arguably fading away, but it deserves some mention.

SCSI Chains

SCSI manifests itself through a **SCSI chain**, a series of SCSI devices working together through a host adapter. The host adapter provides the interface between the SCSI chain and the PC. Figure 9.23 shows a typical PCI host adapter. Many techs refer to the host adapter as the *SCSI controller*, so you should be comfortable with both terms.

• **Figure 9.23**   SCSI host adapter

All SCSI devices can be divided into two groups: internal and external. Internal SCSI devices are attached inside the PC and connect to the host adapter through the latter's internal connector. Figure 9.24 shows an internal SCSI device, in this case a CD-ROM drive. External devices hook to the external connector of the host adapter. Figure 9.25 is an example of an external SCSI device.

Internal SCSI devices connect to the host adapter with a 68-pin ribbon cable (Figure 9.26). This flat, flexible cable functions precisely like a PATA cable. Many external devices connect to the host adapter with a 50-pin high-density (HD) connector. Figure 9.27 shows a host adapter external port. Higher-end SCSI devices use a 68-pin HD connector.

Multiple internal devices can be connected simply by using a cable with enough connectors. Figure 9.28, for example, shows a chain of three SCSI devices, including the host adapter.

• **Figure 9.24**   Internal SCSI CD-ROM drive

Assuming the SCSI host adapter has a standard external port (some controllers don't have external connections at all), plugging in an external SCSI device is as simple as running a cable from device to controller. The external SCSI connectors are D-shaped so you can't plug them in

• **Figure 9.25**   Back of external SCSI device

• **Figure 9.26**   Typical 68-pin ribbon cable

● **Figure 9.27**   50-pin HD port on SCSI host adapter

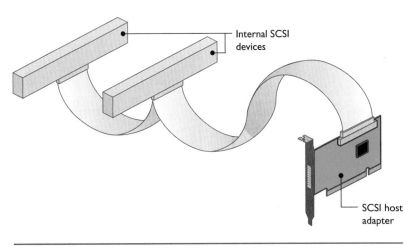

● **Figure 9.28**   Internal SCSI chain with two devices

backward. As an added bonus, some external SCSI devices have two ports, one to connect to the host adapter and a second to connect to another SCSI device. The process of connecting a device directly to another device is called *daisy-chaining*. You can daisy-chain as many as 15 devices to one host adapter. SCSI chains can be internal, external, or both (Figure 9.29).

SCSI IDs

If you're going to connect a number of devices on the same SCSI chain, you must provide some way for the host adapter to tell one device from another. To differentiate devices, SCSI uses a unique identifier called the **SCSI ID**. The SCSI ID number can range from 0 to 15. SCSI IDs are similar to many other PC hardware settings in that a SCSI device can theoretically have any SCSI ID as long as that ID is not already taken by another device connected to the same host adapter.

● **Figure 9.29**   Internal and external devices on one SCSI chain

Some conventions should be followed when setting SCSI IDs. Typically, most people set the host adapter to 7 or 15, but you can change this setting. Note that there is no order for the use of SCSI IDs. It does not matter which device gets which number, and you can skip numbers. Restrictions on IDs apply only within a single chain. Two devices can have the same ID, in other words, as long as they are on different chains (Figure 9.30).

Every SCSI device has some method of setting its SCSI ID. The trick is to figure out how as you're holding the device in your hand. A SCSI device may use jumpers, dip switches, or even tiny dials; every new SCSI device is an adventure as you try to determine how to set its SCSI ID.

Termination

Whenever you send a signal down a wire, some of that signal reflects back up the wire, creating an echo and causing electronic chaos. SCSI chains use **termination** to prevent this problem. Termination simply means putting something on the ends of the wire to prevent this echo. Terminators are usually pull-down resistors and can manifest themselves in many different ways. Most of the devices within a PC have the appropriate termination built in. On other devices, including SCSI chains and some network cables, you have to set termination during installation.

The rule with SCSI is that you *must* terminate *only* the ends of the SCSI chain. You have to terminate the ends of the cable, which usually means that you need to terminate the two devices at the ends of the cable. Do *not* terminate devices that are not on the ends of the cable. Figure 9.31 shows some examples of where to terminate SCSI devices.

Old SCSI equipment allowed SCSI IDs from 0 to 7 only.

SCSI device SCSI ID 6

SCSI device SCSI ID 1

SCSI host adapter SCSI ID 7

SCSI host adapter SCSI ID 7

• **Figure 9.30**   IDs don't conflict between separate SCSI chains.

• **Figure 9.31**   Location of the terminated devices

• **Figure 9.32**   Setting termination

Because any SCSI device might be on the end of a chain, most manufacturers build SCSI devices that can self-terminate. Some devices can detect that they are on the end of the SCSI chain and automatically terminate themselves. Most devices, however, require you to set a jumper or switch to enable termination (Figure 9.32).

■ Protecting Data with RAID

Ask experienced techs "What is the most expensive part of a PC?" and they'll all answer in the same way: "It's the data." You can replace any single part of your PC for a few hundred dollars at most, but if you lose critical data—well, let's just say I know of two small companies that went out of business just because they lost a hard drive full of data.

Data is king; data is your PC's *raison d'être*. Losing data is a bad thing, so you need some method to prevent data loss. Of course, you can do backups, but if a hard drive dies, you have to shut down the computer, reinstall a new hard drive, reinstall the operating system, and then restore the backup. There's nothing wrong with this as long as you can afford the time and cost of shutting down the system.

A better solution, though, would save your data if a hard drive died and enable you to continue working throughout the process. This is possible if you stop relying on a single hard drive and instead use two or more drives to store your data. Sounds good, but how do you do this? Well, first of all, you could install some fancy hard drive controller that reads and writes data to two hard drives simultaneously (Figure 9.33). The data on each drive would always be identical. One drive would be the primary drive and the other drive, called the *mirror* drive, would not be used unless the primary drive failed. This process of reading and writing data at the same time to two drives is called **disk mirroring**.

If you really want to make data safe, you can use a separate controller for each drive. With two drives, each on a separate controller, the system will continue to operate even if the primary drive's controller stops working. This super-drive mirroring technique is called **disk duplexing** (Figure 9.34). Disk duplexing is also much faster than disk mirroring because one controller does not write each piece of data twice.

RAID 1 (mirroring)
• Exactly two (redundant) drives
• Safe but slow
• Both drives are assigned the same drive letter.

SATA RAID Controller

• **Figure 9.33**   Mirrored drives

RAID I (duplexing)
- Exactly two (redundant) drives
- Faster and safer
- Both drives are assigned the same drive letter.

• **Figure 9.34**   Duplexing drives

Even though duplexing is faster than mirroring, they both are slower than the classic one-drive, one-controller setup. You can use multiple drives to increase your hard drive access speed. **Disk striping** (without parity) means spreading the data among multiple (at least two) drives. Disk striping by itself provides no redundancy. If you save a small Microsoft Word file, for example, the file is split into multiple pieces; half of the pieces go on one drive and half on the other (Figure 9.35).

The one and only advantage of disk striping is speed—it is a fast way to read and write to hard drives. But if either drive fails, *all* data is lost. You should not do disk striping—unless you're willing to increase the risk of losing data to increase the speed at which your hard drives save and restore data.

Disk striping with parity, in contrast, protects data by adding extra

RAID 0 (striping)
- Two or more (non-redundant) drives
- Fast, but not really safe
- Both drives are assigned the same drive letter.

• **Figure 9.35**   Disk striping

information, called *parity data*, that can be used to rebuild data if one of the drives fails. Disk striping with parity requires at least three drives, but it is common to use more than three. Disk striping with parity combines the best of disk mirroring and plain disk striping. It protects data and is quite fast. The majority of network servers use a type of disk striping with parity.

RAID

An *array* in the context of RAID refers to a collection of two or more hard drives.

A couple of sharp guys in Berkeley back in the 1980s organized the many techniques for using multiple drives for data protection and increasing speeds as the **redundant array of independent (or inexpensive) disks (RAID)**. They outlined seven levels of RAID, numbered 0 through 6.

- **RAID 0—Disk Striping**   Disk striping requires at least two drives. It does not provide redundancy to data. If any one drive fails, all data is lost.

- **RAID 1—Disk Mirroring/Duplexing**   RAID 1 arrays require at least two hard drives, although they also work with any even number of drives. RAID 1 is the ultimate in safety, but you lose storage space because the data is duplicated; you need two 100-GB drives to store 100 GB of data.

- **RAID 2—Disk Striping with Multiple Parity Drives**   RAID 2 was a weird RAID idea that never saw practical use. It's unused, so ignore it.

- **RAID 3 and 4—Disk Striping with Dedicated Parity**   RAID 3 and 4 combined dedicated data drives with dedicated parity drives. The differences between the two are trivial. Unlike RAID 2, these versions did see some use in the real world but were quickly replaced by RAID 5.

- **RAID 5—Disk Striping with Distributed Parity**   Instead of dedicated data and parity drives, RAID 5 distributes data and parity information evenly across all drives. This is the fastest way to provide data redundancy. RAID 5 is by far the most common RAID implementation and requires at least three drives. RAID 5 arrays effectively use one drive's worth of space for parity. If, for example, you have three 200-GB drives, your total storage capacity is 400 GB. If you have four 200-GB drives, your total capacity is 600 GB.

- **RAID 6—Disk Striping with Extra Parity**   If you lose a hard drive in a RAID 5 array, your data is at great risk until you replace the bad hard drive and rebuild the array. RAID 6 is RAID 5 with extra parity information. RAID 6 needs at least five drives, but in exchange you can lose up to two drives at the same time. RAID 6 is gaining in popularity for those willing to use larger arrays.

<table>
<tr><td>Tech Tip</td></tr>
<tr><td>RAID Lingo
No tech worth her salt says such things as "We're implementing disk striping with parity." Use the RAID level. Say, "We're implementing RAID 5." It's more accurate and very impressive to the folks in the accounting department!</td></tr>
</table>

There is actually a term for a storage system composed of multiple independent disks rather than disks organized by using RAID: *JBOD*, which stands for *just a bunch of disks* (or *drives*).

After these first RAID levels were defined, some manufacturers came up with ways to combine different RAIDs. For example, what if you took two pairs of striped drives and mirrored the pairs? You would get what is called RAID 0+1. Or what if (read this carefully now) you took two pairs of mirrored drives and striped the pairs? You then get what we call RAID 1+0 or what is often called RAID 10. Combinations of different types of single RAID are called *multiple RAID* or *nested RAID* solutions.

Implementing RAID

RAID levels describe different methods of providing data redundancy or enhancing the speed of data throughput to and from groups of hard drives. They do not say *how* to implement these methods. Literally thousands of methods can be used to set up RAID. The method you use depends largely on the level of RAID you desire, the operating system you use, and the thickness of your wallet.

The obvious starting place for RAID is to connect at least two hard drives in some fashion to create a RAID array. For many years, if you wanted to do RAID beyond RAID 0 and RAID 1, the only technology you could use was good-old SCSI. SCSI's chaining of multiple devices to a single controller made it a natural for RAID. SCSI drives make superb RAID arrays, but the high cost of SCSI drives and RAID-capable host adapters kept RAID away from all but the most critical systems—usually big file servers.

In the past few years, substantial leaps in ATA technology have made ATA a viable alternative to SCSI drive technology for RAID arrays. Specialized ATA RAID controller cards support ATA RAID arrays of up to 15 drives—plenty to support even the most complex RAID needs. In addition, the inherent hot-swap capabilities of serial ATA have virtually guaranteed that serial ATA will quickly take over the lower end of the RAID business. Personally, I think the price and performance of serial ATA mean SCSI's days are numbered.

Once you have a number of hard drives, the next question is whether to use hardware or software to control the array. Let's look at both options.

Try This!

Managing Heat with Multiple Drives

Adding three or more fast hard drives into a cramped PC case can be a recipe for disaster to the unwary tech. All those disks spinning constantly create a phenomenal amount of heat. Heat kills PCs! You have to manage the heat inside a RAID-enabled system or risk losing your data, drives, and basic system stability. The easiest way to do this is to add fans, so Try This!

Open up your PC case and look for built-in places to mount fans. How many case fans do you have installed now? What size are they? What sizes can you use? (Most cases use 80-mm fans, but 60- and 120-mm fans are common as well.) Jot down the particulars of your system and take a trip to the local PC store to check out the fans.

Before you get all fan-happy and grab the biggest and baddest fans to throw in your case, don't forget to think about the added noise level. Try to get a compromise between keeping your case cool enough and avoiding early deafness.

Hardware vs. Software

All RAID implementations break down into either hardware or software methods. Software is often used when price takes priority over performance. Hardware is used when you need speed along with data redundancy. Software RAID does not require special controllers; you can use the regular ATA controllers, SATA controllers, or SCSI host adapters to make a software RAID array. But you do need "smart" software. The most common software implementation of RAID is the built-in RAID software that comes with Windows 2000, 2003, and 2008 Server. The Disk Management program in these Windows Server versions can configure drives for RAID 0, 1, or 5, and it works with PATA, SATA, and/or SCSI (Figure 9.36). Disk Management in Windows 2000 Professional, Windows XP, and Windows Vista, in contrast, can only do RAID 0.

You can use Disk Management in Windows 2000, Windows XP Professional, and Windows Vista to create RAID 1 and RAID 5 arrays, but you can use Disk Management only remotely on a Windows 2000, 2003, or 2008 Server OS. In other words, the capability is there, but Microsoft has limited the OS. If you want to use software RAID in Windows 2000, XP (Home or Professional), or Vista, you need to use a third-party tool to set it up.

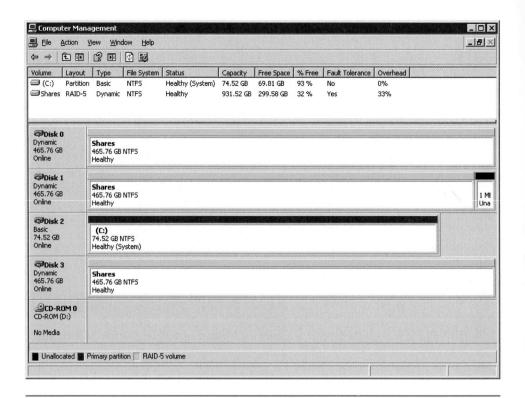

Volume	Layout	Type	File System	Status	Capacity	Free Space	% Free	Fault Tolerance	Overhead
(C:)	Partition	Basic	NTFS	Healthy (System)	74.52 GB	69.81 GB	93 %	No	0%
Shares	RAID-5	Dynamic	NTFS	Healthy	931.52 GB	299.58 GB	32 %	Yes	33%

Disk 0
Dynamic
465.76 GB
Online

Shares
465.76 GB NTFS
Healthy

Disk 1
Dynamic
465.76 GB
Online

Shares
465.76 GB NTFS
Healthy

1 ME
Una

Disk 2
Basic
74.52 GB
Online

(C:)
74.52 GB NTFS
Healthy (System)

Disk 3
Dynamic
465.76 GB
Online

Shares
465.76 GB NTFS
Healthy

CD-ROM 0
CD-ROM (D:)

No Media

■ Unallocated ■ Primary partition ☐ RAID-5 volume

● **Figure 9.36** Disk Management tool of Computer Management in Windows 2003 Server

Windows Disk Management is not the only software RAID game in town. A number of third-party software programs work with Windows or other operating systems.

Software RAID means the operating system is in charge of all RAID functions. It works for small RAID solutions but tends to overwork your operating system easily, creating slowdowns. When you *really* need to keep going, when you need RAID that doesn't even let the users know a problem has occurred, hardware RAID is the answer.

Hardware RAID centers on an *intelligent* controller—either a SCSI host adapter or a PATA/SATA controller that handles all of the RAID functions (Figure 9.37). Unlike a regular PATA/SATA controller or SCSI host adapter, these controllers have chips that have their own processor and memory. This allows the card, instead of the operating system, to handle all of the work of implementing RAID.

Most RAID setups in the real world are hardware-based. Almost all of the many hardware RAID solutions provide *hot-swapping*—the ability to replace a bad drive without disturbing the operating system. Hot-swapping is common in hardware RAID.

Hardware-based RAID is invisible to the operating system and is configured in several ways, depending on the specific chips involved. Most RAID systems have a special configuration utility in Flash ROM that you access after CMOS but before the OS loads. Figure 9.38

● **Figure 9.37** Serial ATA RAID controller

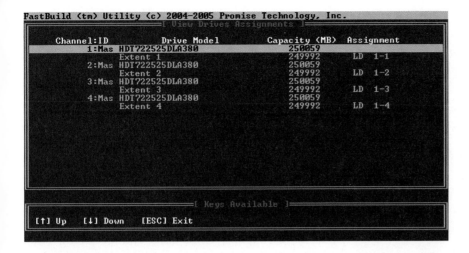

```
FastBuild (tm) Utility (c) 2004-2005 Promise Technology, Inc.
================[ View Drives Assignments ]================
    Channel:ID        Drive Model         Capacity (MB)  Assignment
        1:Mas  HDT722525DLA380              250059
               Extent 1                     249992        LD   1-1
        2:Mas  HDT722525DLA380              250059
               Extent 2                     249992        LD   1-2
        3:Mas  HDT722525DLA380              250059
               Extent 3                     249992        LD   1-3
        4:Mas  HDT722525DLA380              250059
               Extent 4                     249992        LD   1-4




==================[ Keys Available ]==================

  [↑] Up    [↓] Down    [ESC] Exit
```

• **Figure 9.38**   RAID configuration utility

shows a typical firmware program used to configure a hardware RAID solution.

Personal RAID

Due to drastic reductions in the cost of ATA RAID controller chips, in the past few years we've seen an explosion of ATA-based hardware RAID solutions built into mainstream motherboards. While this "ATA RAID on the motherboard" began with parallel ATA, the introduction of serial ATA made motherboards with built-in RAID extremely common.

These personal RAID motherboards might be common but they're not used too terribly often, given that these RAID solutions usually provide only RAID 0 or RAID 1. If you want to use RAID, spend a few extra dollars and buy a RAID 5–capable controller.

RAID controllers aren't just for internal drives; some models can handle multiple eSATA drives configured at any of the RAID levels. If you're feeling lucky, you can create a RAID array using both internal and external SATA drives.

The Future Is RAID

RAID has been with us for about 20 years, but until only recently it was the domain of big systems and deep pockets. During those 20 years, however, a number of factors have come together to make RAID a reality for both big servers and common desktop systems. Imagine a world where dirt-cheap RAID on every computer means no one ever again loses critical data. I get goose bumps just thinking about it!

Beyond A+

Spindle (or Rotational) Speed

Hard drives run at a set spindle speed, measured in *revolutions per minute* (*RPM*). Older drives run at the long-standard speed of 3600 RPM, but new drives are hitting 15,000 RPM. The faster the spindle speed, the faster the controller can store and retrieve data. Here are the common speeds: 4500, 5400, 7200, and 10,000 RPM.

Faster drives mean better system performance, but they can also cause the computer to overheat. This is especially true in tight cases, such as minitowers, and in cases containing many drives. Two 4500-RPM drives might run forever, snugly tucked together in your old case. But slap a hot new 10,000 RPM drive in that same case and watch your system start crashing right and left!

You can deal with these hotrod drives by adding drive bay fans between the drives or migrating to a more spacious case. Most enthusiasts end up doing both. Drive bay fans sit at the front of a bay and blow air across the drive. They range in price from $10 to $100 (U.S.) and can lower the temperature of your drives dramatically. Some cases come with a bay fan built in (Figure 9.39).

Airflow in a case can make or break your system stability, especially when you add new drives that increase the ambient temperature. Hot systems get flaky and lock up at odd moments. Many things can impede the airflow—jumbled-up ribbon cables, drives squished together in a tiny case, fans clogged by dust or animal hair, and so on.

Technicians need to be aware of the dangers when adding a new hard drive to an older system. Get into the habit of tying off ribbon cables, adding front fans to cases when systems lock up intermittently, and making sure any fans run well. Finally, if a client wants a new drive for a system in a tiny minitower with only the power supply fan to cool it off, be gentle, but definitely steer the client to one of the slower drives!

• **Figure 9.39**   Bay fan

Hybrid Hard Drives

Windows Vista supports hybrid hard drives (HHDs), drives that combine flash memory and spinning platters to provide fast and reliable storage, and offers ReadyBoost and Superfetch for faster caching and booting. Samsung has drives with 128-MB and 256-MB flash cache, for example, that shave boot times in half and, because the platters don't have to spin all of the time, add 20–30 minutes more of battery life for portable computers. Adding that much more run time with only a tiny price premium and no extra weight is the Holy Grail of portable computing.

Chapter 9 Review

■ Chapter Summary

After reading this chapter and completing the exercises, you should understand the following about hard drive technologies.

Explain how hard drives work

■ Traditional hard drives contain aluminum platters coated with a magnetic medium and read/write heads that float on a cushion of air. Hard drives store data in a tiny magnetic field called a flux that defines a zero or a one. The switching back and forth of the field is called flux reversal. The incredible storage capacity of today's drives results from Partial Response Maximum Likelihood (PRML) encoding that includes intelligent circuitry to analyze each flux reversal.

■ Two technologies have been used to move read/write heads across the platters: stepper motors and voice coil. Very susceptible to physical deterioration and temperature changes, the now obsolete stepper motors moved the actuator arm in fixed increments or steps, often resulting in data-transfer errors or the inability to access data on a cold drive. The heads had to be parked to a non-data area when not in use to prevent possible damage to the disk surface. Today's drives use a linear or voice coil motor consisting of a permanent magnet surrounding a coil on the actuator arm. Electrical current causes the coil to generate a magnetic field that moves the actuator arm and thus the read/write heads. Containing no data, one side of one platter is used as a map to position the heads directly over the data. Voice coil technology automatically parks the heads when the drive loses power.

■ Disk geometry for a particular hard drive consists of three primary values: heads, cylinders, and sectors per track (sectors/track). There are two read/write heads per platter. A hard drive can have either an even or an odd number of heads. A cylinder defines a group of tracks of the same diameter. Each track is sliced into tiny slivers called sectors, each of which stores 512 bytes of data. Disk geometry uses the number of sectors per track. Combining cylinders, heads, and sectors/track is referred to as CHS. Write precompensation and landing zone, two other geometric values, have no relevance in today's PCs, but most CMOS utilities still support them.

■ Solid-state drives use memory chips to store data and don't have any metal spinning parts. They require less electricity than platter-based drives and offer faster reads and writes. At the time of this writing, they cost substantially more than traditional drives.

Identify and explain the PATA and SATA hard drive interfaces

■ Today's hard drives have either an ATA interface or a SCSI interface. ATA drives may be parallel ATA (PATA) or the newer serial ATA (SATA). A specification of the American National Standards Institute (ANSI), the AT Attachment (ATA) interface (commonly but incorrectly referred to as IDE) used a 40-pin ribbon cable, had a built-in controller, and did not require a low-level format. By 1995, EIDE was the dominant interface. Its features include higher capacities, support for non–hard drive storage devices, a four-device maximum, and improved throughput. The terms ATA, IDE, and EIDE are used interchangeably to describe all PATA devices.

■ PATA drives use a 40-pin plug and a controller that connects them to the external data bus. Although the real controller is built into the hard drive itself, the 40-pin connector on the motherboard is called the controller. Most modern motherboards contain two PATA controllers, each capable of supporting up to two PATA devices. By looking at the motherboard itself or at the motherboard book, you can determine which is the primary controller and which is the secondary. If you are using only one controller, it should be the primary one.

■ Originally, IDE drives used the same BIOS command set introduced years earlier. Maximum values of 1024 cylinders, 16 heads, and 63 sectors per track limited an IDE drive's capacity to 528 million bytes (504 MB). Western Digital developed the LBA sector translation method to accommodate larger EIDE drives. LBA supports drives with up to 256 heads, for a storage capacity limit of 8.4 GB.

- As drive capacity neared the 8.4-GB maximum, Phoenix Technologies broke the limit by coming up with a new set of BIOS commands called Interrupt 13 extensions (INT13). Completely ignoring the CHS values, INT13 supports drives up to 137 GB by reporting a stream of addressable sectors to LBA.

- As drive capacity neared the 137-GB limit, the ANSI ATA committee adopted ATA/ATAPI-6, a new standard that increased the limit to more than 144 petabytes (144,000,000 GB). It uses a 48-bit addressing scheme and an enhanced block mode that transfers up to 65,536 sectors at a time.

- Newer hard drives use direct memory access (DMA) mode to send data directly to RAM, bypassing the CPU. Instead of using the slow DMA controller chip, today's DMA transfers use bus mastering to transfer 32 bits of data. Hard drives typically use one of the following modes: Ultra DMA mode 4 (ATA/66), Ultra DMA mode 5 (ATA/100), and Ultra DMA mode 6 (ATA/133). To use Ultra DMA, you must have a controller and an 80-wire ribbon cable. Some motherboards combine different speeds of ATA controllers, with the higher-speed controller indicated with a bright color. The 80-wire ribbon cable indicates where to connect the master and slave drives. High-end PATA devices can use lower-end controllers, but they will operate at the slower speed.

- Serial ATA (SATA) devices look identical to standard PATA devices (except their data and power connectors), but their thinner seven-wire cables provide better airflow and may be up to a meter (39.4 inches) long. SATA does away with the entire master/slave concept. Each drive connects to one port, so daisy-chaining drives is no longer possible.

- SATA devices are hot-swappable, great for RAID technology. SATA transfers data in serial bursts for up to 30 times the throughput of PATA. SATA drives come in two common varieties, the 1.5 GB and the 3 GB, that have a maximum throughput of 150 MBps and 300 MBps, respectively.

Identify and explain the SCSI hard drive interfaces

- All SCSI chains, which support either 8 or 16 devices including the controller, require proper termination to prevent signal echo. Additionally, each device on a chain requires a unique SCSI ID, which can be set by jumpers, switches, or dials.

- All SCSI devices can be divided into two groups: internal and external. Internal SCSI devices connect to the host adapter with a 68-pin ribbon cable. External devices connect to the host adapter with either a 50-pin HD connector or a 68-pin HD connector. SCSI enables you to daisy-chain devices together to form longer SCSI chains.

- Improper termination or incorrect SCSI ID settings are the two most common causes of SCSI devices not working. The key factor here is that you must terminate only the ends of the SCSI chain.

Describe how to protect data with RAID

- Drive mirroring writes data simultaneously to two hard drives, enabling the system to continue to work if one hard drive dies. A faster and even more effective technique is drive duplexing, which performs mirroring by using separate controllers for each drive. A third way to create redundant data is disk striping with parity. This technique, requiring at least three drives, combines the redundancy of disk mirroring with the speed of disk striping. Although disk striping without parity works very fast, splitting the data across two drives means you'll lose *all* data if either drive fails.

- Numbered 0 through 6, there are seven official levels of RAID, but the most commonly used ones are RAID 0 (disk striping), RAID 1 (disk mirroring or duplexing), and RAID 5 (disk striping with distributed parity).

- RAID may be implemented through hardware or software methods. Although software implementation is cheaper, hardware techniques provide better performance. Windows 2000 Server, Windows Server 2003, and Windows Server 2008 include built-in RAID software for RAID 0, RAID 1, and RAID 5 for either ATA or SCSI. Windows 2000, Windows XP Professional, and Windows Vista include Disk Management for RAID 0. RAID software solutions tend to overwork your operating system, resulting in slowdowns. Hardware RAID is invisible to the OS and is usually hot-swappable. A hardware ATA RAID controller usually requires CMOS configuration. Many motherboards include built-in ATA-based hardware RAID 0 and RAID 1 capabilities.

- SCSI drives were a natural for the multiple-disk RAID. Specialized ATA RAID controller cards support ATA RAID arrays of up to 15 drives. With its hot-swap capabilities, SATA may soon take over lower-end RAID from SCSI.

Key Terms

40-pin ribbon cable *(287)*
80-wire cable *(293)*
Advanced Technology Attachment (ATA) *(286)*
Advanced Technology Attachment Packet Interface
  (ATAPI) *(290)*
ATA/133 *(294)*
ATA/ATAPI-6 *(293)*
cylinder *(284)*
disk duplexing *(300)*
disk mirroring *(300)*
disk striping *(301)*
disk striping with parity *(301)*
DMA modes *(288)*
Enhanced IDE (EIDE) *(288)*
external SATA (eSATA) *(296)*
geometry *(283)*
hard disk drive (HDD) *(281)*
head *(283)*
head actuator *(282)*
host bus adapter (HBA) *(294)*
Integrated Drive Electronics (IDE) *(286)*
Interrupt 13 (INT13) extensions *(293)*

logical block addressing (LBA) *(289)*
parallel ATA (PATA) *(286)*
Partial Response Maximum Likelihood (PRML) *(282)*
PIO modes *(288)*
redundant array of independent (or inexpensive)
  disks (RAID) *(302)*
SATA bridge *(295)*
SCSI chain *(297)*
SCSI ID *(298)*
sector *(284)*
sector translation *(289)*
sectors per track (sectors/track) *(284)*
serial ATA (SATA) *(286)*
Self-Monitoring, Analysis, and Reporting Technology
  (S.M.A.R.T.) *(291)*
small computer system interface (SCSI) *(296)*
solid-state drive (SSD) *(285)*
stepper motor *(282)*
termination *(299)*
track *(284)*
Ultra DMA *(292)*
voice coil *(282)*

Key Term Quiz

Use the Key Terms list to complete the sentences that
follow. Not all terms will be used.

1. An ATA hard drive connects to the controller
   with a(n) _____40_____, while an Ultra DMA
   mode 4 drive uses a(n) _____80_____.

2. A(n) _____cylinder_____ is composed of a group of
   tracks of the same diameter that the read/write
   heads can access without moving.

3. To install a parallel ATA device to a serial ATA
   controller, use a tiny card called a(n) _____SATA Bridge_____

4. LBA, developed by Western Digital, uses
   _____sector trans_____ to get around the limits of 1024
   cylinders, 16 heads, and 63 sectors/track.

5. Seen in RAID 5, _____DS w/ Parity_____ uses at least three
   drives and combines the best features of disk
   mirroring and disk striping.

6. A CD-ROM drive that is _____Atapi_____-compliant
   installs and cables just like an EIDE drive.

7. The ANSI ATA committee adopted the _____Atapi-6_____
   standard, called "Big Drives" by Maxtor, that
   allows drives with more than 144 petabytes.

8. Drives known as _____Ata-133_____ transfer data at
   133 MBps.

9. Drives that use _____DMA_____ bypass the CPU
   and send data directly to memory.

10. Devices known as _____ devices require
    termination at both ends of a chain.

1. Which of the following is *not* used to compute storage capacity in CHS disk geometry?

   A. Sectors per track

   B. Tracks

   C. Heads

   D. Cylinders

2. Which level of RAID is disk striping with distributed parity?

   A. RAID 0

   B. RAID 1

   C. RAID 5

   D. RAID 6

3. Counting both channels, what is the maximum number of drives/devices that EIDE can support?

   A. One

   B. Two

   C. Seven

   D. Four

4. If you install two IDE drives on the same cable, how will the computer differentiate them?

   A. The CMOS setup allows you to configure them.

   B. You must set jumpers to determine which drive functions as master and which functions as slave.

   C. You will set jumpers so each drive has a unique ID number.

   D. The drives will be differentiated by whether you place them before or after the twist in the ribbon cable.

5. What was the maximum hard drive size allowed by BIOS routines for the original AT command set?

   A. 528 MB

   B. 1024 MB

   C. 504 MB

   D. 1028 MB

6. Which of the following terms does *not* describe parallel ATA devices?

   A. IDE

   B. EIDE

   C. SCSI

   D. ATA

7. Shelby wants to add a 100-GB hard drive to her computer. Which of the following will allow her to do so?

   A. CHS

   B. LBA

   C. ECHS

   D. INT13

8. Which of the following techniques provides redundancy by using two disks and two controllers?

   A. Drive mirroring

   B. Drive duplexing

   C. Disk striping

   D. Disk striping with parity

9. How many wires does an Ultra DMA ATA cable have?

   A. 24

   B. 34

   C. 40

   D. 80

10. Which of the following is *not* an advantage of serial ATA (SATA)?

    A. It is hot-swappable.

    B. Thinner cables provide better airflow inside the case.

    C. SATA provides faster data throughput than PATA.

    D. SATA cables must be shorter than PATA cables.

11. What standard did the ANSI ATA committee adopt that increased disk storage capacity to more than 144 petabytes?

    A. ATA/ATAPI-6

    B. LBA

    C. INT13

    D. ECHS

12. Which of the following can SSDs use to retain data integrity when a system loses power or is turned off?
    A. DRAM
    B. RAM drive
    C. NAND
    D. SDRAM

13. Which of the following represent common solid-state drive form factors?
    A. AT, ATX, and BTX
    B. 8-inch, 2.5-inch, and 5.25-inch
    C. 1.8-inch, 2.5-inch, and 3.5-inch
    D. IEEE 1394, USB, and SCSI

■ Essay Quiz

1. Discuss at least three advantages of serial ATA over parallel ATA.

2. Compare and contrast hardware and software RAID implementation.

3. Your friend Blaine has a Pentium 4 computer with a 100-MHz bus. Currently, it has only an 80-GB ATA/100 hard drive and a CD-RW drive. Because he's interested in video, he knows he needs more storage capacity and wants to add a second hard drive. What advice will you give him about selecting a new hard drive?

4. Hard drives include other features and characteristics not included in this chapter. Choose one of the following topics and use the Internet to define and explain it to the class.
   ■ Zone bit recording
   ■ "Pixie dust" hard drives

5. Your office is about to purchase ten new portable computers for the sales force and needs a recommendation. Prepare a short essay that compares and contrasts platter-based and solid-state drives so your boss can pick what's best for the staff.

Lab Projects

• Lab Project 9.1

Visit your local computer store or use the Internet to discover what kinds of hard drives and hard drive interfaces are commonly offered with new computers. Try to determine whether the motherboards offer only parallel ATA interfaces or if they offer serial ATA interfaces, either onboard or through an expansion card. If you were purchasing a new computer, would you select PATA or SATA? Why?

• Lab Project 9.2

Your supervisor has decided to implement RAID on the old company server machine, where everyone stores their work-related data. Come up with two competing RAID setups, one that maximizes security of data at the lowest cost possible and another that maximizes speed but retains some security. Cost is not a factor for the second RAID plan.

Removable Media

10

"Bring my screwdriver and my special CD of town-saving music."

—JIMMY NEUTRON, *JIMMY NEUTRON: BOY GENIUS*

In this chapter, you will learn how to

- ■ **Explain and install floppy disk drives**
- ■ **Demonstrate the variations among flash drives and other tiny drives**
- ■ **Identify optical-media technology**

Removable media refers to any type of mass storage device that you may use in one system and then physically remove from that system and use in another. Removable media has been a part of the personal PC since its first introduction back in 1980. Granted, back then the only removable media available were floppy disks, but being able to move programs and data easily from one machine to another was quickly established as one of the strongest points of the personal computer. Over time, higher-capacity removable media technologies were introduced. Some technologies—CDs, DVDs, Blu-ray Discs, and thumb drives, for example—have become very common. Other technologies (which you may or may not have heard of), such as Iomega Zip drives or HD DVDs, were popular for a time but faded away or were discontinued. The history of PCs has also left a trash heap of removable media technologies that were trumpeted in with fanfare and a lot of money but never really saw any adoption.

Today's highly internetworked computers have reduced the need for removable media as a method of sharing programs and data, but removable media has so many other uses that this hasn't slowed things down a bit. Removable media is the perfect tool for software distribution, data archiving, and system backup. Figure 10.1 shows my software toolbox. As a PC technician, you'll not only need to install, maintain, and troubleshoot removable media on systems for users, but also find yourself turning to removable media as a way to store and run software tools to perform all types of PC support.

This chapter covers the most common types of removable media used today. For the sake of organization, all removable media types are broken down into these groups:

- **Floppy drives**   The traditional floppy drive
- **Flash memory**   From USB thumb drives to flash memory cards
- **Optical discs**   Any shiny disc technology from CD-ROMs and DVDs to Blu-ray Discs
- **External drives**   Any hard drive or optical drive that connects to a PC via an external cable

If you go by the earlier description of removable memory, two other technologies, PC Cards and tape backups, also fit as removable media. PC Cards are a laptop-centric technology and are covered in Chapter 14, "Learning Portable Computing," whereas tape backups are part of the big world of backups and were covered briefly in Chapter 4, "Understanding Windows."

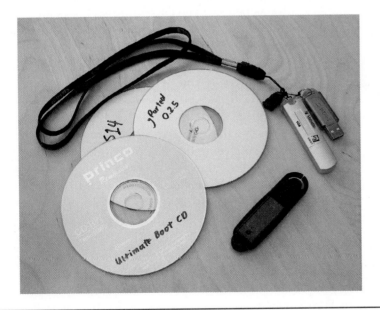

• **Figure 10.1**   Author's toolbox

Chapter 10: Removable Media

Historical/Conceptual

■ Floppy Drives

Good old floppies! These little disks, storing a whopping 1.44 MB of data per disk, have been part of PCs from the beginning. For decades, the PC industry made one attempt after another to replace the floppy with some higher-capacity removable media, only to keep falling back to the floppy disk. Floppy drive technology was well entrenched: motherboard makers found floppies easy to add, all BIOS supported them, and they were almost always the first boot device, so techs loved floppies when they helped boot a system.

Only in the past few years have we finally seen systems without floppy drives due to an industry push called *legacy-free computing*: an initiative forwarded by Microsoft and Intel back in 2001 to rid computers of old technologies such as PS/2 ports, serial ports, parallel ports—and floppy drives (interesting how long it took to start being adopted by PC makers). Thus, the venerable floppy drive will probably soon disappear from PCs. Until then, the floppy drive, that artifact from the Dark Ages of the PC world, will continue to be a viable technology you must know.

Floppy Drive Basics

When you insert a **floppy disk** into a **floppy drive**, the protective slide on the disk opens, revealing the magnetic media inside the plastic casing. A motor-driven spindle snaps into the center of the drive to make it spin. A set of read/write heads then moves back and forth across the disk, reading or writing tracks on the disk as needed. The current floppy disks are 3½ inches wide and store 1.44 MB (Figure 10.2). You use a **3½-inch floppy drive** to access the contents of the disk.

Whenever your system accesses a floppy disk in its floppy drive, a read/write LED on the outside front of the drive flashes on. You should not try to remove the floppy disk from the drive when this light is lit! That light means that the read/write heads are accessing the floppy drive, so pulling the disk out while the light is on can damage the floppy disk. When the light is off, you can push in the small release button on the front of the drive to eject the floppy disk.

• **Figure 10.2**   Floppy drive and floppy disk

The term "floppy" comes from the fact that early floppy disks were actually floppy. You could easily bend one. Newer floppy disks came in much more robust, rigid plastic casings, but the term has stuck—we still call them floppies.

The first PC floppy drives used a 5¼-inch floppy drive format (Figure 10.3). The 5¼-inch measurement actually described the drive, but most users also called the disks for those drives 5¼-inch disks. In the 1970s and early 1980s, before PCs became predominant, you would occasionally see an 8-inch format floppy drive in computers. Fortunately, these never saw any noticeable use in PCs. If you happen to run into an 8-inch drive or disk, keep it! Collectors of old computers pay big money for these old drives.

Around 1986, the 3½-inch drives appeared and, within a few years, came to dominate the floppy world completely. Today, both 3½-inch and

5¼-inch floppy drives have mostly been replaced by CD and DVD burners and USB flash drives. If you are really interested, however, you can still purchase these drives on the Internet or special-order a custom-built system complete with floppy drives pre-installed.

Installing Floppy Drives

All Windows systems reserve the drive letters A: and B: for floppy drives. You cannot name them anything other than A: or B:, but you can configure a floppy to get either drive letter. However, convention dictates that if you have only one floppy drive, you should call it A:. The second floppy drive is then called B:.

Floppy drives connect to the computer via a **34-pin ribbon cable**. If the cable supports two floppy drives, it has a seven-wire twist in the middle to differentiate electronically between the A: and B: drives. Given that the majority of users do not want two floppy drives, many system makers have dropped the twist and saved a couple of pennies on a simpler cable (Figure 10.4).

By default, almost all PCs (well, the ones that still support floppy drives) first try to boot to a floppy before any other boot device, looking for an operating system. This process enables technicians to insert a floppy disk into a sick computer to run programs when the hard drives fail. It also means hackers can insert bootable floppy disks into servers and do bad things. You do have a choice, however, because most systems have special CMOS settings with which you can change this default boot order to something other than the default drive A: and then C:; I'll show you how in a minute.

Inserting Ribbon Cables

Look at the floppy cable in Figure 10.4. Notice the connector on the left side. This connector, identical to the other connector on the same cable, plugs into the floppy controller on the motherboard, as shown in Figure 10.5. Notice how clearly the motherboard has **pin 1** marked in Figure 10.5. Not all motherboards are so clear. Make sure to orient the cable so that the colored stripe on the side of the cable is aligned with pin 1.

Here are a few tips on cable orientation. (By the way, these rules work for all ribbon cables, not just floppy cables.) Ribbon cable connectors usually have a distinct orientation notch in the middle. If your cable connector has an orientation notch and the controller socket has a slot in which the orientation notch fits, your job is easy (Figure 10.6).

Unfortunately, not all connectors use the orientation notch. Try looking in the motherboard book. All motherboard books provide a graphic of the motherboard showing the proper orientation position. Look at other ribbon

● **Figure 10.3**   A 5¼-inch floppy drive and disk

● **Figure 10.4**   Floppy cable for only one drive

• **Figure 10.5**   Plugging a floppy cable into a controller, pin 1 labeled at left

cables on the motherboard. In almost all motherboards, all plugs orient the same way. Last of all, just guess! You will not destroy anything by inserting the cable backward. When you boot up, the floppy drive will not work. This is not a big deal; turn off the system and try again.

After you insert the floppy ribbon cable into the floppy controller, you need to insert the ribbon cable into the floppy drive. Watch out here! You still need to orient the cable by pin 1—all the rules of ribbon cable insertion apply here, too. Before you plug in the floppy ribbon cable to the floppy drive, you need to know which connector on the cable to use; it makes a big difference. The specific connector that you insert into the floppy drive determines its drive letter.

If the floppy drive is installed on the end connector, it becomes the A: drive; if the drive is installed on the middle connector, it is the B: drive (Figure 10.7). If you're installing only one floppy, make sure you install it in the A: drive position.

> In the past, the CompTIA A+ certification exams have been very focused on the pins on cables! Know the number (34) and orientation (pin 1 to pin 1) for the pins on the floppy drive ribbon cable.

• **Figure 10.6**   Floppy controller with notch

Mike Meyers' CompTIA A+ Guide: Essentials

Drive A   Drive B   To Controller

• **Figure 10.7**   Cable placement determines the drive letter.

Power

Floppy drives need electricity to work, just like every other device in the PC. Modern 3½-inch floppy drives use the small **mini power connector**. Be careful! Inserting a mini connector incorrectly is easy, and if you install it incorrectly, you'll destroy the floppy drive and make what we call "The Nasty Smell." Look at Figure 10.8, a bottom view of a properly installed mini connector—note the chamfers (beveled edges) that show correct orientation. The problem lies in the plastic used to make the connector. The plastic connector bends easily, so even the least brawny techs can put the plug in a mini connector backward or hit only three of the four pins.

Great! You have installed a floppy drive! Once you have physically installed the floppy drive, it's time to go into CMOS.

• **Figure 10.8**   Properly installed mini connector

CMOS

After the floppy drive is installed, you need to configure the CMOS settings, which must correspond to the capacities of the drives. Look in your CMOS for a menu called "Standard CMOS Features" (or something similar to that) to see your floppy settings. Most CMOS setups configure the A: drive by default as a 3½-inch, 1.44-MB drive, so in most cases the floppy is already configured. Simply double-check the setting in CMOS; if it's okay, exit without changing anything. Figure 10.9 shows a typical CMOS setting for a single

> ⚠️ Installing *any* power connector incorrectly will destroy whatever device is unfortunate enough to be so abused. However, with the exception of minis, most power connectors are constructed so that it's almost impossible to install them incorrectly unintentionally.

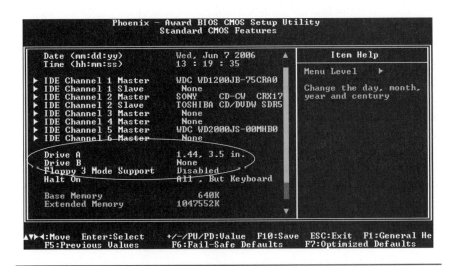

• **Figure 10.9**   CMOS setting for one standard floppy drive

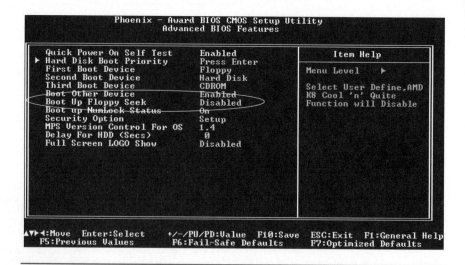

```
          Phoenix - Award BIOS CMOS Setup Utility
                   Advanced BIOS Features

   Quick Power On Self Test      Enabled            Item Help
 ▶ Hard Disk Boot Priority      Press Enter
   First Boot Device            Floppy        Menu Level    ▶
   Second Boot Device           Hard Disk
   Third Boot Device            CDROM         Select User Define,AMD
   Boot Other Device            Enabled       K8 Cool 'n' Quite
   Boot Up Floppy Seek          Disabled      Function will Disable
   Boot up Numlock Status       On
   Security Option              Setup
   MPS Version Control For OS   1.4
   Delay For HDD (Secs)         0
   Full Screen LOGO Show        Disabled




▲▼▶◀:Move   Enter:Select      +/-/PU/PD:Value  F10:Save   ESC:Exit  F1:General Help
     F5:Previous Values           F6:Fail-Safe Defaults   F7:Optimized Defaults
```

• **Figure 10.10**   CMOS Boot Up Floppy Seek option

floppy drive. On the rare occasion that you require a setting other than the typical 3½-inch, 1.44-MB A: drive, simply select the drive (A: or B:) and enter the correct capacity.

Disabling the Boot Up Floppy Seek option tells the PC not to check the floppy disk during the POST, which isn't very handy except for slightly speeding up the boot process (Figure 10.10).

Many CMOS setup utilities have an option called Floppy 3 Mode Support. Refer to Figure 10.9 to see an example of a CMOS with this option. A Mode 3 floppy is a special 1.2-MB format used outside the United States, primarily in Japan. Unless you live in Japan and use Mode 3 floppy disks, ignore this option.

■ Flash Memory

Flash memory, the same flash memory that replaced CMOS technology for your system BIOS, found another home in PCs in the form of removable mass storage devices. Flash memory comes in two families: USB thumb drives and memory cards. USB thumb drives are flash devices that contain a standard USB connection. "Memory card" is a generic term for a number of tiny cards that are used in cameras, PDAs, and other devices. Both of these families can manifest themselves as drives in Windows, but they usually perform different jobs. USB thumb drives have replaced virtually all other rewritable removable media as the way people transfer files or keep copies of important programs. My thumb drives (yes, I have two on me at all times) keep backups of my current work, important photos, and a stack of utilities I need to fix computers. Memory cards are very small and make a great way to store data on small devices and then transfer that data to your PC.

USB Thumb Drives

Moving data between computers is always a pain, and even more so since digital photography and multimedia storage have littered hard drives with huge files that won't fit on a single floppy disk. The latest entry into the floppy disk replacement sweepstakes is a winner: the USB flash memory drive, also known as the **USB thumb drive**, jump drive, or flash drive. These tiny new drives are incredibly popular (Figure 10.11). For a low price in US$, you can get an 8-GB thumb drive that holds as much data as 5600 standard 3½-inch floppy disks.

The smallest thumb drives are slightly larger than an adult thumbnail; others are larger and more rounded. The drives are hot-swappable in Windows 2000/XP/Vista. You simply plug one into any USB port and it appears as a removable storage device in My Computer or Computer. After you plug the drive into a USB port, you can copy or move data to or from your hard disk and then unplug the unit and take it with you. You can read, write, and delete files directly from the drive. Because these are USB devices, they don't need an external power source. The nonvolatile flash memory is solid-state, so it's shock resistant and is supposed to retain data safely for a decade. One big improvement over floppies is cross-platform compatibility—you can transfer files among Macintosh, Windows, and Linux operating systems.

• **Figure 10.11**   USB thumb drives

The latest systems enable you to boot to a thumb drive. With a bootable thumb drive you can replace bootable floppies, CDs, and DVDs with fast flash drives. Making a thumb drive bootable is a bit of a challenge, so most of the classic bootable-utility CD makers have created USB versions that seek out your thumb drive and add an operating system with the utilities you wish to use. Most of these are simply versions of Linux-based live CDs. At this point there's no single magic USB thumb drive to recommend, because bootable USB drives are still quite new, and updated versions come out almost daily. If you just have to try this new technology now, check out the GParted LiveUSB at http://gparted.sourceforge.net and click on the Live CD/USB/PXE link.

Flash Cards

Flash cards are the way people store data on small appliances. Every digital camera, virtually every PDA, and many cell phones come with slots for some type of memory card. Memory cards come in a number of incompatible formats, so let's start by making sure you know the more common ones.

CompactFlash

CompactFlash (CF) is the oldest, most complex, and physically largest of all removable flash media cards (Figure 10.12). Roughly one inch wide, CF cards use a simplified PCMCIA bus (see Chapter 14, "Learning Portable Computing," for details) for interconnection. CF cards come in two sizes: CF I (3.3 mm thick) and CF II (5 mm thick). CF II cards are too thick to fit into CF I slots.

• **Figure 10.12**   CF card

• Figure 10.13   Microdrive

Clever manufacturers have repurposed the CF form factor to create the microdrive (Figure 10.13). **Microdrives** are true hard drives, using platters and read/write heads that fit into the tiny CF form factor. Microdrives are slower and use more power than flash drives and, when they were first introduced, cost much less than an equivalent CF flash card. From the user's standpoint, CF flash cards and microdrives look and act exactly the same way, although the greater power consumption of microdrives makes them incompatible with some devices. These days, microdrives have been surpassed in size, speed, and cost by their flash cousins and have become more difficult to find.

SmartMedia

SmartMedia came out as a competitor to CF cards and for a few years was quite popular in digital cameras (Figure 10.14). The introduction of SD media reduced SmartMedia's popularity, and no new devices use this media.

Secure Digital

Secure Digital (SD) cards are arguably the most common flash media format today. About the size of a small postage stamp, you'll see SD cards in just about any type of device that uses flash media. SD comes in two types: the original SD and SDIO. SD cards store only data. The more advanced SDIO (the "IO" denoting input/output rather than storage) cards also support devices such as GPSs and cameras. If you want to use an SDIO device, you must have an SDIO slot. There is no way to tell an SD slot from an SDIO slot, so read the technical specs for your device!

SD cards also come in three tiny forms called *SD*, *Mini Secure Digital* (*MiniSD*), and *Micro Secure Digital* (*MicroSD*) cards. They're extremely popular in cellular phones that use flash memory, but see little use in other devices. Figure 10.15 shows the three forms of SD cards.

SD cards come in three storage capacities. *Standard SD* cards store from 4 MB to 4 GB, *Secure Digital High Capacity* (*SDHC*) cards store 4 GB to 32 GB, and *Secure Digital Extended Capacity* (*SDXC*) cards have a storage capacity of 32 GB to 2 TB. Early SD card readers and devices cannot read the SDHC or SDXC cards, though the latter standards provide backward compatibility.

• Figure 10.14   SmartMedia

SD cards developed out of an older, slower flash memory technology called *MultiMediaCard* (*MMC*). If you happen to have an MMC card lying around, you can use it in almost any SD card slot. SD cards are a little thicker than MMC cards, though, so the reverse is not true.

• Figure 10.15   SD, MiniSD, and MicroSD cards

Memory Stick

Sony always likes to use proprietary formats, and their **Memory Stick** flash memory is no exception. If you own something from Sony and it uses flash memory, you'll need a Memory Stick (Figure 10.16). There are several Memory Stick formats, including Standard, Pro, Duo, Pro Duo, and Micro.

xD Picture Card

The proprietary **Extreme Digital (xD) Picture Cards** (Figure 10.17) are about half the size of an SD card. They're almost exclusively used in Olympus and Fujifilm digital cameras, although Olympus (the developer of the xD technology) produces a USB housing so you can use an xD Picture Card like any other USB flash memory drive. The xD Picture Cards come in three flavors: original, Standard (Type M), and Hi-Speed (Type H). The Standard cards are slower than the original cards but offer greater storage capacity. The Hi-Speed cards are two to three times faster than the others and enable you to capture full-motion video—assuming the camera has that capability, naturally!

• **Figure 10.16**   Memory Stick

Card Readers

Whatever type of flash memory you use, your PC must have a **card reader** to access the data on the card directly. A number of inexpensive USB card readers are available today (Figure 10.18), and some PCs, especially those tuned to home theater use, often come with built-in readers—handy to have when someone pulls out an SD card and says "Let's look at the pictures I just took!" Of course, if the person just happened to bring her camera and the usually proprietary USB cable along, you could connect the camera to the PC and pull pictures in that way. Just make sure you have spare batteries, too! Wouldn't a card reader be a more elegant solution?

Whichever type of flash memory you have, understand that it acts exactly like a hard drive. If you wish, you can format a memory card as well as copy, paste, and rename files.

• **Figure 10.17**   xD card

■ Optical Discs

CD, DVD, and BD-media drives and discs come in a variety of flavors and formats, enabling you to back up data, record music, master home videos, and much, much more. **Optical disc** is the generic term for all those different types of shiny, 12-centimeter-wide discs that, if you're a slob like me, collect around your computer like pizza boxes. The drives that support them are called **optical drives**. This section examines optical discs and drives in detail.

CD stands for **compact disc**, a medium that was originally designed more than 20 years ago as a replacement for vinyl records. The CD now reigns as the primary method of long-term storage for sound and data. The **digital versatile disc (DVD)** first eliminated VHS cassette tapes from the commercial home movie market, and has also grown into a contender for

• **Figure 10.18**   USB card reader

backups and high-capacity storage. **Blu-ray Disc (BD)** eliminated the High-Definition DVD (HD DVD) format and may very well supersede DVD in the future as the high-definition video and data storage war wages on.

Going beyond those big three household names, the term optical disc refers to technologies such as CD-ROM, CD-R, CD-RW, DVD, DVD+RW, HD DVD, BD-R, BD-RE, and so on. Each of these technologies will be discussed in detail in this chapter—for now, understand that although the term optical disc describes a variety of exciting formats, they all basically boil down to the same physical object: that little shiny disc.

CD-Media

The best way to understand the world of optical discs is to sort out the many types of technologies available, starting with the first: the compact disc. All you're about to read is relevant and fair game for the CompTIA A+ Essentials exam. Begin by looking at how CDs work.

How CDs Work

CDs—the discs that you buy in music stores or may find in software boxes—store data via microscopic pits. CD producers use a powerful laser to burn these pits into a glass master CD. Once the CD producer creates a master, expensive machines create plastic copies, using a very high-tolerance injection-molding process. The copies are coated with a reflective metallic covering and then finished with lacquer for protection. CDs store data on only one side of the disc—we don't flip a CD as we used to flip vinyl records. Did I just sound really old? The data on a CD is near the top of the CD, where the label is located (Figure 10.19).

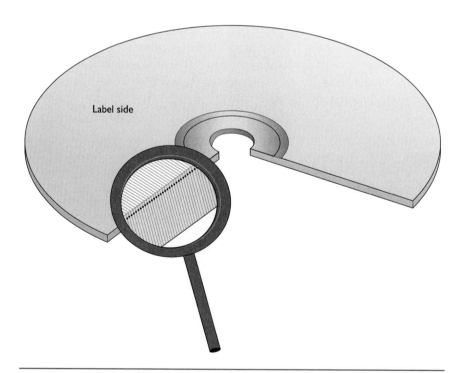

• **Figure 10.19**   Location of the data

Many people believe that scratching a CD on the bottom makes it unreadable. This is untrue. If you scratch a CD on the bottom (the shiny side), just polish out the scratches—assuming that they aren't too deep—and reread the CD. A number of companies sell inexpensive CD-polishing kits. It's the scratches on the *top* of the disc that wreak havoc on CDs. Avoid writing on the top with anything other than a soft-tipped pen, and certainly don't scratch the top!

CD readers (such as the one in your car or the one in your PC) use a laser and mirrors to read the data from the CD. The metallic covering of the CD makes a highly reflective surface; the pits create interruptions in that surface, while the non-pitted spots, called *lands*, leave it intact. The laser picks up on the reflected pattern that the pits and lands create, and the CD drive converts this pattern into binary ones and zeros. Because the pits are so densely packed on the CD, a vast amount of data can be stored: a standard CD holds up to 5.2 billion bits, or 650 million bytes, of data.

Try This!

Repairing a CD-ROM

To revive scratched CD-ROMs and other CD-media in the comfort of your home or office, get a CD polishing kit and familiarize yourself with its operation. Try This!

1. Obtain a CD-polishing kit from your local computer store, or find one online.

2. Take a CD-ROM *that you don't mind potentially ruining* and make light scratches on the bottom of the disc. Be sure not to scratch too heavily! Just try to replicate the everyday wear and tear that you've probably seen on CD-ROMs before. If you have a disc that's already lightly scratched, that's even better.

3. Use the CD-polishing kit, following the provided instructions exactly.

CD Formats

The first CDs were designed for playing music and organized the music in a special format called **CD-Digital Audio (CDDA)**, which we usually just call CD-audio. CD-audio divides the CD's data into variable-length tracks; on music CDs, each song gets one track. CD-audio is an excellent way to store music, but it lacks any error checking, file support, or directory structure, making it a terrible way to store data. For this reason, The Powers That Be created a special method for storing data on a CD, called—are you ready—**CD-ROM**. The CD-ROM format divides the CD into fixed sectors, each holding 2353 bytes.

Most CD-ROM drives also support a number of older, less well-known formats. You may never come across these formats—CD-I, CD-ROM/XA, and so forth—although you may see them listed among compatible formats on the packaging for a new drive or with a program like Nero InfoTool (Figure 10.20). Don't let these oddball formats throw you—with few exceptions, they've pretty much fallen by the wayside. All CD-ROM drives read all of these formats, assuming that the system is loaded with the proper software.

The CD-ROM format is something like a partition in the hard drive world. CD-ROM may define the sectors (and some other information), but it doesn't enable a CD-ROM disc to act like a hard drive, with a file structure, directories, and such. To make a CD-ROM act like a hard drive, there's another layer of formatting that defines the file system used on the drive.

• **Figure 10.20**   Crazy CD formats

At first glance you might think "Why don't CD-ROMs just use a FAT or an NTFS format like hard drives?" Well, first of all, they could. There's no law of physics that prevented the CD-ROM world from adopting any file system. The problem is that the CD makers did not want CD-ROM to be tied to Microsoft's or Apple's or anyone else's file format. In addition, they wanted non-PC devices to read CDs, so they invented their own file system just for CD-ROMs called **ISO-9660**. This format is sometimes referred to by the more generic term, CD File System (CDFS). The vast majority of data CD-ROMs today use this format.

Over the years, extensions of ISO-9660 have addressed certain limitations, such as the characters used in file and directory names, filename length, and directory depth. It's important to know these ISO-9660 extensions:

- **Joliet** Microsoft's extension of ISO-9660. Macintosh and Linux also support Joliet-formatted discs.

- **Rock Ridge** An open standard to provide UNIX file system support for discs; rarely used outside of UNIX systems.

- **El Torito** Added support to enable bootable CD-media. All bootable CDs use the El Torito standard, which is supported by the BIOS on all modern PCs.

- **Apple Extensions** Apple's added support for their HFS file system. Windows systems cannot read these CDs without third-party tools.

It is important to appreciate that all of these file systems are extensions, not replacements for ISO-9660. That means a single CD/DVD can have both regular ISO-9660 information and an extension. For example, it's very common to have a CD-media that is ISO-9660 and Joliet. If you place the CD into a device that cannot read Joliet, it will still be able to read the ISO-9660 information.

CD-ROM Speeds

The first CD-ROM drives processed data at roughly 150,000 bytes per second (150 KBps), copying the speed from the original CD-audio format. Although this speed is excellent for listening to music, the CD-ROM industry quickly recognized that installing programs or transferring files from a CD-ROM at 150 KBps was the electronic equivalent of watching paint dry. Since the day the first CD-ROM drives for PCs hit the market, there has been a desire to speed them up to increase their data throughput. Each increase in speed is measured in multiples of the original 150-KBps drives and given an × to show speed relative to the first (1×) drives. Here's a list of the common CD-ROM speeds, including most of the early speeds that are no longer produced:

1× 150 KBps	10× 1500 KBps	40× 6000 KBps
2× 300 KBps	12× 1800 KBps	48× 7200 KBps
3× 450 KBps	16× 2400 KBps	52× 7800 KBps
4× 600 KBps	24× 3600 KBps	60× 9000 KBps
6× 900 KBps	32× 4800 KBps	72× 10800 KBps
8× 1200 KBps	36× 5400 KBps	

Keep in mind that these are maximum speeds that are rarely met in real-life operation. You can, however, count on a 32× drive to read data faster than an 8× drive. As multipliers continue to increase, so many other factors come into play that telling the difference between a 48× and a 52× drive, for example, becomes difficult. High-speed CD-ROM drives are so inexpensive, however, that most folks buy the fastest drive possible—at least installations go faster!

CD-R

Making CD-ROMs requires specialized, expensive equipment and substantial expertise, so a relatively small number of CD-ROM production companies do it. Yet, since the day the first CD-ROMs came to market, demand has been terrific for a way that ordinary PC users could make their own CDs. The CD industry made a number of attempts to create a technology that would let users record, or *burn*, their own CDs.

In the mid-1990s, the CD industry introduced the **CD-recordable (CD-R)** standard, which enables affordable CD-R drives, often referred to as *CD burners*, to add data to special CD-R discs. Any CD-ROM drive can then read the data stored on the CD-R, and all CD-R drives can read regular CD-ROMs. CD-R discs come in two varieties: a 74-minute disc that holds approximately 650 MB, and an 80-minute variety that holds approximately 700 MB (Figure 10.21). A CD-R burner must be specifically designed to support the longer 80-minute CD-R format, but most drives you'll encounter can do this.

CD-R discs function similarly to regular CD-ROMs, although the chemicals used to make them produce a brightly colored recording side on almost all CD-R discs. CD-ROM discs, in contrast, have a silver recording side. CD-R technology records data by using special organic dyes embedded into the disc. This dye is what gives the CD-R its distinctive bottom color. CD-R burners have a second burn laser, roughly ten times as powerful as the read laser, that heats the organic dye. This causes a change in the reflectivity of the surface, creating the functional equivalent of a CD-ROM's pits.

• **Figure 10.21**   A CD-R disc, with its capacity clearly labeled

Once the CD-R drive burns data onto a CD-R, the data cannot be erased or changed short of destroying the disc itself. Early CD-R drives required that the entire disc be burned in one burn session, wasting any unused part of the CD-R disc. These were called single-session drives. All modern CD-R drives are **multisession drives** so you can go back and burn additional data onto the CD-R disc until the disc is full. Multisession drives also have the capability to "close" a partially filled CD-R so that no more data can be burned onto that disc.

Some music CD players can't handle CD-R discs.

CD-R drives have two speeds that matter: the record speed and the read speed, both expressed as multiples of the 150-KBps speed of the original CD-ROM drives. The record speed, which is listed first, is always equal to or slower than the read speed. For example, a CD-R drive with a specification of 8×24× would burn at 8× and read at 24×.

CD-RW

For all their usefulness, CD-R drives have disappeared from the market. Notice that I didn't say CD-R *discs* have disappeared; more CD-R discs are burned now than ever before. Just as CD-R drives could both burn CD-R discs and read CD-ROMs, a newer type of drive called **CD-rewritable (CD-RW)** took over the burning market from CD-R drives. Although this drive has its own type of CD-RW discs, it also can burn to CD-R discs, which are much cheaper.

CD-RW technology enables you not only to burn a disc, but to *burn over* existing data on a CD-RW disc. This is not something you need for every disc; for example, I create CD-R archives of my completed books to store the text and graphics for posterity—this is data I want to access later but do not need to modify. While I'm working on content for the CD that accompanies this book, however, I may decide to delete an item; I couldn't do that with a CD-R. The CD-RW format, on the other hand, essentially takes CD-media to the functional equivalent of a 650-MB floppy disk. Once again, CD-RW discs look exactly like CD-ROM discs with the exception of a colored bottom side. Figure 10.22 shows all three formats.

A CD-RW drive works by using a laser to heat an amorphous (noncrystalline) substance that, when cooled, slowly becomes crystalline. The crystalline areas are reflective, whereas the amorphous areas are not. Because both CD-R and CD-RW drives require a powerful laser, making a drive that could burn CD-Rs and CD-RWs was a simple process, and plain CD-R drives disappeared almost overnight. Why buy a CD-R drive when a comparably priced CD-RW drive could burn both CD-R and CD-RW discs?

CD-RW drive specs have three multiplier values. The first shows the CD-R write speed, the second shows the CD-RW rewrite speed, and the third shows the read speed. Write, rewrite, and read speeds vary tremendously among the various brands of CD-RW drives; here are just a few representative samples: 8×4×32×, 12×10×32×, and 48×24×48×.

One of the goals with the introduction of CD-RWs was the idea of making a CD-RW act like a hard drive so you could simply drag a file onto the CD-RW (or CD-R) and just as easily drag it off again. This goal was difficult for two reasons: first, the different file formats made on-the-fly conversion risky. Second, CD-RWs don't store data exactly the same way as hard drives and would quickly wear out if data were copied in the same manner.

Two developments, UDF and packet writing, enable you to treat a CD-RW just like a hard drive—with a few gotchas. The not-so-new kid in town with CD-media file formats is the **universal data format (UDF)**. UDF is a replacement for ISO-9660 and all of its various extensions, resulting in a single file format that any drive and operating system can read. UDF has taken over the DVD world (all movie DVDs use this format) and is poised to also become the CD-media file format in the near future. UDF handles very large

> You can rewrite CD-RW discs a limited number of times. The number varies according to the source, but expect a maximum life of about 1000 rewrites, although in real life you'll get considerably fewer.

• **Figure 10.22**   CD-ROM, CD-R, and CD-RW discs

files and is excellent for all rewritable CD-media. UDF has been available for quite a while, but until Windows Vista came out, no version of Windows could write to UDF-formatted discs. They could *read* the discs, but if you wanted to *write* to them in Windows you had to use one of a number of third-party UDF tools such as Roxio's DirectCD and Nero's InCD. UDF also supports a feature called Mount Rainier—better known as packet writing—that works with UDF so you can copy individual files back and forth like a hard drive. With UDF and packet writing, rewritable CD-media is as easy to use as a hard drive.

Windows and CD-Media

Virtually all optical drives are **ATAPI-compliant**, meaning they plug into the ATA controllers on the motherboard, just like a hard drive, so you don't need to install drivers. You just plug in the drive and, assuming you didn't make any physical installation mistakes, the drive appears in Windows (Figure 10.23).

Windows displays an optical drive in My Computer or Computer with the typical optical drive icon and assigns it a drive letter. If you want to put data on a CD-R disc, however, you need special *burner software* to get that data onto the disc. Windows XP comes with burning support—you just drop a CD-R disc into your CD-RW drive, open the drive in My Computer, drag the files you wish to copy, and click Write to Disc. Also, Windows Media Player versions such as 9, 10, and 11 enable you to create music and data CDs within Windows XP. With Windows Vista, you can burn music and data directly to disc. Just put your CD-R into your CD-RW drive and, if AutoPlay is set to detect blank CDs, the OS presents you with the options to burn an audio CD by using Windows Media Player or to burn files to disc by using Windows. Almost every new CD-RW drive comes with some type of burner software as well, so you rarely need to go out and buy your own unless you have a preference for a particular brand. Figure 10.24 shows the opening menu of one that I like, the popular Nero optical disc burning program.

Try This!

Deleting Files from a CD-RW

Windows XP comes with built-in support for CD-Rs and CD-RWs. If you have a CD-RW drive with Windows XP, copy a couple of files onto a CD-RW and burn them to the disc. Now try to delete only one file—you can't! That's because no version of Windows before Vista supports packet writing. Try installing a copy of Roxio's Creator 9 or Nero 2009 and try again on a fresh CD-RW—it works! All third-party UDF tools support packet writing.

• **Figure 10.23**   CD-media drive in Windows

When I buy a new program on CD, the first thing I do is make a backup copy; then I stash the original under lock and key. If I break, melt, or otherwise destroy the backup, I quickly create a new one from the original. I can easily copy the disc, because my system, like many, has both a regular CD-ROM and a CD-RW drive (even though CD-RW drives read CD-ROM discs). I can place a CD in the CD-ROM drive and a CD-R or CD-RW disc in the CD-RW drive. Then I use a disk-copy application to create an exact replica of the CD quickly. CD-RW drives work great for another, bigger type of backup: not the archival "put it on the disc and stash it in the closet" type of

• Figure 10.24   Nero optical disc burning program

backup but rather the daily/weekly backups that most of us do (or should do!) on our systems. Using CD-R discs for these backups is wasteful; once a disc fills up, you throw it away at the next backup. But with CD-RW, you can use the same set of CD-RW discs time and again to perform backups.

Music CDs

Computers do not hold a monopoly on CD burning. Many companies offer consumer CD burners that work with your stereo system. These come in a wide variety of formats, but they're usually dual-deck player/recorder combinations. These recorders do not use regular CD-R or CD-RW discs. Instead, under U.S. law, these home recorders must use a slightly different disc called a **music CD-R**. Makers of music CDs pay a small royalty for each CD (and add it to your price). You can record *to* a music CD-R or CD-RW, but you cannot record *from* one—the idea being to restrict duplication. If you decide to buy one of these burners, make sure to buy the special music CD-Rs. Music CD-Rs are designed specifically for these types of devices and may not work well in a PC.

DVD-Media

For years, the video industry tried to create an optical-media replacement for videotape. The 12-inch-diameter *laserdisc* format originally introduced by Philips gained some ground in the 1980s and 1990s. But the high cost of both the discs and the players, plus various marketing factors, meant there was never a very large laserdisc market. You may still find one of them sitting around, however, or you may know someone who invested in a small collection during the laserdisc's heyday.

The DVD was developed by a large consortium of electronics and entertainment firms during the early 1990s and released as digital *video* discs in 1995. The transformation of DVD to a data storage medium quickly required a name change to digital *versatile* discs. You'll still hear both terms used. The industry also uses the term **DVD-video** to distinguish the movie format from the data formats.

With the exception of the DVD logo stamped on all commercial DVDs (Figure 10.25), DVDs look exactly like CD-media discs; but that's pretty much where the similarities end. DVD has become the fastest growing media format in history and has completely overtaken VHS as the preferred media for video. Additionally, one variant of DVD called DVD-RAM has enjoyed some success as a mass storage medium.

The single best word to describe DVD is *capacity*. All previous optical discs stored a maximum of 700 MB of data or 80 minutes of low-quality video. The lowest-capacity DVD holds 4.37 GB of data, or two hours of standard-definition video. The highest-capacity DVD stores roughly 16 GB of data, or more than eight hours of video! DVD achieves these amazing capacities by using a number of technologies, but three are most important. First, DVD uses smaller pits than CD-media, and packs them much more densely. Second, DVD comes in both *single-sided* (*SS*) and *double-sided* (*DS*) formats. As the name implies, a DS disc holds twice the data of an SS disc, but it also requires you to flip the disc to read the other side. Third, DVDs come in *single-layer* (*SL*) and *dual-layer* (*DL*) formats. DL formats use two pitted layers on each side, each with a slightly different reflectivity index. Table 10.1 shows the common DVD capacities.

• **Figure 10.25**   Typical DVD-video

DVD-Video

The most beautiful trait of DVD-video lies in its capability to store two hours of video on one side. You drop in a DVD-video and get to watch an entire movie without flipping it over. DVD-video supports TV-style 4:3 aspect-ratio screens as well as 16:9 theater screens, but it is up to the producer to decide which to use. Many DVD-video producers distribute DVD movies on DS media with a 4:3 ratio on one side and 16:9 ratio on the other. DVD-video relies on the **MPEG-2** standard of video and audio compression to reach the magic of two hours of video per side. *Moving Picture Experts Group (MPEG)* is a group of compression standards for both audio and video. The MPEG-2 standard offers resolutions of up to 1280 × 720 at 60 frames per second (fps), with full CD-quality audio (standard DVDs only offer 480 vertical resolution, the same as regular television).

Table 10.1	DVD Versions/Capacities
DVD Version	**Capacity**
DVD-5 (12 cm, SS/SL)	4.37 GB, more than two hours of video
DVD-9 (12 cm, SS/DL)	7.95 GB, about four hours of video
DVD-10 (12 cm, DS/SL)	8.74 GB, about four and a half hours of video
DVD-18 (12 cm, DS/DL)	15.90 GB, more than eight hours of video

Tech Tip

MPEG Standards

Reproducing video and sound on the PC provides interesting challenges for developers. How do you take a motion picture from film, translate it into ones and zeros that the CPU understands, process those bits, and then send high-quality video and sound to the monitor and speakers for the pleasure of the computer user? How much data do you think is required to display even a two-minute clip of a car racing through a city street, in all the minute detail of the shops, people, screeching tires, road debris, and so on? For that matter, how do you store *the obviously huge amount of data required to do this?*

To handle these chores, the Moving Pictures Experts Group (MPEG) has released coding standards such as MPEG-1, MPEG-2, and MPEG-4. Each standard provides a different compression algorithm, *which makes the files manageable. The standards also implement various technologies to handle movement, called* motion compensation. *The details of the standards matter a lot to the folks producing the movies and other video and audio content, but here's the short answer that should suffice for the purposes of a PC tech.*

MPEG-1 is the standard on which video and MP3, among other technologies, are based. The most common implementations of this standard provide a resolution of 352 × 240 at 30 fps. This video quality falls just below that of a conventional VHS video.

One very well-known subset of MPEG-1 is better known for audio than video. MPEG-1 Layer 3, better known as MP3 format, dominates the world of audio. MP3 takes an uncompressed audio file and compresses it dramatically, but the algorithm is so tight that the music that comes out of the speakers remains almost completely faithful to the original audio file. To paraphrase a catchphrase from the 1980s—I want my MP3s!

MPEG-2 provides resolutions of 720 × 480 and 1280 × 720 at 60 fps (as well as others), plus CD-quality audio, making it adequate for all major TV standards, even HDTV. MPEG-2 is the standard that covers DVD-ROM technology—it can compress two hours of video into a file no larger than a few gigabytes. Although encoding video into MPEG-2 format requires a computer with some serious firepower, even a modest PC can decompress and play such a video.

The **MPEG-4** *standard is based on MPEG-1, MPEG-2, and Apple's QuickTime technology. MPEG-4 graphics and video files use what's known as* wavelet *compression to create files that are more compact than either JPEG or QuickTime files. This superior compression makes MPEG-4 popular for delivering video and images over the Web. MPEG-4 higher-efficiency standards such as advanced video coding are included with MPEG-4 and used for Blu-ray Discs. And notably, MPEG-4 provides Intellectual Property Management and Protection (IPMP), which supports digital rights management.*

MPEG-7 is designed to complement the previous standards as a fast and efficient multimedia content searching tool.

MPEG-21 is concerned with and focuses on coding and digital rights. MPEG-21 uses a Rights Expression Language (REL) and a Rights Data Dictionary to protect digital material from illicit file sharing.

DVD-ROM

DVD-ROM is the DVD equivalent of the standard CD-ROM data format except that it's capable of storing up to almost 16 GB of data. Almost all DVD-ROM drives also fully support DVD-video, as well as most CD-ROM formats. Most DVD drives sold with PCs are DVD-ROM drives.

Recordable DVD

The IT industry has no fewer than *six* distinct standards of recordable DVD-media: DVD-ROM for general use, DVD-R for authoring, DVD-RW, DVD+R, DVD+RW, and DVD-RAM. Both DVD-R standard discs and DVD+R discs work like CD-Rs. You can write to them but not erase or alter what's written. **DVD-RW**, **DVD+RW**, and DVD-RAM discs can be written and rewritten, just like CD-RW discs. Most DVD drives can read all formats with the exception of DVD-RAM. DVD-RAM is the only DVD format that uses a cartridge, so it requires a special drive (Figure 10.26). DVD-RAM is still around but fading away.

Although there is little if any difference in quality among the standards, the competition between corporations pushing their preferred standards has raged for years. Sony and Phillips, for example, pushed the + series, whereas other manufacturers pushed the – series.

Worse, no recordable DVD drive manufactured before 2003 could write any format except its own. You could plop down US$250 on a brand-new DVD+RW drive and still find yourself unable to edit a disc from your friend who used the DVD-RW format! Half of the time, the drive couldn't even *read* the competing format disc.

The situation is much better today, as DVD±RW combo drives in PCs play just about anyone else's DVDs. The challenge is DVD players. If you want to make a DVD of your family picnic and then play it on the DVD player hooked to your television, take the time to read the documentation for your player to make sure it reads that particular DVD format—not all players read all formats.

Blu-ray Disc-Media

Blu-ray Disc is considered the next generation in optical disc formatting and storage technology after CD and DVD. Because of its near-perfect audio and video quality; mass acceptance by industry-leading computer, electronics, game, music, retail, and motion picture companies; and huge storage capacities of up to 25 GB (single-layer disc) and 50 GB (dual-layer disc), Blu-ray Disc technology is expected to make CD and DVD optical media and devices obsolete.

Blu-ray Discs come in two sizes, standard and mini. The standard size matches that of earlier optical discs, such as CD-R and DVD-RW, and is what you'll see used in computers and for movies (Figure 10.27). The mini-size discs are a lot smaller and, naturally, offer less storage. You'll find mini Blu-ray Discs in very high-end camcorders. Table 10.2 shows the details of the two formats.

Unlike with DVD discs, Blu-ray Disc offers no option at this time of a double-sided disc. I wouldn't be surprised to see this option in the coming years.

Blu-ray Disc technology offers several advantages over DVD aside from raw capacity. First, Blu-ray Disc uses a blue-violet laser (hence the Blu in the name) with a wavelength of 405 nm. (DVD uses a red laser technology with a wavelength of 650 nm.) The 405-nm wavelength is smaller and much more precise, enabling better use of space during the creation process and ultimately resulting in a sharper image. Second, Blu-ray Disc can handle high-definition (HD) video in resolutions far higher than DVD. Finally, Blu-ray Disc supports many more video compression schemes, giving producers more options for putting content on discs.

• **Figure 10.26**   DVD-RAM disc

• **Figure 10.27**   Standard Blu-ray Disc

Table 10.2	Standard and Mini Blu-ray Disc		
Type	**Size**	**Capacity (single layer)**	**Capacity (dual layer)**
Standard disc	12 cm	25 GB	50 GB
Mini disc	8 cm	7.8 GB	15.6 GB

There was a brief battle for supremacy in the high-definition digital war between Blu-ray Disc and a competing high-definition optical disc standard called HD DVD. Major content manufacturers and developers leaned toward Blu-ray Disc, and in early 2008, Toshiba—the primary company behind HD DVD—threw in the towel. HD DVD is no longer being developed or supported.

BD-ROM

BD-ROM (read only) is the Blu-ray Disc equivalent of the standard DVD-ROM data format except, as noted earlier, it can store much more data and produces superior audio and video results. Almost all BD-ROM drives are fully backward compatible and support DVD-video as well as most CD-ROM formats. If you want to display the best possible movie picture quality on your HDTV, you should get a Blu-ray Disc player and use Blu-ray Discs in place of DVDs. Most new computer systems don't come standard with Blu-ray Disc drives installed. You can often custom-order a system with a Blu-ray Disc drive or you can simply install one yourself. Figure 10.28 shows a Blu-ray Disc drive.

BD-R and BD-RE

Blu-ray Discs come in two writable formats, **BD-R** (for **recordable**) and **BD-RE** (for **rewritable**). You can write to a BD-R disc one time. You can write to and erase a BD-RE several times. There are also BD-R and BD-RE versions of mini Blu-ray Discs.

Blu-ray Burners

Most Blu-ray Disc burners cost a lot (at the time of this writing) and are out of the price range for the average consumer, but they will eventually be as common as the average CD-RW or DVD-RW. Blu-ray Disc burners and other Blu-ray Disc drives can be connected internally or externally to a system. It is common for them to be connected externally via Hi-Speed USB 2.0, FireWire, or eSATA or internally through PATA, SATA, SCSI, or USB connections. Operating systems such as Windows 2000, XP, Vista, and Windows 7 all support Blu-ray Disc burners and software. The software you use for burning is totally up to you; however, as always, you should follow the manufactured specifications for the best results. Most multidrive Blu-ray Disc burners offer the following support features:

- **Figure 10.28**   A combination CD/DVD/Blu-ray Disc drive

If you own a PlayStation 3, you already have a Blu-ray Disc player. That's the optical format the game system uses.

- **Media support**   BD-R, BD-RE, DVD-ROM, DVD-RAM, DVD-video, DVD+/-R DL, DVD+/-R, DVD+/-RW, CD-DA, CD-ROM, CD-R, and CD-RW.

- **Write speed (max)**   2× BD-R, 4× DVD+/-R DL, 8× DVD+/-R(8×), and 24× CD-R

- **Rewrite speed (max)**   2× BD-RE, 8× DVD+RW, 6× DVD-RW, 5× DVD-RAM, and 16× CD-RW

- **Read speed (max)**   2× BD-ROM, 8× DVD-ROM, and 32× CD-ROM

- **Compatibility**   Most Blu-ray Disc drives are backward compatible, meaning they can read and play CDs and DVDs. CD and DVD drives and players cannot read or play Blu-ray Discs.

■ Chapter Summary

After reading this chapter and completing the exercises, you should understand the following about floppy disk drives, flash memory, and optical-media technology.

Explain and install floppy disk drives

- Floppy disk drives are becoming a thing of the past as Microsoft and Intel push for legacy-free computing. The small, 1.44-MB-capacity floppy disks are being replaced by higher-capacity removable media.

- Floppy disks are constructed of a flexible magnetic disc housed inside a square plastic case. The case has a sliding protective cover that opens to reveal a portion of the magnetic media when inside a floppy drive. Read/write heads inside the floppy disk drive move back and forth across the media, reading or writing data as necessary.

- During disk access, an LED on the front of the drive lights up. Never eject a floppy disk when this light is on.

- Floppy disks have gone through several stages of improvement, becoming smaller with each phase. Pre-PC computers used an 8-inch floppy. Early PCs used a 5¼-inch floppy. Modern floppy disks, which appeared around 1986, are 3½ inches.

- You may have a maximum of two floppy disk drives in a system, and they must use either the drive letter A: or B:; however, a single floppy disk drive can be configured to use either drive letter. By convention, if your system has only one floppy disk drive, you should configure it as drive A:. A 34-pin ribbon data cable is used to connect the floppy disk drive to the motherboard; a 4-pin mini connector supplies power. Attaching the data cable backward won't damage anything, but the drive won't work. If you attach the power connector incorrectly, you risk damaging the drive.

- Most floppy ribbon cables have three connectors and a twist. The end without the twist connects to the motherboard, matching the red stripe on the cable with pin 1 of the motherboard connector. The drive attached to the middle connector on the cable receives the drive letter B:. The drive attached to

the other end of the cable (after the twist) is assigned the drive letter A:.

- After connecting a floppy disk drive, configure the CMOS settings. Make sure the CMOS setting matches your floppy disk drive size/capacity; for example, 3½ inches and 1.44 MB.

Demonstrate the variations among flash drives and other tiny drives

- Flash memory includes USB thumb drives and memory cards. USB thumb drives contain a standard USB connection and have replaced many other forms of removable media as the way to transfer files. Memory cards, a generic term, are used in digital cameras, PDAs, and other devices.

- Thumb drives store much more data than floppies— sometimes up to the equivalent of thousands of floppy disks. They are hot-swappable in Windows 2000/XP/Vista and don't require an external power source, as they are powered directly from the USB bus. Most new PCs enable you to boot from a USB thumb drive.

- Flash cards, which are used in portable devices such as digital cameras, PDAs, and phones, come in many varieties. The most common types are CompactFlash, SmartMedia, Secure Digital, Memory Stick, and Extreme Digital (xD) Picture Card. CompactFlash cards are the oldest of these. At about 1 inch wide, they use the PCMCIA bus and come in two thicknesses: CF I at 3.3 mm thick and CF II at 5 mm thick. SmartMedia competed directly with CompactFlash and was used mainly in digital cameras. The introduction of Secure Digital has made SmartMedia all but obsolete. Secure Digital is perhaps the most popular flash card today and comes in two types: original SD and SDIO. Smaller versions of Secure Digital cards, MiniSD and MicroSD, are also available. Memory Stick, a proprietary format from Sony, comes in several formats, including Standard, Pro, Duo, Pro Duo, and Micro. xD Picture Cards, developed by Olympus, are about half the size of Secure Digital cards and are used almost exclusively in digital cameras.

- No matter what type of flash card you have, you need a card reader to access it. Some PCs have built-in card readers. External USB card readers are also available. Sometimes a device such as a digital camera or PDA can double as a card reader.

Identify optical-media technology

- CDs store data by using microscopic pits burned into a glass master CD with a powerful laser. Expensive machines create plastic copies of the glass master that are then coated with a reflective metallic coating. CDs store data on one side of the disc only. The CD drive reads the pits and the non-pitted areas (lands) and converts the pattern into ones and zeros.

- CDs come in many varieties. CD-Digital Audio is for playing music, but it lacks error checking, file support, and directory structure. CD-ROM discs are for storing data. They use the ISO-9660 file system, also known as CDFS. Extensions of ISO-9660 have offered improvements to file and directory naming, filename length, and directory depth and include Joliet, Rock Ridge, El Torito, and Apple Extensions.

- CD-ROM speeds have increased substantially from the original 150 KBps. Increased speeds are measured in multiples of 150 KBps, so a 10× CD-ROM has a maximum speed of 1500 KBps.

- CD-recordable (CD-R) discs hold either 650 MB or 700 MB and can store either audio or data. Special organic dyes that give the CD-Rs their distinctive bottom color aid in the burning process. A strong laser in the CD drive heats the dye and changes the reflectivity of the CD-R's surface, resulting in a reflective/less-reflective pattern that is converted to ones and zeros. Once data is burned to a CD-R, the data cannot be erased. With multisession drives, you can burn data to a portion of a disc and then go back later and burn more data to the disc. CD-R discs are rated with two speeds: a write speed followed by a read speed.

- CD-rewritable (CD-RW) discs, unlike CD-Rs, enable you to erase data and burn new data. CD-RWs are rated with three speeds: write speed followed by rewrite speed followed by read speed. The UDF file format (the replacement for ISO-9660) handles large files better than CDFS. Packet writing, a feature used by UDF, allows you to copy files back and forth to a CD-RW like a hard drive.

- Most CD drives are ATAPI compliant and do not need drivers installed for them to work. Windows XP can burn CD-Rs and CD-RWs with no additional software but cannot burn bootable CDs. If you need to create a bootable CD, you need a third-party application such as Ahead's Nero Express. Many companies offer standalone CD burners that attach to your stereo system instead of your PC; however, these machines use a different type of CD called a music CD-R and are not compatible with standard CD-R or CD-RW discs.

- DVDs were released as digital video discs in 1995, but as usage evolved to include data storage, the name was changed to digital versatile disc. The lowest-capacity DVD holds 4.37 GB of data. DVDs offer much higher capacities than CDs, because DVDs use smaller and more densely packed pits, can be burned on both sides of the disc, and can burn two layers of pits per side for a total of four layers. DVD video uses the MPEG-2 video standard and can store two hours of video on a single side.

- DVD-ROM, the DVD equivalent of CD-ROM, can store up to 16 GB of data. Recordable DVD-media comes in many varieties: DVD-ROM for general purpose, DVD-R for authoring, DVD+R, DVD-RW, DVD+RW, and DVD-RAM. You can write to DVD-R and DVD+R but not erase them. You can both burn and erase DVD-RW, DVD+RW, and DVD-RAM.

- Standard Blu-ray Discs have storage capacities of up to 25 GB (single-layer disc) and 50 GB (dual-layer disc) and provide near-perfect picture quality.

- You can write to a BD-R (recordable) disc one time. You can erase and write to a BD-RE (rewritable) several times.

■ Key Terms

3½-inch floppy drive *(314)*
34-pin ribbon cable *(315)*
ATAPI-compliant *(327)*
BD-ROM *(332)*

Blu-ray Disc (BD) *(322)*
Blu-ray Disc recordable (BD-R) *(332)*
Blu-ray Disc rewritable (BD-RE) *(332)*
card reader *(321)*

CD-Digital Audio (CDDA) *(323)*
CD-recordable (CD-R) *(325)*
CD-rewritable (CD-RW) *(326)*
CD-ROM *(323)*
compact disc (CD) *(321)*
CompactFlash (CF) *(319)*
digital versatile disc (DVD) *(321)*
DVD-ROM *(330)*
DVD-RW *(330)*
DVD+RW *(330)*
DVD-video *(329)*
Extreme Digital (xD) Picture Card *(321)*
floppy disk *(314)*
floppy drive *(314)*
ISO-9660 *(324)*

Memory Stick *(321)*
microdrive *(320)*
mini power connector *(317)*
MPEG-2 *(329)*
MPEG-4 *(330)*
multisession drive *(325)*
music CD-R *(328)*
optical disc *(321)*
optical drive *(321)*
pin 1 *(315)*
removable media *(312)*
Secure Digital (SD) *(320)*
SmartMedia *(320)*
universal data format (UDF) *(326)*
USB thumb drive *(319)*

■ Key Term Quiz

Use the Key Terms list to complete the sentences that follow. Not all terms will be used.

1. If you want to burn part of a disc and finish burning it at a later time, you need to select a(n) _____.

2. The first kind of CD disc was the _____ that is still used for music but is inappropriate for data because it lacks any error correction techniques.

3. While a CD-ROM disc holds about 700 MB of data, a(n) _____ stores from 4.37 GB to 15.9 GB, depending on the number of sides and layers used.

4. Floppy drives use a(n) _____ to connect the floppy drive to the motherboard.

5. The red stripe on a floppy drive cable must be oriented to _____ on the controller.

6. Currently, the most popular flash memory cards are _____.

7. The floppy disk is quickly being replaced by the _____ because of its large capacity and portability.

8. DVD video uses the _____ standard of video.

9. DVDs use the _____ file structure.

■ Multiple-Choice Quiz

1. What kind of disc must you use in a non-PC CD burner that works with your stereo system?

   A. CDDA

   B. CD-RW

   C. CD-UDF

   D. Music CD-R

2. What is the minimum capacity of a DVD?

   A. 650 MB

   B. 3.47 GB

   C. 4.37 GB

   D. 7.34 GB

3. If you have two floppy disc drives in your system, which one receives the drive letter A:?

   A. The drive jumpered for master

   B. The drive connected to the primary floppy drive controller

   C. The drive in the middle of the floppy cable

   D. The drive at the end of the floppy cable

4. Which type of flash memory card is currently the oldest?

   A. CompactFlash

   B. Memory Stick

   C. Secure Digital

   D. SmartMedia

5. Which device allows your computer to read flash memory cards?

   A. Scanner

   B. Card reader

   C. Floppy drive

   D. ZIP drive

6. Both CD and DVD drive speeds are based on multiples of the original CD-ROM drive speed. What is that speed?

   A. 100 KBps

   B. 150 KBps

   C. 100 MBps

   D. 150 MBps

7. You are looking for a CD-RW drive that can write CD-Rs at 48×, read CDs at 52×, and write CD-RWs at 32×. Which of the following answers meets your specifications?

   A. 52×48×32

   B. 32×48×52

   C. 48×32×52

   D. 48×52×32

8. What type of DVD can store 15.9 GB of data or more than eight hours of video?

   A. Double-sided, single-layered

   B. Single-sided, single-layered

   C. Single-sided, dual-layered

   D. Double-sided, dual-layered

9. Which of the following kinds of discs is the best choice for performing regular backups?

   A. CD-ROM/XA

   B. CD-Interactive (CD-I)

   C. CD-R

   D. CD-RW

■ Essay Quiz

1. Why do many manufacturers build computers without floppy drives? If you bought a new computer, would you still want a floppy disk on it? Write a short essay defending or attacking the floppy drive.

2. You have been tasked to provide removable media for each of the technicians in your department. One tech wants a card reader and SD cards, and another wants a USB thumb drive. Write a memo outlining the advantages of each technology and make a recommendation.

3. Your department is getting ready to replace the old computers, and your boss, Mrs. Turner, has asked you to investigate what kind of optical drives the new computers should have. Write a memo to your boss listing the device(s) you have selected and justifying your choice(s).

4. Your friend Dudley wants to burn high-definition movies on his desktop system, which currently only has a CD-RW drive. He eventually wants to play back the movies with the highest possible picture quality on his brand-new HDTV. What kind of technology and other considerations would you suggest to Dudley to achieve his goal?

Lab Projects

• Lab Project 10.1

Flash media comes in a bunch of different forms. Take a trip to your local computer store—or even to a drugstore that has digital picture processing—and see what sort of media or flash devices they have available. What are some of the advantages or disadvantages of one form factor over another?

• Lab Project 10.2

Use the Internet to check these sites: www.compaq.com, www.dell.com, and www.gateway.com. What kinds of optical drives do these companies offer with their new computers? Do any of the companies offer multiple optical drives? If so, which ones and what devices? What upgrades for optical drives do the companies offer and how expensive are the upgrades? If you were buying a new PC, which optical drive(s) would you want on your computer? Why?

Installing and Upgrading Windows

chapter

11

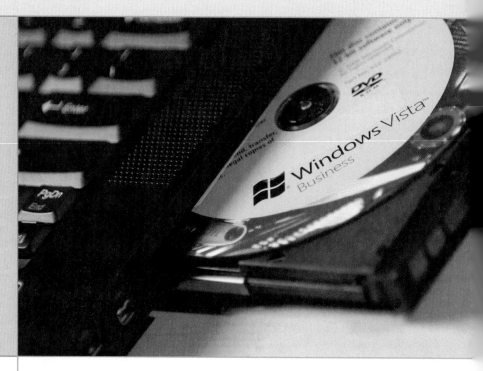

"Microsoft has a new version out…which according to everybody is the 'most reliable Windows ever.' To me, this is like saying that asparagus is 'the most articulate vegetable ever.'"

—DAVE BARRY

In this chapter, you will learn how to

- **Identify and implement pre-installation tasks**
- **Install and upgrade Windows 2000, Windows XP, and Windows Vista**
- **Troubleshoot installation problems**
- **Identify and implement post-installation tasks**
- **Explain the structures created during the installation process**

An **operating system (OS)** provides the fundamental link between the user and the hardware that makes up the PC. Without an operating system, all of the greatest, slickest PC hardware in the world is but so much copper, silicon, and gold wrapped up as a big, beige paperweight (or, if you're a teenaged boy, a big, gleaming, black paperweight with a window and glowing fluorescent lights, possibly shaped like a robot). The operating system creates the interface between human and machine, enabling you to unleash the astonishing power locked up in the sophisticated electronics of the PC to create amazing pictures, games, documents, business tools, medical miracles, and much more.

This chapter takes you through the processes for installing and upgrading Windows. It starts by analyzing the preinstallation tasks, steps not to be skipped by the wise tech. The bulk of the chapter comes in the second section, where you'll learn about installing and upgrading Windows 2000, XP, and Vista. Not all installations go smoothly, so section three looks at troubleshooting installation issues. Section four walks you through the typical post-installation tasks. The chapter finishes by examining what you've created in the installation process, such as where the various operating system (OS) files reside and how they interact to create a seamlessly booting new installation of Windows.

Preparing for Installation or Upgrade

Installing or upgrading an OS is like any good story: it has a beginning, a middle, and an end. In this case, the beginning is the several tasks you need to do before you actually do the installation or upgrade. If you do your homework here, the installation process is a breeze, and the post-installation tasks are minimal.

Don't get discouraged at all of the preparation tasks. They usually go pretty fast, and skipping them can cause you gobs of grief later when you're in the middle of installing and things blow up. Well, maybe there isn't a real explosion, but the computer might lock up and refuse to boot into anything usable. With that in mind, look at the nine tasks you need to complete *before* you insert that CD or DVD. Here's the list; discussion follows:

1. Identify hardware requirements.

2. Verify hardware and software compatibility.

3. Decide what type of installation to perform.

4. Determine how to back up and restore existing data, if necessary.

5. Select an installation method.

6. Determine how to partition the hard drive and what file system to use.

7. Determine your computer's network role.

8. Decide on your computer's language and locale settings.

9. Plan for post-installation tasks.

Identify Hardware Requirements

Hardware requirements help you decide whether a computer system is a reasonable host for a particular operating system. Requirements include the CPU model, the amount of RAM, the amount of free hard disk space, and the video adapter, display, and storage devices that may be required to install and run the operating system. They are stated as minimums or, more recently, as recommended minimums. Although you could install an operating system on a computer with the old minimums that Microsoft published, they were not realistic if you wanted to actually accomplish work. With the last few versions of Windows, Microsoft has published recommended minimums that are much more realistic. You will find the published minimums on the packaging and at Microsoft's Web site (www.microsoft.com). Later in this chapter, I'll also tell you what I recommend as minimums for Windows 2000, Windows XP, and Windows Vista.

Verify Hardware and Software Compatibility

Assuming your system meets the requirements, you next need to find out how well Windows supports the brand and model of hardware and application software you intend to use under Windows. You have two basic sources for this information: Microsoft and the manufacturer of the device or software. How do you actually access this information? Use the Web!

If you're installing Windows XP or Vista, the Setup Wizard automatically checks your hardware and software and reports any potential conflicts. But please don't wait until you are all ready to install to check this out. With any flavor of Windows, *first do your homework*.

Microsoft goes to great lengths to test any piece of hardware that might be used in a system running Windows through their **Windows Logo'd Product List** (Figure 11.1). This list, formerly known as the *Hardware Compatibility List (HCL)*, is the definitive authority as to whether your component is compatible with the OS. Every component listed on the Windows Logo'd Product List Web site has been extensively tested to verify that it works with Windows XP, Windows Vista, or Windows 7 and is guaranteed by Microsoft to work with your installation. The URL for the Windows Logo'd Product List is www.microsoft.com/whdc/hcl/default.mspx. Sadly, Microsoft no longer maintains a compatibility list specifically for Windows 2000, but in general, products compatible with XP will also be compatible with 2000.

When you install a device that's not been tested by Microsoft, a rather scary screen appears (Figure 11.2). This doesn't mean the component won't

> You'll occasionally hear the HCL or Windows Logo'd Product List referred to as the Windows Catalog. The Windows Catalog was a list of supported hardware Microsoft would add to the Windows installation CD. The Windows Logo'd Product List Web site is the modern tech's best source, so use that rather than any printed resources.

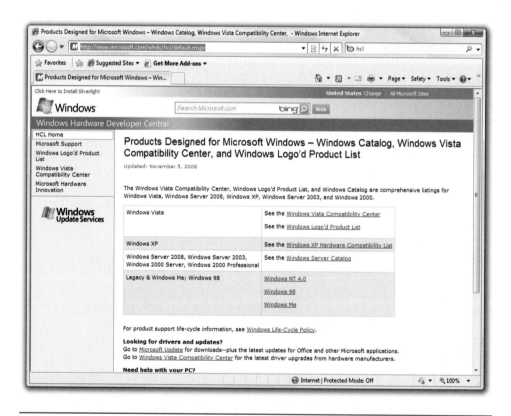

• **Figure 11.1**   Windows Logo'd Product List

work, only that it's not been tested. Not all component makers go through the rather painful process of getting the Microsoft approval so they can list their component in the Windows Logo'd Product List. As a general rule, unless the device is more than five years old, go ahead and install it. If it still doesn't work, you can simply uninstall it later.

Don't panic if you don't see your device on the list; many supported devices aren't on it. Check the optical discs that came with your hardware for proper drivers. Better yet, check the manufacturer's Web site for compatible drivers. Even when the Windows Logo'd Product List lists a piece of hardware, I still make a point of checking the manufacturer's Web site for newer drivers.

When preparing to upgrade, check with the manufacturers of the applications already installed in the previous OS. If there are software compatibility problems with the versions you have, the manufacturer should provide upgrade packs that you can install during the Windows setup process.

• **Figure 11.2**   Untested device in Windows XP

Decide What Type of Installation to Perform

You can install Windows in several ways. A **clean installation** of an OS involves installing it onto an empty hard drive with no previous OS installed. An **upgrade installation** means installing an OS on top of an earlier installed version, thus inheriting all previous hardware and software settings. You can combine versions of Windows by creating a **multiboot installation**. Installing usually involves some sort of optical disc, but other methods also exist. Let's look at all the options.

Clean Installation

A clean installation usually begins with a completely empty hard disk. The advantage to doing a clean installation is that you don't carry problems from the old OS over to the new one, but the disadvantage is that you have to reinstall all applications and reconfigure the desktop and each application to the user's preferences. You perform a clean installation by resetting your CMOS to tell the system to boot from the optical drive before your hard drive. You then boot off of a Windows installation disc, and Windows gives you the opportunity to partition and format the hard drive and then install Windows.

Upgrade Installation

In an upgrade installation, the new OS installs into the same folders as the old OS, or in tech speak, the new installs *on top of* the old. The new OS replaces the old OS but retains all saved data and inherits all of the previous settings (such as font styles, desktop colors and background, and so on), hardware, and applications. You don't have to reinstall your favorite programs!

To begin the upgrade of Windows, you must run the appropriate program from the optical disc. This usually means inserting a Windows installation disc into your system while your old OS is running, which starts the installation program. Then, to do an upgrade, you indicate that the new

CompTIA tests you on knowing how to upgrade a Windows 9x or Windows NT system to Windows 2000 or Windows XP and how to upgrade from Windows XP to Windows Vista. You do not need to know about Windows 9x or NT for the tests, but you do need to know how to upgrade them.

Before starting an OS upgrade, make sure you have shut down all other open applications!

version of Windows should install into a directory that already contains an installation of Windows (it will do this by default). You will be asked whether it is an upgrade or a new installation; if you select new installation, it will remove the existing OS before installing.

If for some reason the Windows 2000 or Windows XP installation program doesn't start automatically, go to My Computer, open the installation disc, and locate WINNT32.EXE. This program starts an upgrade to Windows 2000 or XP. In Windows Vista, open the disc in Windows Explorer and run Setup.exe in the disc's root directory, which starts the Vista upgrade.

Multiboot Installation

A third option that you need to be aware of is the dual boot or multiboot installation. Both Windows 2000 and Windows XP can install in a separate folder from your existing copy of Windows so you can put both operating systems on the same partition. Then every time your computer boots, you'll get a menu asking you which version of Windows you wish to boot. Multiboot requires that you format your active partition with a file system that every operating system you install can use. This hasn't been much of a problem since the Windows 9x family stopped being relevant, because there's really no reason to use anything other than NTFS. Windows Vista doesn't let you define its install folder, so to multiboot Vista and XP, for example, you'd need to install each OS on a different partition.

Other Installation Methods

In medium to large organizations, more advanced installation methods are often employed, especially when many computers need to be configured identically. A common method is to place the source files in a shared directory on a network server. Then, whenever a tech needs to install a new OS, it is a simple task of booting up the computer, connecting to the source location on the network, and starting the installation from there. This method alone has many variations and can be automated with special scripts that automatically select the options and components needed. The scripts can even install the necessary applications at the end of the OS installation—all without user intervention once the installation has been started.

Another type of installation that is very popular for re-creating standard configurations is an **image installation**. An image is a complete copy of a hard disk volume on which an operating system and, usually, all required application software programs have been preinstalled. Images can be stored on optical discs, in which case the tech runs special software on the computer that copies the image onto the local hard drive. Images can also be stored on special network servers, in which case the tech connects to the image server by using special software and copies the image from the server to the local hard drive. A leader in this technology has been Norton Ghost, which is available from Symantec. Other similar programs are Clonezilla and Acronis's True Image.

Beginning with Windows 2000 Server, Microsoft added *Remote Installation Services (RIS)*, which can be used to initiate either a scripted installation or an installation of an image.

Tech Tip

Multiboot Configuration

When configuring a computer for multibooting, there are two basic rules: first, you must format the system partition in a file system that is common to all installed operating systems, and second, you must install the operating systems in order from oldest to newest.

Scripting OS and application installations is a full-time job in many organizations. Many scripting tools and methods are available from both Microsoft and third-party sources.

Determine How to Back Up and Restore Existing Data, If Necessary

Whether you are installing or upgrading, you may need to back up existing user data first, because things can go very wrong either way, and the data on the hard drive might be damaged. You'll need to find out where the user is currently saving data files. If they are saving onto the local hard drive, it must be backed up before the installation or replacement takes place, to preserve the data. However, if all data has been saved to a network location, you are in luck, because the data is safe from damage during installation.

If the user saves data locally, and the computer is connected to a network, save the data, at least temporarily, to a network location until after the upgrade or installation has taken place. If the computer is not connected to a network but the computer has a burnable optical drive, copy the data to DVDs. You can also use an external hard drive, which is a handy thing for any tech to have. Wherever you save the data, you will need to copy or restore any lost or damaged data back to the local hard disk after the installation.

If you plan to migrate a user from one system to another, here's where you might start the process by running the Files and Settings Transfer Wizard (Windows XP) or Windows Easy Transfer (Windows Vista). You'll complete that process during the post-installation tasks. Rather than discuss the process twice, I leave the full discussion on migration for the "Post-Installation Tasks" section later in this chapter.

Select an Installation Method

Once you've backed up everything important, you need to select an installation method. You have two basic choices: insert the installation disc into the drive and go, or install over a network. The latter method falls into the realm of CompTIA Network+ technicians or even network administrators, so this book assumes you'll install from disc.

Determine How to Partition the Hard Drive and What File System to Use

If you are performing a clean installation, you need to decide ahead of time how to partition the disk space on your hard disk drive, including the number and size of partitions and the file system (or systems) you will use. Actually, in the decision process, the file system comes first, and then the space issue follows, as you will see.

This was a much bigger issue back in the days when older operating systems couldn't use newer file systems, but now that every Windows OS that you could reasonably want to install supports NTFS, there's really no reason to use anything else. You still might have a reason to partition your drive, but as for choosing a file system, your work is done for you.

Determine Your Computer's Network Role

The question of your computer's network role comes up in one form or another during a Windows installation. A Windows computer can have one of several roles relative to a network (in Microsoft terms). One role, called *standalone*, is actually a non-network role, and it simply means that the computer does not participate on a network. You can install any version of Windows on a standalone computer, and this is the only role that a Windows XP Home computer can play on a network. Every other modern version of Windows can be a member of either a workgroup or a domain (or, if you're using Windows 7, a HomeGroup). You will learn more about the workgroup and domain member roles in Chapter 16, "Learning Local Area Networking."

Decide on Your Computer's Language and Locale Settings

These settings are especially important for Windows operating systems because they determine how date and time information is displayed and which math separators and currency symbols are used for various locations.

Plan for Post-Installation Tasks

After installing Windows, you may need to install the latest service pack or updates. You may also need to install updated drivers and reconfigure any settings, such as network settings, that were found not to work. You will also need to install and configure any applications (word processor, spreadsheet, database, e-mail, games, etc.) required by the user of the computer. Finally, don't forget to restore any data backed up before the installation or upgrade.

■ Installing and Upgrading Windows

At the most basic level, installing any operating system follows a fairly standard set of steps. You turn on the computer, insert an operating system disc into the optical drive, and follow the installation wizard until you have everything completed. Along the way, you'll accept the **End User License Agreement (EULA)** and enter the product key that says you're not a pirate; the product key is invariably located on the installation disc's case. At the same time, there are nuances between installing Windows 2000 or upgrading to Windows Vista that every CompTIA A+ certified tech must know, so this section goes through many installation processes in some detail.

Installing or Upgrading to Windows 2000 Professional

On the face of it, installing Windows 2000 Professional seems fairly simple. You insert the installation disc, access the setup routine, and go! But that conceptualization does not hold up in practice.

Hardware Requirements

The minimum specs represent what Microsoft says you need so you can install the Windows 2000 Professional OS. However, you need to take these specifications and at least double them if you want to be happy with your system's performance.

Here is a more realistic recommendation for a useful Windows 2000 Professional computer system:

Component	Minimum for a Windows 2000 Professional Computer	Recommended for a Windows 2000 Professional Computer
CPU	Intel Pentium 133 MHz	Intel Pentium II 350 MHz
Memory	64 MB	128 MB
Hard disk	2 GB with 650 MB of free space	6.4 GB with 2 GB of free space
Network	None	Modern network card
Display	Video adapter and monitor with VGA resolution	Video adapter and monitor with SVGA resolution, capable of high-color (16-bit) display
Optical drive	If you don't have an optical drive, you must use a floppy disk drive or install over a network.	If you don't have an optical drive, you must use a floppy disk drive or install over a network.

If your test system(s) exceeds the recommended configuration, all the better. You can never have too fast a processor or too much hard disk space.

Installing or Upgrading to Windows XP Professional

You prepare for installing Windows XP just as you do for installing Windows 2000. Windows XP has a few different aspects to it that are worth considering as a separate issue.

Upgrade Paths

You can upgrade to Windows XP Professional from all of the following versions of Windows:

- Windows 98 (all versions)
- Windows Me
- Windows NT 4.0 Workstation (Service Pack 5 and later)
- Windows 2000 Professional (including service packs)
- Windows XP Home Edition

XP Hardware Requirements

Hardware requirements for Windows XP Professional are higher than for previous versions of Windows, but are still very low by modern hardware standards.

Microsoft XP runs on a wide range of computers, but you need to be sure that your computer meets the minimum hardware requirements as shown here.

Also shown is my recommended minimum for a system running a typical selection of business productivity software.

Component	Minimum for a Windows XP Computer	Recommended for a Windows XP Computer
CPU	Any Intel or AMD 233 MHz or higher processor	Any Intel or AMD 300 MHz or higher processor
Memory	64 MB of RAM (though Microsoft admits XP will be somewhat crippled with only this amount)	512 MB of RAM or higher
Hard disk	1.5 GB of available hard drive space	4 GB of available hard drive space
Network	None	Modern network card
Display	Video card that supports SVGA with at least 800 × 600 resolution	Video card that supports DirectX with at least 1024 × 768 resolution
Optical drive	Any CD- or DVD-media drive	Any CD- or DVD-media drive

Hardware and Software Compatibility

You'll need to check hardware and software compatibility before installing Windows XP Professional—as either an upgrade or a new installation. Of course, if you purchase a computer with Windows XP preinstalled, you're spared this task, but you'll still need to verify that the application software you plan to add to the computer will be compatible. Luckily, Microsoft includes the Upgrade Advisor on the Windows XP disc.

Upgrade Advisor   You would be hard-pressed these days to find a computer incapable of running Windows XP, but if you are ever uncertain about whether a computer you excavated at an archeological dig can run XP, fear not! The **Upgrade Advisor** is the first process that runs on the XP installation disc. It examines your hardware and installed software (in the case of an upgrade) and provides a list of devices and software that are known to have issues with XP. Be sure to follow the suggestions on this list.

You can also run the Upgrade Advisor separately from the Windows XP installation. You can run it from the Windows XP disc. Microsoft used to offer the XP Upgrade Advisor on its Web site, but searching for it now will just redirect you to the Vista Upgrade Advisor (more on that later), so running it from the disc is the way to go nowadays.

Booting into Windows XP Setup

The Windows XP discs are bootable, and Microsoft no longer includes a program to create a set of setup boot disks. This should not be an issue, because PCs manufactured in the past several years can boot from the optical drive. This system BIOS setting, usually described as boot order, is controlled through a PC's BIOS-based Setup program.

In the unlikely event that your lab computer can't be made to boot from its optical drive, you can create a set of six (yes, six!) Windows XP setup boot floppy disks by using a special program you can download from Microsoft's Web site. Note that Microsoft provides separate boot disk programs for XP Home and XP Pro.

Running the Upgrade Advisor

If you have a PC with Windows XP or an older version of Windows, you should know how to run the Upgrade Advisor on your system, so try this:

1. Insert the Windows XP installation disc. If Autorun is enabled, the Welcome to Microsoft Windows XP screen appears. If this does not appear, select Start | Run, enter the following, and then click OK:

   ```
   d:\SETUP.EXE
   ```

   (Where *d* is the drive letter for the optical drive.)

2. At the Welcome to Microsoft Windows XP screen, select Check System Compatibility to start the Upgrade Advisor. On the following page, select Check My System Automatically.

3. In the Upgrade Advisor dialog box, select the first choice if you have an Internet connection. If you don't have an Internet connection, select No, Skip This Step and Continue Installing Windows. (Don't worry, you aren't really going to install yet.)

4. Click Next. The Upgrade Advisor shows the tasks that Dynamic Update is performing, and then it restarts Setup.

5. After Setup restarts, you'll be back at the same page in the Upgrade Advisor. This time, select No, Skip This Step and Continue Installing Windows, and click Next. The Upgrade Report page appears next. You can save the information in a file by clicking Save As and selecting a location.

6. Read the findings that the Upgrade Advisor presents. If a problem was found, click the Full Details button for instructions, and be sure to follow them. When you have recorded any necessary instructions, click Finish.

Registration Versus Activation

During setup, you will be prompted to register your product and activate it. Many people confuse activation with registration, but these are separate operations. **Registration** tells Microsoft who the official owner or user of the product is, providing contact information such as name, address, company, phone number, and e-mail address. Registration is still entirely optional. Activation is a way to combat software piracy, meaning that Microsoft wishes to ensure that each license for Windows XP is used solely on a single computer. It's more formally called **Microsoft Product Activation (MPA)**.

Mandatory Activation Within 30 Days of Installation   Activation is mandatory, but you can skip this step during installation. You have 30 days in which to activate the product, during which time it works normally. If you don't activate it within that time frame, it will be disabled. Don't worry about forgetting, though, because once it's installed, Windows XP frequently reminds you to activate it with a balloon message over the tray area of the taskbar. The messages even tell you how many days you have left.

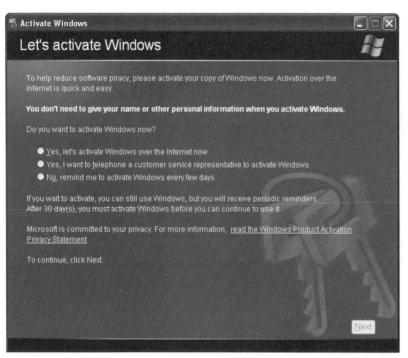

Activation Mechanics Here's how product activation works. When you choose to activate, either during setup or later when XP reminds you to do it, an installation ID code is created from the product ID code that you entered during installation and a 50-digit value that identifies your key hardware components. You must send this code to Microsoft, either automatically if you have an Internet connection or verbally via a phone call to Microsoft. Microsoft then returns a 42-digit product activation code. If you are activating online, you don't have to enter the activation code; it happens automatically. If you are activating over the phone, you must read the installation ID to a representative and enter the resulting 42-digit activation code into the Activate Windows by Phone dialog box.

No personal information about you is sent as part of the activation process. Figure 11.3 shows the dialog box that opens when you start activation by clicking on the reminder message balloon.

• **Figure 11.3** Activation takes just seconds with an Internet connection.

Installing or Upgrading to Windows Vista

Preparing for a Windows Vista installation is not really different from preparing for a Windows 2000 or XP install. There are, of course, a few things to consider before installing or upgrading your system to Vista.

Upgrade Paths

Windows Vista is persnickety about doing Upgrade installs with different editions; although you can upgrade to any edition of Vista from any version of Windows XP, many upgrade paths will require you to do a clean installation of the Vista operating system. Note that you cannot upgrade from Windows 2000 to Vista, but must do a clean installation. Vista's upgrade paths are so complicated that the only way to really explain them is using a grid showing the OS you're trying to upgrade from and the edition of Vista you're upgrading to. Fortunately for you, Microsoft provides such a grid, which I've re-created in Table 11.1.

Hardware Requirements

Windows Vista requires a substantially more powerful computer to run than Windows 2000 or XP. Make sure your computer meets at least the

Table 11.1   Vista's Labyrinthine Upgrade Paths

	Vista Home Basic	Vista Home Premium	Vista Business	Vista Ultimate
XP Professional	Clean Install	Clean Install	Upgrade Install	Upgrade Install
XP Home	Upgrade Install	Upgrade Install	Upgrade Install	Upgrade Install
XP Media Center	Clean Install	Upgrade Install	Clean Install	Upgrade Install
XP Tablet PC	Clean Install	Clean Install	Upgrade Install	Upgrade Install
XP Professional x64	Clean Install	Clean Install	Clean Install	Clean Install
Windows 2000	Clean Install	Clean Install	Clean Install	Clean Install

following minimum hardware requirements suggested by Microsoft, though it would be far better to meet my recommended requirements:

Component	Minimum for a Windows Vista Computer	Recommended for a Windows Vista Computer
CPU	1 GHz 32-bit (x86) or 64-bit (x64) processor	Any dual-core Intel or AMD processor or better
Memory	512 MB of RAM for Vista Basic (for all other editions, 1 GB of RAM)	2 GB of RAM or higher
Hard disk	20 GB hard drive with 15 GB of available hard drive space for Vista Basic (for all other editions, 40 GB hard drive with 15 GB of free space)	100 GB hard drive or greater
Network	Modern network card with Internet access	Modern network card with Internet access
Display	Support for DirectX 9 graphics and 32 MB of graphics memory for Vista Basic (for all other editions, 128 MB of graphics memory, plus pixel shader 2.0 support, the WDDM driver, and 32 bits per pixel)	DirectX 10 capable graphics card with at least 512 MB of graphics memory
Optical drive	Any DVD-media drive	Any DVD-media drive

If you're uncertain about whether your computer will run Vista, you can download and run the Windows Vista Upgrade Advisor from www.microsoft.com/windows/windows-vista/get/upgrade-advisor.aspx, which will tell you if your computer meets Microsoft's minimum requirements.

The CompTIA A+ Essentials exam is likely to test your knowledge regarding the minimum installation requirements for Windows Vista Home Basic, Home Premium, Business, or Ultimate. Know them well!

Hardware and Software Compatibility

Windows Vista is markedly different from Windows XP in many very basic, fundamental ways, and this causes all sorts of difficulty with programs and device drivers designed for Windows XP. When Vista came out, you probably heard a lot of people grumbling about it, and likely they were grumbling about hardware and software incompatibility. Simply put, a lot of old programs and devices don't work in Windows Vista, which is bad news for people who are still running Microsoft Word 97.

Fortunately, Microsoft offers a Windows Vista Compatibility Center where you can check whether a piece of software or hardware will work with Vista. Most programs developed since Vista's release in 2007 should work, but checking the compatibility of any programs you absolutely cannot do without is always a good idea.

Upgrading Issues

A few extra steps before you pop in that installation disc are worth your time. If you plan to upgrade rather than perform a clean installation, follow these steps first:

1. Check out the Windows Logo'd Product List site or the Windows Vista Compatibility Center site, or run a compatibility report by using the Check Upgrade utility provided with Windows 2000 Professional or the Upgrade Advisor for Windows XP or Vista, depending on which OS you're planning on installing. These utilities generate a detailed list of potentially problematic devices and applications. You can run the utility in both 2000 and XP as follows: insert the Windows Installation disc and, from your current OS, open a command prompt or use the Start Run dialog box to run the WINNT32.EXE program with the CHECKUPGRADEONLY switch turned on. The command line will look like this:

   ```
   d:\i386\winnt32 /checkupgradeonly
   ```

   (where d: is the optical drive).

2. Have an up-to-date backup of your data and configuration files handy.

3. Perform a "spring cleaning" on your system by uninstalling unused or unnecessary applications and deleting old files.

4. Perform a disk scan and a disk defragmentation.

5. Uncompress all files, folders, and partitions.

6. Perform a virus scan, and then remove or disable all virus-checking software.

7. Disable virus checking in your system CMOS.

8. Keep in mind that if worse comes to worst, you may have to start over and do a clean installation anyway. This makes step 2 exceedingly important. Back up your data!

The Windows 2000/XP Clean Installation Process

The steps involved in a clean installation of Windows 2000 Professional and Windows XP are virtually identical. The only differences are the order of two steps and some of the art on the screens that appear, so we can comfortably discuss both installations at the same time.

A clean installation begins with your system set to boot to your optical drive and the Windows installation disc in the drive. You start your PC, and assuming you have the boot order right, the installation program starts booting (Figure 11.4). Note at the bottom that it says to press F6 for a third-party SCSI or RAID driver. You only do this if you want to install Windows onto a strange drive and Windows does not already have the driver for that drive. Don't worry about this; Windows has a huge assortment of drivers for just about every hard drive ever made, and in the rare situation where you need a third-party driver, the folks who sell you the SCSI or RAID array will tell you ahead of time.

• **Figure 11.4** Windows Setup text screen

After the system copies a number of files, you'll see the Welcome screen (Figure 11.5). This is an important screen! As you'll see in later chapters, techs often use the Windows installation disc as a repair tool, and this is the screen that lets you choose between installing Windows or repairing an existing installation. Because you're making a new install, just press ENTER.

You're now prompted to read and accept the EULA. Nobody ever reads this—it gives you a stomachache when you see

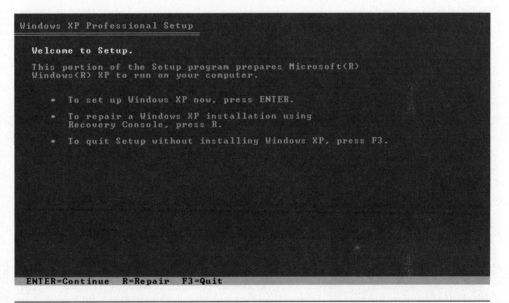

• **Figure 11.5** Welcome text screen

what you're really agreeing to—so just press F8 and move to the next screen to start partitioning the drive (Figure 11.6).

If your hard disk is unpartitioned, you need to create a new partition when prompted. Follow the instructions. In most cases, you can make a single partition, although you can easily make as many partitions as you wish. You can also delete partitions if you're using a hard drive that was partitioned in the past (or if you mess up your partitioning). Note that there is no option to make a primary or extended partition; this tool makes the first partition primary and the rest extended.

After you've made the partition(s), you must select the partition on which to install XP (sort of trivial if you only have one partition), and then you need to decide which file system format to use for the new partition.

Tech Tip

Save Some Space
Many techie types, at least those with big (> 500 GB) hard drives, only partition half of their hard drive for Windows. This makes it easy for them to install an alternative OS (usually Linux) at a later date.

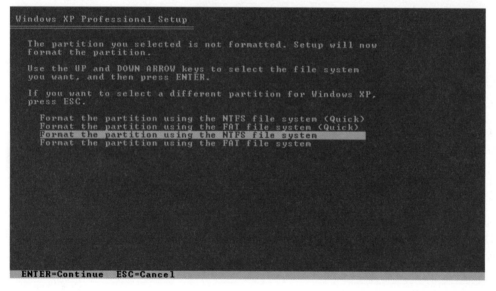

```
Windows XP Professional Setup

  The following list shows the existing partitions and
  unpartitioned space on this computer.

  Use the UP and DOWN ARROW keys to select an item in the list.

    • To set up Windows XP on the selected item, press ENTER.

    • To create a partition in the unpartitioned space, press C.

    • To delete the selected partition, press D.

  8190 MB Disk 0 at Id 0 on bus 0 on atapi [MBR]
          Unpartitioned space                 8189 MB




  ENTER=Install   C=Create Partition   F3=Quit
```

• **Figure 11.6**   Partitioning text screen

```
Windows XP Professional Setup

  The partition you selected is not formatted. Setup will now
  format the partition.

  Use the UP and DOWN ARROW keys to select the file system
  you want, and then press ENTER.

  If you want to select a different partition for Windows XP,
  press ESC.

      Format the partition using the NTFS file system (Quick)
      Format the partition using the FAT file system (Quick)
      Format the partition using the NTFS file system
      Format the partition using the FAT file system




  ENTER=Continue   ESC=Cancel
```

• **Figure 11.7**   Choosing NTFS

Unless you have some weird need to support FAT or FAT32, format the partition by using NTFS (Figure 11.7).

Setup now formats the drive and copies some basic installation files to the newly formatted partition, displaying another progress bar. Go get a book to read while you wait.

After it completes copying the base set of files to the hard drive, your computer reboots, and the graphical mode of Windows setup begins. This is where 2000 and XP begin to vary in appearance, even though they are performing the same steps. The rest of this section shows Windows XP. If you're running a Windows 2000 install, compare it to the screens you see here; it's interesting to see the different presentation doing the same job.

You will see a generic screen during the installation that looks like Figure 11.8. On the left of the screen, uncompleted tasks have a white button, completed tasks have a green button, and the current task has a red button. You'll get plenty of advertising to read as you install.

The following screens ask questions about a number of things the computer needs to know. They include the desired region and language the computer will operate in, your name and organization for personalizing

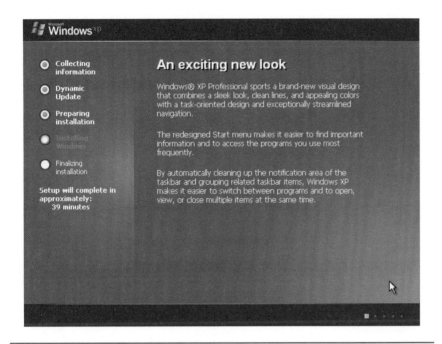

• Figure 11.8   Beginning of graphical mode

your computer, and a valid **product key** for Windows XP (Figure 11.9). Be sure to enter the product key exactly, or you will be unable to continue.

Next, you need to give your computer a name that will identify it on a network. Check with your system administrator for an appropriate name. If you don't have a system administrator, just enter a simple name such as MYPC for now—you can change this at any time—and read up on networking later in this book. You also need to create a password for the Administrator user account (Figure 11.10). Every Windows system has an Administrator user

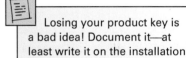

Losing your product key is a bad idea! Document it—at least write it on the installation CD-ROM.

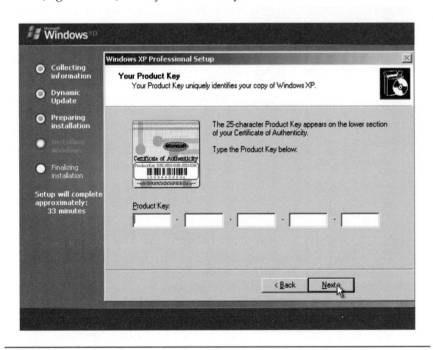

• Figure 11.9   Product key

● **Figure 11.10**   Computer name and Administrator password

account that can do anything on the computer. Techs will need this account to modify and fix the computer in the future.

Last, you're asked for the correct date, time, and time zone. Then Windows tries to detect a network card. If a network card is detected, the network components will be installed and you'll have an opportunity to configure the network settings. Unless you know you need special settings for your network, just select the Typical Settings option (Figure 11.11). Relax; XP will do most of the work for you. Plus you can easily change network settings after the installation.

The big copy of files now begins from the CD-ROM to your hard drive. This is a good time to pick your book up again, because watching the ads is boring (Figure 11.12).

After the files required for the final configuration are copied, XP reboots again. During this reboot, XP determines your screen size and applies the appropriate resolution. This reboot can take several minutes to complete, so be patient.

Once the reboot is complete, you can log on as the Administrator. Balloon messages may appear over the tray area of the taskbar—a common message concerns the display resolution. Click the balloon and allow Windows XP to automatically adjust the display settings.

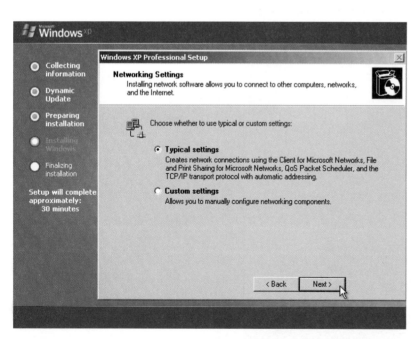

● **Figure 11.11**   Selecting typical network settings

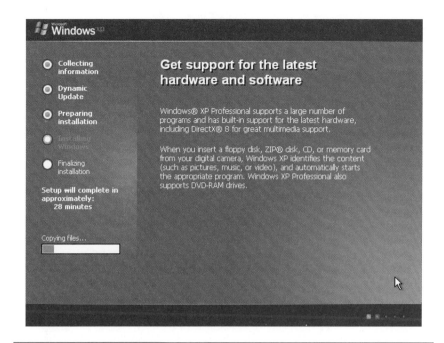

The Big Copy

The final message in the installation process reminds you that you have 30 days left for activation. Go ahead and activate now over the Internet or by telephone. It's painless and quick. If you choose not to activate, simply click the Close button on the message balloon. That's it! You have successfully installed Windows XP and should have a desktop with the default Bliss background, as shown in Figure 11.13.

• Figure 11.13   Windows XP desktop with Bliss background

The Windows Vista Clean Installation Process

With Windows Vista, Microsoft has dramatically changed the installation process. No longer will you spend your time looking at a boring blue ASCII screen and entering commands by keyboard—the Vista installer has a full graphical interface, making it easy to partition drives and install your operating system. If you thought that installing Windows XP seemed a little primitive, you'll love the fancy Vista installer.

Just as when installing Windows 2000 or XP, you need to boot your computer from some sort of Windows installation media. Usually, you'll use a DVD disc, though you can also install Vista from a USB drive, over a network, or even off of several CD-ROMs that you have to specially order from Microsoft. When you've booted into the installer, the first screen you see asks you to set your language, time/currency, and keyboard settings, as in Figure 11.14.

The next screen in the installation process is somewhat akin to the 2000 and XP Welcome screen, in that it enables techs to start the installation disc's repair tools (Figure 11.15). Just like the completely revamped installer, the Vista repair tools are markedly different from the ones for Microsoft's previous operating systems. The 701 Essentials exam doesn't really require you to know a whole lot about these repair tools, so, for now, just click where it says *Repair your computer* to use the repair tools. Because you're just installing Windows in this chapter, click *Install now*.

• **Figure 11.14**   Windows Vista language settings screen

The next screen shows just how wildly different the Vista installation order is. When installing Vista, you enter your product key before you do anything else, as you can see in Figure 11.16. With Windows 2000 and XP, this didn't come until much, much later in the process, and there's a very interesting reason for this change.

Microsoft has dramatically altered the method they use to distribute different editions of their operating system; instead of having different discs for each edition of Windows Vista, every Vista installation disc contains all of the available editions. In Windows 2000 and XP, your product key did very little besides let the installation disc know that you had legitimately purchased the OS. In Vista, your product key not only verifies the legitimacy of your purchase; it also tells the installer which edition you purchased, which, when you think about it, is a lot to ask of a randomly generated string of numbers and letters.

If you leave the product key blank and click the Next button, you will be taken to a screen asking you which version of Vista you would like to install (Figure 11.17). Lest you start to think that you've discovered a way to install Vista without paying for it, you should know that doing this

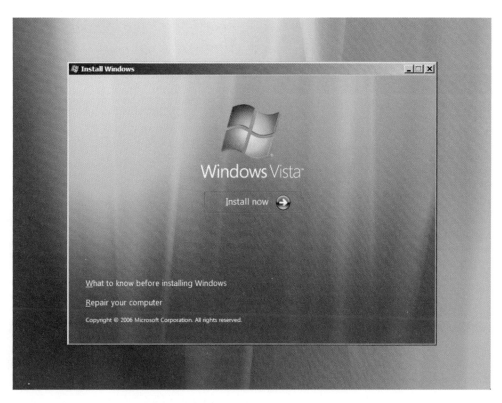

• **Figure 11.15**   The Windows Vista setup Welcome screen

• **Figure 11.16**   The Windows Vista product key screen

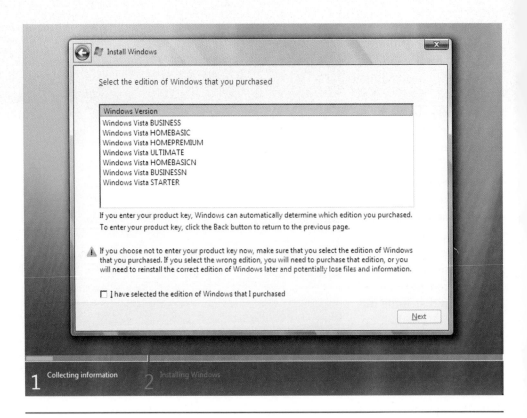

• **Figure 11.17**   Choose the edition of Vista you want to install.

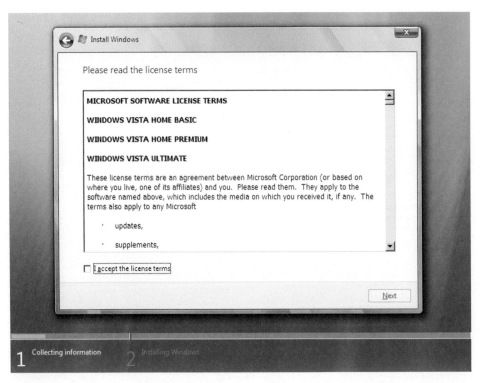

• **Figure 11.18**   The Vista EULA

simply installs a 30-day trial of the operating system. After 30 days, you will no longer be able to boot to the desktop without entering a valid product key that matches the edition of Vista you installed.

After the product key screen (and in Figure 11.18), you'll find Microsoft's new and improved EULA, which you can skip unless you're interested to see what's changed in the world of obtuse legalese since the release of Windows XP.

On the next page, you get to decide whether you'd like to do an upgrade installation or a clean installation (Figure 11.19). As you learned earlier, you have to begin the Vista installation

● **Figure 11.19**   Choose your installation type.

process from within an older OS to use the Upgrade option, so this option will be dimmed for you if you've booted off of the installation disc. To do a clean installation of Vista, edit your partitions, and just generally install the OS like a pro, you choose the Custom (advanced) option.

Choosing the Custom install option brings you to the screen in Figure 11.20. This is the screen where you can partition your hard drives and choose which partition to install Windows to. From this screen, you can click the Advanced button to display a variety of partitioning options, and you can click the Load Driver button to, well,

● **Figure 11.20**   The partitioning screen

● **Figure 11.21**   Browse for drivers.

● **Figure 11.22**   Choose a user picture.

load hard drive drivers (Figure 11.21). The process of loading drivers is much more intuitive than in Windows XP and 2000: you just browse to the location of the drivers you want by using Windows' very familiar browsing window.

Of course, you will most likely never have to load drivers for a drive, and if it is ever necessary, your drive will almost certainly come with a driver disc and documentation telling you that you'll have to load the drivers.

Once you've partitioned your drives and selected a partition to install Vista to, the installation process takes over, copying files, expanding files, installing features, and just generally doing lots of computerish things. This can take a while, so if you need to get a snack or read *War and Peace*, do it during this part of the installation.

When Vista has finished unpacking and installing itself, it asks you to choose a user name and picture (Figure 11.22). This screen also asks you set up a password for your main user account, which is definitely a good idea if you're going to have multiple people using the computer.

After picking your user name and password, and letting Windows know how much you like pictures of kitties, you're

Mike Meyers' CompTIA A+ Guide: Essentials

taken to a screen where you can type in a computer name (Figure 11.23). By default, Windows makes your computer name the same as your user name but with "-PC" appended to it, which in most cases is fine.

This is also the screen where you can change the desktop background that Windows will start up with. You can change this easily later on, so pick whatever you like and click the Next button.

The next page asks you how you want to set up Windows Automatic Updates (Figure 11.24). Most users want to choose the top option, *Use recommended settings*, as it provides the most hassle-free method for updating your computer. The middle option, *Install important updates only*,

• **Figure 11.23** Choose your computer name.

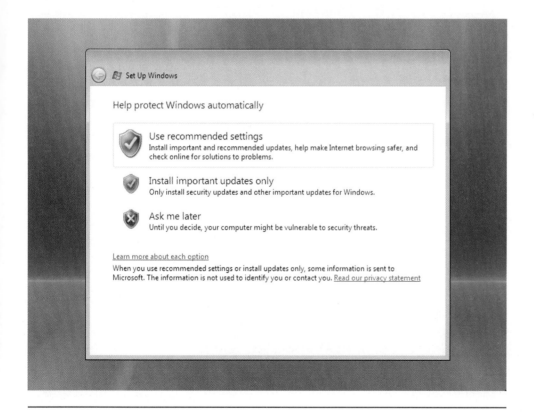

• **Figure 11.24** The automatic updates screen

● **Figure 11.25**   Vista pities the fool who doesn't know what time it is.

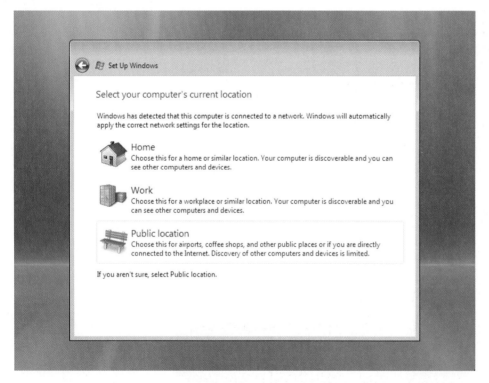

● **Figure 11.26**   Tell Windows what kind of network you're on.

installs only the most critical security fixes and updates and leaves the rest of the updates up to you. This is useful when setting up computers for businesses, as many companies' IT departments like to test out any updates before rolling them out to the employees. You should only select the last option, *Ask me later*, if you can dedicate yourself to checking weekly for updates, as it will not install any automatically.

Next up is the time and date screen, where you can make sure your operating system knows what time it is, as in Figure 11.25. This screen should be pretty self-explanatory, so set the correct time zone, the correct date, and the correct time, and move to the next screen.

If you have your computer connected to a network while running the installer, the next screen will ask you about your current location (Figure 11.26). If you're on a trusted network, such as your home or office network, make the appropriate selection and your computer will be discoverable on the network. If you're on, say, a Starbucks' network, choose *Public location* so the caffeine addicts around you can't see your computer and potentially do malicious things to it.

Once you're past that screen, Windows thanks you for installing it, which is awfully polite for a piece of software, don't you think (Figure 11.27)?

• **Figure 11.27** Aw, shucks, Microsoft Windows Vista. Don't mention it.

Lest you think you're completely through the woods, Windows will run some tests on your computer to give it a performance rating, which, in theory, will tell you how well programs will run on your computer. You'll sometimes see minimum performance ratings on the sides of game boxes, but even then, you're more likely to need plain, old-fashioned minimum system requirements. This process can take anywhere from 5 to 20 minutes, so this is another one of those coffee-break moments in the installation process.

Once the performance test finishes, Vista boots up and you have 30 days to activate your new operating system.

Automating the Installation

As you can see, you may have to sit around for quite a while when installing Windows. Instead of having to sit there answering questions and typing in CD keys, wouldn't it be nice just to boot up the machine and have the installation process finish without any intervention on your part—especially if you have 30 PCs that need to be ready to go tomorrow morning? Fortunately, Windows offers two good options for automating the installation process: scripted installations and disk cloning.

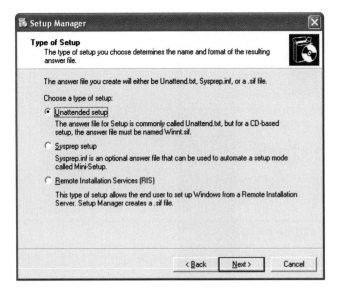

Scripting Windows 2000 and XP Installations with Setup Manager

For automating a Windows 2000 or XP install, Microsoft provides *Setup Manager* to help you create a text file—called an *answer file*—containing all of your answers to the installation questions. Windows doesn't come with Setup Manager, but you can download it from the Microsoft Download Center (www.microsoft.com/downloads) as part of the Windows XP Service Pack 2 Deployment Tools. Setup Manager supports creating answer files for three types of setups: Unattended, Sysprep, and Remote Installation Services (Figure 11.28). The current version of the tool can create answer files for Windows XP Home Edition, Windows XP Professional, and Windows Server 2003 (Standard, Enterprise, or Web Edition); see Figure 11.29.

Setup Manager can create an answer file to completely automate the process, or you can use it to set default options. You'll almost always want to create an answer file that automates the entire process (Figure 11.30).

When running a scripted installation, you have to decide how to make the installation files themselves available to the PC. Although you can boot your new machine from an installation CD, you can save yourself a lot of CD swapping if you just put the installation files on a network share and install your OS over the network (Figure 11.31).

• **Figure 11.28**   Setup Manager can create answer files for three types of setups.

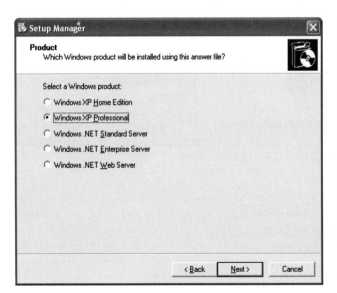

• **Figure 11.29**   Setup Manager can create answer files for five versions of Windows.

• **Figure 11.30**   Setup Manager can create several kinds of answer files.

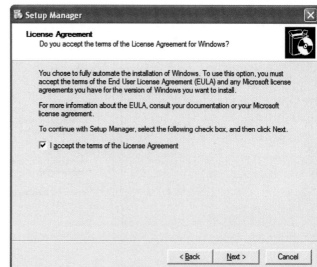

• **Figure 11.31**   Choose where to store the installation files.

• **Figure 11.32**   Don't forget to accept the license agreement.

When you run Setup Manager, you get to answer all those pesky questions. As always, you will also have to "accept the terms of the License Agreement" (Figure 11.32) and specify the product key (Figure 11.33), but at least by scripting these steps you can do it once and get it over with.

Now it's time to get to the good stuff, customizing your installation. Using the graphical interface, decide what configuration options you want to use: screen resolutions, network options, browser settings, regional settings, and so on. You can even add finishing touches to the installation, installing additional programs such as Microsoft Office and Adobe Reader by

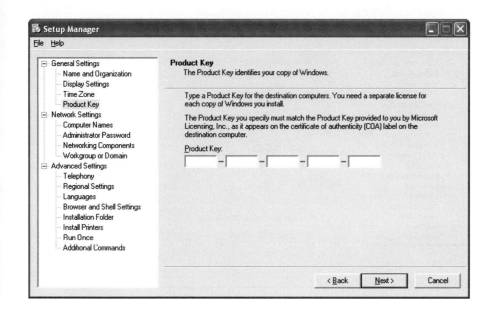

• **Figure 11.33**   Enter the product key.

• **Figure 11.34**   Running additional commands

automatically running additional commands after the Windows installation finishes (Figure 11.34). You can also set programs to run once (Figure 11.35).

Remember that computer names must be unique on the network. If you're going to use the same answer files for multiple machines on the same network, you need to make sure that each machine gets its own unique name. You can either provide a list of names to use, or you can have the Setup program randomly generate names (Figure 11.36).

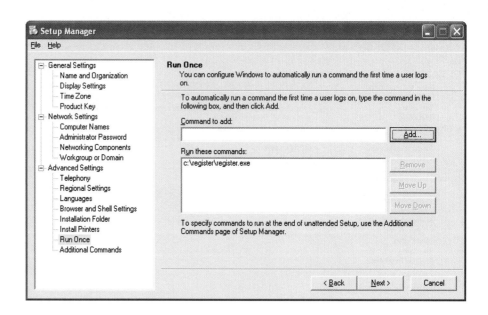

• **Figure 11.35**   Running a program once

● Figure 11.36   Pick your computer names.

When you're finished, Setup Manager prompts you to save your answers as a text file. The contents of the file will look something like this:

```
;SetupMgrTag
[Data]
    AutoPartition=1
    MsDosInitiated="0"
    UnattendedInstall="Yes"

[Unattended]
    UnattendMode=FullUnattended
    OemSkipEula=Yes
    OemPreinstall=No
    TargetPath=\WINDOWS

[GuiUnattended]
    AdminPassword=414c11f760b0064 ... [out to 64 characters]
    EncryptedAdminPassword=Yes
    OEMSkipRegional=1
    TimeZone=85
    OemSkipWelcome=1
    AutoLogon=Yes
    AutoLogonCount=1

[UserData]
    ProductKey=FFFFF-FFFFF-FFFFF-FFFFF-FFFFF
    FullName="Scott"
    OrgName="Total Seminars"
    ComputerName=*
```

```
[Identification]
    JoinDomain=TOTAL
    DomainAdmin=admin09
    DomainAdminPassword=my-password
```

The list goes on for another hundred lines or so, and this is a fairly simple answer file. One thing to note is that if you provide a domain administrator's user name and password for the purpose of automatically adding new PCs to your domain, that user name and password will be in the text file in clear text:

```
[Identification]
    JoinDomain=TOTAL
    DomainAdmin=admin09
    DomainAdminPassword=my-password
```

In that case, you will want to be very careful about protecting your setup files.

Once you have your answer file created, you can start your installation with this command, and go enjoy a nice cup of coffee while the installation runs:

```
D:\i386\winnt32 /s:%SetupFiles% /unattend:%AnswerFile%
```

Tech Tip

Creating a Network-Aware Bootable Disc
If you need help creating a network boot floppy or CD, check out www.netbootdisk.com/bootcd.htm.

For `%SetupFiles%`, substitute the location of your setup files—either a local path (`D:\i386` if you are installing from a CD) or a network path. If you use a network path, don't forget to create a network boot disk so that the installation program can access the files. For `%AnswerFile%`, substitute the name of the text file you created with Setup Manager (usually `unattend.txt`).

Of course, you don't have to use Setup Manager to create your answer file. Feel free to pull out your favorite text editor and write one from scratch. Most techs, however, find it much easier to use the provided tool than to wrestle with the answer file's sometimes arcane syntax.

Automating a Vista Installation with the Automated Installation Kit

As of Windows Vista, Setup Manager is history—as is any method of automating an installation that isn't extremely complicated and intimidating. Microsoft has replaced Setup Manager with the Windows Vista Automated Installation Kit (AIK), a set of tools which, although quite powerful, seem to have made something of a Faustian deal to obtain that power at the expense of usability (Figure 11.37).

Writing a step-by-step guide to creating an answer file in the AIK would almost warrant its own chapter, and as the CompTIA A+ Essentials exam doesn't cover it at all, I'm not going to go into too much gory detail. I will, however, give a brief account of the process involved.

The basic idea behind the AIK is that a tech can create an answer file by using a tool called the Windows System Image Monitor, and then use that answer file to build a Master Installation file that can be burned to DVD. Vista's answer files are no longer simple text documents but .XML files, and

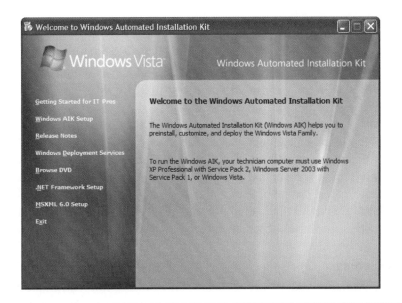

• **Figure 11.37**   The Automated Installation Kit

the process of creating one is much, much more complicated than it used to be. Gone are the days of simply running a wizard and modifying options as you see fit, replaced instead with a method of choosing components (which represent the things you want your automated installation to do, such as create a partition, enter a certain product key, and much, much more) out of a huge, often baffling list and then modifying their settings (Figure 11.38).

Once you've selected and modified all of the components you're interested in, you have to save your answer file, copy it to either a floppy disk or a USB thumb drive, and plug that into a new computer that you're going to install Vista on. When you boot a computer off of the Vista installation disc, it automatically searches all removable media for an answer file, and, finding one, uses it to automatically install itself. If you're only installing Vista to this one computer, you're finished, but if you want to install it to multiple computers, you'll probably want to create a disc image based off of your Master Installation file.

To create such an image, you must use a couple more tools in the AIK—Windows PE and ImageX—to "capture" the installation and create a disc image from it. If the rest of the process seemed a bit complicated, this part is like solving a Rubik's cube with your teeth while balancing on top of a flag pole and juggling. Suffice it to say that

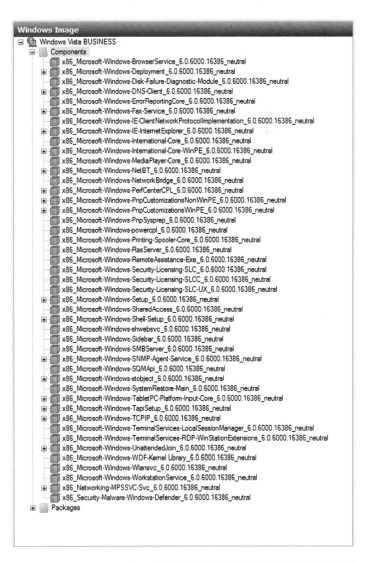

• **Figure 11.38**   The list of components in the Image Monitor

the AIK comes with documentation that tells you how to do this, so with a bit of patience, you can get through it.

After you've created an image from your Master Installation file, you can burn it to discs or share it on a network to set up new computers. All in all, this is an extremely complicated process that will, when you're finished with it, make installing Windows Vista a snap.

Scripted installations are a fine option, but they don't work well in all scenarios. Creating a fully scripted installation, including the installation of all additional drivers, software updates, and applications, can be a time-consuming process involving lots of trial-and-error adjustments. Wouldn't it be easier, at least some of the time, to manually set up one PC exactly the way you want it, and then automatically create exact copies of that installation on other machines? That's where disk cloning comes into play.

Disk Cloning

Disk cloning simply takes an existing PC and makes a full copy of the drive, including all data, software, and configuration files. You can then transfer that copy to as many machines as you like, essentially creating clones of the original machine. In the old days, making a clone was pretty simple. You just hooked up two hard drives and copied the files from the original to the clone by using something like the venerable XCOPY program (as long as the hard drive was formatted with FAT or FAT32). Today, you'll want to use a more sophisticated program, such as Norton Ghost, to make an image file that contains a copy of an entire hard drive and then lets you copy that image either locally or over the network.

Sysprep

Cloning a Windows PC works great for some situations, but what if you need to send the same image out to machines that have slightly different hardware? What if you need the customer to go through the final steps of the Windows installation (creating a user account, accepting the license agreement, etc.)? That's when you need to combine a scripted setup with cloning by using the System Preparation Tool, **Sysprep**, which can undo portions of the Windows installation process.

After installing Windows and adding any additional software (Microsoft Office, Adobe Acrobat, Yahoo Instant Messenger, etc.), run Sysprep (Figure 11.39) and then create your disk image by using the cloning

• **Figure 11.39** Sysprep, the System Preparation Tool

application of your choice. The first time a new system cloned from the image boots, an abbreviated version of setup, Mini-Setup, runs and completes the last few steps of the installation process: installing drivers for hardware, prompting the user to accept the license agreement and create user accounts, and so on. Optionally, you can use Setup Manager to create an answer file to customize Mini-Setup, just as you would with a standard scripted installation.

Tech Tip

RIS

Microsoft offers an even more advanced way of rolling out new systems: Remote Installation Services (RIS). *RIS requires at least Windows Server 2003 and is well beyond the scope of the CompTIA A+ Essentials exam.*

■ Troubleshooting Installation Problems

The term "installation problem" is rather deceptive. The installation process itself almost never fails. Usually, something else fails during the process that is generally interpreted as an "install failure." Let's look at some typical installation problems and how to correct them.

Text Mode Errors

If you're going to have a problem with a Windows installation, this is the place to get one. It's always better to have the error right off the bat as opposed to when the installation is nearly complete. Text mode errors most often take place during clean installations and usually point to one of the following problems:

No Boot Device Present When Booting Off the Startup Disk

Either the startup disk is bad or the CMOS is not set to look at that disk drive first.

Windows Setup Requires XXXX Amount of Available Drive Space

You forgot to format the C: drive, or there's a bunch of stuff on the drive already.

Not Ready Error on Optical Drive

You probably just need to give the optical drive a moment to catch up. Press R for retry a few times. You may also have a damaged installation disc, or the optical drive may be too slow for the system.

A Stop Error (Blue Screen of Death) After the Reboot at the End of Text Mode

This may mean you didn't do your homework in checking hardware compatibility, especially the BIOS. Stop errors are scary, but often fixable, so if you encounter one of these errors during installation, check out the Microsoft Knowledge Base.

Graphical Mode Errors

Once the installation passes the text mode and moves into graphical mode, a whole new crop of problems may arise.

Hardware Detection Errors

Failure to detect hardware properly by any version of Windows Setup can be avoided by simply researching compatibility beforehand. Or, if you decided to skip that step, you might be lucky and only have a hardware detection error involving a noncritical hardware device. You can troubleshoot this problem at your leisure. In a sense, you are handing in your homework late, checking out compatibility and finding a proper driver after Windows is installed.

Every Windows installation depends on Windows Setup properly detecting the computer type (motherboard and BIOS stuff, in particular) and installing the correct hardware support. Microsoft designed Windows to run on several hardware platforms using a layer of software tailored specifically for the hardware, called the **hardware abstraction layer (HAL)**.

Can't Read CAB Files

This is probably the most common of all installation errors. **CAB files** (as in cabinet) are special compressed files, recognizable by their .CAB file extension, that Microsoft uses to distribute copies of Windows. If your system can't read them, first check the installation disc for scratches. Then try copying all of the files from the source directory on the disc (\i386) into a directory on your local hard drive. Then run Windows Setup from there, remembering to use the correct program (WINNT32.EXE). If you can't read any of the files on the installation disc, you may have a defective drive.

Lockups During Installation

Lockups are one of the most challenging problems that can take place during installation, because they don't give you a clue as to what's causing the problem. Here are a few things to check if you get a lockup during installation.

Smart Recovery, Repair Installation

Most system lockups occur when Windows Setup queries the hardware. If a system locks up once during setup, turn off the computer—literally. Unplug the system! Do *not* press CTRL-ALT-DEL. Do *not* click Reset. Unplug it! Then turn the system back on, boot into Setup, and rerun the Setup program. Windows will see the partial installation and either restart the installation process automatically (Smart Recovery) or prompt you to repair the installation. Both of these look at the installation progress and complete the installation.

Optical Drive, Hard Drive

Bad optical discs, optical drives, or hard drives may cause lockups. Check the optical disc for scratches or dirt, and clean it up or replace it. Try a known good disc in the drive. If you get the same error, you may need to replace the drive.

Log Files

Windows generates a number of special text files called **log files** that track the progress of certain processes. Although Windows creates different log files for different purposes, two files most interest us:

- **SETUPLOG.TXT** tracks the complete installation process, logging the success or failure of file copying, Registry updates, reboots, and so on.

- **SETUPAPI.LOG** tracks each piece of hardware as it is installed. This is not an easy log file to read, as it uses Plug and Play code, but it will show you the last device installed before Windows locked up.

Windows stores these log files in the WINNT or Windows directory (the location in which the OS is installed). These operating systems have powerful recovery options, so, honestly, the chances of your ever actually having to read a log file, understand it, and then get something fixed as a result of that understanding are pretty small. What makes log files handy is when you call Microsoft or a hardware manufacturer. They *love* to read these files, and they actually have people who understand them. Don't worry about understanding log files for the CompTIA A+ Essentials exam; just make sure you know the names of the log files and their location. Leave the details to the übergeeks.

■ Post-Installation Tasks

You might think that's enough work for one day, but your task list has a few more things. They include updating the OS with patches and service packs, upgrading drivers, restoring user data files, and migrating and retiring.

Patches, Service Packs, and Updates

Someone once described an airliner as consisting of millions of parts flying in close formation. I think that's also a good description for an operating system. And we can even carry that analogy further by thinking about all of the maintenance required to keep an airliner safely flying. Like an airliner, the parts (programming code) of your OS were created by different people, and some parts may even have been contracted out. Although each component is tested as much as possible, and the assembled OS is also tested, it's not possible to test for every possible combination of events. Sometimes a piece is simply found to be defective. The fix for such a problem is a corrective program called a **patch**.

In the past, Microsoft provided patches for individual problems. They also accumulated patches until they reached some sort of critical mass and then bundled them together as a **service pack.** They still do this. But they also make it easier for you to find and install the appropriate patches and service packs, which, when combined, are called *updates*. They make these updates available at their Web site or on optical disc. Many organizations make the updates available for distribution from network servers. Immediately after installing Windows, install the latest updates on the computer.

Upgrading Drivers

Even if you did all your preinstallation tasks, you may decide to go with the default drivers that come with Windows and then upgrade them to the latest drivers after the fact. This is a good strategy, because installation is a complicated task and you can simplify it by installing old but adequate drivers. Maybe those newest drivers are just a week old—waiting until after the Windows installation to install new drivers gives you a usable driver to go back to if the new driver turns out to be a lemon. In the next chapter, "Learning Input/Output," you'll learn more about working with drivers, including a little driver magic called "Roll Back Driver."

Restoring User Data Files (If Applicable)

Remember when you backed up the user data files before installation? You don't? Well, check again, because now is the time to restore that data. Your method of restoring depends on how you backed up the files in the first place. If you used a third-party backup program, you need to install it before you can restore those files, but if you used the Windows Backup utility (Windows 2000 or XP) or the Backup and Restore Center (Windows Vista), you are in luck, because they are installed by default (with the exception of Windows XP Home edition). If you did something simpler, such as copying to optical discs or a network location, all you have to do is copy the files back to the local hard disk. Good luck!

Migrating and Retiring

Seasons change and so does the state of the art in computing. At a certain point in a computer's life, you'll need to retire an old system. This means you must move the data and users to a new system or at least a new hard drive—a process called **migration**—and then safely dispose of the old system. Microsoft offers a few tools to accomplish this task, and because it's important to know about them for the A+ exam (not to mention for your next new computer purchase), I'm going to go over them.

Files and Settings Transfer Wizard

You've already heard a bit about the **Files and Settings Transfer Wizard (FSTW)** back in Chapter 4, "Understanding Windows," but the Essentials exam expects you to have more than just a passing knowledge of it. When migrating to a new system, you would run the Files and Settings Transfer Wizard on the newer computer (assuming the newer computer is running Windows XP, but more on Vista's migration options later), which would then use the wizard to pull files off of the older one. You start the wizard by going to Accessories | System Tools in Windows XP's All Programs menu. Once you've fired it up, you're presented with the screen in Figure 11.40.

Files and Settings Transfer Wizard

Welcome to the Files and Settings Transfer Wizard

This wizard helps you transfer files and settings from your old computer to your new one.

You can transfer settings for Internet Explorer and Outlook Express, as well as desktop and display settings, dial-up connections, and other types of settings.

The best way to use this wizard for transferring files and settings is to use either a direct cable connection or a network. Learn more about connecting your computers.

Please close any other programs before you continue.

To continue, click Next.

[< Back] [Next >] [Cancel]

• **Figure 11.40**   The Files and Settings Transfer Wizard's initial screen

When you click the Next button on the wizard's first screen, you're asked whether the computer you're using is the new or old computer, as in Figure 11.41.

Note that the old computer can be running any version of Windows all the way back to Windows 95. Older Windows operating systems didn't come with the Files and Settings Transfer Wizard installed, so if you're migrating from an older version of Windows, you'll have to either install the wizard onto the older computer with the XP disc or create a Wizard Disk that will enable you to do the same thing. You're given the option to create such a disk by clicking Next with New computer selected, as in Figure 11.42.

Once you've either created a Wizard Disk (or told the wizard that you're going to install the wizard from the XP CD), you're taken to a screen that asks where to look for the files and settings that you've collected (Figure 11.43). The first two options are slightly outdated, because the first refers to a direct serial connection, now a rarity in the personal computing world, and the second asks for a floppy disc, though you can use it with USB thumb drives as well. The third option is the most likely candidate for a migration, because it enables you to look for your older computer on your home network.

Meanwhile, to actually determine which files and settings are going to be transferred, you need to run the wizard on your old computer. If you're migrating from another Windows XP machine, you need to tell the wizard where it's being run; otherwise, you skip to the next step, which asks how you want to transfer the files (Figure 11.44). The best option is to transfer them over a home network, but you can also save the files on a USB thumb drive or simply on a folder on your computer, though, obviously, that doesn't do a lot for transferring the files.

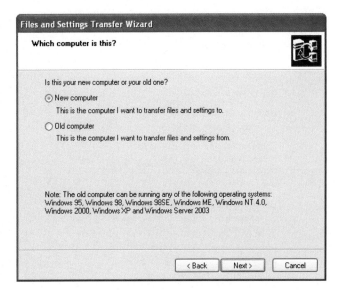

• **Figure 11.41**   Is this the new computer or your old one?

• **Figure 11.42**   Creating a Wizard Disk

• **Figure 11.43**   Where are the files and settings?

When you click Next, the wizard shows its default list of folders and settings to save, but being the savvy PC tech you are, you'll probably want to customize which folders are migrated. You can do that by checking the box that says *Let me select a custom list of files and settings when I click Next* (Figure 11.45).

If you've checked that box, the next page enables you to add additional settings and browse for additional folders, files, or even file types to back up, making it pretty easy to simply back up every .MP3 on your computer (Figure 11.46). Neat, huh?

Once you click Next on that screen, the wizard begins the actual transfer process, which can take quite a lot of time depending on how much stuff you're transferring. This is an excellent time to, for example, read the complete works of Pliny the Elder, or, even more usefully, to memorize all of the previous chapters of this book word-for-word, because you'll probably have plenty of time.

• **Figure 11.44**　How will you transfer the files?

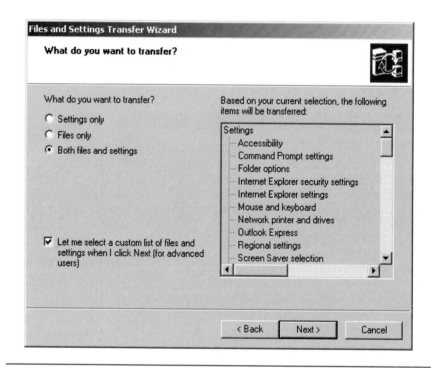

• **Figure 11.45**　The files and settings you're going to transfer

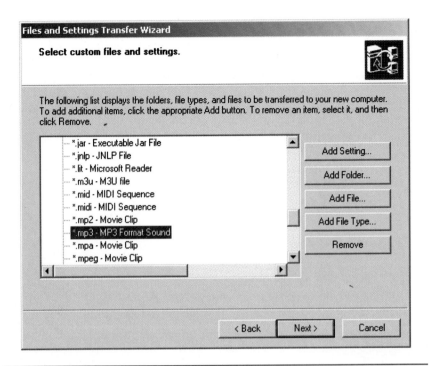

• Figure 11.46 Customizing the transfer

User State Migration Tool

If you're the sort of computer user who demands maximum functionality and power from your operating system, you'll probably want to use the **User State Migration Tool (USMT)**. The USMT has all of the same features as the Files and Settings Transfer Wizard, but with much more control over advanced configurations for the new computer. Its primary use is in businesses, because it has to be run in a Windows Server domain. In practice, if you're migrating a single user, use the FSTW. If you need to migrate multiple users, the USMT is the tool.

Windows Easy Transfer

With Windows Vista and 7, Microsoft has upgraded the Files and Settings Transfer Wizard, calling it **Windows Easy Transfer**. Windows Easy Transfer comes native in Vista/7 and can be downloaded and installed on Windows XP or 2000 as well, though you won't be able to transfer settings from a 2000 computer, only files. Windows Easy Transfer is located in the System Tools subfolder of the Accessories folder in your Programs menu. The first screen of the Windows Easy Transfer simply gives you a bit of information about the process, so there's not really much to do there.

When you click Next, you're taken to a screen that asks if you want to start a new transfer or continue an old one (Figure 11.47). If you've already set up your old computer to transfer the files, select the latter option; if you haven't, select the former.

If you choose to start a new transfer, the process is very similar to the Files and Settings Transfer Wizard: you select whether you're using your new or old computer and then follow the same basic steps as before.

• Figure 11.47   Start a new transfer or continue one?

There are some differences, of course—network security is improved by using Transfer Keys to protect your files from others on the network, there's an option to use a special Easy Transfer cable to transfer your files between USB ports, and the order of some screens is changed around a bit—but if you understand the Files and Settings Transfer Wizard transfer process, Windows Easy Transfer shouldn't be too difficult.

Migration Practices

When talking about migration or retirement in terms of security, you need to answer one question: What do you do with the old system or drive?

All but the most vanilla new installations have sensitive data on them, even if it's simply e-mail messages or notes-to-self that would cause embarrassment if discovered. Most PCs, especially in a work environment, contain a lot of sensitive data. You can't just format C: and hand over the drive.

Follow three principles when migrating or retiring a computer. First, migrate your users and data information in a secure environment. Until you get passwords properly in place and test the security of the new system, you can't consider that system secure. Second, remove data remnants from hard drives that you store or give to charity. Third, recycle the older equipment; don't throw it in the trash. PC recyclers go through a process of deconstructing hardware, breaking system units, keyboards, printers, and even monitors into their basic plastics, metals, and glass for reuse.

The easiest way for someone to compromise or access sensitive data is to simply take it when you're not looking. This is especially true when copying information to a new, unprotected system. Don't set a copy to run while you go out to lunch, but rather be there to supervise and remove any remnant data that might still reside on any mass storage devices, especially hard drives.

You might think that, as easy as it seems to be to lose data, you could readily get rid of data if you tried. That's not the case with magnetic media, though, such as hard drives and flash memory. Cleaning a drive completely is very difficult. Repeated formatting won't do the trick. Partitioning and formatting won't work. Data doesn't necessarily get written over in the same place every time, which means that a solid wipe of a hard drive by writing zeros to all of the clusters still potentially leaves a lot of sensitive and recoverable data, typically called **remnants**, on the drive.

Although you can't make data 100 percent unrecoverable short of physically shredding or pulverizing a drive, you can do well enough for donation purposes by using one of the better drive-wiping utilities, such as Webroot's Window Washer (Figure 11.48). With Window Washer, you can erase your Web browsing history, your recent activity in Windows (such as what programs you ran), and even your e-mail messages permanently. As an added bonus, you can create a bootable disk that enables you to wipe a drive completely.

Recycle

An important and relatively easy way to be an environmentally conscious computer user is to *recycle*. Recycling products such as paper and printer cartridges not only keeps them out of overcrowded landfills but also ensures that the more toxic products are disposed of in the right way. Safely disposing of hardware containing hazardous materials, such as computer monitors, protects both people and the environment.

• **Figure 11.48**   Webroot Window Washer security software

Anyone who's ever tried to sell a computer more than three or four years old learns a hard lesson: they're not worth much if anything at all. It's a real temptation to take that old computer and just toss it in the garbage, but never do that!

First of all, many parts of your computer—such as your computer monitor—contain hazardous materials that pollute the environment. Luckily, thousands of companies now specialize in computer recycling and will gladly accept your old computer. If you have enough computers, they might even pick them up. If you can't find a recycler, call your local municipality's waste authority to see where to drop off your system.

An even better alternative for your old computer is donation. Many organizations actively look for old computers to refurbish and to donate to schools and other organizations. Just keep in mind that the computer can be too old—not even a school wants a computer more than five or six years old.

■ Post-Installation: How All the Pieces Fit Together

You know from previous chapters the locations of many of the user-focused folders that are installed automatically. The Windows desktop, for example, is simply a folder, most commonly found in the user folders section of the C: drive. Similarly, My Documents/Documents is just another folder.

Installation creates a set of Windows-specific files and folders that the OS needs to run a PC. Some of these files and folders are directly on the root of the C: drive; others can be elsewhere. The best way to remember the locations of these files and folders and to know their importance to the OS is by looking at how they interact to boot the PC. Windows 2000 and Windows XP have pretty much the same files and boot process; Windows Vista differs a bit, so we'll look at the latter OS separately.

The 2000/XP Boot Process

Windows 2000 and XP distinguish between the files that start the operating system (called the *system files*) and the rest of the operating system files (usually in the \WINDOWS or \WINNT folders). The system files (memorize these!) consist of three required files: NTLDR, BOOT.INI, and NTDETECT.COM. If you're using a SCSI hard drive, there's a fourth file called NTBOOTDD.SYS. The NTLDR (pronounced *NT loader*) file begins the boot process.

You know from earlier chapters that to make a drive bootable requires an active, primary partition, right? Let's look at the process in a PC with a hard drive partitioned as C: and D:.

The CPU wakes up and runs the system BIOS, and then the BIOS sends out a routine looking for a valid operating system in the boot sector of the primary master hard drive. The master file table (MFT) lives in the boot sector of the C: partition. It points to the location of the Windows 2000/XP system files, also on the C: drive, because that's the bootable drive. Windows calls the primary active partition the *system partition* or the *system volume* (if it's a dynamic disk).

The Windows 2000/XP *boot files* consist of NTOSKRNL.EXE (the Windows kernel), the \WINNT\SYSTEM32\CONFIG\SYSTEM file (which controls the loading of device drivers), and the device drivers. Although these files are the core of the Windows 2000/XP OS, they are not capable of booting, or starting, the system. For that feat, they require NTLDR, NTDETECT.COM, and BOOT.INI—the system files.

The system files start the PC and then, at the end of that process, point the CPU to the location of the boot files. The CPU goes over and chats with NTOSKRNL, and the GUI starts to load. The operating system is then up and running, and you're able to do work.

The odd part about all this is that Microsoft decided to make the OS files mobile. *The Windows operating system files can reside on any partition or volume in the PC.* The \WINDOWS folder, for example, could very well be on drive D:, not drive C:. Whichever drive holds the core OS files is called the *boot partition*. This can lead to a little confusion when you say the system files are on the C: drive and Windows is on the D: drive, but that's just the way it is. The vast majority of Windows 2000/XP systems have the system partition and the boot partition both on the same big C: partition.

You have the process now in general, so let's look more specifically at the makeup and function of the individual files involved in the boot process.

2000/XP System Partition Files

Windows 2000 and XP require the three system files in the root directory of the system partition:

- NTLDR
- BOOT.INI
- NTDETECT.COM

To see these files, go into My Computer and open the C: drive. Go to Tools | Folder Options. Click *Show hidden files and folders*, uncheck the *Hide protected operating system files (Recommended)* option, and click OK. Now when you return to viewing the folder in My Computer, you will see certain critical files that Windows otherwise hides from you to prevent you from accidentally moving, deleting, or changing them in some unintended way (Figure 11.49).

• **Figure 11.49**   My Computer showing the system files

NTLDR

When the system boots up, the master boot record (MBR) or MFT on the hard drive starts the NTLDR program. The **NTLDR** program then launches Windows 2000/XP or another OS. To find the available OSes, the NTLDR program must read the BOOT.INI configuration file. To do so, it loads its own minimal file system, which enables it to read the BOOT.INI file off of the system partition.

BOOT.INI File

The **BOOT.INI** file is a text file that lists the OSes available to NTLDR and tells NTLDR where to find the boot partition (where the OS is stored) for each of them. The BOOT.INI file has sections defined by headings enclosed in brackets. A basic BOOT.INI in Windows XP looks like this:

```
[boot loader]
timeout=30
default=multi(0)disk(0)rdisk(0)partition(1)\WINDOWS
[operating systems]
multi(0)disk(0)rdisk(0)partition(1)\WINDOWS="Microsoft Windows XP
Professional" /fastdetect
```

A more complex BOOT.INI may look like this:

```
[boot loader]
timeout=30
default=multi(0)disk(0)rdisk(0)partition(1)\WINDOWS
[operating systems]
multi(0)disk(0)rdisk(0)partition(1)\WINDOWS="Microsoft Windows XP
Professional" /fastdetect
multi(0)disk(0)rdisk(0)partition(1)\WINNT="Microsoft Windows 2000
Professional" /fastdetect
```

Such a BOOT.INI would result in the boot menu that appears in Figure 11.50.

```
Please select the operating system to start:

    Microsoft Windows 2000 Professional
    Microsoft Windows 2000 Recovery Console
    Previous Operating system on C:

Use ↑ and ↓ to move the highlight to your choice.
Press Enter to choose.
Seconds until highlighted choice will be started automatically: 26




For troubleshooting and advanced startup options for Windows 2000, press F8.
```

• **Figure 11.50**   Boot loader in Windows 2000 with System Recovery Console

This crazy `multi(0)disk(0)rdisk(0)partition(1)` is an example of the Advanced RISC Computing (ARC) naming system. It's a system that's designed to enable your PC to boot Windows from any hard drive, including removable devices. Let's take a quick peek at each ARC setting to see how it works.

`Multi(x)` is the number of the adapter and always starts with 0. The adapter is determined by the boot order you set in your CMOS setting. For example, if you have a single PATA controller and a SATA controller, and you set the system to boot first from the PATA, any drive on that controller will get the value `multi(0)` placed in its ARC format. Any SATA drive will get `multi(1)`.

`Disk(x)` is only used for SCSI drives, but the value is required in the ARC format, so with ATA systems it's always set to `disk(0)`.

`Rdisk(x)` specifies the number of the disk on the adapter. On a PATA drive, the master is `rdisk(0)` and the slave is `rdisk(1)`. On SATA drives, the order is usually based on the number of the SATA connection printed on the motherboard, though some systems allow you to change this in CMOS.

`Partition(x)` is the number of the partition or logical drive in an extended partition. The numbering starts at 1, so the first partition is `partition(1)`, the second is `partition(2)`, and so on.

The `\WINDOWS` is the name of the folder that holds the boot files. This is important to appreciate! The ARC format looks at the folder, so there's no problem running different versions of Windows on a single partition. You can simply install them in different folders. Of course, you have other limitations, such as file system type, but in general, multibooting in Windows is pretty trivial. Better yet, this is all handled during the installation process.

ARC format can get far more complicated. SCSI drives get a slightly different ARC format. For example, if you installed Windows on a SCSI drive, you might see this ARC setting in your BOOT.INI:

```
scsi(0)disk(1)rdisk(0)partition(1)
```

If you want to boot to a SCSI drive, Windows adds a fourth file to your system files called NTBOOTDD.SYS. This file only exists if you want to boot to a SCSI drive. Most people don't boot to a SCSI, so don't worry if you don't see this file with the other three system files.

On rare occasions, you might find yourself needing to edit the BOOT.INI file. Any text editor handily edits this file, but most of us prefer to edit BOOT.INI via the System Setup dialog box. In Windows 2000/XP, open the System applet from the Control Panel. Click the Advanced tab and then click the Startup and Recovery button. The BOOT.INI options show up at the top (Figure 11.51).

BOOT.INI has some interesting switches at the end of the ARC formats that give special instructions on how the operating system should boot. Sometimes Windows puts these in automatically, and sometimes you will add them manually for troubleshooting. Here are a few of the more common ones:

- **/BOOTLOG** Tells Windows to create a log of the boot process and write it to a file called Ntbtlog.txt.

- **/CMDCONS** Tells Windows to start the Recovery Console.

• **Figure 11.51** BOOT.INI

- **/LASTKNOWNGOOD** Tells Windows to boot the Last Known Good set of files.

- **/NOEXECUTE** Newer CPUs come with Data Execute Protection (DEP) to prevent unruly programs from causing system lockups. The setting for this, /NOEXECUTE=OPTIN, is the default on Windows systems.

NTDETECT.COM

If the NTLDR determines that you have chosen to start Windows 2000/XP, it boots the system into protected mode and then calls on **NTDETECT.COM** to detect the installed hardware on the system. NTLDR then refers to the BOOT.INI file to locate the Windows boot files.

Critical Boot Files

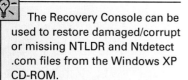

The Recovery Console can be used to restore damaged/corrupt or missing NTLDR and Ntdetect .com files from the Windows XP CD-ROM.

Naming all the critical boot files for Windows 2000/XP is akin to naming every muscle in the human body—completely possible, but time-consuming and without any real benefit. However, a few of the *most* important files certainly deserve a short mention.

Once NTLDR finishes detections, it loads NTOSKRNL.EXE, HAL.DLL, some of the Registry, and some basic device drivers; then it passes control to the NTOSKRNL.EXE file. NTOSKRNL.EXE completes the Registry loading, initializes all device drivers, and starts the WINLOGON .EXE program, which displays the Windows 2000/XP logon screen (Figure 11.52).

Take the time to memorize the primary boot files and the boot process for Windows 2000/XP. Most boot errors are easily repaired if you know which files are used for booting and in which order they load.

• **Figure 11.52** Where do you want to go today?

The Vista/7 Boot Process

Windows Vista has a very different boot process than previous versions of Windows. For one thing, Vista supports both BIOS and UEFI, whereas older versions of Windows did not, so things are a bit more complex right off the bat. Instead of having a unified Windows Vista boot process, there are actually two slightly different boot processes: one for systems using BIOS and one for systems with UEFI.

The very first thing that happens when you power on a system with Windows Vista is that either the BIOS or the UEFI starts up. The difference between BIOS and UEFI systems is in what happens next. In a BIOS-based system, the BIOS uses its boot order to scan partitions, one by one, for a Master Boot Record (MBR). The MBR holds a small bit of file system boot code that scans the system's partition table for the system partition and then loads its boot sector. The boot sector in turn contains code that does nothing but point the boot process toward a file called BOOTMGR (pronounced "boot manager," or

Cross Check

Editing BOOT.INI

In Chapter 4, "Learning Windows," you learned about another tool used to edit the BOOT.INI file in Windows 2000/XP. What tool was that? Does it work in Vista?

"boot mugger" if you're trying to make nerds laugh). On an UEFI system, on the other hand, neither the MBR nor the file system boot code is run, and UEFI simply loads up BOOTMGR directly.

If you've ever run a dual-boot system with Vista on it, you're probably already somewhat familiar with the BOOTMGR; one of its jobs is displaying that "Which operating system do you want to load?" screen and then loading the appropriate operating system. When the BOOTMGR starts, it reads data from a Boot Configuration Data (BCD) file that contains information about the various operating systems installed on the system as well as instructions for how to actually load (bootstrap) them. Once an operating system is selected (or immediately if only one is present), BOOTMGR loads a program called WINLOAD.EXE, which readies your system to load the operating system kernel itself rather like the way you clean up your house before Aunt Edna comes to visit. It does this by loading into memory the hardware abstraction layer, the system Registry, and the drivers for any boot devices before the operating system itself takes over.

Once the operating system process (called NTOSKRNL.EXE) takes over, it loads up all of the various processes and systems that comprise Windows, the Windows Vista logo comes up, and you're happily computing, completely oblivious to all of the complex electronic communication that just took place inside your computer.

No Installation Is Perfect

Even when the installation seems smooth, issues may slowly surface, especially in the case of upgrades. Be prepared to reinstall applications or deal with new functions that were absent in the previous OS. If things really fall apart, you can go back to the previous OS or, if you have an OEM computer (one built by, for example, Dell or HP instead of by you), your computer likely came with either a special recovery partition on its hard drive or a set of recovery discs that you can utilize to restore your operating system to its factory settings. You usually invoke a system recovery by hitting a certain key during boot-up—usually F10 or F11—and then following a set of prompts.

The procedures I've laid out in this chapter may seem like a lot of work—how bad could it be to grab an installation CD/DVD-ROM, fling a copy of Windows onto a system, and, as the saying goes, let the chips fall where they may? Plenty bad, is how bad. Not only is understanding these procedures important for the CompTIA A+ Essentials exam; they can also save your, ah, hide, once you're a working PC tech and you're tasked to install the latest version of Windows on the boss's new computer!

Tech Tip

BOOTMGR Is Missing!
If you use Vista long enough, you may encounter an error message saying that Windows cannot boot because the BOOTMGR is missing. This message is generated when the boot sector code is unable to locate the BOOTMGR, which can be caused by file system corruption, a botched installation, or viruses.

BOOTMGR is also responsible for bringing Windows out of hibernation, so if your computer refuses to wake up, blame BOOTMGR!

Unlike with Windows 2000 and XP, the boot files and the system files must all reside on the same partition in Vista and Windows 7.

Boot Configuration Data (BCD) replaces the boot.ini used in previous operating systems and can be altered by using the command-line tool bcdedit.exe.

Chapter 11 Review

◼ Chapter Summary

After reading this chapter and completing the exercises, you should understand the following about Windows.

Identify and implement preinstallation tasks

- Identify hardware requirements, making sure your computer meets the recommended minimums for CPU, RAM, free hard disk space, video adapter, display, and other components. Check the Windows Logo'd Product List or the Windows Compatibility Center at the Microsoft Web site to verify that the Windows version you're installing supports the hardware and application software you will run.

- A clean OS installation takes place on a new hard drive or one that has been reformatted and repartitioned. You must reinstall all applications and reconfigure user preferences. In an upgrade installation, the new OS is installed in the directory where the old OS was located. The new OS retains the hardware and software settings of the old OS, including user preferences. Before you upgrade, back up any data that the user has saved on the local hard drive.

- Use the most advanced file system your version of Windows supports unless you are planning a multiboot configuration. Windows Vista will not multiboot with another OS on the same partition.

Install and upgrade Windows 2000, Windows XP, and Windows Vista

- You can install Windows 2000 with floppy diskettes or a CD-ROM. Windows XP does not create a set of setup boot disks and does not use a floppy disk by default. If you install from the CD, you must add an optical drive to your PC's boot sequence and boot directly to the Windows 2000 or Windows XP CD-ROM. If this isn't possible in Windows XP, you can download a set of six setup boot floppy disks from the Microsoft Web site.

- You can install Windows Vista/7 from a DVD-ROM, a USB drive, or specially ordered CD-ROMs, from over a network, or by using a disc image.

- During installation, you will be prompted for registration information, including your name, address, and other details. Registration is optional. Designed to prevent a Windows license from being used for more than one PC, Microsoft Product Activation (MPA) is *mandatory* within 30 days of installing Windows XP, Vista, or 7, or the operating system will be disabled. You can activate the OS by using an Internet connection or by calling Microsoft. You give Microsoft an installation code—a 50-digit value that identifies your key hardware components—and Microsoft gives you a 42-digit product activation code.

- To do a clean installation of Windows 2000/XP, boot the computer to the Windows installation disc, which will copy files to your hard drive. You then remove the disc, the system reboots, and Windows loads system devices and displays the Welcome to Setup screen. When prompted, accept the End User License Agreement (EULA). If necessary, create a new partition (default size or smaller). After you select the partition where Windows should be installed and the file system to use (NTFS is recommended), Setup copies files to the Windows folder and appropriate subfolders. Several reboots later and you're good to go.

- Installing Windows Vista/7 is very different from installing 2000 or XP, but most of the concepts are the same. You still boot the computer from the installation disc, accept a EULA, partition your system drive, and enter a product key. You just do all those things in a different order and by using a graphical user interface instead of a primitive text mode.

- The system requirements for Windows Vista are slightly different, depending on whether you're installing the Home Basic edition or any other edition. The non-Basic editions all require a 1-GHz processor, 1 GB of RAM, and 40 GB of hard drive space (with at least 15 MB of free space); a DirectX 9 capable graphics card with at least 128 MB of memory, pixel shader 2.0 support, the WDDM driver, and 32 bits per pixel; a network card with

Internet access; and a DVD drive. Home Basic is similar but only requires 512 MB of RAM, a 20-GB hard drive (again, with 15 GB free), and a basic 32-MB graphics card without any fancy features.

- You can automate the installation process through scripted installations and disk cloning. Windows 2000 and Windows XP can use Setup Manager to help you create an answer file that contains all of the answers to the installation questions, such as computer name, locale, screen resolution, and so on. Windows Vista comes with the Automated Installation Kit (AIK) that you can use to create an answer file. It's a substantially more complex tool than the older Setup Manager.

- With disc cloning, you simply take an existing PC and make a full copy of the drive, including all data, software, and configuration files. You can then transfer that copy to as many machines as you like, essentially creating clones of the original machine.

Troubleshoot installation problems

- Although the installation process itself rarely fails, you may encounter an installation failure caused by something else. Text mode errors during a clean installation may range from "No Boot Device Present" (the startup disk is bad or CMOS is not set to look at the appropriate drive first), to "Drive C: does not contain a Valid FAT Partition" (there is no partition or a partition Windows cannot use), to insufficient space on the drive. If you get a "Not Ready Error on CD-ROM," you could have a damaged installation disc or a slow optical drive that needs to catch up. A stop error (Blue Screen of Death) after the reboot at the end of the text mode points to a hardware incompatibility problem.

- Graphical mode errors indicate a different set of problems than text mode errors. Windows Setup must be able to detect the computer type (especially the motherboard and BIOS) and install the correct hardware abstraction layer (HAL). You may get a hardware detection error if Windows Setup fails to detect a device. If it is a noncritical piece of hardware, you can work on this problem later. This error may be solved by finding the proper driver.

- Probably the most common installation problem is failure to read the compressed Windows OS distribution files called CAB files. Try copying these files to your local hard drive and running the Setup program from there.

- If the system locks up during installation, do *not* press CTRL-ALT-DEL or the Reset button to restart the installation. Instead, unplug the system and then turn it back on so Windows will recognize a partial installation and go to the Safe Recovery mode, where it can often complete the installation. A bad CD-ROM, optical drive, or hard drive can cause an installation lockup.

- During installation, Windows creates several log files. The two files of interest are SETUPLOG.TXT, which tracks the installation process (logging success and failures), and SETUPAPI.LOG, which tracks each piece of hardware as it is installed and shows you the last device installed before Windows locked up. Windows 2000 and XP store these log files in the OS installation directory (usually WINNT or Windows).

Identify and implement post-installation tasks

- The first essential tasks post installation include updating Windows by applying patches you download from Microsoft and updating drivers for hardware to the latest and hopefully most stable versions.

- After updating, you can go through the process of restoring a user's files through the various backup utilities available or by using the Files and Settings Transfer Wizard (FSTW) or Windows Easy Transfer.

- When migrating data to a new computer, it's important to follow three principles: migrate in a secure environment, remove data remnants when disposing of hard drives, and recycle old equipment.

- Completely removing data from a hard drive is difficult, short of physically destroying the drive. Tools such as Webroot's Window Washer are necessary to permanently erase files.

- When getting rid of old computer parts, it's important to recycle or donate them. This is not only helpful to the environment but also to the community.

Explain the structures created during the installation process

- Windows 2000 and XP use three primary system files (NTLDR, BOOT.INI, and NTDETECT.COM) to boot the system. These three files find and boot the operating system (NTOSKRNL.EXE) as well as any files necessary to run the OS.

- NTLDR is responsible for starting the operating system process in Windows 2000 and XP, and it does so by reading the BOOT.INI file, using its own tiny file system.

- The BOOT.INI file stores information about the location of all operating systems installed on the system.

- NTDETECT.COM detects the hardware on a Windows 2000/XP system before the actual OS is loaded.

- The Windows Vista/7 boot process first loads up some code in the MBR, which in turn calls the BOOTMGR. The BOOTMGR uses Boot Configuration Data (BCD) files to present the user with a list of all of the system's installed operating systems. Once an OS has been selected, the BOOTMGR loads a program called WINLOAD.EXE, which prepares the system environment for the operating system before loading the NTOSKRNL.

■ Key Terms

BOOT.INI *(382)*
CAB files *(372)*
clean installation *(341)*
disk cloning *(370)*
End User License Agreement (EULA) *(344)*
Files and Settings Transfer Wizard *(374)*
hardware abstraction layer (HAL) *(372)*
image installation *(342)*
log files *(373)*
Microsoft Product Activation (MPA) *(347)*
migration *(374)*
multiboot installation *(341)*
NTDETECT.COM *(384)*
NTLDR *(382)*

operating system (OS) *(338)*
patch *(373)*
product key *(353)*
registration *(347)*
remnants *(379)*
service pack *(373)*
SETUPAPI.LOG *(373)*
SETUPLOG.TXT *(373)*
Sysprep *(370)*
Upgrade Advisor *(346)*
upgrade installation *(341)*
User State Migration Tool (USMT) *(377)*
Windows Easy Transfer *(377)*
Windows Logo'd Product List *(340)*

■ Key Term Quiz

Use the Key Terms list to complete the sentences that follow. Not all terms will be used.

1. If you do not complete the _____ within 30 days, Windows stops working.

2. If you have a new hard drive with nothing on it, you will likely choose to do a(n)_____.

3. A(n) _____ is a fix for a single problem with the OS, while a(n) _____ is a combination of fixes.

4. If you wish to have only one OS and keep the applications and configuration of the current

system, you should choose to do a(n) _____ of the new OS.

5. Microsoft uses compressed _____ to distribute installation files.

6. The _____ is a list of hardware devices and services that are guaranteed to work on Windows.

7. The Windows XP boot process accesses a list of installed operating systems stored in the _____ file.

8. If you're not sure your system can support Windows Vista, run the _____.

9. Windows creates _____ during the installation, which contains information about all installed hardware.

10. Windows XP and Vista have tools for migrating user files and settings. The tool in Vista is called _____.

■ Multiple-Choice Quiz

1. Which of the following is an advantage of running Windows 2000 on NTFS as opposed to FAT32?
   A. Security
   B. Support for DOS applications
   C. Long filenames
   D. Network support

2. Ricardo's Windows XP installation has failed. What file should he check to see what files failed to copy?
   A. INSTALL.LOG
   B. SETUP.LOG
   C. SETUP.TXT
   D. SETUPLOG.TXT

3. If you do not complete the activation process for Windows XP, Vista, or 7, what will happen to your computer?
   A. Nothing. Activation is optional.
   B. The computer will work fine for 30 days and then Windows will be disabled.
   C. Microsoft will not know how to contact you to provide upgrade information.
   D. You will have to use a floppy disk set to boot to Windows.

4. After you have completed a Windows installation and verified that the system starts and runs okay, what should you do next?
   A. Do nothing. You're through.
   B. Install World of Warcraft and enjoy.
   C. Install productivity applications and restore data.
   D. Install the latest service pack or updates along with any updated drivers.

5. If Windows locks up during the installation, what should you do?
   A. Press CTRL-ALT-DEL to restart the installation process.
   B. Push the Reset button to restart the installation process.
   C. Press the ESC key to cancel the installation process.
   D. Unplug the computer and restart the installation process.

6. You can upgrade directly to Windows Vista from which of these operating systems?
   A. Windows 3.1
   B. Windows XP
   C. Windows 2000
   D. All of the above

7. If you get an error message saying that the Setup program cannot read the CAB files, what should you do?
   A. Copy the CAB files from the Windows installation disc to your local hard drive and run the Setup program from there.
   B. Skip this step because the CAB files are not necessary to install Windows successfully.
   C. Go to the Microsoft Web site and download the latest version of the CAB File Wizard.
   D. Cancel the installation process and keep your old operating system because your hardware does not meet the minimum requirements.

8. If you receive a graphical mode error in a Windows 2000 or XP installation saying that Windows failed to detect a noncritical piece of hardware, what should you do?
   A. You need to remove the hardware device or replace it with one that is compatible with the OS.

B. You can probably solve the problem after the installation is complete by finding the proper driver.

C. You will get a stop error and be unable to complete the installation process.

D. You should reboot the computer and restart the installation.

9. If you are not sure your Windows XP system can support Windows Vista, what should you do?

A. Consult the Windows Catalog.

B. Consult the Windows Logo'd Product List.

C. Run the Vista Upgrade Advisor.

D. Install Vista and hope for the best, because it will probably work.

10. If you are experiencing problems with Windows 2000 and wish to install Windows XP, what type of installation is preferred?

A. Clean installation

B. Upgrade installation

C. Network installation

D. Image installation

11. What does the BOOT.INI file do in the Windows 2000/XP boot process?

A. It takes control of the system from the BIOS.

B. It loads all of the necessary device drivers and hardware devices.

C. It lists the locations of all Windows operating systems on the system.

D. It loads the BOOTMGR.

12. What does the BOOTMGR do in the normal Windows Vista/7 boot process?

A. It loads device drivers and files from the system Registry to prepare for the loading of the operating system.

B. It gathers information about a system's installed operating systems, enables a user to select between them, and then loads WINLOADER.EXE.

C. It manages a system's boot order.

D. It's the name of the operating system process.

13. When the text mode of Windows Setup completes and the computer reboots to continue in graphical mode, what must you enter to continue the installation?

A. Activation key

B. CPU ID

C. Registration information

D. Product key

14. The Norton Ghost software is most helpful with which method of installation?

A. Clean installation

B. Upgrade installation

C. Network installation

D. Image installation

15. Which setting affects the way currency and math separators display?

A. Currency

B. Language

C. Locale

D. Date/Time

■ Essay Quiz

1. You've been tasked to teach some new hires how to do a rollout of the latest version of Windows. Write a short essay that outlines what the newbies need to know to upgrade 10 machines. You can assume that the network roles, language, and local settings will stay the same. Make an argument for a clean, upgrade, or multiboot installation. You can use Windows XP or, if you're feeling adventurous, Windows Vista. If you go for the latter, do a Web search for any special steps or procedures not included in the book. Check my Web site Tech Files for one on Windows Vista installation: www.totalsem.com.

2. The same group of newbies will need help with post-installation tasks, so write a second memo that tells them what to do after installing.

3. Your boss has decided to go higher tech on you and wants the next rollout of 10 Windows machines to be automatic, rather than have techs sit through the whole process. Select one of the three methods outlined in the chapter for automating the installation process and make a case for one over the other two.

4. Your boss decided to upgrade her computer from Windows 2000 to Windows XP Professional, but Windows keeps crashing in the middle. Write a short note discussing what could be happening so you can walk her through the installation troubleshooting over the phone.

5. Take the analysis of the functions of a computer operating system and apply it to a device you might encounter in everyday life. For example, describe the automobile or a washing machine in terms of operating system functions. Be creative!

Lab Projects

• Lab Project 11.1

The chapter mentions a couple of alternative operating systems, including Mac OS X and Linux. Do an Internet search or a tour of your local PC superstore and compare the operating systems available. Are Mac OS X, Linux, and Windows the only operating systems out there?

• Lab Project 11.2

Search the Microsoft Knowledge Base for articles about "Stop Error 0x0A" during a Windows 2000 installation. (Hint: Use the Advanced Search feature!) Based on one of the articles you locate, prepare a five-minute report for the class about the cause of this error and the steps Microsoft recommends to solve it.

• Lab Project 11.3

You know that some printers may work in Windows XP but not with Windows Vista. Check the Windows Logo'd Product List to determine whether the following printers are compatible with Windows Vista:

- HP LaserJet 4100
- HP Photosmart 2000

- HP DeskJet 722C
- Epson Stylus Color 1160
- Canon LBP 660

If you have a different printer, check it also while you're looking at the Windows Logo'd Product List.

Learning Input/Output

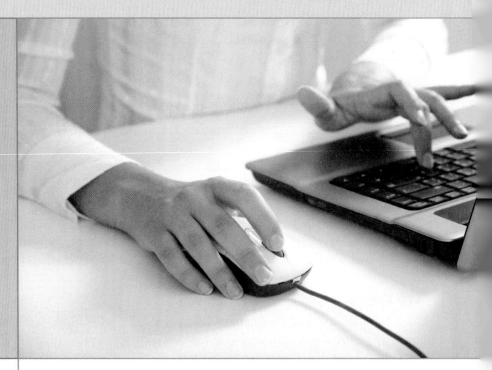

"The Macintosh uses an experimental pointing device called a 'mouse.' There is no evidence that people want to use these things. I don't want one of these new fangled devices."

—JOHN C. DVORAK, 1984

In this chapter, you will learn how to

- ■ **Identify certain common input/output devices on a PC**
- ■ **Describe how certain specialty input/output devices work on a PC**

In Chapter 3, "The Visible PC," you learned how to recognize and connect a number of common devices and the ports they use. This chapter discusses a number of common and not-so-common input/output (I/O) devices that use the ports you've already learned about.

The CompTIA A+ Essentials exam objectives split computer I/O devices into three groups: common, multimedia, and specialty. Common I/O devices, such as keyboards and mice, are found on virtually every PC. Multimedia I/O devices support video and sound functions. Specialty I/O devices run the gamut from common (touch screens) to rare (biometric devices). In fact, the exam deals with an entire set of I/O devices—networking devices—as completely distinct technologies. This book dedicates entire chapters to sound and video, printing, and networking, providing details about dealing with these types of devices and the ports they use. This chapter concentrates on two of the I/O device groups: the common devices and the specialty devices. You'll learn how to identify both the most common and some of the most unusual I/O devices used in today's PCs.

■ Common I/O Devices

So what is a "common" I/O device? I'm hoping you immediately thought of the mouse and the keyboard, two of the most basic, necessary, and abused I/O devices on a computer. Another fairly common input device that's been around a long time is the scanner. To these oldsters, you can add relative newcomers to the world of common devices: digital cameras and Web cameras.

📄 If you want to get picky, these five common I/O devices enable a user only to *input* data; they don't provide any output at all.

Keyboards

Keyboards are both the oldest and still the primary way you input data into a PC. Windows comes with perfectly good drivers for any keyboard, although some fancier keyboards may come with specialized keys that require a special driver be installed to operate properly. About the only issue that might affect keyboard installation is if you're using a USB keyboard: make sure that the USB Keyboard Support option is enabled in your CMOS (Figure 12.1). The other main issue with keyboards has been mostly solved with the proliferation of USB keyboards—older keyboards using the now-outdated PS/2 port had to be installed before the computer was booted. If you tried to plug in a PS/2 keyboard after your computer had started up, it wouldn't work.

• **Figure 12.1**   CMOS USB Keyboard Support option

There's not much to do to configure a standard keyboard. The only configuration tool you might need is the Keyboard Control Panel applet. This tool enables you to change the repeat delay (the amount of time you must hold down a key before the keyboard starts repeating the character), the repeat rate (how quickly the character is repeated after the repeat delay), and the default cursor blink rate. Figure 12.2 shows the default Windows

Tech Tip

Wireless Keyboards and Batteries
Wireless keyboards are a wonderful convenience because they remove the cable between you and the PC, but make sure you keep a complete set of spare batteries around.

• **Figure 12.2**   Keyboard Control Panel applet

Keyboard Properties window—some keyboard makers provide drivers that add extra tabs.

Keyboards might be easy to install, but they do fail occasionally. Given their location—right in front of you—the three issues that cause the most keyboard problems stem from spills, physical damage, and dirt.

Spilling a soda onto your keyboard can make for a really bad day. If you're quick and unplug the keyboard from the PC before the liquid hits the electrical components, you might be able to save the keyboard. It'll take some cleaning, though (keep reading for cleaning tips). More often than not, you'll get a sticky, ill-performing keyboard that is not worth the hassle—just replace it!

Other common physical damage comes from dropping objects onto the keyboard, such as a heavy book (like the one in your hands). This can have bad results! Most keyboards are pretty resilient, though, and can bounce back from the hit.

Clean dirt and grime off the keys by using a cloth dampened with a little water, or if the water alone doesn't do the job, use a bit of isopropyl alcohol on a cloth (Figure 12.3).

Dirty keys might be unsightly, but dirt under the keys might cause the keyboard to stop working completely. When your keys start to stick, grab a bottle of compressed air and shoot some air under the keys. Do this outside or over a trash can—you'll be amazed how much junk gets caught under the keys! If you really mess up a keyboard by dumping a chocolate milkshake on the keys, you're probably going to need to dismantle the keyboard to clean it. This is pretty easy as long as you keep track of where all of the parts go. Keyboards are made of layers of plastic that create the electrical connections when you press a key. Unscrew the keyboard (keep track of the screws!) and gently peel away the plastic layers, using a damp cloth to clean each layer (Figure 12.4). Allow the sheets to dry and then reassemble the keyboard.

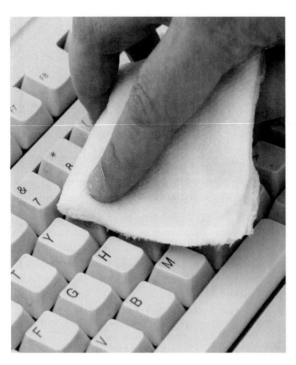

• Figure 12.3   Cleaning keys

Sometimes dirt or foreign objects get under individual keys, requiring you to remove the key to get to the dirt or object. Removing individual keys from a keyboard is risky business, because keyboards are set up in many different ways. Most manufacturers use a process in which keys are placed on a single plastic post. In that case, you may use a screwdriver or other flat tool to safely pop off the key (Figure 12.5). Be careful! You'll need to use a good amount of force and the key will fly across the room. Other keyboard makers (mainly on laptops) use tiny plastic pins shaped like scissors. In that case, beware—if you try prying one of these off, you'll permanently break the key!

The bottom line when it comes to stuck keys is that the keyboard's probably useless with the stuck key, so you might as well try to clean it. Worse comes to worst, you can always buy another keyboard.

• Figure 12.4   Serious keyboard surgery

Mice

Have you ever tried to use Windows without a mouse? It's not fun, but it can be done. All techs eventually learn the Windows navigation hot keys for those times when mice fail, but all in all we do love our mice. Like keyboards, Windows comes with excellent drivers for all standard mice; the exception you're likely to encounter is the more advanced mice that come with extra buttons. Conveniently, the built-in Windows drivers consider a mouse's scroll wheel to be standard equipment and will support it.

You can adjust your mouse settings through the Mouse Control Panel applet. Figure 12.6 shows the Windows 2000 version. Be aware that the Mouse Properties window in Windows 2000 uses a different layout than that of Windows Vista (Figure 12.7) or Windows XP (which are almost identical).

All of the settings you need for adjusting your mouse can be found in the Mouse Properties window. In particular, make sure to adjust the mouse speed, double-click speed, and acceleration to fit your preferences. Mouse speed and double-click speed are obvious, but mouse acceleration needs a bit of explaining as it has changed from Windows 2000 to Windows XP and Windows Vista. Originally, mouse *acceleration* referred to a feature that caused the mouse speed to increase when the mouse moved a relatively large distance across the screen. The Windows 2000 Mouse Properties

• **Figure 12.5**   Prying off a key

> **Tech Tip**
>
> **A Clean Mouse Is a Happy Mouse!**
> *As with keyboards, the biggest troublemaker for mice is dirt. Whenever a mouse stops working or begins to act erratically, always check first for dirt.*

Everything in this section works equally well for trackballs.

• **Figure 12.6**   Windows 2000 Mouse Control Panel applet

• **Figure 12.7**   Windows Vista Mouse Control Panel applet

window included a Motion tab where you could set the mouse speed and acceleration. Windows XP and Vista dropped the Motion tab in favor of an *Enhance pointer precision* checkbox on the Pointer Options tab (Figure 12.8). Enhance pointer precision is a much more advanced form of automatic acceleration. Although it works well, it can cause erratic mouse movements in some applications.

• **Figure 12.8**   Enhance pointer precision checkbox on the Pointer Options tab

Currently, two types of mouse technologies dominate the market: ball mice and optical mice. **Ball mice** use a small round ball, while **optical mice** use LEDs or lasers and a camera to track their movements and thus move the mouse pointer across the screen. The problem with ball mice is that the ball inside the mouse picks up dirt over time and deposits the dirt on internal rollers that contact the ball. Dirt builds up to the point that the mouse stops responding smoothly. If you are struggling with your mouse to point at objects on your screen, you need to clean the mouse. Few mice manufacturers still make ball mice, as they tend to require far more maintenance than optical mice.

To access the internals of a ball mouse, turn it over and remove the protective cover over the mouse ball. The process of removing the cover varies, but it usually involves rotating the collar that surrounds the ball until the collar pops out (Figure 12.9). Be careful—without the collar, the mouse ball will drop out the instant you turn the mouse upright.

Use any nonmetallic tool to scrape the dirt from the roller without scratching or gouging the device. Although you could use a commercial "mouse cleaning kit," I find that a fingernail or a pencil eraser cleans the rollers quite nicely and at much less expense (Figure 12.10). Clean a ball mouse in this way at least every two or three months.

Optical mice require little maintenance and almost never need cleaning, as the optics that make them work are never in contact with the grimy outside world. On the rare occasion where an optical mouse begins to act erratically, try using a cloth or damp cotton swab to clean out any bits of dirt that may be blocking the optics (Figure 12.11).

• **Figure 12.9**   Removing the collar on a ball mouse

• **Figure 12.10**   Cleaning the rollers on a ball mouse

• **Figure 12.11**   Cleaning an optical mouse

Scanners

You can use a scanner to make digital copies of existing paper photos, documents, drawings, and more. Better scanners give you the option of copying directly from a photographic negative or slide, providing images of stunning visual quality—assuming the original photo was halfway decent, of course! In this section, you'll look at how scanners work and then turn to what you need to know to select the correct scanner for you or your clients.

How Scanners Work

All consumer-level scanners—called **flatbed scanners**—work the same way. You place a photo or other object facedown on the glass, close the lid, and then use software to initiate the scan. The scanner runs a bright light along the length of the glass tray once or more to capture the image. Figure 12.12 shows an open scanner.

The scanning software that controls the hardware can be manifested in a variety of ways. Nearly every manufacturer has some sort of drivers and other software to create an interface between your computer and the scanner. When you push the front button on the Epson Perfection scanner, for example, the Epson software opens the Photoshop program as well as its own interface, as shown in Figure 12.13.

• **Figure 12.12**   Scanner open with photograph facedown

• **Figure 12.13**   Epson software with Photoshop open in the background

You can also open your favorite image-editing software first and choose to acquire a file from a scanner. Figure 12.14 shows the process of acquiring an image from a scanner in the popular shareware image-editing software, Paint Shop Pro. As in most such software, you choose File | Import and then select a source. In this case, the scanner uses the traditional TWAIN drivers. **TWAIN** stands for *Technology Without an Interesting Name*—I'm not making this up!—and has been the default driver type for scanners for a long time.

At this point, the drivers and other software controlling the scanner pop up, providing an interface with the scanner (as shown in Figure 12.14). Here you can set the resolution of the image as well as many other options.

How to Choose a Scanner

You must consider five primary variables when choosing a scanner: resolution, color depth, grayscale depth, connection, and scan speed. You can and will adjust the first three during the scanning process, although probably only down from their maximum. You need to decide on the connection before you buy. The scan speed relates to all four of the other variables, and the maximum speed is hard-coded into the scanner.

Configurable Variables Scanners convert the scanned image into a grid of dots. The maximum number of dots determines how well you can capture an image and how the image will look when scaled up in size. Most folks use the term *resolution* to define the grid size. As you might imagine, the higher the resolution, the better the scanned image will look and scale.

Older scanners can create images of only 600 × 600 dots per inch (dpi), while newer models commonly achieve four times that density and high-end machines do much more. Manufacturers cite *two* sets of numbers for a scanner's resolution: the resolution it achieves mechanically—called the **optical resolution**—and the enhanced resolution it can achieve with assistance from some onboard software.

The enhanced resolution numbers are useless. I recommend at least 2400 × 2400 dpi optical resolution or better, although you can get by with a lower resolution for purely Web-destined images.

The **color depth** of a scan defines the number of bits of information the scanner can use to describe each individual dot. This number determines color, shade, hue, and so forth, so a higher number makes a dramatic difference in your picture quality. With binary numbers, each extra bit of information *doubles* the quality. An 8-bit scan, for example, can save up to 256 color variations per dot. A 16-bit scan, in contrast, can save up to 65,536 variations, not the 512 that you might expect!

Modern scanners come in 24-bit, 36-bit, and 48-bit variations. These days, 48-bit scanners are common enough that you shouldn't have to settle for less, even on a budget. Figures 12.15, 12.16, and 12.17 show pretty clearly the difference resolution makes when scanning.

Scanners differ a lot in **grayscale depth**, a number that defines how many shades of gray the scanner can save per dot. This matters if you work with black-and-white images in any significant way, because grayscale depth is usually a much lower number than color depth. Current consumer-level

Tech Tip

Optical Character Recognition
In addition to loading pictures into your computer, many scanners offer a feature called optical character recognition (OCR), *a way to scan a document and have the computer turn the picture into text that you can manipulate by using a word processing program. Many scanners come with OCR software, such as ABBYY FineReader.*

• **Figure 12.14**   Acquiring an image in Paint Shop Pro

● **Figure 12.15**   Earring scanned at 72 dpi and 24-bit color

● **Figure 12.16**   Same earring, scanned at 300 dpi and 24-bit color

● **Figure 12.17**   Same earring, scanned at 1200 dpi and 24-bit color

Sometimes when installing a scanner or other device, Windows will give you an error message warning you about installing unsigned drivers. Microsoft has a program where device manufacturers can submit drivers to be tested by Microsoft, at which point they are given a digital signature that verifies they work. Not all manufacturers bother to do this, however, so if you trust the manufacturer, there probably isn't any harm in ignoring this warning.

scanners come in 8-bit, 12-bit, and 16-bit grayscale varieties. I recommend 16-bit or better.

Connection   Almost all modern scanners plug into the USB port on your PC, although some high-end models offer FireWire as well. Older scanners come in SCSI and parallel varieties.

Scanning Speed   Scanners have a maximum scanning speed defined by the manufacturer. The time required to complete a scan is also affected by the parameters you set; the time increases as you increase the amount of detail captured. A typical low-end scanner, for example, takes upwards of 30 seconds to scan a 4 × 6 photo at 300 dpi. A faster scanner, in contrast, can crank out the same scan in 10 seconds.

Raise the resolution of the scan to 600 dpi at 48-bit resolution, and that faster scanner can take a full minute to complete the scan. Adjust your scanning settings to optimize for your project. Don't always go for the highest possible scan if you don't need the resolution.

Connections matter as well. A good Hi-Speed USB scanner can scan an 8 × 10 image in about 12 seconds at 300 dpi. I made the mistake of taking the scanner to a friend's house to scan some of her jewelry, but she had only a Full-Speed USB port. I plugged the scanner into her PC and it took about 45 seconds to scan each 8 × 10 image. We were up all night finishing the project!

Installation and Scanning Tips

Most USB and FireWire devices require you to install the software drivers before you plug in the device for the first time. I have run into exceptions, though, so I strongly suggest you read the scanner's documentation before you install.

As a general rule, you should obtain the highest quality scan you can manage, and then play with the size and image quality when it's time to include it in a Web site or an e-mail. The amount of RAM in your system—and to a lesser extent, the processor speed—dictates how big a file you can handle.

For example, don't do 8 × 10 scans at 600 dpi if you have only 128 MB of RAM, because the image file alone weighs in at over 93 MB. Because your operating system, scanner software, image-editing program, and a lot of other things are taking up plenty of that RAM already, your system will likely crash.

If you travel a lot, you'll want to make sure to use the locking mechanism for the scanner light assembly. Just be sure to unlock before you try to use it or you'll get a light that's stuck in one position. That won't make for very good scans!

Digital Cameras

Another option available for those not-yet-taken pictures is to put away your point-and-shoot film camera and use a digital camera. **Digital cameras** electronically simulate older film technology and provide a wonderful tool for capturing a moment and then sending it to friends and relatives.

In a short period of time, digital camera prices have gone from levels that made them the province of a few wealthy technogeeks to being competitive with a wide range of electronic consumer goods. Because digital cameras interface with computers, CompTIA A+ certified techs need to know the basics.

Storage Media—Digital Film for Your Camera

Every consumer-grade camera saves the pictures it takes onto some type of *removable storage media*. Think of it as your digital film. Probably the most common removable storage media used in modern digital cameras (and probably your best choice) is the Secure Digital (SD) card (Figure 12.18). About the size of a Wheat Thin (roughly an inch square), you can find these tiny cards with capacities ranging from 64 MB to more than 1 GB. They are among the fastest of the various media types at transferring data to and from a PC, and they're quite sturdy.

• **Figure 12.18**   Secure Digital card

Connection

These days, almost all digital cameras plug directly into a USB port (Figure 12.19). Another common option, though, is to connect only the camera's storage media to the computer, using one of the many digital media readers available.

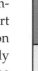

Cross Check

Flash Media

You learned all about the many types of flash media and micro drives in Chapter 10, "Removable Media," so go there now and answer these questions. What's the difference between a thumb drive and an SD card? Can you make a bootable flash-media drive?

You can find readers designed specifically for SD cards, as well as other types. Plenty of readers can handle multiple media formats. Many computers come with a decent built-in digital media reader (Figure 12.20).

Quality

As with scanners, you should consider the amount of information a particular model of camera can capture, which in the digital camera world is expressed as some number of **megapixels**. Instead of light-sensitive film, digital cameras have one CCD (charged coupled device) or CMOS (complementary metal-oxide semiconductor) sensor covered with photosensitive pixels (called *photosites*) to capture the image; the more pixels on the sensor, the higher the resolution of the images it captures.

Not so long ago, a 1-megapixel digital camera was the bleeding edge of digital photographic technology, but now you can find cameras with ten times that resolution for a few hundred dollars. As a basis of reference, a 2-megapixel camera produces snapshot-sized (4 × 6 inch) pictures with print photograph quality, whereas a 5-megapixel unit can produce a high-quality 8 × 10 inch print.

• **Figure 12.19**   Camera connecting to USB port

Another feature of most digital cameras is the capability to zoom in on your subject. The way you ideally want to do this is the way film cameras do it, by using the camera's optics—that's the lens. Most cameras above the basic level have some **optical zoom**—meaning the zoom is built into the lens of the camera—but almost all models include multiple levels of **digital zoom**, accomplished by some very clever software in the camera. Choose your camera based on optical zoom: 3× at a minimum or better if you can afford it. Digital zoom is useless.

• **Figure 12.20**   Digital media reader built into computer

● **Figure 12.21** Typical digital cameras

Form Factor

As was the case with film cameras, size matters on digital cameras. Digital cameras come in several form factors. They range from tiny, ultra-compact models that readily fit in a shirt pocket to monster cameras with huge lenses. Although it's not universally true, the bigger the camera, the more features and sensors it can have. Thus bigger is usually better in terms of quality. In shape, they come in a rectangular package, in which the lens retracts into the body, or as an SLR-type, with a lens that sticks out of the body. Figure 12.21 shows both styles.

Web Cameras

PC cameras, often called **webcams** because their most common use is for Internet video communication, are fairly new to the world of common I/O devices. Too many people run out and buy the cheapest one, not appreciating the vast difference between a discount webcam and more expensive models; nor do they take the time to configure the webcam properly. Let's consider some of the features you should look for when buying webcams and some of the problems you can run into when using them.

The biggest issue with webcams is the image quality. Webcams measure their resolution in pixels. You can find webcams with resolutions of as few as 100,000 pixels and webcams with millions of pixels. Most people who use webcams agree that 1.3 million pixels (megapixels) is pretty much the highest resolution quality you can use before your video becomes so large it will bog down even a broadband connection.

The next issue with webcams is the *frame rate*, which is the number of times the camera "takes your picture" each second. Higher frame rates make for smoother video; 30 frames per second is considered the best. A good camera with a high megapixel resolution and fast frame rate will provide you with excellent video conferencing capabilities. Figure 12.22 shows the author using his headset to chat via webcam using Skype software.

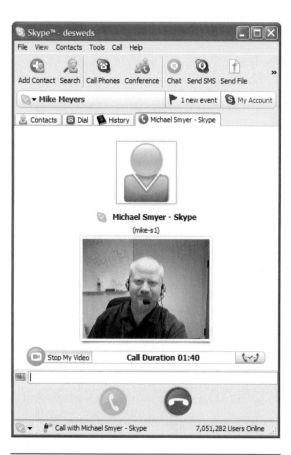

● **Figure 12.22** Video chatting by webcam with Skype

Most people who use online video also want a microphone. Many cameras come with microphones, or you can use your own. Those who do a lot of video chatting may prefer to get a camera without a microphone and then buy a good quality headset with which to speak and listen.

Many cameras now can track you when you move, to keep your face in the picture—a handy feature for fidgety folks using video conferencing! This interesting technology recognizes a human face with little or no "training" and rotates its position to keep your face in the picture. Some companies even add funny extras, which, although not very productive, are good for a laugh (Figure 12.23).

Read more about pixels and frame rates in Chapter 13, "Learning Video and Multimedia."

• **Figure 12.23** This webcam program's animated character mirrors your movements as you conference with friends or coworkers.

Almost all webcams use USB connections. Windows comes with a limited set of webcam drivers, so always make sure to install the drivers supplied with the camera before you plug it in. Most webcams use Hi-Speed USB, so make sure you're plugging your webcam into a Hi-Speed USB port.

Once the camera's plugged in, you'll need to test it. All cameras come with some type of program, but finding the program can be a challenge. Some brands put the program in the system tray, some place it in My Computer, others put it in the Control Panel—and some do all three! Figure 12.24 shows the Control Panel applet that appeared when I installed the webcam driver.

The biggest challenge to using webcams is getting your webcam applications to recognize that your webcam is available and configured for use. Every program does this differently, but conceptually the steps are basically the same (with plenty of exceptions):

1. Tell the program you want to use a camera.

2. Tell the program whether you want the camera to turn on automatically when you chat.

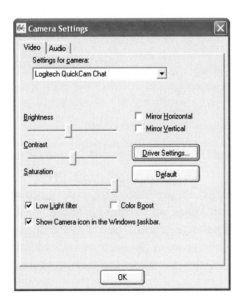

• **Figure 12.24** Camera Settings applet

3. Configure the image quality.

4. Test the camera.

If you're having problems with a camera, always go through the general I/O problems first, as this will clear up most problems. If you're still having trouble getting the camera to work in a program, be sure to turn off all other programs that may be using the camera. Windows allows only one program at a time to use a webcam.

■ Specialty I/O Devices

The CompTIA A+ Essentials exam wants to make sure you're aware of four other types of I/O devices: biometric scanners, bar code readers, touch screens, and KVM switches. Let's look at these fairly specialized devices.

Biometric Devices

If you look up *biometrics* on the popular Wikipedia Web site, you'll get the following definition: "Biometrics (ancient Greek: *bios* ='life,' *metron* ='measure') is the study of automated methods for uniquely recognizing humans based upon one or more intrinsic physical or behavioral traits." (The quote might differ from what you find because Wikipedia changes pretty frequently, but the gist should be the same.)

The field of biometrics also encompasses a number of security devices, such as door locks and security cameras, that don't really fit into the world of PCs. This section concentrates on the types of biometrics that you can actually buy and use on your PC. Within the realm of computers, biometrics includes a huge number of technologies, from thumb drives that read fingerprints to software that does voice recognition.

PCs use biometrics for security. **Biometric devices** scan and remember unique aspects of various body parts such as your retina, iris, head image, or fingerprint, using some form of sensing device such as a retinal scanner. This information is used as a key to prevent unauthorized people from accessing whatever the biometric device is securing. Most biometric devices currently used in PCs secure only themselves. The USB thumb drive in Figure 12.25 has a tiny fingerprint scanner. You slide your finger (any finger you choose) over the drive to unlock the contents of the thumb drive.

Less common are biometric security devices that secure entire computers. The Microsoft fingerprint scanner is a USB device that replaces standard user name and password security. Figure 12.26 shows the scanner built into a keyboard. When a program or Web site asks for a user name and password, you simply press your finger against the fingerprint scanner. It confirms your identity (assuming your fingerprint matches), and then special software that comes with the scanner supplies the program or Web site with your stored user name and password.

● **Figure 12.25** USB thumb drive with fingerprint scanner (*photo courtesy of Lexar Media, Inc.*)

Biometric devices are also used for recognition. Recognition is different from security in that the biometric device doesn't care who you are; it just wants to know what you're doing. The best example of this is voice recognition. Voice recognition programs convert human voice input into commands or text. Voice recognition for PCs has been around for some time. Although it has never achieved enough accuracy to replace a keyboard completely, voice recognition is common in devices that have a limited number of commands to interpret, such as cell phones and PDAs. If you speak the words "Call Mike Meyers" into your smartphone, your phone knows what to do—at least, *my* phone does!

No matter what biometric device you use, you use the same steps to make it work:

1. Install the device.

2. Register your identity with the device by sticking your eye, finger, or other unique body part (Why are you snickering?) into the device so it can scan you.

3. Configure its software to tell the device what to do when it recognizes your scanned identity.

• **Figure 12.26**   Microsoft fingerprint scanner on a keyboard

Bar Code Readers

Bar code readers are designed to read standard **Universal Product Code (UPC)** bar codes (Figure 12.27). We read bar codes for only one reason—to track inventory. Bar code readers enable easy updating of inventory databases stored on PCs. Bar code readers are just about the oldest "specialty" I/O device used with PCs.

Two types of bar code readers are commonly found with PCs: pen scanners and hand scanners. Pen scanners look like an ink pen and must be swiped across the bar code (Figure 12.28). Hand scanners are held in front of the UPC code while a button is pressed to scan. All bar code readers emit a tone to let you know the scan was successful.

Older bar code readers used serial ports, but all of the newer readers use either PS/2 or USB ports. No configuration is usually necessary, other than making sure that the particular bar code reader works with whatever database/point of sale software you use. When in doubt, most people find the PS/2-style bar code readers work best, as they simply act like a keyboard. You plug the reader into your keyboard port and then plug your keyboard into the reader. Then all you need is software that accepts keyboard input (and what one doesn't!), and it will work.

• **Figure 12.27**   Typical UPC code

• **Figure 12.28**   Pen scanner (*photo courtesy of Wasp Barcode Technologies*)

Touch Screens

A **touch screen** is a monitor with some type of sensing device across its face that detects the location and duration of contact, usually by a finger or stylus. All touch screens then supply this contact information to the PC as though it were a click event from a mouse. Touch screens are used in situations for which conventional mouse/keyboard input is either impossible or impractical. Here are a few places you'll see touch screens at work:

- Information kiosks
- PDAs
- Point of sale systems
- Tablet PCs

Touch screens can be separated into two groups: built-in screens like the ones in PDAs, and standalone touch screen monitors like those used in many point of sale systems. From a technician's standpoint, you can think of a standalone touch screen as a monitor with a built-in mouse. All touch screens have a separate USB or PS/2 port for the "mouse" part of the device, along with drivers you install just as you would for any USB mouse.

KVM Switches

A **keyboard, video, mouse (KVM) switch** is a hardware device that most commonly enables multiple computers to be viewed and controlled by a single mouse, keyboard, and screen. Some KVM switches reverse that capability, enabling a single computer to be controlled by multiple keyboards, mice, or other devices. KVM switches are especially useful in data centers where multiple servers are rack mounted, space is limited, and power is a concern. An administrator can use a single KVM switch to control multiple server systems from a single keyboard, mouse, and monitor.

There are many brands and types of KVM switches. Some enable you to connect to only two systems, and some support hundreds. Some even come with audio output jacks to support speakers. Typical KVM switches come with two or more sets of wires that are used for input devices such as PS/2 and/or USB mice and video output (Figure 12.29).

To use a KVM switch, you simply connect a keyboard, mouse, and monitor to the KVM switch and then connect the KVM switch to the desired computers. Once connected and properly configured, assigned keyboard hotkeys—a combination of keys typically assigned by the KVM switch manufacturer—enable you to toggle between the computers connected to the KVM switch. In most cases, you simply tap the SCROLL LOCK key twice to switch between sessions.

Installing a KVM switch is not difficult; the most important point to remember is to connect the individual sets of cables between the KVM ports and each computer one at a time, keeping track of which keyboard, mouse, and video cable go to which computers. (I highly recommend labeling and using twist or zip ties.)

• **Figure 12.29** A typical KVM switch

If you get the connections wrong, the KVM switch won't function as desired. If you connect a mouse and keyboard wires to the correct KVM port, for example, but attach the same computer's video cable to a different port on the KVM switch, you won't get the correct video when you try to switch to that computer. The same holds true for the mouse and keyboard cables. Don't cross the cables!

 Older KVM switches are said to be passive, meaning they don't continuously communicate with all connected systems. This can cause problems if the connected systems automatically reboot after a power surge or loss. Modern-day active KVM switches resolve this issue through *peripheral emulation*, meaning they communicate with and monitor all systems connected to the KVM switch.

Chapter 12 Review

■ Chapter Summary

After reading this chapter and completing the exercises, you should understand the following about input/output.

Identify certain common input/output devices on a PC

■ Keyboards are the oldest type of input device and still the primary way users input data. Although a keyboard works without the installation of additional drivers, you need to install drivers for specialty keyboards, such as keyboards with fancy buttons or other programmable features. If you're using a USB keyboard, make sure to enable USB keyboard support in CMOS Setup.

■ Configure basic keyboard settings in the Keyboard Control Panel applet. You can change the repeat delay, repeat rate, and cursor blink rate. Clean dirty keys with a damp cloth or isopropyl alcohol. Compressed air works well to dislodge hair, dust, and other small objects from the keys. With most keyboards you can pop off individual keys to do some deep cleaning. Some keyboards (such as those on laptops) are not meant to have keys removed and doing so might permanently damage the keyboard.

■ Mice work with the generic Windows drivers. You only need to install mouse drivers if your mouse has special programmable features, such as additional buttons. Various mouse settings can be configured via the Mouse Control Panel applet. Configurable settings include mouse speed, double-click speed, and acceleration.

■ The internal rubber ball on a ball mouse should be cleaned every few months. Rotate the collar on the underside of the mouse to release the rubber ball. Optical mice, which use LEDs or lasers to track movement, may occasionally need their lenses wiped free of grime, but overall outperform and outlive ball mice.

■ Flatbed scanners have a hinged lid and flat glass surface on which you can place material to be scanned. Most scanners come with software to control the hardware and to control the scanning process itself. The scan software allows you to select the color mode and resolution of the scanned document. Scanners use a traditional TWAIN driver to transfer digital images to the PC. Some scanners offer additional features, such as OCR capabilities.

■ When choosing a scanner, consider the scanner's optical resolution (ignore the enhanced resolution), color depth, grayscale depth, connection type, and scan speed. The higher these numbers, the better quality the scanned images will be. Shoot for a minimum 2400 × 2400 dpi optical resolution, 48-bit color depth, 16-bit grayscale depth, and a Hi-Speed USB or FireWire connection.

■ Most digital cameras store images on removable media, such as SD cards. Photos can be transferred to a PC by connecting the camera directly to a USB or FireWire port. Alternatively, if the PC is equipped with a media card reader, the flash memory card can be removed from the camera and inserted directly into the PC's card reader.

■ A 2-megapixel camera will produce 4 × 6 pictures with print photograph quality, while a 5-megapixel camera will produce 8 × 10 pictures with print photograph quality. The more sensors a camera has, the better the image quality, so you'll find that physically larger cameras take better pictures than the tiny ones. Look for a camera with at least 3× optical zoom and ignore the digital zoom that is advertised.

■ Webcams are often used for Internet video communication. A 1.3-megapixel webcam delivers a decent-resolution video without bogging down a broadband connection. Look for a webcam that has a frame rate of about 30 frames per second. Some webcams come with built-in microphones, but if you want high-quality audio without feedback or echo, invest in a microphone headset. After installing the driver and connecting a webcam, be sure to configure it properly so your Internet chat software knows to use the webcam.

Describe how certain specialty input/output devices work on a PC

■ Biometric devices scan various body parts, such as fingerprints or retinas, for authentication, security, and recognition. Some biometric devices control access to an entire PC, while some small devices, such as USB thumb drives, have biometric fingerprint scanners built in to control access to the single device. Voice recognition allows users to speak commands to the computer, such as "Call Mike Meyers" to dial the phone via a modem.

- Bar code readers read the standard Universal Product Code (UPC) bar code. The two types of bar code readers are pen scanners and hand scanners. Pen scanners look like ink pens and must be swiped across the bar code. Hand scanners are aimed at the bar code and when a button or trigger is pressed, the reader scans the bar code. All bar code scanners produce an audible tone to verify that the bar code has been read. Old bar code readers used serial ports, but newer ones use either USB or PS/2 connections.

- Tablet PCs feature touch screens, as do information kiosks, PDAs, and point of sale systems. Touch screens can be operated with either a finger or a stylus. Some devices, such as PDAs, have built-in touch screens, while a point of sale system may use a standalone touch screen monitor.

- KVM switches are hardware devices with which multiple systems can be monitored and controlled by a single mouse, keyboard, and monitor. KVMs are most commonly used in datacenters, enabling administrators to control multiple rack-mounted servers from a single keyboard, mouse, and monitor station.

Key Terms

ball mouse *(397)*
bar code reader *(405)*
biometric device *(404)*
color depth *(399)*
digital camera *(400)*
digital zoom *(401)*
flatbed scanner *(398)*
grayscale depth *(399)*
keyboard, video, mouse (KVM) switch *(406)*

megapixels *(401)*
optical mouse *(397)*
optical resolution *(399)*
optical zoom *(401)*
TWAIN *(399)*
touch screen *(406)*
Universal Product Code (UPC) *(405)*
webcam *(402)*

Key Term Quiz

Use the Key Terms list to complete the sentences that follow. Not all terms will be used.

1. A(n) _____ is useful when scanning a page from a book; a(n) _____ is useful when scanning the price of retail items at a store.

2. A(n) _____ captures digital images on removable media; a(n) _____ transmits digital images across the Internet for video communication.

3. The amount of information a digital camera can capture is measured in _____.

4. A scanner's ability to produce color, hue, and shade is defined by its _____.

5. When comparing digital cameras and their zoom capabilities, pay attention to the _____ and ignore the _____.

6. For moving the mouse pointer, most people prefer a(n) _____ over a(n) _____ because the former is much easier to keep clean.

Multiple-Choice Quiz

1. A user reports that his mouse is jittery. What is the most likely cause?

    A. His optical mouse has the wrong driver installed.

    B. His wireless mouse has a dead battery.

    C. His ball mouse has acquired dirt in the rollers.

    D. He had one too many cups of coffee that morning.

2. Which specifications describe a high-quality webcam that won't bog down an Internet connection?

   A. 5 megapixels at 15 frames per second

   B. 1.3 megapixels at 15 frames per second

   C. 5 megapixels at 40 frames per second

   D. 1.3 megapixels at 30 frames per second

3. Which device is a biometric device?

   A. Bar code reader

   B. Optical mouse

   C. Retinal scanner

   D. Flatbed scanner

4. The number that defines how many shades of gray per dot a scanner can save is referred to as what?

   A. Resolution

   B. DPI

   C. Color depth

   D. Grayscale depth

5. A color depth of 16 bits can store how many color variations per dot?

   A. 16

   B. 32

   C. 512

   D. 65,536

6. While testing a newly installed KVM switch, you can't display the second connected system while tapping the SCROLL LOCK key. What is most likely the problem?

   A. Incorrect KVM UPC code

   B. Crossed video cable

   C. Locked SCROLL LOCK key

   D. Active KVM

7. The smoothness of a Web camera's video is determined by its:

   A. Frame rate

   B. Resolution

   C. Megapixels

   D. Active PPC

8. Most modern keyboards use what type of port?

   A. PS/2

   B. Mini-DIN

   C. KVM

   D. USB

9. Large, professional-level digital cameras that have lenses that stick out from the camera's body are called:

   A. Compact

   B. Web cameras

   C. SLR

   D. Retractable

■ Essay Quiz

1. A friend at the local film school needs a new keyboard. What advice can you give her about the connection style for these devices?

2. Ken asks for your help because he is always forgetting his Windows password. What can you recommend to make logons easier for him?

3. The new head of sales is frustrated because when she tries to use her keyboard, letters continue to print across the screen even if she quickly taps a key, resulting in messages that llllooooooookkkk llllliiiiikkkkeeee tttthhhhiiiissss. How can you walk her through fixing this problem over the phone?

Lab Projects

• Lab Project 12.1

Explore the Keyboard and Mouse Control Panel applets. Change the settings and try to use the devices. Which settings caused the most frustration? Were there any changes you made that you preferred over the original settings?

• Lab Project 12.2

Grab a lab partner and a stopwatch. How many input devices can you two name in 30 seconds? Reset the timer. How many output devices can you two name in 30 seconds? Are any devices considered both input and output?

chapter 13

Learning Video and Multimedia

Ted: Yes, Bill. But, I do not believe we will get Eddie Van Halen until we have a triumphant video.

Bill: Ted, it's pointless to have a triumphant video before we even have decent instruments.

Ted: Well, how can we have decent instruments when we don't really even know how to play?

Bill: That is why we need Eddie Van Halen!

Ted: And that is why we need a triumphant video.

Bill, Ted: EXCELLENT!

—BILL AND TED, *BILL AND TED'S EXCELLENT ADVENTURE*

In this chapter, you will learn how to

- Explain how video displays work
- Select the proper video card
- Describe how to implement sound in a PC
- Explain the function of video capture cards and TV tuners

The term *video* encompasses a complex interaction among numerous parts of the PC, all designed to put a picture on the screen. The **monitor** or **video display** shows you what's going on with your programs and operating system. It's the primary output device for the PC. The video card or **display adapter** handles all of the communication between the CPU and the monitor (Figure 13.1). The operating system needs to know how to handle communication between the CPU and the display adapter, which requires drivers specific for each card and proper setup within Windows. Finally, each application needs to be able to interact with the rest of the video system.

Let's look at monitors and video cards individually. I'll bring them back together as a team later in the chapter so you can understand the many nuances that make video so challenging. Even later in the chapter, you'll look at sound cards, video capture cards, and TV tuners, all of which work together to make the PC a premium multimedia platform. Let's begin with the video display and then move on from there.

Video Displays

To understand displays, you need a good grasp of each component and how they work together to make a beautiful (or not so beautiful) picture on the screen. Different types of displays use different methods and technologies to accomplish this task. Video displays for PCs come in three varieties: CRT, LCD, and projectors. The first two you'll see on the desktop or laptop; the last you'll find in boardrooms and classrooms, splashing a picture onto a screen.

• **Figure 13.1** Typical monitor and video card

CRT Monitors

Cathode ray tube (CRT) monitors were the original computer monitors—those heavy, boxy monitors that take up half your desk. Although for the most part they've been replaced by LCD technology on new systems, plenty of CRT monitors are still chugging away in the field. As the name implies, this type of display contains a large cathode ray tube, a type of airtight vacuum tube. One end of this tube is a slender cylinder that contains three electron guns. The other end of the tube, which is fatter and wider, is the display screen.

Before we begin in earnest, I want to give you a note of warning about the inside of a traditional monitor. I will discuss what can be repaired and what requires more specialized expertise. Make no mistake—the interior of a monitor might appear similar to the interior of a PC because of the printed circuit boards and related components, but the similarity ends there. No PC has voltages exceeding 15,000 to 30,000 V, but most monitors do. So let's get one thing perfectly clear: opening up a monitor can kill you! Even when the power is disconnected, certain components retain a substantial voltage for an extended period of time. You can inadvertently short one of the components and fry yourself—to death. Given this risk, certain aspects of monitor repair lie outside the necessary skill set for a normal PC support person, and definitely outside the CompTIA A+ certification exam domains! I will show you how to address the problems you can fix safely and make sure you understand the ones you need to hand over to a monitor shop.

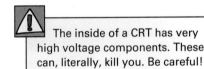

The inside of a CRT has very high voltage components. These can, literally, kill you. Be careful!

The inside of the display screen has a phosphor coating. When power is applied to one or more of the electron guns, a stream of electrons shoots towards the display end of the CRT (Figure 13.2). Along the way, this stream is subjected to magnetic fields generated by a ring of electromagnets called a *yoke* that controls the electron beam's point of impact. When the phosphor coating is struck by the electron beam, it releases its energy as visible light.

When struck by a stream of electrons, a phosphor quickly releases a burst of energy. This happens far too quickly for the human eye and brain connection to register. Fortunately, the phosphors on the display screen have a quality called **persistence**, which means the phosphors continue to glow after being struck by the electron beam. Too much persistence and the image is smeary; too little and the image appears to flicker. The perfect combination of beam and persistence creates the illusion of a solid picture.

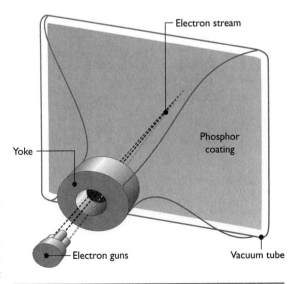

• **Figure 13.2** Electron stream in the CRT

Refresh Rate

The monitor displays video data as the electron guns make a series of horizontal sweeps across the screen, energizing the appropriate areas of the phosphorous coating. The sweeps start at the upper-left corner of the monitor and move across and down to the lower-right corner. The screen is "painted" only in one direction; then the electron guns turn and retrace their path across the screen, to be ready for the next sweep. These sweeps are called **raster lines** (Figure 13.3).

The speed at which the electron beam moves across the screen is known as the **horizontal refresh rate (HRR)**, as shown in Figure 13.4. The monitor draws a number of lines across the screen, eventually covering the screen with glowing phosphors. The number of lines is not fixed, unlike television screens, which have a set number of lines. After the guns reach the lower-right corner of the screen, they turn off and point back to the upper-left corner. The amount of time it takes to draw the entire screen and get the electron guns back to the upper-left corner is called the **vertical refresh rate (VRR)**, shown in Figure 13.5.

The monitor does not determine the HRR or VRR; the video card "pushes" the monitor at a certain VRR and then the monitor sets the corresponding HRR. If the video card is set to push at too low a VRR, the monitor produces a noticeable flicker, causing eyestrain and headaches for users. Pushing the monitor at too high a VRR, however, causes a definite distortion of the screen image and will damage the circuitry of the monitor and eventually destroy it. The number one killer of monitors is improper VRR settings, and the number one reason your office is filled with crabby workers is that the VRR is set too low. All good PC support techs understand this and take substantial time tweaking the VRR to ensure that the video card pushes the monitor at the highest VRR without damaging the monitor—this is the Holy Grail of monitor support!

One raster line

● **Figure 13.3**   Electron guns sweep from left to right

The time it takes to draw one line across the screen and be ready for the next is called the horizontal refresh rate (HRR). This is measured in KHz (thousands of lines per second).

● **Figure 13.4**   Horizontal refresh rate

The number of times per second the electron guns can draw the entire screen and then return to the upper left-hand corner is called the vertical refresh rate (VRR). This is measured in Hz (screens per second).

● **Figure 13.5**   Vertical refresh rate

Phosphors and Shadow Mask

All CRT monitors contain dots of phosphorous or some other light-sensitive compound that glows *red*, *green*, or *blue* (*RGB*) when an electron gun sweeps over it. These **phosphors** are evenly distributed across the front of the monitor (Figure 13.6).

A normal CRT has three electron guns: one for the red phosphors, one for the blue phosphors, and one for the green phosphors. It is important to understand that the electron guns do not fire colored light; they simply fire electrons at different intensities, which then make the phosphors glow. The higher the intensity of the electron stream, the brighter the color produced by the glowing phosphor.

Directly behind the phosphors in a CRT is the **shadow mask**, a screen that allows only the proper electron gun to light the proper phosphors (Figure 13.7). This prevents, for example, the red electron beam from "bleeding over" and lighting neighboring blue and green dots.

The electron guns sweep across the phosphors as a group, turning rapidly on and off as they move across the screen. When the group reaches the end of the screen, it moves to the next line. It is crucial to understand that turning the guns on and off, combined with moving the guns to new lines, creates a mosaic that is the image you see on the screen. The number of times the guns turn on and off, combined with the number of lines drawn on the screen, determines the number of mosaic pieces used to create the image. Each of these individual pieces is called a **pixel**, from the term *picture element*. You can't hold a pixel in your hand; it's just the area of phosphors lit at one instant when the group of guns is turned on. The size of pixels can change, depending on the number of times the group of guns is turned on and off and the number of lines drawn.

Resolution

Monitor **resolution** is always shown as the number of horizontal pixels times the number of vertical pixels. A resolution of 640 × 480, therefore, indicates a horizontal resolution of 640 pixels and a vertical resolution of 480 pixels. If you multiply the values together, you can see how many pixels are on each screen: 640 × 480 = 307,200 pixels per screen. An example of resolution affecting the pixel size is shown in Figure 13.8.

• **Figure 13.6**   A monitor is a grid of red, green, and blue phosphors.

• **Figure 13.7**   Shadow mask

See the "Modes" section later in this chapter for the names of each resolution.

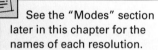

● **Figure 13.8**   Resolution versus pixel size

Some common resolutions are 640 × 480, 800 × 600, 1024 × 768, 1280 × 960, 1280 × 1024, and 1600 × 1200. Notice that most of these resolutions match a 4:3 ratio. This is called the **aspect ratio**. Many monitors are shaped like television screens, with a 4:3 aspect ratio, so most resolutions are designed to match—or at least be close to—that shape. Other monitors, generically called *wide-screen monitors*, have a 16:9 or 16:10 ratio. Two of the common resolutions you'll see with these monitors are 1366 × 768 and 1920 × 1200.

The last important issue is to determine the maximum possible resolution for a monitor. In other words, how small can one pixel be? Well, the answer lies in the phosphors. A pixel must be made up of at least one red, one green, and one blue phosphor to make any color, so the smallest theoretical pixel would consist of one group of red, green, and blue phosphors: a **triad** (Figure 13.9). Various limitations in screens, controlling electronics, and electron gun technology make the maximum resolution much bigger than one triad.

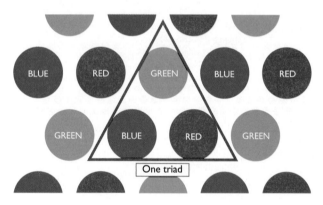

● **Figure 13.9**   One triad

Dot Pitch

The resolution of a monitor is defined by the maximum amount of detail the monitor can render. The dot pitch of the monitor ultimately limits this resolution. The **dot pitch** defines the diagonal distance between phosphorous dots of the same color, and is measured in *millimeters* (*mm*). Because a lower dot pitch means more dots on the screen, it usually produces a sharper, more defined image (Figure 13.10). Dot pitch works in tandem with the maximum number of lines the monitor can support to determine the greatest working resolution of the monitor. It might be possible to place an image at 1600 × 1200 on a 15-inch monitor with a dot pitch of 0.31 mm, but it would not be very readable.

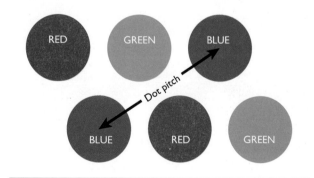

● **Figure 13.10**   Measuring dot pitch

The dot pitch can range from as high as 0.39 mm to as low as 0.18 mm. For most Windows-based applications on a 17-inch monitor, many people find that 0.28 mm is the maximum usable dot pitch that still produces a clear picture.

Bandwidth

Bandwidth defines the maximum number of times the electron gun can be turned on and off per second. Bandwidth is measured in *megahertz (MHz)*. In essence, bandwidth tells us how fast the monitor can put an image on the screen. A typical value for a better-quality 17-inch color monitor would be around 150 MHz, which means that the electron beam can be turned on and off 150 million times per second. The value for a monitor's bandwidth determines the maximum VRR the video card should push the monitor for any given resolution. It reads as follows:

maximum VRR = bandwidth ÷ pixels per page

For example, what is the maximum VRR that a 17-inch monitor with a bandwidth of 100 MHz and a resolution of 1024 × 768 can support? The answer is

maximum VRR = 100,000,000 ÷ (1024 × 768) = 127 Hz

That's a pretty good monitor, as most video cards do not push beyond 120 Hz! At a resolution of 1200 × 1024, the vertical refresh would be

100,000,000 ÷ (1200 × 1024) = 81 Hz

So, we would make sure to set the video card's VRR to 80 Hz or less. If you had a monitor with a bandwidth of only 75 MHz, the maximum VRR at a 1200 × 1024 resolution would be only 61 Hz.

Most monitor makers know that people aren't going to take the time to do these calculations. Instead, they do the calculations for you and create tables of refresh rates at certain resolutions to show what a monitor can do.

Degaussing

From time to time, your beautiful CRT display might get slightly, well, less beautiful. Because of the powerful magnets involved in putting a picture up on your monitor, the monitor's shadow mask will occasionally pick up some wonky magnetic fields, distorting or discoloring the displayed image. Fortunately for you, almost every CRT monitor out there has a **degauss** button that removes unwanted magnetic fields and will have your picture looking fine in no time.

Try This!

Determine the Dot Pitch of Your Monitor

Have you ever wondered what the dot pitch measurement of a CRT monitor is? Well, let's try to figure it out. First, take note of the manufacturer and model name/number of your monitor or of any CRT. You might need this information in a second.

Now, in your best contortionist pose, try to take a look at the back of your monitor. Normally, there is a small metal plate back there that indicates such information as the model number and serial number of your monitor. Sometimes this plate also lists a few monitor specifications, including dot pitch. Did you find it? No? Well then, crawl down off your desk, slowly, and fire up your favorite Web browser.

Search for the Web site of your monitor's manufacturer. See if you can find the technical specifications for your monitor listed on the Web site. Use the manufacturer, model name, and model number information that you wrote down earlier.

Great! Now that you have the basics of CRT monitors, let's turn to LCD monitors. Although the technology differs dramatically between the monitor types, most of the terms used for CRTs also apply to LCD functions.

LCD Monitors

Liquid crystal displays (LCDs) are the most common type of display technology for PCs. LCD monitors have many advantages over CRTs. They are thinner and lighter, use much less power, are virtually flicker free, and don't emit potentially harmful radiation. LCDs still have resolution, refresh rates, and bandwidth, but LCDs also come with their own family of abbreviations, jargon, and terms you need to understand so you can install, maintain, and support LCDs.

How LCDs Work

The secret to understanding LCD panels is to understand the concept of the polarity of light. Anyone who played with a prism in sixth grade or has looked at a rainbow knows that light travels in waves (no quantum mechanics here, please!), and the wavelength of the light determines the color. What you might not appreciate is the fact that light waves emanate from a light source in three dimensions. It's impossible to draw a clear diagram of three-dimensional waves, so instead, let's use an analogy. To visualize this, think of light emanating from a flashlight. Now think of the light emanating from that flashlight as though someone was shaking a jump rope. This is not a rhythmic shaking, back and forth or up and down; it's more as if a person went crazy and was shaking the jump rope all over the place—up, down, left, right—constantly changing the speed.

That's how light really acts. Well, I guess we could take the analogy one step further by saying the person has an infinite number of arms, each holding a jump rope shooting out in every direction to show the three-dimensionality of light waves, but (a) I can't draw that and (b) one jump rope will suffice to explain LCD panels. The varying speeds create wavelengths, from very short to very long. When light comes into your eyes at many different wavelengths, you see white light. If the light came in only one wavelength, you would see only that color. Light flowing through a polarized filter (like sunglasses) is like putting a picket fence between you and the people shaking the ropes. You see all of the wavelengths, but only the waves of similar orientation. You would still see all of the colors, just fewer of them because you only see the waves of the same orientation, making the image darker. That's why many sunglasses use polarizing filters.

Now, what would happen if you added another picket fence but put the slats in a horizontal direction? This would effectively cancel out all of the waves. This is what happens when two polarizing filters are combined at a 90-degree angle—no light passes through.

Now, what would happen if you added a third fence between the two fences with the slats at a 45-degree angle? Well, it would sort of "twist" some of the shakes in the rope so that the waves could then get through. The same thing is true with the polarizing filters. The third filter twists some of the light so that it gets through. If you're really feeling scientific, go to any teachers' supply store and pick up three polarizing filters for about (US)$3 each and try it. It works.

• **Figure 13.11**   Waves of similar orientation

Liquid crystals take advantage of the property of polarization. Liquid crystals are composed of a specially formulated liquid full of long, thin crystals that always want to orient themselves in the same direction, as shown in Figure 13.11. This substance acts exactly like a liquid polarized filter. If you poured a thin film of this stuff between two sheets of glass, you'd get a darn good pair of sunglasses.

Imagine cutting extremely fine grooves on one side of one of those sheets of glass. When you place this liquid in contact with a finely grooved surface, the molecules naturally line up with the grooves in the surface (Figure 13.12).

If you place another finely grooved surface, with the grooves at a 90-degree orientation to the other surface, opposite of the first one, the molecules in contact with that side will attempt to line up with it. The molecules in between, in trying to line up with both sides, will immediately line up in a nice twist (Figure 13.13).

• **Figure 13.12**   Liquid crystal molecules tend to line up together.

• **Figure 13.13**   Liquid crystal molecules twisting

● **Figure 13.14**   No charge, enabling light to pass

LCD pixels are very different from the pixels in a CRT. A CRT pixel's size changes depending on the resolution. The pixels in an LCD panel are fixed and cannot be changed. See the section called "LCD Resolution" later in the chapter for the scoop.

If two perpendicular polarizing filters are then placed on either side of the liquid crystal, the liquid crystal will twist the light and enable it to pass (Figure 13.14).

If you expose the liquid crystal to an electrical potential, however, the crystals will change their orientation to match the direction of the electrical field. The twist goes away and no light passes through (Figure 13.15).

A color LCD screen is composed of a large number of tiny liquid crystal molecules (called **sub-pixels**) arranged in rows and columns between polarizing filters. A translucent sheet above the sub-pixels is colored red, green, or blue. Each tiny distinct group of three sub-pixels—one red, one green, and one blue—forms a physical pixel, as shown in Figure 13.16.

● **Figure 13.15**   Electrical charge, no light is able to pass

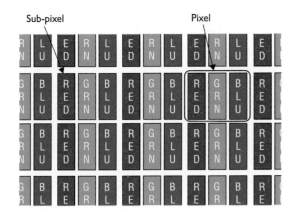

• **Figure 13.16**   LCD pixels

Once all of the pixels are laid out, how do you charge the right spots to make an image? Early LCDs didn't use rectangular pixels. Instead, images were composed of different-shaped elements, each electrically separate from the others. To create an image, each area was charged at the same time. Figure 13.17 shows the number zero, a display made possible by charging six areas to make an ellipse of sorts. This process, called *static charging*, is still quite popular in more basic numeric displays such as calculators.

The static method would not work in PCs due to its inherent inflexibility. Instead, LCD screens use a matrix of wires (Figure 13.18). The vertical wires, the Y wires, run to every sub-pixel in the column. The horizontal wires, the X wires, run along an entire row of sub-pixels. There must be a charge on both the X and the Y wires to make enough voltage to light a single sub-pixel.

If you want color, you have three matrices. The three matrices intersect very close together. Above the intersections, the glass is covered with tiny red, green, and blue dots. Varying the amount of voltage on the wires makes different levels of red, green, and blue, creating colors (Figure 13.19).

We call this usage of LCD technology **passive matrix**. All LCD displays on PCs used only passive matrix for many years. Unfortunately, passive matrix is slow and tends to create a little overlap between individual pixels. This gives a slightly blurred effect to the image displayed. Manufacturers eventually came up with a speedier method of display, called **dual-scan passive matrix**, in which the screen refreshed two lines at a time. Although other LCD technologies have since appeared, dual-scan continues to show up on some lower-end LCD panels.

Thin Film Transistor

A vast improvement over dual scan is called **thin film transistor (TFT)** or **active matrix** (Figure 13.20). Instead of using X and Y wires, one or more tiny transistors control each color dot, providing faster picture display, crisp definition, and much tighter color control. TFT is the LCD of choice today, even though it is much more expensive than passive matrix.

• **Figure 13.17**   Single character for static LCD numeric display

• **Figure 13.18**   An LCD matrix of wires

• **Figure 13.19**   Passive matrix display

You'll also find passive matrix displays in smaller, handheld devices. See Chapter 14, "Learning Portable Computing," for details about handheld computing devices.

● **Figure 13.20**   Active matrix display

LCD Components

The typical LCD projector is composed of three main components: the LCD panel, the backlight(s), and the inverters. The LCD panel creates the image, the **backlights** illuminate the image so you can see it, and the **inverters** send power to the backlights. Figure 13.21 shows a typical layout for the internal components of an LCD monitor.

One of the great challenges to LCD power stems from the fact that the backlights need AC power while the electronics need DC power. The figure shows one of the many ways that LCD monitor makers handle this issue. The AC power from your wall socket goes into an AC/DC transformer that changes the power to DC. The LCD panel uses this DC power.

Note in Figure 13.21 that this monitor has two backlights: one at the top and one at the bottom. Most LCDs have two backlights, although many only have one. All LCD backlights use **cold cathode fluorescent lamp (CCFL)** technology, popular for its low power use, even brightness, and long life. Figure 13.22 shows a CCFL from an LCD panel.

CCFLs need AC power to operate, but given that the transformer converts the incoming AC power to DC, each CCFL backlight needs a device called an inverter to convert the DC power back into AC. Figure 13.23 shows a typical inverter used in an LCD.

Looking once again at Figure 13.21, note the DVI and VGA inputs. DVI is a digital signal, so it connects directly to the LCD's

● **Figure 13.21**   LCD internals

● **Figure 13.22**   CCFL backlight

● **Figure 13.23**   Inverter

logic circuitry. The VGA goes to an analog to digital converter before reaching the LCD logic board.

Keep in mind that Figure 13.21 is a generic illustration. The actual location and interconnections of the components are as variable as the number of LCD panels available today!

LCD Resolution

All LCD monitors have a **native resolution**, such as 1680 × 1050, that enables them to display the sharpest picture possible. As mentioned earlier, the pixels are fixed. You simply cannot run an LCD monitor at a resolution higher than the native one. Worse, because LCDs have no equivalent to a shadow mask, they can't run at a *lower* than native resolution without severely degrading image quality. A CRT can simply use more dots and the filtering and smoothing of the shadow mask to make a picture at a lower resolution look as good and crisp as the same picture at a higher resolution, but an LCD cannot. The LCD has to use an edge-blurring technique called **anti-aliasing** to soften the jagged corners of the pixels when running at lower than native resolution, which simply does not look as good. The bottom line? Always set the LCD at native resolution!

Try This!

Test the Viewing Angle of LCDs

Take a trip to your local computer store to look at LCD displays. Don't be distracted looking at all of the latest graphics cards, sound cards, CPUs, motherboards, and RAM—well, actually, it's okay to look at those things. Just don't forget to look at LCDs!

Stand about two feet in front of an LCD display. Look directly at the image on the screen and consider the image quality, screen brightness, and color. Take a small step to your right. Compare the image you see now to the image you saw previously. Continue taking small steps to the right until you are no longer able to discern the image on the display. You've reached the edge of the viewing angle for that LCD.

Do this test with a few different monitors. Do smaller LCDs, such as 15-inch displays, have smaller viewing angles? Do larger displays have better viewing angles? You might also want to test the vertical viewing angles of some monitors. Try to find an LCD that is on your eye level; then look at it from above and below—does it have a large viewing range vertically?

Two LCD panels that have the same physical size may have different native resolutions.

Brightness

The strength of an LCD monitor's backlights determines the brightness of the monitor. The brightness is measured in **nits**. LCD panels vary from 100 nits on the low end to over 1000 nits or more on the high end. Average LCD panels are around 300 nits, which most monitor authorities consider excellent brightness.

One nit equals one candela/m². One candela is roughly equal to the amount of light created by a candle.

Response Rate

An LCD panel's **response rate** is the amount of time it takes for all of the sub-pixels on the panel to go from pure black to pure white and back again. This is roughly the same concept as the CRT refresh rate, but with one important difference. Once the electron gun on a CRT lights a phosphor, that phosphor begins to fade until it is lit again. Individual LCD sub-pixels hold their intensity until the LCD circuitry changes that sub-pixel, making the problem of flicker nonexistent on LCDs.

Manufacturers measure LCD response rates in milliseconds, with lower being better. A typical lower-end or older LCD has a response rate of 20–25 ms. The screens look fine, but you'll get some ghosting if you try to watch a movie or play a fast-paced video game. In recent years, manufacturers have figured out how to overcome this issue, and you can find many LCD monitors with a response rate of 6–8 ms.

A video card needs to be able to support dual-link DVI to run a 120-Hz monitor or television. See the discussion on DVI later in this chapter for details.

Refresh Rate

The refresh rate for an LCD monitor uses numbers similar to that for a CRT monitor, such as 60 Hz, but the terms mean slightly different things between the two technologies. With CRTs, as you'll recall, the phosphors on the screen start to lose their glow and need to be hit again by the electron guns many times per second to achieve an unwavering or flicker-free image. Each dot on an active matrix LCD, in contrast, has its own transistor to light it up. There's no need to freshen up the dot; it's on or off. Regardless of the refresh rate for the LCD, therefore, there's never any flicker at all.

The refresh rate for an LCD monitor refers to how often a screen can change or update completely. Think of the refresh rate as a metronome or timer and you'll be closer to how it works in an LCD. For most computing issues, 60 Hz is fine and that's been the standard for the industry. Humans see things that change as infrequently as 24 times per second—the standard for motion pictures at the cinema, for example, and the best high-definition (HD) signal—as a full motion video. To be able to change almost three times faster is perfectly acceptable, even in higher-end applications such as fast-moving games.

Monitor manufacturers have released 120-Hz LCD monitors in a response to the convergence of LCDs, televisions, and computers to enable you to see HD movies or standard-definition (SD) content without any problems or visual artifacts on an LCD monitor. The easiest number that provides a whole-number division for both 24 frames per second and 30 frames per second was 120 Hz. The latter is the standard for SD content.

Contrast Ratio

A big drawback of LCD monitors is that they don't have nearly the color saturation or richness of contrast of a good CRT monitor—although LCD technology continues to improve every year. A good contrast ratio—the difference between the darkest and lightest spots that the monitor can display—is 450:1, although a quick trip to a computer store will reveal LCDs with lower levels (250:1) and higher levels (1000:1).

LCD monitor manufacturers market a *dynamic contrast ratio* number for their monitors, which measures the difference between a full-on, all-white screen and a full-off, all-black screen. This yields a much higher number than the standard contrast ratio. My Samsung panels have a 1000:1 contrast ratio, for example, but a 20,000:1 dynamic contrast ratio. Sounds awesome, right? In general, the dynamic contrast ratio doesn't affect viewing on computer monitors. Focus on the standard contrast ratio when making decisions on LCD screens.

Projectors

Projectors are a third option for displaying your computer images and the best choice when displaying to an audience or in a classroom. There are two ways to project an image on a screen: rear-view and front-view. As the name would suggest, a **rear-view projector** (Figure 13.24) shoots an image onto a screen from the rear. Rear-view projectors are always self-enclosed and are very popular for televisions, but are virtually unheard of in the PC world.

A **front-view projector** shoots the image out the front and counts on you to put a screen in front at the proper distance. Front-view projectors connected to PCs running Microsoft PowerPoint have been the cornerstone of every meeting almost everywhere for at least the past ten years (Figure 13.25). This section deals exclusively with front-view projectors that connect to PCs.

Projector Technologies

Projectors that connect to PCs have been in existence for almost as long as PCs themselves. Given all that time, a number of technologies have been used in projectors. The first generation of projectors used CRTs. Each color used a separate CRT that projected the image onto a screen (Figure 13.26). CRT projectors create beautiful images but are expensive, large, and very heavy, and have for the most part been abandoned for more recent technologies.

Given that light shines through an LCD panel, LCD projectors are a natural fit for front projection. LCD projectors are light and very inexpensive compared to CRTs but lack the image quality. LCD projectors are so light that almost all portable projectors use LCD (Figure 13.27).

All projectors share the same issues as their equivalent technology monitors. LCD projectors have a specific native resolution, for example. In addition, you need to understand three concepts specific to projectors: lumens, throw, and lamps.

• **Figure 13.24** Rear-view projector (*photo courtesy of Samsung*)

• **Figure 13.25** Front-view projector (*photo courtesy of Dell Inc.*)

Another type of technology that's seen in projectors but is outside the scope of the CompTIA A+ Essentials exam is called digital light processing (DLP).

• **Figure 13.26** CRT projector

• **Figure 13.27** LCD projector (*photo courtesy of ViewSonic*)

Lumens

The brightness of a projector is measured in lumens. A **lumen** is the amount of light given off by a light source from a certain angle that is perceived by the human eye. The greater the lumen rating of a projector, the brighter the projector will be. The best lumen rating depends on the size of the room and the amount of light in the room. There's no single answer for "the right lumen rating" for a projector, but use this as a rough guide. If you use a projector in a small, darkened room, 1000 to 1500 lumens will work well. If you use a projector in a midsized room with typical lighting, you'll need at least 2000 lumens. Projectors for large rooms have ratings over 10,000 lumens and are very expensive.

Throw

A projector's **throw** is the size of the image at a certain distance from the screen. All projectors have a recommended minimum and maximum throw distance that you need to take into consideration. A typical throw would be expressed as follows. A projector with a 16:9 image-aspect ratio needs to be 11 to 12 feet away from the projection surface to create a 100-inch diagonal screen. A *long throw lens* has about a 1:2 ratio of screen size to distance, so to display a 4-foot screen, you'd have to put the projector 8 feet away. Some *short throw lenses* drop that ratio down as low as 1:1!

Lamps

The bane of every projector is the lamp. Lamps work hard in your projector, as they must generate a tremendous amount of light. As a result, they generate quite a bit of heat, and all projectors come with a fan to keep the lamp from overheating. When you turn off a projector, the fan continues to run until the lamp is fully cooled. Lamps are also expensive, usually in the range of a few hundred dollars (U.S.), which comes as a nasty shock to someone who's not prepared for that price when the lamp dies!

Common Features

CRT or LCD, all monitors share a number of characteristics that you need to know for purchase, installation, maintenance, and troubleshooting.

Size

You need to take care when buying CRT monitors. CRT monitors come in a large number of sizes, all measured in inches (although most metric countries provide the metric equivalent value). All monitors provide two numbers: the monitor size and the actual size of the screen. The monitor size measures from two opposite diagonal corners. The actual screen is measured from one edge of the screen to the opposite diagonal side. This latter measurement is often referred to as the **viewable image size (VIS)**, as shown in Figure 13.28. You will commonly see a size difference of one to two inches between the two measurements. A 17-inch CRT monitor, for example, might have a 15.5-inch VIS.

Monitor size   Viewable image size

• **Figure 13.28**   Viewable image size of a CRT

LCD monitors dispense with the two values and simply express the VIS value. You must consider this issue when comparing LCDs to CRTs. A 15-inch LCD monitor will have about the same viewing area as a 17-inch CRT.

Connections

CRT monitors for PCs all use the famous 15-pin, three-row, DB-type connector (Figure 13.29) and a power plug. The DB connector is also called a *D-shell* or *D-subminiature* connector. Larger or multipurpose monitors may have a few other connectors, but as far as the CRT is concerned, these are the only two you need for video.

Unlike the analog CRTs, LCD monitors need a digital signal. This creates somewhat of an issue. The video information stored on a video card's RAM is clearly digital. All VGA and better video cards include a special chip (or function embedded into a chip that does several other jobs) called the **random access memory digital-to-analog converter (RAMDAC)**. As the name implies, RAMDAC takes the digital signal from the video card and turns it into an analog signal for the analog CRT (Figure 13.30). The RAMDAC can also convert digital to analog.

Well, RAMDACs certainly make sense for analog CRT monitors. However, if you want to plug your LCD monitor into a regular video card, you need a RAMDAC on the LCD monitor to convert the signal from analog to digital (Figure 13.31).

Many LCD monitors use exactly this process. These are called *analog LCD monitors*. The monitor really isn't analog; it's digital, but it takes a standard VGA input. These monitors have one advantage: you may use any

● **Figure 13.29**   A traditional CRT connector

> You'll often hear the terms *flat-panel display* or *LCD panel* to describe LCD monitors. I prefer the term *LCD monitor*, but you should be prepared to hear it a few different ways.

Digital data in RAM

The RAMDAC translates the digital signal to an analog signal.

Analog signal to monitor

● **Figure 13.30**   An analog signal sent to a CRT monitor

The RAMDAC in the LCD converts the analog signal back to digital.

Digital data in RAM

Converts to analog

• **Figure 13.31**   Converting analog back to digital on the LCD

standard VGA video card. But these monitors require adjustment of the analog timing signal to the digital clock inside the monitor. This used to be a fairly painful process, but most analog LCD monitors now include intelligent circuitry to make this process either automatic or very easy.

Why convert the signal from digital to analog and then back to digital? Well, many monitor and video card people agree that it just doesn't make much sense. We now see quite a few digital LCD monitors and digital video cards. They use a completely different connector than the old 15-pin DB connector used on analog video cards and monitors. After a few false starts with connection standards, under names such as P&D and DFP, the digital LCD world, with a few holdouts, moved to the **digital visual interface (DVI)** standard. DVI is actually three different connectors that look very much alike: DVI-D is for digital, DVI-A is for analog (for backward compatibility if the monitor maker so desires), and the DVI-A/D or DVI-I (interchangeable) accepts either a DVI-D or DVI-A. DVI-D and DVI-A are keyed so that they will not connect.

DVI-D and DVI-I connectors come in two varieties, single-link and dual-link. *Single-link DVI* has a maximum bandwidth of 165 MHz, which, translated into practical terms, limits the maximum resolution of a monitor to 1920 × 1080 at 60 Hz or 1280 × 1024 at 85 Hz. *Dual-link DVI* uses more pins to double throughput and thus grant higher resolutions (Figure 13.32). With dual-link, you can have displays up to a whopping 2048 × 1536 at 60 Hz!

Digital connectors are quickly replacing analog in the monitor world. Digital makes both the monitor and the video card cheaper, provides a clearer signal because no conversion is necessary, and makes installation easy. Many monitors and video cards these days only support digital signals,

• **Figure 13.32**   Dual-link DVI-I connector

You can plug a single-link DVI monitor into a dual-link DVI connector and it'll work just fine.

but there are still quite a few of each that provide both digital and analog connections.

The video card people have it easy. They either include both a VGA and a DVI-D connector or use a DVI-I connector. The advantage to DVI-I is that you can add a cheap DVI-I–to-VGA adapter (one usually comes with the video card) like the one shown in Figure 13.33 and connect an analog monitor just fine.

Monitor makers have it tougher. Most LCD monitor makers have made the jump to DVI, but many include a VGA connector for those machines that still need it.

Unless you're buying a complete new system, you'll rarely buy a video card at the same time you buy a monitor. When you're buying a monitor or a video card, make sure that the new device will connect to the other!

• **Figure 13.33** DVI-I–to-VGA adapter

Adjustments

Most adjustments to the monitor take place at installation, but for now, let's just make sure you know what they are and where they are located. Clearly, all monitors have an On/Off button or switch. Also, see if you can locate the Brightness and Contrast buttons. Beyond that, most monitors (at least the only ones you should buy) have an onboard menu system, enabling a number of adjustments. Every monitor maker provides a different way to access these menus, but they all provide two main functions: physical screen adjustment (bigger, smaller, move to the left, right, up, down, and others) and color adjustment. The color adjustment lets you adjust the red, green, and blue guns to give you the best color tones. All of these settings are a matter of personal taste. Make sure the person who will use the computer understands how to adjust these settings (Figure 13.34).

📄 Video cards with two video connectors support dual monitors.

Power Conservation

CRT and LCD monitors differ greatly in the amount of electricity they require. The bottom line is that CRTs use a lot and LCDs use a lot less. Here's the scoop.

Approximately half the power required to run a desktop PC is consumed by the CRT monitor. Monitors that meet the Video Electronics Standards Association (VESA) specification for **display power management signaling (DPMS)** can reduce monitor power consumption by roughly 75 percent. This is accomplished by reducing or eliminating the signals sent by the video card to the monitor during idle periods. By eliminating these pulses, the monitor essentially takes catnaps. The advantage over simply shutting the monitor off is in the time it takes to restore the display.

• **Figure 13.34** Typical menu controls

A typical CRT monitor consumes approximately 120 W. During a catnap or power-down mode, the energy consumption is reduced to below 25 W, while enabling the screen to return to use in less than 10 seconds. Full shut-off is accomplished by eliminating all clocking pulses to the monitor. Although this reduces power consumption to below 15 W, it also requires anywhere from 15 to 30 seconds to restore a usable display.

A typical LCD monitor, in contrast, uses less than half the electricity that a CRT uses. A 19-inch, 4:3 aspect-ratio flat panel, for example, uses around 33 W at peak usage and less than 2 W in DPMS mode. Larger LCDs use more power at peak usage than smaller ones. A 21-inch wide-screen model, for example, might draw ~75 W at peak but drop down to less than 2 W in DPMS mode. Swapping out CRTs with LCDs is a great way to save on your electric bill!

■ Video Cards

The video card, or display adapter, handles the video chores within the PC, processing information from the CPU and sending it out to the monitor. The video card is composed of two major pieces: the video RAM and the video processor circuitry. The video RAM stores the video image. On the first video cards, this RAM was good old dynamic RAM (DRAM), just like the RAM on the motherboard. Today's video cards often have better RAM than your system has! The video processing circuitry takes the information on the video RAM and shoots it out to the monitor. Although early video processing circuitry was little more than an intermediary between the CPU and the video RAM, modern video processors are more powerful than all but the latest CPUs! It's not at all uncommon to see video cards that need fans to cool their onboard processors (Figure 13.35).

This section looks at five aspects that define a video card: display modes, motherboard connection, graphics processor circuitry, video memory, and connections.

Modes

The trick to understanding video cards is to appreciate the beginnings and evolution of video. Video output to computers was around long before PCs were created. At the time PCs became popular, video was almost exclusively text-based, meaning that the only image the video card could place on the monitor was one of the 256 ASCII characters. These characters were made up of patterns of pixels that were stored in the system BIOS. When a program wanted to make a character, it talked to DOS or to the BIOS, which stored the image of that character in the video memory. The character then appeared on the screen.

The beauty of text video cards was that they were simple to use and cheap to make. The simplicity was based on the fact that only 256 characters existed, and no color choices were available—just monochrome text.

You could, however, choose to make the character bright, dim, normal, underlined, or blinking. Positioning the characters was easy, as space on the screen allowed for only 80 characters per row and 24 rows of characters.

Long ago, RAM was very expensive, so video card makers were interested in using the absolute least amount of RAM possible. Making a monochrome text video card was a great

● **Figure 13.35**   Video card with a cooling fan

way to keep down RAM costs. Let's consider this for a minute. First, the video RAM is where the contents of the screen are located. You need enough video RAM to hold all of the necessary information for a completely full screen. Each ASCII character needs 8 bits (by definition), so a monitor with 80 characters/row and 24 rows will need

80 characters × 24 rows = 1920 characters = 15,360 bits or 1920 bytes

The video card would need less than 2000 bytes of memory, which isn't much, not even in 1981 when the PC first came out. Now, be warned that I'm glossing over a few things—where you store the information about underlines, blinking, and so on. The bottom line is that the tiny amount of necessary RAM kept monochrome text video cards cheap.

Very early on in the life of PCs, a new type of video card, called a *graphics video card*, was invented. It was quite similar to a text card. The text card, however, was limited to the 256 ASCII characters, whereas a graphics video card enabled programs to turn any pixel on the screen on or off. It was still monochrome, but programs could access any individual pixel, enabling much more creative control of the screen. Of course, it took more video RAM. The first graphics cards ran at 320 × 200 pixels. One bit was needed for each pixel (on or off), so

320 × 200 = 64,000 bits or 8000 bytes

That's a lot more RAM than was needed for text, but it was still a pretty low amount of RAM—even in the old days. As resolutions increased, however, the amount of video RAM needed to store this information also increased.

After monochrome video was invented, moving into color for both text and graphics video cards was a relatively easy step. The only question was how to store color information for each character (text cards) or pixel (graphics cards). This was easy—just set aside a few more bits for each pixel or character. So now the question becomes, "How many bits do you set aside?" Well, that depends on how many colors you want. Basically, the number of colors determines the number of bits. For example, if you want four colors, you need 2 bits (2 bits per pixel). Then, you could do something like this:

00 = black	01 = cyan (blue)
10 = magenta (reddish pink)	11 = white

So if you set aside 2 bits, you could get 4 colors. If you want 16 colors, set aside 4 bits, which would make 16 different combinations. Nobody ever invented a text mode that used more than 16 colors, so let's start thinking in terms of only graphics mode and bits per pixel. To get 256 colors, each pixel would have to be represented with 8 bits. In PCs, the number of colors—called the **color depth**—is always a power of 2: 4, 16, 256, 64 K, and so on. Note that as more colors are added, more video RAM is needed to store the information. Here are the most common color depths and the number of bits necessary to store the color information per pixel:

2 colors = 1 bit (mono)
4 colors = 2 bits
16 colors = 4 bits
256 colors = 8 bits

64 K colors = 16 bits
16.7 million colors = 24 bits

Most technicians won't say, for example, "I set my video card to show over 16 million colors." Instead, they'll say, "I set my color depth to 24 bits." Talk in terms of bits, not colors. It is assumed that you know the number of colors for any color depth.

You can set the color depth for a Windows 2000 or Windows XP computer in the Display Properties applet on the Settings tab (Figure 13.36). If you set up a typical Windows XP computer, you'll notice that Windows offers you 32-bit color quality, which might make you assume you're about to crank out more than 4 billion colors, but that's simply not the case. The 32-bit color setting offers 24-bit color plus an 8-bit alpha channel. An alpha channel controls the opacity of a particular color. By using an alpha channel, Windows can more effectively blend colors to create the effect of semi-transparent images. In Windows XP, you see this in the drop shadow under a menu; in Windows Vista, almost every screen element can be semi-transparent (Figure 13.37).

Your video card and monitor are capable of showing Windows in a fixed number of different resolutions and color depths. The choices depend on the resolutions and color depths the video card can push to the monitor and the amount of bandwidth your monitor can support. Any single combination of resolution and color depth you set for your system is called a **mode**. For standardization, VESA defines a certain number of resolutions, all derived from the granddaddy of video modes: VGA.

• **Figure 13.36**   Adjusting color settings in Windows XP

• **Figure 13.37**   Semi-transparency in Windows Vista

VGA

With the introduction of the PS/2, IBM introduced the **video graphics array (VGA)** standard. This standard offered 16 colors at a resolution of 640 × 480 pixels. VGA supported such an amazing variety of colors by using an analog video signal instead of a digital one, as was the case prior to the VGA standard. A digital signal is either all on or all off. By using an analog signal, the VGA standard can provide 64 distinct levels for the three colors (RGB)—that is, 64^3 or 262,144 possible colors—although only 16 or 256 can be seen at a time. For most purposes, 640 × 480 and 16 colors defines VGA mode. This is typically the display resolution and color depth referred to on many software packages as a minimum display requirement. Every video card made in the past 15 years can output as VGA, but VGA-only cards are now obsolete.

Beyond VGA

The 1980s were a strange time for video. Until the very late 1980s, VGA was the highest mode defined by VESA, but demand grew for modes that went beyond VGA. This motivated VESA to introduce (over time) a number of new modes with names such as SVGA, XGA, and many others. Even today, new modes are being released! Table 13.1 shows the more common modes.

The video card must have sufficient RAM to support each combination of color depth and resolution. Many years ago this mattered, when video cards had scant megabytes of memory. A video card with only 2 MB of RAM, for example, could handle a high color (16-bit) display at 1024 × 768, but not the same resolution with true color (24-bit). Table 13.2 shows common modes and the minimum video memory needed. All modern video cards can handle true color at any resolution.

> To accommodate rotated LCD monitors in portrait view, the video resolution numbers might be reversed. Rather than 1280 × 1024, for example, you might see 1024 × 1280. The amount of RAM needed remains the same regardless.

Motherboard Connection

Using more color depth slows down video functions. Data moving from the video card to the display has to go through the video card's memory chips and the expansion bus, and this can happen only so quickly. The standard PCI slots used in almost all systems are limited to 32-bit transfers at roughly 33 MHz, yielding a maximum bandwidth of 132 MBps. This sounds like a lot until you start using higher resolutions, high color depths, and higher refresh rates.

Table 13.1	Typical Display Modes		
Video Mode	**Resolution**	**Aspect Ratio**	**Typical Device**
SVGA	800 × 600	4:3	Small monitors
HDTV 720p	1280 × 720	16:9	Lowest resolution that can be called HDTV
SXGA	1280 × 1024	5:4	Native resolution for many desktop LCD monitors
WSXGA	1440 × 900	16:10	Widescreen laptops
SXGA+	1400 × 1050	4:3	Laptop monitors and high-end projectors
UXGA	1600 × 1200	4:3	Larger CRT monitors
HDTV 1080p	1920 × 1080	16:9	Full HDTV resolution
WUXGA	1920 × 1200	16:10	For 24" widescreen monitors

Table 13.2	Common Modes and the Minimum Video Memory Required	
Resolution	16-bit (high color)	24-bit (true color)
640 × 480	1 MB	1 MB
800 × 600	1 MB	2 MB
1024 × 768	2 MB	4 MB
1280 × 1024	4 MB	4 MB
1600 × 1200	4 MB	6 MB

For example, take a typical display at 800 × 600 with a fairly low refresh of 70 Hz. The 70 Hz means the display screen is being redrawn 70 times per second. If you use a low color depth of 256 colors, which is 8 bits ($2^8 = 256$), you can multiply all of the values together to see how much data per second has to be sent to the display:

$$800 \times 600 \times 1 \text{ byte} \times 70 = 33.6 \text{ MBps}$$

If you use the same example at 16 million (24-bit) colors, the figure jumps to 100.8 MBps. You might say, "Well, if PCI runs at 132 MBps, it can handle that!" That statement would be true if the PCI bus had nothing else to do but tend to the video card, but almost every system has more than one PCI device, each requiring part of that throughput. The PCI bus simply cannot handle the needs of many current systems.

• Figure 13.38   AGP

Cross Check

Multiple Actions per Clock Cycle

You've run into devices in the PC that can handle multiple actions during a single clock cycle, right? Refer to Chapters 5, "Learning CPUs," and 6, "Learning RAM," and cross-check your memory. Which CPUs can clock multiply? What advantages does that bring to the PC? Which types of RAM run faster than the system clock?

AGP

Intel answered the desire for video bandwidth even higher than PCI with the **Accelerated Graphics Port (AGP)**. AGP is a single, special port, similar to a PCI slot, that is dedicated to video. You will never see a motherboard with two AGP slots. Figure 13.38 shows an early-generation AGP. AGP is derived from the 66-MHz, 32-bit PCI 2.1 specification. AGP uses a function called *strobing* that increases the signals two, four, and eight times for each clock cycle.

Simply describing AGP as a faster PCI would seriously misrepresent the power of AGP. AGP has several technological advantages over PCI, including the bus, the internal operations, and the capability to handle 3-D texturing.

First, AGP currently resides alone, on its own personal data bus, connected directly to the Northbridge (Figure 13.39). This is important because more advanced versions of AGP outperform every bus on the system except the frontside bus!

• **Figure 13.39**   An AGP bus

Second, AGP takes advantage of pipelining commands, similar to the way CPUs pipeline. Third, AGP has a feature called **sidebanding**—basically a second data bus that enables the video card to send more commands to the Northbridge while receiving other commands at the same time.

Video cards do all kinds of neat stuff with their RAM; for example, video cards store copies of individual windows so they can display the windows at different points on the screen very quickly. A demanding application can quickly max out the onboard RAM on a video card, so AGP provides a pathway so the AGP card can "steal" chunks of the regular system memory to store video information, especially textures. This is generically called a *system memory access* and is quite popular.

AGP has gone through three sets of specifications (AGP1.0, AGP2.0, and AGP3.0), but the official names tend to be ignored. Most techs and consumers refer to the various cards by their strobe multiplier, such as AGP 1×, 2×, 4×, and 8×. The only problem with blurring the distinctions between the specifications comes from the fact that many new motherboards simply don't support the older AGP cards because the older cards require a different physical connection than the new ones.

Some motherboards support multiple types of AGP. Figure 13.40 shows an AGP slot that accommodates everything up to 8×, even the very rare AGP Pro cards. Note that the tab on the slot covers the extra pins required for AGP Pro.

Because many AGP cards will run on older AGP motherboards, you can get away with mixing AGP specifications. To get the best, most stable performance possible, you should use an AGP card that's fully supported by the motherboard.

> **Tech Tip**
>
> **GART and AGP Aperture**
> *Intel couldn't quite bring itself to call AGP's system memory access...err...system memory access, so they use a couple of different terms. The video processor maps out a portion of system memory by using the* Graphics Address Remapping Table (GART). *The size of the re-mapped region is called the AGP aperture. A typical AGP aperture is 32 MB or 64 MB.*

• **Figure 13.40**   AGP 8× slot

The only significant downside to AGP lies in the close connection tolerances required by the cards themselves. It's very common to snap in a new AGP card and power up just to get a no-video-card beep or a system that doesn't boot. Always take the time to ensure that an AGP card is snapped down securely and screwed in before starting the system.

PCIe

AGP is a great way to get video information to and from video cards very quickly, but it has the downside of being a unique connector in a world where saving money is important. AGP, being based on PCI, also uses a parallel interface. When the **PCI Express (PCIe)** interface was developed to replace PCI, the PCIe designers worked hard to make sure it would also replace AGP. PCIe is a natural evolution for video because it is incredibly fast, using a serial communication method. Also, because PCIe is a true expansion bus designed to talk to the CPU and RAM, it also supports all of the little extras found in AGP, such as sidebanding and system memory access. All PCIe video cards use the PCIe ×16 connector (Figure 13.41). PCIe replaced AGP as the primary video interface almost overnight.

Graphics Processor

The graphics processor handles the heavy lifting of taking commands from the CPU and translating them into coordinates and color information that the monitor understands and displays.

Graphics processors are also known as GPUs.

Video card discussion, at least among techs, almost always revolves around the graphics processor they use and the amount of RAM onboard. A typical video card might be called an ATI Radeon X1950 XTX 512 MB, so let's break that down. ATI is the manufacturer, Radeon X1950 XTX is the model of the card as well as the graphics processor, and 512 MB is the amount of video RAM.

• **Figure 13.41**   PCIe video card connected in PCIe slot

Many companies make the hundreds of different video cards on the market, but only two companies produce the vast majority of graphics processors found on video cards: NVIDIA and ATI. NVIDIA and ATI make and sell graphics processors to third-party manufacturers who then design, build, and sell video cards under their own branding. ATI also makes and sells its own line of cards. Figure 13.42 shows an NVIDIA GeForce GTX 260 on a board made by EVGA.

Your choice of graphics processor is your single most important decision in buying a video card. Low-end graphics processors usually work fine for the run-of-the-mill user who wants to write letters or run a Web browser. High-end graphics processors are designed to support the beautiful 3-D games that are so popular today.

NVIDIA and ATI are extremely competitive, and both companies introduce multiple models of graphics processors (and therefore new models of cards) every year. However, unless you're using the Vista Aero glass desktop, all of these extra features you see in video cards are really only for the true driving force in video cards: 3-D gaming. Your PC is capable of providing you with hours of incredible entertainment via a huge number of popular games that immerse you in 3-D environments full of light, shadows, explosions, and other amazing effects that create a fun and beautiful gaming experience.

These 3-D games have special needs to do all this amazing stuff. One need is textures. A *texture* is a small picture that is tiled over and over again on walls, floors, and other surfaces to create the 3-D world. Take a look at the wall in Figure 13.43. It's made up of only three textures that are repeated over and over on the surface.

Games also use hundreds of lighting effects such as transparency (water), shadows, reflection, and bump mapping—the process of laying multiple textures on the same spot to give a more textured (bumpy) look to the surface. These games are where the higher-quality graphics processors really shine.

Choosing a graphics processor is a challenge because the video industry is constantly coming out with new models. One of the best guides is price. The best (and newest) graphics cards usually cost around (US) $400–500. The cheapest cards cost around $50. I usually split the difference and go for a card priced around $180 to $200—such a card will have most of the features you want without breaking your bank account.

If you use your computer only for 2-D programs (most office applications such as word processors, e-mail, and Web browsers are 2-D), most of the features of the more advanced graphics cards will do you little good. If you're not a gamer, you can meet your needs with a cheap, low-end video card.

• **Figure 13.42**   NVIDIA GeForce GTX 260

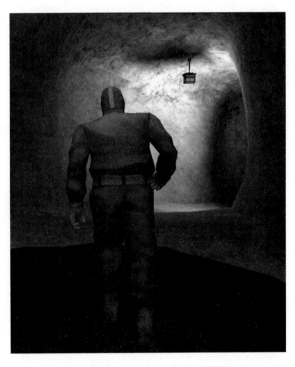

• **Figure 13.43**   Wall of textures

Video Memory

Video memory is crucial to the operation of a PC. It is probably the hardest-working set of electronics on the PC. Video RAM constantly updates to reflect

Try This!

Testing Your Video

Your client needs to know right now whether his system will run the latest game, so turn to the DirectX Diagnostic Tool and give it a go. Although you can open the tool in System Information, you can also run it directly from the Start menu. Go to Start | Run, type in **dxdiag**, and click OK. Or in Vista/7, just Start, type **dxdiag**, and press ENTER.

1. Select the Display tab and then click the Test DirectDraw button.

2. After the DirectDraw test runs, click the Test Direct3D button.

3. How did your system handle the test? If anything failed, you might think about replacing the card!

every change that takes place on the screen. When you're working with heavy-duty applications (such as games), video memory can prove to be a serious bottleneck in three ways: data throughput speed, access speed, and simple capacity.

Manufacturers have overcome these bottlenecks by upping the width of the bus between the video RAM and video processor; using specialized, super-fast RAM; and adding more and more total RAM.

First, manufacturers reorganized the video display memory on cards from the typical 32-bit-wide structure to 64, 128, or even 256 bits wide. Because the system bus is limited to 32 or 64 bits, this would not be of much benefit if video display cards weren't really coprocessor boards. Most of the graphics rendering and processing is handled on the card by the video processor chip rather than by the CPU. The main system simply provides the input data to the processor on the video card. Because the memory bus on the video card is as much as eight times wider than the standard 32-bit pathway (256 bits), data can be manipulated and then sent to the monitor much more quickly (Figure 13.44).

Specialized types of video RAM have been developed for graphics cards, and many offer substantial improvements in video speeds. The single most important feature that separates DRAM from video RAM is that video RAM can read and write data at the same time. Table 13.3 shows a list of common

• **Figure 13.44**   Wide path between video processor and video RAM

Table 13.3	Video RAM Technologies	
Acronym	**Name**	**Purpose**
VRAM	Video RAM	The original graphics RAM
WRAM	Window RAM	Designed to replace VRAM; never caught on
SGRAM	Synchronous Graphics RAM	A version of SDRAM with features to speed up access for graphics
DDR SDRAM	Double Data Rate Synchronous DRAM	Used on budget graphics cards and very common on laptop video cards
DDR2 SDRAM	Double Data Rate version 2, Synchronous DRAM	Popular on video cards until GDDR3; lower voltage than DDR memory
GDDR3 SDRAM	Graphics Double Data Rate, version 3	Similar to DDR2 but runs at faster speeds; different cooling requirements
GDDR4 SDRAM	Graphics Double Data Rate, version 4	Upgrade of GDDR3; faster clock
GDDR5 SDRAM	Graphics Double Data Rate, version 5	Successor to GDDR4; double the input/output rate of GDDR4

video memory technologies used yesterday and today—make sure you know these for the CompTIA A+ Essentials exam!

Finally, many advanced 3-D video cards come with huge amounts of video RAM. It's very common to see cards with 64, 128, 256, or 512 MB or even 1 GB of RAM! Why so much? Even with PCI Express, accessing data in system RAM always takes a lot longer than accessing data stored in local RAM on the video card. The huge amount of video RAM enables game developers to optimize their games and store more essential data on the local video RAM.

Connections

Modern video cards offer connections to one or more PC monitors. Many also sport connectors for non-monitors, such as televisions. The video card in Figure 13.45 has three connectors: VGA, S-Video, and DVI-I. Other connectors enable the video card to connect to composite, component, and even high-definition devices.

• **Figure 13.45**   Video card connectors, VGA, S-Video, and DVI-I

For Standard Monitors

You know about the standard monitor connectors, VGA and DVI, from the monitor discussion earlier. About the only thing to add is that most DVI connections on video cards these days natively support analog signals. You can use a simple DVI-to-VGA adapter, for example, for connecting a VGA cable to a video card.

Apple Macintosh desktop models use a DisplayPort connection rather than VGA or DVI for connecting to a monitor. Dell offers support for DisplayPort as well at the time of this writing. Figure 13.46 shows a DisplayPort jack on a Dell portable.

• **Figure 13.46**   DisplayPort jack

For Multimedia Devices

Video cards can have one or more standard connections plus non-standard connections for hooking the PC to a multimedia device, such as a television, DVD player, or video camera. The earliest type of connector commonly found is the S-Video connector. This provides decent-quality video output or, in some cases, input. More commonly now you see both a proprietary round connector that supports S-Video and a proprietary dongle that adds support for video through either component connection or composite connections. Figure 13.47 shows the similar round ports.

• **Figure 13.47**   S-Video and proprietary round connectors

• **Figure 13.48** Composite and component connection options

• **Figure 13.49** HDMI port on Lenovo laptop

A composite connector provides a video signal through a single cable, whereas a component adapter provides a split signal, red, green, and blue. Figure 13.48 shows the two connector dongles.

The best connections for outputting to television are the Hi-Definition Multimedia Interface (HDMI) connectors. Although a few devices offer HDMI output directly (such as the portable pictured in Figure 13.49), most video cards support HDMI through a special cable that connects to a dual-link DVI port. Figure 13.50 shows an example of such a cable.

• **Figure 13.50** DVI-to-HDMI cable

> Some video cards with built-in television tuners that enable the PC to be a television as well as a computer have a standard coaxial jack for connecting a cable or antenna. You'll learn more about TV tuners later in the chapter.

Sound

Whether you're racing down the virtual track, pixels flying across the screen, hearing the engine roar as you take another turn and press down the accelerator, or you're surfing the Web for lovely scenic nature photos with the sweet, mellifluous music of Mozart filling the room; sound has become an integral component of the computing experience. Setting up and optimizing sound for the PC has become an integral skill for all computer techs.

Correctly setting up sound for a PC requires that you know about quite a few things, because the sound process has many components. For the CompTIA A+ Essentials exam, you really only need a general idea of how sound works inside a PC and a basic idea of what a sound card looks like, so here's a nice, big overview of PC sound.

How Sound Works in a PC

Like the ripples that roll across a pond when you drop a rock in the center, sound flows from a source in invisible but measurable waves that cause the membranes in your ears to vibrate and create noise. The sophistication of the human ear enables most people to differentiate the melodious from the raucous, the loud from the soft. Computers aren't nearly as sophisticated as the human ear and brain, so clear standards are a must for converting music into a format that a PC can use to record and play sound. Computer folks use the terms *capture* and *output* instead of record and play.

Sound-Capture Basics

Virtually every PC today comes with four critical components for capturing and outputting sound: a sound card, speakers, microphone, and recording/playback software. Computers capture (record) sound waves in electronic format through a process called **sampling**. In its simplest sense, sampling means capturing the state or quality of a particular sound wave a set number of times each second. The sampling rate is measured in units of thousands of cycles per second, or kilohertz (KHz). The more often a sound is sampled, the better the reproduction of that sound. Most sounds in the PC world are recorded with a sampling rate of from 11 KHz (very low quality, like a telephone) to 192 KHz (ultra-high quality, better than the human ear).

Sounds vary according to their loudness (**amplitude**), how high or low their tone (**frequency**), and the qualities that differentiate the same note played on different instruments (**timbre**). All the characteristics of a particular sound wave—amplitude, frequency, timbre—need to be recorded and translated into ones and zeros to reproduce that sound accurately within the computer and out to your speakers.

The number of characteristics of a particular sound captured during sampling is measured by the **bit depth** of the sample, the number of bits used to describe the characteristics of a sound. The greater the bit depth used to capture a sample, the more characteristics of that sound can be stored and thus re-created. An 8-bit sample of a Jimi Hendrix guitar solo, for example, captures 2^8 (256) characteristics of that sound per sample. It would sound like a cheap recording of a recording, perhaps a little flat and thin. A 16-bit sample, in contrast, captures 2^{16} (65,536) different characteristics of his solo and reproduces all the fuzzy overtones and feedback that gave Hendrix his unique sound.

The last aspect of sound capture is the number of tracks of sound you capture. Most commonly, you can capture either a single track (**monaural**) or two tracks (**stereo**). More advanced captures record many more sound tracks, but that's a topic for a more advanced sound capture discussion.

The combination of sampling frequency and bit depth determines how faithfully a digital version of a sound captures what your ear would hear. A sound capture is considered **CD quality** when recorded at 44.1 KHz, with 16-bit depth and in stereo. Most recording programs let you set these values before you begin recording. Figure 13.51 shows the configuration settings for the Windows Sound Recorder.

Hey, wait a minute! Did you notice the Format setting in Figure 13.51? What's that? You can save those sampled sounds in lots of different ways—and that's where the term *format* comes into play.

Recorded Sound Formats

The granddaddy of all sound formats is **pulse code modulation (PCM)**. PCM was developed in the 1960s to carry telephone calls over the first digital lines. With just a few minor changes to allow for use in PCs, the PCM format is still alive and well, although it's better known as the *WAV* format so common in the PC world. WAV files are great for storing faithfully recorded sounds and music, but they do so at a price. WAV files can be huge, especially when sampled at high frequency and depth. A four-minute song at 44.1 KHz and 16-bit stereo, for example, weighs in at a whopping 40-plus MB!

Tech Tip

Sound Terminology

Every modern motherboard comes with sound processing capabilities built in. By default, techs talk about built-in sound as either built-in sound or as a sound card, even when there's no expansion card for sound.

• **Figure 13.51**   Sound Recorder settings

WAV and MP3 are only two among a large number of file formats for sound. Not all sound players can play all of these formats; however, many sound formats are nothing more than some type of compressed WAV file, so with the right codec loaded, you can play most sound formats.

Tech Tip

Compressing WAV Files to MP3 Format

Using MP3 compression, you can shrink a WAV file by a factor of 12 without losing much sound quality. When you compress a WAV file into an MP3 file, the key decision is the bit rate. The bit rate is the amount of information (number of bits) transferred from the compressed file to the MP3 decoder in 1 second. The higher the bit rate of an MP3 file, the higher the sound quality. The bit rate of MP3 audio files is commonly measured in thousands of bits per second, abbreviated Kbps. Most MP3 encoders support a range of bit rates from 24 Kbps up to 320 Kbps (or 320,000 bits per second). A CD-quality MP3 bit rate is 128 Kbps.

MIDI files have the file extension .MID in the PC world.

MIDI files are much less popular than other recorded formats on computers, but every Windows computer and every sound card still fully supports MIDI.

What's interesting about sound quality is that the human ear cannot perceive anywhere near the subtle variations of sound recorded at 44.1 KHz and 16-bit stereo. Clever programmers have written algorithms to store full-quality WAV files as compressed files, discarding unnecessary audio qualities of that file. These algorithms—really nothing more than a series of instructions in code—are called compressor/decompressor programs or, more simply, **codecs**. The most famous of the codecs is the Fraunhoffer MPEG-1 Layer 3 codec, more often called by its file extension, **MP3**.

MIDI

Every sound card can produce sounds in addition to playing prerecorded sound files. Every sound card comes with a second processor designed to interpret standardized **musical instrument digital interface (MIDI)** files. It's important to note that a MIDI file is not an independent music file, unlike a WAV file that sounds more or less the same on many different PCs. A MIDI file is a text file that takes advantage of the sound processing hardware to enable the PC to produce sound. Programmers use these small files to tell the sound card what notes to play, how long, how loud, on which instruments, and so forth. Think of a MIDI file as a piece of electronic sheet music, with the instruments built into your sound card.

The beauty of MIDI files is that they're tiny in comparison to equivalent WAV files. The first movement of Beethoven's Fifth Symphony, for example, weighs in at a whopping 78 MB as a high-quality WAV file. The same seven-minute song as a MIDI file, in contrast, slips in at a svelte 60 KB.

MIDI is hardware dependent, meaning the capabilities and quality of the individual sound card make all the difference in the world on the sound produced. Sound cards play MIDI files by using one of two technologies: FM synthesis or wave table synthesis.

FM Synthesis   Early processors used electronic emulation of various instruments—a technique often called **FM synthesis**—to produce music and other sound effects. Software developers could tell the sound processor to reproduce a piano playing certain notes, for example, and a sound resembling a piano would pour forth from the speakers. The problem with FM synthesis is that although the modulation sounds okay for a single note, such as middle C, it sounds increasingly electronic the farther up or down the scale you go from that prime note.

Wave Table Synthesis   To address the odd techno-sound of early sound processors, manufacturers began embedding recordings of actual instruments or other sounds in the sound card. Modern sound cards use these recorded sounds to reproduce an instrument much more faithfully than with FM synthesis. When asked to play a C note on a piano or on a viola, for example, the sound processor grabs a prerecorded WAV file from its memory and adjusts it to match the specific sound and timing requested. This technique is called **wave table synthesis**. The number of instruments a sound card can play at once is called the **polyphony** of that card—typically 64 sounds on better cards. Most modern sound cards have samples of 128 instruments—a veritable symphony orchestra on a chip!

Other File Formats

The WAV, MP3, and MIDI formats may account for the majority of sound files, but plenty of other less common formats are out there. Here are the extensions of some other sound file formats you may run into in the PC world:

- **AAC** Advanced Audio Coding is the native format for songs downloaded into the Apple iTunes music library. The AAC format is part of the MPEG-4 standard, offers better compression algorithms than MP3, and is freely distributed. Apple used to wrap downloaded songs in a Digital Rights Management (DRM) encapsulation called FairPlay that gave them control over distribution of those songs.

- **AIFF** Audio Interchange File Format files are a popular sound format used on Macintosh computers. These files are often seen on Web sites, and you can use the well-known QuickTime Player to play them.

- **ASM** Assembly Language Source files are compressed sound files often seen on the Internet and used in streaming sound (streaming media is discussed later in this chapter).

- **ASX** Microsoft created the ASX format to facilitate streaming audio over the Internet through Windows Media Player. It's more than just a format, though; it acts like a super playlist and enables you to play other sound file types as well. The full name of the format is Microsoft Advanced Streaming Redirector.

- **AU** This popular format is often seen in the Windows world. Many players can play these files, including players on non-Windows systems, such as Sun, Next, UNIX, and Macintosh.

- **OGG** The Vorbis format is an open-source compression codec that competes well with the proprietary AAC and WMA codecs, as well as MP3. Vorbis files are saved with the .OGG filename extension, so you'll hear them (incorrectly) referred to as "Ogg" files.

- **RM** RealMedia files play either just audio or audio and video. They are proprietary to RealMedia, a popular player often used on the Internet. You must have RealMedia Player installed on your computer to play these files.

- **WMA** Windows Media Audio is Microsoft's proprietary compression format.

This list scratches the surface of the 100-plus sound file formats available, but it represents those you're most likely to encounter.

Playing Sounds

A large number of programs can play sounds on a typical Windows computer. First, virtually every Windows computer comes with Windows Media Player, possibly the most popular of all sound players. Figure 13.52 shows the default Media Player for Windows Vista. You can download many other players, of course, including iTunes, Apple's media program for Windows and Mac OS X. This is good, because not all sound players can play all sounds.

Many applications, especially games, play sounds too. In the not-too-distant past, a game or an application sometimes had its own sound format, but most applications and games today use standard WAV, MP3, or MIDI files.

• **Figure 13.52** Windows Media Player

Streaming media is a broadcast of data that is played on your computer and immediately discarded. Streaming media is incredibly popular on the Internet. Streaming media has spawned an entire industry of Internet radio stations. The three most popular streaming media players are Windows Media Player, Winamp, and Apple's iTunes. With the spread of broadband Internet, the quality of streaming radio has improved dramatically. In fact, it is common to see Internet stations streaming 128 Kbps and better MP3 files. Some sites even have surround sound music for those who have the speakers to appreciate it.

Getting the Right Sound Hardware

Modern motherboards come with built-in sound processing, plus you can buy a sound card that plugs into a PCI or PCIe expansion slot or into a USB port. Sound cards come with many features, including two separate sound processors (one for all of the recorded formats such as WAV and another for MIDI), recording capabilities, support for MIDI instruments, and more. All sound cards, from the cheapest to the most expensive, can play music and drive a pair of speakers, so techs need to delve a little deeper to understand the crucial differences among low-, mid-, and high-end sound cards. Sound cards differ in six basic areas: sound standard, processor capabilities, speaker support, recording quality, jacks, and extra features.

But the sound card itself is only one part of the equation. You also need good-quality speakers if you have any intention of listening to music or enjoying some of the more advanced features such as surround sound.

Sound Card Standards

Most sound cards follow one of two standards, AC'97 or Intel High Definition Audio, although no rule says manufacturers must follow these standards.

Tech Tip

Sound Cards

The hardware portion of sound processing equipment in the PC comes either as a chip built into the motherboard or as an expansion card. Techs call both forms sound cards, though technically the first type is not a card at all. Still, the generic term has stuck for the time being.

This applies both to the sound processing hardware built into motherboards and to add-on sound cards.

The **AC'97** standard applies to lower-end audio devices, having been created when most folks listened to stereo sound at best. Both playback and recording capabilities of such sound cards offer adequate quality, certainly enough for the typical office PC. When you want to go beyond average, though, turn to a motherboard or add-on sound card that offers a newer standard.

Intel designed the **Intel High Definition Audio (HDA)** standard to support features such as true surround sound with many discrete speakers. Technically speaking, whereas AC'97 offers support for up to six channels at 48 KHz/20-bit quality, HDA cranks that up to eight channels at 192 KHz/32-bit quality, a substantial improvement. HDA also supports sending multiple streams of audio from one computer to different output devices, so you can enjoy Internet radio in one room, for example, and listen to a CD in another room, both played on the same computer.

Try This!

Play Sounds in Windows

The typical Windows PC comes with a number of applications for playing sound files. Take a tour of a typical Windows system to see these applications. This exercise uses Windows XP, but almost any version of Windows (95 or later) will also work. For this exercise, you need a Windows XP or Vista system with a functioning sound card, microphone, and speakers.

1. Using the file search feature in Windows, locate all of the files on your computer that have the extension .WAV—all versions of Windows come with a number of WAV files. Double-click one of the files to play it. What program is associated with WAV files?

2. Repeat step 1, but this time look for files with the extension .MID. Not all versions of Windows have MIDI files. Double-click one of the files to play it. What program is associated with MIDI files?

3. From the Start button, search for any sound programs that may be on your system. You'll almost certainly run into Windows Media Player and Sound Recorder, but check to see whether any third-party programs are installed.

4. If possible, install a popular sound player such as Winamp or iTunes on your system. Both programs are free. You can get Winamp at www.winamp.com and iTunes at www.apple.com/itunes. Check Winamp's help files to see what types of file formats Winamp supports—a lot of formats!

5. If you have an Internet connection, try running some streaming audio. If you have Windows Media Player versions 7 through 10, go to the Radio Tuner. If you are running Windows Media Player 11 or later, go to the Media Guide. If you have Winamp, try going to www.shoutcast.com. With iTunes, just click the Radio link in the Library.

Processor Capabilities

Sound processor capabilities differ dramatically from the low end to the high end, even though the prices don't reflect the great divide. The sound processor handles the communication among the application, operating system, and CPU and translates commands into sounds coming out of the speakers. Low-end sound processors do little more than translate, which means that the CPU has to do the heavy lifting on the processing front.

Better sound processors, in contrast, shoulder much of the processing burden and bring a series of extra features to the table. By handling a lot of the processing onboard, these better sound processors free up the CPU for other duties and—in effect and in name—*accelerate* the sound process. These decent sound processors also provide excellent sound reproduction, so your MP3s sound as awesome on your PC as they do on your stereo.

Most mid-range and all high-end sound processors offer support for various surround sound standards, enabling equally equipped games and other applications to provide positional audio effects and detailed sound

As they do with new microprocessor models, Intel gave the HDA standard a codename as well. Look for motherboards offering the *Azalia* sound option. That's Intel High Definition Audio.

Tech Tip

Azalia's Not Just for Intel Boards

Most chipset makers have adopted Intel HDA for their better motherboard offerings. That includes direct Intel competitors, such as NVIDIA. Everybody plays Azalia these days!

modeling—features that make PC gaming take on a whole new dimension. You'll learn about the various standards in detail in the "Speakers" section of this chapter, but for now let an example suffice. With properly implemented positional audio, when you're sneaking down the hall, ready to steal the Pasha's treasure, you will hear behind you the sounds of the guards marching up to capture you. Such added realism has many potential benefits beyond games, but games are currently the primary beneficiary of this technology.

• **Figure 13.53**   A sound card with multiple speaker connections

Speaker Support

Every sound card supports two speakers or a pair of headphones, but many better sound cards support five or more speakers in discrete channels. These multiple speakers provide surround sound—popular not only for games but also for those who enjoy playing DVDs on their PCs. The card shown in Figure 13.53, for example, has outputs for many speakers.

Another popular speaker addition is a subwoofer. A **subwoofer** provides the amazing low-frequency sounds that give an extra dimension to all of your sounds, from the surround sound of a game to the music of a simple stereo MP3 file. Almost all modern sound cards support both surround sound and a subwoofer and advertise this with a nomenclature such as Dolby Digital or DTS. Figure 13.54 shows one type of surround speaker system. (You'll learn more about surround sound in the upcoming "Speakers" section.)

• **Figure 13.54**   Surround speakers (*photo courtesy of Klipsch Group, Inc.*)

Recording Quality

Almost every sound card has an input for a powered microphone, but the high-end cards record with substantially lower amounts of noise or other audible artifacts. The measure that describes the relative quality of an input port is **signal-to-noise ratio** and is expressed in **decibels**. The smaller the number, the worse the card is for recording, because you're more likely to get noise. Most sound cards at the low end and in the mid range have a signal-to-noise ratio of 30 to 50 decibels, which makes them unacceptable for recording. High-end cards offer a 96 to 100+ signal-to-noise ratio, a level near what professional musicians use. Check the documentation before you buy or recommend a sound card for recording purposes (Figure 13.55).

Jacks

Virtually every sound card comes with at least three connections: one for a stereo speaker system, one for a microphone, and one for a secondary input called line in. If you look at the back of a motherboard with a built-in sound card, you'll invariably see these three connections. On most systems, the main stereo speaker connector is green, the line in connector is blue, and the microphone connector is pink. You'll often find plenty of other connectors as well (Figure 13.56).

• **Figure 13.55**   The EMU 1820 advertises its excellent 112-decibel signal-to-noise ratio for recording.

Here's a list of some of the standard connectors:

- **Main speaker out**   Just what it sounds like, the main speaker output is where you plug in the standard speaker connector.

- **Line out**   Some cards will have a separate line out connector that is often used to connect to an external device such as a cassette or CD player. This enables you to output sounds from your computer.

- **Line in**   The line in port connects to an external device such as a cassette or CD player to allow you to import sounds into your computer.

- **Rear out**   The rear out connector connects to the rear speakers for surround sound audio output.

Mini-audio
connectors

• **Figure 13.56**   Typical audio connections on a motherboard sound card

- **Analog/digital out** The multifunction analog/digital out connection acts as a special digital connection to external digital devices or digital speaker systems, and it also acts as the analog connection to center and subwoofer channels. (See the upcoming "Speakers" section for a discussion of surround sound.)

- **Microphone** The microphone port connects to an external microphone for voice input.

- **Joystick** The now-obsolete joystick port connects a joystick or a MIDI device to the sound card. The joystick port is a two-row, DB15 female connection, but few motherboards or sound cards include the port these days.

● **Figure 13.57** Breakout box for a SoundBlaster Live! Platinum sound card

Extra Features

With all motherboards including built-in sound these days, expansion sound card makers have responded by adding a host of extra goodies and capabilities to their cards that, for some folks, prove irresistibly tempting. These include a digital output to integrate the PC with a home entertainment unit, DVD receiver, and surround sound speaker connection capabilities; a breakout box that adds recording and output ports in a 5.25-inch bay; and a FireWire connection for direct gaming, file sharing, and immediate MP3 playing from a portable MP3 device. Figure 13.57 shows a version of the Creative Labs SoundBlaster breakout box. These features aren't for everyone, but they are compelling to many consumers.

Speakers

It always blows me away when I walk into someone's study and hear tinny music whining from a $10 pair of speakers connected to a $2000 computer. If you listen to music or play games on your computer, a decent set of speakers can significantly improve the experience. Speakers come in a wide variety of sizes, shapes, technologies, and quality and can stump the uninformed tech who can't easily tell that the $50 set on the right sounds 100 times better than the $25 pair on the left (Figure 13.58).

Speaker Standards The advent of surround sound in the computing world has created a number of speaker standards. You should know these standards so you can choose the speakers that work best for you and your clients.

Stereo is the oldest speaker technology you'll see in the PC world. Stereo speakers are just what you might imagine: two speakers, a left and a right (Figure 13.59). The two speakers share a single jack that connects to the sound card. Most cheap speakers are stereo speakers.

● **Figure 13.58** High-quality speaker set (right) versus another manufacturer's low-end speaker set (left)

A **2.1** speaker system consists of a pair of standard stereo speakers—called **satellites**—combined with a subwoofer (Figure 13.60). The average 2.1 speaker system has a single jack that connects to the sound card and runs into the subwoofer. Another wire runs from the subwoofer to the two stereo speakers. If you want to enjoy great music and don't need surround sound, this is your speaker standard of choice.

Going beyond standard two-channel (stereo) sound has been a goal in the sound world since the 1970s. However, it wasn't until the advent of Dolby Laboratory's **Dolby Digital** sound standard in the early 1990s that surround sound began to take off. The Dolby Digital sound standard is designed to support five channels of sound: front-left, front-right, front-center, rear-left, and rear-right. Dolby Digital also supports a subwoofer—thus, the term **5.1**. Another company, **Digital Theatre Systems (DTS)**, created a competing standard that also supported a 5.1 speaker system. When DVDs were introduced, they included both Dolby Digital and DTS 5.1 standards, making 5.1 speakers an overnight requirement for home theater. If you want to enjoy your DVDs in full surround sound on your PC, you must purchase a full 5.1 speaker system. A number of 5.1 speaker systems are available for PCs. The choice you make is usually determined by what sounds best to you.

Many sound cards also come with a special **Sony/Philips Digital Interface (S/PDIF)** connector that enables you to connect your sound card directly to a 5.1 speaker system or receiver (Figure 13.61). Using a single S/PDIF instead of a tangle of separate wires for each speaker greatly simplifies your sound setup. S/PDIF connections come in two types, optical and coaxial. The optical variety looks like a square with a small door (at right in Figure 13.61). The coaxial is a standard RCA connector (at left), the same type used to connect a CD player to your stereo. It doesn't matter which one you use; just make sure you have an open spot on your receiver or speakers.

Games can also take advantage of 5.1, 6.1, and 7.1 speakers, but they use the DirectX standard. **DirectX** offers numerous commands, also known as APIs, that issue instructions such as "make a sound on the right speaker" or "play music in both the right and left channels." DirectX simplifies the programming needed to create sound and video: rather than having to program

• **Figure 13.59**   Stereo speakers

Only a few 5.1 PC speaker sets come with S/PDIF. In most cases, you'll have to use the regular audio outputs on the sound card. You'll find the connector more common on 6.1 and 7.1 sets.

• **Figure 13.60**   Typical 2.1 speakers

• **Figure 13.61**   S/PDIF connectors

sounds in different ways for each sound card option, games can talk DirectX. The hardware manufacturers simply have to ensure that their sound cards are DirectX compatible.

DirectX version 3 introduced **DirectSound3D (DS3D)**, which offered a range of commands to place a sound anywhere in 3-D space. Known as **positional audio**, it fundamentally changed the way most PC games were played. DS3D could not handle all sound information, but it supported extensions to its instructions for more advanced sound features. This challenged the sound card designers to develop more fully the concept of positional audio. Creative Labs responded by rolling out **environmental audio extensions (EAX)**, a set of audio presets that gave developers the capability to create a convincing sense of environment in entertainment titles and a realistic sense of distance between the player and audio events. Figure 13.62 shows an EAX setup screen.

In late 2000, a number of EAX effects were incorporated into the DirectX audio component of DirectX 8.0. This signaled the acceptance of EAX as the standard for audio effects in gaming. Shortly afterward, Creative Labs started releasing audio cards that were Dolby 5.1 compatible out of the box. This let you plug a 5.1 speaker system directly into your sound card. The sound card automatically decoded the Dolby/DTS sound track when you played a DVD and the EAX effects when you played a game that supports it. All current sound cards support DirectX and EAX.

Microsoft changed the way audio works in Windows Vista from the way it works in previous versions of Windows. Most notably, Vista doesn't support direct hardware access to sound, so DirectSound does not work. Third-party developers have created various workarounds for this lack of support to enable some older games and hardware to function in Windows Vista. Other developers have gotten behind the OpenAL API to provide environmental audio effects in Vista. Specific OpenAL drivers for games have to be included to provide that support.

Not all cards support Dolby Digital/DTS. Most software DVD players and some sound cards support Dolby Digital. DTS support is a little harder to come by. Check the manufacturer's Web site to determine whether your card will work with DTS.

• **Figure 13.62**   EAX setup screen

Speaker Features   Speakers also come with a few other features that you should consider when choosing a set for yourself or your clients. Speakers offer a variety of power sources, controls accessibility, and headphone jacks.

Most speakers have volume controls as well as an on/off switch. Get a system that provides easy access to those controls by placing them on an easy-to-reach speaker or on a special control box.

The problem with headphones is that you need to plug them into the back of the sound card and then tell Windows to output to them from the Sound applet on the Control Panel. Save yourself a lot of hassle and get a speaker system that has a handy microphone jack on one of the speakers or on a control box.

Video Capture

A microphone, sound card, and software enable you to capture audio, but with a camera capable of capturing full motion video as well as sound, you can turn the PC into your very own movie studio. This is called **video capture**. To capture video from a source requires you to have the proper hardware installed to provide an interface with the camcorder or video player and, if the source is analog, provide translation of the signal as well; plus you need a properly configured application to do the capturing. Once captured, you can use an application to edit the video file. Then save it in some form for upload a la YouTube or save it to DVD or other removable media.

Hardware

You need the proper hardware installed to capture video. From a digital signal, such as a modern camcorder that records directly to its own internal solid-state hard drive, you simply run a cable from the FireWire out port on the camcorder to the FireWire port on your computer. If the camcorder doesn't offer FireWire, it'll most likely use Hi-Speed USB. When capturing from an analog source, such as a VHS cassette player or a Hi-8 tape, you'll need some kind of connection and translation hardware.

• Figure 13.63   A video capture device

The Pinnacle blueBox pictured in Figure 13.63, for example, offers two different dedicated video connections (S-Video on the left and the yellow RCA jack next to it), stereo RCA audio jacks, plus a FireWire port (on the expansion card for it) for direct connection to FireWire onboard the camcorder. The breakout box uses a proprietary connection to plug into the PC.

You need a decent-grade computer with lots of free hard drive space and a substantial amount of RAM to import the video and audio streams from an external source. And you'll certainly need a serious processor when it comes time to edit and compile a new video from the source material. There's no simple rule for how much of any resource you'll need. Different projects have different demands on the hardware. If you're setting up a new computer for video capture, the simple rule is to get as powerful a system as possible with as much hard drive and RAM capacity as you can afford.

Once you have the hardware in place, the true heavy lifting in video capture falls on the software.

The FireWire connection seems redundant—just go straight to FireWire on the PC, right? But it's there to accomplish two goals. First, many PCs don't have a FireWire port, so you would either need to add a FireWire expansion card or use a different type of port. Second, Sony produced a series of Hi-8 camcorders some years ago that had FireWire connectors. Some translation has to happen to turn the analog signal digital.

Software

With video editing applications, such as Adobe Premier Elements or Apple Final Cut, you can import video and then work with it directly. Figure 13.64 shows the former software capturing video and audio translated through the Pinnacle blueBox from a Hi-8 camcorder. Most webcams—even those built into portable computers—are analog, rather than digital devices. Thus some software automatically creates break points in the import to make the editing process easier.

The video editing software enables you to take video and audio from one or many sources and arrange clips into a time line. You can add and edit various transitions between clips, shorten clips, and so on. Figure 13.65 shows the storyboard from Final Cut Pro and a how-to video my team produced in-house.

Once you've finished the editing process, you can export to a file for archiving, sending out on optical disc, or posting to a video-sharing site. With an audio file, as discussed earlier, this is a simple process. You pick a format such as MP3 and save the file. Video is far more complicated.

A video is two or more separate tracks—moving picture and audio—that each go through a compression algorithm. Otherwise, the resulting files would be huge, even for short videos. The compressed tracks then get wrapped up into a **container file**, what's often called a **wrapper**. When you receive a file saved in a standard wrapper, such as .MOV for a QuickTime Movie file, you have no way to know for certain which codecs were used to compress the video or audio tracks inside that container file (Figure 13.66).

• **Figure 13.64** Importing video in Adobe Premier Elements

● **Figure 13.65**   Editing in Final Cut Pro

Codecs

Video files use standard audio codecs for the audio tracks, such as WAV or MP3, but vary wildly in the type of video codecs used. Just as with audio codecs, video codecs take a video stream and compress it by using various algorithms. Here are some of the standard video codecs:

- MPEG-2 Part 2, used for DVDs.

- MPEG-4 Part 2, a codec often used for Internet broadcasts; you'll find implementations of it with other names, such as DivX.

● **Figure 13.66**   A standard container file holds multiple tracks, each encoded separately.

- H.264, used for high-definition movies for Blu-ray Discs, among others.

- Windows Media Video (WMV), the family of Microsoft-developed codecs.

- Theora, an open-source codec developed to go with the Vorbis audio codec as part of the Ogg project.

- TrueMotion VP6, used in Adobe Flash; and VP7, used for Skype video conferencing, among others.

- VC-1, a Microsoft-designed codec that competes with H.264 and other higher-end codecs for the hearts and minds of Blu-ray Disc developers. You'll usually find it wrapped in a WMV container file (see the following section).

Wrappers

When both the video and audio streams of your video file are compressed, the file is placed into some sort of container file or wrapper. The key thing to note here is that the wrapper file doesn't necessarily specify how the video or audio tracks were encoded. You can look at two seemingly identical movie files, for example, both saved with the .MOV file extension, and find that one will play audio and video just fine in Windows Media Player, but the other one might play only the audio and not the video because Media Player lacks the specific codec needed to decode the video stream. Here are some of the standard video wrappers:

- ASF, a container used mainly for WMA and WMV streams; note that you can also have a WMV wrapper for a WMV-format file.

- AVI, the standard container file for Windows.

- Flash Video (.FLV), which contains streams encoded with various codecs, such as H.263 or VP6; can also handle H.264 codec. Flash Video has become the dominant standard for displaying video content on the Web through places such as YouTube and Hulu.

- MOV, the standard container file for Apple QuickTime for both Mac OS X and Windows.

- MPEG-2 Transport Stream (MPEG-TS), a container for broadcasting that can handle many streams.

- Ogg, a container file made for the open-source Vorbis and Theora codecs.

■ TV Tuners

With a **TV tuner**, you can have it all in one package: a computer and the latest TV show as well. Most local stations (in the United States, at least) broadcast high-definition signals, so with the proper TV tuner, you can watch your HDTV without any of the artifacting you see with both cable and satellite feeds. Plus you can make use of typical cable or satellite feeds to watch television as you would with a regular TV. Making it all happen requires four components: a tuner device, an antenna or cable connection, a tuning application, and some sort of program guide.

Tuner Hardware

TV tuners come in just about every expansion option available for computers: expansion cards that plug into PCI or PCIe slots on the motherboard; PC Card or ExpressCard for portable computers; or Hi-Speed USB for desktop and laptop computers. Figure 13.67 shows a PCIe version of an ATI tuner card.

To install a TV tuner, follow standard installation procedures.

To pick up a signal on the TV tuner, just as with a standalone television, you need some source. Most can handle a cable TV connection, for example, or an over-the-air antenna. Figure 13.68 shows a USB Hauppauge HDTV tuner card with retractable antenna. For such a small device, it picks up HDTV signals quite well. You'll get the best results for uncompressed HD

TV tuners often include components for video capture, so you can get both devices on one card or expansion device.

• **Figure 13.67** ATI TV tuner card

• **Figure 13.68** Hauppauge TV tuner with retractable antenna

signals by using a serious, mounted-on-the-rooftop metal antenna with lots of tines.

Tuner hardware comes with a standard coaxial connection. You can plug in a cable or satellite source just as you would any regular television.

Tuner Software

Once you've installed the hardware, you need to load the specific application or applications that make the tuner work as a tuner. If you have a copy of Windows Media Center (through either that version of Windows XP or Windows Vista Ultimate), that will often be the tool of choice. Tuner card distributors bundle third-party applications with their cards. Figure 13.69 shows the EyeTV software enabling the computer to show television shows.

• **Figure 13.69** EyeTV tuner application

Chapter 13 Review

■ Chapter Summary

After reading this chapter and completing the exercises, you should understand the following about video and multimedia.

Explain how video displays work

- The term *video* encompasses a complex interaction among numerous parts of the PC, all designed to put a picture on the screen. The monitor is the primary output device for the PC and shows you what's going on with your programs and operating system. The video card or display adapter handles all of the communication between the CPU and the monitor. Video displays come in three varieties: CRT, LCD, and projectors.

- CRT monitors have a tube that contains three electron guns at the slender end and a display screen coated with phosphor at the wide end. The speed of the electron beam across the screen is the horizontal refresh rate (HRR), more commonly referred to as the refresh rate. The vertical refresh rate (VRR) is the time it takes to draw the entire screen and return the electron guns to the upper-left corner.

- Monitors do not determine the HRR or VRR. The video card "pushes" the monitor at a certain VRR that, in turn, determines the HRR. Setting the VRR too low results in screen flicker, which causes headaches and eyestrain. Setting the VRR too high results in image distortion and damage to the monitor's circuitry. The monitor's bandwidth dictates the maximum VRR.

- A monitor is a grid of red, green, and blue light-sensitive dots called phosphors. Normal CRT monitors have three electron guns that fire electrons of different intensities (not colors) at the colored phosphors. A shadow mask prevents electron bleed-over so electrons from any of the three guns hit only their own colored phosphors. The area of phosphors lit at one instant is a pixel and must consist of at least one red, one green, and one blue phosphor; therefore, the smallest pixel, a triad, would consist of three phosphors.

- Resolution is the number of horizontal pixels times the number of vertical pixels. A resolution of 640 × 480 means 640 pixels across and 480 pixels down,

for a total of 307,200 pixels. Many monitors have a resolution that matches a 4:3 aspect ratio. Widescreen monitors have an aspect ratio of 16:9 or 16:10.

- Dot pitch, measured in millimeters (mm), defines the diagonal distance between phosphorous dots of the same color.

- Liquid crystal displays are the most common type of display for PCs. They offer many advantages over CRTs. An LCD monitor is thinner, lighter, uses less power, is virtually flicker-free, and does not emit potentially harmful radiation.

- An LCD screen is composed of tiny liquid crystal molecules called sub-pixels. Although you may find dual-scan passive matrix on some low-end LCD panels, most of today's LCD panels use active matrix or thin film transistor (TFT) technology.

- The typical LCD projector is composed of the LCD panel, backlights, and inverters. The backlights require AC power and the electronics require DC. The AC/DC transformer changes the AC wall current into DC that the LCD panel can use. All LCD backlights use cold cathode fluorescent lamp (CCFL) technology. CCFLs require AC power, so inverters convert the DC back to AC.

- LCD monitors, unlike CRTs, have a native resolution and a fixed pixel size. LCDs cannot run at a resolution higher than their native resolution, and running at a lower resolution results in degraded image quality. Anti-aliasing softens the edges of jagged pixel corners when running at lower resolutions, but as the image quality degrades, you should use the native resolution.

- LCD monitor brightness is determined by its backlights and is measured in nits. An average LCD measures around 300 nits, with higher numbers being brighter and better.

- The time it takes for sub-pixels to go from pure black to pure white and back again is the LCD's response rate. Response rate is measured in milliseconds, with lower numbers being faster and better. An excellent LCD monitor has a response rate somewhere between 6 and 8 ms.

- LCD monitors lack the color saturation and contrast of a CRT, making CRT the choice for graphics artists. Look for an LCD monitor with a contrast ratio of 450:1 or higher.

- Projectors come in two main varieties: rear-view and front-view. Rear-view projectors shoot an image onto the screen from the back and are almost always self-enclosed. They are a popular choice for televisions, but not for PCs. Front-view projectors shoot an image from the front and are widely used during computer presentations.

- LCD projectors, like LCD monitors, have a native resolution and are lightweight, but lack the image quality of a CRT. Projector brightness is measured in *lumens*. Larger numbers are brighter and better, with 1500 lumens being sufficient for a small dark room. The size of the projected image at a certain distance from the screen is the projector's *throw*. LCD projectors come with internal fans that cool the lamp. Lamps are costly to replace and are considered consumable (meaning you can expect to replace them periodically).

- Measured from two opposite diagonal corners, size for CRT monitors is not usually the same as the viewable image size. A 17-inch CRT monitor might have only a 15.5-inch VIS. Because LCD monitors report only VIS, a 15-inch LCD monitor may have approximately the same viewing area as a 17-inch CRT.

- CRT monitors require two connectors: a 15-pin, three-row DB connector and a power plug. Video cards use a RAMDAC, which takes the digital signal from the video card and turns it into an analog signal for the CRT. LCD monitors require a digital signal. Analog LCD monitors reverse the effects of the RAMDAC so you can plug your LCD monitor into the 15-pin VGA connector on the video card.

- The DVI standard allows the digital signal from the PC to be used by the LCD monitor without any digital-to-analog-and-back-to-digital conversion. The DVI standard includes DVI-D, DVI-A, and DVI-I. Both DVI-D and DVI-I come in single-link and dual-link varieties, with dual-link offering significantly higher resolutions.

- Monitors have adjustment controls for brightness, contrast, image size and position, and color adjustment. These controls are usually accessed via an onboard menu system rather than with hardware knobs or dials.

- A CRT monitor accounts for about half of the power consumption of a desktop PC. Monitors using the VESA standard for power-management signaling can cut monitor power consumption by about 75 percent. An LCD monitor uses less than half the electricity a CRT uses.

Select the proper video card

- The video card has two major pieces: the video RAM and the video processing circuitry. The video RAM stores the video image, and the processing circuitry is similar to that of your computer's CPU.

- The combination of a specific resolution and color depth is referred to as a mode. The VGA mode is defined by a resolution of 640 × 480 and 4-bit color depth (16 colors). Modern video cards and monitors are capable of supporting many modes.

- Using more color depth slows down video functions. PCI slots maxed out at a bandwidth of 132 MBps. The Accelerated Graphics Port (AGP) is better suited for video than PCI because it resides alone on its own bus, pipelines commands, and supports sidebanding and system memory access.

- AGP has undergone several specification upgrades, and the cards are normally referred to by their strobe multiplier. Although you can mix some AGP specifications, it is best to use an AGP card that is fully supported by your motherboard.

- PCI Express video cards are becoming more popular and may soon replace AGP on all new systems. Like AGP, PCI Express supports sidebanding and system memory access, but it uses a faster serial communication method than that of the parallel communication method used by AGP.

- Video cards are identified by their manufacturer, model number, graphic processor, and amount of video RAM. Although a number of companies produce video cards, the two major manufacturers of graphics processors are NVIDIA and ATI. The most important decision when buying a video card is the graphics processor, especially if you play 3-D games where texture and layering are important considerations.

- To overcome the bottlenecks of data throughput speed, access speed, and capacity of video RAM, manufacturers use specialized fast RAM and more and more total RAM. Video memory technologies include VRAM, WRAM, SGRAM, DDR SDRAM,

DDR2 SDRAM, GDDR3 SDRAM, GDDR4 SDRAM, and GDDR5 SDRAM.

Describe how to implement sound in a PC

- The process by which sounds are stored in electronic format on your PC is called sampling. Sampling means capturing the state or quality of a particular sound wave a set number of times each second. All the characteristics of a particular sound wave—amplitude, frequency, timbre—need to be recorded and translated into ones and zeros to reproduce that sound accurately within the computer and out to your speakers. Sounds are sampled thousands of times per second. The amount of information stored at each sampling is called the bit depth, and the higher the bit depth, the better the recording.

- The popular WAV file format (as well as most other recorded sound formats) is based on PCM. WAV files can be huge, especially when sampled at high frequency and depth, so compression is a popular way to reduce the file size of recorded sounds. The most popular compressed file type is MP3.

- To play sounds, you must have some form of player software, such as Windows Media Player. Not all players can play all types of sound files. Some file formats, such as RealMedia, require their own proprietary players.

- MIDI files are not recordings like WAV files. A MIDI file is a text file that takes advantage of the sound processing hardware to enable the PC to produce sound. Programmers use these small files to tell the sound card what notes to play, how long, how loud, on which instruments, and so forth.

- Sound cards use either FM synthesis or wave table synthesis to store notes for MIDI. FM synthesis electronically simulates various instruments, whereas wave table synthesis uses pre-recorded instruments.

- A large number of other sound file formats are available, such as AAC and WMA. Sounds can also be found in video formats, applications, and streaming media, such as the Flash videos on YouTube.

- Low-end sound processors do little more than translate, which means that the CPU has to do the heavy lifting on the processing front. Better sound processors, in contrast, shoulder much of the processing burden and bring a series of extra features to the table. Most mid-range and all high-end sound

processors offer support for various surround sound standards, enabling equally equipped games and other applications to provide positional audio effects and detailed sound modeling.

- Every sound card supports two speakers or a pair of headphones, but many better sound cards support five or more speakers in discrete channels. These multiple speakers provide surround sound and thumping bass through a subwoofer.

- Better sound cards have a lower signal-to-noise ratio and support for multiple audio connections, such as a microphone, line in, and S/PDIF. The latter is for high-end audio.

- Speaker standards include stereo (which uses a left speaker and a right speaker), 2.1 (stereo with an additional subwoofer), and surround sound. Do yourself or your client a favor and spend the extra money for good speakers. They don't cost that much more than cheap speakers and they make an enormous difference for the user experience.

- Surround sound is popular for games and DVD/Blu-ray movies. A number of surround sound standards exist, but the most common are Dolby Digital and DTS. The Dolby Digital and DTS standards both require at least five speakers and a subwoofer.

Explain the function of video capture cards and TV tuners

- To capture video from a source requires you to have the proper hardware installed to provide an interface with the camcorder or video player and, if the source is analog, to provide translation of the signal as well. You also need a properly configured application to do the capturing.

- With a fully digital device, you can capture directly to the PC by using a FireWire or USB connection. With analog devices, you need some sort of translation hardware.

- A computer dedicated to video capture and editing needs to be a pretty stout machine, with lots of hard drive space and RAM. The capture and editing software has a major role in determining the quality of the capture and any subsequent video.

- A video is two or more separate tracks—moving picture and audio—that each go through a compression algorithm. The compressed tracks then get wrapped up into a container file or wrapper. A video can be compressed in one of the standard audio codecs, such as MP3, and one of many video codecs, such as H.264. The wrapper can likewise be one of many styles, such as AVI.

- To set up a PC to view television signals requires several components: a tuner device, an antenna or cable connection, a tuning application, and some

sort of program guide. Tuner hardware comes in many forms, such as PCI expansion cards and USB devices. Tuner devices come with a standard coaxial jack for connecting an exterior antenna or cable or satellite connection. Companies bundle specific tuner software and program guides with their cards.

■ Key Terms

2.1 *(448)*

5.1 *(449)*

AC'97 *(445)*

Accelerated Graphics Port (AGP) *(434)*

active matrix *(421)*

amplitude *(441)*

anti-aliasing *(423)*

aspect ratio *(416)*

backlight *(422)*

bandwidth *(417)*

bit depth *(441)*

cathode ray tube (CRT) *(413)*

CD quality *(441)*

codec *(442)*

cold cathode fluorescent lamp (CCFL) *(422)*

color depth *(431)*

container file *(452)*

decibels *(446)*

degauss *(417)*

Digital Theatre Systems (DTS) *(449)*

digital visual interface (DVI) *(428)*

DirectSound3D (DS3D) *(450)*

DirectX *(449)*

display adapter *(412)*

display power management signaling (DPMS) *(429)*

Dolby Digital *(449)*

dot pitch *(416)*

dual-scan passive matrix *(421)*

environmental audio extensions (EAX) *(450)*

FM synthesis *(442)*

frequency *(441)*

front-view projector *(425)*

horizontal refresh rate (HRR) *(414)*

Intel High Definition Audio (HDA) *(445)*

inverter *(422)*

liquid crystal display (LCD) *(418)*

lumen *(426)*

mode *(432)*

monaural *(441)*

monitor *(412)*

MP3 *(442)*

musical instrument digital interface (MIDI) *(442)*

native resolution *(423)*

nit *(423)*

passive matrix *(421)*

PCI Express (PCIe) *(436)*

persistence *(413)*

phosphor *(415)*

pixel *(415)*

polyphony *(442)*

positional audio *(450)*

projector *(424)*

pulse code modulation (PCM) *(441)*

random access memory digital-to-analog converter (RAMDAC) *(427)*

raster line *(414)*

rear-view projector *(424)*

resolution *(415)*

response rate *(423)*

sampling *(441)*

satellite *(448)*

shadow mask *(415)*

sidebanding *(435)*

signal-to-noise ratio *(446)*

Sony/Philips Digital Interface (S/PDIF) *(449)*

stereo *(441)*

streaming media *(444)*

sub-pixel *(420)*

subwoofer *(446)*

thin film transistor (TFT) *(421)*

throw *(426)*

timbre *(441)*

triad *(416)*

TV tuner *(454)*

vertical refresh rate (VRR) *(414)*

video capture *(451)*

video display *(412)*
video graphics array (VGA) *(433)*
viewable image size (VIS) *(426)*

wave table synthesis *(442)*
wrapper *(452)*

■ Key Term Quiz

Use the Key Terms list to complete the sentences that follow. Not all terms will be used.

1. 44.1-KHz stereo is also known as _____ audio.

2. The most common compressed audio format is _____.

3. A series of instructions telling a computer how to read a compressed file is called a(n) _____.

4. To enable a computer to record full motion video and sound, use _____.

5. You can view television channels on your computer by using a(n) _____.

6. Using an aspect ratio of 4:3, the _____ refers to the number of horizontal pixels times the number of vertical pixels.

7. The _____ bus, designed specifically for video cards, connects directly to the Northbridge, but has for the most part been phased out in favor of the _____ bus.

8. The number of sweeps or raster lines that the electron guns make across the screen is called the _____, while the time it takes to draw the entire screen is called the _____.

■ Multiple-Choice Quiz

1. Which of the following resolutions will produce the best-quality picture on the monitor (assuming the monitor is capable of displaying the resolutions well)?

    A. 640 × 480

    B. 800 × 600

    C. 1024 × 768

    D. 1280 × 1024

2. CRT monitors attach to the video card by using a _____ connector.

    A. 9-pin, 2-row, DB

    B. 36-pin Centronics

    C. 15-pin, 3-row, DB

    D. 25-pin, 2-row, DB

3. Which of these dot pitch numbers indicates a better-quality monitor?

    A. .39

    B. .31

    C. .28

    D. .23

4. What advantages do LCD monitors offer over CRT monitors?

    A. Better color and more contrast

    B. Energy efficiency and no emission of potentially harmful radiation

    C. Electron guns fire CMYK instead of RGB

    D. Both A and B

5. CD-quality sound samples are recorded at 44 KHz, with 16-bit depth and what else?

    A. Monaural

    B. Stereo

    C. 5.1

    D. 2.1

6. What is the most common compressed sound format?

    A. MP3

    B. WAV

    C. VOC

    D. TXT

7. Which component of DirectX offered only a range of commands to place a sound anywhere in 3-D space?

   A. DirectSound

   B. DirectSound3D

   C. EAX

   D. A3D

8. What is the name of the direct competitor to Dolby Digital?

   A. DirectSound

   B. DirectSound3D

   C. DTS

   D. Surround Sound

9. To what does the .1 in 5.1 or 2.1 refer?

   A. Volumetric sound positioning

   B. Subwoofer

   C. Subchannels

   D. Reverb positional matrices

■ Essay Quiz

1. Your company is getting ready to replace their computers and monitors. You would like to see all of the new PCs come with LCD monitors. Write a memo to your boss that talks about the advantages of LCD monitors over CRT monitors, but also mentions the advantages of CRTs over LCDs.

2. Detail in your own words how you think sound aided the evolution of the computer. What aspects of sound are necessary to computers? Why is sound needed?

3. Write an essay on the kind of TV tuner you would need for your computer. Detail what you personally would like to accomplish with your computer and how a TV tuner card would help you.

Lab Projects

• Lab Project 13.1

If you just received a $500 bonus and decided to buy a new video system for your computer, what would you select? Go to the local computer store or to Web sites such as www.newegg.com and pick out the best combination of monitor and video card that you can buy with your bonus. Now imagine that you also received a $200 birthday gift and have decided to purchase an even better graphics card and monitor. Which ones will you select now that you have $700 to spend?

• Lab Project 13.2

Take a tour of the Web site for Creative Labs: www.creative.com. What sound-related products are currently featured there? Check out the specs for Creative's various SoundBlaster cards. Do you see sound cards that use an interface other than PCI? Which features are available only on high-end cards? Which model would you choose to upgrade your current system? Which would you choose if you were building a new system?

Learning Portable Computing

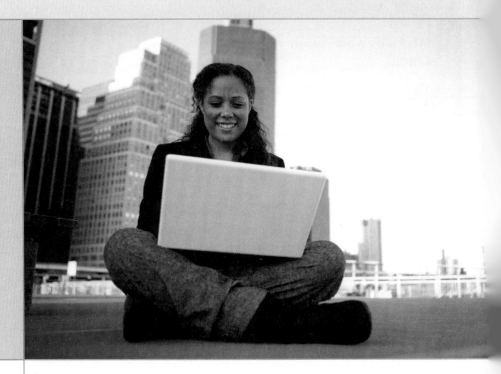

"The great thing about a computer notebook is that no matter how much you stuff into it, it doesn't get bigger or heavier."

—BILL GATES, *BUSINESS @ THE SPEED OF THOUGHT*

In this chapter, you will learn how to

- **Describe the many types of portable computing devices available**
- **Manage and maintain portable computers**
- **Troubleshoot portable computers**

There are times when the walls close in, when you need a change of scenery to get that elusive spark that inspires greatness...or sometimes you just need to get away from your coworkers for a few hours because they're driving you nuts! For many occupations, that's difficult to do. You must have access to your documents and spreadsheets; you can't function without e-mail or the Internet. In short, you need a computer to get your job done.

Portable computing devices combine mobility with accessibility to bring you the best of both worlds; put more simply, portables let you take some or even all of your computing capabilities with you when you go. Some portable computers feature Windows XP/Vista/7 systems with all the bells and whistles and all your Microsoft Office apps for a seamless transition from desk to café table. Even the smallest portable devices enable you to check your appointments and address book, or surf the Web during the endless wait at the doctor's office. This chapter takes an in-depth look at portables, first going through the major variations you'll run into and then hitting the tech-specific topic of maintaining portable computers. Let's get started!

Portable Computing Devices

Note that this chapter does not have a Historical/Conceptual section. Everything in here is on the CompTIA A+ Essentials exam, so pay attention!

All portable devices share certain features. For output, they have LCD screens, although these vary from 20-inch behemoths to microscopic 2-inch screens. Portable computing devices employ sound of varying quality, from simple beeps to fairly nice music reproductions. All of them run on DC electricity stored in batteries, although several different technologies offer a range of battery life, lifespan, and cost. Other than screen, sound, and battery, portable computing devices come in an amazing variety of shapes, sizes, and intended uses.

LCD Screens

Laptops come in a variety of sizes and at varying costs. One major contributor to the overall cost of a laptop is the size of the LCD screen. Most laptops offer a range between 12-inch to 17-inch screens (measured diagonally), while a few offer just over 20-inch screens. Not only are screens getting larger, but also wider screens have become the status quo.

Cross Check

LCD Monitors

Stretching back to the early days of mobile computing, almost every make and model of portable device has used an LCD monitor of some shape or size. You know all about LCD monitors from Chapter 13, "Learning Video and Multimedia." Everything that applies to desktop LCDs applies to screens designed for portable devices as well, so turn to Chapter 13 and cross check your knowledge. What are the variations of LCD screen you'll find today? Which technology offers the best picture? What connectors do you find with LCDs? Are there any special rules about cleaning LCD monitors? (Talk about a leading question!)

Many manufacturers are phasing out the standard 4:3 aspect ratio screen in favor of the widescreen format. **Aspect ratio** is the comparison of the screen width to the screen height. Depending on screen resolution, widescreens can have varying aspect ratios of 10:6, 16:9, 16:9.5, or 16:10. The 16:9 aspect ratio is the standard for widescreen TVs and 16:10 is the standard widescreen computer display.

Laptop LCD screens come in a variety of supported resolutions, described with acronyms such as XGA, WXGA, WSXGA, and more. The *W* in front of the letters indicates widescreen. Table 14.1 lists commonly supported laptop display resolutions.

Laptop screens come with two types of finish: **matte** and **high gloss**. The matte finish was the industry standard for many years and offered a good trade-off between richness of colors and reflection or glare. The better

Table 14.1	Screen Resolutions	
Acronym	**Name**	**Native Resolution**
XGA	eXtended Graphics Array	1024 × 768
WXGA (16x10)	Wide eXtended Graphics Array	1280 × 800
WXGA (16x9)	Wide eXtended Graphics Array	1366 × 768
SXGA	Super eXtended Graphics Array	1280 × 1024
SXGA+	Super eXtended Graphics Array Plus	1400 × 1050
WSXGA+	Widescreen SXGA Plus	1680 × 1050
UXGA	Ultra eXtended Graphics Array	1600 × 1200
WUXGA	Widescreen UXGA	1920 × 1200

screens have a wide viewing angle and decent response time. The major drawback for matte-finished laptop screens is that they wash out a lot in bright light. Using such a laptop at an outdoor café, for example, is almost hopeless during daylight.

Manufacturers released high-gloss laptop screens in 2006, and they've rapidly taken over many store shelves. The high-gloss finish offers sharper contrast, richer colors, and wider viewing angles when compared to the matte screens. Each manufacturer has a different name for high-gloss coatings. Dell calls theirs TrueLife, Acer calls theirs CrystalBrite, and HP calls theirs BrightView. The drawback to the high-gloss screens is that, contrary to what the manufacturers claim, they pick up lots of reflection from nearby objects, including the user! So although they're usable outside during the day, you'll need to contend with increased reflection as well.

Desktop Replacements

When asked about portable computing devices, most folks describe the traditional clamshell **laptop** computer, such as the one shown in Figure 14.1, with built-in LCD monitor, keyboard, and input device (a *touchpad*, in this case). A typical laptop computer functions as a fully standalone PC, potentially even replacing the desktop. The laptop shown in Figure 14.1, for example, has all of the features you expect the modern PC to have, such as a fast CPU, lots of RAM, a high-capacity hard drive, CD-RW and DVD drives, an excellent sound system, and a functioning copy of Windows. Attach it to a network and you can browse the Internet and send e-mail. Considering that it weighs almost as much as a mini-tower PC (or at least it feels like it does when I'm lugging it through the airport!), such a portable can be considered a **desktop replacement**, because it does everything most people want to do with a desktop PC and doesn't compromise performance just to make the laptop a few pounds lighter or the battery last an extra hour.

• **Figure 14.1**   A notebook PC

To get around not having a desktop's full-size keyboard, most portables have a special Function (FN) key on the keyboard that, when pressed, adds an additional option to certain keys on the keyboard. Figure 14.2 shows a

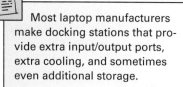
Most laptop manufacturers make docking stations that provide extra input/output ports, extra cooling, and sometimes even additional storage.

• **Figure 14.2**   Laptop keyboard showing Function (FN) key that enables you to access additional key options, as on the F2 key

close-up of a typical keyboard with the Function key; note the other options you can access with the Function key, such as indicated on the F2 key.

For input devices, desktop replacements (and other portables) used trackballs in the early days, often plugged in like a mouse and clipped to the side of the case. Other models with trackballs placed them in front of the keyboard at the edge of the case nearest the user, or behind the keyboard at the edge nearest the screen.

The next wave to hit the laptop market was IBM's **TrackPoint** device, a joystick the size of a pencil eraser, situated in the center of the keyboard. With the TrackPoint, you can move the pointer around without taking your fingers away from the "home" typing position. You use a forefinger to push the joystick around, and then click or right-click, using two buttons below the SPACEBAR. This type of pointing device has since been licensed for use by other manufacturers, and it continues to appear on laptops today.

But by far the most common laptop pointing device found today is the **touchpad** (Figure 14.3)—a flat, touch-sensitive pad just in front of the keyboard. To operate a touchpad, you simply glide your finger across its surface to move the pointer, and tap the surface once or twice to single- or double-click. You can also click by using buttons just below the pad. Most people get the hang of this technique after just a few minutes of practice. The main advantage of the touchpad over previous laptop pointing devices is that it uses no moving parts—a fact that can really extend the life of a hard-working laptop. Some modern laptops actually provide both a TrackPoint-type device and a touchpad, to give the user a choice.

Tech Tip

What's In a Name?
No industry standard exists for the vast majority of styles of portable computing devices, so manufacturers let their marketing folks have fun with naming. What's the difference between a portable, a laptop, and a notebook? Nothing. One manufacturer might call its four-pound portable system with a 12-inch LCD a notebook, while another manufacturer might call its much larger desktop-replacement portable a notebook as well. A laptop refers in general to the clamshell, keyboard-on-the-bottom and LCD-screen-at-the-top design that is considered the shape of mobile PCs.

Desktop Extenders

Manufacturers offer **desktop extender** portable devices that don't replace the desktop but rather extend it by giving you a subset of features of the typical desktop that you can take away from the desk. Figure 14.4 shows a portable with a good but small 13.4-inch-wide screen. The system has 2 GB of RAM, a 2-GHz processor, a 60-GB hard drive, and a battery that enables you to do work on it for more than five hours while disconnected from the wall socket. Even though it plays music and has a couple of decent tiny speakers, you can't game on this computer (Solitaire, perhaps, but definitely not Crysis!). But it weighs only five pounds, nearly half the weight of the typical desktop replacement portable.

Desktop extenders enable you to go mobile. When I'm on a roll writing, for example, I don't want to stop. But sometimes I do want to take a break from the office and stroll over to my favorite café for a latté or a pint of fine ale. At moments like these, I don't need a fully featured laptop with a monster 15- or 17-inch screen, but just a good word processing system—and perhaps the ability to surf the Internet on the café's wireless network so I can ~~goof off~~ research other important topics once I finish my project for the day. A lightweight laptop with a 12- or 13-inch screen, a reasonably fast processor, and gobs of RAM does nicely.

• **Figure 14.3** Touchpad on a laptop

• **Figure 14.4**   Excellent mid-sized portable computer

Netbooks

Netbooks are computers that fill the gap between PDAs and the smaller laptops. These machines usually have displays in the 6- to 10-inch range, modest-sized hard drives, and CPUs geared more for minimal power usage than raw speed. With netbooks, the focus is on small size and low price compared to their more full-featured cousins. This segment of the market is ever evolving, though, and there is quite a bit of blurring between the various classes of laptops.

A prime example of the netbook is the Asus Eee PC, shown in Figure 14.5 sitting on a full-sized laptop. This netbook has a 9-inch screen, a 1.6-GHz Intel Atom CPU, a small solid-state drive, and runs a customized Linux distribution. A key distinguishing feature of these netbooks is the use of Intel's Atom processor. The Atom CPU is very useful for keeping power usage down but has much less computing power than its more power-hungry siblings.

• **Figure 14.5**   Asus Eee PC sitting on a normal laptop

Therefore, most netbooks run either Windows XP or some form of Linux that is better suited for their limited resources.

PDAs and Smartphones

Having a few computing essentials on hand at all times eases the day and makes planning and scheduling much more likely to succeed. Several companies, such as Palm, Apple, HTC, RIM, and Hewlett-Packard, manufacture tiny handheld portable computing devices that hold such data as your address book, appointment schedules, music, movies, and more. Such machines are called **personal digital assistants (PDAs)**, or smartphones if they have calling capabilities. All modern PDAs have many applications, such as Web browsers for surfing the Web on the go, some sort of note-taking application for jotting down quick notes, and many more. Figure 14.6 shows an Apple iPhone smartphone.

PDAs don't run Windows XP or Vista but rather require specialized OSes such as Windows Mobile, Google Android, Apple iPhone OS, Palm WebOS, and various forms of Linux. All of these OSes provide a GUI that enables you to interact with the device by touching the screen directly. Many of today's PDAs use handwriting recognition combined with modified mouse functions, usually in the form of a pen-like **stylus** to make a type of input called **pen-based computing**. To make an application load, for example, you would slide the stylus out of its holder in the PDA case and touch the appropriate icon with the stylus tip.

At the time that this book went to press, some netbooks had started shipping with Windows 7 Starter OS, a stripped-down version of Windows 7 designed to use resources such as RAM and CPU processing as lightly as possible.

• **Figure 14.6**   Apple iPhone

Sync

PDAs make excellent pocket companions because you can quickly add a client's address or telephone number, verify the day's schedule before going to your next meeting, and check your e-mail. Best of all, you can then update all the equivalent features on your desktop PC automatically! PDAs synchronize with your primary PC so you have the same essential data on both machines. Many PDAs come with a cradle, a place to rest your PDA and recharge its battery. The cradle connects to the PC most often through a USB port. You can run software to synchronize the data between the PDA and the main PC. Setting up for a PDA running Windows Mobile, for example, requires you to install a program called Activesync if you're using Windows XP. Vista and Windows 7 drop Activesync and use the built-in *Windows Mobile Device Center* (*WMDC*). This software handles all the synchronization chores. You simply place the PDA in the properly connected cradle to synchronize. Figure 14.7 shows a PDA in the middle of a sync operation.

Sadly, the heavy Windows-only attitude of the CompTIA A+ exams means you won't get any questions about the Apple iPhone. All the same, the iPhone is a *great* example of what a smartphone should be; I own one.

PDA to PDA Communication

Just about every PDA comes with a way to move data from one PDA to another. The original technology for this is called IrDA and the process is called *beaming*. IrDA uses infrared light just like a TV remote to transmit the data between devices. You can use beaming to quickly transfer contact info or small pictures, but larger files take much longer because of IrDA's slow speed.

• **Figure 14.7**   A sync operation

Chapter 17, "Learning Wireless," goes into more detail on all these technologies.

• **Figure 14.8**   SD and Micro SD cards

Tech Tip

Memory Cards

Memory cards made the leap in 2003 from the exclusive realm of tiny devices such as PDAs and digital photographic cameras to full-featured portable PCs and even desktop models. Many laptop PCs sport SD card slots, for example, and you can expect nearly every Sony PC—portable or otherwise—made in 2003 and later to offer a Memory Stick port.

Today, the primary way to move data between PDAs is with radio waves, be it Bluetooth, Wi-Fi, or what CompTIA calls **Cellular WAN**. Bluetooth can be thought of as the most direct replacement for the old IrDA tech. When you wish to transfer files between two Bluetooth devices, you first make each device *discoverable*, which allows other devices in the area to see that it exists. On the sending device, you then select the PDA you wish to send to. The receiving device asks you if you wish to accept the file, and once that's granted, you simply stand there and wait for a moment while the PDAs transfer data. Slick!

With Wi-Fi and Cellular WAN, your PDA acts just like any other computer on a network. You will have an IP address and—depending on the OS your PDA is running—the capability to share files and data. Most PDAs today use a touch screen for entering data and use IrDA, Wi-Fi, and/or Bluetooth connections to communicate with other devices.

PDA Storage

Almost every PDA has both internal flash ROM memory of 1 MB or more and some sort of removable and upgradeable storage medium. Secure Digital (SD) technology has the strongest market share among the many competing standards, but you'll find a bunch of different memory card types out there. SD is by far the most popular, with the cards coming in a variety of physical sizes (SD, Mini SD, and Micro SD) and fitting in a special SD slot. You'll find capacities ranging from 4 MB up to 32 GB—on a card the size of a postage stamp! Figure 14.8 shows some typical memory cards.

Tablet PCs

Tablet PCs combine the handwriting benefits of PDAs with the full-fledged power of traditional portable PCs to create a machine that perfectly meets the needs of many professions. Unlike PDAs and smartphones, tablet PCs use a full-featured PC operating system such as Microsoft Vista Home Premium and up.

Instead of (or in addition to) a keyboard and mouse, tablet PCs provide a screen that doubles as an input device. With a special pen, called a *stylus*, you can actually write on the screen (Figure 14.9). Just make sure you don't grab your fancy Cross ballpoint pen accidentally and start writing on the screen! Unlike many PDA screens, most tablet PC screens are not pressure sensitive—you have to use the stylus to write on the screen. Tablet PCs come in two main form factors: *convertibles*, which include a keyboard that you can fold out of the way, and *slates*, which do away with the keyboard entirely. The convertible tablet PC in Figure 14.9, for example, looks and functions just like the typical clamshell laptop shown back in Figure 14.1. But here it's shown with the screen rotated 180 degrees and snapped flat so it functions as a slate. Pretty slick!

In applications that aren't "tablet-aware," the stylus acts just like a mouse, enabling you to select items, double-click, right-click, and so on. To input text with the stylus, you can either tap keys on a virtual keyboard (Figure 14.10), write in the writing utility

• **Figure 14.9**   A tablet PC

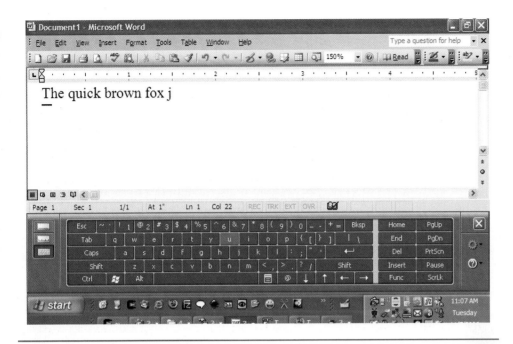

● **Figure 14.10**   The virtual keyboard

(Figure 14.11), or use speech recognition software. With a little practice, most users find the computer's accuracy in recognizing their handwriting to be sufficient for most text input, although speedy touch-typists will probably still want to use a keyboard when typing longer documents.

Tablet PCs work well when you have limited space or have to walk around and use a laptop. Anyone who has ever tried to type with one hand while walking around the factory floor and holding the laptop with the other hand will immediately appreciate the beauty of a tablet PC. In this

Tech Tip

Power Corrupts, and in This Case, It's Good
Handwriting recognition and speech recognition are two technologies that benefit greatly from increased CPU power. As multicore CPUs become more common, get ready to see more widespread adoption of these technologies.

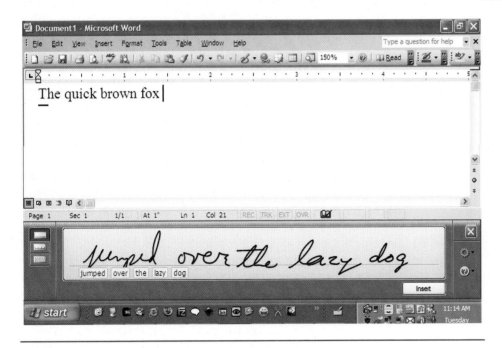

● **Figure 14.11**   The writing pad

scenario, tablet PCs are most effective when combined with applications designed to be used with a stylus instead of a keyboard. An inventory control program, for example, might present drop-down lists and radio buttons to the user, making a stylus the perfect input tool. With the right custom application, tablet PCs become indispensable tools.

Microsoft encourages software developers to take advantage of a feature they call *digital ink*, which allows applications to accept pen strokes as input without first converting the pen strokes into text or mouse-clicks. In Microsoft Journal, which comes with Windows-based tablet PCs, you can write on the screen just as though you were writing on a paper legal pad (Figure 14.12). Many other applications, including Microsoft Office, allow

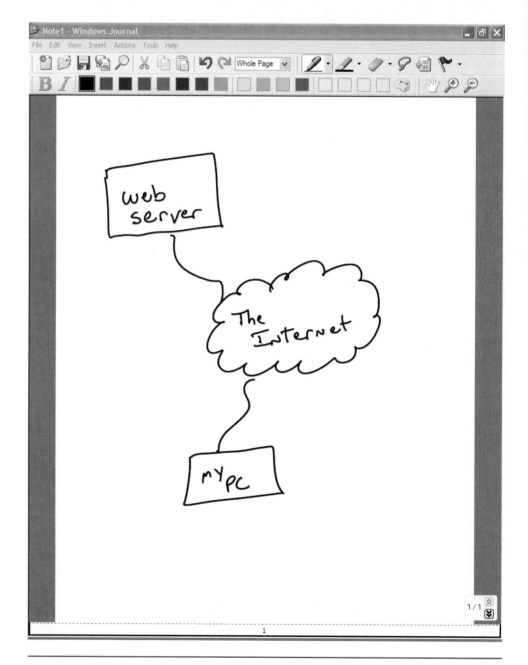

• **Figure 14.12**   Microsoft Journal preserves pen strokes as digital ink.

Mike Meyers' CompTIA A+ Guide: Essentials

you to add ink annotations. Imagine sitting on an airplane reviewing a Microsoft Word document and simply scribbling your comments on the screen (Figure 14.13). No more printing out hard copy and breaking out the red pen for me! Imagine running a PowerPoint presentation and being able to annotate your presentation as you go. In the future, look for more applications to support Microsoft's digital ink.

Many useful third-party applications are designed specifically to take advantage of the tablet PC form factor. In fields such as law and medicine, where tablet PCs have been especially popular, the choices are endless. One handy

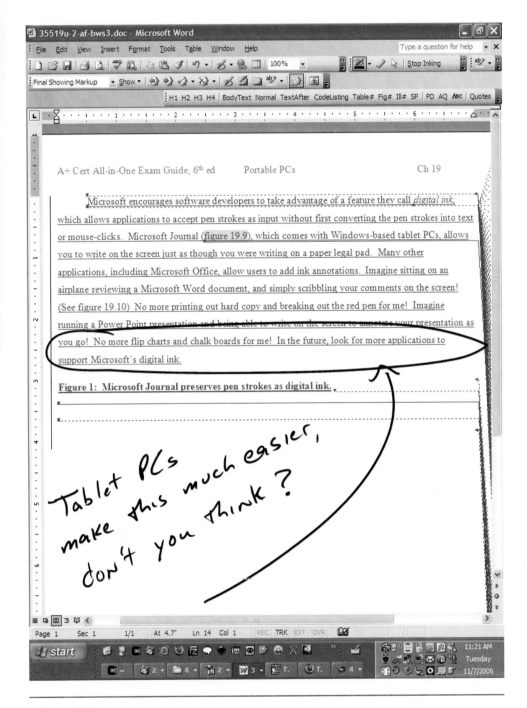

• **Figure 14.13**   Microsoft Office supports digital ink.

Chapter 14: Learning Portable Computing

free utility that anyone who spends time in front of an audience (teachers, salespeople, cult leaders, and so on) will appreciate is InkyBoard (www.cfcassidy.com/Inkyboard). InkyBoard provides a virtual dry-erase board, eliminating the need to find a flip chart or dry-erase board when holding meetings. Ever wished you could have a record of everything that was written on the chalkboard in a class (or business meeting)? If the professor had used InkyBoard, creating and distributing a copy would be a snap.

Portable Computer Device Types

Sorting through all the variations of portable computing devices out there would take entirely too much ink (and go well beyond CompTIA A+). Table 14.2 lists the seven most common styles of portable computing devices, some of their key features, and the intended use or audience for the product. This table is in no way comprehensive, but lists the highlights.

Table 14.2	Portable Computing Devices			
	Screen Size	**Weight**	**Features**	**Uses**
Desktop replacements	14–20 inch+	8–12+ lbs	Everything on a desktop.	Mobile multimedia editing, presentations, mobile gaming.
Desktop extenders	10–14 inch	4–7 lbs	Almost everything you'll find on a desktop. Better battery life than desktop replacements.	Presentations, note-taking in class or meetings, traveling companion for business folks.
Netbooks	6–10 inch	2–3 lbs	Ultimate mobility without sacrificing full PC status. Excellent battery life. No optical drives, limited SSD storage or modest HDD storage.	Long-term traveling companion and small enough to fit in a purse or backpack. Perfect for Web browsing or doing e-mail on the road.
Tablet PCs	10–12 inch	4 lbs	Pen-based interface so you can use them like a paper notepad; no optical drives but integrated wireless networking.	Niche market for people who need handwritten notes that have to be transcribed to the PC.
Ultra mobile PCs	4–7 inch	1–2 lbs	A variation of tablet PCs, UMPCs have Windows XP (Tablet or Home edition), pen-based or touch pad interface, and no optical drives.	More of a niche market than tablet PCs, UMPCs have been overshadowed by netbooks.
PDAs	Up to 4 inches	1 lb	Light, multifunctional devices that carry address book, scheduler, and such features as MP3 and video playback.	Help busy people stay organized. Classic PDAs (without telephone functions) are rare today except for specialized uses (hospitals, point-of-sale).
Smartphones	Up to 4 inches	< 1 lb	Tiny PDAs built into a cell phone; offer Web browsing, SMS, and other Internet connectivity features.	Reduce the number of gadgets some folks carry. Have all but replaced standard PDAs.

Variations

Portables come in such a dizzying variety of sizes, styles, features, and shapes that a simple table in a book cannot do justice to the ingenuity and engineering of the manufacturers of these devices. Only a hands-on field trip can bring home the point for you, so Try This!

1. Visit your local computer or electronics store and tour the portable computing devices.

2. How many variations of laptops are there? Do any offer funky features, such as a swivel screen, portrait-to-landscape mode, or touch screen capabilities?

3. How many variations of PDA do you see? What operating systems do they run?

4. What other devices do you find? What about tablet PCs?

5. If you want to wander into the realm of extremes, check out www.dynamism.com. This company specializes in bringing Japanese-only products to the English-speaking market. You'll find the hottest desktop replacement laptops and the sleekest subnotebooks at the site, with all the details beautifully converted from native Japanese to English.

■ Managing and Maintaining Portable Computers

Most portable PCs come from the factory solidly built and configured. Manufacturers know that few techs outside their factories know enough to work on them, so they don't cut corners. From a tech's standpoint, your most common work on managing and maintaining portables involves taking care of the batteries and extending the battery life through proper power management, keeping the machine clean, and avoiding excessive heat.

Everything you normally do to maintain a PC applies to portable PCs. You need to keep current on Windows patches and service packs and use stable, recent drivers. Run Check Disk with some frequency, and definitely defragment the hard drive. Disk Cleanup is a must if the laptop runs Windows XP or Windows Vista. That said, let's look at issues specifically involving portables.

Batteries

Manufacturers use three types of batteries for portable PCs, and each battery type has its own special needs and quirks. Once you have a clear understanding of the quirks, you can *usually* spot and fix battery problems. The three types of batteries commonly used in mobile PCs are **Nickel-Cadmium (Ni-Cd)**, **Nickel-Metal Hydride (Ni-MH)**, and **Lithium-Ion (Li-Ion)** batteries. Manufacturers have also started working with **fuel cell** batteries, although most of that work is experimental at this writing.

You *must* use disposal companies or battery recycling services to dispose of the highly toxic Ni-Cd batteries.

● Figure 14.15   Ni-MH battery

Nickel-Cadmium

Ni-Cds were the first batteries commonly used in mobile PCs, which means the technology was full of little problems. Probably most irritating was a little thing called **battery memory**, or the tendency of a Ni-Cd battery to lose a significant amount of its rechargeability if it was charged repeatedly without being totally discharged. A battery that originally kept a laptop running for two hours would eventually only keep that same laptop going for 30 minutes or less. Figure 14.14 shows a typical Ni-Cd battery.

To prevent memory problems, a Ni-Cd battery had to be discharged completely before each recharging. Recharging was tricky as well, because Ni-Cd batteries disliked being overcharged. Unfortunately, there was no way to verify when a battery was fully charged without an expensive charging machine, which none of us had. As a result, most Ni-Cd batteries lasted an extremely short time before having to be replaced. A quick fix was to purchase a **conditioning charger**. These chargers would first totally discharge the Ni-Cd battery and then generate a special "reverse" current that, in a way, cleaned internal parts of the battery so it could be recharged more often and would run longer on each recharge. Ni-Cd batteries would, at best, last for 1000 charges, and far fewer with poor treatment. Ni-Cds were extremely susceptible to heat and would self-discharge over time if not used. Leaving a Ni-Cd in the car in the summer was guaranteed to result in a fully discharged battery in next to no time!

But Ni-Cd batteries didn't stop causing trouble after they died. The highly toxic metals inside the batteries made it unacceptable simply to throw them in the trash. Ni-Cd batteries should be disposed of via specialized disposal companies. This is very important! Even though Ni-Cd batteries aren't used in PCs very often anymore, many devices, such as cellular and cordless phones, still use Ni-Cd batteries. Don't trash the environment by tossing Ni-Cds in a landfill. Turn them in at the closest special disposal site; most recycling centers are glad to take them. Also, many battery manufacturers/distributors will take them. The environment you help preserve just might be yours—or your kids'!

Nickel-Metal Hydride

Ni-MH batteries (Figure 14.15) were the next generation of mobile PC batteries and are still quite common today. Basically, Ni-MH batteries are Ni-Cd batteries without most of the headaches. Ni-MH batteries are much less susceptible to memory problems, can tolerate overcharging better, can take more recharging, and can last longer between rechargings. Like Ni-Cds, Ni-MH batteries are susceptible to heat, but at least they are considered less toxic to the environment. A special disposal is still a good idea. Unlike Ni-Cds, it's usually better to recharge an Ni-MH with shallow recharges as opposed to a complete discharge/recharge. Ni-MH is a popular replacement battery for Ni-Cd systems.

Lithium-Ion

The most common type of battery used today is Li-Ion (Figure 14.16). Li-Ion batteries are powerful, completely immune to memory problems, and last at least twice as long as comparable Ni-MH batteries on one charge. Sadly, they can't handle as many charges as Ni-MH types, but today's users are usually more than glad to give up total battery lifespan in return for longer periods between charges. Li-Ion batteries will explode if they are overcharged, so all Li-Ion batteries sold with PCs have built-in circuitry to prevent accidental overcharging. Lithium batteries can only be used on systems designed to use them. They can't be used as replacement batteries.

• **Figure 14.16**   Li-Ion battery

Other Portable Power Sources

In an attempt to provide better maintenance for laptop batteries, manufacturers have developed a new type of battery called the **smart battery**. Smart batteries tell the computer when they need to be charged, conditioned, or replaced.

The Care and Feeding of Batteries

In general, keep in mind the following basics. First, always store batteries in a cool place. Although a freezer is in concept an excellent storage place, the moisture, metal racks, and food make it a bad idea. Second, use a charger for your Ni-Cd and Ni-MH batteries that also conditions the batteries; they'll last longer. Third, keep battery contacts clean with a little alcohol or just a dry cloth. Fourth, *never* handle a battery that has ruptured or broken; battery chemicals are very dangerous. Finally, always recycle old batteries.

Power Management

Many different parts are included in the typical laptop, and each part uses power. The problem with early laptops was that every one of these parts used power continuously, whether or not the system needed that device at that time. For example, the hard drive continued to spin even when it was not being accessed, and the LCD panel continued to display even when the user walked away from the machine.

The optimal situation would be a system where the user could instruct the PC to shut down unused devices selectively, preferably by defining a maximum period of inactivity that, when reached, would trigger the PC to shut down the inactive device. Longer periods of inactivity would eventually enable the entire

Try This!

Recycling Old Portable PC Batteries

Got an old portable PC battery lying around? Well, you need to get rid of it, and there are some pretty nasty chemicals in that battery, so you can't just throw it in the trash. Sooner or later, you'll probably need to deal with such a battery, so Try This!

1. Do an online search to find the battery recycling center nearest to you.

2. Sometimes, you can take old laptop batteries to an auto parts store that disposes of old car batteries—I know it sounds odd, but it's true! See if you can find one in your area that will do this.

3. Many cities offer a hazardous materials disposal or recycling service. Check to see if and how your local government will help you dispose of your old batteries.

system to shut itself down, leaving critical information loaded in RAM, ready to restart if a wake-up event (such as moving the mouse or pressing a key) told the system to restart. The system would have to be sensitive to potential hazards, such as shutting down in the middle of writing to a drive, and so on. Also, this feature could not add significantly to the cost of the PC. Clearly, a machine that could perform these functions would need specialized hardware, BIOS, and operating system to operate properly. This process of cooperation among the hardware, the BIOS, and the OS to reduce power use is known generically as *power management*.

System Management Mode

Intel began the process of power management with a series of new features built into the 386SX CPU. These new features not only enabled the CPU to slow down or stop its clock without erasing the register information, but also enabled power saving in peripherals. These features were collectively called **System Management Mode (SMM)**. All modern CPUs have SMM. Although a power-saving CPU was okay, power management was relegated to special "sleep" or "doze" buttons that would stop the CPU and all of the peripherals on the laptop. To take real advantage of SMM, the system needed a specialized BIOS and OS to go with the SMM CPU. To this end, Intel put forward the **Advanced Power Management (APM)** specification in 1992 and the **Advanced Configuration and Power Interface (ACPI)** standard in 1996.

Requirements for APM/ACPI

To function fully, APM and ACPI require a number of items. First is an SMM-capable CPU. As virtually all CPUs are SMM-capable, this is easy. Second is an APM-compliant BIOS that enables the CPU to shut off the peripherals when desired. The third requirement is devices that will accept being shut off. These devices are usually called Energy Star devices, which signals their compliance with the EPA's Energy Star standard. To be an Energy Star device, a peripheral must be able to shut down without actually turning off and be able to show that it uses much less power than the non–Energy Star equivalent. Last, the system's OS must know how to request that a particular device be shut down, and the CPU's clock must be slowed down or stopped.

ACPI goes beyond the APM standard by supplying support for hot-swappable devices—always a huge problem with APM. This feature aside, it is a challenge to tell the difference between an APM system and an ACPI system at first glance.

APM/ACPI Levels

APM defined four power-usage operating levels for a system. These levels are intentionally fuzzy to give manufacturers considerable leeway in their use; the only real difference among them is the amount of time each takes to return to normal usage. These levels are as follows:

- **Full On**   Everything in the system is running at full power. There is no power management.

- **APM Enabled**   CPU and RAM are running at full power. Power management is enabled. An unused device may or may not be shut down.

Don't limit your perception of APM, ACPI, and Energy Star just to laptops. Virtually all desktop systems and many appliances also use the power management functions.

- **APM Standby** CPU is stopped. RAM still stores all programs. All peripherals are shut down, although configuration options are still stored. (In other words, to get back to APM Enabled, you won't have to reinitialize the devices.)

- **APM Suspend** Everything in the PC is shut down or at its lowest power-consumption setting. Many systems use a special type of Suspend called **hibernation**, where critical configuration information is written to the hard drive. Upon a wake-up event, the system is reinitialized, and the data is read from the drive to return the system to the APM Enabled mode. Clearly, the recovery time between Suspend and Enabled will be much longer than the time between Standby and Enabled.

ACPI, the successor to APM, handles all these levels plus a few more, such as "soft power on/off," that enables you to define the function of the power button. You should familiarize yourself with the following ACPI global (G) and sleeping (S) system power state specifications for both the CompTIA A+ Essentials exam and your own practical application:

- **G0 (S0)** Working state.

- **G1** Sleeping state mode. Further subdivided into four *S* states:

  - **S1** CPU stops processing. Power to CPU and memory (RAM) is maintained.

  - **S2** CPU is powered down.

  - **S3** Sleep or Standby mode. Power to RAM still on.

  - **S4** Hibernation mode. Information in RAM is stored to nonvolatile memory or drive and powered off.

- **G2 (S5)** Soft power off mode. Certain devices used to wake a system—such as keyboard, LAN, USB, and other devices—remain on, while most other components are powered to a mechanical off state (G3).

- **G3** Mechanical off mode. The system and all components, with the exception of the real-time clock (RTC), are completely powered down.

Configuration of APM/ACPI

You configure APM/ACPI via CMOS settings or through Windows. Windows settings override CMOS settings. Although the APM/ACPI standards permit a great deal of flexibility, which can create some confusion among different implementations, certain settings apply generally to CMOS configuration. First is the ability to initialize power management; this enables the system to enter the APM Enabled mode. Often CMOS then presents time frames for entering Standby and Suspend modes, as well as settings to determine which events take place in each of these modes.

Many CMOS versions present settings to determine wake-up events, such as directing the system to monitor a modem or a NIC (Figure 14.17). You'll see this feature as *Wake on LAN* or something similar. A true ACPI-compliant CMOS provides an ACPI setup option. Figure 14.18 shows a typical modern BIOS that provides this setting.

```
                Phoenix - AwardBIOS CMOS Utility
                             Power

          APM Configuration                             Select Menu

    Restore on AC Power Loss      [Power-Off]    Item Specific Help▶▶
    PWR Button < 4 secs           [Instant-Off]
    Power Up On PCI/PCIE Devices  [Disabled]     Set the Data, Time
    USB Resume from S5            [Disabled]     resume by Alarm.
    Power On By RTC Alarm         [Enabled]
    Date(of Month) Alarm          [ 5]
    Alarm Time(hh:mm)              2 :  9 :  5
    Power Up By PS/2 Mouse        [Disabled]
    Power Up By PS/2 Keyboard     [Disabled]




    F1:Help      ↑↓:Select Item   -/+: Change Value      F5:Setup Defaults
    ESC:Exit     ▶◀:Select Menu   Enter: Select SubMenu  F10:Save and Exit
```

● **Figure 14.17**   Setting a wake-up event in CMOS

> In Windows XP you can also access your power options by right-clicking on the desktop, selecting Properties, and then clicking the Power button in the Monitor power section of the Screen Saver tab. In Windows Vista, right-click the Desktop, select Personalize, select Screen Saver, and then click on the *Change power settings* link.

APM/ACPI settings can be found in the Windows 2000/XP/Vista Control Panel applet Power Options. In Windows XP, the Power Options applet has several built-in *power schemes* such as Home/Office and Max Battery that put the system into Standby or Suspend after a certain interval (Figure 14.19). You can also require the system to go into Standby after a set period of time or to turn off the monitor or hard drive after a time, thus creating your own custom power scheme. This is technically called adjusting the **sleep timers**.

Windows Vista's built-in power schemes are similar to Windows XP's, though you can better control power utilization by customizing a Balanced, Power saver, or High performance power plan (Figure 14.20). You can customize a power saver plan for your laptop, for example, and configure it to turn off the display at a certain time interval while on battery or plugged in and configure it to put the computer to sleep as desired (Figure 14.21).

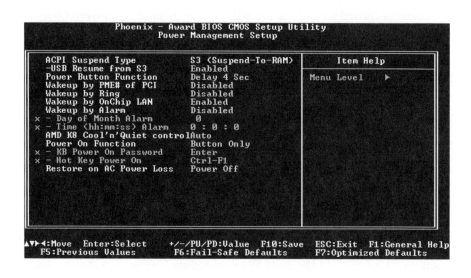

```
                Phoenix - Award BIOS CMOS Setup Utility
                        Power Management Setup

    ACPI Suspend Type          S3 <Suspend-To-RAM>        Item Help
    ─USB Resume from S3         Enabled
    Power Button Function       Delay 4 Sec          Menu Level    ▶
    Wakeup by PME# of PCI       Disabled
    Wakeup by Ring              Disabled
    Wakeup by OnChip LAN        Enabled
    Wakeup by Alarm             Disabled
  x - Day of Month Alarm        0
  x - Time (hh:mm:ss) Alarm     0 : 0 : 0
    AMD K8 Cool'n'Quiet control Auto
    Power On Function           Button Only
  x - KB Power On Password      Enter
  x - Hot Key Power On          Ctrl-F1
    Restore on AC Power Loss    Power Off




  ▲▼▶◀:Move  Enter:Select    +/-/PU/PD:Value  F10:Save  ESC:Exit  F1:General Help
     F5:Previous Values       F6:Fail-Safe Defaults      F7:Optimized Defaults
```

● **Figure 14.18**   CMOS with ACPI setup option

• Figure 14.19   The Windows XP Power Options applet's Power Schemes tab

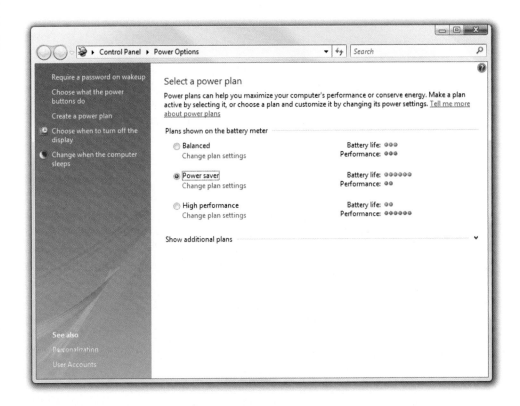

• Figure 14.20   Windows Vista's Balanced, Power saver, or High performance power plans

Chapter 14: Learning Portable Computing

• **Figure 14.21**   Customizing a laptop power plan in Windows Vista

Another feature, Hibernate mode, takes everything in active memory and stores it on the hard drive just before the system powers down. When the PC comes out of hibernation, Windows reloads all the files and applications into RAM. Figure 14.22 shows the Power Options Properties applet in Windows XP.

• **Figure 14.22**   Windows XP hibernation settings in the Power Options applet

Cleaning

Most portable PCs take substantially more abuse than a corresponding desktop model. Constant handling, travel, airport food on the run, and so on can radically shorten the life of a portable if you don't take action. One of the most important things you should do is clean the laptop regularly. Use an appropriate screen cleaner (not a glass cleaner!) to remove fingerprints and dust from the fragile LCD panel. A lint-free cloth should more than suffice in most cases.

Try This!

Adjusting Your System's Power Management

Go into the Power Options applet and take a look at the various settings. What is the current power scheme for your computer? If you're using a laptop with Windows XP, is your system still using the Home/Office Desktop power scheme? If this is the case, change the power scheme to Portable/Laptop. If you're using a laptop with Windows Vista, check to see if you are running a Balanced or High performance power plan. If you are, change the power plan to Power saver and familiarize yourself with some of the advanced power settings (click on the *Change advanced power settings* link).

Try changing the individual settings for each power scheme. For instance, set a new value for the System Standby setting—try making your computer go into standby after five minutes. Don't worry; you aren't going to hurt anything if you fiddle with these settings.

If you've had the laptop in a smoky or dusty environment, try compressed air for cleaning. Compressed air works great for blowing out the dust and crumbs from the keyboard and for keeping PC Card sockets clear. Don't use water on your keyboard! Even a minor amount of moisture inside the portable can toast a component.

Laptop cooling fans tend to get dirty over time. Clean them occasionally using an anti-static vacuum. Never use canned air!

Heat

To manage and maintain a healthy portable PC, you need to deal with issues of heat. Every portable has a stack of electronic components crammed into a very small space. Unlike their desktop brethren, portables don't have lots of freely moving air space that enables fans to cool everything down. Even with lots of low-power-consumption devices inside, portable PCs crank out a good deal of heat. Excessive heat can cause system lockups and hardware failures, so you should handle the issue wisely. Try this as a starter guide.

- Use power management, even if you're plugged into the AC outlet. This is especially important if you're working in a warm (more than 80 degrees Fahrenheit) room.

- Keep air space between the bottom of the laptop and the surface on which it rests. Putting a laptop on a soft surface, such as a pillow on your lap, creates a great heat-retention system—not a good thing! Always use a hard, flat surface.

- Don't use a keyboard protector for extended amounts of time.

- Listen to your fan, assuming the laptop has one. If it's often running very fast—you can tell by the high-pitched whirring sound— examine your power management settings and your environment, and change whatever is causing heat retention.

- Speaking of fans, be alert to a fan that suddenly goes silent. Fans do fail on laptops, causing overheating and failure. All laptop fans can be replaced easily.

Protect the Machine

Although prices continue to drop for basic laptops, a fully loaded system is still pricey. To protect your investment, you'll want to adhere to certain best practices. You've already read tips in this chapter to deal with cleaning and heat, so let's look at the "portable" part of portable computers.

Tripping

Pay attention to where you run the power cord when you plug in a laptop. One of the primary causes of laptop destruction is people tripping over the power cord and knocking the laptop off of a desk. This is especially true if you plug in at a public place such as a café or airport. Remember, the life you save could be your portable PC's!

Storage

If you aren't going to use your laptop or PDA for a while, storing it safely will go a long way toward keeping it operable when you do power it up again. Investing in a quality case is worth the extra few dollars—preferably one with ample padding. Smaller devices such as PDAs are well protected inside small shock-resistant aluminum cases that clip onto your belt, while laptops do fine in well-padded cases or backpacks. Not only will this protect your system on a daily basis when transporting it from home to office, but it will keep dust and pet hair away as well. Lastly, protect from battery leakage by removing the battery if you'll be storing your device for an extended time.

Travel

If traveling with a laptop, take care to protect yourself from theft. If possible, use a case that doesn't look like a computer case. A well-padded backpack makes a great travel bag for a laptop and appears less tempting to would-be thieves. Don't forget to pack any accessories you might need, like modular devices, spare batteries, and AC adapters. Make sure to remove any disks, such as CD/DVD or floppies, from their drives. Most importantly—back up any important data before you leave!

Make sure to have at least a little battery power available. Heightened security at airports means you might have to power on your system to prove it's really a computer and not a transport case for questionable materials. And never let your laptop out of your sight. If a security checkpoint involves putting your laptop through an x-ray machine, request a manual search instead. The x-ray won't harm your computer like a metal detector would, but if the laptop gets through the line at security before you do, someone else might walk away with it. If flying, stow your laptop under the seat in front of you where you can keep an eye on it.

If you travel to a foreign country, be very careful about the electricity. North America uses ~115-V power outlets, but the most of the rest of the world uses ~230-V outlets. Many portable computers have **auto-switching power supplies**, meaning they detect the voltage at the outlet and adjust accordingly. For these portables, a simple plug converter will do the trick. Other portable computers, however, have *fixed-input power supplies*, which means they run only on ~115-V or ~230-V power. For these portables, you need a full-blown electricity converting device, either a step-down or step-up *transformer*. You can find converters and transformers at electrical parts stores, such as Radio Shack in the United States.

Shipping

Much of the storage and travel advice can be applied to shipping. Remove the batteries and the optical discs from their drives. Pack the laptop well and disguise the container as best you can. Back up any data and verify the warranty coverage. Ship with a reputable carrier and always request a tracking number and, if possible, delivery signature. It's also worth the extra couple of bucks to pay for the shipping insurance. And when the clerk asks what's in the box, it's safer to say "electronics" rather than "a new 20-inch laptop computer."

 Be sure to remove all thumb drives and PC Cards before shipping a laptop.

Security

The fact is, if someone really wants to steal your laptop, they'll find a way. There are, however, some things you can do to make yourself, and your equipment, less desirable targets. As you've already learned, disguise is a good idea. Although you don't need to camouflage your laptop or carry it in a brown grocery bag on a daily basis, an inconspicuous carrying case will draw less attention.

Another physical deterrent is a laptop lock. Similar to a steel bicycle cable, there is a loop on one end and a lock on the other. The idea is to loop the cable around a solid object, such as a bed frame, and secure the lock to the small security hole on the side of the laptop. Again, if someone really wants to steal your computer, they'll find a way. They'll dismantle the bed frame if they're desperate. The best protection is to be vigilant and not let the computer out of your sight.

An alternative to physically securing a laptop with a lock is to use a software tracking system. Software makers, such as Computer Security Products, Inc., at www.computersecurity.com, offer tracking software that transmits a signal to a central office if the computer is stolen and connected to a phone line or the Internet. The location of the stolen PC can be tracked, and sensitive files can even be deleted automatically with the aid of the stealth signal.

PC Cards

The **Personal Computer Memory Card International Association (PCMCIA)** establishes standards involving portable computers, especially when it comes to expansion cards, which are generically called PC Cards. **PC Cards** are roughly credit card–sized devices that enhance and extend the functions of a portable PC. PC Cards are as standard on today's mobile computers as the hard drive. PC Cards are easy to use, inexpensive, and convenient. Figure 14.23 shows a typical PC Card.

Almost every portable PC has one or two PC Card slots, into which you insert a PC Card. Each card has at least one function, but many have two, three, or more! You can buy a PC Card that offers connections for removable media, for example, such as combination SD and CompactFlash card readers.

• **Figure 14.23**   PC Card

• **Figure 14.24** PC Card slots

You can also find PC Cards that enable you to plug into multiple types of networks. All PC Cards are hot-swappable, meaning you can plug them in without powering down the PC.

PCMCIA has established two versions of PC Cards, one using a parallel bus and the other using a serial bus. Each version, in turn, offers two technology variations as well as several physical varieties. This might sound complicated at first, but here's the map to sort it all out.

Parallel PC Cards

Parallel PC Cards come in two flavors, **16-bit** and **CardBus**, and each flavor comes in three physical sizes, called Type I, Type II, and Type III. The 16-bit PC Cards, as the name suggests, are 16-bit, 5-V cards that can have up to two distinct functions or devices, such as a modem/network card combination. CardBus PC Cards are 32-bit, 3.3-V cards that can have up to eight (!) functions on a single card. Regular PC Cards fit into and work in CardBus slots, but the reverse is not true. CardBus totally dominates the current PC Card landscape, but you might still run into older 16-bit PC Cards.

Type I, II, and III cards differ only in the thickness of the card (Type I being the thinnest, and Type III the thickest). All PC Cards share the same 68-pin interface, so any PC Card will work in any slot that accepts that card type. Type II cards are by far the most common of PC Cards. Therefore, most laptops have two Type II slots, one above the other, so the computer can accept two Type I or II cards or one Type III card (Figure 14.24).

Although PCMCIA doesn't require that certain sizes perform certain functions, most PC Cards follow their recommendations. Table 14.3 lists the sizes and typical uses of each type of PC Card.

ExpressCard

ExpressCard, the high-performance serial version of the PC Card, has begun to replace PC Card slots on newer laptop PCs. Although ExpressCard offers significant performance benefits, keep in mind that ExpressCard and PC Cards are incompatible. You cannot use your PC Card in your new laptop's ExpressCard socket. The PC Card has had a remarkably long life in portable PCs, and you can still find it on some new laptops, but get ready to replace all of your PC Card devices. ExpressCard comes in two widths: 54 mm and 34 mm. Figure 14.25 shows a 34-mm and a 54-mm ExpressCard. Both cards are 75 mm long and 5 mm thick, which makes them shorter than all previous PC Cards and the same thickness as a Type II PC Card.

Table 14.3	PC Card Types and Their Typical Uses			
Type	**Length**	**Width**	**Thickness**	**Typical Use**
Type I	85.6 mm	54.0 mm	3.3 mm	Flash memory
Type II	85.6 mm	54.0 mm	5.0 mm	I/O (modem, NIC, and so on)
Type III	85.6 mm	54.0 mm	10.5 mm	Hard drives

• **Figure 14.25**   34-mm and 54-mm ExpressCards

Keeping Your PC Cards Healthy
PC Cards typically come with a hard plastic storage case. Always be sure to use this case to store the cards when you're not using them. If dust, dirt, or grime gets into the array of contacts at the end of the card, the card won't work when you try to use it next. Also, be careful when using PC Cards that extend out of the PC Card slot past the edge of your laptop. One dark night I set my laptop on the floor with a PC Card NIC sticking out of it while I went to get a drink of water. On my way back, I accidentally stepped on the card sticking out of my laptop and nearly snapped it in half. Luckily, my laptop wasn't damaged, but the card was toast!

ExpressCards connect to either the Hi-Speed USB 2.0 bus or a PCI Express bus. These differ phenomenally in speed. The amazingly slow-in-comparison USB version has a maximum throughput of 480 Mbps. The PCIe version, in contrast, roars in at 2.5 Gbps in unidirectional communication. Very nice!

Table 14.4 shows the throughput and variations for the parallel and serial PC Cards currently or soon to be on the market.

Software Support for PC Cards

The PCMCIA standard defines two levels of software drivers to support PC Cards. The first and lower level is known as **socket services**. Socket services are device drivers that support the PC Card socket, enabling the system to detect when a PC Card has been inserted or removed, and providing the necessary I/O to the device. The second and higher level is known as **card services**. The card services level recognizes the function of a particular PC Card and provides the specialized drivers necessary to make the card work.

In today's laptops, the socket services are standardized and are handled by the system BIOS. Windows itself handles all card services and has a large preinstalled base of PC Card device drivers, although most PC Cards come with their own drivers.

ExpressCards don't require either socket or card services, at least not in the way PC Cards do. The ExpressCard modules automatically configure the software on your computer, which makes them truly plug and play.

Table 14.4	PC Card Speeds
Standard	**Maximum Theoretical Throughput**
PC Card using 16-bit bus	160 Mbps
CardBus PC Card using PCI bus	1056 Mbps
ExpressCard using USB 2.0 bus	480 Mbps
ExpressCard using PCIe bus	2.5 Gbps

See Chapter 16, "Learning Local Area Networking," for the scoop on dial-up networking and Ethernet.

Mobile NICs and Mini PCI

Every laptop made in the past few years comes with networking capabilities built in. They have Ethernet ports for plugging into a wired network and Wi-Fi for wireless networking, and some have Cellular WAN radios so you can access the Internet over a cell phone network. Laptops run Windows just like a desktop system, so they have all the networking software ready to go.

Many of these integrated network cards are installed in a Mini PCI slot on the laptop motherboard. The **Mini PCI** bus is an adaptation of the standard PCI bus and was developed specifically for integrated communications peripherals such as modems and network adapters. Built-in networking support means you don't need an additional PC Card to provide a network adapter. The Mini PCI bus also provides support for other integrated devices, such as Bluetooth, modems, audio, or hard drive controllers. One great aspect of Mini PCI is that if some new technology eclipses the current wireless technology or some other technology that uses the bus, you can upgrade by swapping a card.

Officially released in 1999, Mini PCI is a 32-bit, 33-MHz bus and is basically PCI v2.2 with a different form factor. Like PCI, it supports bus mastering and DMA. Mini PCI cards are about a quarter the size of regular PCI cards and can be as small as 2.75 inches by 1.81 inches by .22 inch. They can be found in small products such as laptops, printers, and set-top boxes.

To extend battery life, you can toggle built-in communication devices such as Wi-Fi and Bluetooth adapters on and off without powering down the computer. Many laptops come with a physical switch along the front or side edge to allow you to power the communications adapter on or off. Similarly, you can often use a keyboard shortcut for this, generally by pressing the Function (FN) key along with some other key. The FN key, when pressed, allows other keys to accomplish specific tasks. For example, on my laptop, pressing FN-F2 toggles my Wi-Fi adapter on and off; pressing FN-F10 ejects my CD-ROM drive.

A typical reason to upgrade a Mini PCI Wi-Fi NIC is to gain access to improved security options such as better encryption.

■ Troubleshooting Portable Computers

Many of the troubleshooting techniques you learned about for desktop systems can be applied to laptops. For example, take the proper precautions before and during disassembly. Use the proper hand tools, and document, label, and organize each plastic part and screw location for reassembly. Additionally, here are some laptop-specific procedures to try.

Laptop Won't Power On

- Verify AC power by plugging another electronic device into the wall outlet. If the other device receives power, the outlet is good.
- If the outlet is good, connect the laptop to the wall outlet and try to power on. If no LEDs light up, you may have a bad AC adapter. Swap it out with a known-good power adapter.

- A faulty peripheral device might keep the laptop from powering up. Remove any peripherals such as USB or FireWire devices.

Screen Doesn't Come On Properly

- If the laptop is booting (you hear the beeps and the drives), first make sure the display is turned on. Press the FN key and the key to activate the screen a number of times until the laptop display comes on. If that doesn't work, check the LCD cutoff switch—on many laptops, this is the small nub somewhere near the screen hinge that shuts the monitor off when you close the laptop—and make sure it isn't stuck in the down position.

- If the laptop display is very dim, you may have lost an inverter. The clue here is that inverters never go quietly. They can make a nasty hum as they are about to die and an equally nasty popping noise when they actually fail. Failure often occurs when you plug in the laptop's AC adapter, as the inverters take power directly from the AC adapter. It's also possible that the backlights in the LCD panel have died, though this is much less common than a bad inverter.

- If the screen won't come on or is cracked, most laptops have a port for plugging in an external monitor, which you can use to log into your laptop.

Wireless Networking Doesn't Work

- Check along the front, rear, or side edges of the laptop for a physical switch that toggles the internal wireless adapter on and off.

- Try the special key combination for your laptop to toggle the wireless adapter. You usually press the FN key in combination with another key.

- You might simply be out of range. Physically walk the laptop over to the wireless router or access point to ensure there are no out-of-range issues.

Handwriting Is Not Recognized

- If your PDA or tablet PC no longer recognizes your handwriting or stylus, you may need to retrain the digitizer. Look for an option in your PDA OS settings to align the screen. On Windows-based tablet PCs, you will find a similar option under Start | Settings | Control Panel.

Keypad Doesn't Work

- If none of the keys work on your laptop, there's a good chance you've unseated the keypad connector. These connectors are quite fragile and are prone to unseating from any physical stress on the laptop. Check the manufacturer's disassembly procedures to locate and reseat the keypad.

- If you're getting numbers when you're expecting to get letters, the number lock (NUMLOCK) function key is turned on. Turn it off.

Tech Tip

Battery Won't Charge

If you have a laptop with a battery that won't charge up, it could be one of two things: the battery might be cooked or the AC adapter isn't doing its job. To troubleshoot, replace the battery with a known-good battery. If the new battery works, you've found the problem. Just replace the battery. Alternatively, remove the battery and run the laptop on AC only. If that works, you know the AC adapter is good. If it doesn't, replace the AC adapter.

Touchpad Doesn't Work

- A shot of compressed air does wonders for cleaning pet hair out of the touchpad sensors. You'll get a cleaner shot if you remove the keyboard before using the compressed air. Remember to be gentle when lifting off the keyboard and make sure to follow the manufacturer's instructions.

- The touchpad driver might need to be reconfigured. Try the various options in the Control Panel | Mouse applet.

Chapter 14 Review

Chapter Summary

After reading this chapter and completing the exercises, you should understand the following about portable computers.

Describe the many types of portable computing devices available

- All portable devices share certain features: video output using LCD screens, some kind of PC sound, and DC battery power. There's no industry standard for naming the vast majority of styles of portable computing devices.

- A laptop refers in general to the clamshell, keyboard-on-the-bottom and LCD-screen-at-the-top design that is considered the shape of mobile PCs. Most notebooks are laptops in the 8½ × 11–inch range. The traditional clamshell laptop computer features a built-in LCD monitor, keyboard, and input device and functions as a fully standalone PC. A portable PC can be considered a desktop replacement if it does everything most people want to do with a desktop PC.

- Desktop extender portable devices don't replace the desktop but rather extend it by giving you a subset of features that you can take away from the desk. They are usually smaller and lighter than desktop replacement portables. Netbook portables (sometimes called subnotebooks, though the terms aren't necessarily synonymous) normally weigh less than three pounds and are less than an inch in thickness. These machines usually have smaller displays, lower-capacity hard drives, and CPUs that operate at lower speeds than their more full-sized brethren.

- Personal digital assistants (PDAs) are tiny handheld portable computing devices that hold such data as your address book and appointment schedules. Small enough to fit into a pocket, today's PDAs are pen-based computers, using a pen-like stylus and handwriting recognition. PDAs require specialized OSes such as Windows Mobile, PocketPC, PalmOS, or Linux. All of these OSes provide a GUI that enables you to interact with the device by touching the screen directly. PDAs synchronize with your PC, most often by using a cradle and USB port, so you have the same essential data on both machines.

- Over the years, input devices for portables have ranged from trackballs that clipped to the case or were built in near the keyboard, to IBM's TrackPoint pencil eraser–sized joystick embedded in the keyboard. The most common laptop pointing device found today, the touchpad, is a flat, touch-sensitive pad that you slide your finger across to move the cursor or pointer around the screen, and tap on to perform "mouse clicks."

Manage and maintain portable computers

- Portable computers use three types of batteries: Nickel-Cadmium (Ni-Cd), Nickel-Metal Hydride (Ni-MH), and Lithium-Ion (Li-Ion).

- The first batteries used in mobile PCs were Nickel-Cadmium (Ni-Cd). If a Ni-Cd battery was not completely discharged before each recharge, it lost a significant amount of its rechargeability, a condition referred to as battery memory. At best, Ni-Cd batteries would last for 1000 charges, but they were very susceptible to heat. Because of the toxic metals inside these batteries, they had to be disposed of via specialty disposal companies. Although no longer used in PCs, Ni-Cd batteries are still found in cellular and cordless phones.

- The second generation of mobile PC batteries, the Nickel-Metal Hydride (Ni-MH) batteries are less susceptible to memory problems, tolerate overcharging better, take more recharging, and last longer between rechargings, but they are still susceptible to heat.

- Although some portable PCs still use Ni-MH batteries, Lithium-Ion (Li-Ion) is more common today. This third-generation battery takes fewer charges than Ni-MH, but it lasts longer between charges. Because Li-Ion batteries can explode if they are overcharged, they have circuitry to prevent overcharging.

- A new type battery called the smart battery tells the computer when it needs to be charged, conditioned, or replaced.

- Batteries should be stored in a cool place, but not in the freezer because of moisture, metal racks, and food. Condition Ni-Cd and Ni-MH batteries to make them last longer. You can clean battery contacts with alcohol or a dry cloth. Because batteries contain dangerous chemicals, never handle one that has ruptured. Always recycle old batteries rather than disposing of them in the trash.

■ The process of cooperation among the hardware, the BIOS, and the OS to reduce power use is known generically as power management. Early laptops used power continuously, regardless of whether the system was being used at the time. With power management features, today's laptops can automatically turn off unused devices or can shut down the entire system, leaving the information in RAM ready for a restart. Performing these power management functions requires specialized hardware, BIOS, and an operating system that supports power management.

■ Starting with the 386SX, Intel introduced System Management Mode (SMM), a power management system that would make the CPU and all peripherals go to "sleep." In 1992, Intel introduced the improved Advanced Power Management (APM) specification, followed by the Advanced Configuration and Power Interface (ACPI) standard in 1996.

■ To use APM or ACPI, the computer must have an SMM-capable CPU, an APM-compliant BIOS, and devices that can be shut off. Referred to as Energy Star devices, these peripherals can shut down without actually turning off. The OS must also know how to request that a particular device be shut down. ACPI extends power-saving to include hot-swappable devices.

■ Virtually all laptops and desktops use power management functions. APM defines four power-usage levels, including Full On, APM Enabled, APM Standby, and APM Suspend. ACPI, the successor to APM, handles all these levels plus a few more, totaling four Global (G) and seven total (S) states. Support for APM has been discontinued in Windows Vista, which uses ACPI.

■ Configure APM/ACPI through CMOS or through the Power Options Control Panel applet in Windows 2000/XP/Vista, with Windows settings overriding CMOS settings. Many CMOS versions allow configuration of wake-up events, such as having the system monitor a modem or particular IRQ.

■ Hibernation writes information from RAM to the hard drive. Upon waking up, the data is returned to RAM, and programs and files are in the same state they were in when the computer entered hibernation.

■ Use an appropriate screen cleaner (not glass cleaner) to clean the LCD screen. Use compressed air around the keyboard and PC Card sockets. Never use water around the keyboard.

■ To combat the inevitable heat produced by a portable computer, always use power management, keep an air space between the bottom of the laptop and the surface on which it rests, don't use a keyboard protector for an extended period of time, and be aware of your fan.

■ Store your portable computer in a quality case when traveling. Laptops benefit from a cushy carrying case, while hard aluminum cases keep your PDA from getting banged up. Well-padded backpacks not only keep your laptop protected but also make your system less conspicuous to would-be thieves. When traveling, don't forget accessories such as AC power cords, additional batteries, or modular devices. Remove all discs from drives and make sure you have enough battery power to boot up for security personnel. If shipping your computer, go with a reputable carrier, keep your tracking number, and request a delivery signature. Use a laptop lock or a software tracking system to protect your laptop when traveling.

■ PC Cards are roughly credit-card-sized devices that enhance and extend the functions of a portable PC. Still commonly known by their older name, PCMCIA cards, PC Cards are as standard on today's mobile computers as the hard drive. Almost every portable PC has one or two PC Card slots. All PC Cards are hot-swappable.

■ Parallel PC Cards come in two flavors, 16-bit and CardBus; and each flavor comes in three different physical sizes, called Type I, Type II, and Type III. Type I, II, and III cards differ only in the thickness of the card (Type I being the thinnest and Type III the thickest). Type II cards are by far the most common. All parallel PC Cards share the same 68-pin interface. The 16-bit PC Cards are 16-bit, 5-V cards that can have up to two distinct functions or devices, such as a modem/network card combination. CardBus PC Cards are 32-bit, 3.3-V cards that can have up to eight different functions on a single card. The 16-bit PC Cards will fit into and work in CardBus slots, but the reverse is not true.

- The serial ExpressCard comes in two widths: 54 mm and 34 mm. Both cards are 75 mm long and 5 mm thick, which makes them shorter than all previous PC Cards and the same thickness as a Type II PC Card. ExpressCards connect to either the Hi-Speed USB 2.0 bus (480 Mbps) or a PCI Express bus (2.5 Gbps).

- The PCMCIA standard defines two levels of software drivers to support PC Cards. The first and lower level is known as socket services. Socket services are device drivers that support the PC Card socket, enabling the system to detect when a PC Card has been inserted or removed and providing the necessary I/O to the device. The second and higher level is known as card services. The card-services level recognizes the function of a particular PC Card and provides the specialized drivers necessary to make the card work. In today's laptops, the socket services are standardized and are handled by the system BIOS. Windows itself handles all card services and has a large preinstalled base of PC Card device drivers, although most PC Cards come with their own drivers.

- Most laptops now come with integrated wireless networking support by way of a built-in Wi-Fi adapter usually installed in a Mini PCI slot on the laptop motherboard. The Mini PCI bus is an adaptation of the standard PCI bus and was developed specifically for integrated communications peripherals such as modems and network adapters. To extend battery life, built-in communication devices such as Wi-Fi and Bluetooth adapters can be toggled on and off without powering down the computer.

Troubleshoot portable computers

- If your laptop won't power on, try a different wall outlet. If it still fails to power up, remove all peripheral devices and try again.

- If the screen doesn't come on properly, verify that the laptop is configured to use the built-in LCD screen by pressing the appropriate key to cycle through the internal and external monitors. If you hear a popping sound, you may have blown an inverter. If the screen is definitely broken, you may use an external monitor to access the laptop.

- If wireless networking is not working, check for the physical switch on the side of the laptop that toggles power to the internal network card. If your laptop doesn't have a switch, check for a key combination or function key that toggles power. You also may be out of range. Physically walk the laptop closer to the wireless router or access point.

- If your PDA or tablet PC fails to recognize handwriting, retrain the digitizer. PDAs often have a setting to "align the screen," while tablet PC users can check the Control Panel for the appropriate applet.

- If the keypad or touchpad doesn't work, try a shot of compressed air, reseat the physical internal connection, or reconfigure the driver settings through the Control Panel Keyboard or Mouse applets.

■ Key Terms

16-bit *(484)*

Advanced Configuration and Power Interface (ACPI) *(476)*

Advanced Power Management (APM) *(476)*

aspect ratio *(463)*

auto-switching power supply *(482)*

battery memory *(474)*

card services *(485)*

CardBus *(484)*

Cellular WAN *(468)*

conditioning charger *(474)*

desktop extender *(465)*

desktop replacement *(464)*

ExpressCard *(484)*

fuel cell *(473)*

hibernation *(477)*

high gloss *(463)*

laptop *(464)*

Lithium-Ion (Li-Ion) *(473)*

matte *(463)*

Mini PCI *(486)*

Nickel-Cadmium (Ni-Cd) *(473)*

Nickel-Metal Hydride (Ni-MH) *(473)*

PC Card *(483)*

PCMCIA card *(484)*

pen-based computing *(467)*

Personal Computer Memory Card International Association (PCMCIA) *(483)*

personal digital assistant (PDA) *(467)*
sleep timer *(478)*
smart battery *(475)*
socket services *(485)*
stylus *(467)*

System Management Mode (SMM) *(476)*
tablet PC *(468)*
touchpad *(465)*
TrackPoint *(465)*

■ Key Term Quiz

Use the Key Terms list to complete the sentences that follow. Not all terms will be used.

1. PC Cards require two levels of software drivers: _____ to allow the laptop to detect when a PC Card has been inserted or removed and _____ to provide drivers to make the card work.

2. Although _____ were the first batteries for mobile PCs, they are limited now to cellular and cordless phones because of their problems with battery memory.

3. The _____ tells the computer when it needs to be charged, conditioned, or replaced.

4. John read an ad recently for a(n) _____ portable PC that had everything he could possibly want on a PC, desktop or portable.

5. With the 386SX, Intel introduced _____, the first power management system with the ability to make the CPU and all peripherals go to sleep.

6. Many newer laptops feature _____ screens offering richer color, higher contrast, and wider viewing angles.

7. A(n) _____ combines the best of PDAs and fully featured laptops.

■ Multiple-Choice Quiz

1. What infrared process enables you to transfer data from one PDA to another wirelessly?

   A. Beaming

   B. Flashing

   C. Panning

   D. Sending

2. Which of the following APM power levels writes information from RAM to the hard drive and then copies the data back to RAM when the computer is activated again?

   A. Full On

   B. APM Enabled

   C. APM Standby

   D. Hibernation

3. Where do you configure APM/ACPI in Windows XP?

   A. The Power Options applet in the Control Panel

   B. The Display applet in the Control Panel

   C. The Power Management applet in the Control Panel

   D. The Power and Devices applet in the Control Panel

4. Which of the following input devices will you most likely find on a portable PC?

   A. TrackPoint

   B. Touchpad

   C. Trackball

   D. Mouse

5. Which buses do ExpressCards use?

   A. Hi-Speed USB and FireWire

   B. Hi-Speed USB and PCI Express

   C. PCI and PCI Express

   D. Mini PCI and Parallel

6. Convertibles and slates describe what type of device?

   A. Multicore processor

   B. Clamshell laptop computer

C. PDA

D. Tablet PC

7. Which bus was developed specifically for integrated communications peripherals such as modems and network adapters?

A. FireWire

B. Mini PCI

C. PCI

D. USB

8. What is a small portable computer designed to fill the gap between PDAs and laptops called?

A. Desktop extender

B. Desktop replacement

C. Netbook

D. Tablet PC

9. If the fan suddenly goes silent in your laptop, what should you do?

A. Keep using it; everything is probably OK.

B. Blow into the laptop's exhaust vent.

C. Unplug your laptop and then plug it back in.

D. Replace the fan.

■ Essay Quiz

1. At the upcoming training seminar for new techs, your boss wants to make sure they understand and use power management settings. You've been asked to prepare a short presentation showing the range of power management settings available in Windows 2000, XP, and Vista and demonstrating how to set them. What will you include in your presentation?

2. You've been tasked to advise your group on current portable computer technology so they can purchase ten new laptops by the end of the quarter. In a short essay, weigh the pros and cons of getting desktop replacements versus smaller laptops that would come with docking stations.

3. Your boss has a new portable computer and is planning to take it with him on a business trip to Paris. He's not all that tech-savvy or much of a traveler, so write a memo that tells him what to do or avoid while traveling, especially overseas.

Lab Project

• Lab Project 14.1

This chapter mentioned that, although they are more expensive, portable PCs typically provide less processing power, and smaller hard drives, and in general are not as full-featured as desktop computers. Use the Internet to check sites such as www.ibm.com, www.gateway.com, www.dell.com, and www.hp.com to compare the best equipped, most powerful laptop you can find with the best equipped, most powerful desktop computer you can find. How do their features and prices compare? Now find a less expensive laptop and try to find a desktop computer that is as similar as possible in terms of capabilities, and compare their prices.

chapter

15

Learning Printing

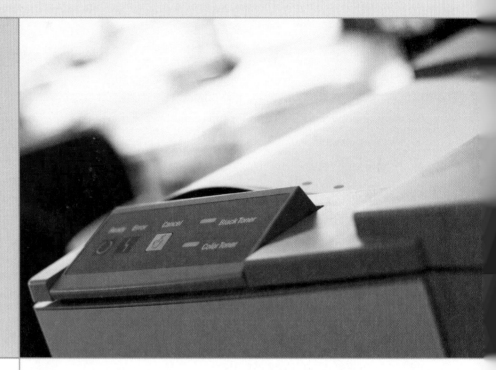

"Faster! Faster! Faster would be better!"

—Capt. Malcolm Reynolds, *Serenity*

In this chapter, you will learn how to

- **Describe current printer technologies**
- **Install a printer on a Windows PC**
- **Recognize and fix basic printer problems**

Despite all of the talk about the "paperless office," printers continue to be a vital part of the typical office. In many cases, PCs are used exclusively for the purpose of producing paper documents. Many people simply prefer dealing with a hard copy. Programmers cater to this preference by using metaphors such as *page*, *workbook*, and *binder* in their applications. The CompTIA A+ certification strongly stresses the area of printing and expects a high degree of technical knowledge of the function, components, maintenance, and repair of all types of printers.

Printer Technologies

No other piece of your computer system is available in a wider range of styles, configurations, and feature sets than a printer, or at such a wide price variation. What a printer can and can't do is largely determined by the type of printer technology it uses—that is, how it gets the image onto the paper. Modern printers can be categorized into several broad types: impact, inkjet, dye-sublimation, thermal, laser, and solid ink.

Impact Printers

Printers that create an image on paper by physically striking an ink ribbon against the paper's surface are known as **impact printers**. Even though *daisy-wheel* printers (essentially an electric typewriter attached to the PC instead of directly to a keyboard) have largely disappeared, their cousins, **dot-matrix printers**, still soldier on in many offices. Although dot-matrix printers don't deliver what most home users want—high-quality and flexibility at a low cost—they're still widely found in businesses for two reasons: dot-matrix printers have a large installed base, and they can be used for multipart forms because they actually strike the paper. Impact printers tend to be relatively slow and noisy, but when speed, flexibility, and print quality are not critical, they provide acceptable results. PCs used for printing multipart forms, such as *point of sale* (*POS*) machines that need to print receipts in duplicate, triplicate, or more, represent the major market for new impact printers, although many older dot-matrix printers remain in use.

Dot-matrix printers use a grid, or matrix, of tiny pins, also known as **printwires**, to strike an inked printer ribbon and produce images on paper (Figure 15.1). The case that holds the printwires is called a **printhead**. Using either 9 or 24 pins, dot-matrix printers treat each page as a picture broken up into a dot-based raster image. The 9-pin dot-matrix printers are generically called *draft quality*, while the 24-pin printers are known as *letter quality* or **near-letter quality (NLQ)**. The BIOS for the printer (either built into the printer or a printer driver) interprets the raster image in the same way a monitor does, "painting" the image as individual dots. Naturally, the more pins, the higher the resolution. Figure 15.2 illustrates the components common to dot-matrix printers. Many dot-matrix printers use continuous-feed paper with holes on its sides that are engaged by metal sprockets to pull the paper through—this is known as *tractor-feed paper* because the sprockets are reminiscent of the wheels on a tractor.

● **Figure 15.1**   An Epson FX-880+ dot-matrix printer

Inkjet Printers

Inkjet printers (also called *ink-dispersion printers*), like the one shown in Figure 15.3, are relatively simple devices consisting of a printhead mechanism, support electronics, a transfer mechanism to move the printhead back and forth, and a paper feed component to drag, move, and eject paper (Figure 15.4). They work by ejecting ink through tiny tubes. Most inkjet printers use heat to move the ink, while a few use a mechanical method. The heat-method printers use tiny resistors or electroconductive plates at the end of each tube

Platen   Printhead   Ribbon

Electronics   Power supply   Traverse assembly

• **Figure 15.2**   Inside a dot-matrix printer

• **Figure 15.3**   Typical inkjet printer

that literally boil the ink; this creates a tiny air bubble that ejects a droplet of ink onto the paper, thus creating a portion of the image (Figure 15.5).

The ink is stored in special small containers called **ink cartridges**. Older inkjet printers had two cartridges: one for black ink and another for colored ink. The color cartridge had separate compartments for cyan (blue), magenta (red), and yellow ink, to print colors by using a method known as CMYK (you'll read more about CMYK later in this chapter). If your color cartridge ran out of one of the colors, you had to purchase a whole new color cartridge or deal with a messy refill kit.

Printer manufacturers began to separate the ink colors into three separate cartridges so that printers came with four cartridges: one for each color and a fourth for black (Figure 15.6). This not only was more cost-effective for the user, but also resulted in higher quality printouts. Today you can find color inkjet printers with six, eight, or more color cartridges. In addition to the basic CMYK inks, the other cartridges provide for green, blue,

Electronics   Storage/cleaning/maintenance position

Traverse assembly   Ink cartridges

Print area

Traverse guides   Printhead and cartridge caddy   Power supply

• **Figure 15.4**   Inside an inkjet printer

Paper

Sprayed ink
forms characters.

Color InkJet

Ink droplets

Horizontal
plates

Nozzle

Vertical
plates

Ink fountain

Electrically charged
plates control direction
of inkjet spray.

● **Figure 15.5**   Detail of the inkjet printhead

gray, light cyan, dark cyan, and more. Typically, the more ink cartridges a printer uses, the higher the quality of the printed image—and the higher the cost of the printer.

The two key features of an inkjet printer are the **print resolution**—that is, the density of ink, which affects print quality—and the print speed. Resolution is measured in **dots per inch (dpi)**; higher numbers mean that the ink dots on the page are closer together, so your printed documents will look better. Resolution is most important when you're printing complex images such as full-color photos, or when you're printing for duplication and you care that your printouts look good. Print speed is measured in **pages per minute (ppm)**, and this specification is normally indicated right on the printer's box. Most printers have one (faster) speed for monochrome printing—that is, using only black ink—and another for full-color printing.

● **Figure 15.6**   Inkjet ink cartridges

Another feature of inkjet printers is that they can support a staggering array of print media. Using an inkjet printer, you can print on a variety of matte or glossy photo papers, iron-on transfers, and other specialty media; some printers can print directly onto specially coated optical discs, or even fabric. Imagine running a T-shirt through your printer with your own custom slogan (how about "I'm CompTIA A+ Certified!"). The inks have improved over the years, too, now delivering better quality and longevity than ever. Where older inks would smudge if the paper got wet or start to fade after a short time, modern inks are smudge proof and of archival quality—for example, some inks by Epson are projected to last up to 200 years.

Dye-Sublimation Printers

The term *sublimation* means to cause something to change from a solid form into a vapor and then back into a solid. This is exactly the process behind *dye-sublimation printing*, sometimes called *thermal dye transfer* printing. **Dye-sublimation printers** are used mainly for photo printing, high-end desktop publishing, medical and scientific imaging, and other applications for which fine detail and rich color are more important than cost and speed. Smaller, specialized printers called *snapshot* printers use dye sublimation specifically for printing photos at a reduced cost compared to their full-sized counterparts.

The dye-sublimation printing technique is an example of the so-called CMYK (**c**yan, **m**agenta, **y**ellow, blac**k**) method of color printing. It uses a roll of heat-sensitive plastic film embedded with page-sized sections of cyan (blue), magenta (red), and yellow dye; many also have a section of black dye. A printhead containing thousands of heating elements, capable of precise temperature control, moves across the film, vaporizing the dyes and causing them to soak into specially coated paper underneath before cooling and reverting to a solid form. This process requires one pass per page for each color. Some printers also use a final finishing pass that applies a protective laminate coating to the page. Figure 15.7 shows how a dye-sublimation printer works.

Documents printed through the dye-sublimation process display *continuous-tone* images, meaning that the printed image is not constructed of pixel dots but a continuous blend of overlaid differing dye colors. This is in contrast to other print technologies' *dithered* images, which use closely packed, single-color dots to simulate blended colors. Dye-sublimation printers produce high-quality color output that rivals professional photo lab processing.

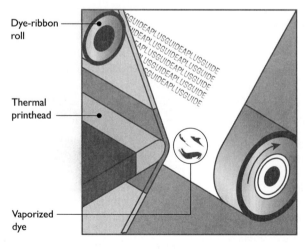

Dye-ribbon roll

Thermal printhead

Vaporized dye

• **Figure 15.7**   The dye-sublimation printing process

Thermal Printers

Thermal printers use a heated printhead to create a high-quality image on special or plain paper. You'll see two kinds of thermal printers in use. The first is the *direct thermal* printer, and the other is the *thermal wax transfer* printer. Direct thermal printers burn dots into the surface of special heat-sensitive paper. If you remember the first generation of fax machines, you're already familiar with this type of printer. Many retail businesses still use it as a receipt printer. Thermal wax printers work similarly to dye-sublimation printers, except that instead of using rolls of dye-embedded film, the film is coated with colored wax. The thermal printhead passes over the film ribbon and melts the wax onto the paper. Thermal wax printers don't require special papers like dye-sublimation printers, so they're more flexible and somewhat cheaper to use, but their output isn't quite as good because they use color dithering.

Laser Printers

Using a process called *electro-photographic imaging*, **laser printers** produce high-quality and high-speed output of both text and graphics. Figure 15.8 shows a typical laser printer. Laser printers rely on the photoconductive properties of certain organic compounds. *Photoconductive* means that particles of these compounds, when exposed to light (that's the "photo" part), will *conduct* electricity. Laser printers usually use lasers as a light source because of their precision. Some lower-cost printers use LED arrays instead.

• **Figure 15.8** Typical laser printer

The first laser printers created only monochrome images. Today, you can also buy a color laser printer, although the vast majority of laser printers produced today are still monochrome. Although a color laser printer can produce complex full-color images such as photographs, they really shine for printing what's known as *spot color*—for example, eye-catching headings, lines, charts, or other graphical elements that dress up an otherwise plain printed presentation.

Critical Components of the Laser Printer

The CompTIA A+ Essentials exam takes a keen interest in the particulars of the laser printing process, so it pays to know your way around a laser printer. Let's take a look at the many components of laser printers and their functions (Figure 15.9).

Toner Cartridge The **toner cartridge** in a laser printer is so named because of its most obvious activity: supplying the toner that creates the image on the page (Figure 15.10). To reduce maintenance costs, however, many other laser printer parts, especially those that suffer the most wear and tear, have been incorporated into the toner cartridge. Although this makes replacement of individual parts nearly impossible, it greatly reduces the need for replacement; those parts that are most likely to break are replaced every time you replace the toner cartridge.

Photosensitive Drum The **photosensitive drum** is an aluminum cylinder coated with particles of photosensitive compounds. The drum itself is grounded to the power supply, but the coating is not. When light hits these

Tech Tip

Hidden Costs

*Some printers use **consumables**—such as ink—at a much faster rate than others, prompting the industry to rank printers in terms of their cost per page. Using an inexpensive printer (laser or inkjet) costs around 4 cents per page, while an expensive printer can cost more than 20 cents per page—a huge difference if you do any volume of printing. This hidden cost is particularly pernicious in the sub $100 inkjet printers on the market. Their low prices often entice buyers, who then discover that the cost of consumables is outrageous—these days, a single set of color and black inkjet cartridges can cost as much as the printer itself, if not more!*

System board — Toner cartridge — High-voltage power supply

Printer memory

Gearbox/motors — Fuser assembly — Sub-logic board — Paper tray — Primary power supply

• **Figure 15.9**   Components inside a laser printer

Color laser printers have four toner cartridges: black, cyan, magenta, and yellow.

• **Figure 15.10**   Laser printer's toner cartridge

particles, whatever electrical charge they may have "drains" out through the grounded cylinder.

Erase Lamp   The **erase lamp** exposes the entire surface of the photosensitive drum to light, making the photosensitive coating conductive. Any electrical charge present in the particles bleeds away into the grounded drum, leaving the surface particles electrically neutral.

Primary Corona   The **primary corona** wire, located close to the photosensitive drum, never touches the drum. When the primary corona is charged with an extremely high voltage, an electric field (or corona) forms, enabling voltage to pass to the drum and charge the photosensitive particles on its surface. The *primary grid* regulates the transfer of voltage, ensuring that the surface of the drum receives a uniform negative voltage of between ~600 and ~1000 volts (V).

Laser   The **laser** acts as the writing mechanism of the printer. Any particle on the drum struck by the laser becomes conductive and its charge is drained away into the grounded core of the drum. The entire surface of the drum has a uniform negative charge of between ~600 and ~1000 V following its charging by the primary corona wire. When particles are struck by the laser, they are discharged and left with a ~100-V negative charge. Using the laser, we can "write" an image onto the drum. Note that the laser writes a positive image to the drum.

Toner   The **toner** in a laser printer is a fine powder made up of plastic particles bonded to iron particles. The *toner cylinder* charges the toner with a negative charge of between ~200 and ~500 V. Because that charge falls between the original uniform negative charge of the photosensitive drum (~600 to ~1000 V) and the charge of the particles on the drum's surface hit by the laser (~100 V), particles of toner are attracted to the areas of the photosensitive drum that have been hit by the laser (that is, areas that have a *relatively* positive charge with reference to the toner particles).

The toner used in laser printers is typically carbon melt mixed with a polyester resin.

Transfer Corona   To transfer the image from the photosensitive drum to the paper, the paper must be given a charge that will attract the toner particles off of the drum and onto the paper. The **transfer corona** is a thin wire, usually protected by other thin wires, that applies a positive charge to the paper, drawing the negatively charged toner particles to the paper. The paper, with its positive charge, is also attracted to the negatively charged drum. To prevent the paper from wrapping around the drum, a **static charge eliminator** removes the charge from the paper.

In most laser printers, the transfer corona is outside the toner cartridge, especially in large, commercial-grade machines. The transfer corona is prone to a build-up of dirt, toner, and debris through electrostatic attraction, and it must be cleaned. It is also quite fragile—usually finer than a human hair. Most printers with an exposed transfer corona provide a special tool to clean it, but you can also—very delicately—use a cotton swab soaked in 90 percent denatured alcohol (don't use rubbing alcohol because it contains emollients). As always, never service any printer without first turning it off and unplugging it from its power source.

Fuser Assembly   The **fuser assembly** is almost always separate from the toner cartridge. It is usually quite easy to locate as it is close to the bottom of the toner cartridge and usually has two rollers to fuse the toner. Sometimes the fuser is somewhat enclosed and difficult to recognize because the rollers are hidden from view. To help you determine the location of the fuser, think about the data path of the paper and the fact that fusing is the final step of printing.

The toner is merely resting on top of the paper after the static charge eliminator has removed the paper's static charge. The toner must be permanently attached to the paper to make the image permanent. Two rollers, a pressure roller and a heated roller, are used to fuse the toner to the paper. The pressure roller presses against the bottom of the page, and the heated roller presses down on the top of the page, melting the toner into the paper. The heated roller has a nonstick coating such as Teflon to prevent the toner from sticking to the heated roller.

Power Supplies   All laser printers have at least two separate power supplies. The first power supply is called the primary power supply, or sometimes just the power supply. This power supply, which may actually be more than one power supply, provides power to the motors that move the paper, the system electronics, the laser, and the transfer corona. The high-voltage power supply usually provides power only to the primary corona. The extremely high voltage of the high-voltage power supply makes it one of the most dangerous devices in the world of PCs! Before opening a printer to insert a new toner cartridge, it is imperative that you *always turn off* a laser printer!

Cross Check

High Voltage—Keep Away!

The power supply inside a laser printer is not the only dangerous high-voltage toy in the world of PC equipment. You've learned about two other potentially hazardous electrical components that you should approach with caution.

1.   What are they?

2.   Which of these three items is potentially the most deadly?

To refresh your memory, check out Chapter 8, "Learning PC Power," and Chapter 13, "Learning Video and Multimedia."

Turning Gears   A laser printer has many mechanical functions. First, the paper must be picked up. Next, the photosensitive roller must be turned and the laser, or a mirror, must be moved from left to right. The toner must be evenly distributed, and the fuser assembly must squish the toner into the paper. Finally, the paper must be kicked out of the printer and the assembly cleaned to prepare for the next page.

All of these functions are served by complex gear systems. In most laser printers, these gear systems are packed together in discrete units generically called *gear packs* or *gearboxes*. Most laser printers have two or three gearboxes that you can remove relatively easily in the rare case when one of them fails. Most gearboxes also have their own motor or solenoid to move the gears.

System Board   Every laser printer contains at least one electronic board. On this board is the main processor, the printer's ROM, and the RAM used to store the image before it is printed. Many printers divide these functions among two or three boards dispersed around the printer. An older printer may also have an extra ROM chip and/or a special slot where you can install an extra ROM chip, usually for special functions such as PostScript.

On some printer models you can upgrade the contents of these ROM chips (the *firmware*) by performing a process called *flashing* the ROM. Flashing is a lot like upgrading the system BIOS, which you learned about in Chapter 7, "Learning Motherboards." Upgrading the firmware can help fix bugs, add new features, or update the fonts in the printer.

Of particular importance is the printer's RAM. When the printer doesn't have enough RAM to store the image before it prints, you get a memory overflow problem. Also, some printers store other information in the RAM, including fonts or special commands. Adding RAM is usually a simple job—just snapping in a SIMM or DIMM stick or two—but getting the *right* RAM is important. Call or check the printer manufacturer's Web site to see what type of RAM you need. Although most printer companies will happily sell you their expensive RAM, most printers can use generic DRAM like the kind you use in a PC.

Ozone Filter   The coronas inside laser printers generate ozone (O_3). Although not harmful to humans in small amounts, even tiny concentrations of ozone will cause damage to printer components. To counter this problem, most laser printers have a special ozone filter that needs to be vacuumed or replaced periodically.

Sensors and Switches   Every laser printer has a large number of sensors and switches spread throughout the machine. The sensors are used to detect a broad range of conditions such as paper jams, empty paper trays, or low toner levels. Many of these sensors are really tiny switches that detect open doors and so on. Most of the time these sensors/switches work reliably, yet occasionally they become dirty or broken, sending a false signal to the printer. Simple inspection is usually sufficient to determine if a problem is real or just the result of a faulty sensor/switch.

Solid Ink

Solid ink printers use just what you'd expect—solid inks. The technology was originally developed by Tektronix, whose printer division was acquired by Xerox. Solid ink printers use solid sticks of nontoxic "ink" that produce more vibrant color than other print methods. The solid ink is melted and absorbed into the paper fibers; it then solidifies, producing a continuous-tone output. Unlike dye-sublimation printers, all colors are applied to the media in a single pass, reducing the chances of misalignment. Solid ink sticks do not rely on containers like ink for inkjet printers and can be "topped off" midway through a print job by inserting additional color sticks without taking the printer offline.

These printers are fast, too! A full-color print job outputs the first page in about six seconds. Of course, all that speed and quality comes at a price. Xerox's base model starts at about twice the cost of a laser printer, with the expensive model selling for about six times the cost! Solid ink printers become a bit more affordable when you factor in the cost of consumables. A single stick of ink costs about as much as an inkjet cartridge, for example, but with a print capacity of 1000 pages, that completely beats the cost of inkjet cartridges over time.

Printer Languages

Now that you've learned about the different types of print devices and techniques, it's time to take a look at how they communicate with the PC. How do you tell a printer to make a letter *A* or to print a picture of your pet iguana? Printers are designed to accept predefined printer languages that handle both characters and graphics. Your software must use the proper language when communicating with your printer, so that your printer can output your documents onto a piece of paper. Following are the more common printer languages.

ASCII

You might think of the **American Standard Code for Information Interchange (ASCII)** language as nothing more than a standard set of characters, the basic alphabet in upper- and lowercase with a few strange symbols thrown in. ASCII actually contains a variety of control codes for transferring data, some of which can be used to control printers. For example, ASCII code 10 (or 0A in hex) means "Line Feed," and ASCII code 12 (0C) means "Form Feed." These commands have been standard since before the creation of IBM PCs, and all printers respond to them. If they did not, the PRT SCR (print screen) key would not work with every printer. Being highly standardized has advantages, but the control codes are extremely limited. Printing high-end graphics and a wide variety of fonts requires more advanced languages.

PostScript

Adobe Systems developed the **PostScript** page description language in the early 1980s as a device-independent printer language capable of high-resolution graphics and scalable fonts. PostScript interpreters are embedded in the printing device. Because PostScript is understood by printers at a hardware level, the majority of the image processing is done by the printer and not the PC's CPU, so PostScript printers print faster. PostScript defines the page as a single raster image; this makes PostScript files extremely portable—they can be created on one machine or platform and reliably printed out on another machine or platform (including, for example, high-end typesetters).

Hewlett-Packard Printer Control Language (PCL)

Hewlett-Packard developed its **printer control language (PCL)** as a more advanced printer language to supersede simple ASCII codes. PCL features a set of printer commands greatly expanded from ASCII. Hewlett-Packard designed PCL with text-based output in mind; it does not support advanced graphical functions. The most recent version of PCL, PCL6, features scalable fonts and additional line-drawing commands. Unlike PostScript, however, PCL is not a true page description language; it uses a series of commands to define the characters on the page. Those commands must be supported by each individual printer model, making PCL files less portable than PostScript files.

Windows GDI and XPS

Windows 2000/XP use the **graphical device interface (GDI)** component of the operating system to handle print functions. Although you *can* use an external printer language such as PostScript, most users simply install printer drivers and let Windows do all the work. The GDI uses the CPU rather than the printer to process a print job and then sends the completed job to the printer. When you print a letter with a TrueType font in Windows, for example, the GDI processes the print job and then sends bitmapped images of each page to the printer. The printer sees a page of TrueType text, therefore, as a picture, not as text. As long as the printer has a capable-enough raster image processor and plenty of RAM, you don't need to worry about the printer language in most situations. We'll revisit printing in Windows in more detail later in this chapter.

Windows Vista supports GDI printing, but it also includes a new printing subsystem called the **XML Paper Specification (XPS) print path**. XPS provides several improvements over GDI, including enhanced color management (which works with Windows Color System) and better print layout fidelity. The XPS print path requires a driver that supports XPS. Additionally, some printers natively support XPS, eliminating the requirement that the output be converted to a device-specific printer control language before printing.

Printer Connectivity

Most printers connect to one of two ports on the PC: a DB-25 parallel port or a USB port. The parallel connection is the classic way to plug in a printer, but most printers today use USB. You'll need to know how to support the more obscure parallel ports, cables, and connections as well as the plug-and-play USB connections.

Parallel Communication and Ports

The **parallel port** was included in the original IBM PC as a faster alternative to serial communication. The IBM engineers considered serial communication, limited to 1 bit at a time, to be too slow for the "high-speed" devices of the day (for example, dot-matrix printers). The standard parallel port has been kept around for backward compatibility despite several obvious weaknesses.

Parallel ports may be far faster than serial ports, but they are slow by modern standards. The maximum data transfer rate of a standard parallel port is still only approximately 150 kilobytes per second (KBps). Standard parallel communication on the PC also relies heavily on software, eating up a considerable amount of CPU time that could be used better.

Parallel ports are hindered by their lack of true bidirectional capability. Although one-way communication was acceptable for simple line printers and dot-matrix printers, parallel communication also became popular for a wide range of external devices that required two-way communication. Although it is possible to get two-way communication out of a standard parallel port, the performance is not impressive.

Although the phrase "Centronics standard" was common in the heyday of parallel ports, no such animal actually existed. Prior to the development of IEEE 1284, a very loose set of standards was adopted by manufacturers in an attempt to reduce incompatibility issues somewhat.

IEEE 1284 Standard

In 1991, a group of printer manufacturers proposed to the *Institute of Electrical and Electronics Engineers* (*IEEE*) that a committee be formed to create a standard for a backward-compatible, high-speed, bidirectional parallel port for the PC. The committee was the IEEE 1284 committee (hence the name of the standard).

The **IEEE 1284 standard** requires the following:

- Support for five distinct modes of operation: *compatibility mode, nibble mode, byte mode, EPP,* and *ECP*

- A standard method of negotiation for determining which modes are supported both by the host PC and by the peripheral device

- A standard physical interface (that is, the cables and connectors)

- A standard electrical interface (that is, termination, impedance, and so on)

Because only one set of data wires exists, all data transfer modes included in the IEEE 1284 standard are half-duplex: data is transferred in only one direction at a time.

Many techs confuse the concept of duplex printing—a process that requires special printers capable of printing on both sides of a sheet of paper—with bidirectional printing. They are two different things!

Tech Tip

IEEE 1284 Transfer Modes
The five modes of operation for parallel printing specified in the IEEE 1284 standard (compatibility, nibble, byte, EPP, ECP) are inching closer to obsolescence as USB printers take over the market. If you find yourself needing to optimize the performance of a legacy parallel printer, you can look up these modes by name, using various Web search tools.

Parallel Connections, Cabling, and Electricity

Although no true standard exists, *standard parallel cable* usually refers to a printer cable with the previously mentioned male **DB-25 connector** on one end and a 36-pin **Centronics connector** on the other (Figure 15.11). The shielding (or lack thereof) of the internal wiring and other electrical characteristics of a standard parallel printer cable are largely undefined except by custom. In practice, these standard cables are acceptable for transferring data at 150 KBps, and for distances of less than 6 feet, but they would be dangerously unreliable for some transfer modes.

For more reliability at distances up to 32 feet (10 meters), use proper IEEE 1284–compliant cabling. The transfer speed drops with the longer cables, but it does work, and sometimes the trade-off between speed and distance is worth it.

Installing a parallel cable is a snap. Just insert the DB-25 connector into the parallel port on the back of the PC and insert the Centronics connector into the printer's Centronics port, and you're ready to go to press!

• **Figure 15.11** Standard parallel cable with 36-pin Centronics connector on one end and DB-25 connector on the other

Some printers come with both USB and parallel connections, but this has become very rare. If you need a parallel printer for a system, be sure to confirm that the particular model you want will work with your system!

In almost all cases, you must install drivers before you plug a USB printer into your computer. You'll learn about installing printer drivers later in this chapter.

USB Printers

New printers now use USB connections that you can plug into any USB port on your computer. USB printers don't usually come with a USB cable, so you need to purchase one when you purchase a printer. (It's quite a disappointment to come home with your new printer only to find you can't connect it because it didn't come with a USB cable.) Most printers use the standard USB type A connector on one end and the smaller USB type B connector on the other end, although some use two type A connectors. Whichever configuration your USB printer has, just plug in the USB cable—it's literally that easy!

FireWire Printers

Some printers offer FireWire connections in addition to or instead of USB connections. A FireWire printer is just as easy to connect as a USB printer, because FireWire is also hot-swappable and hot-pluggable. Again, make sure you have the proper cable, as most printers don't come with one. If your printer has both connections, which one should you use? The answer is easy if your PC has only USB and not FireWire. If you have a choice, either connection is just as good as the other, and the speeds are comparable. If you already have many USB devices, you may want to use the FireWire printer connection, to leave a USB port free for another device.

Network Printers

Connecting a printer to a network isn't just for offices anymore. More and more homes and home offices are enjoying the benefits of network printing. It used to be that to share a printer on a network—that is, to make it available to all network users—you would physically connect the printer to a single computer and then share the printer on the network. The downside to this was that the computer to which the printer was connected had to be left on for others to use the printer.

Today, the typical **network printer** comes with its own onboard network adapter that uses a standard RJ-45 Ethernet cable to connect the printer directly to the network by way of a router. The printer can typically be assigned a static IP address, or it can acquire one dynamically from a DHCP server. (Don't know what a router, IP address, or DHCP server is? Take a look at Chapter 16, "Learning Local Area Networking.") Once connected to the network, the printer acts independent of any single PC. Some of the more costly network printers come with a built-in Wi-Fi adapter to connect to the network wirelessly. Alternatively, some printers offer Bluetooth interfaces for networking.

Even if a printer does not come with built-in Ethernet, Wi-Fi, or Bluetooth, you can purchase a standalone network device known as a *print server* to connect your printer to the network. These print servers, which can be Ethernet or Wi-Fi, enable one or several printers to attach via parallel port or USB. So take that ancient ImageWriter dot-matrix printer and network it—I dare you!

Other Printers

Plenty of other connection types are available for printers. We've focused mainly on parallel, USB, FireWire, and networked connections. Be aware that you may run into an old serial port printer or a SCSI printer. Although this is unlikely, know that it's a possibility.

■ Installing a Printer in Windows

You need to take a moment to understand how Windows handles printing, and then you'll see how to install, configure, and troubleshoot printers in these operating systems.

The CompTIA A+ Essentials exam tests you on installing and troubleshooting printers, so read these sections carefully!

To Windows 2000, XP, and Vista/7, a printer is not a physical device; it is a *program* that controls one or more physical printers. The *physical* printer is called a print device to Windows (although I continue to use the term "printer" for most purposes, just like almost every tech on the planet). Printer drivers and a spooler are still present, but in Windows 2000/XP and Vista/7, they are integrated into the printer itself (Figure 15.12). This arrangement gives Windows amazing flexibility. For example, one printer can support multiple print devices, enabling a system to act as a print server. If one print device goes down, the printer automatically redirects the output to a working print device.

The general installation, configuration, and troubleshooting issues are basically identical in all modern versions of Windows. Here's a review of a typical Windows printer installation. I'll mention the trivial differences among Windows 2000, XP, and Vista as I go along.

Setting Up Printers

Setting up a printer is so easy that it's almost scary. Most printers are plug and play, so installing a printer is reduced to simply plugging it in and loading the driver if needed. If the system does not detect the printer or if the printer is not plug and play, click Start | Printers and Faxes in Windows XP to open the Printers applet; in Windows 2000, click Start | Settings | Printers. For Windows Vista, you need to open the Control Panel and find

● **Figure 15.12**   Printer driver and spooler in Windows

Figure 15.13 Choosing local or network printer in Windows XP

the Printer menu item—it is either by itself or, in Category View, under Hardware. You can also find the icon for this applet in the Control Panel of Windows 2000/XP.

As you might guess, you install a new printer by clicking the Add a Printer icon (somehow Microsoft has managed to leave the name of this applet unchanged through all Windows versions since 9x). This starts the Add Printer Wizard. After a pleasant intro screen, you must choose to install either a printer plugged directly into your system or a network printer (Figure 15.13). You also have the *Automatically detect and install my Plug and Play printer* option, which you can use in many cases when installing a USB printer.

If you choose a local printer (see Chapter 16, "Learning Local Area Networking," for a discussion of networked printers), the applet next asks you to select a port; select the one where you installed the new printer (Figure 15.14). Once you select the port, Windows asks you to specify the type of printer, either by selecting the type from the list or by using the Have Disk option, just as you would for any other device (Figure 15.15). Note the handy Windows Update button, which you can use to get the latest printer driver from the Internet. When you click Next on this screen, Windows installs the printer.

Figure 15.16 shows a typical Windows XP Printers and Faxes screen on a system with one printer installed. Note the small checkmark in the icon's corner; this shows that the device is the default printer. If you have multiple printers, you can change the default printer by selecting the printer's properties and checking Make Default Printer.

In addition to the regular driver installation outlined previously, some installations use printer emulation. *Printer emulation* simply means using a substitute printer driver for a printer, as opposed to using one made exclusively for that printer. You'll run into printer emulation in two

Figure 15.14 Selecting a port in Windows XP

Figure 15.15 Selecting a printer model/driver in Windows XP

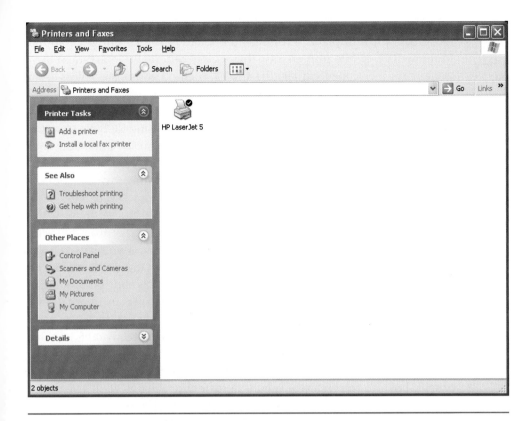

circumstances. First, some new printers do not come with their own drivers. They instead emulate a well-known printer (such as an HP LaserJet 4) and run perfectly well on that printer driver. Second, you may see emulation in the "I don't have the right driver!" scenario. I keep about three different HP LaserJet and Epson ink jet printers installed on my PC because I know that with these printer drivers, I can print to almost any printer. Some printers may require you to set them into an *emulation mode* to handle a driver other than their native one.

Optimizing Print Performance

Although a quality printer is the first step toward quality output, your output relies on factors other than the printer itself. What you see on the screen may not match what comes out of the printer, so calibration is important. Using the wrong type of paper can result in less than acceptable printed documents. Configuring the printer driver and spool settings can also affect your print jobs.

Calibration

If you've ever tweaked that digital photograph so it looks perfect onscreen, only to discover that the final printout was darker than you had hoped, consider calibrating your monitor. **Calibration** matches the print output of your printer to the visual output on your monitor and governs that through software. All three parts need to be set up properly for you to print what you see consistently.

Tech Tip

Readme Files

You've seen how to get your system to recognize a printer, but what do you do when you add a brand-new printer? Like most peripherals, the printer will include an installation CD-ROM that contains various useful files. One of the most important but least used tools on this CD-ROM is the Readme file. This file, generally in TXT format, contains the absolute latest information on any idiosyncrasies, problems, or incompatibilities related to your printer or printer driver. Usually, you can find it in the root folder of the installation CD-ROM, although many printer drivers install the Readme file on your hard drive so you can access it from the Start menu. The rule here is read first to avoid a headache later!

Computer monitors output in RGB—that is, they compose colors using red, green, and blue pixels, as discussed in Chapter 13, "Learning Video and Multimedia"—while printers mix their colors differently to arrive at their output. As mentioned earlier, the CMYK method composes colors from cyan (blue), magenta (red), yellow, and black.

The upshot of all this is that the printer tries to output—by using CMYK (or another technique)—what you see on the screen using RGB. Because the two color modes do not create color the same way, you see color shifts and not-so-subtle differences between the onscreen image and the printed image. By calibrating your monitor, you can adjust the setting to match the output of your printer. You can do this manually through "eyeballing" it or automatically by using calibration hardware.

To calibrate your monitor manually, obtain a test image from the Web (try sites such as www.DigitalDog.net) and print it out. If you have a good eye, you can compare this printout to what you see on the screen and make the adjustments manually through your monitor's controls or display settings.

Another option is to calibrate your printer by using an International Color Consortium (ICC) color profile, a preference file that instructs your printer to print colors a certain way—for example, to match what is on your screen. Loading a different color profile results in a different color output. Color profiles are sometimes included on the installation CD-ROM with a printer, but you can create or purchase custom profiles as well. The use of ICC profiles is not limited to printers; you can also use them to control the output of monitors, scanners, or even digital cameras. Windows Vista includes *Windows Color System* (WCS) to help build color profiles for use across devices. WCS is based on a new standard that Microsoft calls *color infrastructure and translation engine* (CITE).

■ Troubleshooting Printers

As easy as printers are to set up, they are equally robust at running, assuming that you install the proper drivers and keep the printer well maintained. But printer errors do occasionally develop. This section takes a look at the most common print problems with Windows.

Printers of all stripes share some common problems, such as print jobs that don't print, strangely sized prints, and misalignment. Other issues include consumables, sharing multiple printers, and crashing on power-up. Let's take a look at these general troubleshooting issues, but start with a recap of the tools of the trade.

Tools of the Trade

Before you jump in and start to work on a printer that's giving you fits, you'll need some tools. You can use the standard computer tech tools in your toolkit, plus a couple of printer-specific devices. Here are some that will come in handy:

- A multimeter for troubleshooting electrical problems such as faulty wall outlets
- Various cleaning solutions, such as denatured alcohol

- An extension magnet for grabbing loose screws in tight spaces and cleaning up iron-based toner

- An optical disc or USB thumb drive with test patterns for checking print quality

- Your trusty screwdriver—both a Phillips-head and flat-head, because if you bring just one kind, it's a sure bet that you'll need the other

Many printers allow you to print a test page either via the controls on the printer or through Windows. Make sure you read your printer's manual to find out how to do this, because printing a test page is often a vital trouble-shooting tool.

Print Job Never Prints

If you click Print but nothing comes out of the printer, first check all the obvious things. Is the printer on? Is it connected? Is it online? Does it have paper? Assuming the printer is in good order, it's time to look at the spooler. You can see the spooler status either by double-clicking the printer's icon in the Printers applet or by double-clicking the tiny printer icon in the notification area if it's present. If you're having a problem, the printer icon will almost always be there. Figure 15.17 shows the print spooler open.

Print spoolers can easily overflow or become corrupt due to a lack of disk space, too many print jobs, or one of a thousand other factors. The status window shows all of the pending print jobs and enables you to delete, start, or pause jobs. I usually just delete the affected print job(s) and try again.

Print spoolers are handy. If the printer goes down, you can just leave the print jobs in the spooler until the printer comes back online. Some versions of Windows require you to select Resume Printing manually, but others automatically continue the print job(s). If you have a printer that isn't coming on anytime soon, you can simply delete the print job in the spooler window and try another printer.

If you have problems with the print spooler, you can get around them by changing your print spool settings. Go into the Printers and Faxes applet, right-click the icon of the printer in question, and choose Properties. In the resulting Properties window (Figure 15.18), choose the *Print directly to the printer* radio button and click OK; then try sending your print job again. Note that this window also offers you the choice of printing immediately—that is, starting to print pages as soon as the spooler has enough information to feed to the printer—or holding off on printing until the entire job is spooled.

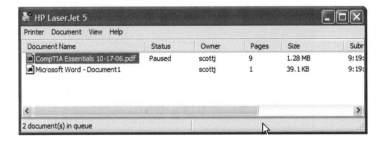

• **Figure 15.17**   Print spooler

● **Figure 15.18**   Print spool settings

Another possible cause for a stalled print job is that the printer is simply waiting for the correct paper! Laser printers in particular have settings that tell them what size paper is in their standard paper tray or trays. If the application sending a print job specifies a different paper size—for example, it wants to print a standard No. 10 envelope, or perhaps a legal sheet, but the standard paper tray holds only 8.5 × 11 letter paper—the printer usually pauses and holds up the queue until someone switches out the tray or manually feeds the type of paper that this print job requires. You can usually override this pause, even without having the specified paper, by pressing the OK or GO button on the printer.

The printer's default paper tray and paper size options will differ greatly depending on the printer type and model. To find these settings, go into the printer's Properties window from the Printers and Faxes applet, and then select the Device Settings tab. This list of settings includes Form To Tray Assignment, where you can specify which tray (in the case of a printer with multiple paper trays) holds which size paper.

Strange Sizes

A print job that comes out a strange size usually points to a user mistake in setting up the print job. All applications have a Print command and a Page Setup interface. The Page Setup interface enables you to define a number of print options, which vary from application to application. Figure 15.19 shows the Page Setup options for Microsoft Word. Make sure the page is set up properly before you blame the printer for a problem.

● **Figure 15.19**   Page Setup options for Microsoft Word

If you know the page is set up correctly, recheck the printer drivers. If necessary, uninstall and reinstall the printer drivers. If the problem persists, you may have a serious problem with the printer's print engine, but that comes up as a likely answer only when you continually get the same strangely sized printouts using a variety of applications.

Misaligned or Garbage Prints

Misaligned or garbage printouts invariably point to a corrupted or incorrect driver. Make sure you're using the right driver (it's hard to mess this up, but not impossible) and then uninstall and reinstall the printer driver and print a test page. If the problem persists, you may be asking the printer to do something it cannot do. For example, you may be printing to a PostScript printer with a PCL driver. Check the printer type to verify that you haven't installed the wrong type of driver for that printer!

Tech Tip

Check the MSDS

When in doubt about what to do with a component, check with the manufacturer for a **material safety data sheet (MSDS)**. *These standardized forms provide detailed information about the potential environmental hazards associated with different components and proper disposal methods. For example, surf to www.hp.com/hpinfo/ globalcitizenship/environment/ productdata/index.html to find the latest MSDS for all Hewlett-Packard products. This isn't just a printer issue—you can find an MSDS for most PC components. When in doubt about how to get rid of any PC component, check with the manufacturer for an MSDS.*

MSDSs contain important information regarding hazardous materials, such as safe use procedures and emergency response instructions. An MSDS is typically posted anywhere a hazardous chemical is used.

Chapter 15 Review

■ Chapter Summary

After reading this chapter and completing the exercises, you should understand the following aspects of printers.

Describe current printer technologies

- Impact printers create an image on paper by physically striking an ink ribbon against the paper's surface. The most commonly used impact printer technology is dot matrix. Dot-matrix printers have a large installed base in businesses, and they can be used for multipart forms because they actually strike the paper. Dot-matrix printers use a grid, or matrix, of tiny pins, also known as printwires, to strike an inked printer ribbon and produce images on paper. The case that holds the printwires is called a printhead. Dot-matrix printers come in two varieties: 9-pin (draft quality) and 24-pin (letter quality).

- Inkjet printers include a printhead mechanism, support electronics, a transfer mechanism to move the printhead back and forth, and a paper feed component to drag, move, and eject paper. They eject ink through tiny tubes. The heat or pressure used to move the ink is created by tiny resistors or electroconductive plates at the end of each tube.

- Ink is stored in ink cartridges. Older color printers used two cartridges: one for black and one for cyan, magenta, and yellow. Newer printers come with four, six, eight, or more cartridges.

- The quality of a print image is called the print resolution. The resolution is measured in dots per inch (dpi), which has two values: horizontal and vertical. An example of a resolution is 600 × 600 dpi. Printing speed is measured in pages per minute (ppm). Modern inkjet printers can print on a variety of media, including glossy photo paper, optical discs, or fabric.

- Dye-sublimation printers are used to achieve excellent print quality, especially in color, but they're expensive. Documents printed through the dye-sublimation process display continuous-tone images, meaning that each pixel dot is a blend of the dye colors. This is in contrast to other print technologies' dithered images, which use closely packed, single-color dots to simulate blended colors.

- Two kinds of thermal printers create either quick one-color printouts such as faxes or store receipts (direct thermal) or higher-quality color prints (thermal wax transfer).

- Using a process called electro-photographic imaging, laser printers produce high-quality and high-speed output. Laser printers usually use lasers as a light source because of their precision, but some lower-cost printers may use LED arrays instead. The toner cartridge in a laser printer supplies the toner that creates the image on the page; many other laser printer parts, especially those that suffer the most wear and tear, have been incorporated into the toner cartridge. Although the majority of laser printers are monochrome, you can find color laser printers capable of printing photographs.

- Be aware of the cost of consumables when purchasing a printer. Some less expensive printers may seem like a good deal, but ink or toner cartridge replacements can cost as much as the entire printer.

- The photosensitive drum in a laser printer is an aluminum cylinder coated with particles of photosensitive compounds. The erase lamp exposes the entire surface of the photosensitive drum to light, making the photosensitive coating conductive and leaving the surface particles electrically neutral. When the primary corona is charged with an extremely high voltage, an electric field (or corona) forms, enabling voltage to pass to the drum and charge the photosensitive particles on its surface; the surface of the drum receives a uniform negative voltage of between ~600 and ~1,000 V.

- The laser acts as the writing mechanism of the printer. When particles are struck by the laser, they are discharged and left with a ~100-V negative charge. The toner in a laser printer is a fine powder made up of plastic particles bonded to iron particles. The toner cylinder charges the toner with a negative charge of between ~200 and ~500 V.

Because that charge falls between the original uniform negative charge of the photosensitive drum (~600 to ~1000 V) and the charge of the particles on the drum's surface hit by the laser (~100 V), particles of toner are attracted to the areas of the photosensitive drum that have been hit by the laser. The transfer corona applies a positive charge to the paper, drawing the negatively charged toner particles on the drum to the paper. The toner is merely resting on top of the paper after the static charge eliminator has removed the paper's static charge. Two rollers, a pressure roller and a heated roller, are used to fuse the toner to the paper.

- All laser printers have at least two separate power supplies. The primary power supply, which may actually be more than one power supply, provides power to the motors that move the paper, the system electronics, the laser, and the transfer corona. The high-voltage power supply usually only provides power to the primary corona; it is one of the most dangerous devices in the world of PCs. Always turn off a laser printer before opening it up.

- A laser printer's mechanical functions are served by complex gear systems packed together in discrete units generically called gear packs or gearboxes. Most laser printers have two or three. Every laser printer has sensors that detect a broad range of conditions, such as paper jams, empty paper trays, or low toner levels.

- Every laser printer contains at least one electronic system board (many have two or three) that contains the main processor, the printer's ROM, and the RAM used to store the image before it is printed. When the printer doesn't have enough RAM to store the image before it prints, you get a memory overflow problem. Most printers can use generic DRAM like the kind you use in your PC, but check with the manufacturer to be sure.

- Because even tiny concentrations of ozone (O_3) will cause damage to printer components, most laser printers have a special ozone filter that needs to be vacuumed or replaced periodically.

- Solid ink printers use sticks of solid ink to produce extremely vibrant color. The inks are melted, absorbed into the paper fibers, and then solidify, producing continuous-tone output in a single pass. The solid ink sticks may be inserted midway through a print job if a certain color needs to be topped off.

- ASCII contains a variety of control codes for transferring data, some of which can be used to control printers; ASCII code 10 (or 0A in hex) means "Line Feed," and ASCII code 12 (0C) means "Form Feed." These commands have been standard since before the creation of IBM PCs, and all printers respond to them; however, the control codes are extremely limited. Utilizing high-end graphics and a wide variety of fonts requires more advanced languages.

- Adobe Systems' PostScript page description language is a device-independent printer language capable of high-resolution graphics and scalable fonts. Because PostScript is understood by printers at a hardware level, the majority of the image processing is done by the printer and not the PC's CPU, so PostScript printers print faster. PostScript defines the page as a single raster image; this makes PostScript files extremely portable.

- Hewlett-Packard's printer control language (PCL) features a set of printer commands greatly expanded from ASCII, but it does not support advanced graphical functions. PCL6 features scalable fonts and additional line-drawing commands. PCL uses a series of commands to define the characters on the page, rather than defining the page as a single raster image like PostScript.

- Windows 2000/XP use the graphical device interface (GDI) component of the operating system to handle print functions. The GDI uses the CPU rather than the printer to process a print job and then sends the completed job to the printer. As long as the printer has a capable-enough raster image processor (RIP) and plenty of RAM, you don't need to worry about the printer language at all in most situations. Windows Vista/7 includes support for the XML Paper Specification (XPS) print path, which requires an XPS-compatible driver. Some devices support XPS natively.

- Most printers connect to one of two ports on the PC: a DB-25 parallel port or a USB port. The parallel connection is the classic way to plug in a printer, but most new printers use USB. The parallel port was included in the original IBM PC as a faster alternative to serial communication and has been kept around for backward compatibility. Parallel ports are slow by modern standards, with a maximum data transfer rate of 150 KBps. Parallel ports lack true bidirectional capability. A standard parallel connection normally manifests as a female

DB-25 connector on the PC and a corresponding male connector on the printer cable. Eight wires are used as grounds, four for control signals, five for status signals, and eight for data signals going from the PC to the device. The parallel connector on the printer side is called a Centronics connector.

- IEEE 1284 was developed as a standard for a backward-compatible, high-speed, bidirectional parallel port for the PC. It requires support for compatibility, nibble mode, byte mode, EPP, and ECP; a standard method of negotiating compatible modes between printer and PC; standard cables and connectors; and a standard electrical interface.

- USB is the most popular type of printer connection today. USB printers rarely come with the necessary USB cable, so you may need to purchase one at the same time you purchase the printer. FireWire printers are less prevalent than USB but offer easy connectivity, high speed, and hot-swapping capability.

- Network printers come with their own network card and connect directly to a network. This can be an RJ-45 port for an actual cable, or it can be a wireless network card. Some printers offer Bluetooth adapters for networking. To connect a printer with a network card directly to a network, use a print server.

Install a printer on a Windows PC

- In Windows 2000/XP/Vista, a printer is not a physical device; it is a program that controls one or more physical printers. The physical printer is called a print device. Print drivers and a spooler are still present, but in 2000/XP/Vista they are integrated into the printer itself.

- Select Start | Printers and Faxes in Windows XP to open the Printers applet; in Windows 2000, select Start | Settings | Printers. In Windows Vista select the Printers item from the Control Panel. This applet can also be found in the Control Panel of Windows 2000/XP. You install a new printer by clicking the Add Printer icon to start the Add Printer Wizard. You must choose to install a local or a network printer; and you must select a port for a local printer. You must specify the printer type from the wizard's list, or use the Have Disk option. Windows XP and Vista's applet features a Windows Update button you can use to get the latest printer driver from the Internet.

- One printer will always be the default printer. If you have more than one printer installed, you can make any printer the default printer. The icon for the default printer has a small checkmark in the corner. If you have multiple printers, you can change the default printer by selecting the printer's properties and checking Make Default Printer.

- Printer emulation means to use a substitute printer driver for a printer, as opposed to one made exclusively for that printer. Some printers are designed to emulate other, more widely supported models. If you don't have the specific driver for a printer, you can often use the driver from a similar model.

- Your monitor creates colors by using RGB, while a printer outputs in CMYK. This difference can lead to a printed page differing greatly in color and tone from what you see on the monitor. Calibrating your monitor to your printer is an important step in printing the colors you see on your screen. Manually calibrate your monitor by eyeballing it, use ICC color profiles to instruct the printer to output colors a certain way, or use calibration hardware and software to automate the process. Windows Vista includes Windows Color System to help build color profiles for use across devices.

Recognize and fix basic printer problems

- When troubleshooting a printer, first check all the obvious things. Is the printer on? Is it connected? Is it online? Does it have paper? Then check the spooler status either by double-clicking the printer's icon in the Printers applet, or by double-clicking the tiny printer icon in the system tray if it's present. You may be able to bypass spooler problems by changing the printer properties setting to *Print directly to the printer*.

- A print job that comes out a strange size usually points to a user mistake in setting up the print job. Use the program's Page Setup feature to fix these problems. If you know the page is set up correctly, recheck the printer drivers. Misaligned or garbage printouts invariably point to a corrupted or incorrect driver.

- Printer manufacturers will supply an MSDS for each of their products; they provide detailed information about the potential environmental hazards associated with different components and proper disposal methods. This isn't just a printer issue—you can find an MSDS for most PC components.

■ Key Terms

American Standard Code for Information Interchange (ASCII) *(503)*
calibration *(509)*
Centronics connector *(505)*
consumable *(499)*
DB-25 connector *(505)*
dot-matrix printer *(495)*
dots per inch (dpi) *(497)*
dye-sublimation printer *(498)*
erase lamp *(500)*
fuser assembly *(501)*
graphical device interface (GDI) *(504)*
IEEE 1284 standard *(505)*
impact printer *(495)*
ink cartridge *(496)*
inkjet printer *(495)*
laser *(500)*
laser printer *(499)*
material safety data sheet (MSDS) *(513)*

near-letter quality (NLQ) *(495)*
network printer *(506)*
pages per minute (ppm) *(497)*
parallel port *(504)*
photosensitive drum *(499)*
PostScript *(503)*
primary corona *(500)*
print resolution *(497)*
printer control language (PCL) *(504)*
printhead *(495)*
printwire *(495)*
solid ink printer *(502)*
static charge eliminator *(501)*
thermal printer *(499)*
toner *(500)*
toner cartridge *(499)*
transfer corona *(501)*
XML Paper Specification (XPS) print path *(504)*

■ Key Term Quiz

Use the Key Terms list to complete the sentences that follow. Not all terms will be used.

1. The _____ requires support for compatibility mode, nibble mode, byte mode, EPP, and ECP.

2. A standard parallel printer cable normally has a male _____ on one end and a 36-pin _____ on the other.

3. Laser printers use lasers to create the print image on a(n) _____.

4. The _____ on a standard laser printer contains a pressure roller and a heated roller.

5. The resolution of a printer is measured in _____.

6. A printer's speed is rated in _____.

7. The _____ is responsible for cleaning the photosensitive drum of electrical charge.

■ Multiple-Choice Quiz

1. What is the approximate maximum data transfer rate of a standard parallel port?

   A. 50 KBps

   B. 150 KBps

   C. 500 KBps

   D. 2 MBps

2. Janet just bought a new computer. She wants to install her three-year-old inkjet printer on the new system but has lost the driver CD. She can't

get on the Internet to download the latest drivers. What should she do for drivers?

   A. Install a driver for a similar printer.

   B. She's stuck until she can get on the Internet.

   C. She can use the Windows built-in drivers.

   D. She can install the printer without drivers.

3. The dye-sublimation printing technique is an example of what method of color printing?

   A. CMYK

   B. Thermal wax transfer

C. RGB

D. Direct thermal

4. The output from your inkjet printer appears much darker than what you see on your screen. What is the problem?

A. You are using a paper weight that is not supported in the MSDS.

B. The printer and monitor need to be calibrated.

C. The color ink cartridges are almost empty.

D. The black ink cartridge is almost empty.

5. What is the best way to make a printer available to everyone on your network and maintain the highest level of availability?

A. Use a FireWire printer connected to a user's PC and share that printer on the network.

B. Use a USB printer connected to a user's PC and share that printer on the network.

C. Use a network printer connected directly to the network.

D. Use a mechanical switch box with the printer.

6. What do you use to manage print jobs?

A. Print spooler

B. Material safety data sheet

C. Page Setup

D. Printhead

7. John just installed a second printer on his system. When he prints in Microsoft Word, the job goes to the wrong printer. What does he need to do to get print jobs always to go to one printer or the other?

A. He needs to set the primary printer.

B. He needs to set the main printer.

C. He needs to set the default printer.

D. He needs to set the system printer.

8. What document tells you how to properly dispose of potentially harmful products?

A. Environmental disposal form

B. Material safety data sheet

C. Material disposal data sheet

D. Hazardous waste compliance sheet

9. What is print speed measured in?

A. mph

B. f/s

C. pph

D. ppm

Essay Quiz

1. Your department needs a number of color inkjet printers. At your organization, though, all purchases are handled through professional buyers. Sadly, they know nothing about color inkjet printers. You need to submit a Criteria for Purchase form to your buyers. This is the standard form that your organization gives to buyers so they know what to look for in the products they buy. What are the top three purchasing criteria that you think they need to consider? Write the criteria as simply and clearly as possible.

2. Interview a person who uses a computer for work. Ask what the person does and then write a short description of the type of printer that would most suit that person's needs. Explain why this printer would be the best choice.

3. You have been tasked to make a recommendation for a printer purchase for a busy office of ten people. Make a case for purchasing either an inkjet or laser printer, providing enough information to compare the two technologies. You can choose the type of business, so recommend the appropriate printer, such as a laser printer to an office that primarily produces text documents. Make your recommendation opposite to the one you made for essay question #2.

4. Write a short essay comparing and contrasting inkjet printers with the three less-common print technologies: dye-sublimation, thermal, and solid ink.

Lab Project

• Lab Project 15.1

Laser printers often have rather complex maintenance procedures and schedules. Select a laser printer—preferably one that you actually have on hand—and locate and compile, on paper, all of the following information about your printer:

- Maintenance schedule
- List of error codes
- Maintenance procedures
- Location of the latest drivers for Windows

chapter 16

Learning Local Area Networking

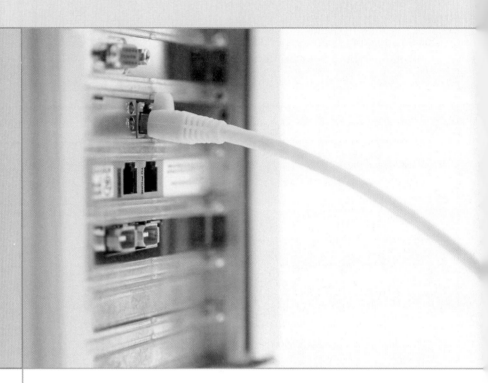

"I'm interested in upgrading my 28.8 kilobaud Internet connection to a 1.5 megabit fiberoptic T1 line. Will you be able to provide an IP router that's compatible with my token ring Ethernet LAN configuration?"

—COMIC BOOK GUY, *THE SIMPSONS*

In this chapter, you will learn how to

- **Explain networking technologies**
- **Explain network organization and protocols**
- **Configure TCP/IP**
- **Troubleshoot networks**

Networks dominate the modern computing environment. A vast percentage of businesses have PCs connected in a small local area network (LAN), and big businesses simply can't survive without connecting their many offices into a single wide area network (WAN). Even the operating systems of today demand networks. Windows XP, Vista, and 7, for example, come out of the box *assuming* you'll attach them to a network of some sort just to make them work past 30 days (product activation), and they get all indignant if you don't.

Because networks are so common today, every good tech needs to know the basics of networking technology, operating systems, implementation, and troubleshooting. Accordingly, this chapter teaches you how to build and troubleshoot a basic network.

A Brief History of Networking Technologies

When the first network designers sat down at a café to figure out how to get two or more PCs to share data and peripherals, they had to write a lot of details on little white napkins to answer even the most basic questions. The first big question was: *How*? It's easy to say, "Well, just run a wire between them!" Although most networks do manifest themselves via some type of cable, this barely touches the thousands of questions that come into play here. Here are a few of the *big* questions:

- How will each computer be identified? If two or more computers want to talk at the same time, how do you ensure that all conversations are understood?

- What kind of wire? What gauge? How many wires in the cable? Which wires do which things? How long can the cable be? What type of connectors?

- If more than one PC accesses the same file, how can they be prevented from destroying each other's changes to that file?

- How can access to data and peripherals be controlled?

Clearly, making a modern PC network entails a lot more than just stringing up some cable! Most commonly, you have a **client** machine, a PC that requests information or services. It needs a **network interface card (NIC)** that defines or labels the client on the network. A NIC also helps break files into smaller data units, called **packets**, to send across the network, and it helps reassemble the packets it receives into whole files. Second, you need some medium for delivering the packets between two or more PCs—most often this is a wire that can carry electrical pulses; sometimes it's radio waves or other wireless methods. Third, your PC's operating system has to be able to communicate with its own networking hardware and with other machines on the network. Finally, modern PC networks often employ a **server** machine that provides information or services. Figure 16.1 shows a typical network layout.

This section of the chapter looks at the inventive ways network engineers found to handle the first two of the four issues. After a brief look at core technology, the chapter dives into four specific types of networks. You'll dig into the software side of things later in the chapter.

Topology

If a bunch of computers connect together to make a network, some logic or order must influence the way they connect. Perhaps each computer connects to a single main line that snakes around the office. Each computer might have its own cable, with all of the cables coming together to a central point. Or maybe all of the cables from all of the computers connect to a main loop that moves data along a track, picking up and dropping off data like a circular subway line.

A network's *topology* describes the way that computers connect to each other in that network. The most common network topologies are called *bus*, *ring*, *star*, and *mesh*. Figure 16.2 shows the four types: a **bus topology**, where

Windows Vista Business workstations

Windows Server 2008

• **Figure 16.1**   A typical network

all computers connect to the network via a main line called a *bus cable*; a **ring topology**, where all computers on the network attach to a central ring of cable; a **star topology**, where the computers on the network connect to a central wiring point (usually called a *hub*); and a **mesh topology**, where each computer has a dedicated line to every other computer—the mesh topology is mostly used in wireless networks. There are also **hybrid topologies**, such as star bus or star ring, that combine aspects of the other topologies to capitalize on their strengths and minimize their weaknesses. You'll look at the most important hybrid topology, star bus, in a moment, but for now, make sure you know the four main topologies!

If you're looking at Figure 16.2 and thinking that a mesh topology looks amazingly resilient and robust, it is—at least on paper. Because every computer physically connects to every other computer on the network, even if half of the PCs crash, the network functions as well as ever (for the survivors). In a practical sense, however, implementing a true mesh topology network would be an expensive mess. For example, even for a tiny network with only 10 PCs, you would need *45* separate and distinct pieces of cable to connect every PC to every other PC. What a mesh mess! Because of this, mesh topologies have never been practical in a cabled network.

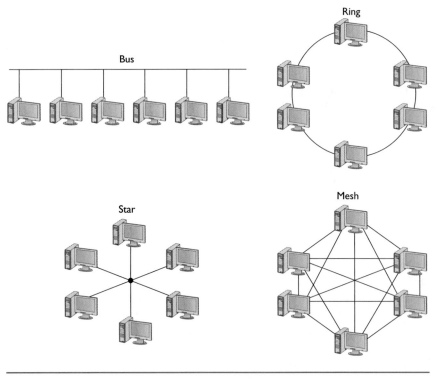

• **Figure 16.2**   Clockwise from top left: bus, ring, mesh, and star topologies

Although a topology describes the method by which systems in a network connect, the topology alone doesn't describe all of the features necessary to make a cabling system work. The term *bus topology*, for example, describes a network that consists of some number of machines connected to the network via the same piece of cable. Notice that this definition leaves a lot of questions unanswered. What is the cable made of? How long can it be? How do the machines decide which machine should send data at a specific moment? A network based on a bus topology can answer these questions in a number of different ways.

Most techs make a clear distinction between the *logical topology* of a network—how the network is laid out on paper, with nice straight lines and boxes—and the physical topology. The *physical topology* describes the typically messy computer network, with cables running diagonally through the ceiling space or snaking their way through walls. If someone describes the topology of a particular network, make sure you understand whether they're talking about the logical or physical topology.

Over the years, manufacturers and standards bodies created several specific network technologies based on different topologies. A *network technology* is a practical application of a topology and other critical technologies to provide a method to get data from one computer to another on a network.

Network Communication

If there was nothing more to computer networking than simply choosing how to wire a bunch of computers together, then this chapter would already be over. However, as you might expect, it's considerably more complex than that. The computers not only have to be hooked up to one another, but also must have a means of transmitting data to one another in a way that every computer in the network can understand. This section looks at how that's done.

Packets/Frames and NICs

Data is moved from one PC to another in discrete chunks called *packets* or *frames*. The terms *packet* and *frame* are interchangeable. Every NIC in the world has a built-in identifier, a binary address unique to that single network card, called a **media access control (MAC) address**. You read that right—every network card in the world has its own unique MAC address! The MAC address is 48 bits long, providing more than 281 *trillion* MAC addresses, so there are plenty of MAC addresses to go around. MAC addresses may be binary, but we represent them by using 12 hexadecimal characters. These MAC addresses are burned into every NIC, and some NIC makers print the MAC address on the card. Figure 16.3 shows the System Information utility description of a NIC, with the MAC address highlighted.

• **Figure 16.3** MAC address

Hey! I thought we were talking about packets? Well, we are, but you need to understand MAC addresses to understand packets. The many varieties of packets share certain common features (Figure 16.4). First, packets contain the MAC address of the network card to which the data is being sent. Second, they have the MAC address of the network card that sent the data. Third is the data itself (at this point, we have no idea what the data is—certain software handles that question), which can vary in size depending on the type of frame. Finally, some type of data check—such as a **cyclic redundancy check (CRC)**—is performed and information is stored in the packet to enable the receiving network card to verify if the data was received in good order.

This discussion of packets raises the question, how big is the packet? Or more specifically, how much data do you put into each packet? How do you ensure that the receiving PC understands the *way* the data was broken down by the sending machine and can thus put the pieces back together? The problem in answering these questions is that they encompass so many items. When the first networks were created, *everything* from the frames to the connectors to the type of cable had to be invented from scratch.

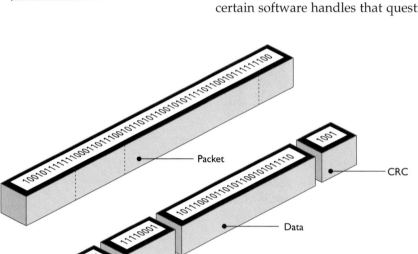

Packet

CRC

Data

Sender MAC

Recipient MAC

• **Figure 16.4**   Generic packet/frame

To make a successful network, you need the sending and receiving PCs to use the same hardware protocol. A **hardware protocol** defines many aspects of a network, from the topology, to the packet type, to the cabling and connectors used. A hardware protocol defines everything necessary to get data from one computer to another. Over the years, many hardware protocols have been implemented, with such names as Token Ring, FDDI, and ARCnet, but one hardware protocol dominates the modern PC computing landscape: Ethernet.

Introducing Ethernet

A consortium of companies composed of Digital Equipment, Intel, and Xerox invented the first network in the mid 1970s. More than just creating a network, they wrote a series of standards that defined everything necessary to get data from one computer to another. This series of standards was called **Ethernet**, and it is the dominant standard for today's networks. Ethernet comes in two main flavors defined by cabling type: unshielded twisted pair and fiber optic. Because all flavors of Ethernet use the same packet type, you can have any combination of hardware devices and cabling systems on an Ethernet network and all of the PCs will be able to communicate just fine.

Most modern Ethernet networks employ one of three technologies (and sometimes all three), **10BaseT**, **100BaseT**, or **1000BaseT**. As the numbers in the names suggest, 10BaseT networks run at 10 Mbps, 100BaseT networks run at 100 Mbps, and 1000BaseT networks—called Gigabit Ethernet—run at

1000 Mbps, or 1 Gbps. All three technologies—sometimes referred to collectively as *10/100/1000BaseT* or just plain Ethernet—use a *star bus* topology and connect via a type of cable called **unshielded twisted pair (UTP)**.

Earlier forms of Ethernet used coaxial cable: 10Base5 used RG-8 coaxial cables with DB-15 connectors called AUI connectors and could run up to 500 meters. 10Base2 used RG-62 cable with BNC connectors and could run up to 185 meters.

Star Bus

Imagine taking a bus network and shrinking the bus down so it will fit inside a box. Then, instead of attaching each PC directly to the wire, you attach them via cables to special ports on the box (Figure 16.5). The box with the bus takes care of all of the tedious details required by a bus network. The bus topology would look a lot like a star topology, wouldn't it?

The central box with the bus is called a hub or switch. The **hub** provides a common point for connection for network devices. Hubs can have a wide variety of ports. Most consumer-level hubs have four or eight, but business-level hubs can have 32 or more ports. A hub is the old-style device, rarely used in today's networks. A **switch** is a far superior and far more common version of a hub. Figure 16.6 shows a typical consumer-level switch.

Different networks come in different speeds. One common speed is 100 Megabits per second (Mbps). We call this speed a **bandwidth**. If you put 32 PCs on a 32-port 100-Mbps hub, you have 32 PCs sharing the 100-Mbps bandwidth. A switch addresses that problem by making each port its own separate network. Each PC gets to use the full bandwidth available. The bottom line? Swap out your old hubs for newer switches and you'll dramatically improve your network performance.

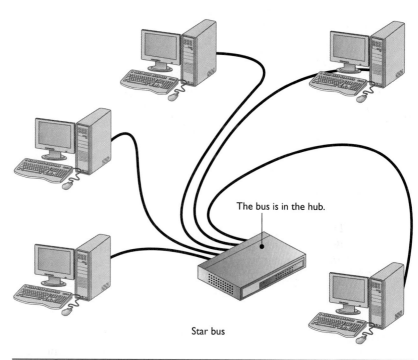

The bus is in the hub.

Star bus

• **Figure 16.5**   Star bus

• **Figure 16.6**   A switch

Cheap and centralized, a star bus network does not go down if a cable breaks. True, the network would go down if the hub itself failed, but that is rare. Even if a hub fails, replacing a hub in a closet is much easier than tracing a bus running through walls and ceilings and trying to find a break!

Unshielded Twisted Pair

Unshielded twisted pair (UTP) cabling is the specified cabling for 10/100/1000BaseT and is the predominant cabling system used today. Many types of twisted pair cabling are available, and the type used depends on the needs of the network. Twisted pair cabling consists of AWG 22–26 gauge wire twisted together into color-coded pairs. Each wire is individually insulated and encased as a group in a common jacket.

CAT Levels   UTP cables come in categories that define the maximum speed at which data can be transferred (also called *bandwidth*). The major categories (CATs) are as follows:

CAT 1	Standard phone line	CAT 2	Data speeds up to 4 Mbps (ISDN and T1 lines)
CAT 3	Data speeds up to 16 Mbps	CAT 4	Data speeds up to 20 Mbps
CAT 5	Data speeds up to 100 Mbps	CAT 5e	Data speeds up to 1 Gbps
CAT 6	Data speeds up to 10 Gbps		

The CAT level should be clearly marked on the cable, as Figure 16.7 shows.

The *Telecommunication Industry Association/Electronics Industries Alliance* (*TIA/EIA*) establishes the UTP categories, which fall under the TIA/EIA 568 specification. Currently, most installers use CAT 5e or CAT 6 cable. Although many networks run at 10 Mbps, the industry standard has shifted to networks designed to run at 100 Mbps and faster. Because only CAT 5 or better handles these speeds, just about everyone is installing the higher rated cabling, even if they are running at speeds that CAT 3 or CAT 4 would do. Consequently, it is becoming more difficult to get anything but CAT 5, CAT 5e, or CAT 6 cables.

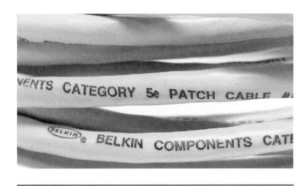

● **Figure 16.7**   Cable markings for CAT level

Shielded Twisted Pair

Shielded twisted pair (STP), as its name implies, consists of twisted pairs of wires surrounded by shielding to protect them from EMI, or electromagnetic interference. STP is pretty rare, primarily because there's so little need for STP's shielding; it only really matters in locations with excessive electronic noise, such as a shop floor area with lots of lights, electric motors, or other machinery that could cause problems for other cables.

Implementing 10/100/1000BaseT

The 10BaseT, 100BaseT, and 1000BaseT cabling standards require two pairs of wires: a pair for sending and a pair for receiving. 10BaseT runs on CAT 3, CAT 4, or CAT 5 cable. 100BaseT requires at least CAT 5 to run. 1000BaseT is a special case because it needs all four pairs of wires in a CAT 5e or CAT 6 cable. These cables use a connector called an **RJ-45** connector. The *RJ* (*registered jack*) designation was invented by Ma Bell (the phone company, for you youngsters) years ago and is still used today. Currently only two types of RJ connectors are used for networking: RJ-11 and RJ-45 (Figure 16.8). **RJ-11** is the connector that hooks your telephone to the telephone jack. It supports up to two pairs of wires, though most phone lines use only one pair. The other pair is used to support a second phone line. RJ-11 connectors are primarily used for dial-up networking (see Chapter 18, "Learning the Internet") and are not used in any common LAN installation, although a few weird (and out of business) "network in a box" companies used them. RJ-45 is the standard for UTP connectors. RJ-45 has connections for up to four pairs and is visibly much wider than RJ-11. Figure 16.9 shows the position of the #1 and #8 pins on an RJ-45 jack.

The TIA/EIA has two standards for connecting the RJ-45 connector to the UTP cable: the TIA/EIA 568A and the TIA/EIA 568B. Both are acceptable. You do not have to follow any standard as long as you use the same pairings on each end of the cable; however, you will make your life simpler if you choose a standard. Make sure that all of your cabling uses the same standard and you will save a great deal of work in the end. Most importantly, *keep records!*

Like all wires, the wires in UTP are numbered. However, a number does not appear on each wire. Instead, each wire has a standardized color. Table 16.1 shows the official TIA/EIA Standard Color Chart for UTP.

• **Figure 16.8** RJ-11 and RJ-45

Table 16.1	**UTP Cabling Color Chart**					
Pin	568A	568B	Pin	568A	568B
1	White/Green	White/Orange	5	White/Blue	White/Blue
2	Green	Orange	6	Orange	Green
3	White/Orange	White/Green	7	White/Brown	White/Brown
4	Blue	Blue	8	Brown	Brown

• **Figure 16.9** RJ-45 pin numbers

Multispeed Cards All Ethernet networks share the same language, so you can easily have mixed or combined networks. All it takes is a network card capable of running at multiple speeds or even over multiple cables. Most NICs built into motherboards today, for example, are Gigabit autosensing cards (Figure 16.10). If you plug into a 100BaseT network, they automatically run at 100 Mbps. If you plug into a 1000 Mbps network, they quickly ramp up and run at 1000 Mbps.

Tech Tip

Plenum versus PVC Cabling

Most workplace installations of network cable go up above the ceiling and then drop down through the walls to present a nice port in the wall. The space in the ceiling, under the floors, and in the walls through which cable runs is called the plenum *space. The potential problem with this cabling running through the plenum space is that the protective sheathing for networking cables, called the* jacket, *is made from plastic, and if you get any plastic hot enough, it creates smoke and noxious fumes. Standard network cables usually use PVC (polyvinyl chloride) for the jacket, but PVC produces noxious fumes when burned. Fumes from cables burning in the plenum space can quickly spread throughout the building, so you want to use a more fire-retardant cable in the plenum space. Plenum-grade cable is simply network cabling with a fire-retardant jacket and is required for cables that go in the plenum space. Plenum-grade cable costs about three to five times more than PVC, but you should use it whenever you install cable in a plenum space.*

Tech Tip

Crossover Cables

*You can actually hook two network cards together without a hub by using a special UTP cable called a **crossover cable**. A crossover cable is a standard UTP cable but with one RJ-45 connector using the 568A standard and the other using the 568B. This reverses the signal between sending and receiving wires and thus does the job of a hub or switch. Crossover cables work great as a quick way to network two PCs. You can purchase a crossover cable at any computer store.*

• **Figure 16.10**   NIC built into motherboard

Duplex and Half-Duplex   All modern NICs can run in **full-duplex** mode, meaning they can send and receive data at the same time. The vast majority of NICs and switches use a feature called *autosensing* to accommodate very old devices that might attach to the network and need to run in half-duplex mode. Half-duplex means that the device can send and receive, but not at the same time. An obvious example of a half-duplex device is the walkie-talkies you played with as a kid that required you to press and hold the orange button to transmit—at which time you couldn't hear anything. Half-duplex devices are exceedingly rare in modern computers, but you need to understand this option. Some NICs just can't handle full-duplex communication when you plug them directly into another NIC by using a crossover cable—that is, no switch. Dropping both NICs down from full-duplex or autosensing can sometimes enable these odd NICs to communicate.

Link Lights   All NICs made today have some type of light-emitting diode (LED) *status indicator* that gives information about the state of the NIC's link to whatever's on the other end of the connection. Even though you know the lights are actually LEDs, get used to calling them **link lights**, as that's the term all network techs use. NICs can have between one and four different link lights, and the LEDs can be any color. These lights give you clues about what's happening with the link and are one of the first items to check whenever you think a system is disconnected from the network (Figure 16.11).

Hubs and switches also have link lights, enabling you to check the connectivity at both ends of the cable. If a PC can't access a network, always first check the link lights. Multispeed devices usually have a link light that tells you the speed of the connection. In Figure 16.12, the light for port 2 on the top photo is orange, for example, signifying that the other end of the cable is plugged into either a 10BaseT or 100BaseT NIC. The same port connected to a Gigabit NIC—that's the lower picture—displays a green LED.

• **Figure 16.11**   Mmmm, pretty lights!

A properly functioning link light is steadily on when the NIC is connected to another device. No flickering, no on and off, just on. A link light that is off or flickering shows a connection problem.

Another light is the **activity light**. This little guy turns on when the card detects network traffic, so it makes an intermittent flickering when operating properly. The activity light is a lifesaver for detecting problems, because in the real world, the connection light sometimes lies to you. If the connection light says the connection is good, the next step is to try to copy a file or do something else to create network traffic. If the activity light does not flicker, you have a problem.

No standard governs how NIC manufacturers use their lights; as a result, they come in an amazing array of colors and layouts. When you encounter a NIC with a number of LEDs, take a moment to try to figure out what each one means. Although different NICs have different ways of arranging and using their LEDs, the functions are always the same: link, activity, and speed.

• **Figure 16.12**   Multispeed lights

> Though no real standard exists for NIC LEDs, CompTIA will test you on some more-or-less de facto LED meanings. You should know that a solid green light means connectivity, a flashing green light means intermittent connectivity, no green light means no connectivity, and a flashing amber light means there are collisions on the network (which is sometimes okay). Also, know that the first things you should check when having connectivity issues are your NIC's LEDs.

Fiber Optic Ethernet

Fiber optic cable is a very attractive way to transmit Ethernet network packets. First, because it uses light instead of electricity, fiber optic cable is immune to electrical problems such as lightning, short circuits, and static. Second, fiber optic signals travel much farther, up to 2000 meters (compared with 100 meters on UTP) with some standards. Most fiber Ethernet networks use *62.5/125 multimode* fiber optic cable. All fiber Ethernet networks that use these cables require two cables. Figure 16.13 shows three of the more common connectors used in fiber optic networks. Square *SC* connectors are shown in the middle and on the right, and the round *ST* connector is on the left.

Like many other fiber optic connectors, the SC and ST connectors are half-duplex, meaning data flows only one way—hence the need for two cables in a fiber installation. Other half-duplex connectors you might run into are FC/PC, SMA, D4, MU, and LC. They look similar to SC and ST connectors but offer variations in size and connection. Newer and higher-end fiber installations use full-duplex connectors, such as the MT-RJ connectors.

> ST, SC, LC, and MT-RJ fiber connectors will likely be questioned on the Essentials exam.

The two most common fiber optic standards are called 1000BaseSX and 10GBaseSR. The major difference is the speed of the network (there are also some important differences in the way systems interconnect, and so on). Fiber optic cabling is delicate, expensive, and difficult to use, so it is usually reserved for use in data centers and is rarely used to connect desktop PCs.

Coax/BNC

Early versions of Ethernet ran on **coaxial cable** instead of UTP. Coax consists of a center cable (core) surrounded by insulation. This in turn is covered with a *shield* of

• **Figure 16.13**   Typical fiber optic cables with connectors braided cable. The inner core actually carries the signal. The shield effectively eliminates outside interference. The entire cable is then surrounded by a protective insulating cover. This type of coax looks like a skinny version of the RG-59 or RG-6 coax used by your cable television, but it is quite different. The RG rating is clearly marked on the cable. If it isn't, the cable should say something like "Thinnet" or "802.3" to let you know you have the right cable. To connect the cable to individual machines, a twist-on *BNC connector* is used.

Parallel/Serial

It would be unfair not to give at least a token nod to using the parallel or serial ports on a pair of PCs to make a direct cable connection. All versions of Windows have complete support for allowing two, and no more than two, systems to network together, using either parallel or serial cables. You need crossover versions of IEEE 1284 cables for parallel and RS-232 cables for serial. These should be considered only as a last resort option, given the incredibly slow speeds of parallel and especially serial cable transmission compared to that of Ethernet. You should never use direct cable connections unless no other viable alternative exists.

FireWire

You can connect two computers by using FireWire cables. Apple designed FireWire to be network aware, so the two machines will simply recognize each other and, assuming they're configured to share files and folders, you're up and running.

USB

You can also connect two computers by using USB, but it's not quite as elegant as FireWire. The most common way is to plug a USB NIC into each PC and then run a UTP crossover cable between the Ethernet ports. You also can buy a special USB crossover cable to connect the two machines. Finally, at least one company makes a product that enables you to connect with a normal USB cable, called USB Duet.

◼ Network Organization

Apart from the various physical media used to connect networks and the methods used to transmit data through them, all networks can be broken down into three basic organizational groups: client/server, peer-to-peer, and domain-based. Let's take a look at traditional network organization.

Client/Server

In a **client/server network**, one machine is dedicated as a resource to be shared over the network. This machine will have a dedicated network operating system (NOS), optimized for sharing files. This special OS includes powerful caching software that enables high-speed file access. It will have extremely high levels of protection and an organization that permits extensive control of the data. This machine is called a *dedicated server*. All of the other machines that use the data are called *clients* (because it's what they usually are) or *workstations*.

The client/server system dedicates one machine to act as a server, whose purpose is to serve up resources to the other machines on the network. These servers do not run Windows XP or Vista. They use highly sophisticated and expensive NOSes that are optimized for the sharing and administration of network resources. Dedicated server operating systems include Windows Server 2008, big UNIX systems such as IBM AIX and HP-UX, and some versions of Linux.

The terms *client* and *server* are, to say the least, freely used in the Windows world. Keep in mind that a *client* generally refers to any process (or in this context, computer system) that can request a resource or service, and a *server* is any process (or system) that can fulfill the request.

Peer-to-Peer

Some networks do not require dedicated servers—every computer can perform both server and client functions. A **peer-to-peer network** enables any or all of the machines on the network to act as a server. Peer-to-peer networks are much cheaper than client/server networks because the software costs less and does not require that you purchase a high-end machine to act as the dedicated server. The most popular peer-to-peer NOSes today are the various versions of Windows and Macintosh OS X.

The biggest limiting factor to peer-to-peer networking is that it's simply not designed for a large number of computers. Windows has a built-in limit (ten) to the number of users who can concurrently access a shared file or folder. Microsoft recommends that peer-to-peer workgroups not exceed 15 PCs. Beyond that, creating a domain-based network makes more sense (see the following section).

Security is the other big weakness of peer-to-peer networks. Each system on a peer-to-peer network maintains its own security.

With the Windows Professional/Business versions, you can tighten security by setting NTFS permissions locally, but you are still required to place a local account on every system for any user who's going to access resources. So even though you get better security in a Windows Professional/Business peer-to-peer network, system administration entails a lot of running around to individual systems to create and delete local users every time someone joins or leaves the workgroup. In a word: bleh.

Peer-to-peer workgroups are little more than a pretty way to organize systems to make navigating through Windows networks a little easier (Figure 16.14). In reality, workgroups have no security value. Still, if your networking needs are limited—such as a small home network—peer-to-peer networking is an easy and cheap solution.

• Figure 16.14 Multiple workgroups in a network

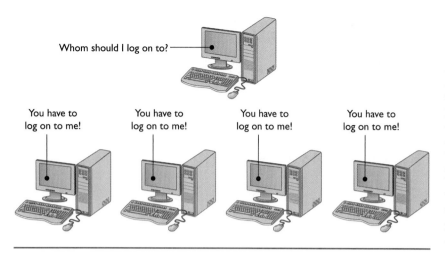

• **Figure 16.15** Multiple logins in a peer-to-peer network

• **Figure 16.16** A domain controller eliminates the need for multiple logins.

Domain-Based

One of the similarities between the client/server network model and peer-to-peer networks is that each PC in the network maintains its own list of user accounts. If you want to access a server, you must log on. When only one server exists, the logon process takes only a second and works very well. The trouble comes when your network contains multiple servers. In that case, every time you access a different server, you must repeat the logon process (Figure 16.15). In larger networks containing many servers, this becomes a time-consuming nightmare not only for the user, but also for the network administrator.

A **domain-based network** provides an excellent solution for the problem of multiple logins. In a domain-based environment, one or more dedicated servers called *domain controllers* hold the security database for all systems. This database holds a list of all users and passwords in the domain. When you log on to your computer or to any computer, the logon request goes to an available domain controller to verify the account and password (Figure 16.16).

Modern domain-based networks use what is called a **directory service** to store user and computer account information. Large Microsoft-based networks use the *Active Directory* (*AD*) directory service. Think of a directory service as a big, centralized index, similar to a telephone book, that each PC accesses to locate resources in the domain.

Server versions of Microsoft Windows look and act similar to the workstation versions, but they come with extra networking capabilities, services, and tools so they can take on the role of domain controller, file server, *remote access services* (*RAS*) server, application server, Web server, and so on. A quick glance at the options you have in Administrative Tools shows how much more full-featured the server versions are

Cross Check

Administrative Tools

Windows comes with a set of utilities called Administrative Tools, as you know from previous chapters. Refer to Chapter 4, "Understanding Windows," and answer these questions.

1. How do you access Administrative Tools?

2. Which tool or tools might be useful for working with networks?

3. More specifically, which tool would help you analyze network performance?

● Figure 16.17 Administrative Tools in Windows Vista Business

compared to the workstation versions of Windows. Figure 16.17 shows the
Administrative Tools options on a typical Windows Vista workstation.
These should be familiar to you. Figure 16.18 shows the many extra tools
you need to work with Windows 2008 Server.

● Figure 16.18 Administrative Tools in Windows Server 2008

Every Windows system contains a special account called the **administrator account**. This one account has complete and absolute power over the entire system. When you install Windows, you must create a password for the administrator account. Anyone who knows the administrator password can install/delete any program, read/change/delete any file, run any program, and change any system setting. As you might imagine, you should protect the administrator password carefully. Without it, you cannot create additional accounts (including additional accounts with administrative privileges) or change system settings. If you lose the administrator password (and no other account with administrative privileges exists), you have to reinstall Windows completely to create a new administrator account—so don't lose it!

In Windows XP, open the Properties window for My Computer and select the Computer Name tab, as shown in Figure 16.19. This shows your current selection. Windows Vista and 7 show the computer name right on the System Properties dialog box and give you a link to the 2000/XP-style dialog box (Figure 16.20). Clicking the Network ID button opens the Network Identification Wizard, but most techs just use the Change button, which brings up the Computer Name/Domain Changes dialog box (Figure 16.21). Clicking the Change button does the same thing as clicking the Network ID button except that the wizard does a lot of explaining that you don't need if you know what you want to do. Make sure you have a valid domain account or you won't be able to log in to a domain.

At this point, you've prepared the OS to network in general, but now you need to talk to the specific hardware. For that, you need to load protocols.

Protocols

Simply moving data from one machine to another is hardly sufficient to make a complete network; many other functions need to be handled. For example, if a file is being copied from one machine to another, something must keep track of all of the packets so the file can be properly reassembled. If many machines are talking to the same machine at once, that machine must somehow keep track of which packets it sends to or receives from each of the other PCs.

Another issue arises if one of the machines in the network has its network card replaced. Up to this point, the only way to distinguish one machine from another was by the MAC address on the network card. To solve this, each machine must have a name, an identifier for the network, which is "above" the MAC address. Each machine, or at least one of them, needs to keep a list of all of the MAC addresses on the network and the names of the machines, so that packets and names can be correlated. That way, if a PC's network card is replaced, the network, after some special queries, can update the list to associate the name of the PC with its new network card's MAC address.

Network protocol software takes the incoming data received by the network card, keeps it organized, sends it to the application that needs it, and then takes outgoing data from the application and hands it to the NIC to be sent out over the network. All networks use some protocol. Although many protocols exist, one dominates the world of PCs—TCP/IP.

• **Figure 16.21**   Using the Change button

NetBEUI/NetBIOS

Before we talk about TCP/IP, we need to discuss a little history. During the 1980s, IBM developed **NetBIOS Extended User Interface (NetBEUI)**, the default protocol for Windows for Workgroups, LANtastic, and Windows 95. NetBEUI offers small size, easy configuration, and a relatively high speed, but it can't be used for routing. Its inability to handle routing limits NetBEUI to networks smaller than about 200 nodes.

You can connect multiple smaller networks into a bigger network, turning a group of LANs into one big WAN, but this raises a couple of issues with network traffic. A computer needs to be able to address a packet so that it goes to a computer within its own LAN or to a computer in another LAN in the WAN. If every computer saw every packet, the network traffic would quickly spin out of control! Plus, the machines that connect the LANs—called **routers**—need to be able to sort those packets and send them along to the proper LAN. This process, called *routing*, requires routers and a routing-capable protocol to function correctly.

NetBEUI was great for a LAN, but it lacked the extra addressing capabilities needed for a WAN. A new protocol was needed, one that could handle routing.

A *node* is any device that has a network connection—usually this means a PC, but other devices can be nodes. For example, many printers now connect directly to a network and can therefore be deemed nodes. I use the term *node* extensively in the rest of the chapter in place of *PC* or *networked computer*. This is especially true when I talk about wireless technologies, because that's the term the manufacturers use.

Novell developed the *Internetwork Packet Exchange/ Sequenced Packet Exchange* (*IPX/SPX*) protocol exclusively for its NetWare products. The IPX/SPX protocol is speedy, works well with routers, and takes up relatively little RAM when loaded. Although once popular, it has all but disappeared in favor of TCP/IP. Microsoft implements a version of IPX/SPX called *NWLink*.

TCP/IP

Transmission Control Protocol/Internet Protocol (**TCP/IP**) was originally developed for the Internet's progenitor, the *Advanced Research Projects Agency Network* (*ARPANET*) of the U.S. Department of Defense. In 1983, TCP/IP became the built-in protocol for the popular BSD (Berkeley Software Distribution) UNIX, and other flavors of UNIX quickly adopted it as well. TCP/IP is the best protocol for larger networks with more than 200 nodes. The biggest network of all, the Internet, uses TCP/IP as its protocol. Windows also uses TCP/IP as its default protocol.

■ Configuring TCP/IP

TCP/IP is the primary protocol of most modern networks, including the Internet. For a PC to access the Internet, it must have TCP/IP loaded and configured properly. TCP/IP has become so predominant that most network folks use it even on networks that do not connect to the Internet. So whether you are installing a modem for a dial-up connection to the Internet or setting up 500 computers on their own private *intranet*, you must understand some TCP/IP basics. Although TCP/IP is powerful, it is a bit of a challenge to set up. This section first guides you through the basic components of the protocol, after which you'll look at specific TCP/IP settings and what they do.

Network Addressing

Any network address must provide two pieces of information: it must uniquely identify the machine and it must locate that machine within the larger network. In a TCP/IP network, the IP address identifies the PC and the network on which it resides.

Tech Tip

IPv6

The IP addresses I'm showing you here are technically IP version 4, or IPv4, addresses, but this type of addressing has a bit of a problem—namely, that we're running out of possible IP addresses, and there won't be any left in a few years. No big deal. Now, before you go running out into the streets shouting about the impending demise of the Internet or start hoarding canned food in your basement, let me tell you about the solution. IP version 6, the newest version of the Internet protocol, which will save us all from an Internetless world, uses a 128-bit address instead of IPv4's 32-bit address. What this means is that there are more possible addresses than with IPv4. A lot more. My favorite illustration is to think of all of the molecules that make up the Earth, and divide them by 7. That's how many possible IPv6 addresses there are. The drawback is that IPv6 addresses are not quite as svelte and easy to remember as in IPv4. For example, an IPv6 address looks like this: 2001:0db8:85a3:0000:0000: 8a2e:0370:7334. Not quite as easy to work with as 192.168.1.1, eh? IPv6 also handles routing and various other things differently than IPv4, but the main things to know are that the IP addresses look remarkably different and there are enough of them to last for a while. There's no solid plan yet for when everyone is going to switch to IPv6, but it'll be a big change when it happens.

IP Addresses

In a TCP/IP network, the systems don't have names but rather use IP addresses. The **IP address** is the unique identification number for your system on the network. Part of the address identifies the network, and part identifies the local computer (host) address on the network. IP addresses consist of four sets of eight binary numbers (octets), each set separated by a period. This is called *dotted-decimal notation*. So, instead of a computer being called SERVER1, it gets an address like so:

202.34.16.11

Written in binary form, the address would look like this:

```
11001010.00100010.00010000.00001011
```

To make the addresses more comprehensible to users, the TCP/IP folks decided to write the decimal equivalents:

```
00000000 = 0
00000001 = 1
00000010 = 2
...
11111111 = 255
```

IP addresses are divided into class licenses that correspond with the potential size of the network: Class A, Class B, and Class C. Class A licenses were intended for huge companies and organizations, such as major multinational corporations, universities, and governmental agencies. Class B licenses were assigned to medium-size companies, and Class C licenses were designated for smaller LANs. Class A networks use the first octet to identify the network address and the remaining three octets to identify the host. Class B networks use the first two octets to identify the network address and the remaining two octets to identify the host. Class C networks use the first three octets to identify the network address and the last octet to identify the host. Table 16.2 lists range (class) assignments.

Table 16.2	Class A, B, and C Addresses		
Network Class	Address Range	No. of Network Addresses Available	No. of Host Nodes (Computers) Supported
A	1–126	129	16,777,214
B	128–191	16,384	65,534
C	192–223	2,097,152	254

You'll note that the IP address ranges listed in Table 16.2 skip from 126.x.x.x to 128.x.x.x. That's because the 127 address range (that is, 127.0.0.1–127.255.255.255) is reserved for network testing (loopback) operations. (We usually just use the address 127.0.0.1 for loopback purposes and call it the *localhost* address, but any address that starts off with *127* will work just as well.) That's not the only reserved range, either! Each network class has a specific IP address range reserved for *private* networks—traffic from these networks doesn't get routed to the Internet at large. Class A's private range goes from 10.0.0.1 to 10.255.255.255. Class B has two private address ranges: 172.16.0.1 up to 172.16.255.255 for manually configured addresses and 169.254.0.1 to 169.254.255.254 (link-local addresses). Class C's private addresses range from 192.168.0.0 to 192.168.255.255.

Pinging the loopback is the best way to test whether a NIC is working properly. To test a NIC's loopback, the other end of the cable must be in a working switch or you must use a loopback device such as a loopback adapter/plug.

Subnet Mask

The **subnet mask** is a value that distinguishes which part of the IP address is the network address and which part of the address is the host address. The subnet mask blocks out (or masks) the network portions (octets) of an IP address. Certain subnet masks are applied by default. The default subnet mask for Class A addresses is 255.0.0.0; for Class B, it's 255.255.0.0; and for Class C, 255.255.255.0. For example, in the Class B IP address 131.190.4.121 with a subnet mask of 255.255.0.0, the first two octets (131.190) make up the network address, and the last two (4.121) make up the host address.

The CompTIA A+ Essentials exam does not require you to break down IP addresses and subnet masks into their binary equivalents or to deal with non-standard subnet masks such as 255.255.240.0, but you should know what IP addresses and subnet masks are and how to configure your PC to connect to a TCP/IP network.

A New Kind of Port

The term "port" has several meanings in the computer world. Commonly, port defines the connector socket on an Ethernet NIC, where you insert an RJ-45 jack. That's how I've used the term for the most part in this book. It's now time to see another use of the word port.

In TCP/IP, *ports* are 16-bit numbers between 0 and 65,535, assigned to a particular TCP/IP session. All TCP/IP packets (except for some really low-level maintenance packets) contain port numbers that the two communicating computers use to determine not only the kind of session—and thus what software protocol—to use to handle the data in the packet, but also how to get the packet or response back to the sending computer.

Each packet has two ports assigned, a destination port and an ephemeral port. The **destination port** is a fixed, predetermined number that defines the function or session type. Common TCP/IP session types use destination port numbers in the range 0–1023. The **ephemeral port** is an arbitrary number generated by the sending computer; the receiving computer uses the ephemeral port as a destination address so that the sending computer knows which application to use for the returning packet. Ephemeral ports usually fall in the 1024–5000 range, but this varies slightly among the different operating systems.

Ports enable one computer to serve many different services, such as a Web server and e-mail server, at the same time. We will discuss the most common ports and the associated services in Chapter 18, "Learning the Internet."

TCP/IP Services

TCP/IP is a different type of protocol. It adds a number of special sharing functions unique only to it, lumped together under the umbrella term *TCP/IP services*. The most famous TCP/IP service is called *Hypertext Transfer Protocol* (*HTTP*), the language of the World Wide Web. If you want to surf the Web, you must have TCP/IP. But TCP/IP supplies many other services beyond just HTTP. By using a service called Telnet, for example, you can access a remote system as though you were actually in front of that machine.

Another example is a handy utility called PING. **PING** enables one machine to check whether it can communicate with another machine. Figure 16.22 shows an example of PING running on a

```
Administrator: C:\Windows\system32\cmd.exe

C:\>ping www.totalsem.com

Pinging www.totalsem.com [209.29.33.25] with 32 bytes of data:
Reply from 209.29.33.25: bytes=32 time=60ms TTL=53
Reply from 209.29.33.25: bytes=32 time=60ms TTL=53
Reply from 209.29.33.25: bytes=32 time=60ms TTL=53
Reply from 209.29.33.25: bytes=32 time=66ms TTL=53

Ping statistics for 209.29.33.25:
    Packets: Sent = 4, Received = 4, Lost = 0 (0% loss),
Approximate round trip times in milli-seconds:
    Minimum = 60ms, Maximum = 66ms, Average = 61ms

C:\>
```

• **Figure 16.22**   PING in action

Windows Vista system. Isn't it interesting that many TCP/IP services run from a command prompt? Good thing you know how to access one! I'll show you other services in a moment.

The goal of TCP/IP is to link any two hosts (remember, a host is just a computer in TCP/IP lingo), whether the two computers are on the same LAN or on some other network within the WAN. The LANs within the WAN are linked together with a variety of connections, ranging from basic dial-up connections to dedicated high-speed (and expensive) data lines (Figure 16.23). To move traffic between networks, you use routers (Figure 16.24). Each host sends traffic to the router only when that data is destined for a remote network, cutting down on traffic across the more expensive WAN links. The host makes these decisions based on the destination IP address of each packet.

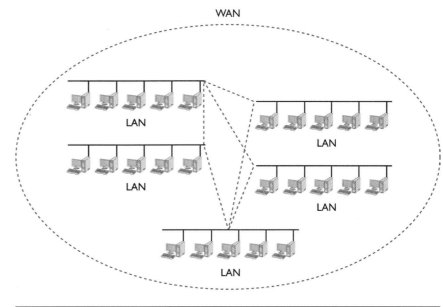

• **Figure 16.23** WAN concept

TCP/IP Settings

TCP/IP has a number of unique settings that you must set up correctly to ensure proper network functioning. Unfortunately, these settings can be quite confusing, and there are quite a few of them. Not all settings are used for every type of TCP/IP network, and it's not always obvious where you go to set them.

• **Figure 16.24** Typical router

Windows makes this fairly easy by letting you configure both dial-up and network connections by using the Network Connections dialog box (Figure 16.25). To get there, right-click My Network Places (Windows 2000/XP) or Network (Windows Vista/7) and select Properties. In Vista/7, you have to click the *Manage network connections* button, but in 2000 and XP, you simply select the connection you wish to configure and then set its TCP/IP properties. Windows labels most wired networks Local Area Connection, so that's probably the one you should look for.

The CompTIA A+ Essentials exam assumes that someone else, such as a tech

• **Figure 16.25** Network Connections dialog box showing dial-up and LAN connections

support person or some network guru, will tell you the correct TCP/IP settings for the network. Your only job is to understand roughly what they do and to know where to enter them so the system works. Following are some of the most common TCP/IP settings.

Configuring TCP/IP

By default, TCP/IP is configured to receive an IP address automatically from a DHCP server on the network (and automatically assign a corresponding subnet mask). As far as the CompTIA A+ Essentials exam is concerned, Network+ techs and administrators give you the IP address, subnet mask, and default gateway information and you plug them into the PC. That's about it, so here's how to do it manually:

1. In Windows XP, open the Control Panel and double-click the Network Connections applet. Double-click the Local Area Connection icon. In Windows 2000, click Start | Settings | Network and Dial-up Connections, and double-click the Local Area Connection icon. In Windows Vista/7, right-click on Network and then click *Manage network connections*. After that, double-click the Local Area Network icon.

2. Click the Properties button, highlight Internet Protocol (TCP/IP), and click the Properties button. In Windows Vista/7, you should highlight Internet Protocol Version 4 (TCP/IPv4) because Vista and 7 both have IPv4 and IPv6 installed by default.

3. In the dialog box, click the radio button next to *Use the following IP address*.

4. Enter the IP address in the appropriate fields.

5. Press the TAB key to skip down to the Subnet mask field. Note that the subnet mask is entered automatically, although you can type over this if you want to enter a different subnet mask (see Figure 16.26).

6. Optionally, enter the IP address for a default gateway (a router or another computer system that will forward transmissions beyond your network).

7. Optionally, enter the IP addresses of a primary and a secondary DNS server.

8. Click the OK button to close the dialog box.

9. Click the Close button to exit the Local Area Connection Status dialog box.

10. Windows will alert you that you must restart the system for the changes to take effect.

Default Gateway

A computer that wants to send data to another machine outside its LAN is not expected to know exactly how to reach every other computer on the Internet. Instead, all IP hosts know the address of at least one router to which they pass all of the data packets they need to send outside the LAN. This router is called the **default gateway**, which is just another way of saying "the local router" (Figure 16.27).

• **Figure 16.26**   Setting up IP

Domain Name Service (DNS)

Knowing that users could not remember lots of IP addresses, early Internet pioneers came up with a way to correlate those numbers with more human-friendly computer designations. Special computers, called **domain name service (DNS)** servers, keep databases of IP addresses and their corresponding names. For example, a machine called TOTALSEMINAR1 will be listed in a DNS directory with a corresponding IP address, such as 209.34.45.163. So instead of accessing the \\209.34.45.163\FREDC share to copy a file, you can ask to see \\TOTALSEMINAR1\FREDC. Your system will then query the DNS server to get TOTALSEMINAR1's IP address and use that to find the right machine. Unless you want to type in IP addresses all the time, a TCP/IP network will need at least one DNS server (Figure 16.28).

The Internet has regulated domain names. If you want a domain name that others can access on the Internet, you must register your domain name and pay a small yearly fee. In most cases, your ISP can handle this for you. Originally, DNS names all ended with one of the following seven domain name qualifiers, called *top-level domains* (*TLDs*):

● **Figure 16.27**   Setting a default gateway

.com General business   **.org** Nonprofit organizations
.edu Educational organizations **.gov** Government organizations
.mil Military organizations   **.net** Internet organizations
.int International

As more and more countries joined the Internet, an entire new level of domains was added to the original seven to indicate a DNS name in a particular country, such as .uk for the United Kingdom. It's common to see DNS names such as www.bbc.co.uk or www.louvre.fr. The *Internet Corporation for Assigned Names and Numbers* (*ICANN*) announced the creation of several more new domains, including .name, .biz, .info, and others. Given the explosive growth of the Internet, these are unlikely to be the last ones! For the latest developments, check ICANN's Web site at www.icann.org.

WINS

Before Microsoft came fully on board with Internet standards such as TCP/IP, the company implemented its own type of name server: *Windows Internet Name Service* (*WINS*). WINS enables NetBIOS network names such as SERVER1 to be correlated to IP addresses, just as DNS does, except these names are *Windows* network names such as SERVER1, not fully qualified domain Internet names (FQDNs) such as server1.example.com. NetBIOS names must be unique and contain 15 or fewer characters, but other than that there isn't much to it. Assuming that a

● **Figure 16.28**   Adding two DNS servers in Windows Vista

WINS server exists on your network, all you have to do to set up WINS on your PC is type in the IP address for the WINS server (Figure 16.29). Networks based on Windows 2000/XP/Vista/7 don't use WINS; they use an improved "dynamic" DNS (DDNS) that supports both Internet names and Windows names. On older networks that still need to support the occasional legacy Windows NT 4.0 server, you may need to configure WINS, but on most TCP/IP networks you can leave the WINS setting blank.

DHCP

The last feature that most TCP/IP networks support is **dynamic host configuration protocol (DHCP)**. To understand DHCP, you must first remember that every machine must be assigned an IP address, a subnet mask, a default gateway, and at least one DNS server (and maybe a WINS server). These settings can be added manually by using the TCP/IP Properties window. When you set the IP address manually, the IP address will not change and is called a **static IP address** (Figure 16.30).

• **Figure 16.29**   Setting up WINS to use DHCP

DHCP enables you to create a pool of IP addresses that are given temporarily to machines. DHCP is especially handy for networks of a lot of laptops that join and leave the network on a regular basis. Why give a machine that is on the network for only a few hours a day a static IP address? For that reason, DHCP is quite popular. If you add a NIC to a Windows system, the default TCP/IP settings are set to use DHCP. When you accept those automatic settings, you're really telling the machine to use DHCP (Figure 16.31).

• **Figure 16.30**   Setting a static IP address

• **Figure 16.31**   Automatically obtain an IP address

Troubleshooting Networks

The "Troubleshooting Networks" section covers a range of questions you're likely to see on the "Operational Procedure" exam domain. See also Chapter 20, "The Complete PC Technician," for more on the topic.

Once you go beyond a single PC and enter the realm of networked computers, your troubleshooting skills need to take a giant leap up in quality. Think of the complexity added with networks. Suddenly you have multiple PCs with multiple users who could, at the drop of a hat, do all kinds of inadvertent damage to a fully functional PC. Networked PCs have a layer of networked hardware and resource sharing that adds a completely new dimension to a user's cry for help, "I can't print!"

Where can the problem lie in a *non-networked situation* if a person cannot print? Here are the obvious ones:

- Printer is not connected to the PC.
- Printer is out of ink.
- PC doesn't have the proper driver loaded.
- PC points by default to a printer other than the one that the user thinks should print.

That's about it. Maybe the parallel port configuration is wrong in CMOS or the USB drivers aren't correct, but still.... Now do the same thing with a *networked situation* where a user can't print. Here are the obvious *extra* issues, because all of the local machine issues apply as well:

- Print server is down.
- Printer is locked by another user.
- The client PC doesn't have network connectivity.
- The NIC driver is bad or incorrect.
- The client PC doesn't have the proper printer drivers installed for the networked printer.
- The cable between the client PC's NIC and the nearest switch is bad.
- The port to which the cable connects is bad.
- The switch failed.
- Somebody in an office down the hall spilled coffee on the printer, inside the mechanism, and then didn't fess up to the accident.

That's a lot of variables, and they just scratch the surface of possibilities. You live in a networked world—it's time to elevate your troubleshooting skills and methodologies to the next level. This section offers a series of steps you can use when performing any type of PC or network troubleshooting. You'll look at ways to apply your tech skills and general communication skills to get to the bottom of a problem and get that problem fixed.

Verify the Symptom

The one thing that all PC problems have in common is a symptom. If something odd wasn't happening (or not happening) to users as they tried to do whatever they need to do on their computers, you wouldn't have a problem at all, would you? Unfortunately, the vast majority of users out there aren't CompTIA A+ certified technicians. As a tech, you need to overcome a rather

Look for lots of questions on communication with users on the Essentials exam.

nasty communication gap before you can begin to consider a fix. Let's bridge that gap right now.

It usually starts with a phone call:

You: "Tech Support, this is Mike. How can I help you?"

User: "Uh, hi, Mike. This is Tom over in Accounting. I can't get into the network. Can you help me?"

Tom just started over in the Accounting department this week and has been a pain in the rear end so far. Ah, the things you might want to say to this person: "No. I only help non-pain-in-the-rear accountants." Or how about this? "Let me check my appointment schedule.... Ah, yes. I can check on your problem in two weeks. Monday at 4:00 P.M. okay for you?"

But, of course, you had the audacity to choose the beloved profession of IT tech support, so you don't get to say the things that you might want to say. Rather, you need to take a position of leadership and get to the bottom of the problem, and that means understanding the symptom. Take a deep breath, smile, and get to work. You have two issues to deal with at this point. First, if you're working with a user, you must try to get the user to describe the symptom. Second, whether you're working on a system alone or you're talking to a user on the telephone, you must verify that the symptom is legitimate.

Getting a user to describe a symptom is often a challenge. Users are not techs and as a result their perception of the PC is very different than yours. But by the same token, most users know a bit about PCs, and you want to take advantage of a user's skill and experience whenever you can. A personal example of verifying the symptom: Once I got a call from a user telling me that his "screen was blank." I told him to restart his system. To which he responded, "Shouldn't I shut down the PC first?" I said, "I thought you just told me the screen was blank!" He replied, "That's right. There's nothing on the screen but my desktop."

When Does It Happen?

Once you know the symptom, you need to try to inspect the problem yourself. This doesn't mean you need to go to the system; many real problems are easily fixed by the user, under your supervision. But you must understand when the problem occurs so that you can zero in on where to look for the solution. Does it happen at boot? It might be a CMOS/BIOS issue. Is it taking place as the OS loads? Then you need to start checking initialization files. Does it take place when the system runs untouched for a certain amount of time? Then maybe the power management could come into play.

What Has Changed?

Systems that run properly tend to continue to run properly. Systems that have undergone a hardware or software change have a much higher chance of not running properly than a system that has not been changed. If something has gone wrong, talk to the user to determine whether anything in particular has occurred since the system last worked properly. Has new software been installed? Did the user add some new RAM? Change the Windows Domain? Run a Windows Update? Drop the monitor on the floor? Not only do you need to consider those types of changes, but you must also make sure that any unrelated changes don't send you down the wrong path.

The fact that someone installed a new floppy drive yesterday probably doesn't have anything to do with the printer that isn't working today.

Last, consider side effects of changes that don't seem to have anything to do with the problem. For example, I once had a customer whose system kept freezing up in Windows. I knew he had just added a second hard drive, but the system booted up just fine and ran normally—except it would freeze up after a few minutes. The hard drive wasn't the problem. The problem was that he unplugged the CPU fan in the process of installing it. When I discover a change has been made, I like to visualize the process of the change to consider how that change may have directly or indirectly contributed to a problem. In other words, if you run into a situation where a person added a NIC to a functioning PC that now won't boot, you need to think about what part of the installation process could be fouled up to cause a PC to stop working.

Check the Environment

I use the term *environment* in two totally different fashions in this book. The first way is the most classic definition: the heat, humidity, dirt, and other outside factors that can affect the operation of the system. The other definition is more technical and addresses the computing environment of the system and other surrounding systems: What type of system do they run? What OS? What is their network connection? What are the primary applications they use? What antivirus program do they run? Do other people use the system?

Answering these questions gives you an overview of what is affecting this system both internally and externally. A quick rundown of these issues can reveal possible problems that might not be otherwise recognized. For example, I once got a call from a user complaining she had no network connection. I first checked the NIC to ensure it had link lights (always the first thing to check to ensure a good physical connection!) only to discover that she had no link lights—someone had decided to turn on a space heater, which destroyed the cable!

Reproducing the Problem

My official rule on problems with a PC is this: "If a problem happens only once, it is not a problem." PCs are notorious for occasionally locking up, popping errors, and displaying all types of little quirks that a quick reboot fixes, and they don't happen again. Why do these things happen? I don't know, although I'm sure if someone wanted me to guess I could come up with a clever explanation. But the majority of PCs simply don't have redundancy built in, and it's okay for them to occasionally hiccup.

A problem becomes interesting to me if it happens more than once. If it happens twice, the chances are much higher that it will happen a third time. I want to see it happen that third time—under my supervision. I will direct the user to try to reproduce the problem while I am watching to see what triggers the failure. This is a huge clue to helping you localize the real problem. Intermittent failures are the single most frustrating events that take place in a technician's life. But do remember that many seemingly intermittent problems really aren't intermittent—you have simply failed to reproduce the events exactly enough to see the consistency of the problem. Always take the time to match every step that leads to a problem to try to re-create the same error.

Isolating the Symptom

With so many bits and pieces to a PC, you must take the time to try to isolate the symptom to ensure your fix is going to the software or hardware that really needs it. In hardware, that usually means removing suspect parts until only one possible part remains. In software, that usually means removing background programs, booting into Safe Mode, or trying to create a situation where only the suspected program is running.

Isolation takes on a whole new meaning with networks. One of the greatest tools in networking is isolation—does this problem happen on other systems, on other workgroups, on other PCs running DHCP? Whenever a problem takes place in networking, isolation is the key to determining the problem.

Separating Hardware from Software

Many problems that occur on a PC are difficult to isolate given that it is difficult to determine whether the problem lies in the software or the hardware. If you find yourself in this situation, you can take a few steps to help you zero in on which side of the PC to suspect.

Known Good Hardware

The absolute best way to know whether a problem is hardware or software related is to replace the suspected piece of hardware with a known good part. If you can't tell whether a Windows page fault comes from bad RAM or a software incompatibility, quickly replacing the RAM with known good RAM should help you determine whether the RAM or the software is to blame.

Cable and Loopback Test

A bad NIC can also generate a "can't see the network" problem. Use whatever utility was provided with your OS to verify that the NIC works. If you have a NIC with diagnostic software, run it—this software will check the NIC's circuitry. The NIC's female connector is a common failure point, so NICs that come with diagnostic software often include a special test called a loopback test. A loopback test sends data out of the NIC and checks to see if it comes back. Some NICs perform only an internal loopback that tests the circuitry that sends and receives, but not the actual connecting pins. A true external loopback requires a **loopback plug** inserted into the NIC's port (Figure 16.32). If a NIC is bad, replace it—preferably with an identical NIC so you don't have to reinstall drivers.

The network cable is a common source of network troubles. You can use a cable tester if you suspect a cable problem. With the right equipment, diagnosing a bad cabling run is easy. Anyone with a network should own a midrange cable tester such as the Fluke MicroScanner. With a little practice, you can easily determine not only whether a cable is disconnected, but also where the disconnection takes place. Sometimes patience is required, especially if the cable runs aren't labeled, but you will find the problem.

• **Figure 16.32**　Loopback plug

Uninstall/Reinstall

If you can do so easily, try uninstalling the suspected software and reinstalling. Many hardware/software problems magically disappear with a simple uninstall/reinstall.

Patching/Upgrading

Many hardware or software problems take place due to incompatibilities between the two suspect sides. Try upgrading drivers. Download patches or upgrades to software, especially if the hardware and the software are more than two years apart in age.

Virus Check

Last (maybe I should have put this first), always check for viruses. Today's viruses manifest so many different symptoms that failure to check for them is a study in time wasting. I recently got a new hard drive that started to make a nasty clicking noise—a sure sign of a failing hard drive. However, I ran an extensive virus check and guess what—it was a virus! Who would have thought? I checked with the hard drive maker's Web site, and my fears were confirmed. It just goes to show you—even the best of techs can be caught by the simplest problems.

Research

Once you have your mind wrapped around the problem, it's time to fix it. Unless the problem is either simple (network cable unplugged) or something you've seen before and know exactly how to fix, you'll almost certainly need to research it. The Internet makes this easy. I use one of my favorite tricks when I get some bizarre error text: I type the error message into my search engine—that would be Google, of course—and most times find a quick fix!

Make the Fix and Test

Once you have a good idea as to the problem and how to fix it, it's time to do the fix. Always make backups—or at least warn the user of the risk to the system. If possible, try to remember how the system was configured before the fix so you can go back to square one if the fix fails to work. After you perform the fix, do whatever you need to do to make sure the system is again working properly. Make sure the user sees that the system is working properly and can sign off on your work.

OSI Seven-Layer Model

A lot of people think about networks and troubleshoot networking issues by using the OSI seven-layer model. Using this model (or my four-layer model, described in the next section of this chapter) helps you isolate problems and then implement solutions. Here are the seven layers of the OSI model:

- **Layer 1** Physical
- **Layer 2** Data Link
- **Layer 3** Network
- **Layer 4** Transport
- **Layer 5** Session
- **Layer 6** Presentation
- **Layer 7** Application

The Physical layer turns binary code into a physical signal and back into ones and zeros.

Basic switches reside at Layer 2 (Data Link) of the OSI model. They provide filtering based on MAC. More advanced switches that can perform InterVLAN and protocol support operate at Layer 3 (Layer 3 switch). Routers are often called Layer 3 switches.

• Figure 16.34 OSI seven-layer model

The *Physical layer* defines the physical form taken by data when it travels across a cable. Devices that work at the physical layer include NICs and hubs. Figure 16.33 shows a sending NIC turning a string of ones and zeros into an electrical signal, and a receiving NIC turning it back into the same ones and zeros.

The *Data Link layer* defines the rules for accessing and using the Physical layer. MAC addresses and Ethernet's CSMA/CD operate at the Data Link layer.

The *Network layer* defines the rules for adding information to the data packet that controls how routers move it from its source on one network to its destination on a different network. The IP protocol that handles IP addressing works on Layer 3.

The *Transport layer*, Layer 4, breaks up data it receives from the upper layers (that is, Layers 5–7) into smaller pieces for transport within the data packets created at the lower layers. In TCP/IP networks, the protocols that typically handle this transition between upper and lower layers are TCP and UDP.

The *Session layer* manages the connections between machines on the network. Protocols such as NetBIOS and sockets enable a computer to connect to a server, for example, and send and receive e-mail or download a file. Each different task you can perform on a server would require a different kind of session.

The *Presentation layer* presents data from the sending system in a form that a receiving system can understand. Most Layer 6 functions are handled by the same software that handles Layer 7 functions.

The *Application layer* is where you (or a user) get to interact with the computers. These are programs that make networking happen, such as Web browsers and e-mail applications. Chapter 18, "Learning the Internet," covers these applications in a lot more detail.

The key to using the OSI seven-layer model is to ask the traditional troubleshooting question: what can the problem be? If Jill can't browse a Web site, for example, could this be a Layer 7 issue? Sure: if her browser software was messed up, this could stop her from browsing. It could also be a lower-level problem, though, and you need to run through the questions. Can she do anything over the network? If her NIC doesn't show flashing link lights, that could point all the way down to the Physical layer and a bad NIC, cable, or hub.

If she has good connectivity to the overall network but can't ping the Web server, that could point to a different problem altogether. Figure 16.34 shows the OSI seven-layer model graphically.

The only drawback to the OSI seven-layer model, in my view, is that it's too complex. I like to conceptualize network issues into fewer layers—four to be precise. Let's take a look.

Mike's Four-Layer Model

Network problems, by the very nature of the complexity of a network, usually make for more complex problems. Given that, I have created a four-step process that I modestly call "Mike's Four-Layer Model." These four things go through my mind every time I have a problem. I think about four distinct categories to help me isolate the symptoms and make the right fix.

Hardware

Hardware is probably the most self-explanatory of the four categories. This covers the many ways data can be moved from one PC to another. Does the system have a good connection? How's the cabling? This also covers network cards: are they installed properly and tested? Plus, the Hardware category hits on all of those interesting boxes, such as hubs, switches, and repeaters, among which all of the wires in the network run. If you can see it, it's under this category.

Protocols

This category covers the protocols, such as TCP/IP or NetBEUI. Is the protocol installed? Is it configured properly? Does any particular system's configuration prevent it from working with another system?

Network

The network category has two parts: servers and clients. Network operating systems must differentiate systems that act as server from those that do not. If a system is a server, some process must take place to tell it to share resources. Additionally, if a system is intended to share, it must be given a name. This category also includes defining and verifying users and groups; does your system need them? Do the right accounts exist, and are they working properly?

Shared Resources

Once all of the systems, users, and groups are working properly, you need to identify the resources they will share. If a drive or folder is to be shared, the OS must provide a way to identify that drive or folder as available for sharing. The rules for naming shared resources are called *naming conventions*. A great example would be a system that offers its D:\FRED directory for sharing. This D:\FRED directory needs a network name, such as FRED_FILES. This network name is displayed to all of the devices on the network.

Sharing a resource is only half the battle. Individual systems need to be able to access the shared resources. The network needs a process whereby a PC can look out on the network and see what is available. Having found those available resources, the PC then needs to make them look and act as though they were local resources. A network also needs to control access to resources. A laser printer, for example, might be available for sharing, but only for the Accounting department, excluding other departments.

Chapter 16 Review

Chapter Summary

After reading this chapter and completing the exercises, you should understand the following about local area networking.

Explain networking technologies

- A PC connected to a network, called a client machine, must have a NIC. The PC must be able to initiate and carry out the exchange of data with other client machines and with one or more server machines, using either a cable or some type of wireless transmission method.

- The most common network topologies include bus, ring, star, and mesh. Logical topology refers to how the network is laid out on paper. Physical topology refers to the actual hardware (clients, servers, cables).

- Data is sent in discrete chunks called packets or frames. The built-in 48-bit MAC address, unique to each NIC, is vital to the creation and function of data packets. Each data packet includes certain vital elements: the MAC of the recipient's NIC, the MAC of the sender's NIC, the data itself, and a CRC that enables the recipient to verify that the data arrives intact.

- A hardware protocol defines many aspects of a network, from the packet type to the cabling and connectors used—in short, everything necessary to get data from one computer to another. The hardware protocol that dominates the modern computing landscape is Ethernet.

- The two main types of Ethernet are based on the cable type: UTP and fiber optic. All Ethernet uses the same packet type, so any combination of hardware devices and cabling systems can work on an Ethernet network.

- Most modern Ethernet networks use either 100BaseT or 1000BaseT, both of which use UTP cable. 100BaseT runs at 100 Mbps; 1000BaseT runs at 1000 Mbps (or 1 Gbps). These two technologies, known collectively as 100/1000BaseT, use a star bus topology, which employs hubs or switches to make termination simpler and avoid the vulnerabilities of a bus topology.

- UTP cables come in different categories intended for different uses. CAT 1 cable is standard phone wire. Most UTP networks today use CAT 5e (maximum speed 1 Gbps) or CAT 6 cable (maximum speed 10 Gbps). 100BaseT requires a minimum of CAT 5 (maximum speed 100 Mbps) to run, while 1000BaseT requires a minimum of CAT 5e.

- UTP cables use the RJ-45 connector, which is essentially a wider version of the familiar RJ-11 phone connector. Two TIA/EIA standards, 568A and 568B, dictate acceptable ways to arrange the eight UTP cable wires in an RJ-45 jack. You should choose a wiring standard and stick with it to avoid network headaches.

- Standard network cables use PVC for the jacket, which emits toxic fumes when burned. Plenum-grade cables use a fire-retardant jacket and should be used when cables are installed in a plenum space.

- In an Ethernet network, each PC connects to a hub or switch via one of the hub's or switch's ports. The maximum distance from the hub or switch to a connected device is 100 meters. Hubs and switches act as repeaters, boosting signals as they pass on data, so they require a reliable power source.

- Fiber optic Ethernet transmits light instead of electricity, achieving much greater maximum distances than other forms of Ethernet. Most fiber networks use LEDs to send light signals and use multimode fiber optic cabling. Networks that use laser light use single-mode fiber optic cabling. Laser light and single-mode cabling are used most often for very long distance connections.

- Most fiber optic cables use one of two connectors: the square SC type or the round ST type.

Explain network organization and protocols

- The three types of network organization are client/server, peer-to-peer, and domain-based. All Windows PCs can function as network clients and servers.

- A client/server network dedicates one machine to act as a server. The server has a dedicated NOS optimized for sharing files, with powerful caching software that enables high-speed file access, extremely high levels of protection, and an organization that permits extensive control of the data.

- A peer-to-peer network enables any or all of the machines on the network to act as a server. Every computer can perform both server and client functions. A peer-to-peer network comprising only client machines requires you to place a local account on every system, which the system administrator must add and delete individually.

- In a domain-based network environment, the security database for all systems is centralized on one or more servers called domain controllers. This database holds a single list of all users and passwords. When you log on to any computer in the network, the logon request goes to an available domain controller for verification.

- Every Windows system contains a very special account called administrator that has complete and absolute power over the entire system. When you install Windows, you must create a password for the administrator account. Anyone who knows the administrator password has the ability to read any file and run any program.

- Network protocol software takes the incoming data received by the network card, keeps it organized, sends it to the application that needs it, and then takes outgoing data from the application and hands it to the NIC to be sent out over the network. All networks use some protocol; most networks today use TCP/IP.

- IBM developed NetBEUI, the default protocol for Windows for Workgroups, LANtastic, and Windows 95. NetBEUI was small and relatively high speed, but it couldn't be used for routing.

Configure TCP/IP

- Systems in a TCP/IP network use IP addresses rather than names. IP addresses are four sets of eight binary numbers (octets) separated by periods (dotted-octet notation). The first part of the address identifies the network; the second part identifies the local computer (host) address. The subnet mask is a value that distinguishes which part of the IP address is the network address and which part is the host address. The subnet mask blocks out (masks) the network portions (octets) of an IP address.

- A traditional TCP/IP network divides IP addresses into classes, which correspond with the potential size of the network: Class A, Class B, and Class C. Class A networks use the first octet to identify the network address, and the remaining three octets to identify the host. Class B networks use two and two. Class C networks use three and one.

- TCP/IP adds a number of special sharing functions unique only to it, called TCP/IP services, such as HTTP, the language of the World Wide Web. Another example is Telnet, which enables you to access a remote system as though you were actually in front of that machine.

- TCP/IP uses a 16-bit number called a port number to control the connection between two systems. Each packet has two ports assigned, a destination port and an ephemeral port. The destination port is a fixed, predetermined number that defines the type of server connected, such as port 80 for a Web server. The ephemeral port is an arbitrary number generated by the sending computer; the receiving computer uses the ephemeral port as a destination address so that the sending computer knows which application to use for the returning packet.

- The goal of TCP/IP is to link together multiple LANs to make a WAN. You use routers to move traffic between networks. Each host sends traffic to the router only when that data is destined for a remote network, cutting down on traffic across the more expensive WAN links.

- On a Windows system, you can configure both dial-up and network connections by using the Network Connections dialog box. Simply select the connection you wish to configure, and then set its TCP/IP properties.

- A computer that wants to send data to a machine outside its LAN is not expected to know all of the IP addresses of all of the computers on the Internet. Instead, all IP machines know the name of one computer, called the default gateway, to which they pass the data they need to send outside the LAN. The default gateway is the local router.

- DNS servers keep databases of IP addresses and their corresponding names. Virtually all TCP/IP networks require you to set up DNS server names.

- If you want an Internet domain name that others can access on the Internet, you must register your domain name and pay a small yearly fee. Originally, DNS names all ended with one of the following top-level domains: .com, .org, .edu, .gov, .mil, .net, and .int.

- DHCP automatically assigns IP address settings (including IP, subnet mask, default gateway, DNS servers, and WINS server, if necessary). If you add a NIC to a Windows system, the TCP/IP settings are set to use DHCP. A manually assigned IP address is known as a static IP address.

Troubleshoot networks

- The one thing that all PC problems have in common is a symptom. If you're working with a user, you must try to get the user to describe the symptom. Then you must verify that the symptom is legitimate. Try to inspect the problem yourself. Find out when it occurs so that you can zero in on where to look for the solution.

- Systems are much more likely to have problems after a hardware or software change; check to see if that has happened since the system last worked properly. When you discover a change has been made, try to visualize the process of the change to consider how that change may have directly or indirectly contributed to a problem.

- Check the environment to get an overview of what is affecting this system both internally and externally. The larger environment—heat, humidity, dirt, and other outside factors—may affect the operation of the system, as may the computing environment of this system and other surrounding systems, including the type of system, OS, network connection, primary applications, antivirus program, and other users.

- If a problem happens twice, the chances are much higher that it will happen a third time. Direct the user to try to reproduce the problem while you watch to see what triggers the failure. Many seemingly intermittent problems really aren't intermittent—you just haven't reproduced the events exactly.

- Take the time to try to isolate the symptom to ensure that your fix is going to the software or hardware that really needs it. Remove suspect pieces of hardware until only one possible "bad apple" remains. Remove background programs, boot into Safe Mode, or try to create a situation in which only the suspected program is running. Isolation is one of the greatest tools in networking.

- If you aren't sure whether a problem lies in the software or in the hardware, you can take a few steps to help you zero in on which side of the PC to suspect. The best step is to replace the suspected piece of hardware with a known good part and then try uninstalling the suspected software and reinstalling. Try upgrading drivers. Download patches or upgrades to software, especially if the hardware and the software are more than two years apart in age, and always check for viruses.

- Once you've discovered the problem, unless it is either simple (network cable unplugged) or something you've seen before and know exactly how to fix, you'll need to research it. The Internet makes this easy. One of my favorite tricks is to type the error into my search engine, because most times I can find a quick fix.

- Make backups—or at least warn the user of the risk—before you try a fix. If possible, try to remember how the system was set up before the fix so you can go back to square one if the fix fails to work. After you perform the fix, do whatever you need to do to make sure the system is working properly. Make sure the user experiences the system working properly and can sign off on your work.

- You can use the OSI seven-layer model to troubleshoot network problems. The Physical layer defines the physical form taken by data when it travels across a cable. The Data Link layer defines the rules for accessing and using the Physical layer. The Network layer defines the rules for adding information to the data packet that controls how routers move it from its source on one network to its destination on a different network.

- The Transport layer breaks up data it receives from the upper layers into smaller pieces for transport within the data packets created at the lower layers. The Session layer manages the connections between machines on the network. The Presentation layer presents data from the sending system in a form that a receiving system can understand. The Application layer is where you (or a user) get to interact with the computers.

- Mike's Four-Layer Model is an approach to network troubleshooting. First, check the hardware, including connections, NICs, and hubs/switches/routers. Second, check that the protocols, such as TCP/IP, are installed and properly configured. Third, check the network setup, whether it includes a server or is peer-to-peer. Finally, check the shared resources. Have you identified the appropriate resources and made them available for sharing to all relevant users? Are the individual systems set up to access the shared resources?

■ Key Terms

■ Key Term Quiz

Use the Key Terms list to complete the sentences that follow. Not all terms will be used.

1. Every network card has a unique built-in identifier called a(n) _____.

2. The _____ hardware protocol dominates the modern computing landscape.

3. The _____ is a value that distinguishes which part of an IP address is the network address and which part is the host address.

4. A(n) _____ helps break files into packets to send across the network, and reassemble packets it receives into whole files.

5. The command-line utility called _____ enables one machine to check whether it can communicate with another machine.

6. A center cable surrounded by insulation and covered with a shield of braided cable is called _____.

7. The _____ connector is the standard connector used for UTP Ethernet installations.

8. A person logged in to the _____ on a Windows system can read any file and run any program on the system.

■ Multiple-Choice Quiz

1. James needs to connect his Windows XP system to a Windows 2000 network domain. Which of the following will get him to the screen he needs?

   A. Control Panel | Client for Microsoft Networks | Log on to Windows NT domain

   B. Right-click My Computer | Properties | Client for Microsoft Networks | Network ID

   C. Control Panel | Network Connections | Network Identification | Log on to Windows NT domain

   D. Right-click My Computer | Properties | Computer Name | Network ID

2. What is the meaning of the networking term *topology*?

   A. The choice of network protocol

   B. The cabling specification of a network

   C. The physical layout of a network

   D. A network that uses hubs

3. What transmits the sender's MAC address, recipient's MAC address, data, and CRC when two computers communicate across a network?

   A. Packet

   B. IP unit

   C. CSMA

   D. Token

4. You need to change the TCP/IP settings of the local area connection of a Windows XP machine on your Microsoft network. How do you get to the screen where you can perform this task? (Select all that apply.)

   A. Start | right-click My Network Places | Properties | Local Area Connection

   B. Start | Settings | Network and Dial-up Connections | Local Area Connection

   C. Start | Control Panel | Network Connections | Local Area Connection

   D. Right-click My Computer | Properties | Network Connections | Local Area Connection

5. What *minimum* level of cabling must be used to support Gigabit networks?

   A. CAT 3

   B. CAT 5

   C. CAT 5e

   D. CAT 6

6. You need to run 1000BaseT through an area with a great deal of electronic noise. What type of copper cable should you use?

   A. 1330nm multimode fiber

   B. STP

   C. UTP

   D. Coax

7. What is the technology that enables a single computer to run multiple servers by using TCP/IP?

   A. Services

   B. Doors

   C. Ports

   D. Parallel Serving

8. A small plug that allows you to test a NIC's circuitry is called a(n) _____.

   A. Loopback plug

   B. Port tester

   C. Multimeter

   D. Integrated network and logic probe

9. You are down under your desk organizing some wires when you notice that the activity light on your NIC is blinking erratically. Is there a problem?

   A. Yes, the activity light should be on steadily when the computer is running.

   B. Yes, the activity light should be blinking steadily, not randomly.

   C. No, the light blinks when there is network traffic.

   D. No, the light blinks to show bus activity.

10. Which layer of the OSI model describes the cabling of a network?

    A. Layer 1

    B. Layer 2

    C. Layer 3

    D. Layer 7

Essay Quiz

1. A client wants to implement a network in her building, but she can't decide on the technology to use. She inherited the building with some networking stuff in place, namely CAT 5e strung through the walls and the ceiling to a central wiring area. All of the offices have RJ-45 outlets for workstations. Write an essay detailing the technologies she could install by using the existing equipment and why she might select one over the other(s). Include an explanation of the equipment she has already installed.

2. You are a tech for a small company and you get a call from Jessica, who cannot access the network anymore from her workstation. What techniques would you use to help troubleshoot her system and get her back working?

3. There are different classifications of IP addresses and ways to assign them. Write a short essay on the difference between Class A, B, and C addresses, and how to choose either static or dynamic addressing.

Lab Projects

• Lab Project 16.1

The PC is not the only device that can connect to an Ethernet network. Do an Internet search or take a trip to your local computer store and compile a list of network devices. What did you find? How would they be used?

• Lab Project 16.2

Nearly every hardware manufacturer wants you to upgrade to their latest networking gear and they keep adding new features to entice you. Do a search through the bigger companies' product lists and compare the Linksys, Netgear, Microsoft, and D-Link devices:

www.linksysbycisco.com
www.netgear.com
www.microsoft.com
www.dlink.com

Learning Wireless

chapter

17

"The wireless telegraph is not difficult to understand. The ordinary telegraph is like a very long cat. You pull the tail in New York, and it meows in Los Angeles. The wireless is the same, only without the cat."

—ALBERT EINSTEIN

In this chapter, you will learn how to

■ **Discuss wireless networking components**

■ **Analyze and explain wireless networking standards**

Wireless networks have been popular for many years now, but unlike wired networks, so much of how wireless works continues to elude people. Part of the problem might be that a simple wireless network is so inexpensive and easy to configure that most users and techs never really get into the *hows* of wireless. The chance to get away from all the cables and mess and just *connect* has a phenomenal appeal. Well, let's change all that and dive deeply into wireless networking.

Wireless Networking Components

Instead of a physical set of wires running between network nodes, wireless networks use either radio waves or beams of infrared light to communicate with each other. Various kinds of wireless networking solutions have come and gone in the past. The wireless radio wave networks you'll find yourself supporting these days are based on the IEEE 802.11 wireless Ethernet standard, marketed as Wi-Fi, and on Bluetooth technology. Wireless networks using infrared light are limited to those that use the Infrared Data Association (IrDA) protocol. Finally, the cell phone companies have gotten into the mix and offer access to the Internet through cellular networks with technologies such as EDGE and 3G.

Wireless networking capabilities of one form or another are built into many modern computing devices. Infrared *transceiver* ports have been standard issue on portable computers, PDAs, and high-end printers for years, although they're absent from most of the latest PCs and portables. Figure 17.1 shows the infrared transceiver ports on an older laptop and PDA. Wireless Ethernet and, to a lesser extent, Bluetooth capabilities are now ubiquitous as integrated components, or you can easily add them by using USB, PCI, PCI Express, or PC Card adapters. Figure 17.2 shows a desktop PCI Wi-Fi adapter. You can also add wireless network capabilities by using external USB wireless network adapters, as shown in Figure 17.3.

Wireless networking is not limited to PCs. Most handheld computers, PDAs, and smartphones have wireless capabilities built in or available as add-on options. Figure 17.4 shows a smartphone accessing the Internet over a Wi-Fi connection.

• **Figure 17.1**   Infrared transceiver ports on a laptop and PDA

• **Figure 17.2**   Wireless PCI add-on card

• **Figure 17.3**   External USB wireless NIC

• Figure 17.4 Smartphone with wireless capability

> Wireless access points are commonly known as WAPs, APs, or simply wireless routers.

> Wireless networks use the carrier sense multiple access/collision avoidance (CSMA/CA) standard, while wired Ethernet networks use carrier sense multiple access/collision detection (CSMA/CD).

To extend the capabilities of a wireless Ethernet network, such as connecting to a wired network or sharing a high-speed Internet connection, you need a **wireless access point (WAP)**. A WAP centrally connects wireless network nodes in the same way that a hub connects wired Ethernet PCs. Many WAPs also act as switches and Internet routers, such as the Linksys device shown in Figure 17.5.

Wireless communication via Bluetooth comes as a built-in option on newer PCs and peripheral devices, or you can add it to an older PC via an external USB Bluetooth adapter. Figure 17.6 shows a Bluetooth adapter with a Bluetooth-enabled mouse and keyboard.

Wireless Networking Software

Wireless devices use the same networking protocols and client that their wired counterparts use, and they operate by using the **carrier sense multiple access/collision avoidance (CSMA/CA)** networking scheme. The *collision avoidance* aspect differs slightly from the *collision detection* standard used in wired Ethernet. Wireless nodes listen in on the wireless medium to see if another node is currently broadcasting data. If so, it waits a random amount of time before retrying. So far, this method is exactly the same as the method used by wired Ethernet networks. Because wireless nodes have a more difficult time detecting data collisions, however, they offer the option of using the *Request to Send/Clear to Send (RTS/CTS)* protocol. When enabled, a transmitting node that determines that the wireless medium is clear to use sends an RTS frame to the receiving node. The receiving node responds with a CTS frame, telling the sending node that it's okay to transmit. Then, once the data is sent, the transmitting node waits for an acknowledgment (ACK) from the receiving node before sending the next data packet. Very elegant, but keep in mind that using RTS/CTS introduces significant overhead to the process and can impede performance.

• Figure 17.5 Linksys device that acts as wireless access point, switch, and router

• Figure 17.6 External USB Bluetooth adapter, keyboard, and mouse

In terms of configuring wireless networking software, you need to do very little. Wireless network adapters are plug and play, so any modern version of Windows immediately recognizes one when installed, prompting you to load any needed hardware drivers. You will, however, need a utility to set parameters such as the network name.

Windows XP and later built-in tools for configuring these settings, but for previous versions of Windows, you need to rely on configuration tools provided by the wireless network adapter vendor. Figure 17.7 shows a typical wireless network adapter configuration utility. Using this utility, you can determine your link state and signal strength, configure your wireless networking *mode* (discussed next), and set security encryption, power saving options, and so on.

Wireless Network Modes

The simplest wireless network consists of two or more PCs communicating directly with each other without cabling or any other intermediary hardware. More complicated wireless networks use a WAP to centralize wireless communication and bridge wireless network segments to wired network segments. These two methods are called ad hoc mode and infrastructure mode.

Ad hoc Mode

Ad hoc mode is sometimes called *peer-to-peer mode*, with each wireless node in direct contact with every other node in a decentralized free-for-all, as shown in Figure 17.8. Two or more wireless nodes communicating in ad hoc mode form what's called an *Independent Basic Service Set (IBSS)*. Ad hoc mode networks are suited for small groups of computers (less than a dozen or so) that need to transfer files or share printers. Ad hoc networks are also good for temporary networks such as study groups or business meetings.

Infrastructure Mode

Wireless networks running in **infrastructure mode** use one or more WAPs to connect the wireless network nodes to a wired network segment, as shown in Figure 17.9. A single WAP servicing a given area is called a *Basic Service Set (BSS)*. This service area can be extended by adding more WAPs. This is called, appropriately, an *Extended Basic Service Set (EBSS)*.

• **Figure 17.7**   Wireless configuration utility

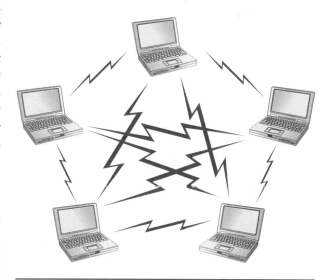

• **Figure 17.8**   Wireless ad hoc mode network

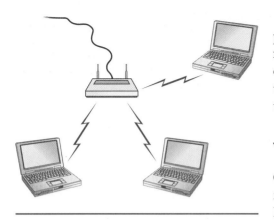

• **Figure 17.9**   Wireless infrastructure mode network

Wireless networks running in infrastructure mode require more planning and are more complicated to configure than ad hoc mode networks, but they also give you finer control over how the network operates. Infrastructure mode is better suited to networks that need to share dedicated resources such as Internet connections and centralized databases.

Wireless Networking Security

One of the major complaints against wireless networking is that it offers weak security. In many cases, all you need to do to access a wireless network is walk into a WAP's coverage area, turn on your wireless device, and connect! Furthermore, data packets are floating through the air instead of safely wrapped up inside network cabling. What's to stop an unscrupulous PC tech with the right equipment from grabbing those packets out of the air and reading that data himself?

Wireless networks use three methods to secure access to the network itself and secure the data that's being transferred. The **service set identifier (SSID)** parameter—also called the *network name*—is used to define the wireless network. This is very handy when you have a number of wireless networks in the same area.

SSID

One of the main security weaknesses with wireless networks is that, out of the box, *no* security is configured at all. Wireless devices *want* to be heard, and WAPs are usually configured to broadcast their presence to their maximum range and welcome all other wireless devices that respond.

Changing the default SSID for the WAP is the first step in setting up a new wireless network.

Always change the default SSID to something unique, and change the password right away. Configuring a unique SSID name and password is the very least that you should do to secure a wireless network. The default SSID names and passwords are well known and widely available online. This is intended to make setting up a wireless network as easy as possible, but can cause problems in places with a lot of overlapping wireless networks. Each wireless network node and access point needs to be configured with the same unique SSID name. This SSID name is then included in the header of every data packet broadcast in the wireless network's coverage area. Data packets that lack the correct SSID name in the header are rejected.

Another trick often seen in wireless networks is to tell the wireless device not to broadcast the SSID. People not authorized to access the network will have a harder time knowing it's there.

MAC Address Filtering

Most WAPs also support **MAC address filtering**, a method that enables you to limit access to your wireless network based on the physical, hard-wired address of the units' wireless NIC. MAC address filtering is a handy way of creating a type of "accepted users" list to limit access to your wireless network, but it works best when you have a small number of users. A table stored in the WAP lists the MAC addresses that are permitted to participate

Many techs shorten the term "MAC address filtering" to simply "MAC filtering." Either term works.

in the wireless network. Any data packets that don't contain the MAC address of a node listed in the table are rejected.

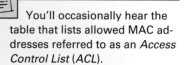

You'll occasionally hear the table that lists allowed MAC addresses referred to as an *Access Control List* (*ACL*).

WEP

Early on, Wi-Fi developers introduced the **Wired Equivalent Privacy (WEP)** protocol to attempt to ensure that data is secured while in transit over the airwaves. WEP encryption uses a standard 40-bit encryption to scramble data packets. Many vendors also support 104-bit encryption. Note that some vendors advertise 128-bit encryption, but they actually use a 104-bit encryption key. Unfortunately, WEP encryption includes a flaw that makes it extremely vulnerable to attack. Although better than no encryption at all, keep in mind that WEP will not keep out a knowledgeable intruder.

One important note to consider is that WEP doesn't provide complete end-to-end encryption. WEP provides encryption only between the WAP and the wireless device. Encryption is stripped from the data packet as it travels "up" through the subsequent network layers. For true end-to-end encryption, you need to upgrade to WPA or WPA2.

WPA

The **Wi-Fi Protected Access (WPA)** protocol addresses the weaknesses of WEP and acts as a security protocol upgrade to WEP. WPA offers security enhancements such as an encryption key integrity-checking feature and user authentication through the industry-standard *Extensible Authentication Protocol* (*EAP*). EAP provides a huge security improvement over WEP encryption. After all, MAC addresses are fairly easy to "sniff" out, because they're transmitted in unencrypted, clear text format. User names and passwords are encrypted and therefore much more secure. Even with these enhancements, WPA was intended only as an interim security solution until the IEEE 802.11i security standard was finalized and implemented.

WPA2

Today, Mac OS X and Microsoft Windows support the full IEEE 802.11i standard, more commonly known as **Wi-Fi Protected Access 2 (WPA2)**, to lock down wireless networks. WPA2 uses the Advanced Encryption Standard (AES), among other improvements, to provide a secure wireless environment. If you haven't upgraded to WPA2, you should.

Speed and Range Issues

Wireless networking data throughput speeds depend on several factors. Foremost is the standard that the wireless devices use. Depending on the standard used, wireless throughput speeds range from a measly 2 Mbps to a snappy 100+ Mbps. One of the other factors affecting speed is the distance between wireless nodes (or between wireless nodes and centralized access points). Wireless devices dynamically negotiate the top speed at which they can communicate without dropping too many data packets. Speed decreases as distance increases, so the maximum throughput speed is achieved only at extremely close range (less than 25 feet or so). At the outer reaches of a device's effective range, speed may decrease to around 1 Mbps before it drops out altogether.

Tech Tip

Increasing Wireless Range
You can increase range in a couple of ways. You can install multiple WAPs to permit "roaming" between one WAP's coverage area and another's—an EBSS, described earlier in this chapter. Or you can install a replacement antenna that increases a single WAP's signal strength, thus increasing its range. If that is still not enough, signal boosters are available that can give you even more power.

Speed is also affected by interference from other wireless devices operating in the same frequency range—such as cordless phones or baby monitors—and by solid objects. So-called *dead spots* occur when something capable of blocking the radio signal comes between the wireless network nodes. Large electrical appliances such as refrigerators are *very* effective at blocking a wireless network signal. Other culprits include electrical fuse boxes, metal plumbing, air conditioning units, and similar objects.

Wireless networking range is difficult to define, and you'll see most descriptions listed with qualifiers, such as "*around* 150 feet" and "*about* 300 feet." This is simply because, like throughput speed, range is greatly affected by outside factors. Interference from other wireless devices affects range, as does interference from solid objects. The maximum ranges listed in the next section are those presented by wireless manufacturers as the theoretical maximum ranges. In the real world, you'll experience these ranges only under the most ideal circumstances. True effective range is probably about half what you see listed.

■ Wireless Networking Standards

To help you gain a better understanding of wireless network technology, here is a brief look at the standards used.

IEEE 802.11-Based Wireless Networking

The **IEEE 802.11** wireless Ethernet standard, more commonly known as **Wi-Fi**, defines methods by which devices may communicate by using *spread-spectrum* radio waves. Spread-spectrum broadcasts data in small, discrete chunks over the frequencies available within a certain frequency range.

The 802.11-based wireless technologies broadcast and receive on one of two license-free industrial, scientific, and medical (ISM) radio bands: 2.4 GHz and 5.8 GHz. Even though the ISM band is 5.8 GHz, we just say "5 GHz" for reasons I can't answer. Over the years, the original 802.11 standard has been extended to 802.11a, 802.11b, 802.11g, and 802.11n variations used in Wi-Fi wireless networks. Each of these versions of 802.11 uses one of the two

Tech Tip

Spread-Spectrum Broadcasting

The 802.11 standard defines three spread-spectrum broadcasting methods: direct-sequence spread-spectrum (DSSS), frequency-hopping spread-spectrum (FHSS), and orthogonal frequency-division multiplexing (OFDM). DSSS sends data out on multiple frequencies at the same time, while FHSS sends data on one frequency at a time, constantly shifting (or hopping) frequencies. OFDM, the most common broadcast method, uses multiple data streams, each of which is constantly shifting (or hopping) frequencies. DSSS uses considerably more bandwidth than FHSS or OFDM, around 22 MHz as opposed to 1 MHz, respectively. DSSS is capable of greater data throughput, but DSSS is more prone to interference than FHSS. HomeRF wireless networks, now obsolete, were the only types that used FHSS; all the other 802.11-based wireless networking standards use DSSS or OFDM.

Wi-Fi is by far the most widely adopted wireless networking type today. Not only do millions of private businesses and homes have wireless networks, but many public places such as coffee shops and libraries also offer Internet access through wireless networks.

ISM bands, with the exception of 802.11n, which uses one but may use both. Don't worry; I'll break this down for you in a moment.

Newer wireless devices can communicate with older wireless devices, so if you are using an 802.11n WAP, all of your 802.11g devices can use it. The exception to this is 802.11a, which requires that all of the equipment directly support it. The following paragraphs describe the important specifications of each of the popular 802.11-based wireless networking standards.

802.11a   Despite the "a" designation for this extension to the 802.11 standard, **802.11a** was actually on the market *after* 802.11b. The 802.11a standard differs from the other 802.11-based standards in significant ways. Foremost is that it operates in the 5-GHz frequency range. This means that devices that use this standard are less prone to interference from other devices that use the same frequency range. 802.11a also offers considerably greater throughput than 802.11 and 802.11b, at speeds up to 54 Mbps, though its actual throughput is no more than 25 Mbps in normal traffic conditions. Although its theoretical range tops out at about 150 feet, its maximum range will be lower in a typical office environment. Despite the superior speed of 802.11a, it isn't as widely adopted in the PC world as some of the following 802.11 versions.

802.11b   **802.11b** was the first standard to take off and become ubiquitous in wireless networking. The 802.11b standard supports data throughput of up to 11 Mbps (with actual throughput averaging 4 to 6 Mbps)—on par with older wired 10BaseT networks—and a maximum range of 300 feet under ideal conditions. In a typical office environment, its maximum range is lower. The main downside to using 802.11b is, in fact, that it uses a very popular frequency. The 2.4-GHz ISM band is already crowded with baby monitors, garage door openers, microwaves, and wireless phones, so you're likely to run into interference from other wireless devices.

802.11g   **802.11g** came out in 2003, taking the best of 802.11a and b and rolling them into a single standard. 802.11g offers data transfer speeds equivalent to 802.11a, up to 54 Mbps, with the wider 300-foot range of 802.11b. More important, 802.11g runs in the 2.4-GHz ISM band, so it is backward compatible with 802.11b, meaning that the same 802.11g WAP can service both 802.11b and 802.11g wireless nodes. 802.11g is incredibly popular and is only just now starting to lose out to the newest version of 802.11, 802.11n.

802.11n The **802.11n** standard brings several improvements to Wi-Fi networking, including faster speeds and new antenna technology implementations.

The 802.11n specification requires all but handheld devices to use multiple antennae to implement a feature called **multiple in/multiple out (MIMO)**, which enables the devices to make multiple simultaneous connections. With up to four antennae, 802.11n devices can achieve amazing speeds. (The official standard supports throughput of up to 600 Mbps, although practical implementation drops that down substantially.)

Many 802.11n WAPs employ *transmit beamforming*, a multiple-antennae technology that helps get rid of dead spots—or at least make them not so bad. The antennae adjust the signal once the WAP discovers a client to optimize the radio signal.

Like 802.11g, 802.11n WAPs can run in the 2.4-GHz ISM band, supporting earlier, slower 802.11b/g devices. However, 802.11n also has a more powerful, so-called *dual-band*. To use dual-band 802.11n, you need a more advanced (and more expensive) WAP that runs at both 5 GHz and 2.4 GHz simultaneously; some support 802.11a devices as well as 802.11b/g devices. Nice!

Table 17.1 compares the important differences among the versions of 802.11.

Know the differences among 802.11a, 802.11b, 802.11g, and 802.11n.

Table 17.1	Comparison of 802.11 Standards			
Standard	**802.11a**	**802.11b**	**802.11g**	**802.11n**
Max. throughput	54 Mbps	11 Mbps	54 Mbps	100+ Mbps
Max. range	150 feet	300 feet	300 feet	300+ feet
Frequency	5 GHz	2.4 GHz	2.4 GHz	2.4 and 5 GHz
Security	SSID, MAC filtering, industry-standard WEP, WPA	SSID, MAC filtering, industry-standard WEP, WPA	SSID, MAC filtering, industry-standard WEP, WPA	SSID, MAC filtering, industry-standard WEP, WPA
Compatibility	802.11a	802.11b	802.11b, 802.11g	802.11b, 802.11g, 802.11n, (802.11a in some cases)
Spread-spectrum method	DSSS	OFDM	OFDM	OFDM
Communication mode	Ad hoc or infrastructure	Ad hoc or infrastructure	Ad hoc or infrastructure	Ad hoc or infrastructure
Description	Products that adhere to this standard are considered Wi-Fi certified. Eight available channels. Less prone to interference than 802.11b and 802.11g.	Products that adhere to this standard are considered Wi-Fi certified. Fourteen channels available in the 2.4-GHz band (only 11 of which can be used in the U.S. due to FCC regulations). Three non-overlapping channels.	Products that adhere to this standard are considered Wi-Fi certified. Improved security enhancements. Fourteen channels available in the 2.4-GHz band (only 11 of which can be used in the U.S. due to FCC regulations). Three non-overlapping channels.	Same as 802.11g but adds the 5-GHz band that 802.11a uses. 802.11n can also make use of multiple antennae (MIMO) to increase its range and speed.

Other Wireless Standards

The 802.11 standards are the big players in home networking, but they're far from the only way to cut the cords. There are many other wireless standards that use all sorts of different methods to provide wireless communication, from infrared beams to cellular signals. Let's take a look at a few of these other methods.

Infrared Wireless Networking

Wireless networking using infrared technology is largely overlooked these days, probably because of the explosion of interest in the newer and faster wireless standards. But it is still a viable method to transfer files on some older devices.

Communication through infrared devices is enabled via the **Infrared Data Association (IrDA)** protocol. The IrDA protocol stack is a widely supported industry standard and has been included in all versions of Windows since Windows 95.

In speed and range, infrared isn't very impressive. Infrared devices are capable of transferring data at up to 4 Mbps—not too shabby, but hardly stellar. The maximum distance between infrared devices is 1 meter. Infrared links are direct line-of-sight and are susceptible to interference. Anything that breaks the beam of light can disrupt an infrared link: a badly placed can of Mountain Dew, a coworker passing between desks, or even bright sunlight hitting the infrared transceiver can cause interference.

Infrared is designed to make a point-to-point connection between two devices only in ad hoc mode. No infrastructure mode is available. You can, however, use an infrared access point device to enable Ethernet network communication using IrDA. Infrared devices operate at half-duplex, meaning that while one is talking, the other is listening—they can't talk and listen at the same time. IrDA has a mode that emulates full-duplex communication, but it's really half-duplex. The IrDA protocol offers exactly nothing in the way of encryption or authentication. Infrared's main security feature is the fact that you have to be literally within arm's reach to establish a link. Clearly, infrared is not the best solution for a dedicated network connection, but for a quick file transfer or print job without getting your hands dirty, it'll do in a pinch.

Table 17.2 lists infrared's important specifications.

Bluetooth

Bluetooth wireless technology (named for ninth-century Danish king Harald Bluetooth) is designed to create small wireless networks preconfigured to do

Apple computers also support IrDA, as do Linux PCs.

Many modern laptops still come with a little infrared window, but don't let that fool you into thinking the laptop has IrDA networking. These IR receivers are for use with remotes so you can use the laptop just like a TV or DVD player.

Table 17.2	Infrared Specs
Standard	**Infrared (IrDA)**
Max. throughput	Up to 4 Mbps
Max. range	1 meter (39 inches)
Security	None
Compatibility	IrDA
Communication mode	Point-to-point ad hoc

very specific jobs. Some great examples are audio devices such as headsets that connect to your smartphones, **personal area networks (PANs)** that link two PCs for a quick-and-dirty wireless network, and input devices such as keyboards and mice. Bluetooth is *not* designed to be a full-function networking solution, nor is it meant to compete with Wi-Fi. If anything, Bluetooth has replaced infrared as a means to connect PCs to peripherals.

Bluetooth, like any technology, has been upgraded over the years to make it faster and more secure. Two major versions of Bluetooth are widespread today. The first generation (versions 1.1 and 1.2) supports speeds around 1 Mbps. The second generation (2.0 and 2.1) is backward compatible with its first-generation cousins and adds support for more speed by introducing Enhanced Data Rate (EDR), which pushes top speeds to around 3 Mbps.

The IEEE organization has made first-generation Bluetooth the basis for its 802.15 standard for wireless PANs. Bluetooth uses the FHSS broadcasting method, switching between any of the 79 frequencies available in the 2.45-GHz range. Bluetooth hops frequencies some 1600 times per second, making it highly resistant to interference.

Generally, the faster and further a device sends data, the more power it needs to do so, and the Bluetooth designers understood a long time ago that some devices (such as a Bluetooth headset) could save power by not sending data as quickly or as far as other Bluetooth devices may need. To address this, all Bluetooth devices are configured for one of three classes that define maximum power usage in milliwatts (mW) and maximum distance:

Class 1	100 mW	100 meters
Class 2	2.5 mW	10 meters
Class 3	1 mW	1 meter

Bluetooth is *not* designed to be a full-fledged wireless networking solution. Bluetooth is made to replace the snake's nest of cables that currently connects most PCs to their various peripheral devices—keyboard, mouse, printer, speakers, scanner, and the like—but you won't be swapping out your 802.11-based networking devices with Bluetooth-based replacements anytime soon.

Having said that, Bluetooth-enabled wireless networking is comparable to other wireless technologies in a few ways:

- Like infrared, Bluetooth is acceptable for quick file transfers where a wired connection (or a faster wireless connection) is unavailable.

- Almost all wireless headsets are now Bluetooth.

- Bluetooth's speed and range make it a good match for wireless print server solutions.

Bluetooth hardware comes either integrated into many newer portable electronic gadgets such as PDAs and cell phones or as an adapter added to an internal or external expansion bus. Bluetooth networking is enabled through ad hoc–styled PC-to-PC (or PDA-, handheld computer–, or cell phone–to-PC) connections, or in an infrastructure-like mode through Bluetooth access points. Bluetooth access points are very similar to 802.11-based access points, bridging wireless Bluetooth PAN segments to wired LAN segments.

Cellular

A **cellular wireless network** enables you to connect to the Internet through a network-aware PDA, cell phone, or smartphone. Using an add-on PC Card or USB dongle, you can connect any laptop to a cellular network as well. Figure 17.10 shows an AT&T USBConnect Mercury 3G device for just that purpose.

In areas with broad cell phone coverage, such as big cities, cellular wireless networks offer high-speed access (around 1.5-Mbps download speeds) anywhere you go. Carriers use many protocols to provide the higher speeds, and collectively they are known as 3G. Just fire up your smartphone or portable computer and start surfing the Web! In remote areas where the 3G networks have not been built out, the speed drops down to something closer to modem connection speeds. (See Chapter 18, "Learning the Internet," for the scoop on modems.)

Cellular networks use various protocols to connect, such as Global System for Mobile Communications (GSM), General Packet Radio Service (GPRS), and Code Division Multiple Access (CDMA). The 3G networks make use of protocols such as UMTS/HSPA (AT&T), EV-DO (Verizon), and UMTS (T-Mobile). These protocols are handled seamlessly by the software and hardware. What end users see is TCP/IP, just as if they connected through a wired network.

• **Figure 17.10**   AT&T USBConnect Mercury 3G

■ Chapter Summary

After reading this chapter and completing the exercises, you should understand the following about wireless networking.

Discuss wireless networking components

- The wireless radio wave networks you'll find yourself supporting these days are those based on the IEEE 802.11 wireless Ethernet standard Wi-Fi and on the newer Bluetooth technology. Many cellular phone providers also provide Internet access through their networks. Wireless networks using infrared light use the IrDA protocol.

- Wireless networking capabilities of one form or another are built into many modern computing devices. Wireless Ethernet and Bluetooth are almost ubiquitous as integrated components or can easily be added by using USB, PCI, PCI Express, or PC Card adapters. Many handheld computers, smartphones, and PDAs have wireless capabilities built in or available as add-on options.

- To extend the capabilities of a wireless Ethernet network, such as connecting to a wired network or sharing a high-speed Internet connection, you need a WAP. A WAP centrally connects wireless network nodes in the same way that a hub connects wired Ethernet PCs.

Analyze and explain wireless networking standards

- Wireless devices use the same networking protocols and client that their wired counterparts use, and they operate by using the CSMA/CA networking scheme, where nodes check before broadcasting. Wireless nodes also use the RTS/ CTS protocol. When enabled, a transmitting node that determines that the wireless medium is clear to use sends an RTS frame to the receiving node. The receiving node responds with a CTS frame, telling the sending node that it's okay to transmit. Then, once the data is sent, the transmitting node waits for an acknowledgment (ACK) from the receiving node before sending the next data packet.

- You will need a utility to set parameters such as your SSID. Windows XP and up have built-in tools for this, but otherwise you must rely on

configuration tools provided by the wireless network adapter vendor.

- The simplest wireless network consists of two or more PCs communicating directly with each other without cabling or any other intermediary hardware (ad hoc mode). More complicated (and more common) wireless networks use a WAP to centralize wireless communication and bridge wireless network segments to wired network segments (infrastructure mode).

- Ad hoc networks are also good for temporary networks such as study groups or business meetings.

- Infrastructure mode is better suited to business networks or networks that need to share dedicated resources such as Internet connections and centralized databases.

- Out of the box, wireless networks have no security configured at all. Wireless devices want to be heard, and WAPs are usually configured to broadcast their presence to their maximum range and welcome all other wireless devices that respond. Further, data packets are floating through the air instead of safely wrapped up inside network cabling.

- Most WAPs support MAC address filtering, a method that enables you to limit access to your wireless network based on the physical, hard-wired address of the unit's wireless network adapter.

- Enabling WEP encrypts your data to secure it while in transit over the airwaves, but the WEP encryption standard itself is flawed and cannot be relied upon to protect your data against a knowledgeable and motivated attacker.

- WPA and WPA2 address the weaknesses of WEP and act as a sort of security protocol upgrade to WEP-enabled devices. WPA and WPA2 offer security enhancements such as an encryption key integrity-checking feature and user authentication through the industry-standard EAP.

- Depending on the standard used, wireless throughput speeds range from a measly 2 Mbps to a snappy 100+ Mbps. Wireless devices dynamically negotiate the top speed at which they can communicate without dropping too many data packets.

- Wireless networking speed and range are greatly affected by outside factors, such as interference from other wireless devices or solid objects. A wireless device's true effective range is probably about half the theoretical maximum listed by the manufacturer.

- 802.11a differs from the other 802.11-based standards in significant ways. Foremost, it operates in a different frequency range, 5 GHz, so 802.11a devices are less prone to interference. 802.11a also offers considerably greater throughput than 802.11 and 802.11b, at speeds up to 54 Mbps, but its range tops out at only about 150 feet. 802.11a isn't widely adopted in the PC world.

- The 802.11b standard supports data throughput of up to 11 Mbps—on par with older wired 10BaseT networks—and a range of up to 300 feet under ideal conditions.

- The 802.11g standard offers data transfer speeds equivalent to 802.11a, up to 54 Mbps, with the wider 300-foot range of 802.11b. Because 802.11g is backward compatible with 802.11b, the same 802.11g WAP can service both 802.11g and 802.11b wireless nodes.

- 802.11n ups the speed even more to 100+ Mbps and extends the range to greater than 300 feet by using MIMO (multiple in/multiple out) with extra antennae. You can also configure it to use the less crowded 5-GHz band if you are using a dual-mode WAP.

- Wireless networking using infrared (IR) technology is enabled via the Infrared Data Association—IrDA—protocol stack, a widely supported industry standard, and has been included in all versions of Windows since Windows 95. IR is designed to make only a point-to-point connection between two devices in ad hoc mode of up to 4 Mbps, at a maximum distance of 1 meter.

- Bluetooth wireless technology is designed to create small wireless personal area networks (PANs) that link PCs to peripheral devices such as PDAs and printers, input devices such as keyboards and mice, and even consumer electronics such as cell phones, home stereos, televisions, home security systems, and so on. Bluetooth is not designed to be a full-function networking solution.

- Cellular wireless networks enable you to connect to the Internet through a smartphone or portable computer with an access card with download speeds of around 1.5 Mbps. Cellular networks use various protocols, including GSM, GPRS, and CDMA. The current high-speed cellular network protocols are collectively called 3G.

■ Key Terms

802.11a *(563)*	**infrastructure mode** *(559)*
802.11b *(563)*	**MAC address filtering** *(560)*
802.11g *(563)*	**multiple in/multiple out (MIMO)** *(564)*
802.11n *(564)*	**personal area network (PAN)** *(566)*
ad hoc mode *(559)*	**service set identifier (SSID)** *(560)*
Bluetooth *(565)*	**Wi-Fi** *(562)*
carrier sense multiple access/collision avoidance (CSMA/CA) *(558)*	**Wi-Fi Protected Access (WPA)** *(561)*
	Wi-Fi Protected Access 2 (WPA2) *(561)*
cellular wireless network *(567)*	**Wired Equivalent Privacy (WEP)** *(561)*
IEEE 802.11 *(562)*	**wireless access point (WAP)** *(558)*
Infrared Data Association (IrDA) *(565)*	

■ Key Term Quiz

Use the Key Terms list to complete the sentences that follow. Not all terms will be used.

1. A protocol for setting up wireless PANs and connecting to some peripherals is called _____.

2. Establishing a unique _____ or network name helps ensure that only wireless network devices configured similarly are permitted access to the network.

3. The wireless Ethernet standard that operates at a maximum of 54 Mbps on the 2.4-GHz frequency is _____.

4. Computers are in _____ when they connect directly together without using a WAP.

5. Of the three common wireless encryption protocols, _____ is the *least* secure.

6. If you need to share an Internet connection or connect to a wired network through your wireless network, you would use _____.

7. The _____ feature enables devices on 802.11n networks to make multiple simultaneous connections, allowing for a theoretical throughput of 600 Mbps.

8. 802.11 implements _____, which proactively avoids network packet collisions rather than simply detecting them when they occur.

■ Multiple-Choice Quiz

1. Two wireless nodes that are communicating directly with each other, without any intermediary systems or hardware, are using what wireless mode?

    A. Ad hoc

    B. Bluetooth

    C. Infrastructure

    D. 802.11

2. What device centrally connects wireless network nodes in the same way that a hub connects wired Ethernet PCs?

    A. Bluetooth adapter

    B. Wireless NIC

    C. SSID

    D. WAP

3. What is the approximate range of an 802.11b/g network?

    A. ~1000 ft

    B. ~300 ft

    C. ~150 ft

    D. ~500 ft

4. Which encryption method used on wireless networks is the most secure?

    A. WEP

    B. Wi-Fi

    C. WINS

    D. WPA2

5. What can limit wireless connectivity to a list of accepted users based on the hard-wired address of their wireless NIC?

    A. Encryption

    B. MAC filtering

    C. NWLink

    D. WEP

6. Which wireless standard combines the longest range with the most throughput?

    A. 802.11a

    B. 802.11b

    C. 802.11g

    D. 802.11n

7. Personal area networks are created by what wireless technology?

    A. Bluetooth

    B. IrDA

    C. Wi-Fi

    D. Cellular wireless

8. What is the best technology if you need Internet access from anywhere in the country?

    A. Bluetooth

    B. IrDA

    C. Wi-Fi

    D. Cellular wireless

9. What is the technical name of a wireless network?

    A. SSID

    B. BSSID

    C. SSD

    D. WPA

10. What is the approximate range of a Class 2 Bluetooth PAN?

- **A.** ~100 m
- **B.** ~10 m
- **C.** ~5 m
- **D.** ~1 m

11. Which of the following wireless standards lets you connect to the Internet from almost anywhere?

- **A.** 802.11g
- **B.** 802.11n
- **C.** Cellular
- **D.** Bluetooth

■ Essay Quiz

1. Some friends of yours insist that wireless network standard 802.11a was available before 802.11b. They also say 802.11a is "better" than 802.11b. Find the pages in this chapter that discuss these standards, and jot down some notes to explain the facts.

2. Prepare a short memo to your instructor (or friend) that outlines the basic differences between WEP and WPA encryption methods. Use any standard memo format you are familiar with.

Lab Projects

• Lab Project 17.1

You just received a nice tax return and want to expand your home network. Your current wired home network setup consists of two Intel Pentium 4–class desktop PCs with 10/100-Mbps NICs and a relative's older laptop with both an RJ-45 port and 802.11b wireless built in. The main Internet connection coming into your home enters your more powerful desktop system first and then spreads out to a 100-Mbps switch from there. With your own money to be spent buying equipment, you seek a solution that will satisfy your needs for a long time.

You want to buy your new equipment locally so you can set it up right away. Use the Internet to explore prices and equipment in local stores. Also check out reviews of the items you are interested in obtaining. After you have done sufficient research, prepare an itemized price list with your choices arranged like the following table:

ITEM	STORE/MODEL	PRICE	QUANTITY	TOTAL
Wireless NICs, PCI				
Wireless NICs, PC Card				
Wireless Access Point				
Other				
TOTALS				

• Lab Project 17.2

You have been tasked with expanding your company's wireless network. Your IT Manager asked you to create a presentation that explains wireless routers and their functions. She specifically said to focus on the 802.11g and 802.11n wireless network standards. Create a brief, yet informative PowerPoint presentation that includes comparisons of these two technologies. You may include images of actual wireless bridges from vendor Web sites as needed, being sure to cite your sources. Include any up-to-date prices from your research as well.

Learning the Internet

"The Internet is a great way to get on the Net."

—BOB DOLE

In this chapter, you will learn how to

■ **Explain how the Internet works**

■ **Connect to the Internet**

■ **Explain VPNs**

Imagine coming home from a long day at work building and fixing PCs, sitting down in front of your shiny new computer, double-clicking the single icon that sits dead center on your monitor...and suddenly you're enveloped in an otherworldly scene, where 200-foot trees slope smoothly into snow-white beaches and rich blue ocean. Overhead, pterodactyls soar through the air while you talk to a small chap with pointy ears and a long robe about heading up the mountain in search of a giant monster.... TV show from the SciFi channel? Spielberg's latest film offering? How about an interactive game played by millions of people all over the planet on a daily basis by connecting to the Internet? If you guessed the last one, you're right.

This chapter covers the skills you need as a PC tech to help people connect to the Internet. It starts with a brief section on how the Internet works, along with the concepts of connectivity, and then it goes into the specifics on the many different types of Internet connections. Let's get started!

◼ How the Internet Works

Thanks to the Internet, people can communicate with one another over vast distances, often in the blink of an eye. As a PC tech, you need to know how PCs communicate with the larger world for two reasons. First, knowing the process and pieces involved in the communication enables you to troubleshoot effectively when that communication goes away. Second, you need to be able to communicate knowledgeably with a network technician who comes in to solve a more complex issue.

Internet Tiers

You probably know that the Internet is millions and millions of computers all joined together to form the largest network on Earth, but not many folks know much about how these computers are organized. To keep everything running smoothly, the Internet is broken down into groups called **tiers**. The main tier, called *Tier 1*, consists of nine companies called *Tier 1 providers*. The Tier 1 providers own long-distance, high-speed fiber-optic networks called *backbones*. These backbones span the major cities of the earth (not all Tier 1 backbones go to all cities) and interconnect at special locations called *network access points* (*NAPs*). Anyone wishing to connect to any of the Tier 1 providers must pay large sums of money. The Tier 1 providers do not charge each other.

Tier 2 providers own smaller, regional networks and must pay the Tier 1 providers. Most of the famous companies that provide Internet access to the general public are Tier 2 providers. *Tier 3 providers* are even more regional and connect to Tier 2 providers.

The piece of equipment that makes this tiered Internet concept work is called a backbone router. *Backbone routers* connect to more than one other backbone router, creating a big, interwoven framework for communication. Figure 18.1 illustrates the decentralized and interwoven nature of the Internet. The key reason for interweaving the backbones of the Internet was to provide alternative pathways for data if one or more of the routers went down. If Jane in Houston sends a message to her friend Polly in New York City, for example, the shortest path between Jane and Polly in this hypothetical situation is this: Jane's message originates at Rice University in Houston, bounces to Emory University in Atlanta, flits through Virginia Commonwealth University in Richmond, and then zips into SUNY in New York City (Figure 18.2). Polly happily reads the message and life is great. The Internet functions as planned.

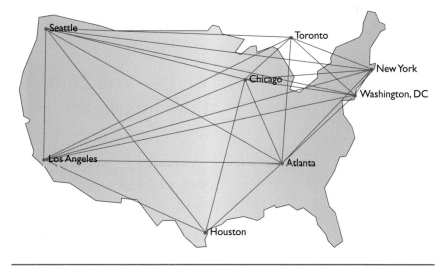

• **Figure 18.1**   Internet Tier 1 connections

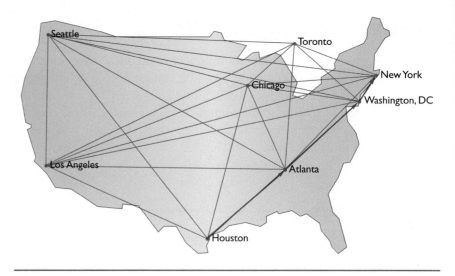

• **Figure 18.2**   Message traveling from Houston to NYC

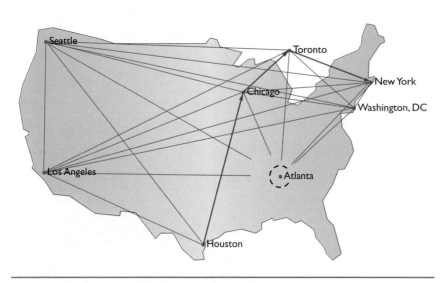

• **Figure 18.3**   Rerouted message from Houston to NYC

But what happens if the entire southeastern United States experiences a huge power outage and Internet backbones in every state from Virginia to Florida go down? Jane's message would bounce back to Rice and the Rice computers. Being smart cookies, the routers would reroute the message to nodes that still functioned—say, Rice to University of Chicago, to University of Toronto, and then to SUNY (Figure 18.3). It's all in a day's work for the highly redundant and adaptable Internet. At this point in the game (2010), the Internet simply cannot go down fully—barring, of course, a catastrophe of Biblical proportions.

TCP/IP—The Common Language of the Internet

As you know from all the earlier chapters in this book, hardware alone doesn't cut it in the world of computing. You need software to make the machines run and create an interface for humans. The Internet is no exception. TCP/IP provides the basic software structure for communication on the Internet.

Because you spent a good deal of Chapter 16, "Learning Local Area Networking," working with TCP/IP, you should have an appreciation for its adaptability and, perhaps more importantly, its extendability. TCP/IP provides the addressing scheme for computers that communicate on the Internet through IP addresses, such as 192.168.4.1 or 16.45.123.7. As a protocol, though, TCP/IP is much more than just an addressing system. TCP/IP provides the framework and common language for the Internet. And it offers a phenomenally wide-open structure for creative purposes. Programmers can write applications built to take advantage of the TCP/IP structure and features, creating what are called TCP/IP services. The cool thing about TCP/IP services is that they're limited only by the imagination of the programmers.

There are many different TCP/IP services, and you don't need to know most of them for the Essentials exam, but I must mention one service that you've most likely worked with yourself, whether you knew it by that term or not. The most famous service is the **Hypertext Transfer Protocol (HTTP)**, the service that provides the structure for the **World Wide Web** ("the Web," for short), the graphical face of the Internet. Using your **Web browser**—a program specifically designed to retrieve, interpret, and display Web pages—an almost endless variety of information and entertainment is just a click away. I can't tell you how many times I've started to look up something on the Web, and suddenly it's two hours later and I still haven't looked up what I started out wanting to know, but I don't actually care, because I've learned some amazing stuff! But then when I do go look it up, in just minutes I can find information it used to take *days* to uncover. The Web can arguably claim the distinction of being both the biggest time-waster and the biggest time-saver since the invention of the book!

At this point, you have an enormous, beautifully functioning network. All the backbone routers connect with fiber and thick copper cabling backbones, and TCP/IP enables communication and services for building applications for humans to interface across the distances. What's left? Oh, that's right: how do you tap into this great network and partake of its goodness?

Internet Service Providers

Every Tier 1 and Tier 2 provider leases connections to the Internet to companies called **Internet service providers (ISPs)**. ISPs essentially sit along the edges of the Tier 1 and Tier 2 Internet and tap into the flow. You can, in turn, lease some of the connections from the ISP and thus get on the Internet.

ISPs come in all sizes. Comcast, the huge cable television provider, has multiple, huge-capacity connections into the Internet, enabling its millions of customers to connect from their local machines and surf the Web. Contrast Comcast with Unísono, an ISP in San Miguel de Allende, Mexico (Figure 18.4). Billed as the "Best Internet Service in San Miguel," it services only a small (but delightful) community and the busy tourist crowd.

Microsoft calls the connections ISPs make to the Internet *access points*, which I think is a very bad name. You'd think we'd be able to come up with new terms for things! Instead, some folks in this industry continue rebranding things with the same phrases or catchwords, only serving to confuse already bewildered consumers.

Connection Concepts

Connecting to an ISP requires two things to work perfectly: hardware for connectivity, such as a modem and a working cable line; and software, such as protocols to govern the connections and the data flow (all configured in Windows) and applications to take advantage of the various TCP/IP services. Once you have a contract with an ISP to grant you access to the Internet, the ISP gives you TCP/IP configuration numbers and data so you can set up your software to connect directly to a router at the ISP that becomes your gateway to the Internet. The router to which you connect at the

● **Figure 18.4** Unísono homepage

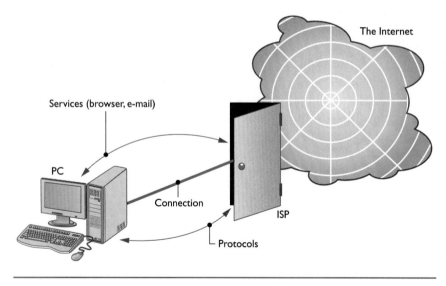

Services (browser, e-mail)

The Internet

PC

Connection

ISP

Protocols

● **Figure 18.5** Simplified Internet connectivity

ISP, by the way, is often referred to as the **default gateway**. Once you configure your software correctly, you can connect to the ISP and get to the greater Internet. Figure 18.5 shows a standard PC-to-ISP-to-Internet connection. Note that various protocols and other software manage the connectivity between your PC and the default gateway.

■ Connecting to the Internet

PCs commonly connect to an ISP by using one of seven technologies that fit into four categories: dial-up, both analog and ISDN; dedicated, such as DSL, cable, and LAN; wireless; and satellite. Analog dial-up is the slowest of the bunch and requires a telephone line and a special networking device called a modem. ISDN uses digital dial-up and has much greater speed. All the others use a regular Ethernet NIC like you played with in Chapter 16, "Learning Local Area Networking." Satellite is the odd one out here; it may use either a modem or a NIC, depending on the particular configuration you have, although most folks will use a NIC. Let's take a look at all these various connection options.

Dial-up

A dial-up connection to the Internet requires two pieces to work: hardware to dial the ISP, such as a modem or ISDN terminal adapter; and software to govern the connection, such as Microsoft's **Dial-Up Networking (DUN)**. Let's look at the hardware first, and then we'll explore software configuration.

The CompTIA A+ Essentials exam expects you to know two very common Internet terms, which I'll be using during this chapter: bandwidth and latency. **Bandwidth** refers to the amount of data a connection is capable of transmitting per second, and **latency** is the amount of time a packet takes to get to its destination and is measured in milliseconds.

Modems

At some point in the early days of computing, some bright guy or gal noticed a colleague talking on a telephone, glanced down at a PC, and then put two and two together: why not use telephone lines for data communication? The basic problem with this idea is that traditional telephone lines use analog signals, while computers use digital signals (Figure 18.6). Creating a dial-up network required equipment that could turn digital data into an analog signal to send it over the telephone line, and then turn it back into digital data when it reached the other end of the connection. A device called a modem solved this dilemma.

Modems enable computers to talk to each other via standard commercial telephone lines by converting analog signals to digital signals, and vice versa. The term *modem* is short for modulator/demodulator, a description of transforming the signals. Telephone wires transfer data via analog signals that continuously change voltages on a wire. Computers hate analog signals. Instead, they need digital signals, voltages that are either on or off, meaning the wire has voltage present or it does not. Computers, being binary by nature, use only two states of voltage: zero volts and positive volts. Modems take analog signals from telephone lines and turn them into digital signals that the PC can understand (Figure 18.7). Modems also take digital signals from the PC and convert them into analog signals for the outgoing telephone line.

A modem does what is called *serial communication*: It transmits data as a series of individual ones and zeros. The CPU can't process data this way. It needs parallel communication,

Analog: Increasing and decreasing waves of electricity

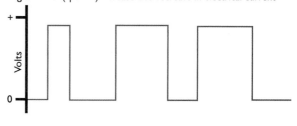
Digital: A set (specific) increase and decrease in electrical current

● **Figure 18.6** Analog signals used by a telephone line versus digital signals used by the computer

● **Figure 18.7** Modem converting analog signal to digital signal

• **Figure 18.8**   CPUs can't read serial data.

0 1 0 1 1 0 1 0

• **Figure 18.9**   The UART chip converts serial data to parallel data that the CPU can read.

2 It uses a serial port's UART.

1 An external modem has no UART.

• **Figure 18.10**   An external modem uses the PC's serial port.

transmitting and receiving data in discrete 8-bit chunks (Figure 18.8). The individual serial bits of data are converted into 8-bit parallel data that the PC can understand through the **universal asynchronous receiver/transmitter (UART)** chip (Figure 18.9).

There are many types of UARTs, each with different functions. All serial communication devices are really little more than UARTs. *External* modems can convert analog signals to digital ones and vice versa, but they must rely on the serial ports to which they're connected for the job of converting between serial and parallel data (Figure 18.10). Internal modems can handle both jobs because they have their own UART built in (Figure 18.11).

Phone lines have a speed based on a unit called a **baud**, which is one cycle per second. The fastest rate that a phone line can achieve is 2400 baud. Modems can pack multiple bits of data into each baud; a 33.6 kilobits per second (Kbps) modem, for example, packs 14 bits into every baud: $2400 \times 14 = 33.6$ Kbps. Thus, it is technically incorrect to say, "I have a 56-K baud modem." The correct statement is, "I have a 56-Kbps modem." But don't bother; people have used the term "baud" instead of **bits per second (bps)** so often for so long that the terms have become functionally synonymous.

Modern Modem Standards: V.90 vs. V.92 The fastest data transfer speed a modem can handle is based on its implementation of one of the international standards for modem technology: the **V standards**. Set by the International Telecommunication Union (ITU), the current top standards are V.90 and V.92. Both standards offer download speeds of just a hair under 56 Kbps, but they differ in upload speeds: up to 33.6 Kbps for V.90, and up to 48 Kbps for V.92 modems. To get anywhere near the top speeds of a V.90 or V.92 modem requires a comparable modem installed on the other line and connecting telephone lines in excellent condition. In practice, you'll rarely get faster throughput than about 48 Kbps for downloads and 28 Kbps for uploads.

Flow Control (Handshaking)   Flow control, also known as **hand-shaking**, is the process by which two serial devices verify a conversation. Imagine people talking on a CB radio. When one finishes speaking, he will say "over." That way the person listening can be sure that the sender is finished speaking before she starts. Each side of the conversation is verified. During a file transfer, two distinct conversations take place that require flow control: local (between modem and COM port) and end-to-end (between modems).

The modems themselves handle end-to-end flow control. PCs can do local flow control between the modem and COM port in two ways: hardware and software. Hardware flow control employs extra wires in the serial connection between the modem and the COM port to let one device tell the other that it is ready to send or receive data. These extra wires are called *ready to send* (*RTS*) and *clear to send* (*CTS*), so hardware handshaking is often called RTS/CTS. Software flow control uses a special character called XON to signal that data flow is beginning, and another special character called XOFF to signal that data transmission is finished; therefore, software handshaking is often called XON/XOFF. Software handshaking is slower and not as dependable as hardware handshaking, so you rarely see it.

Bells and Whistles   Although the core modem technology has changed little in the past few years, modem manufacturers have continued to innovate on many peripheral fronts—pardon the pun. You can walk into a computer store nowadays, for example, and buy a V.92 modem that comes bundled with an excellent fax machine and a digital answering machine. You can even buy modems that you can call remotely that will wake up your PC (Figure 18.12). What will they think up next?

Modem Connections   Internal modems connect to the PC very differently from how external modems connect. Almost all internal modems connect to a PCI or PCI Express expansion bus slot inside the PC, although cost-conscious manufacturers may use smaller modems that fit in special expansion slots designed to support multiple communications features such as modems, NICs, and sound cards (Figure 18.13). Older AMD motherboards used Audio/Modem Riser (AMR) or Advanced Communication Riser (ACR) slots, while Intel motherboards used Communication and Networking Riser (CNR) slots.

External modems connect to the PC through an available serial port (the old way) or USB port (Figure 18.14). Many older PCs came with 9-pin serial ports, whereas most external modems designed to connect to a serial port come with a 25-pin connector. That means you will probably need a 9-to-25-pin converter, available at any computer store, to connect your external modem. Serial ports are now quite rare as virtually all computers today have two or more USB ports.

Don't fret about USB versus serial for your modem connection, as the very low speeds of data communication over a modem make the physical type of the connection unimportant. Even the slow, aging serial interface more than adequately handles 56-Kbps data transfers. If you have the option, choose a USB modem, especially one with a volume control knob. USB offers simple

• **Figure 18.11**   An internal modem has UART built in.

You can test a modem by plugging in a physical device called a *loopback plug*, and then running diagnostics.

• **Figure 18.12**   Some of the many features touted by the manufacturer of the SupraMax modem

AMR, ACR, and CNR slots have gone away, though you'll still find them on older systems. Current systems use built-in components or PCIe ×1 slots for modems, sound cards, and NICs.

• **Figure 18.13** A CNR modem

• **Figure 18.14** A USB modem

plug and play and easy portability between machines, plus such modems require no external electrical source, getting all the power they need from the USB connection.

Dial-up Networking

The software side of dial-up networks requires configuration within Windows to include information provided by your ISP. The ISP provides a dial-up telephone number or numbers, as well as your user name and initial password. In addition, the ISP will tell you about any special configuration options you need to specify in the software setup. The full configuration of dial-up networking is beyond the scope of this book, but you should at least know where to go to follow instructions from your ISP. Let's take a look at the Network and Internet Connections applet in Windows XP.

Network Connections   To start configuring a dial-up connection in Windows XP, open the Control Panel. In Category View, select Network and Internet Connections from the Pick a category menu and then choose *Set up or change your Internet connection* from the Pick a task menu. The Internet Properties dialog box opens with the Connections tab displayed (Figure 18.15). All your work will proceed from here.

Click the Setup button to run the New Connection Wizard (Figure 18.16), and then work through the screens. At this point, you're going to need information provided by your ISP to configure your connection properly. When you finish the configuration, you'll see a new Connect To option on the Start menu if

• **Figure 18.15** The Connections tab in the Internet Properties dialog box

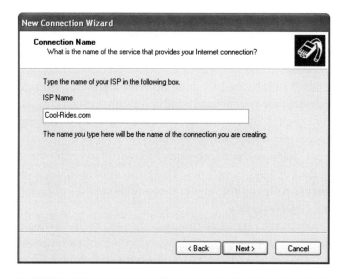

• **Figure 18.16**   The New Connection Wizard

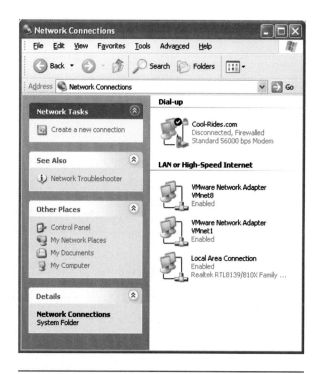

• **Figure 18.17**   Connection options in Network Connections

your system is set up that way. If not, open up Network Connections, and your new dial-up connection will be available. Figure 18.17 shows the option to connect to a fictitious ISP, Cool-Rides.com.

PPP   Dial-up links to the Internet have their own special hardware protocol called **Point-to-Point Protocol (PPP)**. PPP is a streaming protocol developed especially for dial-up Internet access. To Windows, a modem is nothing more than a special type of network adapter. Modems have their own configuration entry in the Network Connections applet.

Most dial-up "I can't connect to the Internet"–type problems are user errors. Your first area of investigation is the modem itself. Use the modem's properties to make sure the volume is turned up. Have the user listen to the connection. Does she hear a dial tone? If she doesn't, make sure the modem's line is plugged into a good phone jack. Does she hear the modem dial and then hear someone saying, "Hello? Hello?" If so, she probably dialed the wrong number! Wrong password error messages are fairly straightforward—remember that the password may be correct but the user name may be wrong. If she still fails to connect, it's time to call the network folks to see what is not properly configured in the Dial-up Networking settings.

ISDN

A standard telephone connection comprises many pieces. First, the phone line runs from your phone out to a network interface box (the little box on the side of your house) and into a central switch belonging to the telephone company. (In some cases, intermediary steps are present.) Standard metropolitan areas have a large number of central offices, each with a central switch. Houston, Texas, for example, has nearly 100 offices in the general metro area. These central switches connect to each other through high-capacity *trunk lines*. Before 1970, the entire phone system was analog; over time, however, phone companies began to upgrade their trunk lines to digital systems. Today, the entire telephone system, with the exception of the line from your phone to the central office, and sometimes even that, is digital.

During this upgrade period, customers continued to demand higher throughput from their phone lines. The old telephone line was not expected to produce more than 28.8 Kbps (56-Kbps modems, which were a *big* surprise to the phone companies, didn't appear until 1995). Needless to say, the phone companies were very motivated to come up with a way to generate higher capacities. Their answer was actually fairly straightforward: make the entire phone system digital. By adding special equipment at the central office and the user's location, phone companies can now achieve a throughput of up to 64 Kbps per line (see the paragraphs following) over the same copper wires already used by telephone lines. This process of sending telephone transmission across fully digital lines end-to-end is called **integrated services digital network (ISDN)** service.

ISDN service consists of two types of channels: Bearer, or B, channels and Delta, or D, channels. B channels carry data and voice information at 64 Kbps. D channels carry setup and configuration information and carry data at 16 Kbps. Most providers of ISDN allow the user to choose either one or two B channels. The more common setup is two B/one D, usually called a *basic rate interface* (*BRI*) setup. A BRI setup uses only one physical line, but each B channel sends 64 Kbps, doubling the throughput total to 128 Kbps. ISDN also connects much faster than modems, eliminating that long, annoying mating call you get with phone modems. The monthly cost per B channel is slightly more than a regular phone line, and usually a fairly steep initial fee is levied for the installation and equipment. The big limitation is that you usually need to be within about 18,000 feet of a central office to use ISDN.

The physical connections for ISDN bear some similarity to analog modems. An ISDN wall socket usually looks something like a standard RJ-45 network jack. The most common interface for your computer is a device called a *terminal adapter* (*TA*). TAs look much like regular modems, and like modems, they come in external and internal variants. You can even get TAs that are also hubs, enabling your system to support a direct LAN connection.

> Another type of ISDN, called a primary rate interface (PRI), is composed of twenty-three 64-Kbps B channels and one 64-Kbps D channel, giving it a total throughput of 1.5 megabits per second. PRI ISDN lines are also known as T1 lines.

DSL

Digital subscriber line (DSL) connections to ISPs use a standard telephone line but special equipment on each end to create always-on Internet connections at blindingly fast speeds, especially when compared with analog dial-up connections. Service levels vary around the United States, but the typical upload speed is ~768 Kbps, while download speed comes in at a very sweet ~3+ Mbps!

DSL requires little setup from a user standpoint. A tech comes to the house to install the DSL receiver, often called a DSL modem (Figure 18.18), and possibly hook up a wireless router. The receiver connects to the telephone line and the PC (Figure 18.19). The tech (or the user, if knowledgeable) then configures the DSL modem and router (if there is one) with the settings provided by the ISP, and that's about it! Within moments, you're surfing at blazing speeds. You don't need a second telephone line. You don't need to wear a special propeller hat or anything. The only kicker is that your house has to be within a fairly short distance from a main phone service switching center, something like 18,000 feet.

> The two most common forms of DSL you'll find are *asynchronous* (*ADSL*) and *synchronous* (*SDSL*). ADSL lines differ between slow upload speed (such as 384 Kbps, 768 Kbps, and 1 Mbps) and faster download speed (usually 3–7 Mbps). SDSL has the same upload and download speeds, but telecom companies charge a lot more for the privilege. DSL encompasses many such variations, so you'll often see it referred to as *x*DSL.

• **Figure 18.18**   A DSL receiver

Cable

Cable offers a different approach to high-speed Internet access, using regular cable TV cables to serve up lightning-fast speeds. It offers faster service than most DSL connections, with a 1–10 Mbps upload and 6–50+ Mbps download. Cable Internet connections are theoretically available anywhere you can get cable TV.

Cable Internet connections start with an RG-6 or RG-59 cable coming into your house. The cable connects to a cable modem that then connects to a NIC in your PC via UTP Ethernet cable. Figure 18.20 shows a typical cable setup. One nice advantage of cable over DSL is that if you have a TV tuner card in your PC, you can use the same cable connection (with a splitter) to watch TV on your PC. Both DSL and cable modem Internet connections can be used by two or more computers if they are part of a LAN, including those in a home.

• **Figure 18.19**   DSL connections

LAN

Most businesses connect their internal local area network (LAN) to an ISP via some hardware solution that Network+ techs deal with. Figure 18.21

> The term *modem* has been warped and changed beyond recognition in modern networking. Both DSL and cable fully digital Internet connections use the term *modem* to describe the box that takes the incoming signal from the Internet and translates it into something the PC can understand.

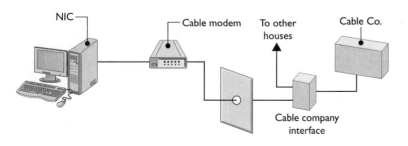

• **Figure 18.20**   Cable connections

shows a typical small-business wiring closet with routers that connect the LAN to the ISP. You learned about setting up and configuring a LAN in Chapter 16, "Learning Local Area Networking," so there's no need to go through any basics here. To complete a LAN connection to the Internet, you need to add a second NIC or a modem to one of the PCs and then configure that PC as the default connection. We'll revisit this idea in a moment with Internet Connection Sharing.

Wireless

Every once in a while a technology comes along that, once the kinks are smoothed out, works flawlessly, creating a magical computing experience. Unfortunately, the various wireless networking technologies out there today don't fulfill that dream yet. When they work, it's like magic. You walk into a coffee shop, sit down, and flip open your laptop computer. After firing up your Internet browser, suddenly you're quaffing lattes and surfing Web sites—with no wires at all.

Suffice it to say that connecting to the Internet via wireless means that you must connect to a cellular network or to a LAN that's wired to an ISP. The local Internet café purchases high-speed Internet service from the cable or telecom company, for example, and then connects a wireless access point (WAP) to its network. When you walk in with your portable PC with wireless NIC and open a Web browser, the wireless NIC communicates with the *fully wired* DHCP server via the WAP and you're surfing on the Internet. It appears magically wireless, but the LAN to ISP connection still uses wires.

Cellular networking is even more seamless. Anywhere you can connect with your cell phone, you can connect with your cellular network–aware portable or laptop computer.

• **Figure 18.21**   A wiring closet

Satellite

Satellite connections to the Internet get the data beamed to a satellite dish on your house or office; a receiver handles the flow of data, eventually sending it through an Ethernet cable to the NIC in your PC. I can already sense people's eyebrows raising. "Yeah, that's the download connection. But what about the upload connection?" Very astute, me hearties! The early days of satellite required you to connect via a modem. You would upload at the slow 26- to 48-Kbps modem speed, but then get superfast downloads from the dish. It worked, so why complain? You really can move to that shack on the side of the Himalayas to write the great Tibetan novel and still have DSL- or cable-speed Internet connectivity. Sweet!

Satellite might be the most intriguing of all the technologies used to connect to the Internet today. As with satellite television, though, you need to have the satellite dish point at the satellites (toward the south if you live in the United States). The only significant issue to satellite is that the distance the signal must travel creates a small delay called the *satellite latency*. This latency is usually unnoticeable unless the signal degrades in foul weather such as rain and snow.

Windows Internet Connection Sharing

Internet Connection Sharing (ICS) enables one system to share its Internet connection with other systems on the network, providing a quick and easy method for multiple systems to use one Internet connection. Modern Windows versions (Windows 2000 through Windows 7) also provide this handy tool. Figure 18.22 shows a typical setup for ICS. Note the terminology used here. The PC that connects to the Internet and then shares that connection via ICS with other machines on a LAN is called the *ICS host* computer. PCs that connect via LAN to the ICS host computer are simply called client computers.

To connect multiple computers to a single ICS host computer requires several things in place. First, the ICS host computer has to have a NIC dedicated to the internal connections. If you connect via dial-up, for example, the ICS host computer uses a modem to connect to the Internet. It also has a NIC that plugs into a switch. Other PCs on the LAN likewise connect to the switch. If you connect via some faster service, such as DSL that uses a NIC cabled to the DSL receiver, you'll need a second NIC in the ICS host machine to connect to the LAN and the client computers.

• **Figure 18.22**   Typical ICS setup

Setting up ICS in Windows is very simple. If you are using Windows 2000 or XP, right-click My Network Places and choose Properties. If you are using Windows Vista or 7, open the Network and Sharing Center and click on *Manage network connections* (Vista) or *Change adapter settings* (7) in the left-hand task list. Now access the Properties dialog box of the connection you wish to share.

Click the Sharing tab (Windows 2000, Vista, and 7) or the Advanced tab (Windows XP), and select *Enable Internet connection sharing for this connection* (Windows 2000) or *Allow other network users to connect through this computer's Internet connection* (Windows XP–7, Figure 18.23). Clients don't need any special configuration but should simply be set to DHCP for their IP address and other configurations.

Common Internet Ports

Once you've established a connection between the PC and the ISP, you can do nothing on the Internet without applications designed to use one or more TCP/IP services, such as Web browsing and e-mail. TCP/IP has the following commonly used services:

- World Wide Web (HTTP and HTTPS)
- E-mail (POP and SMTP)
- Newsgroups
- FTP

• **Figure 18.23**   Enabling Internet Connection Sharing in Windows Vista

Table 18.1	TCP/IP Service Port Numbers
TCP/IP Service	**Port Number**
HTTP	80
HTTPS	443
FTP	20, 21
POP	110
SMTP	25
TELNET	23

- TELNET
- VoIP

Each of these services (sometimes referred to by the overused term *TCP/IP protocols*) operates by using defined ports, requires a special application, and has special settings. As a quick reference, Table 18.1 has some common port numbers CompTIA would like you to know.

Virtual Private Networks

Remote connections have been around for a long time, long before the Internet existed. The biggest drawback about remote connections was the cost to connect. If you were on one side of the continent and had to connect to your LAN on the other side of the continent, the only connection option was a telephone. Or, if you needed to connect two LANs across the continent, you ended up paying outrageous monthly charges for a private connection. The introduction of the Internet gave people wishing to connect to their home networks a very cheap connection option, but with one problem: the whole Internet is open to the public. People wanted to stop using dial-up and expensive private connections and use the Internet instead, but they wanted to do it securely.

Those clever network engineers worked long and hard and came up with several solutions to this problem. Standards have been created that use encrypted tunnels between a computer (or a remote network) to create a private network through the Internet (Figure 18.24), resulting in what is called a **Virtual Private Network (VPN)**.

- **Figure 18.24**   VPN connecting computers across the United States

An encrypted tunnel requires endpoints—the ends of the tunnel where the data is encrypted and decrypted. In the SSH tunnel you've seen thus far, the client for the application sits on one end and the server sits on the other. VPNs do the same thing. Either some software running on a computer or, in some cases, a dedicated box must act as an endpoint for a VPN (Figure 18.25).

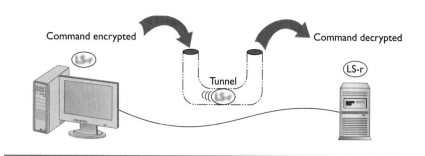

• **Figure 18.25**   Typical tunnel

To make VPNs work requires a protocol that uses one of the many **tunneling** protocols available and adds the capability to ask for an IP address from a local DHCP server to give the tunnel an IP address that matches the subnet of the LAN. The connection keeps the IP address to connect to the Internet, but the tunnel endpoints must act like NICs (Figure 18.26). Let's look at one of the protocols, PPTP.

• **Figure 18.26**   Endpoints must have their own IP addresses.

PPTP VPNs

So how do we make IP addresses appear out of thin air? Microsoft got the ball rolling with the **Point-to-Point Tunneling Protocol (PPTP)**, an advanced version of a protocol used for dial-up Internet called PPP that handles all of this right out of the box. The only trick is the endpoints. In Microsoft's view, a VPN is intended for individual clients (think employees on the road) to connect back to the office network, so Microsoft places the PPTP endpoints on the client and a special remote access server program called Routing and Remote Access Service (RRAS), originally only available on Windows Server, on the server (Figure 18.27).

On the Windows client side, you right-click on My Network Places and click on Create a New Connection (Windows 2000–XP) or right-click on Network and select *Set up a connection or network* (Windows Vista) from the Network and Sharing Center. This presents you with a dialog box where you can enter all your VPN server information. Your network administrator will most likely provide this to you. The result is a virtual network card that, like any other NIC, gets an IP address from the DHCP server back at the office (Figure 18.28).

When your computer connects to the RRAS server on the private network, PPTP creates a secure tunnel through the Internet back to the private LAN. Your client takes on an IP address of that network, as if your computer were plugged into the LAN back at the office. Even your Internet traffic will go through your office first. If you open your Web browser, your client will go across the Internet to the office LAN and then use the LAN's Internet connection! Because of this, Web browsing is very slow over a VPN.

A system connected to a VPN looks as though it's on the local network but performs much slower than if the system were connected directly back at the office.

• **Figure 18.27** RRAS in action

• **Figure 18.28** VPN connection in Windows

Beyond A+

The areas covered by the CompTIA A+ Essentials exam do a great job on the more common issues of dealing with the Internet, but a few hot topics (although beyond the scope of the CompTIA A+ Essentials exam) are so common and important that you need to know them: online gaming, chatting, and file sharing.

Online Gaming

One of the more exciting and certainly more fun aspects of the Internet is online gaming. Competing online against a real person or people makes for some pleasant gaming. Enjoying classics such as Hearts and Backgammon with another human can be challenging and fun. Another popular genre of online gaming is the "first-person shooters" format. These games place you in a small world with up to 32 other players. A great example is Valve Software's Counter-Strike: Source (Figure 18.29).

No discussion of online gaming is complete without talking about the most amazing game type of all: the massively multiplayer online role-playing game (MMORPG). Imagine being an elfin wizard, joined by a band of friends, all going on adventures together in worlds so large that it would take a real 24-hour day to journey across them! Imagine that in this same world, 2000 to 3000 other players, as well as thousands of game-controlled characters, are participating! Plenty of MMORPGs are out there, but the most popular today is World of Warcraft (Figure 18.30).

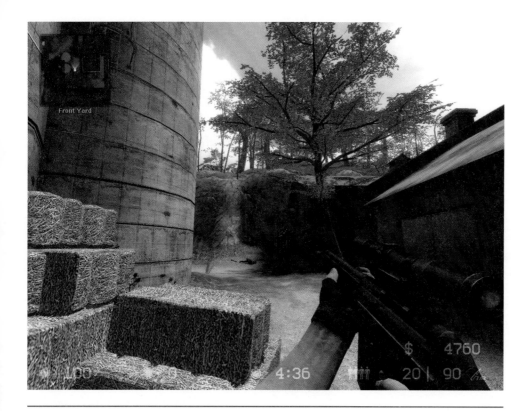

• Figure 18.29   Counter-Strike: Source

Each of these games employs good old TCP/IP to send information, us-ing ports reserved by the game. For instance, the Quake series of games uses port 26000, while DirectX uses ports 47624 and 2300–2400.

• Figure 18.30   My editor playing World of Warcraft

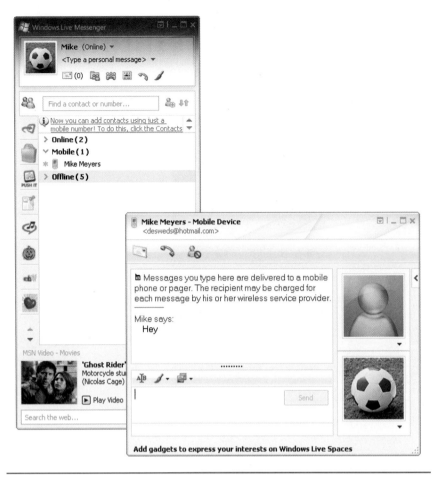

Chatting

If there's one thing we human beings love to do, it's chat. The Internet provides a multitude of ways to do so, whether by typing or actual talking. Keep in mind that chatting occurs in real time. As fast as you can type or talk, whoever is at the other end hears or sees what you have to say. To chat, however, you need some form of chat software. The oldest family of chat programs is based on the Internet Relay Chat (IRC) protocol, and the single most common IRC chat program is probably mIRC. IRC protocols allow for a number of other little extras as well, such as being able to share files.

Today, companies such as AOL, Yahoo!, and Microsoft have made their own chat programs that not only provide text chat but also add features such as voice and video, turning your PC into a virtual replacement for your telephone! Figure 18.31 shows the popular Microsoft Windows Live Messenger software.

• **Figure 18.31** Windows Live Messenger in action

File Sharing

The last extra Internet function to discuss is also probably the most controversial: file sharing. File sharing basically consists of a whole bunch of computers with one program loaded, such as Lime Wire or Shareaza. The file-sharing program enables each of the computers running that program to offer files to share, such as MP3 music files and MPEG movies. Once all of the file-sharing computers log on to the Internet, any of them can download any file offered by any other in the group.

File sharing through such *distributed* sharing software becomes almost anonymous and free—and that's the problem. You can share *anything*, even copyright-protected music, movies, and more. The music industry in particular has come out swinging to try to stop file-sharing practices. As a result, the music industry is working on a way to shut down those persons who share lots of files. But software developers have countered, creating Internet protocols such as BitTorrent to handle the distribution and make the file sharers much more difficult to find and punish. Figure 18.32 shows one of the more popular BitTorrent protocol programs called μTorrent (the μ is the symbol for "micro," so you pronounce it "micro torrent"). BitTorrent has many legitimate uses as well—its protocol is extremely efficient for the

590

Mike Meyers' CompTIA A+ Guide: Essentials

● **Figure 18.32**　μTorrent

distribution of large files and has become the method of choice for distributing Linux distributions and large open-source applications such as Apache and OpenOffice.

These example programs just scratch the surface of the many applications that use the Internet. One of the more amazing aspects of TCP/IP is that its basic design is around 30 years old. We use TCP/IP in ways completely outside the original concept of its designers, yet TCP/IP continues to show its power and flexibility. Pretty amazing!

Chapter 18 Review

■ Chapter Summary

After reading this chapter and completing the exercises, you should understand the following about the Internet.

Explain how the Internet works

■ A PC tech needs to know how PCs communicate with the world for two reasons: (1) to troubleshoot when a process or piece stops working, and (2) to communicate knowledgeably with a network technician who comes in to solve a more complex issue.

■ The Internet is broken down into three tiers. Tier 1 providers own the fiber-optic backbones that interconnect at network access points. Backbone routers create an interwoven framework for redundant communications.

■ TCP/IP provides the basic software structure for Internet communications. It provides IP addresses and the naming scheme for computers on the Internet. This protocol suite also offers a variety of other services, including HTTP, which provides structure for the Web.

■ Internet service providers (ISPs) lease connections to the Internet from Tier 1 and Tier 2 providers. In turn, ISPs lease connections to allow individuals and companies to access the Internet. ISPs may serve customers nationwide, such as Comcast, or they may be limited to a small community of users.

■ Connecting to the Internet requires hardware for connectivity and software to govern the connection and data flow. The router that connects you to your ISP is your default gateway.

Connect to the Internet

■ Seven technologies are commonly used to connect a PC to an ISP. These technologies fit into four categories: (1) dial-up (analog and ISDN), (2) dedicated (DSL, cable, and LAN), (3) wireless, and (4) satellite. Analog dial-up, the slowest connection, uses a telephone line and a modem. ISDN is a much faster digital dial-up method. With the exception of satellite, which may use either a modem or a NIC, all the other technologies use an Ethernet NIC.

■ A dial-up connection needs hardware, such as a modem or ISDN terminal adapter, and software, such as Microsoft's DUN.

■ A modem converts digital signals from the PC into analog signals that travel on telephone lines, and vice versa. An example of serial communication, the modem transmits data as a series of ones and zeros. On the other hand, the computer processes data by using parallel communication or data in discrete 8-bit chunks. A UART chip converts serial to parallel and parallel to serial. An external modem uses the UART chip in the computer's serial port, while an internal modem has its own built-in UART.

■ Phone lines measure speed in bauds, or cycles per second. However, the fastest baud rate a phone line can achieve is 2400 baud. Today's modems pack multiple bits of data into each baud. Although not technically correct, people use the term *baud* instead of *bps* so often that the terms have become synonymous.

■ The International Telecommunication Union (ITU) sets V standards to define the fastest data transfer speed a modem can handle. Currently V.90 and V.92 are the highest standards, downloading data at just a little under 56 Kbps. Upload speeds differ, with 33.6 Kbps being the fastest for V.90 and 48 Kbps proving the fastest for V.92 modems.

■ Modems may be internal or external. The less-expensive internal modems usually connect to a PCI or PCI Express expansion bus slot. Some motherboards include special expansion slots used for multiple communications features such as modems, NICs, and sound cards. AMD calls such slots ACRs, while Intel has named them CNR slots. Many motherboards come with integrated modems. External modems attach to the PC's serial port or USB port. Most motherboards today include two or more USB ports. It is a good idea to choose a USB modem because you won't need an external electrical source and it will likely include a volume control knob.

■ Windows includes configuration options to set up dial-up networks. Windows XP uses the Network and Internet Connections applet, Windows 2000 calls this feature Network and Dial-up Connections, and Vista uses the *Set up a connection or network* wizard. To configure dial-up networking, you'll need information from your ISP. Dial-up links to the Internet use the PPP streaming hardware protocol.

- If you can't connect to the Internet, look at the modem's properties to make sure the volume is turned up. Listen, too, for a befuddled voice on the other end that would indicate your modem is dialing the wrong number. Other things to check: be sure the line is plugged into a good phone jack, and make sure the number and password are correct. If you still can't connect to the Internet, call the network technicians to check that the dial-up networking settings are correct.

- An ISDN consists of two types of channels: Bearer, or B, channels that carry data and voice at 64 Kbps, and Delta, or D, channels that transmit setup and configuration information at 16 Kbps. Users can use one or two B channels, but the most common setup is the BRI, consisting of two B channels and one D channel to provide a throughput total of 128 Kbps. Except for the steep cost of installation and equipment, ISDN lines are only slightly more expensive than regular phone lines, but this service is limited to an area within about 18,000 feet of a central office. ISDN uses a terminal adapter that looks like a regular modem and may be either external or internal.

- DSL modems connect to an ISP by using a standard telephone line and special connections on each end. Although service levels vary, typical upload speed is ~768 Kbps with a download speed of ~3+ Mbps. A tech usually comes to the house to install a DSL receiver (often called a DSL modem) as well as a NIC in the PC. DSL is usually limited to about 18,000 feet from a main phone service switching center.

- Cable TV companies offer high-speed Internet access, with an upload speed of about 1–10 Mbps up and download transmission rates of 6-50+ Mbps. With a TV tuner card, cable enables you to watch TV on your PC.

- Wireless Internet service requires connecting to a LAN that's wired to an ISP. The other wireless option is a satellite connection. Although early satellite technology required uploads through a slow modem (26–48 Kbps) and fast downloads through the dish, newer technology uses the modem only for the initial setup, sending both downloads and uploads through the dish.

- ICS enables multiple systems to use one Internet connection. Included in all current Windows versions, ICS uses an ICS host computer connected to the Internet that then shares the connection via a LAN with client computers. The ICS host computer must have a NIC or modem to connect to the Internet and a NIC that plugs into a hub. The other PCs then connect to the hub.

Explain VPNs

- VPNs, or Virtual Private Networks, enable you to connect over the public Internet and access a remote network as if you were physically plugged into it. PPTP is the protocol used by Microsoft to provide this service. It works by creating virtual network cards that have their own IP address that match what the LAN uses.

■ Key Terms

bandwidth *(577)*
baud *(578)*
bits per second (bps) *(578)*
default gateway *(576)*
Dial-Up Networking (DUN) *(577)*
digital subscriber line (DSL) *(582)*
handshaking *(579)*
Hypertext Transfer Protocol (HTTP) *(575)*
integrated services digital network (ISDN) *(582)*
Internet Connection Sharing (ICS) *(585)*
Internet service provider (ISP) *(575)*
latency *(577)*

modem *(577)*
Point-to-Point Protocol (PPP) *(581)*
Point-to-Point Tunneling Protocol (PPTP) *(587)*
tier *(573)*
tunneling *(587)*
universal asynchronous receiver/transmitter (UART) *(578)*
V standards *(578)*
Virtual Private Network (VPN) *(586)*
Web browser *(575)*
World Wide Web *(575)*

Key Term Quiz

Use the Key Terms list to complete the sentences that follow. Not all terms will be used.

1. The time it takes for a packet to travel to its destination and back is called _____.

2. Internet Explorer is a(n) _____.

3. Although some people use the term to refer to modem speed, _____ actually means the number of cycles per second, while _____ is a more accurate measurement of actual data throughput.

4. Set by the International Telecommunication Union (ITU), _____ define the fastest data transfer speed a modem can handle.

5. The service that provides the structure for the World Wide Web, allowing documents to be sent across the Web, is _____.

6. Dial-up links to the Internet use a streaming hardware protocol called _____.

7. A(n) _____ enables you to access a remote network over the Internet securely.

Multiple-Choice Quiz

1. Which statements about integrated services digital network (ISDN) are true? (Select three.)

   A. An ISDN connection uses either an internal or an external terminal adapter (TA).

   B. BRI has two B channels and one D channel for a throughput total of 128 Kbps.

   C. PRI has 23 B channels and 1 D channel for a total throughput of 1.5 Mbps.

   D. ISDN consists of end-to-end high-speed analog lines.

2. What is the name for the router that your PC uses to connect to your Internet service provider?

   A. Loopback address

   B. Backbone

   C. IP address

   D. Default gateway

3. To configure dial-up networks with Windows XP, which applet should you use?

   A. Network and Internet Connections

   B. Network Neighborhood

   C. Internet Connection Sharing

   D. Remote Assistance

4. A Virtual Private Network creates a(n) _____ through the Internet.

   A. Tunnel

   B. BRI

   C. Connection

   D. SSH session

5. What port is used by the HTTP protocol?

   A. 80

   B. 20

   C. 21

   D. 110

6. Which of the following Internet connection methods enables you to watch television on your computer if you have a TV tuner card?

   A. DSL

   B. Satellite

   C. Cable

   D. ISDN

7. What is the name for the extremely fast networking connections through which Internet transmissions take place?

   A. Gateways

   B. Tier 1 providers

   C. Backbones

   D. ISPs

8. A new client lives in a rural area, outside the connectivity radius of the local cable company and definitely more than 20,000 feet away from the nearest switching center for the phone company. Which Internet option offers the client the best performance?

   A. Cable

   B. Dial-up

   C. DSL

   D. Satellite

1. Sean is planning to take some distance education courses next term. He currently uses a regular phone line and a modem to connect to the Internet. He's consulted you to figure out what his options are for a faster connection. Review his options, explaining the advantages and disadvantages, along with any restrictions that may prevent his receiving the service.

Lab Project

• Lab Project 18.1

Are all high-speed Internet connections created equal? Test them to find out! Speakeasy.net hosts one of the best Internet sites for testing the speed of an Internet connection: www.speakeasy.net/speedtest/

Test three to five Internet connections that you can easily get to, such as your home, a friend's house, your school, a library, and an Internet café. How do the connections compare? If you can, find out which technology the connections use. Which one seems to offer the best connection in your area?

Learning Computer Security

In this chapter, you will learn how to

- **Describe key security concepts**
- **Define and describe various forms of malicious software**
- **Explain how to protect computers from malicious software and how to recover affected computers**

Your PC is under siege. Through your PC, a malicious person can gain valuable information about you and your habits. He can steal your files. He can run programs that log your keystrokes and thus gain account names and passwords, credit card information, and more. He can run software that takes over much of your computer processing time and use it to send spam or steal from others. The threat is real and right now. Worse, he's doing one or more of these things to your clients as I write these words. You need to secure your computer, your users, and your data from these attacks.

■ Security Concepts

When most people think of computer security, they think of Internet attacks, viruses, and all sorts of real or imagined electronic threats. In their minds, protecting themselves against these threats is paramount to all else, but, as with most things in life, it's important to learn the basics before you move on to more advanced things. Specifically, techs should learn to protect their equipment from physical theft, how to properly classify and protect their data, and how to create proper passwords and authentication schemes. These security fundamentals serve as a basis for all other computer security.

Data Classification and Compliance

Larger organizations, such as government entities, benefit greatly from organizing their data according to its sensitivity—what's called **data classification**—and making certain that computer hardware and software stay as uniform as possible. In addition, many government and internal regulations apply fairly rigorously to this type of organizations.

Data classification systems vary by the organization, but a common scheme classifies documents as public, internal use only, highly confidential, top secret, and so on. Using a classification scheme enables employees such as techs to know very quickly what to do with documents, the drives containing documents, and more. Your strategy for recycling a computer system left from a migrated user, for example, will differ a lot if the data on the drive was classified as internal use only or top secret.

Compliance means, in a nutshell, that members of an organization or company must abide by or comply with all of the rules that apply to the organization or company. Statutes with funny names such as Sarbanes-Oxley impose certain behaviors or prohibitions on what people can and cannot do in the workplace.

From a technician's point of view, the most common compliance issue revolves around software, such as what sort of software users can be allowed to install on their computers or, conversely, why you have to tell a user that he can't install the latest application that may help him do the job more effectively because that software isn't on the approved list. This can lead to some uncomfortable confrontations, but it's part of a tech's job.

The concepts behind compliance in IT are not, as some might imagine at first blush, to stop you from being able to work effectively. Rather they're designed to stop users with not quite enough technical skill or knowledge from installing malicious programs or applications that will destabilize their systems. This keeps technical support calls down and enables techs to focus on more serious problems.

Access Control

Access is the key. If you can control access to the data, programs, and other computing resources, you've secured your systems. **Access control** is composed of four interlinked areas that a good security-minded tech should think about: physical security, authentication, users and groups, and security policies. Much of this you know from previous chapters, but this section should help tie it all together as a security topic.

Some criminals attempt to gain access to a secure system by pretending to be someone else, either in person, over the phone, or in an e-mail. For example, a hacker might call an employee inside an organization they want to attack pretending to be tech support in order to ask for that employee's user name and password. This type of attack is called **social engineering**, and it's one of the most common methods for discovering passwords.

Secure Physical Area and Lock Down Your System

The first order of security is to block access to the physical hardware from people who shouldn't have access. This isn't rocket science. Lock the door. Don't leave a PC unattended when logged in. In fact, don't ever leave a system logged in, even as a limited user. God help you if you walk away from a server still logged in as an administrator. You're tempting fate.

For that matter, when you see a user's computer logged in and unattended, do the user and your company a huge favor and lock the computer. Just walk up and press WINDOWS LOGO KEY-L on the keyboard to lock the system. It works in all versions of Windows.

Authentication

Security starts with properly implemented **authentication**, which means in essence how the computer determines who can or should access it. And once accessed, what that user can do. A computer can authenticate users through software or hardware, or a combination of both.

Software Authentication: Proper Passwords   It's still rather shocking to me to power up a friend's computer and go straight to his or her desktop, or with my married-with-kids friends, to click one of the parents' user account icons and not be prompted for a password. This is just wrong! I'm always tempted to assign passwords right then and there—and not tell them the passwords, of course—so they'll see the error of their ways when they try to log in next. I don't do it but always try to explain gently the importance of good passwords.

There's not a person alive today who doesn't have to remember the password to something or other, even if it's just their email, so I won't belabor the point here. Suffice it to say that you need to make certain that all of your users have proper passwords. Don't let them write passwords down or tape them to the underside of their mouse pads either!

It's not just access to Windows that you need to think about. There's always the temptation for people to hack the system and do mean things, such as changing CMOS settings, opening up the case, and even stealing hard drives. Any of these actions render the computer inoperable to the casual user until a tech can undo the damage or replace components. All modern CMOS setup utilities come with a number of tools to protect your computer, such as drive lock, intrusion detection, and of course system access passwords such as the one shown in Figure 19.1. Refer to Chapter 7, "Learning Motherboards," to refresh yourself on what you can do at a BIOS level to protect your computer.

• **Figure 19.1**   CMOS access password request

Hardware Authentication Smart cards and biometric devices enable modern systems to authenticate users with more authority than mere passwords. **Smart cards** are credit-card-sized cards with circuitry that can identify the bearer of the card. Smart cards are relatively common for such tasks as authenticating users for mass transit systems, for example, but are fairly uncommon in computers. Figure 19.2 shows a smart card and keyboard combination.

People can guess or discover passwords, but forging someone's fingerprints is a lot harder. The keyboard in Figure 19.3 authenticates users on a local machine by using fingerprints. Other devices that will do the trick are key fobs, retinal scanners, and PC cards for laptop computers. Devices that require some sort of physical, flesh-and-blood authentication are called **biometric devices**.

• **Figure 19.2** Keyboard-mounted smart card reader being used for a commercial application (*photo courtesy of Cherry Corp.*)

Clever manufacturers have developed key fobs and smart cards that use radio frequency identification (RFID) to transmit authentication information so users don't have to insert something into a computer or card reader. The Privaris plusID combines, for example, a biometric fingerprint fob with an RFID tag that makes security as easy as opening a garage door remotely! Figure 19.4 shows a plusID device.

NTFS, not FAT32!

The file system on a hard drive matters a lot when it comes to security. On a Windows machine with multiple users, you simply must use NTFS or you have no security at all. Not just primary drives but also any secondary drives in computers in your care should be formatted as NTFS, with the exception of removable drives such as the one you use to back up your system.

When you run into a multiple-drive system that has a second or third drive formatted as FAT32, you can use the *CONVERT* command-line utility to go from FAT to NTFS. The syntax is pretty straightforward. To convert a D: drive from FAT or FAT32 to NTFS, for example, you'd type the following:

```
CONVERT D: /FS:NTFS
```

How's this for full disclosure? Microsoft does not claim that the keyboard in Figure 19.3 offers any security at all. In fact, the documentation specifically claims that the fingerprint reader is an accessibility tool, not a security device. Because it enables a person to log on to a local machine, though, I think it falls into the category of authentication devices.

plusID

PRIVARIS

• **Figure 19.3** Microsoft keyboard with fingerprint accessibility

• **Figure 19.4** plusID (*photo courtesy of Privaris, Inc.*)

You can substitute a mount name in place of the drive letter in case you have a mounted volume. The command has a few extra switches as well, so at the command prompt, type a **/?** after the CONVERT command to see all of your options.

Users and Groups

Windows uses user accounts and groups as the bedrock of access control. A user account is assigned to a group, such as Users, Power Users, or Administrators, and by association gets certain permissions on the computer. Using NTFS enables the highest level of control over data resources.

Assigning users to groups is a great first step in controlling a local machine, but this feature really shines once you go to a networked environment. Let's go there now.

User Account Control Through Groups

Access to user accounts should be restricted to the assigned individuals, and those who configure the permissions to those accounts must remember the Principle of Least Privilege: Accounts should have permission to access only the resources they need and no more. Tight control of user accounts is critical to preventing unauthorized access. Disabling unused accounts is an important part of this strategy, but good user account control goes far deeper than that. One of your best tools for user account control is groups. Instead of giving permissions/rights to individual user accounts, give them to groups; this makes keeping track of the permissions assigned to individual user accounts much easier. Figure 19.5 shows me giving permissions to a group for a folder in Windows Vista. Once a group is created and its permissions set, you can then add user accounts to that group as needed. Any user account that becomes a member of a group automatically gets the permissions assigned to that group. Figure 19.6 shows me adding a user to a newly created group in the same Windows Vista system.

Groups are a great way to achieve increased complexity without increasing the administrative burden on network administrators because all network operating systems combine permissions. When a user is a member of more than one group, which permissions does that user have with respect to any particular resource? In all network operating systems, the permissions of the groups are *combined*, and the result is what you call the **effective permissions** the user has to access the resource. As an example, if Rita is a member of the Sales group, which has List Folder Contents permission to a folder, and she is also a member of the Managers group, which has Read and Execute permissions to the same folder, Rita will have both List Folder Contents *and* Read and Execute permissions to that folder.

Watch out for *default* user accounts and groups—they can become secret backdoors to your network! All network operating systems have a default Everyone group that can be used to sneak into shared resources easily. This Everyone group, as its name implies, literally includes anyone who connects to that resource. Windows gives full control to the Everyone group by default, for example, so make sure you know to lock this down!

• **Figure 19.5** Giving a group permissions for a folder in Windows Vista

All of the default groups—Everyone, Guest, Users—define broad groups of users. Never use them unless you intend to permit all of those folks to access a resource. If you use one of the default groups, remember to configure them with the proper permissions to prevent users from doing things you don't want them to do with a shared resource!

All of these groups and organizational units only do one thing for you: They let you keep track of your user accounts, so you know they are only available for those who need them, and they can only access the resources you want them to use.

• **Figure 19.6**   Adding a user to a newly created group in Windows Vista

Security Policies

Although permissions control how users access shared resources, there are other functions you should control that are outside the scope of resources. For example, do you want users to be able to access a command prompt on their Windows system? Do you want users to be able to install software? Would you like to control what systems a user can log into or at what time of day a user can log in? All network operating systems provide you with some capability to control these and literally hundreds of other security parameters, under what Windows calls *policies*. I like to think of policies as permissions for activities as opposed to true permissions, which control access to resources.

A policy is usually applied to a user account, a computer, or a group. Let's use the example of a network composed of Windows XP Professional systems with a Windows 2003 Server system. Every Windows XP system has its own local policies program, which enables policies to be placed on that system only. Figure 19.7 shows the tool you use to set local policies on an individual system, called **Local Security Settings**, being used to deny the user account Danar the capability to log on locally.

Local policies work great for individual systems, but they can be a pain to configure if you want to apply the same settings to more than one PC on your network. If you want to apply policy settings *en masse*, you need to step up to Windows Active Directory domain-based **Group Policy**. By using Group Policy, you can exercise deity-like—Microsoft prefers to use the term *granular*—control over your network clients.

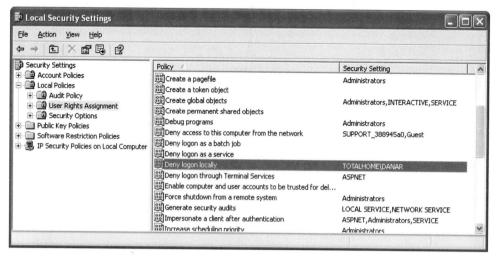

• **Figure 19.7** Local Security Settings

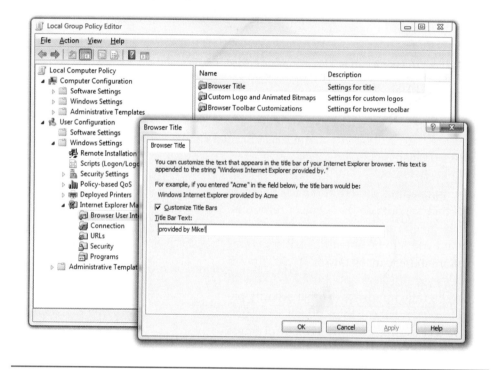

• **Figure 19.8** Using Group Policy to make IE title say "provided by Mike!"

Want to set default wallpaper for every PC in your domain? Group Policy can do that. Want to make certain tools inaccessible to everyone except authorized users? Group Policy can do that, too. Want to control access to the Internet, redirect home folders, run scripts, deploy software, or just remind folks that unauthorized access to the network will get them nowhere fast? Group Policy is the answer. Figure 19.8 shows Group Policy; I'm about to change the default title on every instance of Internet Explorer on every computer in my domain!

That's just one simple example of the settings you can configure by using Group Policy. You can apply literally hundreds of tweaks through Group Policy, from the great to the small, but don't worry too much about familiarizing yourself with each and every one. Group Policy settings are a big topic on most of the Microsoft certification tracks, but for the purposes of the CompTIA A+ Essentials exam, you simply have to be comfortable with the concept behind Group Policy.

Although I could never list every possible policy you can enable on a Windows system, here's a list of some commonly used ones:

- **Prevent Registry Edits** If you try to edit the Registry, you get a failure message.

- **Prevent Access to the Command Prompt** Keeps users from getting to the command prompt by turning off the Run command and the MS-DOS Prompt shortcut.

- **Log on Locally** Defines who may log on to the system locally.

- **Shut Down System** Defines who may shut down the system.

- **Minimum Password Length** Forces a minimum password length.

- **Account Lockout Threshold** Sets the maximum number of logon attempts a person can make before being locked out of the account.

- **Disable Windows Installer** Prevents users from installing software.

- **Printer Browsing** Enables users to browse for printers on the network, as opposed to using only assigned printers.

Although the CompTIA A+ Essentials exam doesn't expect you to know how to implement policies on any type of network, you are expected to understand that policies exist, especially on Windows networks, and that they can do amazing things to control what users can do on their systems. If you ever try to get to a command prompt on a Windows system only to discover the Run command is dimmed, blame it on a policy, not the computer!

■ Malicious Software

The beauty of the Internet is the ease of accessing resources just about anywhere on the globe, all from the comfort of your favorite chair. This connection, however, runs both ways, and people from all over the world can potentially access your computer from the comfort of their evil lairs. The Internet is awash with malicious software—*malware*—that is, even at this moment, trying to infect your systems. Malware consists of computer programs designed to break into computers or cause havoc on computers. The most common types of malware are grayware, spam, viruses, Trojan horses, and worms. You need to understand the different types of malware so you can combat them for you and your users successfully.

Grayware

Programs that intrude unwanted into your computing experience but don't actually do any damage to your systems or data—what's called **grayware**—can make that computing experience less than perfect. On most systems, the Internet Web browser client is the most often used piece of software. Over the years, Web sites have come up with more and more ways to try to get you to see what they want you to see: their advertising. When the Web first got underway, we were forced to look at an occasional banner ad. In the past few years, Web site designers have become much more sophisticated, creating a number of intrusive and irritating ways to get you to part with your money in one form or another.

There are basically three irritating grayware types: pop-ups, spyware, and adware. **Pop-ups** are those surprise browser windows that appear automatically when you visit a Web site, proving themselves irritating and unwanted and nothing else. **Spyware**, meanwhile, defines a family of programs that run in the background on your PC, each sending information about your browsing habits to the company that installed it on your system. **Adware** is not generally as malicious as spyware, but it works similarly to display ads on your system. As such, these programs download new ads and generate undesirable network traffic. Of the three, spyware is much less noticeable but far more nefarious. At its worst, spyware can fire up pop-up windows of competing products on the Web site you're currently viewing. For example, you might be perusing a bookseller's Web site, only to have a pop-up from a competitor's site appear.

Pop-Ups

Getting rid of pop-ups is actually rather tricky. You've probably noticed that most of these pop-up browser windows don't look like browser windows at all. They have no menu bar, button bar, or address window, yet they are separate browser windows. HTML coding permits Web site and advertising designers to remove the usual navigation aids from a browser window so all you're left with is the content. In fact, as I'll describe in a minute, some pop-up browser windows are deliberately designed to mimic similar pop-up alerts from the Windows OS. They might even have buttons similar to Windows' own exit buttons, but you might find that when you click them, you wind up with more pop-up windows instead! What to do?

The first thing you need to know when dealing with pop-ups is how to close them without actually having to risk clicking them. As I said, most pop-ups have removed all navigation aids, and many are also configured to appear on your monitor screen in a position that places the browser window's exit button—the little X button in the upper-right corner—outside of your visible screen area. Some even pop up behind the active browser window and wait there in the background. Most annoying! To remedy this, use alternate means to close the pop-up browser window. For instance, you can right-click the browser window's taskbar icon to generate a pop-up menu of your own. Select Close, and the window should go away. You can also press ALT-TAB to bring the browser window in question to the forefront and then press ALT-F4 to close it.

Most Web browsers have features to prevent pop-up ads in the first place, but I've found that these types of applications are sometimes *too* thorough. That is, they tend to prevent *all* new browser windows from opening, even those you want to view. Still, they're free to try, so have a look to see if they suit your needs. Applications such as AdSubtract control a variety of Internet annoyances, including pop-up windows, cookies, and Java applets, and are more configurable—you can specify what you want to allow on any particular domain address—but the fully functional versions usually cost at least something, and that much control is too confusing for most novice-level users.

Spyware

Some types of spyware go considerably beyond the level of intrusion. They can use your computer's resources to run *distributed computing* applications, capture your keystrokes to steal passwords, reconfigure your dial-up settings to use a different phone number at a much higher connection charge, or even use your Internet connection and e-mail address list to propagate itself to other computers in a virus-like fashion! Are you concerned yet?

Setting aside the legal and ethical issues—and there are many—you should at least appreciate that spyware can seriously impact your PC's performance and cause problems with your Internet connection. The threat is real, so what practical steps can you take to protect yourself? Let's look at how to prevent spyware installation and how to detect and remove any installed spyware.

How does this spyware get into your system in the first place? Obviously, sensible people don't download and install something that they know is going to compromise their computers. Makers of spyware know this, so they bundle their software with some other program or utility that purports to give you some benefit.

What kind of benefit? How about free access to MP3 music files? A popular program called Kazaa does that. How about a handy *e-wallet* utility that remembers your many screen names, passwords, and even your credit-card numbers to make online purchases easier and faster? A program called Gator does that, and many other functions as well. How about browser enhancements, performance boosters, custom cursor effects, search utilities, buddy lists, file savers, or media players? The list goes on and on, yet they all share one thing: they're simply window-dressing for the *real* purpose of the software. So you see, for the most part, spyware doesn't need to force its way into your PC. Instead, it saunters calmly through the front door. If the graphic in Figure 19.9 looks familiar, you might have installed some of this software yourself.

• **Figure 19.9**   Gator Corporation's acknowledgment warning

Some spyware makers use more aggressive means to get you to install their software. Instead of offering you some sort of attractive utility, they use fear tactics and deception to try to trick you into installing their software. One popular method is to use pop-up browser windows crudely disguised as Windows' own system warnings (Figure 19.10). When clicked, these may trigger a flood of other browser windows, or may even start a file download.

The lesson here is simple: *Don't install these programs!* Careful reading of the software's license agreement before you install a program is a good idea, but realistically, it does little to protect your PC. With that in mind, here are a couple of preventive measures you can take to keep parasitic software off of your system.

If you visit a Web site and are prompted to install a third-party application or plug-in that you've never heard of, *don't install it*. Well-known and reputable plug-ins, such

• **Figure 19.10**   A spyware pop-up browser window, disguised as a Windows alert

as Adobe's *Shockwave* or *Flash*, are safe, but be suspicious of any others. Don't click *anywhere* inside of a pop-up browser window, even if it looks just like a Windows alert window or DOS command-line prompt—as I just mentioned, it's probably fake and the Close button is likely a hyperlink. Instead, use other means to close the window, such as pressing ALT-F4 or right-clicking the browser window's icon on the taskbar and selecting Close.

You can also install spyware detection and removal software on your system and run it regularly. Let's look at how to do that.

Some spyware makers are reputable enough to include a routine for uninstalling their software. Gator, for instance, makes it fairly easy to get rid of their programs; just use the Windows Add/Remove Programs applet in the Control Panel. Others, however, aren't quite so cooperative. In fact, because spyware is so—well, *sneaky*—it's entirely possible that your system already has some installed that you don't even know about. How do you find out?

Windows comes with Windows Defender, a fine tool for catching most spyware, but it's not perfect. The better solution is to back up Windows Defender with a second spyware removal program. There are several on the market, but two that I highly recommend are Lavasoft's Ad-Aware (Figure 19.11) and PepiMK's Spybot Search & Destroy.

Both of these applications work exactly as advertised. They detect and delete spyware of all sorts—hidden files and folders, cookies, Registry keys and values, you name it. Ad-Aware is free for personal use, while Spybot Search & Destroy is shareware (Figure 19.12). Many times I've used both programs at the same time because one tends to catch what the other misses.

• **Figure 19.11**   Lavasoft's Ad-Aware

Spam

E-mail that comes into your Inbox from a source that's not a friend, family member, or colleague, and that you didn't ask for, can create huge problems for your computer and you. This unsolicited e-mail, called **spam**, accounts for a huge percentage of traffic on the Internet. Spam comes in many flavors, from legitimate businesses

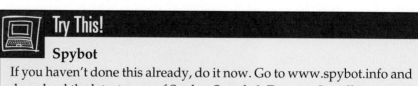

Try This!

Spybot

If you haven't done this already, do it now. Go to www.spybot.info and download the latest copy of Spybot Search & Destroy. Install it on your computer and run it. Did it find any spyware that slipped in past your defenses?

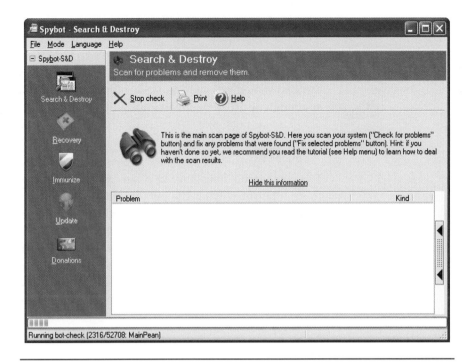

Running bot-check (2316/52708: MainPean)

• **Figure 19.12** Spybot Search & Destroy

trying to sell you products to scammers who just want to take your money. Hoaxes, pornography, and get-rich-quick schemes pour into the Inboxes of most e-mail users. They waste your time and can easily offend.

You can use several options to cope with the flood of spam. The first option is defense. Never post your e-mail address on the Internet. One study tested this theory and found that *over 97 percent* of the spam received during the study went to e-mail addresses they had posted on the public Internet.

Filters and filtering software can block spam at your mail server and at your computer. AOL implemented blocking schemes in 2004, for example, that dropped the average spam received by its subscribers by a large percentage, perhaps as much as 50 percent. You can set most e-mail programs to block e-mail from specific people—good to use if someone is harassing you—or to specific people. You can block by subject line or keywords. Most people use a third-party anti-spam program instead of using the filters in their e-mail program.

 Try This!

Fight Spam Right!

Spam filtering software that you purchase and put on your computer can help, but you have to do some research to see which software offers the best performance. You want to avoid software that causes *false positives*—mislabeling acceptable e-mail as spam—because you miss legitimate e-mail messages from family and friends. So, fire up your trusty Web browser and do some searching.

Start by going to Google and searching for **anti-spam software reviews**. One of the first sites that should come up takes you to *PC Magazine*'s review list, which is kept up to date. What's the current Editor's Choice? What other options do you have?

Viruses

Just as a biological virus gets passed from person to person, a computer **virus** is a piece of malicious software that gets passed from computer to computer (Figure 19.13). A computer virus is designed to attach itself to a program on your computer. It could be your e-mail program, your word

You've got virus!

Hey, new mail comin' your way!

• **Figure 19.13**   You've got mail!

Be sure to know the difference between viruses and spyware. Too many people use the terms interchangeably, and they're very different things.

processor, or even a game. Whenever you use the infected program, the virus goes into action and does whatever it was designed to do. It can wipe out your e-mail or even erase your entire hard drive! Viruses are also sometimes used to steal information or send spam e-mails to everyone in your address book.

Trojans

Trojans are true, freestanding programs that do something other than what the person who runs the program thinks they will do, much as the Trojan horse did in antiquity. An example of a *Trojan virus* is a program that a person thinks is an antivirus program but is actually a virus. Some Trojans are quite sophisticated. It might be a game that works perfectly well, but causes some type of damage when the user quits the game.

Worms

Similar to a Trojan, a **worm** is a complete program that travels from machine to machine, usually through computer networks. Most worms are designed to take advantage of security problems in operating systems and install themselves on vulnerable machines. They can copy themselves over and over again on infected networks and can create so much activity that they overload the network by consuming bandwidth, in worst cases even bringing chunks of the entire Internet to a halt.

You can do several things to protect yourself and your data against these threats. First, make sure you are running up-to-date virus software—especially if you connect to the Internet via an always-on broadband connection. You should also be protected by a firewall, either as part of your network hardware or by means of a software program. (See the sections on antivirus programs and firewalls later in this chapter.)

Because worms most commonly infect systems through security flaws in operating systems, the next defense against them is to make sure you have the latest security patches installed on your version of Windows. A *security patch* is an addition to the operating system to patch a hole in the operating system code. You can download security patches from the Microsoft Update Web site (Figure 19.14).

Microsoft's Windows Update tool is handy for Windows users as it provides a simple method to ensure that your version's security is up to date. The one downside is that not everyone remembers to run Windows Update. Don't wait until something goes wrong on your computer or you hear on the news that another nasty program is running rampant across the Internet. Run Windows Update weekly (or even better, automatically) as a part of your normal system maintenance. Keeping your patches up to date is called *patch management*, and it goes a long way toward keeping your system safe.

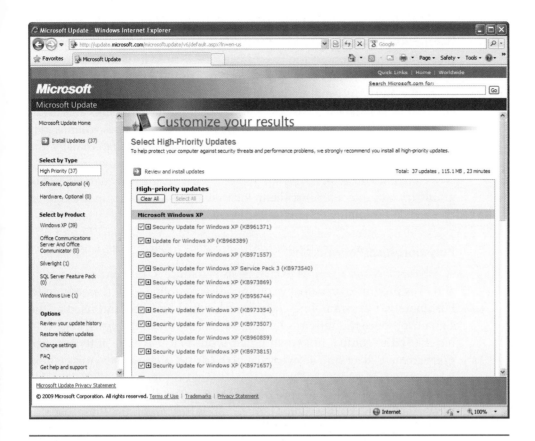

• **Figure 19.14**   Microsoft Update

Virus Prevention and Recovery

The only way to protect your PC permanently from getting a virus is to disconnect from the Internet and never permit any potentially infected software to touch your precious computer. Because neither scenario is likely these days, you need to use a specialized antivirus program to help stave off the inevitable virus assaults. When you discover infected systems, you need to know how to stop the spread of the virus to other computers and how to fix infected computers.

Antivirus Programs

An **antivirus program** protects your PC in two ways. It can be both sword and shield, working in an active seek-and-destroy mode and in a passive sentry mode. When ordered to seek and destroy, the program scans the computer's boot sector and files for viruses and, if it finds any, presents you with the available options for removing or disabling them. Antivirus programs can also operate as **virus shields** that passively monitor your computer's activity, checking for viruses only when certain events occur, such as a program executing or a file being downloaded.

Antivirus programs use different techniques to combat different types of viruses. They detect boot sector viruses simply by comparing the drive's boot sector to a standard boot sector. This works because most boot sectors are basically the same. Some antivirus programs make a backup copy of the boot sector. If they detect a virus, the programs use that backup copy to replace the infected boot sector. Executable viruses are a little more difficult to find because they can be on any file in the drive. To detect executable viruses, the antivirus program uses a library of signatures. A **signature** is the code pattern of a known virus. The antivirus program compares an executable file to its library of signatures. There have been instances where a perfectly clean program coincidentally held a virus signature. Usually the antivirus program's creator provides a patch to prevent further alarms.

Now that you understand the types of viruses and how antivirus programs try to protect against them, let's review a few terms that are often used when describing certain traits of viruses.

Polymorphics/Polymorphs

A **polymorph virus** attempts to change its signature to prevent detection by antivirus programs, usually by continually scrambling a bit of useless code. Fortunately, the scrambling code itself can be identified and used as the signature—once the antivirus makers become aware of the virus. One technique used to combat unknown polymorphs is to have the antivirus program create a checksum on every file in the drive. A *checksum* in this context is a number generated by the software based on the contents of the file rather than the name, date, or size of that file. The algorithms for creating these checksums vary among different antivirus programs (they are also usually kept secret to help prevent virus makers from coming up with ways to beat them). Every time a program is run, the antivirus program calculates a new checksum and compares it with the earlier calculation. If the checksums are different, it is a sure sign of a virus.

Stealth

The term "stealth" is more of a concept than an actual virus function. Most **stealth virus** programs are boot sector viruses that use various methods to hide from antivirus software. The AntiEXE stealth virus hooks on to a little-known but often-used software interrupt, for example, running only when that interrupt runs. Others make copies of innocent-looking files.

Virus Prevention Tips

The secret to preventing damage from a malicious software attack is to keep from getting a virus in the first place. As discussed earlier, all good antivirus programs include a virus shield that scans e-mail, downloads, running programs, and so on automatically (Figure 19.15).

• **Figure 19.15**   A virus shield in action

Use your antivirus shield. It is also a good idea to scan PCs daily for possible virus attacks. All antivirus programs include terminate-and-stay resident programs (TSRs) that run every time the PC is booted. Last but not least, know the source of any software before you load it. Although the chance of commercial, shrink-wrapped software having a virus is virtually nil (there have been a couple of well-publicized exceptions), that illegal copy of Unreal Tournament you borrowed from a local hacker should definitely be inspected with care.

Keep your antivirus program updated. New viruses appear daily, and your program needs to know about them. The list of virus signatures your antivirus program can recognize is called the **definition file**, and you must keep that definition file up to date so your antivirus software has the latest signatures. Fortunately, most antivirus programs update themselves automatically. Further, you should periodically update the core antivirus software programming—called the *engine*—to employ the latest refinements the developers have included.

Virus Recovery Tips

When the inevitable happens and either your computer or one of your user's computers gets infected by a computer virus, you need to follow certain steps to stop the problem from spreading and get the computer back up safely into service. Try this five-step process.

1. Recognize
2. Quarantine
3. Search and destroy
4. Remediate
5. Educate

Recognize and Quarantine

The first step is to recognize that a potential virus outbreak has occurred. If you're monitoring network traffic and one computer starts spewing e-mail, that's a good sign. Or users might complain that a computer that was running snappily the day before seems very sluggish.

Many networks employ software such as the open-source PacketFence that automatically monitors network traffic and can cut a machine off the network if that machine starts sending suspicious packets. You can also quarantine a computer manually by disconnecting the network cable. Once you're sure the machine isn't capable of infecting others, you're ready to find the virus and get rid of it.

 Be sure to turn off System Restore before cleaning up a virus—otherwise Windows might keep a copy of the virus in the system backup files!

Search and Destroy

Once you've isolated the infected computer (or computers), you need to get to a safe boot environment and run your antivirus software. You can try Windows Safe Mode first, because it doesn't require anything but a reboot. If that doesn't work, or you suspect a boot sector virus, you need to turn to an external bootable source, such as a bootable CD or flash memory drive.

avast! Simple User Interface

Tools   Settings   Help

http://www.avast.com

Area to scan

☐ Local Hard Disks   ☐ Floppies
☐ Folders   ☐ CD/DVD
Selected paths:

Type of scan

Quick   Standard   Thorough

☐ Test archives

Information

Current version of virus database: 090820-0, 08/20/09
Resident Protection: Standard
Date of last scan: Not done yet
Virus recovery database (VRDB):   Not done yet
Automatic Updates: Database only

Scan

Start scan   Stop scan   Go to Background

● **Figure 19.16**   avast! Virus Cleaner Tool

Get into the habit of keeping around an antivirus CD-R—a bootable CD-R disc with a copy of an antivirus program. If you suspect a virus, use the disc, even if your antivirus program claims to have eliminated the virus. Turn off the PC and reboot it from the antivirus disc. (You might have to change CMOS settings to boot to an optical disc.) This will put you in a clean boot environment that you know is free from any boot sector viruses. If you only support fairly recent computers, most have an option to boot to a USB flash drive, so you can put a boot environment on a thumb drive for even faster startup speeds.

You have several options for creating the bootable CD-R or flash drive. First, some antivirus software comes in a bootable version, such as the avast! Virus Cleaner Tool (Figure 19.16).

Second, you can download a copy of Linux that offers a LiveCD option such as Ubuntu. With a LiveCD, you boot to the CD and install a complete working copy of the operating system into RAM, never touching or accessing the hard drive, to give you full Internet-ready access to many online antivirus sites. (You'll obviously need Internet access for those tools.) Kaspersky Labs provides a nice option at www.kaspersky.com.

Finally, you can download and burn a copy of the Ultimate Boot CD. It comes stocked with several antivirus programs, so you wouldn't need any other tool. Find it at www.ultimatebootcd.com. The only downside is that the antivirus engines will be out of date, as will their virus encyclopedias.

Once you get to a boot environment, run your antivirus program's most comprehensive virus scan. Then check all removable media that were exposed to the system, as well as any other machine that might have received data from it or that is networked to the cleaned machine. A virus or other malicious program can often lie dormant for months before anyone knows of its presence.

E-mail is still a common source of viruses, and opening infected e-mails is a common way to get infected. Viewing an e-mail in a preview window opens the e-mail message and exposes your computer to some viruses. Download files only from sites you know to be safe, and of course avoid the

Tech Tip

BartPE and Windows PE

For those who like to create custom tools, you can make your own boot environment and stock it with the latest antivirus software of your choice. Use one of two preinstalled environment (PE) tools, BartPE and Windows PE.

BartPE is a third-party tool written by Bart Lagerweij that enables you to create a graphical bootable version of Windows XP, complete with software. You need a legitimate copy of Windows XP (Home or Professional) to create the bootable media, as BartPE pulls from the Windows setup files. You can then add various plug-ins to get antivirus support. Find it here: www.nu2.nu/pebuilder.

Microsoft made available Windows PE 2.0 (Windows PE 3.0 for Windows 7 should be available by the time you read this) for Windows Vista for installation assistance on multiple computers. The boot environment created also enables you to run some software, though it's not as easy as in BartPE. Download Windows PE from Microsoft.

less reputable corners of the Internet, which are the most likely places to pick up computer infections.

Remediate

Virus infections can do a lot of damage to a system, especially to sensitive files needed to load Windows, so you might need to remediate formerly infected systems after cleaning off the drive or drives. **Remediation** simply means that you fix things the virus harmed. This can mean replacing corrupted Windows Registry files or even startup files.

If you can't start Windows after the virus scan is finished, you need to boot to a Windows 2000/XP installation disc, run Setup, select Repair, and then select Recovery Console to boot to the Recovery Console in Windows 2000/XP. If you're running Vista or 7, just boot into a repair environment off of the installation media

Once in the Recovery Console, you'll have access to tools to repair the boot sector (or *boot blocks*, as CompTIA calls them) through the FIXMBR and FIXBOOT commands. You can run BOOTCFG to rebuild a corrupted BOOT.INI file. EXPAND will enable you to grab any replacement files from the Windows CAB files.

With the Windows Vista repair environment, you have access to more repair tools, such as Startup Repair, System Restore, Windows Complete PC Restore, and the command prompt (Figure 19.17). Run the appropriate option for the situation and you should have the machine properly remediated in a jiffy.

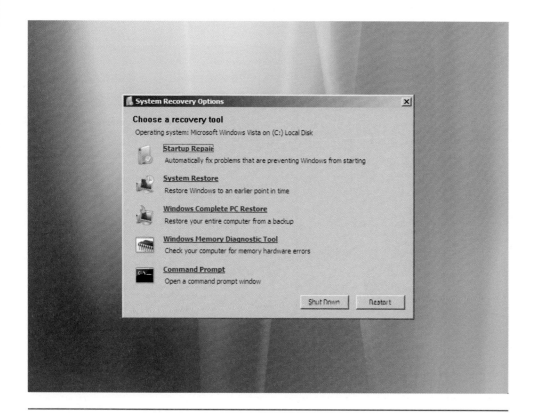

• **Figure 19.17** System Recovery Options in Windows Vista

Educate

The best way to keep from having to deal with malware and grayware is education. It's your job as the IT person to talk to users, especially the ones whose systems you've just spent the last hour cleaning of nasties, about how to avoid these programs. Show them samples of dangerous e-mails they should not open, Web sites to avoid, and the types of programs they should not install and use on the network. Any user who understands the risks of questionable actions on their computers will usually do the right thing and stay away from malware.

Finally, have your users run antivirus and antispyware programs regularly. Schedule them while interfacing with the user so you know it will happen.

Firewalls

Firewalls are an essential tool in the fight against malicious programs on the Internet. **Firewalls** are devices or software that protect an internal network from unauthorized access to and from the Internet at large. Hardware firewalls use a number of methods to protect networks, such as hiding IP addresses and blocking TCP/IP ports. Most SOHO networks use a hardware firewall, such as the Linksys router shown in Figure 19.18. These devices do a great job.

Every version of Windows since Windows XP Service Pack 2 comes with an excellent software firewall, called the Windows Firewall (Figure 19.19). It can also handle the heavy lifting of port blocking, security logging, and more.

> Almost all routers come with built-in firewalls that enable you to create Access Control Lists (ACLs). An ACL might filter by port number, IP address, MAC address, time of day, day of the week, or even Web addresses.

• **Figure 19.18**   Linksys router as a firewall

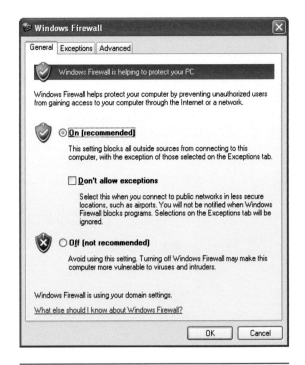

• **Figure 19.19**   Windows Firewall

● Figure 19.20   Control Panel, Category View

You can access the Windows Firewall by opening the Windows Firewall applet in the Control Panel. If you're running the Control Panel in Category View, click the Security Center icon (Figure 19.20) and then click the Windows Firewall option in the Windows Security Center dialog box. Figure 19.21 illustrates the Exceptions tab on the Windows Firewall, showing the applications allowed to use the TCP/IP ports on my computer.

● Figure 19.21   Essential programs (doesn't everyone need to run Half-Life 2?)

■ Chapter Summary

After reading this chapter and completing the exercises, you should understand the following about computer security.

Describe key security concepts

■ Data classification systems vary by the organization, but a common scheme classifies documents as public, internal use only, highly confidential, top secret, and so on. Using a classification scheme enables employees such as techs to know very quickly what to do with documents, drives containing documents, and more.

■ Compliance means that members of an organization or company must abide by or comply with all of the rules that apply to the organization or company. From a technician's point of view, the most common compliance issue revolves around software, such as what sort of software users can be allowed to install on their computers. Compliance keeps technical support calls down and enables techs to focus on more serious problems.

■ Controlling access to programs, data, and other computing resources is the key to securing your system. Access control includes four interlinked areas requiring your attention: physical security, authentication, users and groups, and security policies.

■ Store computers with sensitive data in a locked room and never walk away from your computer while logged in. Log out or lock the computer by pressing WINDOWS LOGO KEY-L.

Define and describe various forms of malicious software

■ Malware includes grayware, spam, viruses, Trojan horses, and worms—all of which can wreak havoc on your system.

■ Irritating Web browser problems include pop-ups, spyware, and adware. Many pop-ups remove the navigation aids from the browser window or mimic Windows dialog boxes. To safely close a pop-up, right-click the pop-up's taskbar icon and choose Close, or press ALT-TAB until the pop-up window is active and then press ALT-F4 to close it.

■ Spyware can use your computer's resources to run distributed computing applications, capture keystrokes to steal passwords, or worse. Spyware typically disguises itself as a useful utility, so be vigilant about what you install. Some spyware can be removed via Add or Remove Programs, but for stubborn spyware, use a third-party tool such as Lavasoft's Ad-Aware or PepiMK's Spybot Search & Destroy.

■ Unsolicited e-mail is called spam. Never post your e-mail address on the Internet; over 97 percent of spam comes from e-mail addresses posted online. Spam filters can block spam at the mail server or at your computer. You can set most e-mail programs to block e-mail sent from specific people or to a specific person.

■ A virus is a piece of malicious software that is passed from computer to computer and is designed to attach itself to another program on your computer. Trojans are freestanding programs that do something other than the user expects it to do when run, such as expecting a game to run but erasing CMOS settings instead. A worm is a freestanding program that takes advantage of security flaws and copies itself over and over again, thereby bogging down a network.

Explain how to protect computers from malicious software and how to recover affected computers

■ To help protect a computer from malware, make sure to run up-to-date antivirus software, use a firewall, and apply all security patches for your software and operating system. Run Windows Update automatically, or at least weekly if you choose to configure it for manual updates.

■ Antivirus software works in active mode to scan your file system for viruses and in passive mode by monitoring your computer's activity and checking for viruses in response to an action, such as running a program or downloading a file. The software detects boot sector viruses by comparing the drive's boot sector to a standard boot sector. To detect executable viruses, a library of virus signatures is used.

- Polymorph viruses attempt to change their signature to prevent detection by antivirus software. Fortunately, the scrambled code itself can be used as a signature. A checksum, based on file contents, can be created for every file on the drive. If the checksum changes, it is a sign of a virus infection. Most stealth viruses are boot sector viruses that hide from antivirus software.

- The best way to prevent damage from a virus is to keep from getting a virus in the first place. Use your passive antivirus shield, scan the PC daily, know where software has come from before you load it, and keep your antivirus definitions updated. Don't view e-mail messages in a preview pane, and only download files from sites you know to be safe.

- When the inevitable happens and either your computer or one of your user's computers is infected by a computer virus, you need to follow a process to stop the problem from spreading and get the computer back up safely into service.

- First, recognize the symptoms of a computer virus attack, such as a suddenly very sluggish computer. Follow up by quarantining the infected computer to make certain the virus doesn't spread. Third, boot the computer in Safe Mode or an alternative safe boot environment and run your antivirus software. To finish up, remediate the formerly infected machine by fixing boot sector problems and so on, and educate your users so infection doesn't happen again.

- Hardware firewalls protect networks by hiding IP addresses and blocking TCP/IP ports. Windows XP and later come with a built-in software firewall that is accessible from the Control Panel Security Center applet.

■ Key Terms

access control *(597)*
adware *(603)*
antivirus program *(609)*
authentication *(598)*
biometric devices *(599)*
compliance *(597)*
data classification *(597)*
definition file *(611)*
effective permissions *(600)*
firewall *(614)*
grayware *(603)*
Group Policy *(601)*
Local Security Settings *(601)*

polymorph virus *(610)*
pop-up *(603)*
remediation *(613)*
signature *(610)*
smart cards *(599)*
social engineering *(598)*
spam *(606)*
spyware *(603)*
stealth virus *(610)*
Trojan *(608)*
virus *(607)*
virus shield *(609)*
worm *(608)*

■ Key Term Quiz

Use the Key Terms list to complete the sentences that follow. Not all terms will be used.

1. Mary's company routinely labels data according to its sensitivity or potential danger to the company if someone outside accesses the data. This is an example of _data classification_.

2. A(n) _trojan_ masquerades as a legitimate program, yet does something different from what is expected when executed.

3. Antivirus software uses an updatable _definition f[ile]_ to identify a virus by its _signature_.

4. A(n) _firewall_ protects against unauthorized access from the Internet.

5. A virus that changes its signature to prevent detection is called a(n) _polymorph_.

6. A(n) _worm_ is a complete program that travels from machine to machine, usually through computer networks.

1. Zander downloaded a game off the Internet and installed it, but as soon as he started to play he got a Blue Screen of Death. Upon rebooting, he discovered that his My Documents folder had been erased. What happened?

   A. He installed spyware.

   B. He installed a Trojan.

   C. He broke the Group Policy.

   D. He broke the Local Security Settings.

2. What is true about virus shields?

   A. They automatically scan e-mails, downloads, and running programs.

   B. They protect against spyware and adware.

   C. They are effective in stopping pop-ups.

   D. They can reduce the amount of spam by 97 percent.

3. A user calls to complain that his computer seems awfully sluggish. All he's done so far is open his e-mail. What should the tech do first?

   A. Educate the user about the dangers of opening e-mail.

   B. Quarantine the computer so the suspected virus does not spread.

   C. Run antivirus software on the computer.

   D. Remediate the infected system.

4. Which of the following are good examples of remediation? (Select two.)

   A. Boot to the Recovery Console in Windows XP and run FIXMBR or FIXBOOT to repair boot sector damage.

   B. Boot to the repair environment in Windows Vista and run System Restore.

   C. Boot to a safe environment and run antivirus software.

   D. Remove a computer suspected of having a virus from the network, effectively quarantining the computer.

5. Which of the following are examples of grayware? (Select two.)

   A. Adware

   B. Spyware

   C. Trojan

   D. Virus

6. A user calls and complains that the technician who fixed his computer removed some software he used to listen to music on the Internet. A check of approved software does not include the LimeWire application, so what should the supervisor do?

   A. Applaud the technician for proper compliance.

   B. Educate the user about the legal issues involved with music downloads.

   C. Add the LimeWire application to the approved software list and make the technician apologize and reinstall the software.

   D. Check with the user's supervisor about adding LimeWire to the approved software list.

7. Cindy wants to put a policy in place at her company with regard to virus prevention or at least limitation. What policies would offer the best solution?

   A. Install antivirus software on every computer. Instruct users on how to run it.

   B. Install antivirus software on every computer. Set the software up to scan regularly.

   C. Install antivirus software on every computer. Set the software up to update the definitions and engine automatically. Set the software up to scan regularly.

   D. Install antivirus software on every computer. Set the software up to update the definitions and engine automatically. Set the software up to scan regularly. Educate the users about what sites and downloads to avoid.

8. What excellent piece of computer protection software was introduced in Windows XP Service Pack 2?

   A. Windows AntiVirus

   B. Windows Firewall

   C. Windows Ad-Aware

   D. Windows Defender

■ Essay Quiz

1. Your boss is considering getting an Internet connection for the office so employees have access to e-mail, but she is concerned about hackers getting into the company server. What can you tell your boss about safeguards you will implement to keep the server safe?

2. An intern in your IT department has asked for your help in understanding the differences between a virus, a worm, and a Trojan horse. What advice can you offer?

Lab Project

• Lab Project 19.1

You know you must run antivirus and antispyware software on any computer connected to the Internet, and many companies will sell you good, bad, and indifferent software. Using the Internet, find free antivirus and free antispyware programs and make sure these are legitimate and reputable programs and not spyware masquerading as legitimate programs! What free antivirus did you find? What free antispyware did you find? How do you know these are reputable? Would you install these on your own personal computer? Why or why not?

The Complete PC Technician

"As no man is born an artist, so no man is born an angler."

—Izaak Walton, *The Compleat Angler* (1653)

In this chapter, you will learn how to

- **Describe how computers work**
- **Implement a troubleshooting methodology**
- **Describe a technician's toolkit**

When a mission-critical computer goes down, regardless of the industry, people get upset. Workers can't work, so they feel guilty. Employers can't get product out on time, so they feel anxious. Supervisors blame employees for fouling things up, or at least the employees fear such blame, even if they did not break the machine.

Into this charged atmosphere comes the tech, ready to fix the computer and move on to the next challenge. Accomplishing this task, though, requires three things: First, a good tech must know the broken machine inside and out—how it's *supposed* to work when working properly. Second, the tech has to calm the workers and supervisors, and get answers to questions to gain relevant information about the problem. Third, the tech must troubleshoot the problem and fix the machine.

This chapter starts with an overview of how computers work and then dives into a section on dealing with customers and how to get them to tell you what you need to know and smile about it. The chapter wraps up with a proven troubleshooting methodology to help you figure out the source of problems and point you to the fix quickly.

■ How Computers Work

You've spent a lot of time going through this book, reading about technologies and components in great detail. Each chapter contained troubleshooting information and methodologies for the components explained in that chapter. In Chapter 5, "Learning CPUs," for example, you learned all about CPUs, from how they work to some of the many different types available. Knowing a CPU's features as well as the difference between the available brands will help you make informed decisions when buying a CPU. In Chapter 9, "Hard Drive Technologies," you learned more about hard drives than you probably ever thought you would. With each chapter, you added more and more information about the pieces that make up the personal computer today.

In this chapter, I want you to distill that knowledge, to think about the computer as a coherent machine. Each of the computer's components works together to enable people to produce some amazing things.

To master the art of troubleshooting as a PC tech, you need to approach a technical problem and answer one question: "What can it be? What can be causing this problem?" (Okay, that was two questions, but you get the idea.) Because every process involves multiple components, you must understand the interconnectedness of those components. If Jane can't print, for example, what could it be? Connectivity? Drivers? Paper jam? Slow network connection? Frozen application? Solar flares? Let's look at the process.

Way back in Chapter 3, "The Visible PC," you learned about the four parts of the computing process: input, processing, output, and storage. Let's take a moment to review the computing process, this time to see how you can use it to help you fix computers.

When you run a program, your computer goes through three of the four stages of the **computing process**: input, processing, and output (Figure 20.1). Input requires specific devices, such as the keyboard and mouse, that enable you to tell the computer to do something, such as open a program or type a word. The operating system (OS) provides an interface and tools so that the microprocessor and other chips can process your request. The image on the monitor or sound from the speakers effectively tells you that the computer has interpreted your command and spit out the result. The fourth stage, storage, comes into play when you want to save a document and when you first open programs and other files.

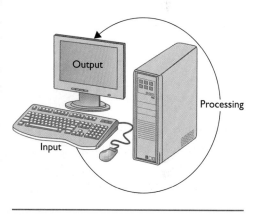

● **Figure 20.1**   Input, processing, and output

Cross Check

Printing Process

You learned all about the printing process in Chapter 15, "Learning Printing," but now think in terms of the computing process. Does the computing process translate when applied to printers? How? If a user can't print, how does knowledge of the computing process help you troubleshoot the printing process?

placeholder

Chapter 20: The Complete PC Technician

Chapter 20: The Complete PC Technician   621

Making this process work, though, requires the complex interaction of many components, including multiple pieces of hardware and layers of software. As a tech, you need to understand all the components and how they work together so that when something doesn't work right, you can track down the source and fix it. A look at a modern program reveals that even a seemingly simple action or change on the screen requires many things to happen within the computer.

Games such as Second Life (Figure 20.2) are huge, taking up multiple gigabytes of space on an Internet server. They simply won't fit into the RAM in most computers, so developers have figured out ways to minimize RAM usage.

In Second Life, for example, you move through the online world in a series of more or less seamlessly connected areas. Crossing a bridge from one island to another triggers the game to quickly update the information you're about to see on the new island, so you won't be out of the action and the illusion of being in the game world remains intact. Here's what happens when you press the W key on your keyboard and your character steps across the invisible zone line.

The keyboard controller reads the grid of your keyboard and, on discovering your input, sends the information to the CPU through the wires of the motherboard (Figure 20.3). The CPU understands the keyboard controller because of a small program that was loaded into RAM from the ROM BIOS on the motherboard when the PC booted up.

The CPU and the application determine what should happen in the game, and on discovering that your character is about to cross the zone line,

Second Life is a massively multiplayer online role-playing game (MMORPG) that offers a unique twist on the genre. You can create just about anything you can imagine, as far as your time and talent can take you. Second Life has a functioning economy that spills out into the real world, meaning you can buy and sell things within the game and turn that into real U.S. dollars, although the more common scenario is to spend real money to get virtual possessions.

• **Figure 20.2**   Second Life

Cross Check

Input Process

You learned about keyboards and many other input devices in Chapter 12, "Learning Input/Output," but now apply the computing process to input devices for troubleshooting purposes. Obviously, keyboards do the "input" part of the computing process, but what can the problem be if you press a key and nothing happens? What other input devices can you recall from Chapter 12, "Learning Input/Output"? If they seem not to work, where in the computing process could the problem lie?

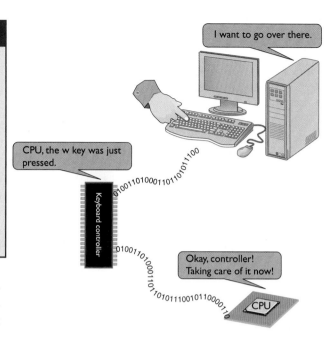

• **Figure 20.3** Keyboard to CPU

they trigger a whole series of actions. The application sends the signal to the OS that it needs a specific area loaded into RAM. The OS sends a signal to the CPU that it needs data stored on the hard drive plus information stored on the Second Life servers. The CPU then sends the commands to the hard drive controller for it to grab the proper stored data and send it to RAM, while at the same time sending a command to the NIC to download the updated information (Figure 20.4).

• **Figure 20.4** CPU to hard drive and NIC

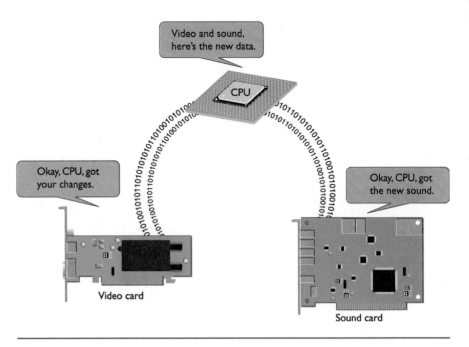

The hard drive controller tells the hard drive to cough up the data—megabytes worth—and then sends that data through the motherboard to the memory controller, which puts it into RAM and communicates with the CPU when it's finished. The network card and network operating system communicate with the Second Life servers and download the necessary updated information. The CPU then uses the application and OS to process the new data, sending video data to the video card and sound data to the sound card, again through the wires on the motherboard (Figure 20.5).

The video card processor puts the incoming data into its RAM, processes the data, and then sends out commands to the monitor to update the screen. The sound card processor likewise processes the data and sends out commands to the speakers to play a new sound (Figure 20.6).

For all of this to work, the PC has to have electricity, so the direct current (DC) provided by the power supply and the alternating current (AC) provided to the power supply must both be the proper voltage and amperage.

Finally, because Second Life is a network application, the OS has to send information through the NIC and onto the Internet to update everyone

Tech Tip

Video Counts

Windows Vista has raised the bar on video demands in a big way, so the video card in your users' systems can make a remarkable difference in their experience. Vista uses the video card to produce many of the cool visual effects of the interface. This means that a low-end video card in an otherwise serviceable machine can cause Vista to misbehave. Unless your client is gaming, there's no reason to drop $300+ on a video card, but assembling or recommending a system with yesterday's video is not necessarily a good thing!

Cross Check

Hard Drive Technologies

You learned about several hard drive technologies way back in Chapter 9, "Hard Drive Technologies," so turn there now and see if you can answer these questions. If an application stumbles or hesitates on the "load from the hard drive" section of the computing process, what could be the problem? Which of the available hard drive technologies offers better throughput? What would you recommend to a client who wanted to upgrade?

else's computer. That way, the other characters in the game world see you move forward a step (Figure 20.7).

What do you see or hear with all these electrons zipping all over the place? Out of a seemingly blank vista (Figure 20.8), a castle begins to appear, building itself piece by piece as your computer processes the new information and updates the video screen. You hear music begin to play from your speakers. Within a few seconds, with the data describing the new island fully downloaded and processed, the world on your monitor looks very different (Figure 20.9). That's when all goes well. Many megabytes of data have flowed from your hard drive and across the Internet, been processed by multiple processors, and sent to the monitor and the speakers.

To keep the action continuous and unbroken, Second Life, like many current online games, uses a process of continuous or **stream loading**: your computer constantly downloads updated information and data from the Second Life servers, so the world you see changes with every step you take. When done right, stream loading can do some amazing things. In the GameCube game Zelda, for example, the game anticipates where you will go next and loads that new area into RAM before you take the step. You can be in one area and use a telescope to zoom in on

• **Figure 20.6**   Updating the screen and speakers

• **Figure 20.7**   PC to Second Life servers

● **Figure 20.8**   New area loading

● **Figure 20.9**   Castle completed

another fully developed area (Figure 20.10), making the experience amazingly seamless, just like real life.

Anytime you have a problem on a computer that's not immediately and clearly obvious (such as not powering up due to not having a power cord plugged in), you should use the computing process to help you zero in on the problem. But the computing process only defines the pieces and their interaction; good troubleshooting requires more than just rummaging around to find the problem. You need to combine the computing process with a troubleshooting theory to get the job done.

■ Troubleshooting Theory

• **Figure 20.10**   Zelda zoomed

Troubleshooting theory is nothing more than a set of mental steps you use along with the computing process to diagnose and fix a computer. Troubleshooting theory includes talking to users to determine how and when the problem took place, determining a cause, testing, verification, and documentation. Techs use a number of good troubleshooting theories. Luckily for those taking the CompTIA A+, CompTIA clearly defines their vision of troubleshooting theory in the 220-701 exam:

2.1 Given a scenario, explain the troubleshooting theory

- ■ Identify the problem
    - ■ Question the user and identify user changes to computer and perform backups before making changes
- ■ Establish a theory of probable cause (question the obvious)
- ■ Test the theory to determine cause
    - ■ Once theory is confirmed determine next steps to resolve problem
    - ■ If theory is not confirmed re-establish new theory or escalate
- ■ Establish a plan of action to resolve the problem and implement the solution
- ■ Verify full system functionality and if applicable implement preventative measures
- ■ Document findings, actions and outcomes

• Figure 20.11 Tech asking nicely

Identify the Problem

There's a reason you're standing in front of a computer to repair it: something happened that the user of the computer has identified as "not good" and that's why you're here. The first step to **identifying any problem** is talking to the user. Get the user to show you what's not good. Is it an error code? Is something not accessible? Is a device not responding? Then ask the user that classic tech question (remember your communication skills here!): "Has anything recently changed on the computer that might have made this problem appear?" What you're really saying is: "Have you jacked with the computer? Did you install some evil program? Did you shove in a USB drive so hard you broke the connection?" Of course, you never say these things, simply ask nicely without accusing so the user can help you fix the problem (Figure 20.11).

In most troubleshooting situations, it's important to back up critical files before making changes to a system. To some extent, this is a matter of proper ongoing maintenance, but if some important bit of data disappears and you don't have a backup, you know who the user will blame, don't you?

If you run into a partially functional system where you might have to re-install the OS but can access the hard drive, you should definitely back up essential data, such as e-mail, browser favorites, important documents, and any data not stored on a regularly backed-up server. Because you can boot to a copy of Windows and go to the Recovery Console, you should never lose essential data, barring full-blown hard drive death.

The CompTIA A+ Essentials exam assumes that all techs should back up systems *every time* before working on them, even though that's not how it works in the real world.

Dead hard drives retain their data, so you can recover it—if you're willing to pay a lot of money. Having a good backup in place makes a lot more economic sense!

When taking a service call over the phone, first ask for the user's name and the problem.

Establish a Theory of Probable Cause (Question the Obvious)

Now it's time to analyze the issue and come up with a theory as to what is wrong—a **theory of probable cause**. Personally, I prefer the word "guess" at this point because very few errors are so obvious that you'll know what to do. Fall back on your knowledge of the computing process to localize the issue based on the symptoms. Keep your guesses…err…theories…simple. One of the great problems for techs is their tendency to overlook the obvious problems in their desire to dig into the system (Figure 20.12).

Outside the Case

Take a moment to look for clues before you open up the case. Most importantly, use all your senses in the process.

What do you see? Is a connector mangled, or a plastic part clearly damaged? Even if that connector or part works fine, the physical abuse could provide extra information. If the user can't connect to a network, check the cable. Was something rolled over it that could have broken the thin, internal wires? Is that a jelly smear near the jammed optical drive door? (No pun intended, really!) A visual examination of the external computer is important.

When you put your hand on the system unit, does it feel hot? Can you feel or hear the vibrations of the fans? If not, that would be a clue to an overheating or overheated computer. Modern computers can run when overly hot, but generally run very sluggishly. If you run through basic malware fixes, but a computer still runs poorly, think about excessive heat as a potential problem.

If you spend a moment listening to the PC, you might get some clues to problem sources. As you may have noticed while working with computers, a properly running hard drive doesn't make a lot of sound; just a regular hum from the spinning platters. If you hear clicking or grinding sounds from a drive, that's a very bad sign and a very important clue! Excessive thrashing or disk access can likewise lead to some potential problem areas, such as insufficient RAM or a badly fragmented drive.

Finally, don't forget your nose. If you smell the unmistakable odor of ozone, you know that's the smell electronic components give off when they cook or are simply running much too hot.

Inside the Case

Use all your senses when you go inside the system unit as well. Do you see any physical damage? Check the motherboard capacitors if you have a dead PC. Properly working capacitors should be nice and flat on top. They definitely shouldn't look like partly melted batteries or be bulging at the seams. Fans should be spinning. The power supply shouldn't be blistering hot. You should be able to localize sounds better with the case off, and any smell of cooking components will definitely be stronger.

• **Figure 20.12**   Ford the Tech misses the obvious.

As you do your inspection, both outside and inside the case, don't jump to conclusions too quickly. When you see a problem that looks obvious, stop and give yourself an "Are you sure?" moment. Consider the possibility that a problem you've seen 50 times before might *not* be the same thing. Of course, it probably *is* the same problem, but that moment of consideration might save you trouble later.

Okay, so you've decided on a theory that makes sense. It's time to see if your theory *is* actually the problem at hand—give it a test to see if it fixes the problem.

Remember, many components have electrical risk. CRT monitors are under high vacuum and can implode if you drop them!

Test the Theory to Determine Cause

The biggest challenge to fixing a computer is that the theory and the fix pretty much prove themselves at the same time. Let's go back to the situation where the power plug isn't in the wall. You observe that nothing happens when the PC power button is pressed. You check the back of the power supply and see that the power cable is plugged in. You then look at the wall outlet...not plugged in! So you quickly plug it in and *tada*! It works! You're a hero! In this simple case, your theory and your test are done in virtually the same move (Figure 20.13).

Of course, most problems aren't that easy. In many cases, **testing your theory** does nothing more than verify that something is broken. Let's say you install an update for your video driver. You reboot, log in to Windows, and suddenly the screen freaks out. Ah, a bad video driver, right? So to test, you reboot the computer and press F8 to get the boot options menu. You select VGA Mode (2000/XP) or Low Resolution Mode (Vista/7) and reboot. Now the computer boots up just fine. You know the problem, but how do you fix it? Roll back the video driver? Reinstall an older driver? Try downloading another copy of the new driver and installing the video driver again? Any of these solutions may be the right one. Choose one and go for it (Figure 20.14).

Uh oh, your first guess was wrong: the video is still messed up. No worries, just try another one of your theories. In most cases you'll just pick another and try again, but sometimes there's a point where the problem is bigger than you. It might be a problem on a server that you're not authorized to configure. It might be a problem with a user account, and techs in your company aren't allowed to change user accounts. It might be a

• **Figure 20.13**   Ford the Tech is a hero!

• **Figure 20.14**   Ford the Tech takes a chance!

Mike Meyers' CompTIA A+ Guide: Essentials

problem with an in-house program and you don't have the skills to fix it. In these cases, you must *escalate* the problem.

Escalation is the process your company (or sometimes just you) goes through when you—the person assigned to repair a problem—are not able to get the job done. It's okay to escalate because no one can fix every problem. All companies should have some form of escalation policy. It might mean calling your boss. It might mean filling out and sending some in-house form to another department. Escalation is sometimes a more casual process. You might want to start researching the problem online; you might want to refer to in-house documentation to see if this problem has appeared in the past. (See "Document Findings, Actions, and Outcomes" later in this chapter.) You may want to call a coworker to come check it out (Figure 20.15).

• **Figure 20.15**   Ford the Tech asks for help from Scott.

Verify and Prevent

Fantastic! Through either your careful work or escalation, you've solved the problem, or so you think. Remember two items here. First, even though you think it's fixed, the user/customer might not think it's fixed. Second, try to do something to prevent the problem from happening again in the future, if possible.

If a user calls complaining of no response from IT support, always escalate the problem!

Verify Full System Functionality   **Verifying** full system functionality is CompTIA's way to tell you to make sure the user is happy. Let's say a user can't print. You determine that the printer spool is stalled due to a locked-up laser printer. You reset the printer and the jobs all start printing. Job done, right? Well, during your theory testing, you switched the default printer to another laser printer on the third floor. The user doesn't know how to set the default printer back to the one you just fixed.

The best way to verify full system functionality is to have the user do whatever she needs to do on the repaired system for a few minutes while you watch. Any minor errors (such as incorrect default printers) will quickly become apparent, and you might learn some interesting aspects of how the user does her job. Knowing what your users do is critical for good techs to help them do their jobs better (Figure 20.16).

If Applicable, Implement Preventive Measures   A very smart tech once told me, "A truly good support tech's work goal should be to never have to get out of his chair." That's a pretty tall order, but it makes sense to me. Do whatever you can to keep this problem from repeating. For some problems, there are obvious actions to take, such as making sure anti-malware is installed so a computer doesn't get

• **Figure 20.16**   Ford the Tech sticks around and watches.

• Figure 20.17   Ford documents a successful fix.

infected again. Sometimes there's no action to take at all: nothing can prevent a hard drive that decides to die. But you can take one more critical action in almost every case: education. Take advantage of the time with the user to informally train him about the problem. Show him the dangers of malware or tell him that sometimes hard drives just die. The more your users know, the less time you'll spend out of your chair.

Document Findings, Actions, and Outcomes

I think the famous historian George Santayana would have made a great PC technician when he said, "Those who cannot remember the past are condemned to repeat it." As a tech, the last step of every troubleshooting job should be documentation. This documentation might be highly formalized in some organizations, or it might just be a few notes you jot down for your own use, but you must document! What was the problem? What did you do to fix it? What worked? What didn't? The best guide to use for documentation is: "What would I have liked to have known about this problem before I walked up to it?" Good documentation is the strongest sign of a good PC tech (Figure 20.17).

Documenting problems helps you track the troubleshooting history of a machine over time, enabling you to make longer-term determinations about retiring it or changing out more parts. If you and fellow techs fix a specific problem with Mary's machine several times, for example, you might decide to swap out her whole system rather than fix it a fourth time.

Documenting helps fellow techs if they have to follow up on a task you didn't finish or troubleshoot a machine you've worked on previously. The reverse is also true. If you get a call about Frank's computer, for example, and check the records to find other service calls on his computer, you might find that the fix for a particular problem is already documented. This is especially true for user-generated problems. Having documentation of what you did also means you don't have to rely on your memory when your coworker asks what you did to fix the weird problem with Jane's computer a year ago!

Documenting also comes into play when you or a user has an accident onsite. If your colleague Joe drops a monitor on his foot and breaks both the monitor and his foot, for example, you need to fill out an *incident report*, just as you would with any kind of accident: electrical, chemical, or physical. An **incident report** should detail what happened and where it happened. This helps your supervisors take the appropriate actions quickly and efficiently.

■ Tech Toolkit

Way back in Chapter 2, "Operational Procedures," you learned the basic parts of a **tech toolkit**—a Phillips-head screwdriver and a few other useful tools, such as a Torx wrench and a pair of tweezers. Any good tech makes a point to carry around at least these tools (Figure 20.18). Over time, you'll add more tools as your experience grows. But your toolkit won't stop at Phillips screwdrivers and Torx wrenches. You should include two other types of tools in your tech toolkit: utilities and field replaceable units (FRUs).

Utilities

Windows comes with plenty of handy utilities, but there are times when you need to use stronger tools than these. The PC industry has thousands of third-party utilities that techs might use to diagnose and repair PCs. Sadly, there is no single selection of tools I can tell you to get: the tools one experienced tech uses differ from the tools I use based on experience, skills, and job functions. That doesn't mean you haven't been hearing my opinions! Throughout this book you've seen quite a few third-party utilities, and many of them are on the CD that comes with your book for you to use right away. Given that you already have my opinion on so many tools, let's instead talk about the types of third-party tools you'll find in most tech toolkits.

Many techs like to challenge me on the idea of carrying around tools. They say, "I know what I like; I'll just download them!" Well, sometimes you don't have Internet access and sometimes you need tools ready to go (see malware cleaners). Granted, there are a number of tools that I would never carry on me. For example, device drivers change so often that keeping a copy on disk is a waste of time. The tools I'm listing here are the ones I promise you want on disk, ready to go when you run into trouble.

• Figure 20.18   Typical technician toolkit

 Tech Tip

Tech Forums
The Tech Forums on the Total Seminars Web site (www.totalsem .com/forums) has an entire section dedicated to nothing more than what we call "Cool Tools." If you want an opinion on hundreds of tech utilities, come over to the Tech Forums and see what we like…and what we dislike.

Malware Cleaners

Ask any tech who works for Best Buy's Geek Squad, "What do you spend the most time doing on jobs?" and they will reply, "Cleaning malware." The first tech utilities you want in your toolkit are malware cleaners. To truly do it right, put your malware cleaners on a bootable optical disc because malware can sometimes attack a malware cleanup tool as you install. If you're not sure what to try first, grab a copy of the Ultimate Boot CD and try some of their fine cleanup tools.

Anti-Malware

After you clean the machine, make sure you have a copy of an anti-malware program that you can install so the user's machine doesn't get corrupted again. We talked about some of the popular freeware versions, but plenty of techs strongly prefer the pay versions and keep copies to sell to their customers.

Boot Tools

You need a tool that's better than the System Configuration utility at controlling what programs autostart on your Windows PC. OK, in this case, one tool stands out so strongly that you have to get it: Mark Russinovich's superb AUTORUNS. It's vastly superior to the built-in System Configuration utility and gives you incredible control of everything that's autostarting. Sure there are others, but I love AUTORUNS. Get it at www.sysinternals.com.

Password Clearer

If you lose a Windows password, especially the Administrator password, and you can't log on to a system, you're in trouble. A number of tools let you reset any user's passwords. These programs don't let you *see* a password, only reset them, so if you have a user with encrypted folders, those won't be recoverable. None of these programs are easy to use, but when the alternative is not logging in, they will save you. Pretty much all of these programs run from a boot CD.

ZIP File Tool

Windows can read many compressed file formats (such as ZIP), but so many others are in use that it's often a good idea to have your own copy handy. I like 7-Zip (www.7-zip.org/), but there are plenty of equally popular alternatives.

Backup

Odds are good that from time to time you'll need to do a backup for a system. I keep an external hard drive with a backup tool so I can go in fast and make backups of the most critical files.

Don't Forget Your Thumb Drives!

I guess I'm showing my age when I talk about putting all these tools on CD media. Sorry, I'm old. Almost all of these tools work equally well on USB thumb drives. I keep my tools on CD media because I still run into the occasional system that doesn't have CMOS settings for a bootable thumb drive.

Field Replaceable Units (FRUs)

Always carry several **field replaceable units (FRUs)**—a fancy way to say *spare parts*—when going to a job site or workstation. Having several known good components on hand enables you to swap out a potentially bad piece of hardware to see if that's the problem. Different technicians will have different FRUs. A printer specialist might carry a number of fusers, for example. Your employer will also have a big effect on what is an FRU and what is not. I generally carry a couple of RAM sticks (DDR, DDR2, and DDR3), a PCI video card, a NIC, and a spare power supply.

 The CompTIA A+ Essentials exam expects you to know that FRUs are computer components such as cards, memory, hard drives, processors, or power supplies that can be easily replaced in the field.

Tech Tip

Why PCI?

I keep a PCI video card in my kit because every computer made in the past ten years has PCI slots. If you run into a system with video problems, you can almost always simply slap in the PCI video card and discover quickly whether the AGP or PCIe video card or card slot is a problem. If the computer boots up with the PCI video card but fails on the PCIe card, for example, you know that either the PCIe card or the slot is causing the problem.

Chapter 20 Review

■ Chapter Summary

After reading this chapter and completing the exercises, you should understand the following about working as a tech.

Describe how computers work

- Good techs must know how their systems are supposed to work when working properly, must be able to calm workers and supervisors and get answers to relevant questions, and must be able to troubleshoot and fix computer problems. A question you must be able to answer is, "What can be causing this problem?"

- When you run a program, computers work through three stages of the four-stage computing process: input, processing, and output. Input requires special input devices such as a keyboard or mouse. The operating system provides the interface and tools so the CPU and other chips can process requests. The output devices, such as the monitor, speakers, and printer, tell you the computer has interpreted your commands. For all this to work, the PC must have electricity and proper AC/DC voltage and amperage.

- When you press a keyboard key, the keyboard controller reads the grid of your keyboard, discovers your input, and then sends the information to the CPU. The CPU understands the keyboard controller because of a small program that was loaded into RAM from the ROM BIOS on the motherboard when the PC booted up.

- Good techs understand the components involved in inputting, processing, and outputting, including the devices that store data, such as hard drives.

Implement a troubleshooting methodology

- The first step in fixing a computer problem is to identify the problem by talking to the client. To determine what the computer is doing or not doing, first allow the client to describe the situation, then ask leading questions to elicit answers.

- Most people feel defensive when asked to explain computer problems, so it is your job to put them at ease by asking the right kinds of questions. Questions such as "What did you do?" generally aren't much help. A better question might be, "When did it last work?" By taking the user explicitly out of the question, you show that you won't accuse them or judge their actions.

- Refrain from using computer jargon, acronyms, or abbreviations. Users are unlikely to be familiar with them and may get confused and think you are talking down to them. Ask simple questions that don't use technical lingo. Have the user physically show you the problem, demonstrating what is happening or what is not happening.

- Once you have ascertained the problem the user is having with the computer, it is important to back up critical data. Unless the hard drive is dead, you should have no reason to lose any data that was accessible before.

- Once you have secured the user's data, you need to establish a theory of probable cause. In other words, look at the machine and determine why it's not working correctly. Don't overlook the obvious, such as a disconnected power or network cable. Use all of your senses: look for damaged components, feel for excessive heat or lack of vibration, listen for any unusual or telltale sounds, and sniff the air for the unmistakable smell of ozone.

- If you run into something more complex than a disconnected cord, don't be afraid to try multiple solutions. Take a chance and see if it works. If you have run out of ideas, escalate the problem; no one person can solve all problems.

- After you have successfully solved the user's problem, have the user sit down and perform the task. This enables you to verify full system functionality with the user.

- Once everything is verified and the customer is happy, make sure to document your findings thoroughly. Keeping records is important. If you or a colleague encounters a similar problem in the future, the answer will be readily available.

Describe a technician's toolkit

- Troubleshooting is more art than science, and as such, there is no step-by-step list of actions to follow. You need to be flexible.

- A well-stocked tech toolkit consists of a Phillips-head screwdriver, flat-head screwdriver, Torx wrench, nut driver, tweezers, grabber tool, flashlight, magnifying glass, and anti-static wrist strap. You should also carry several FRUs. The FRUs you carry will depend on what kind of tech you are, but the FRUs most techs should carry include a few sticks each of DDR, DDR2, and DDR3 RAM, PCI video card, NIC, and power supply.

- Malware is the most common source of consumer computer problems today. Make sure your kit is well stocked with antivirus and other (preferably boot-time) malware removers.

- Lost logon passwords are a common problem, so your kit should include some form of password clearing utility. Remember, these just clear the existing password; they do not show it to you.

- Other handy tools to have are zip/archive extractors and backup utilities. Having these and the rest of your kit and a handy bootable thumb drive can make your job much easer onsite.

◼ Key Terms

computing process *(621)*
document *(632)*
escalate *(631)*
field replaceable unit (FRU) *(634)*
identify the problem *(628)*
incident report *(632)*

stream loading *(625)*
tech toolkit *(632)*
test the theory *(630)*
theory of probable cause *(628)*
troubleshooting theory *(627)*
verify *(631)*

◼ Key Term Quiz

Use the Key Terms list to complete the sentences that follow. Not all terms will be used.

1. A "spare part" you carry with you, such as an extra stick of RAM or a video card, is called a(n) _____.

2. A Phillips-head screwdriver and a few other useful tools should be in your _____.

3. Understanding the _____ enables you to troubleshoot problems more efficiently.

4. When asking questions to *identify the problem* remember to use a nonaccusatory tone.

5. Better online applications use *stream loading* to download updated information and data constantly.

6. Once you have determined the problem with the machine and come up with probable causes, you should *test the theory*

7. Once you have successfully repaired the machine, it is important to *verify* with the user that everything is working correctly.

8. If you can't solve a troubleshooting problem, the next step is to *escalate* the problem to a higher-level tech.

9. A(n) *theory of probable cause* is your guess at what is wrong with the machine.

10. A(n) *incident report* gives the details about an accident on the job site.

◼ Multiple-Choice Quiz

1. At what point during a repair should you escalate the problem?

   A. After the user describes the first problem

   B. As soon as you understand the problem

   C. As soon as you have a solution

   D. When you have tried all your theories and still can't resolve the problem

2. While working at the help desk, you get a call from a distraught user who says she has a blank screen. What would be useful follow-up questions? (Select two.)

   A. Is the computer turned on?

   B. Is the monitor turned on?

C. Did you reboot?

D. What did you do?

3. While working at the help desk, you get a call from Sharon in accounting. She's lost a file that she knows she saved to her hard drive. Which of the following statements would direct Sharon to open her My Documents folder in the most efficient and professional manner?

   A. Sharon, check My Documents.

   B. Sharon, a lot of programs save files to a default folder, often to a folder called My Documents. Let's look there first. Click on the Start button and move the mouse until the cursor hovers over My Documents. Then click the left mouse button and tell me what you see when My Documents opens.

   C. Probably just defaulted to My Docs. Why don't you open Excel or whatever program you used to make the file, and then open a document, and point it to My Documents.

   D. Look Sharon, I know you're a clueless noob when it comes to computers, but how could somebody lose a file? Just open up My Documents, and look there for the file.

4. What tool should be in every technician's toolkit?

   A. Pliers

   B. Hammer

   C. Flat-head screwdriver

   D. Phillips-head screwdriver

5. Al in marketing calls in for tech support, complaining that he has a dead PC. What is a good first question or questions to begin troubleshooting the problem?

   A. Did the computer ever work?

   B. When did the computer last work?

   C. When you say "dead," what do you mean? What happens when you press the power button?

   D. What did you do?

6. While working at the help desk, you get a call from Bryce in Sales complaining that he can't print and every time he clicks on the network shared drive, his computer stops and freezes. He says he thinks it's his hard driver. What would be a good follow-up question or statement?

A. Bryce, you're an idiot. Don't touch anything. I'll be there in five minutes.

B. Okay, let's take this one step at a time. You seem to have two problems, one with printing and the second with the network shared drive, right?

C. First, it's not a hard *driver*, but a hard *drive*. It doesn't have anything to do with the network share or printing, so that's just not right.

D. When could you last print?

7. Phoebe's computer was recently updated during the companywide patch push. Now all Phoebe gets is a black screen. What should you check first?

   A. Take the monitor back to the maintenance room and check it with known good hardware.

   B. Check to make sure the monitor is properly plugged into the system unit and is getting power.

   C. Replace Phoebe's video card.

   D. Take Phoebe's computer back to the maintenance room and reimage it.

8. You've just installed new printer drivers into Roland's computer for the big networked laser printer. What should you do to complete the assignment?

   A. Document that you installed new printer drivers.

   B. Tell Roland to print a test page.

   C. Print a test page and go to the printer to verify the results. Assuming everything works, you're finished.

   D. Print a test page and go to the printer to verify the results. Document that you installed new printer drivers successfully.

9. After examining Paul's computer, you think the problem has something to do with his video card, but you're not certain. Should you try your uncertain fix, escalate the problem, or something else?

   A. Escalate; you need to be 100% correct before you attempt a fix.

   B. Stall for time and hope the problem fixes itself.

   C. Calmly explain to Paul that his computer cannot be fixed.

   D. Take a chance and try your first guess.

10. Upon responding to a coworker's request for help, you find her away from her desk and Microsoft Excel on the screen with a spreadsheet open. How do you proceed?

  A. Go find the coworker and ask her to exit her applications before touching her computer.

  B. Exit Excel, save changes to the document, and begin troubleshooting the computer.

  C. Exit Excel without saving changes to the document and begin troubleshooting the computer.

  D. Use the Save As command to save the file with a new name, exit Excel, and begin troubleshooting the computer.

11. You have been working all afternoon on a user's workstation and you have finally fixed the user's problem. What should you do now?

  A. Tell the user the computer is fixed and leave.

  B. Invite the user to sit down and use the computer to make sure the problem is completely gone from the user's perspective.

  C. Tell the user the machine is fixed, go back to your office and document the problem.

  D. As you leave for the tenth time, complain to the user that you are tired of always fixing his computer.

12. Which of the following makes a good field replaceable unit?

  A. Video card

  B. 20-inch CRT monitor

  C. Set of 2.1 speakers

  D. Printer

13. After replacing a keyboard a user has spilled coffee on for the fifth time, what should you say to the user?

  A. I can't guarantee the new keyboard will work if it gets dirty.

  B. I can't guarantee the new keyboard will work if you continue to spill coffee on it.

  C. These keyboards are expensive. Next time we replace one because you spilled coffee, it's coming out of your paycheck.

  D. You need to be more careful with your coffee.

14. When is it appropriate to yell at a user?

  A. When he screws up the second time

  B. When he interrupts your troubleshooting

  C. When he screws up the fifth time

  D. Never

15. Once you figure out what can be causing a computer to malfunction, what's your next step?

  A. Escalate the problem to a higher-level tech.

  B. Talk to the user about stream loading and other geeky things because your knowledge will put him or her at ease.

  C. Test your theory, starting with the obvious.

  D. Write an incident report to document the problem.

■ Essay Quiz

1. A friend is considering turning his computer hobby into a career and has asked your advice on outfitting himself as a freelance computer technician. What tools can you recommend to your friend?

2. A user phones you at your desk and reports that after pressing the power button on his computer and hearing the hard drive spin up, his screen remains blank. What questions can you ask to determine the problem? Remember, avoid an accusing tone.

3. Briefly explain the various steps in troubleshooting theory.

Lab Projects

• Lab Project 20.1

Think of items you would like to always have on hand as FRUs. Using the Internet, find prices for these items. Make a list of your items and their individual costs; then find the total cost for your equipment.

• Lab Project 20.2

Visit your local computer store or hardware store and purchase the items for a hardware tech toolkit. You may want to include a variety of screwdrivers, an anti-static wrist strap, tweezers, or other items.

• Lab Project 20.3

Create a software tech toolkit on CD or a USB flash drive loaded with a variety of drivers for NICs and video cards. Include free/open-source antivirus software, anti-spyware software, and any other software tools you think might be useful.

Mapping to the CompTIA A+ Essentials Objectives

CompTIA A+ Essentials Objectives Map

Topic	Chapter(s)
Domain 1.0 Hardware	
1.1 Categorize storage devices and backup media	
FDD	3, 9
HDD	3, 9
Solid state vs. magnetic	9
Optical drives	3, 10
CD / DVD / RW / Blu-Ray	3, 10
Removable storage	4, 9, 10, 12
Tape drive	4, 10
Solid state (e.g. thumb drive, flash, SD cards, USB)	9
External CD-RW and hard drive	9
Hot swappable devices and non-hot swappable devices	10
1.2 Explain motherboard components, types, and features	
Form Factor	7
ATX / BTX	7
micro ATX	7
NLX	7
I/O interfaces	3, 12, 13, 15, 16
Sound	3, 13
Video	3, 13
USB 1.1 and 2.0	3, 12
Serial	3, 12
IEEE 1394 / Firewire	3, 12
Parallel	3, 15
NIC	3, 16
Modem	3, 12
PS/2	12
Memory slots	3, 6
RIMM	6
DIMM	3, 6

Topic	Chapter(s)
SODIMM	6
SIMM	6
Processor sockets	3, 5, 7
Bus architecture	5, 7
Bus slots	7, 14
PCI	7
AGP	7
PCIe	7
AMR	7
CNR	7
PCMCIA	14
PATA	9
IDE	9
EIDE	9
SATA, eSATA	3, 9, 10
Contrast RAID (levels 0, 1, 5)	9
Chipsets	5, 7
BIOS / CMOS / Firmware	7
POST	7
CMOS battery	7
Riser card / daughterboard	7
1.3 Classify power supplies' types and characteristics	
AC adapter	8
ATX proprietary	8
Voltage, wattage, and capacity	8
Voltage selector switch	8
Pins (20, 24)	8
1.4 Explain the purpose and characteristics of CPUs and their features	
Identify CPU types	5
AMD	5
Intel	5
Hyperthreading	5
Multi core	5
Dual core	5
Triple core	5
Quad core	5
Onchip cache	5
L1	5
L2	5
Speed (real vs. actual)	5
32 bit vs. 64 bit	5

Topic	Chapter(s)
1.8 Install and configure peripherals and input devices	
Mouse	12
Keyboard	12
Bar code reader	12
Multimedia (e.g. web and digital cameras, MIDI, microphones)	12
Biometric devices	12
Touch screen	12
KVM switch	12
1.9 Summarize the function and types of adapter cards	
Video	7, 13
PCI	7, 13
PCIe	7, 13
AGP	7, 13
Multimedia	13
Sound card	13
TV tuner cards	13
Capture cards	13
I/O	3, 9, 12, 15
SCSI	3, 9
Serial	3, 12
USB	3, 12
Parallel	3, 15
Communications	16
NIC	16
Modem	16
1.10 Install, configure, and optimize laptop components and features	
Expansion devices	14
PCMCIA cards	14
PCI Express cards	14
Docking station	14
Communication connections	14, 16
Bluetooth	14
Infrared	14
Cellular WAN	14
Ethernet	14, 16
Modem	14, 16
Power and electrical input devices	8, 14
Auto-switching	8
Fixed input power supplies	8
Batteries	8, 14
Input devices	14
Stylus / digitizer	14
Function keys	14
Point devices (e.g. touchpad, point stick / track point)	14

Topic	Chapter(s)
1.11 Install and configure printers	
Differentiate between printer types	15
Laser	15
Inkjet	15
Thermal	15
Impact	15
Local vs. network printers	15
Printer drivers (compatibility)	15
Consumables	15
Domain 2.0 Troubleshooting, Repair and Maintenance	
2.1 Given a scenario, explain the troubleshooting theory	
Identify the problem	20
Question the user and identify user changes to computer and perform backups before making changes	20
Establish a theory of probable cause (question the obvious)	20
Test the theory to determine cause	20
Once theory is confirmed determine next steps to resolve problem	20
If theory is not confirmed re-establish new theory or escalate	20
Establish a plan of action to resolve the problem and implement the solution	20
Verify full system functionality and if applicable implement preventative measures	20
Document findings, actions and outcomes	20
2.2 Given a scenario, explain and interpret common hardware and operating system symptoms and their causes	
OS-related symptoms	4, 7, 8, 11, 12, 15
Bluescreen	11
System lock-up	8
Input/output device	12
Application install	4
Start or load	11
Windows specific printing problems	15
Print spool stalled	15
Incorrect / incompatible driver	15
Hardware-related symptoms	5, 7, 8, 10, 16, 20
Excessive heat	5, 8, 20
Noise	5, 20
Odors	10, 20
Status light indicators	16
Alerts	4, 7, 8
Visible damage (e.g. cable, plastic)	5, 20
Use documentation and resources	15, 20
User / installation manuals	15
Internet / web based	20
Training materials	20

Topic	Chapter(s)
2.3 Given a scenario, determine the troubleshooting methods and tools for printers	
Manage print jobs	15
Print spooler	15
Printer properties and settings	15
Print a test page	15
2.4 Given a scenario, explain and interpret common laptop issues and determine the appropriate basic troubleshooting method	
Issues	14
Power conditions	14
Video	14
Keyboard	14
Pointer	14
Stylus	14
Wireless card issues	14
Methods	14
Verify power (e.g. LEDs, swap AC adapter)	14
Remove unneeded peripherals	14
Plug in external monitor	14
Toggle Fn keys or hardware switches	14
Check LCD cutoff switch	14
Verify backlight functionality and pixelation	14
Check switch for built-in WIFI antennas or external antennas	14
2.5 Given a scenario, integrate common preventative maintenance techniques	
Physical inspection	5
Updates	4, 7, 19
Driver	7
Firmware	7
OS	4
Security	19
Scheduling preventative maintenance	4
Defrag	4
Scandisk	4
Check disk	4
Startup programs	4
Use of appropriate repair tools and cleaning materials	5, 19, 21, 22
Compressed air	5, 14
Lint-free cloth	14
Computer vacuum and compressors	5, 14
Power devices	8
Appropriate source such as power strip, surge protector, or UPS	8
Ensuring proper environment	14
Backup procedures	4

Topic	Chapter(s)
Domain 3.0 Operating Systems and Software – Unless otherwise noted, operating systems referred to within include Microsoft Windows 2000, Windows XP Professional, XP Home, XP MediaCenter, Windows Vista Home, Home Premium, Business and Ultimate.	
3.1 Compare and contrast the different Windows Operating Systems and their features	
Windows 2000, Windows XP 32 bit vs. 64 bit, Windows Vista 32 bit vs. 64 bit	4, 5
Side bar, Aero, UAC, minimum system requirements, system limits	4
Windows 2000 and newer – upgrade paths and requirements	11
Terminology (32 bit vs. 64 bit – x86 vs. x64)	4, 5
Application compatibility, installed program locations (32 bit vs. 64 bit), Windows compatibility mode	4
User interface, start bar layout	4
3.2 Given a scenario, demonstrate proper use of user interfaces	
Windows Explorer	4
My Computer	4
Control Panel	4
Command prompt utilities	16, 18
telnet	18
ping	16
ipconfig	16
Run line utilities	4, 13
msconfig	4
msinfo32	4
Dxdiag	13
Cmd	4
REGEDIT	4
My Network Places	4
Taskbar / systray	4
Administrative tools	4
Performance monitor, Event Viewer, Services, Computer Management	4
MMC	4
Task Manager	4
Start Menu	4
3.3 Explain the process and steps to install and configure the Windows OS	
File systems	4, 11
FAT32 vs. NTFS	4, 11
Directory structures	4
Create folders	4
Navigate directory structures	4
Files	4, 14
Creation	11
Extensions	4, 13

Topic	Chapter(s)
Attributes	4
Permissions	4
Verification of hardware compatibility and minimum requirements	11
Installation methods	11
Boot media such as CD, floppy or USB	10, 11
Network installation	11
Install from image	11
Recover CD	4
Factory recovery partition	11
Operating system installation options	11
File system type	11
Network configuration	11
Repair install	11
Disk preparation order	11
Format drive	11
Partition	11
Start installation	11
Device Manager	4, 7
Verify	7
Install and update devices drivers	7
Driver signing	4
User data migration – User State Migration Tool (USMT)	11
Virtual memory	4
Configure power management	14
Suspend	14
Wake on LAN	14
Sleep timers	14
Hibernate	14
Standby	14
Demonstrate safe removal of peripherals	12
3.4 Explain the basics of boot sequences, methods, and startup utilities	
Disk boot order / device priority	11
Types of boot devices (disk, network, USB, other)	11
Boot options	4
Safe Mode	4, 19
Boot to restore point	4
Recovery options	4
Automated System Recovery (ASR)	4
Emergency Repair Disk (ERD)	4
Recovery Console	4

Topic	Chapter(s)
Domain 4.0 Networking	
4.1 Summarize the basics of networking fundamentals, including technologies, devices, and protocols	
Basics of configuring IP addressing and TCP/IP properties (DHCP, DNS)	16
Bandwidth and latency	18
Status indicators	16
Protocols (TCP/IP, NETBIOS)	16
Full-duplex, half-duplex	16
Basics of workgroups and domains	16
Common ports: HTTP, FTP, POP, SMTP, TELNET, HTTPS	18
LAN / WAN	16
Hub, switch and router	16
Identify Virtual Private Networks (VPN)	18
Basics class identification	16
4.2 Categorize network cables and connectors and their implementations	
Cables	16
Plenum / PVC	16
UTP (e.g. CAT3, CAT5 / 5e, CAT6)	16
STP	16
Fiber	16
Coaxial cable	16
Connectors	16
RJ45	16
RJ11	16
4.3 Compare and contrast the different network types	
Broadband	18
DSL	18
Cable	18
Satellite	18
Fiber	18
Dial-up	18
Wireless	17
All 802.11 types	17
WEP	17
WPA	17
SSID	17
MAC filtering	17
DHCP settings	16, 18
Bluetooth	17
Cellular	17

Topic	Chapter(s)
Domain 5.0 Security	
5.1 Explain the basic principles of security concepts and technologies	
Encryption technologies	17
Data wiping / hard drive destruction / hard drive recycling	11
Software firewall	19
Port security	19
Exceptions	19
Authentication technologies	12, 19
User name	19
Password	19
Biometrics	12
Smart cards	19
Basics of data sensitivity and data security	19
Compliance	19
Classifications	19
Social engineering	19
5.2 Summarize the following security features	
Wireless encryption	17
WEPx and WPAx	17
Client configuration (SSID)	17
Malicious software protection	19
Viruses	19
Trojans	19
Worms	19
Spam	19
Spyware	19
Adware	19
Grayware	19
BIOS Security	7
Drive lock	7
Passwords	7
Intrusion detection	7
TPM	7
Password management / password complexity	19
Locking workstation	4, 7
Hardware	7
Operating system	4, 19
Biometrics	12
Fingerprint scanner	12

Topic	Chapter(s)
Domain 6.0 Operational Procedure	
6.1 Outline the purpose of appropriate safety and environmental procedures and given a scenario apply them	
ESD	2
EMI	2
Network interference	2
Magnets	2
RFI	2
Cordless phone interference	2
Microwaves	2
Electrical safety	8, 13, 14, 15
CRT	13
Power supply	8
Inverter	14
Laser printers	15
Matching power requirements of equipment with power distribution and UPSs	8
Material Safety Data Sheets (MSDS)	15
Cable management	2
Avoiding trip hazards	2
Physical safety	2
Heavy devices	2
Hot components	2
Environmental – consider proper disposal procedures	15
6.2 Given a scenario, demonstrate the appropriate use of communication skills and professionalism in the workplace	
Use proper language – avoid jargon, acronyms, slang	2
Maintain a positive attitude	2
Listen and do not interrupt a customer	2
Be culturally sensitive	2
Be on time	2
If late contact the customer	2
Avoid distractions	2
Personal calls	2
Talking to co-workers while interacting with customers	2
Personal interruptions	2
Dealing with a difficult customer or situation	2
Avoid arguing with customers and/or being defensive	2
Do not minimize customers' problems	2
Avoid being judgmental	2
Clarify customer statements	2
Ask open-ended questions to narrow the scope of the problem	2
Restate the issue or question to verify understanding	2

Topic	Chapter(s)
Set and meet expectations / timeline and communicate status with the customer	2
Offer different repair / replacement options if applicable	2
Provide proper documentation on the services provided	2
Follow up with customer / user at a later date to verify satisfaction	2
Deal appropriately with customers' confidential materials	2

About the CD

Mike Meyers has put together a bunch of resources that will help you prepare for the CompTIA A+ Essentials exam and that you will find invaluable in your career as a PC Tech. The CD-ROM included with this book comes complete with a sample version of the Total Tester practice exam software with one full practice exam, all the Chapter Review questions from the book, a searchable electronic copy of the book, a document from CompTIA with a list of acronyms that you should know for the CompTIA A+ Essentials exam, a complete list of the objectives for the CompTIA A+ Essentials exam, a copy of several freeware and shareware programs that Mike talks about in the book, and a sample of LearnKey's online training featuring Mike Meyers. The practice test and video software are easy to install on any Windows 98/NT/2000/XP/Vista/7 computer, and must be installed to access the Total Tester practice exam and LearnKey video sample. The eBook and CompTIA A+ acronyms and objectives lists are Adobe Acrobat files. If you don't have Adobe Acrobat Reader, it is available for installation on the CD-ROM.

System Requirements

The software on the CD-ROM requires Windows 98 or higher, Internet Explorer 5.0 or above, and 50 MB of hard disk space for full installation. To access the online training from LearnKey, you must have Windows Media Player 9, which will be automatically installed when you launch the online training.

Installing and Running Total Tester

If your computer's CD-ROM drive is configured to Autorun, the CD-ROM will automatically start upon inserting the disk. If the Autorun feature does not launch the CD's splash screen, browse to the CD-ROM and double-click the Launch.exe icon.

From the splash screen, you may install Total Tester by clicking the *Install A+ Practice Exams* button. This will begin the installation process, create a program group named Total Seminars, and put an icon on your desktop. To run Total Tester, go to Start | Programs | Total Seminars or just double-click the icon on your desktop.

To uninstall the Total Tester software, go to Start | Settings | Control Panel | Add/Remove Programs and select the A+ Total Tester program. Select Remove, and Windows will completely uninstall the software.

About Total Tester

The best way to prepare for the CompTIA A+ Essentials exam is to read the book and then test your knowledge and review. We have included a sample of Total Seminars' practice exam software to help you test your knowledge as you study. Total Tester provides you with a simulation of the actual exam. There is a suite called A+ 701 split that contains a sample 701 exam that can be taken in either practice or final mode. Practice mode provides an assistance window with hints, references to the book, an explanation of the answer, and the ability to check your answer as you take the test. Both practice and final modes provide an overall grade and a grade broken down by certification objective. There is also a suite called A+ 701 review. This suite has five exams. Each exam covers Chapter Review question from four chapters. To launch a test, select Suites from the menu at the top, then select an exam. Additional practice exams are available for both of the CompTIA A+ exams. Visit our Web site at www.totalsem.com or call 800-446-6004 for more information.

◾ Accessing the eBook, CompTIA A+ Acronyms, and CompTIA A+ Exam Objectives Lists

You will find these documents useful in your preparation for the exam. To access these PDF documents, first be sure you have a copy of Adobe Acrobat Reader installed. If you don't have Acrobat Reader installed on your system, you can install it from the CD-ROM by clicking the *Install Adobe Acrobat Reader* button. Once you have installed Acrobat Reader, simply select the document you want to view from the CD-ROM's splash screen to open and view the document.

◾ Shareware and Freeware

Mike has put together copies of some of his favorite freeware and shareware programs that are mentioned in this book. The CD-ROM includes a list with short descriptions of the programs. To use these programs, select the Shareware and Freeware option on the CD-ROM splash screen. The next menu lists each program. Select a program and follow the installation instructions to load the utility on your system.

◾ LearnKey Online Training

If you like Mike's writing style, you will love listening to him in his LearnKey video training. The CD-ROM includes sample videos of Mike covering several different topics. Check out Mike's video training. If you like it, you can purchase the full 21 hours of interactive video training by contacting Mike's company, Total Seminars, at www.totalsem.com or 800-446-6004. The *Install LearnKey demo* button will launch a wizard to install the software on your computer. Follow the instructions on the wizard to complete the installation. To run the LearnKey demo, use Start | Programs | LearnKey or just double-click the icon on your desktop. Enter a user name and password to begin your video training.

■ Technical Support

For questions regarding the Total Tester software, visit www.totalsem.com or e-mail support@totalsem.com, or visit http://mhp.softwareassist.com/. For customers outside the United States, e-mail international_cs@mcgraw-hill.com.

LearnKey Technical Support

For technical problems with the software (installation, operation, or uninstalling the software) and for questions regarding LearnKey Video Training, e-mail techsupport@learnkey.com.

GLOSSARY

10BaseT Ethernet LAN designed to run on UTP cabling. 10BaseT runs at 10 megabits per second. The maximum length for the cabling between the NIC and the hub (or switch, repeater, etc.) is 100 meters. It uses baseband signaling. No industry standard spelling exists, so sometimes written 10BASE-T or 10Base-T.

100BaseT Generic term for an Ethernet cabling system designed to run at 100 megabits per second on UTP cabling. It uses baseband signaling. No industry standard spelling exists, so sometimes written 100BASE-T or 100Base-T.

1000BaseT Gigabit Ethernet on UTP.

2.1 Speaker setup consisting of two stereo speakers combined with a subwoofer.

3.5-inch floppy drive All modern floppy disk drives are of this size; the format was introduced in 1986 and is one of the longest surviving pieces of computer hardware.

34-pin ribbon cable Type of cable used by floppy disk drives.

3-D graphics Video technology that attempts to create images with the same depth and texture as objects seen in the real world.

40-pin ribbon cable PATA cable used to attach EIDE devices (such as hard drives) or ATAPI devices (such as optical drives) to a system. (*See* PATA.)

5.1 speaker system Four satellite speakers plus a center speaker and a subwoofer.

8.3 naming system File-naming convention that specified a maximum of eight characters for a filename, followed by a 3-character file extension. Has been replaced by LFN (long filename) support.

80-wire ribbon cable PATA cable used to attach fast EIDE devices (such as ATA/100 hard drives) or ATAPI devices (such as optical drives) to a system. (*See* PATA.)

802.11a Wireless networking standard that operates in the 5-GHz band with a theoretical maximum throughput of 54 Mbps.

802.11b Wireless networking standard that operates in the 2.4-GHz band with a theoretical maximum throughput of 11 Mbps.

802.11g Wireless networking standard that operates in the 2.4-GHz band with a theoretical maximum throughput of 54 Mbps and is backward compatible with 802.11b.

802.11n Wireless networking standard that can operate in both the 2.4-GHz and 5-GHz bands and uses MIMO to achieve a theoretical maximum throughput of 100+ Mbps.

A/V sync Process of synchronizing audio and video.

AC (alternating current) Type of electricity in which the flow of electrons alternates direction, back and forth, in a circuit.

AC'97 Sound card standard for lower-end audio devices; created when most folks listened to stereo sound at best.

access control Security concept using physical security, authentication, users and groups, and security policies.

ACPI (Advanced Configuration and Power Interface) Power management specification that far surpasses its predecessor, APM, by providing support for hot-swappable devices and better control of power modes.

activation Process of confirming that an installed copy of a Microsoft product (most commonly Windows or a Microsoft Office application) is legitimate. Usually done at the end of software installation.

active matrix Type of liquid crystal display that replaced the passive matrix technology used in most portable computer displays. Also called *TFT* (*thin film transistor*).

active partition On a hard drive, primary partition that contains an operating system.

active PFC (power factor correction) Circuitry built into PC power supplies to reduce harmonics.

ad hoc mode   Decentralized wireless network mode, otherwise known as peer-to-peer mode, where each wireless node is in meshed contact with every other node.

Add or Remove Programs   Applet allowing users to manually add or remove a program from the system.

address bus   Wires leading from the CPU to the memory controller chip (usually the Northbridge) that enable the CPU to address RAM. Also used by the CPU for I/O addressing. An internal electronic channel from the microprocessor to random access memory, along which the addresses of memory storage locations are transmitted. Like a post office box, each memory location has a distinct number or address; the address bus provides the means by which the microprocessor can access every location in memory.

address space   Total amount of memory addresses that an address bus can contain.

administrative shares   Administrator tool to give local admins access to hard drives and system root folders.

Administrative Tools   Group of Control Panel applets, including Computer Management, Event Viewer, and Reliability and Performance Monitor.

Administrator account   User account, created when the OS is first installed, that is allowed complete, unfettered access to the system without restriction.

Administrators group   List of members with complete administrator privileges.

ADSL (asymmetric digital subscriber line)   Fully digital, dedicated connection to the telephone system that provides average download speeds of 7 Mbps and upload speeds of 512 Kbps.

Advanced Startup Options menu   Menu that can be reached during the boot process that offers advanced OS startup options, such as boot in Safe mode or boot into Last Known Good Configuration.

adware   Type of malicious program that downloads ads to a user's computer, generating undesirable network traffic.

Aero   The Windows Vista desktop environment. Aero adds some interesting aesthetic effects such as window transparency and Flip 3D.

AGP (Accelerated Graphics Port)   32/64-bit expansion slot designed by Intel specifically for video that runs at

66 MHz and yields a throughput of at least 254 Mbps. Later versions (2×, 4×, 8×) give substantially higher throughput.

algorithm   Set of rules for solving a problem in a given number of steps.

ALU (arithmetic logic unit)   CPU logic circuits that perform basic arithmetic (add, subtract, multiply, and divide).

AMD (Advanced Micro Devices)   CPU and chipset manufacturer that competes with Intel. Produces the popular Phenom, Athlon, Sempron, Turion, and Duron microprocessors; also produces video card processors under its ATI brand.

AMI (American Megatrends, Inc)   Major producer of BIOS software for motherboards, as well as many other computer-related components and software.

amperes (amps or A)   Unit of measure for amperage, or electrical current.

amplitude   Loudness of a sound card.

AMR (Audio/Modem Riser)   Proprietary slot used on some motherboards to provide a sound inference–free connection for modems, sound cards, and NICs.

analog   Device that uses a physical quantity, such as length or voltage, to represent the value of a number. By contrast, digital storage relies on a coding system of numeric units.

anti-aliasing   In computer imaging, blending effect that smoothes sharp contrasts between two regions— e.g., jagged lines or different colors. Reduces jagged edges of text or objects. In voice signal processing, process of removing or smoothing out spurious frequencies from waveforms produced by converting digital signals back to analog.

anti-static bag   Bag made of anti-static plastic into which electronics are placed for temporary or long-term storage. Used to protect components from electrostatic discharge.

anti-static mat   Special surface on which to lay electronics. These mats come with a grounding connection designed to equalize electrical potential between a workbench and one or more electronic devices. Used to prevent electrostatic discharge.

anti-static wrist strap   Special device worn around the wrist with a grounding connection designed to equalize electrical potential between a technician and an electronic device. Used to prevent electrostatic discharge.

antivirus program Software designed to combat viruses by either seeking out and destroying them or passively guarding against them.

API (application programming interface) Software definition that describes operating system calls for application software; conventions defining how a service is invoked.

APIPA (Automatic Private IP Addressing) Feature of Windows that automatically assigns an IP address to the system when the client cannot obtain an IP address automatically.

APM (advanced power management) BIOS routines that enable the CPU to turn selected peripherals on and off.

applet Generic term for a program in the Windows Control Panel.

archive To copy programs and data onto a relatively inexpensive storage medium (disk, tape, etc.) for long-term retention.

archive attribute Attribute of a file that shows whether the file has been backed up since the last change. Each time a file is opened, changed, or saved, the archive bit is turned on. Some types of backups turn off this archive bit to indicate that a good backup of the file exists on tape.

ARP (Address Resolution Protocol) Protocol in the TCP/IP suite used with the command-line utility of the same name to determine the MAC address that corresponds to a particular IP address.

ASCII (American Standard Code for Information Interchange) Industry-standard 8-bit characters used to define text characters, consisting of 96 upper- and lowercase letters, plus 32 nonprinting control characters, each of which is numbered. These numbers were designed to achieve uniformity among computer devices for printing and the exchange of simple text documents.

aspect ratio Ratio of width to height of an object. Standard television has a 4:3 aspect ratio.

ASR (Automated System Recovery) Windows XP tool designed to recover a badly corrupted Windows system; similar to ERD.

assertive communication Means of communication that is not pushy or bossy but is also not soft. Useful in dealing with upset customers as it both defuses their anger and gives them confidence that you know what you're doing.

AT (Advanced Technology) Model name of the second-generation, 80286-based IBM computer. Many aspects of the AT, such as the BIOS, CMOS, and expansion bus, have become de facto standards in the PC industry. The physical organization of the components on the motherboard is called the AT form factor.

ATA (AT Attachment) Type of hard drive and controller designed to replace the earlier ST506 and ESDI drives without requiring replacement of the AT BIOS—hence, AT attachment. These drives are more popularly known as IDE drives. (*See* IDE.) The **ATA/33** standard has drive transfer speeds up to 33 MBps; the **ATA/66** up to 66 MBps; the **ATA/100** up to 100 MBps; and the **ATA/133** up to 133 MBps. (*See* Ultra DMA.)

ATA/ATAPI-6 Also known as ATA-6 or "Big Drive." Replaced the INT13 extensions and allowed for hard drives as large as 144 petabytes (144 million GBs).

ATAPI (ATA packet interface) Series of standards that enable mass storage devices other than hard drives to use the IDE/ATA controllers. Popular with optical drives. (*See* EIDE.)

ATAPI-compliant Devices that utilize the ATAPI standard. (*See* ATAPI.)

Athlon Name used for a popular series of CPUs manufactured by AMD.

ATTRIB.EXE Command used to view the specific properties of a file; can also be used to modify or remove file properties, such as read-only, system, or archive.

attributes Values in a file that determine the hidden, read-only, system, and archive status of the file.

ATX (AT eXtended) Popular motherboard form factor that generally replaced the AT form factor.

authentication Any method a computer uses to determine who can access it.

authorization Any method a computer uses to determine what an authenticated user can do.

autodetection Process through which new disks are automatically recognized by the BIOS.

Automatic Updates   Feature allowing updates to Windows to be retrieved automatically over the Internet.

AutoPlay   Windows 2000/XP/Vista/7 setting, along with autorun.inf, enabling Windows to automatically detect media files and begin using them. (*See* AUTORUN.INF.)

AUTORUN.INF   File included on some media that automatically launches a program or installation routine when the media is inserted/attached to a system.

autosensing   Better quality sound cards use autosensing to detect a device plugged into a port and to adapt the features of that port.

auto-switching power supply   Type of power supply able to detect the voltage of a particular outlet and adjust accordingly.

Award Software   Major producer of BIOS software for motherboards.

backlight   One of three main components used in LCDs to illuminate an image.

backside bus   Set of wires that connect the CPU to Level 2 cache. First appearing in the Pentium Pro, all modern CPUs have a backside bus. Some buses run at the full speed of the CPU, whereas others run at a fraction. Earlier Pentium IIs, for example, had backside buses running at half the speed of the processor. (*See also* frontside bus and external data bus.)

Backup or Restore Wizard   Utility contained within Windows that allows users to create system backups and set system restore points.

ball mouse   Input device that enables users to manipulate a cursor on the screen by using a ball and sensors that detect the movement and direction of the ball.

bandwidth   Piece of the spectrum occupied by some form of signal, such as television, voice, fax data. Signals require a certain size and location of bandwidth to be transmitted. The higher the bandwidth, the faster the signal transmission, allowing for a more complex signal such as audio or video. Because bandwidth is a limited space, when one user is occupying it, others must wait their turn. Bandwidth is also the capacity of a network to transmit a given amount of data during a given period.

bank   Total number of SIMMs or DIMMs that can be accessed simultaneously by the chipset. The "width" of the external data bus divided by the "width" of the SIMM or DIMM sticks. DIMM slots must be populated to activate dual- or triple-channel memory.

bar code reader   Tool to read Universal Product Code (UPC) bar codes.

basic disks   Hard drive partitioned in the "classic" way with a master boot record (MBR) and partition table. (*See also* dynamic disks.)

baud   One analog cycle on a telephone line. In the early days of telephone data transmission, the baud rate was often analogous to bits per second. Due to advanced modulation of baud cycles as well as data compression, this is no longer true.

BD-RE (Blu-ray Disc-REwritable)   Blu-ray Disc equivalent of the rewritable DVD, allows writing and rewriting several times on the same BD. (*See* Blu-ray Disc.)

BD-ROM   Blu-ray Disc equivalent of a DVD-ROM or CD-ROM. (*See* Blu-ray Disc.)

beaming   Term used to describe transferring data from one PDA to another by means of IrDA.

beep codes   Series of audible tones produced by a motherboard during the POST. These tones identify whether the POST has completed successfully or whether some piece of system hardware is not working properly. Consult the manual for your particular motherboard for a specific list of beep codes.

binary numbers   Number system with a base of 2, unlike the number systems most of us use that have bases of 10 (decimal numbers), 12 (measurement in feet and inches), and 60 (time). Binary numbers are preferred for computers for precision and economy. An electronic circuit that can detect the difference between two states (on–off, 0–1) is easier and more inexpensive to build than one that could detect the differences among ten states (0–9).

biometric device   Hardware device used to support authentication; works by scanning and remembering unique aspects of a user's various body parts (e.g., retina, iris, face, or fingerprint) by using some form of sensing device such as a retinal scanner.

BIOS (basic input/output system)   Classically, software routines burned onto the system ROM of a PC. More commonly seen as any software that directly controls a particular piece of hardware. A set of programs encoded in read-only memory (ROM) on computers.

These programs handle startup operations and low-level control of hardware such as disk drives, the keyboard, and monitor.

bit Single binary digit. Also, any device that can be in an on or off state.

BitLocker Drive Encryption Drive encryption software offered in Windows Vista/7 Ultimate and Enterprise editions. BitLocker requires a special chip to validate hardware status and to ensure that the computer hasn't been hacked.

bit depth Number of colors a video card is capable of producing. Common bit depths are 16-bit and 32-bit, representing 65,536 colors and 16.7 million colors, respectively.

Bluetooth Wireless technology designed to create small wireless networks preconfigured to do specific jobs, but not meant to replace full-function networks or Wi-Fi.

Blu-ray Disc (BD) Optical disc format that stores 25 or 50 GB of data, designed to be the replacement media for DVD. Competed with HD DVD.

boot To initiate an automatic routine that clears the memory, loads the operating system, and prepares the computer for use. Term is derived from "pull yourself up by your bootstraps." PCs must do that because RAM doesn't retain program instructions when power is turned off. A cold boot occurs when the PC is physically switched on. A warm boot loads a fresh OS without turning off the computer, lessening the strain on the electronic circuitry. To do a warm boot, press the CTRL-ALT-DELETE keys twice in rapid succession (the three-fingered salute).

boot sector First sector on a PC hard drive or floppy disk, track 0. The boot-up software in ROM tells the computer to load whatever program is found there. If a system disk is read, the program in the boot record directs the computer to the root directory to load the operating system.

BOOT.INI Text file used during the boot process that provides a list of all OSs currently installed and available for NTLDR. Also tells where each OS is located on the system. Used in Windows XP and earlier Microsoft operating systems.

bootable disk Disk that contains a functional operating system; can also be a floppy disk, USB thumb drive, or optical disc.

bootstrap loader Segment of code in a system's BIOS that scans for an operating system, looks specifically for a valid boot sector, and, when one is found, hands control over to the boot sector; then the bootstrap loader removes itself from memory.

bps (bits per second) Measurement of how fast data is moved from one place to another. A 56K modem can move ~56,000 bits per second.

broadband Commonly understood as a reference to high-speed, always-on communication links that can move large files much more quickly than a regular phone line.

browser Program specifically designed to retrieve, interpret, and display Web pages.

BSoD (Blue Screen of Death) Infamous error screen that appears when Windows encounters an unrecoverable error.

BTX (Balanced Technology eXtended) Motherboard form factor designed as an improvement over ATX.

buffered/registered DRAM Usually seen in motherboards supporting more than four sticks of RAM, it is required to address interference issues caused by the additional sticks.

buffer underrun Inability of a source device to provide a CD-burner with a constant stream of data while burning a CD-R or CD-RW.

bug Programming error that causes a program or a computer system to perform erratically, produce incorrect results, or crash. The term was coined when a real bug was found in one of the circuits of one of the first ENIAC computers.

burn Process of writing data to a writable optical disc, such as a DVD-R.

burn-in failure Critical failure usually associated with manufacturing defects.

bus Series of wires connecting two or more separate electronic devices, enabling those devices to communicate.

bus mastering Circuitry allowing devices to avoid conflicts on the external data bus.

bus topology Network configuration wherein all computers connect to the network via a central bus cable.

byte   Unit of eight bits; fundamental data unit of personal computers. Storing the equivalent of one character, the byte is also the basic unit of measurement for computer storage.

CAB files   Short for cabinet files. These files are compressed and most commonly used during OS installation to store many smaller files, such as device drivers.

cache (disk)   Special area of RAM that stores the data most frequently accessed from the hard drive. Cache memory can optimize the use of your systems.

cache (L1, L2, L3, etc.)   Special section of fast memory, usually built into the CPU, used by the onboard logic to store information most frequently accessed by the CPU.

calibration   Process of matching the print output of a printer to the visual output of a monitor.

card reader   Device with which you can read data from one of several types of flash memory.

card services   Uppermost level of PCMCIA services. Card services level recognizes the function of a particular PC Card and provides the specialized drivers necessary to make the card work. (*See also* socket services.)

CardBus   32-bit PC cards that can support up to eight devices on each card. Electrically incompatible with earlier PC cards (3.3 V versus 5 V).

CAT 5   Category 5 wire; a TIA/EIA standard for UTP wiring that can operate up to 100 megabits per second.

CAT 5e   Category 5e wire; TIA/EIA standard for UTP wiring that can operate up to 1 gigabit per second.

CAT 6   Category 6 wire; TIA/EIA standard for UTP wiring that can operate up to 10 gigabits per second.

catastrophic failure   Occurs when a component or whole system will not boot; usually related to a manufacturing defect of a component. Could also be caused by overheating and physical damage to computer components.

CCFL (cold cathode fluorescent lamp)   Light technology used in LCDs and flatbed scanners. CCFLs use relatively little power for the amount of light they provide.

CD (CHDIR)   Shorthand for "Change Directory." Allows you to change the focus of the command prompt from one directory to another.

CD (compact disc)   Originally designed as the replacement for vinyl records, CDs have become the primary method of long-term storage of music and data.

CD quality   CD-quality audio has a sample rate of 44.4 KHz and a bit rate of 128 bits.

CDDA (CD-Digital Audio)   Special format used for early CD-ROMs and all audio CDs; divides data into variable length tracks. A good format to use for audio tracks but terrible for data because of lack of error checking.

CD-R (compact disc recordable)   CD technology that accepts a single "burn" but cannot be erased after the one burn.

CD-ROM (compact disc/read only memory)   Read-only compact storage disk for audio or video data. Recordable devices, such as CD-Rs, are updated versions of the older CD-ROM players. CD-ROMs are read by using CD-ROM drives.

CD-RW (compact disc rewritable)   CD technology that accepts multiple reads/writes like a hard drive.

Celeron   Lower-cost brand of Intel CPUs.

Cellular WAN   Technology that allows laptops and other mobile devices to access the Internet over a cell phone network.

cellular wireless networks   Networks that enable cell phones, PDAs, and other mobile devices to connect to the Internet.

Centrino   Marketing name for an Intel laptop solution including the mobile processor, support chips and wireless networking.

Centronics connector   Connector used with older printers.

certification   License that demonstrates competency in some specialized skill.

Certified Cisco Network Associate (CCNA)   One of the certifications demonstrating a knowledge of Cisco networking products.

CHAP (Challenge Handshake Authentication Protocol)   Common remote access protocol; serving system challenges the remote client, usually by means of asking for a password.

chassis intrusion detection   Feature offered in some chassis that trips a switch when the chassis is opened.

chipset Electronic chips, specially designed to work together, that handle all of the low-level functions of a PC. In the original PC, the chipset consisted of close to 30 different chips; today, chipsets usually consist of one, two, or three separate chips embedded into a motherboard.

CHKDSK (Checkdisk) Hard drive error detection and, to a certain extent, correction utility in Windows. Originally a DOS command (CHKDSK.EXE); also the executable for the graphical Error-checking tool.

clean installation Operating system installed on a fresh drive, following a reformat of that drive. Often the only way to correct a problem with a system when many of the crucial operating system files have become corrupted.

client Computer program that uses the services of another computer program. Software that extracts information from a server; your auto-dial phone is a client, and the phone company is its server. Also, a machine that accesses shared resources on a server.

client/server Relationship in which client software obtains services from a server on behalf of a person.

client/server network Network that has dedicated server machines and client machines.

clock cycle Single charge to the clock wire of a CPU.

clock-multiplying CPU CPU that takes the incoming clock signal and multiples it inside the CPU to let the internal circuitry of the CPU run faster.

clock speed Speed at which a CPU executes instructions, measured in MHz or GHz. In modern CPUs, the internal speed is a multiple of the external speed. (*See also* clock-multiplying CPU.)

clock (CLK) wire Charge on the CLK wire to tell the CPU that another piece of information is waiting to be processed.

cluster Basic unit of storage on a floppy or hard disk. Multiple sectors are contained in a cluster. When Windows stores a file on a disk, it writes those files into dozens or even hundreds of contiguous clusters. If there aren't enough contiguous open clusters available, the operating system finds the next open cluster and writes there, continuing this process until the entire file is saved. The FAT or MFT tracks how the files are distributed among the clusters on the disk.

CMOS (complementary metal-oxide semiconductor) Originally, the type of nonvolatile RAM that held information about the most basic parts of your PC, such as hard drives, floppies, and amount of DRAM. Today, actual CMOS chips have been replaced by Flash-type nonvolatile RAM. The information is the same, however, and is still called CMOS—even though it is now almost always stored on Flash RAM.

CMOS setup program Program enabling you to access and update CMOS data.

CNR (Communications and Network Riser) Proprietary slot used on some motherboards to provide a sound inference–free connection for modems, sound cards, and NICs.

coaxial cable Cabling in which an internal conductor is surrounded by another, outer conductor, thus sharing the same axis.

code Set of symbols representing characters (e.g., ASCII code) or instructions in a computer program (a programmer writes source code, which must be translated into executable or machine code for the computer to use).

codec (compressor/decompressor) Software that compresses or decompresses media streams.

color depth Term to define a scanner's ability to produce color, hue, and shade.

COM port(s) Serial communications ports available on your computer. When used as a program extension, .COM indicates an executable program file limited to 64 KB.

command A request, typed from a terminal or embedded in a file, to perform an operation or to execute a particular program.

command prompt Text prompt for entering commands.

command-line interface User interface for an OS devoid of all graphical trappings.

CompactFlash (CF) One of the older but still popular flash media formats. Its interface uses a simplified PC Card bus, so it also supports I/O devices.

compatibility modes Feature of Windows 2000 and beyond to allow software written for previous versions of Windows to operate in newer operating systems.

compliance   Concept that members of an organization must abide by the rules of that organization. For a technician, this often revolves around what software can or cannot be installed on an organization's computer.

component failure   Occurs when a system device fails due to manufacturing or some other type of defect.

compression   Process of squeezing data to eliminate redundancies, allowing files to use less space when stored or transmitted.

CompTIA A+ 220-701 (Essentials)   One half of the CompTIA A+ exam, concentrating on understanding terminology and technology, how to do fundamental tasks, and basic Windows operating system support.

CompTIA A+ 220-702 (Practical Application)   The other half of the CompTIA A+ exam, covering advanced troubleshooting and configuration.

CompTIA A+ certification   Industry-wide, vendor-neutral computer certification program that demonstrates competency as a computer technician.

CompTIA Network+ certification   Industry-wide, vendor-neutral certification for network technicians, covering network hardware, installation, and troubleshooting.

Computer (Vista)   Default interface in Windows Vista and 7 for Windows Explorer; displays drives and network locations. (*See* My Computer.)

Computer Administrator   One of three types of user accounts, the Administrator account has access to all resources on the computer.

Computer Management   Applet in Windows' Administrative Tools that contains several useful snap-ins, such as Device Manager and Disk Management.

computing process   Four parts of a computer's operation: input, processing, output, and storage.

Computing Technology Industry Association (CompTIA)   Nonprofit IT trade association that administers the CompTIA A+ and CompTIA Network+ exams.

conditioning charger   Battery charger that contains intelligent circuitry that prevents portable computer batteries from being overcharged and damaged.

connectors   Small receptacles used to attach cables to a system. Common types of connectors include USB, PS/2, and DB-25.

consumables   Materials used up by printers, including paper, ink, ribbons, and toner cartridges.

container file   File containing two or more separate, compressed tracks, typically an audio and a moving picture track. Also known as a wrapper.

context menu   Small menu brought up by right-clicking on objects in Windows.

Control Panel   Collection of Windows applets, or small programs, that can be used to configure various pieces of hardware and software in a system.

controller card   Card adapter that connects devices, such as a disk drive, to the main computer bus/motherboard.

convergence   Measure of how sharply a single pixel appears on a CRT; a monitor with poor convergence produces images that are not sharply defined.

copy backup   Type of backup similar to Normal or Full, in that all selected files on a system are backed up. This type of backup does not change the archive bit of the files being backed up.

COPY command   Command in the command-line interface for making a copy of a file and pasting it in another location.

Core   Name used for the family of Intel CPUs that succeeded the Pentium 4.

counter   Used to track data about a particular object when using the Performance console.

CPU (central processing unit)   "Brain" of the computer. Microprocessor that handles primary calculations for the computer. CPUs are known by names such as Core i5 and Phenom.

CRC (cyclic redundancy check)   Very accurate mathematical method used to check for errors in long streams of transmitted data. Before data is sent, the main computer uses the data to calculate a CRC value from the data's contents. If the receiver calculates a CRC value different from the received data, the data was corrupted during transmission and is re-sent. Ethernet packets have a CRC code.

C-RIMM or CRIMM (continuity RIMM)   Passive device added to populate unused banks in a system that uses Rambus RIMMs.

crossover cable Special UTP cable used to connect hubs or to connect network cards without a hub. Crossover cables reverse the sending and receiving wire pairs from one end to the other.

CRT (cathode ray tube) Tube of a monitor in which rays of electrons are beamed onto a phosphorescent screen to produce images. Also a shorthand way to describe a monitor that uses CRT rather than LCD technology.

CSMA/CA (carrier sense multiple access with collision avoidance) Networking scheme used by wireless devices to transmit data while avoiding data collisions, which wireless nodes have difficulty detecting.

CSMA/CD (carrier sense multiple access with collision detection) Networking scheme used by Ethernet devices to transmit data and resend data after detecting data collisions.

cylinder Single track on all the platters in a hard drive. Imagine a hard drive as a series of metal cans, nested one inside another; a single can would represent a cylinder.

daily backup Backup of all files that have been changed on that day without changing the archive bits of those files. Also called *daily copy backup*.

daisy-chaining Method of connecting several devices along a bus and managing the signals for each device.

data classification System of organizing data according to its sensitivity. Common classifications include public, highly confidential, and top secret.

data structure Scheme that directs how an OS stores and retrieves data on and off a drive. Used interchangeably with the term file system. (*See also* file system.)

DB connectors D-shaped connectors used for a variety of connections in the PC and networking world. Can be male (with prongs) or female (with holes) and have a varying number of pins or sockets. Also called *D-sub, D-subminiature,* or *D-shell connectors.*

DB-15 A two- or three-row DB connector (female) used for 10Base5 networks, MIDI/joysticks, and analog video.

DB-25 connector DB connector (female), commonly referred to as a parallel port connector.

DC (direct current) Type of electricity in which the flow of electrons is in a complete circle in one direction.

DDR SDRAM (double data rate SDRAM) Type of DRAM that makes two processes for every clock cycle. (*See also* DRAM.)

DDR2 SDRAM Type of SDRAM that sends four bits of data in every clock cycle. (*See also* DDR SDRAM.)

DDR3 SDRAM Type of SDRAM that transfers data at twice the rate of DDR2 SDRAM.

debug To detect, trace, and eliminate errors in computer programs.

decibels Unit of measurement typically associated with sound. The higher the number of decibels, the louder the sound.

dedicated server Machine that is not used for any client functions, only server functions.

default gateway In a TCP/IP network, the nearest router to a particular host. This router's IP address is part of the necessary TCP/IP configuration for communicating with multiple networks using IP.

definition file List of virus signatures that an antivirus program can recognize.

defragmentation (DEFRAG) Procedure in which all the files on a hard disk are rewritten on disk so that all parts of each file reside in contiguous clusters. The result is an improvement in disk speed during retrieval operations.

degauss Procedure used to break up the electromagnetic fields that can build up on the cathode ray tube of a monitor; involves running a current through a wire loop. Most monitors feature a manual degaussing tool.

DEL (Erase) command Command in the command-line interface used to delete/erase files.

desktop User's primary interface to the Windows operating system.

desktop extender Portable computer that offers some of the features of a full-fledged desktop computer but with a much smaller footprint and lower weight.

desktop replacement Portable computer that offers the same performance as a full-fledged desktop computer; these systems are normally very heavy to carry and often cost much more than the desktop systems they replace.

device driver   Program used by the operating system to control communications between the computer and peripherals.

Device Manager   Utility that enables techs to examine and configure all the hardware and drivers in a Windows PC.

DHCP (Dynamic Host Configuration Protocol)   Protocol that enables a DHCP server to set TCP/IP settings automatically for a DHCP client.

differential backup   Similar to an incremental backup. Backs up the files that have been changed since the last backup. This type of backup does not change the state of the archive bit.

digital camera   Camera that simulates film technology electronically.

digital certificate   Form in which a public key is sent from a Web server to a Web browser so that the browser can decrypt the data sent by the server.

digital zoom   Software tool to enhance the optical zoom capabilities of a digital camera.

digitally signed driver   All drivers designed specifically for Windows are digitally signed, meaning they are tested to work stably with these operating systems.

DIMM (dual inline memory module)   32- or 64-bit type of DRAM packaging, similar to SIMMs, with the distinction that each side of each tab inserted into the system performs a separate function. DIMMs come in a variety of sizes, with 184- and 240-pin being the most common on desktop computers.

dipole antennae   Standard straight-wire antennae that provide the most omnidirectional function.

DIR command   Command used in the command-line interface to display the entire contents of the current working directory.

directory   Another name for a folder.

directory service   Centralized index that each PC accesses to locate resources in the domain.

DirectX   Set of APIs enabling programs to control multimedia, such as sound, video, and graphics. Used in Windows Vista to draw the Aero desktop.

Disk Cleanup   Utility built into Windows that can help users clean up their disks by removing temporary Internet files, deleting unused program files, and more.

disk cloning   Taking a PC and making duplicates of the hard drive, including all data, software, and configuration files and transferring it to another PC. (*See* image installation.)

disk duplexing   Type of disk mirroring using two separate controllers rather than one; faster than traditional mirroring.

Disk Management   Snap-in available with the Microsoft Management Console that enables techs to configure the various disks installed in a system; available in the Computer Management Administrative Tool.

disk mirroring   Process by which data is written simultaneously to two or more disk drives. Read and write speed is decreased but redundancy in case of catastrophe is increased.

disk quota   Application allowing network administrators to limit hard drive space usage.

disk striping   Process by which data is spread among multiple (at least two) drives. Increases speed for both reads and writes of data. Considered RAID level 0 because it does not provide fault tolerance.

disk striping with parity   Method for providing fault tolerance by writing data across multiple drives and then including an additional drive, called a parity drive, that stores information to rebuild the data contained on the other drives. Requires at least three physical disks: two for the data and a third for the parity drive. This provides data redundancy at RAID levels 3–5 with different options.

disk thrashing   Hard drive that is constantly being accessed due to lack of available system memory. When system memory runs low, a Windows system will utilize hard disk space as "virtual" memory, thus causing an unusual amount of hard drive access.

display adapter   Handles all the communication between the CPU and the monitor. Also known as a video card.

Display applet   Tool in Windows 2000 and Windows XP used to adjust display settings, including resolution, refresh rate, driver information, and color depth.

DMA (direct memory access) modes   Technique that some PC hardware devices use to transfer data to and from the memory without using the CPU.

DMA controller Resides between the RAM and the devices and handles DMA requests.

DNS (domain name system) TCP/IP name resolution system that translates a host name into an IP address.

DNS domain Specific branch of the DNS name space. First-level DNS domains include .COM, .GOV, and .EDU.

docking station Device that provides a portable computer extra features such as a DVD drive or PC Card, in addition to legacy and modern ports. Similar to a port replicator.

document Steps a technician uses to solve a problem: To record the relevant information. For a technician, this would be recording each troubleshooting job: what the problem was, how it was fixed, and other helpful information.

Documents folder Windows Vista/7 folder for storing user-created files. Replaces the My Documents folder previously used in Windows 2000/XP. (*See* My Documents.)

Dolby Digital Technology for sound reductions and channeling methods used for digital audio.

domain Groupings of users, computers, or networks. In Microsoft networking, a domain is a group of computers and users that share a common account database, called a SAM, and a common security policy. On the Internet, a domain is a group of computers that share a common element in their hierarchical name. Other types of domains exist—e.g., broadcast domain, etc.

domain-based network Network that eliminates the need for logging in to multiple servers by using domain controllers to hold the security database for all systems.

DOS (Disk Operating System) First popular operating system available for PCs. A text-based, single-tasking operating system that was not completely replaced until the introduction of Windows 95.

dot pitch Value relating to CRTs, showing the diagonal distance between phosphors measured in millimeters.

dot-matrix printer Printer that creates each character from an array of dots. Pins striking a ribbon against the paper, one pin for each dot position, form the dots. May be a serial printer (printing one character at a time) or a line printer.

double-sided RAM RAM stick with RAM chips soldered to both sides of the stick. May only be used with motherboards designed to accept double-sided RAM. Very common.

DPI (dots per inch) Measure of printer resolution that counts the dots the device can produce per linear (horizontal) inch.

DPMS (Display Power-Management Signaling) Specification that can reduce CRT power consumption by 75 percent by reducing/eliminating video signals during idle periods.

DRAM (dynamic random access memory or dynamic RAM) Memory used to store data in most personal computers. DRAM stores each bit in a "cell" composed of a transistor and a capacitor. Because the capacitor in a DRAM cell can only hold a charge for a few milliseconds, DRAM must be continually refreshed, or rewritten, to retain its data.

DriveLock CMOS program enabling you to control the ATA security mode feature set. Also known as *drive lock*.

driver signing Digital signature for drivers used by Windows to protect against potentially bad drivers.

DS3D (DirectSound3D) Introduced with DirectX 3.0, DS3D is a command set used to create positional audio, or sounds that appear to come from in front, in back, or to the side of a user. (*See also* DirectX.)

DSL (digital subscriber line) High-speed Internet connection technology that uses a regular telephone line for connectivity. DSL comes in several varieties, including asynchronous (ADSL) and synchronous (SDSL), and many speeds. Typical home-user DSL connections are ADSL with a download speed of 7 Mbps and an upload speed of 512 Kbps.

D-subminiature *See* DB connectors.

DTS (Digital Theatre Systems) Technology for sound reductions and channeling methods, similar to Dolby Digital.

dual boot Refers to a computer with two operating systems installed, enabling users to choose which operating system to load on boot. Can also refer to kicking a device a second time just in case the first time didn't work.

DualView   Microsoft feature enbling Windows to use two or more monitors simultaneously.

dual-channel architecture   Using two sticks of RAM (either RDRAM or DDR) to increase throughput.

dual-channel memory   Form of DDR, DDR2, and DDR3 memory access used by many motherboards that requires two identical sticks of DDR, DDR2, or DDR3 RAM.

dual-core   Dual-core CPUs have two execution units on the same physical chip but share caches and RAM.

dual-scan passive matrix   Manufacturing technique for increasing display updates by refreshing two lines at a time.

dumpster diving   To go through someone's trash in search of information.

DUN (Dial-Up Networking)   Software used by Windows to govern the connection between the modem and the ISP.

duplexing   Similar to mirroring in that data is written to and read from two physical drives, for fault tolerance. Separate controllers are used for each drive, both for additional fault tolerance and additional speed. Considered RAID level 1. Also called *disk duplexing* or *drive duplexing*.

Duron   Lower-cost version of AMD's Athlon series of CPUs.

DVD (digital versatile disc)   Optical disc format that provides for 4–17 GB of video or data storage.

DVD-ROM   DVD equivalent of the standard CD-ROM.

DVD-RW   Rewritable DVD media.

DVD-Video   DVD format used exclusively to store digital video; capable of storing over 2 hours of high-quality video on a single DVD.

DVI (Digital Visual Interface)   Special video connector designed for digital-to-digital connections; most commonly seen on PC video cards and LCD monitors. Some versions also support analog signals with a special adapter.

Dxdiag (DirectX Diagnostics)   Diagnostic tool for getting information about and testing a computer's DirectX version.

dye-sublimation printers   Printer that uses a roll of heat-sensitive plastic film embedded with dyes, which are vaporized and then solidified onto specially coated paper to create a high-quality image.

dynamic disks   Special feature of Windows that enables users to span a single volume across two or more drives. Dynamic disks do not have partitions; they have volumes. Dynamic disks can be striped, mirrored, and striped or mirrored with parity.

EAX (Environment Audio eXtensions)   3-D sound technology developed by Creative Labs but now supported by most sound cards.

ECC (error correction code)   Special software, embedded on hard drives, that constantly scans the drives for bad sectors.

ECC RAM/DRAM (error correction code DRAM)   RAM that uses special chips to detect and fix memory errors. Commonly used in high-end servers where data integrity is crucial.

effective permissions   User's combined permissions granted by multiple groups.

EFI (Extensible Firmware Interface)   Firmware created by Intel and HP that replaced traditional 16-bit BIOS and added several new enhancements.

EFS (encrypting file system)   Encryption tool found in NTFS 5.

EIA/TIA   *See* TIA/EIA.

EIDE (enhanced IDE)   Marketing concept of hard drive–maker Western Digital, encompassing four improvements for IDE drives, including drives larger than 528 MB, four devices, increase in drive throughput, and non–hard drive devices. (*See* ATAPI, PIO mode.)

electrostatic discharge (ESD)   Movement of electrons from one body to another. A real menace to PCs, as it can cause permanent damage to semiconductors.

eliciting answers   Communication strategy designed to help techs understand a user's problems better. Works by listening to a user's description of a problem and then asking cogent questions.

e-mail (electronic mail)   Messages, usually text, sent from one person to another via computer. Can also be sent automatically to a group of addresses (mailing list).

electromagnetic interference (EMI) Electrical interference from one device to another, resulting in poor performance of the device being interfered with. Examples: Static on your TV while running a blow dryer, or placing two monitors too close together and getting a "shaky" screen.

emergency repair disk (ERD) Saves critical boot files and partition information and is the main tool for fixing boot problems in Windows 2000.

encryption Making data unreadable by those who do not possess a key or password.

erase lamp Component inside laser printers that uses light to make the coating of the photosensitive drum conductive.

Error-checking Windows XP/Vista/7 name for the Checkdisk and ScanDisk tools.

eSATA Serial ATA-based connector for external hard drives and optical drives.

escalate Process used when person assigned to repair a problem is not able to get the job done, such as sending the problem to someone else.

Ethernet Name coined by Xerox for the first standard of network cabling and protocols. Based on a bus topology.

Ethic of Reciprocity Golden Rule: Do unto others as you would have them do unto you.

EULA (end-user license agreement) Agreement that accompanies a piece of software, to which user must agree before using the software. Outlines the terms of use for the software and also lists any actions on the part of the user that violate the agreement.

event auditing Feature of Event Viewer's Security section that creates an entry in the Security Log when certain events happen, such as a user logging on.

Event Viewer Utility made available as an MMC snap-in that enables users to monitor various system events, including network bandwidth usage and CPU utilization.

EXPAND Command-line utility program included with Windows used to access files within CAB files.

expansion bus Set of wires going to the CPU, governed by the expansion bus crystal, directly connected to expansion slots of varying types (PCI, AGP, PCIe, etc.). Depending on the type of slots, the expansion bus runs at a percentage of the main system speed (8.33–133 MHz).

expansion bus crystal Controls the speed of the expansion bus.

expansion slots Connectors on a motherboard that enable users to add optional components to a system. (*See also* AGP and PCI.)

ExpressCard Serial PC Card designed to replace CardBus PC Cards. ExpressCards connect to either a Hi-Speed USB (480 Mbps) or PCI Express (2.5 Gbps) bus.

extended partition Type of non-bootable hard disk partition. May only have one extended partition per disk. Purpose is to divide a large disk into smaller partitions, each with a separate drive letter.

extension Three or four letters that follow a filename and identify the type of file. Common file extensions are .ZIP, .EXE, and .DOC.

external data bus (EDB) Primary data highway of all computers. Everything in your computer is tied either directly or indirectly to the external data bus. (*See also* frontside bus and backside bus.)

fast user switching Account option that is useful when multiple users share a system; allows users to switch without logging off.

FAT (file allocation table) Hidden table that records how files on a hard disk are stored in distinct clusters; the only way DOS knows where to access files. Address of first cluster of a file is stored in the directory file. FAT entry for the first cluster is the address of the second cluster used to store that file. In the entry for the second cluster for that file is the address for the third cluster, and so on until the final cluster, which gets a special end-of-file code. There are two FATs, mirror images of each other, in case one is destroyed or damaged.

FAT32 File allocation table that uses 32 bits for addressing clusters. Commonly used with Windows 98 and Windows Me systems. Some Windows 2000 Professional and Windows XP systems also use FAT32, although most modern Windows systems use the more robust NTFS.

FDISK Disk-partitioning utility included with Windows.

fiber optics High-speed channel for transmitting data, made of high-purity glass sealed within an opaque tube. Much faster than conventional copper wire such as coaxial cable.

file Collection of any form of data that is stored beyond the time of execution of a single job. A file may contain program instructions or data, which may be numerical, textual, or graphical information.

file allocation unit Another term for cluster. (*See also* cluster.)

file association Windows term for the proper program to open a particular file; for example, file association for opening .MP3 programs might be Winamp.

file format How information is encoded in a file. Two primary types are binary (pictures) and ASCII (text), but within those are many formats, such as BMP and GIF for pictures. Commonly represented by a suffix at the end of the filename; for example, .txt for a text file or .exe for an executable.

file server Computer designated to store software, courseware, administrative tools, and other data on a local- or wide-area network. It "serves" this information to other computers via the network when users enter their personal access codes.

file system Scheme that directs how an OS stores and retrieves data on and off a drive; FAT32 and NTFS are both file systems. Used interchangeably with the term "data structure." (*See also* data structure.)

filename Name assigned to a file when the file is first written on a disk. Every file on a disk within the same folder must have a unique name. Filenames can contain any character (including spaces), except the following: \ / : * ? " < > |

firewall Device that restricts traffic between a local network and the Internet.

FireWire (IEEE 1394) Interconnection standard to send wide-band signals over a serialized, physically thin connector system. Serial bus developed by Apple and Texas Instruments; enables connection of 63 devices at speeds up to 800 megabits per second.

firmware Embedded programs or code stored on a ROM chip. Generally OS-independent, thus allowing devices to operate in a wide variety of circumstances without direct OS support. The system BIOS is firmware.

Flash ROM ROM technology that can be electrically reprogrammed while still in the PC. Overwhelmingly the most common storage medium of BIOS in PCs today, as it can be upgraded without a need to open the computer on most systems.

flatbed scanner Most popular form of consumer scanner; runs a bright light along the length of the tray to capture an image.

FlexATX Motherboard form factor. Motherboards built in accordance with the FlexATX form factor are very small, much smaller than microATX motherboards.

Flip 3D In the Aero desktop environment, a three-dimensional replacement for ALT-TAB. Accessed by pressing the WINDOWS KEY-TAB key combination.

floppy disk Removable storage media that can hold between 720 KB and 1.44 MB of data.

floppy drive System hardware that uses removable 3.5-inch disks as storage media.

flux reversal Point at which a read/write head detects a change in magnetic polarity.

FM synthesis Producing sound by electronic emulation of various instruments to more-or-less produce music and other sound effects.

folders list Toggle button in Windows Explorer for Windows 2000 and XP that displays the file structure on the left side of the window. In Windows Vista and 7, the folders list is active by default.

form factor Standard for the physical organization of motherboard components and motherboard size. Most common form factors are ATX and BTX.

FORMAT command Command in the command-line interface used to format a storage device.

formatting Magnetically mapping a disk to provide a structure for storing data; can be done to any type of disk, including a floppy disk, hard disk, or other type of removable disk.

FPU (floating point unit) Formal term for math coprocessor (also called a *numeric processor*) circuitry inside a CPU. A math coprocessor calculates by using a floating point math (which allows for decimals). Before the Intel 80486, FPUs were separate chips from the CPU.

fragmentation Occurs when files and directories get jumbled on a fixed disk and are no longer contiguous. Can significantly slow down hard drive access times and can be repaired by using the DEFRAG utility included with each version of Windows. (*See also* defragmentation (DEFRAG).)

freeware   Software that is distributed for free, with no license fee.

frequency   Measure of a sound's tone, either high or low.

frontside bus   Wires that connect the CPU to the main system RAM. Generally running at speeds of 66–133 MHz. Distinct from the expansion bus and the backside bus, though it shares wires with the former.

front-view projector   Shoots the image out the front and counts on you to put a screen in front at the proper distance.

FRU (field replaceable unit)   Any part of a PC that is considered to be replaceable "in the field," i.e., a customer location. There is no official list of FRUs—it is usually a matter of policy by the repair center.

FTP (File Transfer Protocol)   Protocol used when you transfer a file from one computer to another across the Internet. FTP uses port numbers 20 and 21.

fuel cells   Power source that uses chemical reactions to produce electricity. Lightweight, compact, and stable devices expected to replace batteries as the primary power source for portable PCs.

full-duplex   Any device that can send and receive data simultaneously.

Full-Speed USB   USB standard that runs at 12 Mbps.

fuser assembly   Mechanism in laser printers that uses two rollers to fuse toner to paper during the print process.

gain   Ratio of increase of radio frequency output provided by an antenna, measured in decibels (dB).

GDI (graphical device interface)   Component of Windows that utilizes the CPU rather than the printer to process a print job as a bitmapped image of each page.

general protection fault (GPF)   Error code usually seen when separate active programs conflict on resources or data.

geometry   Numbers representing three values: heads, cylinders, and sectors per track; define where a hard drives stores data.

giga   Prefix for the quantity 1,073,741,824 or for 1 billion. One gigabyte would be 1,073,741,824 bytes, except with hard drive labeling, where it means 1 billion bytes. One gigahertz is 1 billion hertz.

GPU (graphics processing unit)   Specialized processor that helps CPU by taking over all of the 3-D rendering duties.

grayscale depth   Number that defines how many shades of gray the scanner can save per dot.

grayware   Program that intrudes into a user's computer experience without damaging any systems or data.

group   Collection of user accounts that share the same access capabilities.

Group Policy   Means of easily controlling the settings of multiple network clients with policies such as setting minimum password length or preventing Registry edits.

Guest/Guest groups   Very limited built-in account type for Windows.

GUI (graphical user interface)   Interface that enables user to interact with computer graphically, by using a mouse or other pointing device to manipulate icons that represent programs or documents, instead of using only text as in early interfaces. Pronounced "gooey."

HAL (hardware abstraction layer)   Part of the Windows OS that separates system-specific device drivers from the rest of the NT system.

handshaking   Procedure performed by modems, terminals, and computers to verify that communication has been correctly established.

hang   When a computer freezes and does not respond to keyboard commands, it is said to "hang" or to have "hung."

hang time   Number of seconds a too-often-hung computer is airborne after you have thrown it out a second-story window.

hardware   Physical computer equipment such as electrical, electronic, magnetic, and mechanical devices. Anything in the computer world that you can hold in your hand. A floppy drive is hardware; Microsoft Word is not.

hardware protocol   Defines many aspects of a network, from the packet type to the cabling and connectors used.

HBA (host bus adapter)   Connects SATA devices to the expansion bus. Also known as the SATA controller.

HD (Hi-Definition) Multimedia transmission standard that defines high-resolution images and 5.1, 6.1, and 7.1 sound.

HDA (High-Definition Audio) Intel-designed standard to support features such as true surround sound with many discrete speakers.

HDD (hard disk drive) Data-recording system using solid disks of magnetic material turning at high speeds to store and retrieve programs and data in a computer.

HDMI (Hi-Definition Multimedia Interface) Single multimedia connection that includes both high-definition video and audio. One of the best connections for outputting to television. Also contains copy protection features.

heads Short for read/write heads; used by hard drives to store data.

heat dope See thermal compound.

hex (hexadecimal) Base-16 numbering system using 10 digits (0 through 9) and six letters (A through F). In the computer world, shorthand way to write binary numbers by substituting one hex digit for a four-digit binary number (e.g., hex 9 = binary 1001).

hibernation Power management setting in which all data from RAM is written to the hard drive before going to sleep. Upon waking up, all information is retrieved from the hard drive and returned to RAM.

hidden attribute File attribute that, when used, does not allow DIR command to show a file.

hierarchical directory tree Method by which Windows organizes files into a series of folders, called *directories*, under the root directory. (*See also* root directory.)

high gloss Laptop screen finish that offers sharper contrast, richer colors, and wider viewing angles than a matte finish, but is also much more reflective.

high-level formatting Format that sets up a file system on a drive.

high-voltage anode Component in a CRT monitor that has very high voltages of electricity flowing through it.

Hi-Speed USB USB standard that runs at 480 Mbps.

honesty Telling the truth—a very important thing for a tech to do.

host On a TCP/IP network, single device that has an IP address—any device (usually a computer) that can be the source or destination of a data packet. In the mainframe world, computer that is made available for use by multiple people simultaneously.

hot-swappable Any hardware that may be attached to or removed from a PC without interrupting the PC's normal processing.

HotSync (synchronization) Program used by PalmOS-based PDAs to synchronize files between a PDA and a desktop computer.

HRR (horizontal refresh rate) Amount of time it takes for a CRT to draw one horizontal line of pixels on a display.

HTML (Hypertext Markup Language) ASCII-based, script-like language for creating hypertext documents such as those on the World Wide Web.

HTTP (Hypertext Transfer Protocol) Extremely fast protocol used for network file transfers in the WWW environment.

HTTPS (Hypertext Transfer Protocol Secure) Secure form of HTTP used commonly for Internet business transactions or any time when a secure connection is required. (*See also* HTTP.)

hub Electronic device that sits at the center of a star topology network, providing a common point for the connection of network devices. Hubs repeat all information out to all ports and have been replaced by switches, although the term is still commonly used.

hyperthreading CPU feature that enables a single pipeline to run more than one thread at once.

I/O (input/output) General term for reading and writing data to a computer. "Input" includes data from a keyboard, pointing device (such as a mouse), or loaded from a disk. "Output" includes writing information to a disk, viewing it on a CRT, or printing it to a printer.

I/O addressing Using the address bus to talk to system devices.

I/O Advanced Programmable Interrupt Controller (IOAPIC) Typically located in the Southbridge, the IOAPIC acts as the traffic cop for interrupt requests to the CPU.

I/O base address First value in an I/O address range.

ICH (I/O controller hub)   Official name for Southbridge chip found in Intel's chipsets.

icon   Small image or graphic, most commonly found on a system's desktop, that launches a program when selected.

ICS (Internet Connection Sharing)   Allowing a single network connection to be shared among several machines. ICS was first introduced with Windows 98.

IDE (Integrated Drive Electronics)   PC specification for small- to medium-sized hard drives in which the controlling electronics for the drive are part of the drive itself, speeding up transfer rates and leaving only a simple adapter (or "paddle"). IDE only supported two drives per system of no more than 504 megabytes each, and has been completely supplanted by Enhanced IDE. EIDE supports four drives of over 8 gigabytes each and more than doubles the transfer rate. The more common name for PATA drives. Also known as *intelligent drive electronics*. (*See* PATA.)

Identify the problem.   To question the user and find out what has been changed recently or is no longer working properly. (One of the steps a technician uses to solve a problem.)

IEC-320   Connects the cable supplying AC power from a wall outlet into the power supply.

IEEE (Institute of Electronic and Electrical Engineers)   Leading standards-setting group in the United States.

IEEE 1284   IEEE standard governing parallel communication.

IEEE 1394   IEEE standard governing FireWire communication. (*See also* FireWire.)

IEEE 1394a   FireWire standard that runs at 400 Mbps.

IEEE 1394b   FireWire standard that runs at 800 Mbps.

IEEE 802.11   Wireless Ethernet standard more commonly known as Wi-Fi.

image file   Bit-by-bit image of data to be burned on CD or DVD—from one file to an entire disc—stored as a single file on a hard drive. Particularly handy when copying from CD to CD or DVD to DVD.

image installation   Operating system installation that uses a complete image of a hard drive as an installation media. Helpful when installing an operating system on a large number of identical PCs.

impact printer   Uses pins and inked ribbons to print text or images on a piece of paper.

impedance   Amount of resistance to an electrical signal on a wire. Relative measure of the amount of data a cable can handle.

incident report   Record of the details of an accident, including what happened and where it happened.

incremental backup   Backs up all files that have their archive bits turned on, meaning that they have been changed since the last backup. Turns the archive bits off after the files have been backed up.

Information Technology (IT)   Field of computers, their operation, and their maintenance.

infrastructure mode   Wireless networking mode that uses one or more WAPs to connect the wireless network nodes to a wired network segment.

inheritance   NTFS feature that passes on the same permissions in any sub-folders/files resident in the original folder.

ink cartridge   Small container of ink for inkjet printers.

inkjet printer   Uses liquid ink, sprayed through a series of tiny jets, to print text or images on a piece of paper.

installation disc   Typically a CD-ROM or DVD that holds all the necessary device drivers.

instruction set   All of the machine-language commands that a particular CPU is designed to understand.

integrity   Always doing the right thing.

interface   Means by which a user interacts with a piece of software.

Interrupt 13 (INT13) extensions   Improved type of BIOS that accepts EIDE drives up to 137 GB.

interrupt/interruption   Suspension of a process, such as the execution of a computer program, caused by an event external to the computer and performed in such a way that the process can be resumed. Events of this kind include sensors monitoring laboratory equipment or a user pressing an interrupt key.

inverter   Device used to convert DC current into AC. Commonly used with CCFLs in laptops and flatbed scanners.

IP (Internet Protocol) Internet standard protocol that provides a common layer over dissimilar networks; used to move packets among host computers and through gateways if necessary. Part of the TCP/IP protocol suite.

IP address Numeric address of a computer connected to the Internet. An IPv4 address is made up of 4 octets of 8-bit binary numbers translated into their shorthand numeric values. An IPv6 address is 128 bits long. The IP address can be broken down into a network ID and a host ID. Also called *Internet address*.

IPCONFIG Command-line utility for Windows servers and workstations that displays the current TCP/IP configuration of the machine. Similar to WINIPCFG and IFCONFIG.

IPSec (Internet Protocol Security) Microsoft's encryption method of choice for networks consisting of multiple networks linked by a private connection, providing transparent encryption between the server and the client.

IrDA (Infrared Data Association) Protocol that enables communication through infrared devices, with speeds of up to 4 Mbps.

IRQ (interrupt request) Signal from a hardware device, such as a modem or a mouse, indicating that it needs the CPU's attention. In PCs, IRQs are sent along specific IRQ channels associated with a particular device. IRQ conflicts were a common problem in the past when adding expansion boards, but the plug-and-play specification has removed this headache in most cases.

ISA (Industry Standard Architecture) Industry Standard Architecture design was found in the original IBM PC for the slots that allowed additional hardware to be connected to the computer's motherboard. An 8-bit, 8.33-MHz expansion bus was designed by IBM for its AT computer and released to the public domain. An improved 16-bit bus was also released to the public domain. Replaced by PCI in the mid-1990s.

ISDN (integrated services digital network) Standard from the CCITT (Comité Consultatif Internationale de Télégraphie et Téléphonie) that defines a digital method for communications to replace the current analog telephone system. ISDN is superior to POTS telephone lines because it supports up to 128 Kbps transfer rate for sending information from computer to computer. It also allows data and voice to share a common phone line. DSL reduced demand for ISDN substantially.

ISO 9660 CD format to support PC file systems on CD media. Supplanted by the Joliet format.

ISO file Complete copy (or image) of a storage media device, typically used for optical discs.

ISP (Internet service provider) Company that provides access to the Internet, usually for money.

jack (physical connection) Part of a connector into which a plug is inserted. Also referred to as ports.

Joliet Extension of the ISO 9660 format. Most popular CD format to support PC file systems on CD media.

joystick Peripheral often used while playing computer games; originally intended as a multipurpose input device.

joule Unit of energy describing (in this book) how much energy a surge suppressor can handle before it fails.

jumper Pair of small pins that can be shorted with a shunt to configure many aspects of PCs. Usually used in configurations that are rarely changed, such as master/slave settings on IDE drives.

Kerberos Authentication encryption developed by MIT to enable multiple brands of servers to authenticate multiple brands of clients.

kernel Core portion of program that resides in memory and performs the most essential operating system tasks.

keyboard Input device. Three common types of keyboards: those that use a mini-DIN (PS/2) connection, those that use a USB connection, and those that use wireless technology.

Knowledge Base Large collection of documents and FAQs that is maintained by Microsoft. Found on Microsoft's Web site, the Knowledge Base is an excellent place to search for assistance on most operating system problems.

KVM (keyboard, video, mouse switch) Hardware device that enables multiple computers to be viewed and controlled by a single mouse, keyboard, and screen.

LAN (local area network) Group of PCs connected via cabling, radio, or infrared that use this connectivity to share resources such as printers and mass storage.

laptop Traditional clamshell portable computing device with built-in LCD monitor, keyboard, and trackpad.

laser Single-wavelength, in-phase light source that is sometimes strapped to the head of sharks by bad guys. Note to henchmen: Lasers should never be used with sea bass, no matter how ill-tempered they might be.

laser printer Electro-photographic printer in which a laser is used as the light source.

Last Known Good Configuration Option on the Advanced Startup Options menu that allows your system to revert to a previous configuration to troubleshoot and repair any major system problems.

latency Amount of delay before a device may respond to a request; most commonly used in reference to RAM.

LBA (logical block addressing) Translation (algorithm) of IDE drives promoted by Western Digital as a standardized method for breaking the 504-MB limit in IDE drives. Subsequently adopted universally by the PC industry and now standard on all EIDE drives.

LCD (liquid crystal display) Type of display commonly used on portable PCs. Also have mostly replaced CRTs as the display of choice for most desktop computer users, due in large part to rapidly falling prices and increasing quality. LCDs use liquid crystals and electricity to produce images on the screen.

LED (light-emitting diode) Solid-state device that vibrates at luminous frequencies when current is applied.

Level 1 (L1) cache First RAM cache accessed by the CPU, which stores only the absolute most-accessed programming and data used by currently running threads. Always the smallest and fastest cache on the CPU.

Level 2 (L2) cache Second RAM cache accessed by the CPU. Much larger and often slower than the L1 cache, and accessed only if the requested program/data is not in the L1 cache.

Level 3 (L3) cache Third RAM cache accessed by the CPU. Much larger and slower than the L1 and L2 caches, and accessed only if the requested program/data is not in the L2 cache. Seen only on high-end CPUs.

Li-Ion (lithium-ion) Battery commonly used in portable PCs. Li-Ion batteries don't suffer from the memory effects of Ni-Cd batteries and provide much more power for a greater length of time.

limited account/user User account in Windows XP that has limited access to a system. Accounts of this type cannot alter system files, cannot install new programs, and cannot edit settings by using the Control Panel.

Linux Open-source UNIX-clone operating system.

Local Security Settings Windows tool used to set local security policies on an individual system.

local user account List of users allowed access to a system.

Local Users and Groups Tool enabling creation and changing of group memberships and accounts for users.

log files Files created in Windows to track the progress of certain processes.

logical drives Sections of a hard drive that are formatted and assigned a drive letter, each of which is presented to the user as if it were a separate drive.

login screen First screen of the Windows interface, used to log in to the computer system.

loopback plug Device used during loopback tests to check the female connector on a NIC.

Low-Speed USB USB standard that runs at 1.5 Mbps.

LPT port Commonly referred to as a printer port; usually associated with a local parallel port.

LPX First slimline form factor; replaced by NLX form factor.

lumens Unit of measure for amount of brightness on a projector or other light source.

Mac (Also **Macintosh**.) Apple Computers' flagship operating system, currently up to OS Xv10.6 "Snow Leopard" and running on Intel-based hardware.

MAC (Media Access Control) address Unique 48-bit address assigned to each network card. IEEE assigns blocks of possible addresses to various NIC manufacturers to help ensure that the address is always unique. The Data Link layer of the OSI model uses MAC addresses for locating machines.

MAC address filtering Method of limiting wireless network access based on the physical, hard-wired address of the units' wireless NIC.

machine language Binary instruction code that is understood by the CPU.

maintenance kits Commonly replaced printer components provided by many manufacturers.

mass storage Hard drives, CD-ROMs, removable media drives, etc.

matte Laptop screen finish that offers a good balance between richness of colors and reflections, but washes out in bright light.

MBR (master boot record) Tiny bit of code that takes control of the boot process from the system BIOS.

MCC (memory controller chip) Chip that handles memory requests from the CPU. Although once a special chip, it has been integrated into the chipset on all PCs today.

MCH (memory controller hub) Intel-coined name for what is now commonly called the Northbridge.

MD (MKDIR) command Command in the command-line interface used to create directories.

mega- Prefix that usually stands for the binary quantity 1,048,576 (2^{20}). One megabyte is 1,048,576 bytes. One megahertz, however, is a million hertz. Sometimes shortened to *Meg*, as in "a 286 has an address space of 16 Megs."

megapixel Term used typically in reference to digital cameras and their ability to capture data.

memory Device or medium for temporary storage of programs and data during program execution. Synonymous with storage, although it most frequently refers to the internal storage of a computer that can be directly addressed by operating instructions. A computer's temporary storage capacity is measured in kilobytes (KB), megabytes (MB), or gigabytes (GB) of RAM (random-access memory). Long-term data storage on disks is also measured in kilobytes, megabytes, gigabytes, and terabytes.

memory addressing Taking memory address from system RAM and using it to address nonsystem RAM or ROM so the CPU can access it.

Memory Stick Sony's flash memory card format; rarely seen outside of Sony devices.

mesh topology Network topology where each computer has a dedicated line to every other computer, most often used in wireless networks.

MFT (master file table) Enhanced file allocation table used by NTFS. (*See also* FAT.)

microATX Variation of the ATX form factor, which uses the ATX power supply. MicroATX motherboards are generally smaller than their ATX counterparts but retain all the same functionality.

microBTX Variation of the BTX form factor. MicroBTX motherboards are generally smaller than their BTX counterparts but retain all the same functionality.

microprocessor "Brain" of a computer. Primary computer chip that determines relative speed and capabilities of the computer. Also called *CPU*.

Microsoft Windows Logo Program Testing program for hardware manufacturers, designed to ensure compatibility with the Windows OS.

MIDI (musical instrument digital interface) Interface between a computer and a device for simulating musical instruments. Rather than sending large sound samples, a computer can simply send "instructions" to the instrument describing pitch, tone, and duration of a sound. MIDI files are therefore very efficient. Because a MIDI file is made up of a set of instructions rather than a copy of the sound, modifying each component of the file is easy. Additionally, it is possible to program many channels, or "voices" of music to be played simultaneously, creating symphonic sound.

migration Moving users from one operating system or hard drive to another.

MIMO (multiple in/multiple out) Feature of 802.11n devices that enables the simultaneous connection of up to four antennae, allowing for increased throughput.

mini-audio connector Very popular, 1/8-inch diameter connector used to transmit two audio signals; perfect for stereo sound.

mini connector One type of power connector from a PC power supply unit. Supplies 5 and 12 volts to peripherals. Also known as a floppy connector,

mini PCI Specialized form of PCI designed for use in laptops.

mini power connector Connector used to provide power to floppy disk drives.

mini-DIN Small connection most commonly used for keyboards and mice. Many modern systems implement USB in place of mini-DIN connections. Also called *PS/2*.

mirrored volume   Volume that is mirrored on another volume. (*See also* mirroring.)

mirroring   Reading and writing data at the same time to two drives for fault tolerance purposes. Considered RAID level 1. Also called *drive mirroring*.

MMC (Microsoft Management Console)   Means of managing a system, introduced by Microsoft with Windows 2000. The MMC allows an Administrator to customize management tools by picking and choosing from a list of snap-ins. Available snap-ins include Device Manager, Users and Groups, and Computer Management.

MMX (multimedia extensions)   Specific CPU instructions that enable a CPU to handle many multimedia functions, such as digital signal processing. Introduced with the Pentium CPU, these instructions are used on all ×86 CPUs.

mode   Any single combination of resolution and color depth set for a system.

modem (modulator/demodulator)   Device that converts a digital bit stream into an analog signal (modulation) and converts incoming analog signals back into digital signals (demodulation). Analog communications channel is typically a telephone line, and analog signals are typically sounds.

module   Small circuit board that DRAM chips are attached to. Also known as a "stick."

Molex connector   Computer power connector used by CD-ROM drives, hard drives, and case fans. Keyed to prevent it from being inserted into a power port improperly.

monaural   Describes recording tracks from one source (microphone) as opposed to stereo, which uses two sources.

monitor   Screen that displays data from a PC. Can use either a cathode ray tube (CRT) or a liquid crystal display (LCD) to display images.

motherboard   Flat piece of circuit board that resides inside your computer case and has a number of connectors on it. You can use these connectors to attach a variety of devices to your system, including hard drives, CD-ROM drives, floppy disk drives, and sound cards.

motherboard book   Valuable resource when installing a new motherboard. Normally lists all the specifications about a motherboard, including the type of memory and type of CPU that should be used with the motherboard.

mount point   Drive that functions like a folder mounted into another drive.

mouse   Input device that enables users to manipulate a cursor on the screen to select items.

MOVE command   Command in the command-line interface used to move a file from one location to another.

MP3   Short for MPEG, Layer 3. MP3 is a type of compression used specifically for turning high-quality digital audio files into much smaller, yet similar sounding, files.

MPA (Microsoft Product Activation)   Introduced by Microsoft with the release of Windows XP, Microsoft Product Activation prevents unauthorized use of Microsoft's software by requiring users to activate the software.

MPEG-2 (Moving Picture Experts Group)   Standard of video and audio compression offering resolutions up to 1280 × 720 at 60 frames per second.

MPEG-4 (Moving Picture Experts Group)   Standard of video and audio compression offering improved compression over MPEG-2.

MS-CHAP   Microsoft's variation of the CHAP protocol, which uses a slightly more advanced encryption protocol. Windows Vista uses MS-CHAP v2 (version 2), and does not support MS-CHAP v1 (version 1).

MSCONFIG (System Configuration utility)   Executable file that runs the Windows System Configuration utility, which enables users to configure a system's boot files and critical system files. Often used for the name of the utility, as in "just run MSCONFIG."

MSDS (material safety data sheet)   Standardized form that provides detailed information about potential environmental hazards and proper disposal methods associated with various PC components.

MSINFO32   Provides information about hardware resources, components, and the software environment. Also known as System Information.

multiboot   OS installation in which multiple operating systems are installed on a single machine. Can also refer to kicking a device several times in frustration.

multimedia extensions Originally an Intel CPU enhancement designed for graphics-intensive applications (such as games). It was never embraced but eventually led to improvements in how CPUs handle graphics.

multimeter Device used to measure voltage, amperage, and resistance.

multisession drive Recordable CD drive capable of burning multiple sessions onto a single recordable disc. A multisession drive also can close a CD-R so that no further tracks can be written to it.

multitasking Process of running multiple programs or tasks on the same computer at the same time.

Music CD-R CD using a special format for home recorders. Music CD-R makers pay a small royalty to avoid illegal music duplication.

My Computer Applet that allows users to access a complete list of all fixed and removable drives contained within a system.

My Documents Introduced with Windows 98 and used in Windows 2000 and Windows XP, the My Documents folder provides a convenient place for users to store their documents, log files, and any other type of files.

My Network Places Folder in Windows XP that enables users to view other computers on their network or workgroup.

native resolution Resolution on an LCD monitor that matches the physical pixels on the screen. CRTs do not have fixed pixels and therefore do not have a native resolution.

NET Command in Windows that allows users to view a network without knowing the names of the other computers on that network.

NetBIOS (Network Basic Input/Output System) Protocol that operates at the Session layer (Layer 5) of the OSI seven-layer model. This protocol creates and manages connections based on the names of the computers involved.

network Collection of two or more computers interconnected by telephone lines, coaxial cables, satellite links, radio, and/or some other communication technique. Group of computers that are connected and that communicate with one another for a common purpose.

Also, the name of Vista's version of the My Network Places folder.

network ID Number that identifies the network on which a device or machine exists. This number exists in both IP and IPX protocol suites.

network printer Printer that connects directly to a network.

NIC (network interface card) Expansion card that enables a PC to physically link to a network.

Ni-Cd (nickel-cadmium) Battery that was used in the first portable PCs. Heavy and inefficient, these batteries also suffered from a memory effect that could drastically shorten the overall life of the battery. (*See also* Ni-MH, Li-Ion.)

Ni-MH (nickel-metal hydride) Battery used in portable PCs. Ni-MH batteries had fewer issues with the memory effect than Ni-Cd batteries. Ni-MH batteries have been replaced by lithium-ion batteries. (*See also* Ni-Cd, Li-Ion.)

nit Value used to measure the brightness of an LCD displays. A typical LCD display has a brightness of between 100 and 400 nits.

NLQ (near-letter quality) Designation for dot-matrix printers that use 24-pin printheads.

NLX Second form factor for slimline systems. Replaced the earlier LPX form factor. (NLX apparently stands for nothing; it's just a cool grouping of letters.)

NMI (non-maskable interrupt) Interrupt code sent to the processor that cannot be ignored. Typically manifested as a BSOD.

NNTP (Network News Transfer Protocol) Protocol run by news servers that enable newsgroups.

non-system disk or disk error Error that occurs during the boot process. Common causes for this error are leaving a non-bootable floppy disk, CD, or other media in the drive while the computer is booting.

nonvolatile Memory that retains data even if power is removed.

normal backup Full backup of every selected file on a system. Turns off the archive bit after the backup.

Northbridge Chip that connects a CPU to memory, the PCI bus, Level 2 cache, and AGP activities. Communicates with the CPU through the frontside bus. Newer CPUs feature an integrated Northbridge.

NOS (network operating system) Standalone operating system or part of an operating system that provides basic file and supervisory services over a network. Although each computer attached to the network has its own OS, the NOS describes which actions are allowed by each user and coordinates distribution of networked files to the user who requests them.

notification area Contains icons representing background processes, the system clock and volume control. Located by default at the right edge of the Windows taskbar. Most users call this area the system tray.

NSLOOKUP Command-line program in Windows used to determine exactly what information the DNS server is providing about a specific host name.

NTDETECT.COM One of the critical Windows NT/2000/XP startup files.

NTFS (NT file system) Robust and secure file system introduced by Microsoft with Windows NT. NTFS provides an amazing array of configuration options for user access and security. Users can be granted access to data on a file-by-file basis. NTFS enables object-level security, long filename support, compression, and encryption.

NTFS permissions Restrictions that determine the amount of access given to a particular user on a system using NTFS.

NTLDR Windows NT/2000/XP boot file. Launched by the MBR or MFT, NTLDR looks at the BOOT.INI configuration file for any installed operating systems.

NVIDIA One of the foremost manufacturers of graphics cards and chipsets.

object System component that is given a set of characteristics and can be managed by the operating system as a single entity.

object access auditing Feature of Event Viewer's Security section that creates an entry in the Security Log when certain objects are accessed, such as a file or folder.

ohm(s) Electronic measurement of a cable's impedance.

OpenGL One of two popular APIs used today for video cards. Originally written for UNIX systems but now ported to Windows and Apple systems. (*See also* DirectX.)

optical disc/media Types of data discs (such as DVDs, CDs, Blu-ray Discs, etc.) that are read by a laser.

optical drive Drive used to read/write to optical discs, such as CDs or DVDs.

optical mouse Pointing device that uses light rather than electronic sensors to determine movement and direction the mouse is being moved.

optical resolution Resolution a scanner can achieve mechanically. Most scanners use software to enhance this ability.

optical zoom Mechanical ability of most cameras to "zoom" in as opposed to the digital ability.

option ROM Alternative way of telling the system how to talk to a piece of hardware. Option ROM stores BIOS for the card onboard a chip on the card itself.

OS (operating system) Series of programs and code that create an interface so users can interact with a system's hardware, for example, DOS, Windows, and Linux.

OS X Current operating system on Apple Macintosh computers. Based on a UNIX core, early versions of OS X ran on Motorola-based hardware; current versions run on Intel-based hardware. Pronounced "ten" rather than "ex."

OSI seven-layer model Architecture model based on the OSI protocol suite that defines and standardizes the flow of data between computers. The seven layers are: **Layer 1 The Physical layer** Defines hardware connections and turns binary into physical pulses (electrical or light). Repeaters and hubs operate at the Physical layer. **Layer 2 The Data Link layer** Identifies devices on the Physical layer. MAC addresses are part of the Data Link layer. Bridges operate at the Data Link layer. **Layer 3 The Network layer** Moves packets between computers on different networks. Routers operate at the Network layer. IP and IPX operate at the Network layer. **Layer 4 The Transport layer** Breaks data down into manageable chunks. TCP, UDP, SPX, and NetBEUI operate at the Transport layer. **Layer 5 The Session layer** Manages connections between machines. NetBIOS and Sockets operate at the Session layer. **Layer 6 The Presentation layer** Can also manage data encryption; hides the differences between various types of computer systems. **Layer 7 The Application layer** Provides tools for programs to use to access the network (and the lower layers). HTTP, FTP, SMTP, and POP3 are all examples of protocols that operate at the Application layer.

overclocking   To run a CPU or video processor faster than its rated speed.

P1 power connector   Provides power to ATX motherboards.

P4 12V connector   Provides additional 12-volt power to motherboards that support Pentium 4 and later processors.

P8 and P9 connectors   Provides power to AT-style motherboards.

packet   Basic component of communication over a network. Group of bits of fixed maximum size and well-defined format that is switched and transmitted as a single entity through a network. Contains source and destination address, data, and control information.

page fault   Minor memory-addressing error.

page file   Portion of the hard drive set aside by Windows to act like RAM. Also known as virtual memory or swap file.

PAN (personal area network)   Small wireless network created with Bluetooth technology and intended to link PCs and other peripheral devices.

parallel port   Connection for the synchronous, high-speed flow of data along parallel lines to a device, usually a printer.

parallel processing   When a multicore CPU processes more than one thread.

parental controls   Tool to allow monitoring and limiting of user activities; designed for parents to control the content their children can access.

parity   Method of error detection where a small group of bits being transferred is compared to a single parity bit set to make the total bits odd or even. Receiving device reads the parity bit and determines if the data is valid, based on if the parity bit is odd or even.

parity RAM   Earliest form of error-detecting RAM; stored an extra bit (called the *parity bit*) to verify the data.

partition   Section of the storage area of a hard disk. Created during initial preparation of the hard disk, before the disk is formatted.

partition table   Table located in the boot sector of a hard drive that lists every partition on the disk that contains a valid operating system.

partitioning   Electronically subdividing a physical hard drive into groups called *partitions* (or *volumes*).

passive matrix   Technology for producing colors in LCD monitors by varying voltages across wire matrices to produce red, green, or blue dots.

password   Key used to verify a user's identity on a secure computer or network.

Password Authentication Protocol (PAP)   Oldest and most basic form of authentication. Also the least safe, because it sends all passwords in clear text.

password reset disk   Special type of floppy disk with which users can recover a lost password without losing access to any encrypted, or password-protected, data.

PATA (parallel ATA)   Implementation that integrates the controller on the disk drive itself. (*See also* ATA, IDE, SATA.)

patch   Small piece of software released by a software manufacturer to correct a flaw or problem with a particular piece of software.

path   Route the operating system must follow to find an executable program stored in a subdirectory.

PC bus   Original 8-bit expansion bus developed by IBM for PCs; ran at a top speed of 4.77 MHz. Also known as the XT bus.

PC Card   Credit-card–sized adapter cards that add functionality in many notebook computers, PDAs, and other computer devices. Come in 16-bit and CardBus parallel format and ExpressCard serial format. (*See also* PCMCIA.)

PC tech   Someone with computer skills who works on computers.

PCI (Peripheral Component Interconnect)   Design architecture for the expansion bus on the computer motherboard, which enables system components to be added to the computer. Local bus standard, meaning that devices added to a computer through this port will use the processor at the motherboard's full speed (up to 33 MHz) rather than at the slower 8 MHz speed of the regular bus. Moves data 32 or 64 bits at a time rather than the 8 or 16 bits the older ISA buses supported.

PCIe (PCI Express)   Serialized successor to PCI and AGP, which uses the concept of individual data paths called *lanes*. May use any number of lanes, although single lanes (×1) and 16 lanes (×16) are the most common on motherboards.

PCI-X (PCI Extended)   Enhanced version of PCI, 64 bits wide. Typically seen in servers and high-end systems.

PCL   Printer control language created by Hewlett-Packard and used on a broad cross-section of printers.

PCM (Pulse Code Modulation)   Sound format developed in the 1960s to carry telephone calls over the first digital lines.

PCMCIA (Personal Computer Memory Card International Association)   Consortium of computer manufacturers who devised the PC Card standard for credit-card–sized adapter cards that add functionality in many notebook computers, PDAs, and other computer devices. (*See also* PC Card.)

PDA (personal digital assistant)   Handheld computer that blurs the line between calculators and computers. Early PDAs were calculators that enabled users to program in such information as addresses and appointments. Modern PDAs, such as the Palm and PocketPC, are fully programmable computers. Most PDAs use a pen/stylus for input rather than a keyboard. A few of the larger PDAs have a tiny keyboard in addition to the stylus.

Pearson VUE   One of the two companies that administers the CompTIA A+ exams, along with Prometric.

peer-to-peer networks   Network in which each machine can act as both a client and a server.

Pentium   Name given to the fifth and later generations of Intel microprocessors; has a 32-bit address bus, 64-bit external data bus, and dual pipelining. Also used for subsequent generations of Intel processors—the Pentium Pro, Pentium II, Pentium III, and Pentium 4. Pentium name was retired after the introduction of the Intel Core CPUs.

pen-based computing   Input method used by many PDAs that combines handwriting recognition with modified mouse functions, usually in the form of a pen-like stylus.

Performance console   Windows tool used to log resource usage over time.

Performance Logs and Alerts   Snap-in enabling the creation of a written record of most everything that happens on the system.

Performance Options   Tool allowing users to configure CPU, RAM, and virtual memory settings.

peripheral   Any device that connects to the system unit.

permission propagation   Term to describe what happens to permissions on an object when you move or copy it.

persistence   Phosphors used in CRT screens continuing to glow after being struck by electrons, long enough for the human eye to register the glowing effect. Glowing too long makes the images smeary, and too little makes them flicker.

Personalization applet   Windows Vista/7 applet with which users can change display settings such as resolution, refresh rate, color depth, and desktop features.

PGA (pin grid array)   Arrangement of a large number of pins extending from the bottom of the CPU package. There are many variations on PGA.

Phillips-head screwdriver   Most important part of a PC tech's toolkit.

Phoenix Technologies   Major producer of BIOS software for motherboards.

phosphor   Electro-fluorescent material that coats the inside face of a cathode ray tube (CRT). After being hit with an electron, it glows for a fraction of a second.

photosensitive drum   Aluminum cylinder coated with particles of photosensitive compounds. Used in a laser printer and usually contained within the toner cartridge.

picoBTX   Variation of the BTX form factor. picoBTX motherboards are generally smaller than their BTX or microBTX counterparts but retain the same functionality.

pin 1   Designator used to ensure proper alignment of floppy disk drive and hard drive connectors.

ping (packet Internet groper)   Slang term for a small network message (ICMP ECHO) sent by a computer to check for the presence and aliveness of another. Used to verify the presence of another system. Also the command used at a prompt to ping a computer.

PIO mode   Series of speed standards created by the Small Form Factor Committee for the use of PIO by hard drives. Modes range from PIO mode 0 to PIO mode 4.

pipeline   Processing methodology where multiple calculations take place simultaneously by being broken into a series of steps. Often used in CPUs and video processors.

pixel (picture element)   In computer graphics, smallest element of a display space that can be independently assigned color or intensity.

plug   Hardware connection with some sort of projection that connects to a port.

plug and play (PnP)   Combination of smart PCs, smart devices, and smart operating systems that automatically configure all necessary system resources and ports when you install a new peripheral device.

polygons   Multi-sided shapes used in 3-D rendering of objects. In computers, video cards draw large numbers of triangles and connect them to form polygons.

polymorph virus   Virus that attempts to change its signature to prevent detection by antivirus programs, usually by continually scrambling a bit of useless code.

polyphony   Number of instruments a sound card can play at once.

POP3 (Post Office Protocol)   Refers to the way e-mail software such as Eudora gets mail from a mail server. When you obtain a SLIP, PPP, or shell account, you almost always get a POP account with it. It is this POP account that you tell your e-mail software to use to get your mail. Also called *point of presence*.

pop-up   Irritating browser window that appears automatically when you visit a Web site.

port (networking)   In networking, the number used to identify the requested service (such as SMTP or FTP) when connecting to a TCP/IP host. Examples: 80 (HTTP), 20 (FTP), 69 (TFTP), 25 (SMTP), and 110 (POP3).

port (physical connection)   Part of a connector into which a plug is inserted. Physical ports are also referred to as jacks.

port replicator   Device that plugs into a USB port or other specialized port and offers common PC ports, such as serial, parallel, USB, network, and PS/2. By plugging your notebook computer into the port replicator, you can instantly connect the computer to nonportable components such as a printer, scanner, monitor, or full-sized keyboard. Port replicators are

typically used at home or in the office with the nonportable equipment already connected.

positional audio   Range of commands for a sound card to place a sound anywhere in 3-D space.

POST (power-on self test)   Basic diagnostic routine completed by a system at the beginning of the boot process to make sure a display adapter and the system's memory are installed; it then searches for an operating system. If it finds one, it hands over control of the machine to the OS.

PostScript   Language defined by Adobe Systems, Inc. for describing how to create an image on a page. The description is independent of the resolution of the device that will actually create the image. It includes a technology for defining the shape of a font and creating a raster image at many different resolutions and sizes.

potential   Amount of static electricity stored by an object.

power conditioning   Ensuring and adjusting incoming AC wall power to as close to standard as possible. Most UPS devices provide power conditioning.

power good wire   Used to wake up the CPU after the power supply has tested for proper voltage.

power supply fan   Small fan located in a system power supply that draws warm air from inside the power supply and exhausts it to the outside.

power supply unit   Provides the electrical power for a PC. Converts standard AC power into various voltages of DC electricity in a PC.

Power User(s) Group   Second most powerful account and group type in Windows after Administrator/Administrators.

ppm (pages per minute)   Speed of a printer.

PPP (Point-to-Point Protocol)   Enables a computer to connect to the Internet through a dial-in connection and enjoy most of the benefits of a direct connection.

primary corona   Wire located near the photosensitive drum in a laser printer, that is charged with extremely high voltage to form an electric field, enabling voltage to pass to the photosensitive drum, thus charging the photosensitive particles on the surface of the drum.

primary partition   Partition on a Windows hard drive designated to store the operating system.

print resolution   Quality of a print image.

print spooler   Area of memory that queues up print jobs that the printer will handle sequentially.

printer   Output device that can print text or illustrations on paper. Microsoft uses the term to refer to the software that controls the physical print device.

printhead   Case that holds the printwires in a dot-matrix printer.

printed circuit boards   Copper etched onto a nonconductive material and then coated with some sort of epoxy for strength.

printwires   Grid of tiny pins in a dot-matrix printer that strike an inked printer ribbon to produce images on paper.

PRML (Partial Response Maximum Likelihood)   Advanced method of RLL that uses powerful, intelligent circuitry to analyze each flux reversal on a hard drive and to make a best guess as to what type of flux reversal it just read. This allows a dramatic increase in the amount of data a hard drive can store.

product key   Code used during installation to verify legitimacy of the software.

program/programming   Series of binary electronic commands sent to a CPU to get work done.

Programs and Features   Windows Vista/7 replacement for the Add or Remove Programs applet.

projector   Device for projecting video images from PCs or other video sources, usually for audience presentations. Available in front and rear view displays.

Prometric   One of the two companies that administers the CompTIA A+ exams, along with Pearson VUE.

prompt   A character or message provided by an operating system or program to indicate that it is ready to accept input.

proprietary   Technology unique to a particular vendor.

protocol   Agreement that governs the procedures used to exchange information between cooperating entities. Usually includes how much information is to be sent, how often it is sent, how to recover from transmission errors, and who is to receive the information.

proxy server   Device that fetches Internet resources for a client without exposing that client directly to the Internet. Usually accept requests for HTTP, FTP, POP3, and SMTP resources. Often caches, or stores, a copy of the requested resource for later use. Common security feature in the corporate world.

public folder   Folder that all users can access and share with all other users on the system or network.

queue   Area where objects wait their turn to be processed. Example: the printer queue, where print jobs wait until it is their turn to be printed.

Quick Launch toolbar   Enables you to launch commonly used programs with a single click.

QVGA   Video display mode of 320 × 240.

RAID (redundant array of inexpensive devices)   Six-level (0–5) way of creating a fault-tolerant storage system:
Level 0   Uses byte-level striping and provides no fault tolerance.
Level 1   Uses mirroring or duplexing.
Level 2   Uses bit-level striping.
Level 3   Stores error-correcting information (such as parity) on a separate disk, and uses data striping on the remaining drives.
Level 4   Level 3 with block-level striping.
Level 5   Uses block-level and parity data striping.

RAID-5 volume   Striped set with parity. (*See also* RAID.)

rails   Separate DC paths within an ATX power supply.

RAM (random access memory)   Memory that can be accessed at random; that is, which you can write to or read from without touching the preceding address. This term is often used to mean a computer's main memory.

RAMDAC (random access memory digital-to-analog converter)   Circuitry used on video cards that support analog monitors to convert the digital video data to analog.

raster image   Pattern of dots representing what the final product should look like.

raster line   Horizontal pattern of lines that form an image on the monitor screen.

RD (RMDIR)   Command in the command-line interface used to remove directories.

RDRAM (Rambus DRAM) Patented RAM technology that uses accelerated clocks to provide very high-speed memory.

read-only attribute File attribute that does not allow a file to be altered or modified. Helpful when protecting system files that should not be edited.

rear-view projector Projector that shoots an image onto a screen from the rear. Rear-view projectors are usually self-enclosed and very popular for TVs, but are virtually unheard of in the PC world.

Recovery Console Command-line interface boot mode for Windows that is used to repair a Windows 2000 or Windows XP system suffering from massive OS corruption or other problems.

Recycle Bin When files are deleted from a modern Windows system, they are moved to the Recycle Bin. To permanently remove files from a system, they must be emptied from the Recycle Bin.

REGEDIT.EXE Program used to edit the Windows Registry.

register Storage area inside the CPU used by the onboard logic to perform calculations. CPUs have many registers to perform different functions.

registration Usually optional process that identifies the legal owner/user of the product to the supplier.

Registry Complex binary file used to store configuration data about a particular system. To edit the Registry, users can use the applets found in the Control Panel or REGEDIT.EXE or REGEDT32.EXE.

Reliability and Performance Monitor Windows Vista's extended Performance applet.

remediation Repairing damage caused by a virus.

remnant Potentially recoverable data on a hard drive that remains despite formatting or deleting.

Remote Assistance Feature of Windows that enables users to give anyone control of his or her desktop over the Internet.

Remote Desktop Connection Windows tool used to enable a local system to graphically access the desktop of a remote system.

REN (RENAME) command Command in the command-line interface used to rename files and folders.

resistance Difficulty in making electricity flow through a material, measured in ohms.

resistor Any material or device that impedes the flow of electrons. Electronic resistors measure their resistance (impedance) in ohms. *See* ohm(s).

resolution Measurement for CRTs and printers expressed in horizontal and vertical dots or pixels. Higher resolutions provide sharper details and thus display better-looking images.

resources Data and services of a PC.

respect What all techs should feel for their customers.

response rate Time it takes for all of the sub-pixels on the panel to go from pure black to pure white and back again.

restore point System snapshot created by the System Restore utility that is used to restore a malfunctioning system. (*See also* System Restore.)

RET (resolution enhancement technology) Technology that uses small dots to smooth out jagged edges that are typical of printers without RET, producing a higher-quality print job.

RFI (radio frequency interference) Another form of electrical interference caused by radio-wave emitting devices, such as cell phones, wireless network cards, and microwave ovens.

RG-58 Coaxial cabling used for 10Base2 networks.

RIMM Individual stick of Rambus RAM. The letters don't actually stand for anything; they just rhyme with SIMM and DIMM.

RIP (raster image processor) Component in a printer that translates the raster image into commands for the printer.

riser card Special adapter card, usually inserted into a special slot on a motherboard, that changes the orientation of expansion cards relative to the motherboard. Riser cards are used extensively in slimline computers to keep total depth and height of the system to a minimum. Sometimes called a daughterboard.

RJ (registered jack) connector UTP cable connector, used for both telephone and network connections. RJ-11 is a connector for four-wire UTP; usually found in telephone connections. RJ-45 is a connector for eight-wire UTP; usually found in network connections.

RJ-11   *See* RJ (registered jack) connector.

RJ-45   *See* RJ (registered jack) connector.

ROM (read-only memory)   Generic term for nonvolatile memory that can be read from but not written to. This means that code and data stored in ROM cannot be corrupted by accidental erasure. Additionally, ROM retains its data when power is removed, which makes it the perfect medium for storing BIOS data or information such as scientific constants.

root directory   Directory that contains all other directories.

root keys   Five main categories in the Windows Registry:

    HKEY_CLASSES_ROOT
    HKEY_CURRENT_USER
    HKEY_USERS
    HKEY_LOCAL_MACHINE
    HKEY_CURRENT_CONFIG

router   Device connecting separate networks; forwards a packet from one network to another based on the network address for the protocol being used. For example, an IP router looks only at the IP network number. Routers operate at Layer 3 (Network) of the OSI seven-layer model.

RS-232C   Standard port recommended by the Electronics Industry Association for serial devices.

Run dialog box   Command box in which users can enter the name of a particular program to run; an alternative to locating the icon in Windows.

S.M.A.R.T. (Self-Monitoring, Analysis, and Reporting Technology)   Monitoring system built into hard drives.

S/PDIF (Sony/Philips Digital Interface Format)   Digital audio connector found on many sound cards. Users can connect their computers directly to a 5.1 speaker system or receiver. S/PDIF comes in both a coaxial and an optical version.

Safe Mode   Important diagnostic boot mode for Windows that only runs very basic drivers and turns off virtual memory.

sampling   Capturing sound waves in electronic format.

SATA (serial ATA)   Serialized version of the ATA standard that offers many advantages over PATA (parallel ATA) technology, including thinner cabling, keyed connectors, and lower power requirements.

SATA bridge   Adapter that allows PATA devices to be connected to a SATA controller.

SATA power connector   15-pin, L-shaped connector used by SATA devices that support the hot-swappable feature.

satellites   Two or more standard stereo speakers to be combined with a subwoofer for a speaker system (i.e., 2.1, 5.1, etc.).

scan code   Unique code corresponding to each key on the keyboard sent from the keyboard controller to the CPU.

SCSI (small computer system interface)   Powerful and flexible peripheral interface popularized on the Macintosh and used to connect hard drives, CD-ROM drives, tape drives, scanners, and other devices to PCs of all kinds. Normal SCSI enables up to seven devices to be connected through a single bus connection, whereas Wide SCSI can handle 15 devices attached to a single controller.

SCSI chain   Series of SCSI devices working together through a host adapter.

SCSI ID   Unique identifier used by SCSI devices. No two SCSI devices may have the same SCSI ID.

SD (Secure Digital)   Very popular format for flash media cards; also supports I/O devices.

SDRAM (synchronous DRAM)   DRAM that is synchronous, or tied to the system clock and thus runs much faster than traditional FPM and EDO RAM. This type of RAM is used in all modern systems.

SEC (single-edge cartridge)   CPU package where the CPU was contained in a cartridge that snapped into a special slot on the motherboard called Slot 1.

sector   Segment of one of the concentric tracks encoded on the disk during a low-level format. A sector holds 512 bytes of data.

sector translation   Translation of logical geometry into physical geometry by the onboard circuitry of a hard drive.

sectors per track (sectors/track)   Combined with the number of cylinders and heads, defines the disk geometry.

serial port   Common connector on a PC. Connects input devices (such as a mouse) or communications devices (such as a modem).

server   Computer that shares its resources, such as printers and files, with other computers on a network. Example: Network File System Server that shares its disk space with a workstation that does not have a disk drive of its own.

service pack   Collection of software patches released at one time by a software manufacturer.

SetupAPI.log   Log file that tracks the installation of all hardware on a system.

Setuplog.txt   Log file that tracks the complete installation process, logging the success or failure of file copying, Registry updates, and reboots.

SFC (system file checker)   Scans, detects, and restores Windows system files, folders, and paths.

shadow mask   CRT screen that allows only the proper electron gun to light the proper phosphors.

shared documents   Windows pre-made folder accessible by all users on the computer.

shared memory   Means of reducing the amount of memory needed on a video card by borrowing from the regular system RAM, which reduces costs but also decreases performance.

share-level security   Security system in which each resource has a password assigned to it; access to the resource is based on knowing the password.

shareware   Program protected by copyright; holder allows (encourages!) you to make and distribute copies under the condition that those who adopt the software after preview pay a fee to the holder of the copyright. Derivative works are not allowed, although you may make an archival copy.

shunt   Tiny connector of metal enclosed in plastic that creates an electrical connection between two posts of a jumper.

SID (security identifier)   Unique identifier for every PC that most techs change when cloning.

sidebanding   Second data bus for AGP video cards; enables the video card to send more commands to the Northbridge while receiving other commands at the same time.

signal-to-noise ratio   Measure that describes the relative quality of an input port.

signature   Code pattern of a known virus; used by antivirus software to detect viruses.

SIMM (single in-line memory module)   DRAM packaging distinguished by having a number of small tabs that install into a special connector. Each side of each tab is the same signal. SIMMs come in two common sizes: 30-pin and 72-pin.

simple file sharing   Allows users to share locally or across the network but gives no control over what others do with shared files.

simple volume   Volume created when setting up dynamic disks. Acts like a primary partition on a dynamic disk.

single-sided RAM   Has chips on only one side as opposed to double-sided RAM.

slimline   Motherboard form factor used to create PCs that were very thin. NLX and LPX were two examples of this form factor.

slot covers   Metal plates that cover up unused expansion slots on the back of a PC. Useful in maintaining proper airflow through a computer case.

smart battery   Portable PC battery that tells the computer when it needs to be charged, conditioned, or replaced.

smart card   Hardware authentication involving a credit-card-sized card with circuitry that can be used to identify the bearer of that card.

SmartMedia   Format for flash media cards; no longer used with new devices.

SMM (System Management Mode)   Special CPU mode that enables the CPU to reduce power consumption by selectively shutting down peripherals.

SMTP (Simple Mail Transport Protocol)   Main protocol used to send electronic mail on the Internet.

snap-ins   Small utilities that can be used with the Microsoft Management Console.

social engineering   Using or manipulating people inside the networking environment to gain access to that network from the outside.

socket services Device drivers that support the PC Card socket, enabling the system to detect when a PC Card has been inserted or removed, and providing the necessary I/O to the device.

SODIMM (small outline DIMM) Memory used in portable PCs because of its small size.

soft power Characteristic of ATX motherboards, which can use software to turn the PC on and off. The physical manifestation of soft power is the power switch. Instead of the thick power cord used in AT systems, an ATX power switch is little more than a pair of small wires leading to the motherboard.

software Single group of programs designed to do a particular job; always stored on mass storage devices.

solid ink printers Printer that uses solid sticks of nontoxic "ink."

sound card Expansion card that can produce audible tones when connected to a set of speakers.

Southbridge Part of a motherboard chipset; handles all the inputs and outputs to the many devices in the PC.

spam Unsolicited e-mails from both legitimate businesses and scammers that accounts for a huge percentage of traffic on the Internet.

spanned volume Volume that uses space on multiple dynamic disks.

SPD (serial presence detect) Information stored on a RAM chip that describes the speed, capacity, and other aspects of the RAM chip.

speaker Device that outputs sound by using magnetically driven diaphragm.

sprite Bitmapped graphic such as a BMP file used by early 3-D games to create the 3-D world.

spyware Software that runs in the background of a user's PC, sending information about browsing habits back to the company that installed it onto the system.

SRAM (static RAM) RAM that uses a flip-flop circuit rather than the typical transistor/capacitor of DRAM to hold a bit of information. SRAM does not need to be refreshed and is faster than regular DRAM. Used primarily for cache.

SSH (Secure Shell) Terminal emulation program similar to Telnet, except that the entire connection is encrypted.

SSD (solid state drive) Data storage device that uses solid state memory to store data.

SSID (service set identifier) Parameter used to define a wireless network; otherwise known as the network name.

SSL (Secure Sockets Layer) Security protocol used by a browser to connect to secure Web sites.

standard account/user User account in Windows Vista that has limited access to a system. Accounts of this type cannot alter system files, cannot install new programs, and cannot edit some settings by using the Control Panel without supplying an administrator password. Replaces the Limited accounts in Windows XP.

standouts Small connectors that screw into a computer case. A motherboard is then placed on top of the standouts, and small screws are used to secure it to the standouts.

star topology Network topology where the computers on the network connect to a central wiring point, usually called a *hub*.

Start button Button on the Windows taskbar that enables access to the Start menu.

Start menu Menu that can be accessed by clicking the Start button on the Windows taskbar. Enables you to see all programs loaded on the system and to start them.

static charge eliminator Device used to remove a static charge.

static IP address Manually set IP address that will not change.

stealth virus Virus that uses various methods to hide from antivirus software.

stepper motor One of two methods used to move actuator arms in a hard drive. (*See also* voice coil motor.)

stereo Describes recording tracks from two sources (microphones) as opposed to monaural, which uses one source.

stick Generic name for a single physical SIMM, RIMM, or DIMM.

STP (shielded twisted pair) Cabling for networks, composed of pairs of wires twisted around each other at specific intervals. Twists serve to reduce interference (also called *crosstalk*)—the more twists, the less interference. Cable has metallic shielding to protect the wires from external interference.

streaming media   Broadcast of data that is played on your computer and immediately discarded.

stream loading   Process a program uses to constantly download updated information.

stripe set   Two or more drives in a group that are used for a striped volume.

strong password   Password containing at least eight characters, including letters, numbers, and punctuation symbols.

stylus   Pen-like input device used for pen-based computing.

subnet mask   Value used in TCP/IP settings to divide the IP address of a host into its component parts: network ID and host ID.

sub-pixel   Tiny liquid crystal molecules arranged in rows and columns between polarizing filters used in LCDs.

subwoofer   Powerful speaker capable of producing extremely low-frequency sounds.

super I/O chip   Chip specially designed to control low-speed, legacy devices such as the keyboard, mouse, and serial and parallel ports.

surge suppressor   Inexpensive device that protects your computer from voltage spikes.

SVGA (super video graphics array)   Video display mode of 800 × 600.

swap file   See page file.

switch   Device that filters and forwards traffic based on some criteria. A bridge and a router are both examples of switches.

SXGA   Video display mode of 1280 × 1024.

SXGA+   Video display mode of 1400 × 1050.

syntax   The proper way to write a command-line command so that it functions and does what it's supposed to do.

Sysprep   Windows tool that makes cloning of systems easier by making it possible to undo portions of the installation.

System BIOS   Primary set of BIOS stored on an EPROM or Flash chip on the motherboard. Defines the BIOS for all the assumed hardware on the mother-

board, such as keyboard controller, floppy drive, basic video, and RAM.

system bus speed   Speed at which the CPU and the rest of the PC operates; set by the system crystal.

system crystal   Crystal that provides the speed signals for the CPU and the rest of the system.

system disk   Any device with a functional operating system.

system fan   Any fan controlled by the motherboard but not directly attached to the CPU.

System Management Mode (SMM)   Provided CPUs the ability to turn off high-power devices (monitors, hard drives, etc.). Originally for laptops; later versions are incorporated in all AMD and Intel CPUs.

System Monitor   Utility that can evaluate and monitor system resources, such as CPU usage and memory usage.

system resources   In classic terms, the I/O addresses, IRQs, DMA channels, and memory addresses. Also refers to other computer essentials such as hard drive space, system RAM, and processor speed.

System Restore   Utility in Windows that enables you to return your PC to a recent working configuration when something goes wrong. System Restore returns your computer's system settings to the way they were the last time you remember your system working correctly—all without affecting your personal files or e-mail.

System ROM   ROM chip that stores the system BIOS.

System Tools   Menu containing tools such as System Information and Disk Defragmenter, accessed by selecting Start | Programs or All Programs | Accessories | System Tools.

system tray   Contains icons representing background processes and the system clock. Located by default at the right edge of the Windows taskbar. Accurately called the *notification area*.

system unit   Main component of the PC, in which the CPU, RAM, CD-ROM, and hard drive reside. All other devices—the keyboard, mouse, and monitor—connect to the system unit.

Tablet PC   Small portable computer distinguished by the use of a touch screen with stylus and handwriting recognition as the primary modes of input. Also the name of the Windows XP-based operating system designed to run on such systems.

tailgating   Form of infiltration and social engineering that involves following someone else through a door as if you belong.

take ownership   Special permission allowing users to seize control of a file or folder and potentially preventing others from accessing the file/folder.

Task Manager   Shows all running programs, including hidden ones, accessed by pressing CTRL-SHIFT-ESC. Able to shut down an unresponsive application that refuses to close normally.

taskbar   Contains the Start button, the system tray, the Quick Launch bar, and buttons for running applications. Located by default at the bottom of the desktop.

TCP/IP (Transmission Control Protocol/Internet Protocol)   Communication protocols developed by the U.S. Department of Defense to enable dissimilar computers to share information over a network.

tech toolkit   Tools a PC tech should never be without, including a Phillips-head screwdriver, a pair of tweezers, a flat-head screwdriver, a hemostat, a Torx wrench, a parts retriever, and a nut driver or two.

telephone scams   Social engineering attack in which the attacker makes a phone call to someone in an organization to gain information.

TELNET   Terminal emulation program for TCP/IP networks that allows one machine to control another as if the user were sitting in front of it.

tera-   Prefix that usually stands for the binary number 1,099,511,627,776 (2^{40}). When used for mass storage, it's often shorthand for a trillion bytes.

terminal   Dumb device connected to a mainframe or computer network that acts as a point for entry or retrieval of information.

terminal emulation   Software that enables a PC to communicate with another computer or network as if the PC were a specific type of hardware terminal.

termination   Using terminating resistors to prevent packet reflection on a network cable.

terminator   Resistor that is plugged into the end of a bus cable to absorb the excess electrical signal, preventing it from bouncing back when it reaches the end of the wire. Terminators are used with coaxial cable and on the ends of SCSI chains. RG-58 coaxial cable requires resistors with a 50-ohm impedance.

Test the theory   Attempt to resolve the issue by either confirming the theory and learning what needs to be done to fix the problem, or by not confirming the theory and forming a new one or escalating. (One of the steps a technician uses to solve a problem.)

texture   Small picture that is tiled over and over again on walls, floors, and other surfaces to create the 3-D world.

TFT (thin film transistor)   Type of LCD screen. (*See also* active matrix.)

theory of probable cause   One possible reason why something is not working; a guess.

thermal compound   Paste-like material with very high heat-transfer properties. Applied between the CPU and the cooling device, it ensures the best possible dispersal of heat from the CPU. Also called *heat dope*.

thermal printer   Printers that use heated printheads to create high-quality images on special or plain paper.

thermal unit   Combination heat sink and fan designed for BTX motherboards; blows hot air out the back of the case instead of just into the case.

thread   Smallest logical division of a single program.

throttling   Power reduction/thermal control capability allowing CPUs to slow down during low activity or high heat build-up situations. Intel's version is known as SpeedStep, AMD's as PowerNow!

throw   Size of the image a projector displays at a certain distance from the screen.

TIA/EIA   Telecommunications Industry Alliance/Electronic Industries Alliance. Trade organization that provides standards for network cabling and other electronics.

tiers   Levels of Internet providers, ranging from the Tier 1 backbones to Tier 3 regional networks.

timbre   Qualities that differentiate the same note played on different instruments.

toner   A fine powder made up of plastic particles bonded to iron particles, used by laser printers to create text and images.

toner cartridge Object used to store the toner in a laser printer. (*See also* laser printer, toner.)

touchpad Flat, touch-sensitive pad that serves as a pointing device for most laptops.

touch screen Monitor with a type of sensing device across its face that detects the location and duration of contact, usually by a finger or stylus.

TRACERT Command-line utility used to follow the path a packet takes between two hosts. Also called TRACEROUTE.

traces Small electrical connections embedded in a circuit board.

track Area on a hard drive platter where data is stored. A group of tracks with the same diameter is called a *cylinder*.

trackball Pointing device distinguished by a ball that is rolled with the fingers.

TrackPoint IBM's pencil-eraser-sized joystick used in place of a mouse on laptops.

transfer corona Thin wire, usually protected by other thin wires, that applies a positive charge to the paper during the laser printing process, drawing the negatively charged toner particles off of the drum and onto the paper.

transparency (Windows Vista Aero) Effect in the Aero desktop environment that makes the edges of windows transparent.

triad Group of three phosphors—red, green, blue—in a CRT.

Trojan Program that does something other than what the user who runs the program thinks it will do.

troubleshooting theory Steps a technician uses to solve a problem: identify the problem, establish a theory of probable cause, test the theory, establish a plan of action, verify functionality, and document findings.

TV tuner Typically an add-on device that allows users to watch television on a computer.

TWAIN (Technology Without an Interesting Name) Programming interface that enables a graphics application, such as a desktop publishing program, to activate a scanner, frame grabber, or other image-capturing device.

UAC (User Account Control) Windows Vista feature that enables Standard accounts to do common tasks and provides a permissions dialog when Standard and Administrator accounts do certain things that could potentially harm the computer (such as attempt to install a program).

UART (universal asynchronous receiver/transmitter) Device that turns serial data into parallel data. The cornerstone of serial ports and modems.

UDF (universal data format) Replaced the ISO-9660 formats, allowing any operating system and optical drive to read UDF formatted disks.

UEFI (Unified Extensible Firmware Interface) Consortium of companies that established the UEFI standard that replaced the original EFI standard.

Ultra DMA Hard drive technology that enables drives to use direct memory addressing. Ultra DMA mode 3 drives—called *ATA/33*—have data transfer speeds up to 33 MBps. Mode 4 and 5 drives—called *ATA/66* and *ATA/100*, respectively—transfer data at up to 66 MBps for mode 4 and 100 MBps for mode 5. Both modes 4 and 5 require an 80-wire cable and a compatible controller to achieve these data transfer rates.

unauthorized access Anytime a person accesses resources in an unauthorized way. This access may or may not be malicious.

Unicode 16-bit code that covers every character of the most common languages, plus several thousand symbols.

unsigned driver Driver that has not gone through the Windows Hardware Quality Labs or Microsoft Windows Logo Program to ensure compatibility.

UPC (Universal Product Code) Bar code used to track inventory.

Upgrade Advisor The first process that runs on the XP installation CD. It examines your hardware and installed software (in the case of an upgrade) and provides a list of devices and software that are known to have issues with XP. It can also be run separately from the Windows XP installation, from the Windows XP CD. The Upgrade Advisor is also available for Windows Vista and Windows 7.

upgrade installation Installation of Windows on top of an earlier installed version, thus inheriting all previous hardware and software settings.

UPS (uninterruptible power supply) Device that supplies continuous clean power to a computer system the whole time the computer is on. Protects against power outages and sags.

URL (uniform resource locator) An address that defines the location of a resource on the Internet. URLs are used most often in conjunction with HTML and the World Wide Web.

USB (universal serial bus) General-purpose serial interconnect for keyboards, printers, joysticks, and many other devices. Enables hot-swapping devices.

USB host controller Integrated circuit that is usually built into the chipset and controls every USB device that connects to it.

USB hub Device that extends a single USB connection to two or more USB ports, almost always directly from one of the USB ports connected to the root hub.

USB root hub Part of the host controller that makes the physical connection to the USB ports.

USB thumb drive Flash memory device that uses the standard USB connection.

User account Container that identifies a user to an application, operating system, or network, including name, password, user name, groups to which the user belongs, and other information based on the user and the OS or NOS being used. Usually defines the rights and roles a user plays on a system.

User Accounts applet Windows XP (and later versions) applet that replaced the Users and Passwords applet of Windows 2000.

user interface Visual representation of the computer on the monitor that makes sense to the people using the computer, through which the user can interact with the computer.

user profiles Settings that correspond to a specific user account and may follow users regardless of the computers where they log on. These settings enable the user to have customized environment and security settings.

User's Files Windows Vista's redux of the My Documents folder structure. It is divided into several folders such as Documents, Pictures, Music, and Video.

Users and Passwords applet Windows 2000 application that allowed management of user accounts and passwords.

Users group List of local users not allowed, among other things, to edit the Registry or access critical system files. They can create groups, but can only manage the groups they create.

USMT (User State Migration Tool) Advanced application for file and settings transfer of multiple users.

UTP (unshielded twisted pair) Popular type of cabling for telephone and networks, composed of pairs of wires twisted around each other at specific intervals. The twists serve to reduce interference (also called *crosstalk*). The more twists, the less interference. Unlike its cousin, STP, UTP cable has no metallic shielding to protect the wires from external interference. 1000BaseT uses UTP, as do many other networking technologies. UTP is available in a variety of grades, called categories, as follows:

Category 1 UTP Regular analog phone lines—not used for data communications.

Category 2 UTP Supports speeds up to 4 megabits per second.

Category 3 UTP Supports speeds up to 16 megabits per second.

Category 4 UTP Supports speeds up to 20 megabits per second.

Category 5 UTP Supports speeds up to 100 megabits per second.

Category 5e UTP Supports speeds up to 1000 megabits per second.

Category 6 UTP Supports speeds up to 10 gigabits per second.

V standards Standards established by CCITT for modem manufacturers to follow (voluntarily) to ensure compatible speeds, compression, and error correction.

verify Making sure that a problem has been resolved and will not return. (One of the steps a technician uses to solve a problem.)

vertices Used in the second generation of 3-D rendering, vertices have a defined X, Y, and Z position in a 3-D world.

VESA (Video Electronics Standards Association) Consortium of computer manufacturers that standardized improvements to common IBM PC components. VESA is responsible for the Super VGA video standard and the VLB bus architecture.

VGA (video graphics array) Standard for the video graphics adapter that was built into IBM's PS/2 computer. It supports 16 colors in a 640 × 480 pixel video display and quickly replaced the older CGA (Color Graphics Adapter) and EGA (Extended Graphics Adapter) standards.

video capture Computer jargon for the recording of video information, such as TV shows or movies.

video card Expansion card that works with the CPU to produce the images displayed on your computer's display.

video display *See* monitor.

virus Program that can make a copy of itself without your necessarily being aware of it. Some viruses can destroy or damage files. The best protection is to back up files regularly.

virus definition or data file Files that enable the virus protection software to recognize the viruses on your system and clean them. These files should be updated often. They are also called *signature files*, depending on the virus protection software in use.

virus shield Passive monitoring of a computer's activity, checking for viruses only when certain events occur.

VIS (viewable image size) Measurement of the viewable image that is displayed by a CRT rather than a measurement of the CRT itself.

voice coil motor One of two methods used to move actuator arms in a hard drive. (*See also* stepper motor.)

VoIP (Voice over Internet Protocol) Collection of protocols that make voice calls over a data network possible.

volatile Memory that must have constant electricity to retain data. Alternatively, any programmer six hours before deadline after a non-stop, 48-hour coding session, running on nothing but caffeine and sugar.

volts (V) Measurement of the pressure of the electrons passing through a wire, or voltage.

volume Physical unit of a storage medium, such as tape reel or disk pack, that is capable of having data recorded on it and subsequently read. Also refers to a contiguous collection of cylinders or blocks on a disk that are treated as a separate unit.

volume boot sector First sector of the first cylinder of each partition; stores information important to its partition, such as the location of the operating system boot files.

voucher Means of getting a discount on the CompTIA A+ exams.

VPN (virtual private network) Encrypted connection over the Internet between a computer or remote network and a private network.

VRM (voltage regulator module) Small card supplied with some CPUs to ensure that the CPU gets correct voltage. This type of card, which must be used with a motherboard specially designed to accept it, is not commonly seen today.

VRR (vertical refresh rate) The amount of time it takes for a CRT to draw a complete screen. This value is measured in hertz, or cycles per second. Most modern CRTs have a VRR of 60 Hz or better.

wait state Occurs when the CPU has to wait for RAM to provide code. Also known as pipeline stalls.

WAP (Wireless Access Point) Device that centrally connects wireless network nodes.

wattage (watts or W) Measurement of the amps and volts needed for a particular device to function.

wave table synthesis Technique that supplanted FM synthesis, wherein recordings of actual instruments or other sounds are embedded in the sound card as WAV files. When a particular note from a particular instrument or voice is requested, the sound processor grabs the appropriate prerecorded WAV file from its memory and adjusts it to match the specific sound and timing requested.

Web browser Program designed to retrieve, interpret, and display Web pages.

webcam PC camera most commonly used for Internet video.

Welcome screen   Login screen for Windows XP. Enables users to select their particular user account by clicking on their user picture.

WEP (Wired Equivalent Privacy)   Wireless security protocol that uses a standard 40-bit encryption to scramble data packets. Does not provide complete end-to-end encryption and is vulnerable to attack.

Wi-Fi   Common name for the IEEE 802.11 wireless Ethernet standard.

wildcard   Character used during a search to represent search criteria. For instance, searching for ***.doc** will return a list of all files with a .doc extension, regardless of the filename. The * is the wildcard in that search.

Windows 2000   Windows version that succeeded Windows NT; it came in both Professional and Server versions.

Windows 9x   Term used collectively for Windows 95, Windows 98, and Windows Me.

Windows Explorer   Windows utility that enables you to manipulate files and folders stored on the drives in your computer.

Windows Logo'd Product List   List of products that have passed the Microsoft Windows Logo Program and are compatible with Windows operating system. Formerly called the *Hardware Compatibility List* (or *HCL*).

Windows NT   Precursor to Windows 2000, XP, and Vista, which introduced many important features (such as HAL and NTFS) used in all later versions of Windows.

Windows sidebar   User interface feature in Windows Vista that enables users to place various gadgets, such as clocks, calendars, and other utilities, on the right side of their desktop.

Windows Update   Microsoft application used to keep Windows operating systems up to date with the latest patches or enhancements. (*See* Automatic Updates.)

Windows Vista   Version of Windows; comes in many different editions for home and office use, but does not have a Server edition.

Windows XP   Version of Windows that replaced both the entire Windows 9x line and Windows 2000; does not have a Server version.

worm   Very special form of virus. Unlike other viruses, a worm does not infect other files on the computer. Instead, it replicates by making copies of itself on other systems on a network by taking advantage of security weaknesses in networking protocols.

WPA (Wi-Fi Protected Access)   Wireless security protocol that uses encryption key integrity-checking and EAP and is designed to improve on WEP's weaknesses.

WPA 2 (Wi-Fi Protected Access 2)   Wireless security protocol, also known as IEEE 802.11i. Uses the Advanced Encryption standard and replaces WPA.

WQUXGA   Video display mode of 2560 × 1600.

wrapper   *See* container file.

WSXGA   Video display mode of 1440 × 900.

WSXGA+   Video display mode of 1680 × 1050.

WUXGA   Video display mode of 1920 × 1200.

WVGA   Video display mode of 800 × 480.

WWW (World Wide Web)   System of Internet servers that support documents formatted in HTML and related protocols. Can be accessed by using Gopher, FTP, HTTP, Telnet, and other tools.

www.comptia.org   CompTIA's Web site.

WXGA   Video display mode of 1280 × 800.

x64   Describes 64-bit operating systems and software.

x86   Describes 32-bit operating systems and software.

XCOPY command   Command in the command-line interface used to copy multiple directories at once, which the COPY command could not do.

xD (Extreme Digital) picture card   Very small flash media card format.

Xeon   Line of Intel CPUs designed for servers.

XGA (extended graphics array)   Video display mode of 1024 × 768.

XPS (XML Paper Specification) print path   Improved printing subsystem included in Windows Vista. Has enhanced color management and better print layout fidelity.

XT bus   *See* PC bus.

ZIF (zero insertion force) socket   Socket for CPUs that enables insertion of a chip without the need to apply pressure. Intel promoted this socket with its overdrive upgrades. The chip drops effortlessly into the socket's holes, and a small lever locks it in.

AMD Opteron CPUs, 169, 172
AMD Phenom Black Edition, 172
AMD Phenom CPUs, 171–172
AMD Phenom II CPUs, 172
AMD Phenom X3, 172
AMD Phenom X4, 172
AMD Sempron CPUs, 165, 170
AMD64 extensions, 170
American Megatrends (AMI), 210, 211
American National Standards
  Institute (ANSI), 286
American Power Conversion
  (APC), 266
American Standard Code for
  Information Interchange language.
  See ASCII
AMI (American Megatrends), 210, 211
amperage, 259
amperes (amps/A), 259, 260
amplitude, 441
AMR (audio modem riser) slot,
  249, 579
analog dial-up, 576–577
analog LCD monitors, 427, 428
analog sources (video), 451
analog/digital out connection, 448
ANSI (American National Standards
  Institute), 286
answer files, 364–369, 371
anti-aliasing, 423
AntiEXE virus, 610
anti-malware utilities, 633
anti-static bags, 28, 29
anti-static mats, 28
anti-static tools, 27–29
anti-static wrist straps, 27–28
antivirus programs, 609–610
AOL, 607
APC (American Power
  Conversion), 266
APM (Advanced Power
  Management), 474–480
APM Enabled power usage level, 476
APM Standby power usage level, 477
APM Suspend power usage level, 477
appearance, 19
Apple Extensions, 324
Apple Macintosh operating system,
  39, 40, 63, 438
applets, 89. *See also specific applets*
Application layer (OSI seven-layer
  model), 548
applications, 39. *See also specific
  applications*
Applications and Background
  Services button, 116–117
Applications tab (Task Manager), 117
ARC (Advanced RISC Computing)
  naming system, 383
Archive attributes, 126
arithmetic logic units (ALUs), 151
ARPANET, 536
ASCII, 430, 431, 503

ASF files, 454
Ask me later option (Automatic
  Updates feature), 362
ASM (Assembly Language Source)
  files, 443
aspect ratio, 416, 463
ASR (Automated System Recovery),
  124, 125
Assembly Language Source (ASM)
  files, 443
assertive communication, 23
Asus Eee PC, 466
ASX files, 443
asynchronous DSL (ADSL), 582
AT buses, 225
AT motherboards, 239–241, 243
ATA hard drives, 286–296, 303
ATA (AT Attachment) interface, 286
ATA RAID controller chips, 305
ATA Security Mode Feature Set,
  216–217
ATA-1 hard drives, 286–288
ATA-2 hard drives, 288–291
ATA-3 hard drives, 291–292
ATA-4 hard drives, 292
ATA-5 hard drives, 293
ATA-6 hard drives, 293–294
ATA-7 hard drives, 294–296
ATA/66 cable, 293
ATA/133, 294
ATA/ATAPI-6. *See* ATA-6
ATA/I33, 294
ATAPI (Advanced Technology
  Attachment Packet Interface),
  290, 291
ATAPI-compliant (term), 327
ATI, 437
ATI TV tuner cards, 454, 455
attributes, backup options and, 126
ATX 12V 1.3 power supplies, 269, 270
ATX 12V 2.0 power supplies, 271–272
ATX form factor, 241–243, 270
ATX power supplies, 269–273
AU files, 443
audio connectors, 46
Audio Interchange File Format
  (AIFF), 443
authentication, 561, 598–599
Authorization of Work form, 21
Automated Installation Kit (AIK),
  368–370
Automated System Recovery (ASR),
  124, 125
Automatic Update Setup Wizard, 102
Automatic Updates feature,
  102–103, 361
AutoPlay option, 327
auto-range meters, 263
Autorun feature, 110
AUTORUN.INF file, 110
AUTORUNS tool, 633–634
autosensing, 528

auto-switching power supplies,
  261, 482
AUX connectors, 269, 271
avast! Virus Cleaner Tool, 612
AVI files, 454
Award BIOS, 211–214
Azalia sound option, 445

■ B

backbone routers, 573
backbones, 573
backlights (LCD monitors), 422
backside bus, 162
backup:
    with CDs, 327, 328
    data, 343
    NTBackup, 122–127
    personal data, 122
    tape, 125, 313
    and troubleshooting, 628
Backup (Windows 2000), 122
Backup and Restore Center,
  127–128, 374
backup tools, 634
Backup Utility (Windows XP),
  122–127
Backup Wizard, 123, 125
backward compatibility, 209, 226, 228,
  271, 293, 295, 504
Balanced Technology eXtended (BTX)
  form factor, 243–244, 272
ball mice, 397
bandwidth, 229, 417, 525, 526
banks (DIMM slots), 188
bar code readers, 405
BartPE tool, 612
basic input/output services. *See* BIOS
basic rate interface (BRI) setup, 582
Basic Service Set (BSS), 559
batteries, 266, 393, 473–475
battery memory, 474
battery recycling services, 474
baud, 578
BCD (Boot Configuration Data)
  files, 385
BD media. *See* Blu-ray Disc
BD-R (BD-recordable) discs, 332
BD-RE (BD-rewritable) discs, 332
beaming, 467
beep codes, 220
Berkeley Software Distribution (BSD)
  UNIX, 536
betamaxing, 190
bidirectional printing, 505
Big Drive, 293
binary numbering system, 142,
  150–151, 231–232
biometric devices, 404–405, 599
    BIOS (basic input/output
      services), 217–218
    AT BIOS, 288, 292

and CPUs/motherboards,
207–209
and device drivers, 219
flashing the, 171
on IBM PC AT, 286
and installation errors, 371
locations of, 219
and logical geometry, 290
and POST cards, 220
and power options, 477, 478
socket services in, 485
and soft power, 269
storage of, 207
system BIOS support, 209
and updating CMOS, 210–214
in Windows 2000/XP boot
process, 380
in Windows Vista/7 boot
process, 384–385
in Windows XP Setup boot
process, 346
bit depth, 441
bit rate, 442
Bit Torrent, 590, 591
BitLocker Drive Encryption, 217
bits, 147–148, 150
bits per second (bps), 578
Blaster worm, 101
blue screen of death, 371
Bluetooth, 468, 506, 557, 558, 565–566
Blu-Ray burners, 332
Blu-ray Disc (BD) media, 56, 322,
331–332, 453
BNC connections, 530
boot blocks, 613
Boot Configuration Data (BCD)
files, 385
boot files, 381, 384, 385
boot options, 214
boot partition, 381
boot processes:
from antivirus discs, 611–612
for clean installations,
350–351, 356
from floppy disks, 315
post-installation, 380–385
power-on self test, 221–222
from thumb drives, 319
into Windows XP Setup, 346
boot sector, 222
boot sector viruses, 609–610
boot tools, 633–634
Boot Up Floppy Seek option
(CMOS), 318
bootable disks, 222, 368
BOOTCFG, 613
BOOT.INI files, 108, 380, 382–384
/BOOTLOG switch, 383
BOOTMGR files, 384–385
bootstrap loader, 222
bps (bits per second), 578
branch predication, 158
branches, 147

BRI (basic rate interface) setup, 582
brightness, 423, 426, 429, 430
broadband Internet, 444, 584
BSD (Berkeley Software Distribution)
UNIX, 536
BSS (Basic Service Set), 559
BTX (Balanced Technology eXtended)
form factor, 243–244, 272
buffered DRAM, 196–197
built-in touch screens, 406
burners/burning, 325–327, 332
bus cable, 522
bus mastering devices, 237
bus topology, 521–522
byte mode, 505
bytes, 53, 147, 150

C

CAB file errors, 372
cable Internet connections, 583
cache, 157–158
camcorders, 451
Camera Settings applet, 403
cameras:
digital, 400–402
web, 402–404, 452
card readers, 321
card services, 485
CardBus PC cards, 484
carrier sense multiple access/collision
avoidance (CSMA/CA)
standard, 558
carrier sense multiple access/collision
detection (CSMA/CD)
standard, 558
CAS (column array strobe), 195
case, of PC system unit, 51–52
CAT levels, of UTP, 526
cathode ray tube monitors. See CRT
monitors
cathode ray tube (CRT) projectors, 425
CCFL (cold cathode fluorescent lamp)
technology, 422
CCleaner (program), 104
CCNA (Certified Cisco Network
Associate) certifications, 4
CD burners, 325
CD File System (CDFS), 324
CD quality sound capture, 441
CD readers, 323
CDDA (CD-Digital Audio) format, 323
CD-Digital Audio (CDDA) format, 323
CDFS (CD File System), 324
CD-R (recordable) discs, 56, 325, 328
CD-ROM (for this book), 11, 13,
652–654
CD-ROM (in general), 56, 323–324
CD-ROM drives, 297
CD-ROM speeds, 324–325
CD-RW (rewritable) discs, 56,
325–327

CD-RW (rewritable) drives,
290, 291
CDs (compact discs), 55–56, 322–328
Celeron-M chips, 174
Cellular WAN, 468
cellular wireless networks, 567
central processing units. See CPUs
Centrino solutions, 167
Centronics connectors, 505
certifications, 1–4. See also CompTIA
A+ certification
Certified Cisco Network Associate
(CCNA) certifications, 4
Certiport's IC³ certification, 3
CF (CompactFlash), 319–320
CFX12V power supply, 272
chains (SCSI devices), 296–298
chamfers, 267
Change/Remove button, 111
chassis intrusion detection, 215
chatting, on Internet, 589
Check Disk tool, 107
Check for updates... (setting), 103
Check Upgrade utility, 350
checksums, 610
chipsets, 203, 205, 223, 244–249
CHKDSK command, 104
CHKDSK.EXE, 107
CHS (cylinder, head, and sector)
information, 284
circuit breakers, 260
Cisco certification, 2, 4
CITE (color infrastructure and
translation engine), 510
CL2 latency, 195
CL3 latency, 195
Class A networks, 537
Class B networks, 537
Class C networks, 537
class objects, 93
classic direct memory access
(DMA), 237
clean installations, 341, 343, 371
of Windows Vista, 348, 349,
356–363
of Windows XP/2000, 350–355
Clear All button, 102
clear to send (CTS) wires, 579
client machines, in networks, 521, 531
client/server LANs, 530–531
clock, 144–146, 189
clock chips, 145, 146, 158–159
clock cycles, 144, 195
clock doubling, 159
clock multiplying CPUs, 158–159, 163
clock speed:
of CPUs, 144–145
and DDR speed, 191, 193, 194
of Pentium CPU, 158–159, 163
clock wires, 144
Clonezilla, 342
/CMDCONS switch, 383

nested RAID solutions, 302
NetBEUI (NetBIOS Extended User Interface) protocols, 535
NetBIOS, 535, 541–542
netbooks, 466–467, 472
NetBurst core, 165
Network (Windows Vista), 88–89
network access points (NAPs), 573
Network and Internet Connections applet, 580–581
Network and Sharing Center (Windows Vista), 587
network bootable disks, 368
network cables, 546
network cards, 535
network connections, 506
Network Connections dialog box, 539
Network Identification Wizard, 534
network interface cards. *See* NICs
Network layer (OSI seven-layer model), 548
network name, 560
network operating system (NOS), 530–531
network printers, 506
network role, 344
network settings (Windows XP), 354
Networking (Domain 4.0), 648
networking devices, 392
networks and networking. *See also* LAN (local area network); wireless networks
    CompTIA Network+ certification, 3
    connectors for, 48
    defined, 1
    in Mike's Four-Layer Model, 549
    on portable computers, 486, 487
    scripting installation from, 364
    technology for, 523
    vendor-specific certification for, 2
    virtual private, 586–588
    for Windows 2000 Professional, 344
    for Windows Vista, 349
    and Windows Vista installations, 362
    for Windows XP Professional, 346
    wireless, for portable computers, 487
    worms in, 608
neutral wires, 261
Never check for updates (setting), 103
New Connection Wizard, 580, 581
New Techs, 11, 213
nibble mode (IEEE 1284 Standard), 505
nibbles, 148
Ni-Cd (nickel-cadmium) batteries, 473, 474
niche-market power supplies, 272

nickel metal hydride (Ni-MH) batteries, 473, 474
nickel-cadmium (Ni-Cd) batteries, 473, 474
NICs (network interface cards), 48
    in computing process, 623–625
    defined, 521
    duplex and half-duplex mode, 528
    in LANs, 523–524
    link lights on, 528–529
    multispeed, 527, 528
    testing loopback of, 537, 546
Ni-MH (nickel metal hybrid) batteries, 473, 474
nits (brightness), 423
NLQ (near-letter quality), 495
NLX form factor, 240–241
No Boot Device Present When Booting Off the Startup Disk error, 371
nodes, 535
/NOEXECUTE switch, 384
non-user specific configurations, 94
nonvolatile flash memory, 286
nonvolatile ROM chips, 208
normal backups, 126
Northbridge, 203, 223, 228, 245, 246, 434
Norton Ghost, 342, 370
NOS (network operating system), 530–531
Not Ready error, 371
Notepad, 81
notetaking, 13
notification area (taskbar), 81
Notify me... (setting), 103
Novell, 536
NTBackup, 122–127
    backup options, 125–127
    Backup Wizard, 125
    tape backups, 125
    Windows 2000 Emergency Repair Disk, 123, 124
    Windows XP Automated System Recovery, 124, 125
Ntblog.txt files, 383
NTBOOTDD.SYS files, 380, 383
NTDETECT.COM files, 380, 384
NTFS (NT File System), 65, 68, 69, 531, 599, 600
NTLDR (NT loader) files, 380
NTLDR program, 382
NTOSKRNL.EXE, 381, 384, 385
number lock function key, 487
NVIDIA, 245
NVIDIA GeForce 9400 mGPU, 248
NVIDIA GeForce GTX 260, 437
NVIDIA nForce 980a SLI, 247
NWLink, 536

▓ O

OCR (optical character recognition), 399
OEM computers, 385

OFDM (orthogonal frequency-division-multiplexing) broadcasting, 562
OGG files, 443, 453, 454
ohms (Ω), 260
Old Techs, 11–13
OLGA (organic land grid array), 168
Olympus, 321
onboard devices, 46–47
online gaming, 588–589
online UPS (uninterruptible power supply), 265
Only Back Up the System State data button (Backup Wizard), 125
OpenAL API, 450
operating system (OS). *See also specific operating systems*
    in computing process, 40–41, 623, 624
    defined, 39
    installing and upgrading, 338
    network, 530–531
    reinstalling, 124
    restoring previous, 385
Operating Systems and Software (Domain 3.0), 8, 646–647
Operational Procedure (Domain 6.0), 650–651
operational procedures, 7, 18–33
    communication, 23–27
    professionalism, 19–23
    safety and tools, 27–32
optical character recognition (OCR), 399
optical discs, 82, 110–111, 313, 321–332. *See also specific optical discs*
optical drives:
    defined, 55, 321
    installation errors on, 371, 372
    Not Ready errors on, 371
    for PC system unit, 55–56
    for Windows 2000 Professional, 344
    for Windows Vista, 349
    for Windows XP Professional, 346
optical mice, 397
optical resolution, 399, 400
optical zoom, 401
Optimized Defaults options, 216
option ROM, 218
organic land grid array (OLGA), 168
orthogonal frequency-division-multiplexing (OFDM) broadcasting, 562
OS. *See* operating system
OSI Seven-Layer model, 547–548
out-of-order processing, 161
output, 41, 621. *See also* input/output devices
overclocking, 145, 176, 194, 214
overheating, 629
ozone filter (printing), 502

■ P

PAC (pin array cartridge), 168
packet writing, 327
PacketFence, 611
packets, 521, 523–524
page file, 97–100
Page Setup interface, 512
pages per minute (PPM), 497
PANs (personal area networks), 566
paper size options (printing), 512
paper tray options (printing), 512
paperwork, 21
paragraphs (bits), 148
Parallel Advanced Technology
    Attachment hard drives. *See* PATA
    hard drives
parallel communication, 504–505,
    577–578
parallel connections, 505, 530
parallel PC cards, 484
parallel ports, 50, 504–505
parallel processing, 170
parity RAM, 196
Partial Response Maximum
    Likelihood (PRML) encoding, 282
`Partition (x)` ARC setting, 383
partition files, 381–384
partitioning (hard drive), 343, 351, 359
parts retriever, 32
passive matrix display, 421
password clearers, 634
passwords:
    for administrator accounts, 534
    in answer files, 368
    avoiding learning, 20–21
    drive lock, 216–217
    and security, 598
    Windows policy for, 603
    in Windows Vista installation
      process, 360
PATA (Parallel Advanced Technology
    Attachment) hard drives, 55, 286,
    304, 383
patch management, 608
patches, 100–103, 370, 373, 546
patterns (address buses), 149–151
PC buses, 224–225
PC cameras. *See* web cameras
PC cards, 296, 313, 483–486
PC techs, 0–15
    CompTIA A+ certification, 2–4
    CompTIA A+ certification
      exams, 4–13
    and computing process, 41–42
    computing process and
      troubleshooting by, 621–627
    skills of, 1
    toolkits of, 32, 632–634
    traits of, 19–23
    troubleshooting theory, 627–632
PCBs (printed circuit boards), 239
PC-DOS, 88
PCI cards, 557

PCI (peripheral component
    interconnect) expansion buses, 227,
    237, 579
PCI Express (PCIe) connections, 272, 436
PCI Express (PCIe) expansion buses,
    228–230, 237, 485, 579
PCI Extended (PCI-X) expansion
    buses, 228
PCI video cards, 634
PCL6, 504
PCMCIA (Personal Computer
    Memory Card International
    Association), 483, 484
PCMCIA buses, 319
PCMCIA cards. *See* PC cards
PCs (personal computers), 38–58
    complete PC system, 42–51
    computing process, 39–42
    system unit, 51–56
    tablet, 468–472
    ultra mobile, 472
PDAs (personal digital assistants),
    467–468, 472, 557, 567
Pearson VUE, 8
peer-to-peer local area networks, 531
peer-to-peer mode, 559
P8/P9 power socket, 240
pen scanners, 405
pen-based computing, 467, 468
Pentium 4, 71, 165–167, 190
Pentium chip (original), 160–161
Pentium CPUs, 154–160
    cache, 157–158
    clock speed and multipliers,
      158–159, 163
    MMX, 162–163
    pipelining, 155–157
    32-bit processing, 155
    voltages, 159–160
Pentium D CPUs, 170
Pentium II CPUs, 163–164
Pentium M, 171
Pentium Pro CPUs, 160–162
Pentium Xeon, 169
perfect flat CRT monitors, 414
Performance console, 118–120
Performance Logs and Alerts, 119–120
Performance Options, 116–117
performance rating (PR) numbers,
    165, 363
Performance tab (Task Manager), 117
peripheral emulation, 407
peripherals, 42, 267–268, 566
permissions, 111, 600–601
perpendicular recording, 282
persistence (CRT monitors), 413
personal area networks (PANs), 566
Personal Computer Memory Card
    International Association
    (PCMCIA), 483, 484
personal computers. *See* PCs
personal data, 122
personal RAID, 305
Personal Video Recorder (PVR), 69

P4 power connectors, 271
PGA (pin grid array) packages, 53, 153
Philips, 328, 330
Phillips-head screwdrivers, 32
Phoenix Technologies, 210, 211, 213, 293
phosphors, 413–415, 423
photoconductivity, 499
photosensitive drum, 499, 500
photosites, 401
physical access control, 598
physical geometry, 289, 290
Physical layer (OSI seven-layer
    model), 548
physical safety, 30–31
physical topologies, 523
picoBTX form factor, 243
PICs, 234
pin 1, 315, 316
pin array cartridge (PAC), 168
pin grid array (PGA) packages, 53, 153
PING utility, 538
Pinnacle blueBox, 451, 452
PIO modes, 287, 288
pipeline stalls, 156
pipelining, 155–157
Piriform, 104
pixels, 401, 414–416, 420, 421
platter-based hard disk drives, 281–285
platters, 281, 283, 289, 306
playback, 445
plenum-grade cabling, 527
plug and play (PnP), 215, 216, 507, 508
plug-ins, 605–606
plugs, 43
plusID devices, 599, 600
PnP. *See* plug and play
PnP/PCI Configurations screen,
    215, 216
point of sale (POS) machines, 495
Pointer options tab, 396
Point-to-Point Protocol (PPP), 581
Point-to-Point Tunneling Protocol
    (PPTP), 587–588
policies (Windows), 601–603
polymorph viruses, 610
polyphony, 442
P1 power connectors, 267
POP service, 586
pop-ups, 603–606
portable computers, 462–491
    DDR SDRAM for, 190
    desktop extenders, 465–466, 472
    desktop replacements,
      464–465, 472
    LCD screens for, 463–464, 487
    managing and maintaining,
      473–486
    Mini PCI for, 228
    netbooks, 466–467, 472
    PDAs and smartphones, 467, 472
    support for external SATA
      devices with, 296
    tablet PCs, 468–472
    troubleshooting, 486–488

portrait view (LCD monitors), 433
ports, 43, 538, 585–586. *See also specific ports*
POS (point of sale) machines, 495
positional audio, 450
POST. *See* power-on self test
POST cards, 220–221
post-installation boot processes, 380–385
post-installation tasks, 373–380
PostScript language, 503
potential, electrical, 27
power, 258–260, 429, 430. *See also power supplies*
power conditioning, 264–266
power connectors, 317
power good, 222
power management (portable computers), 475–481
Power Management Setup screen, 215, 216
Power Options applet, 478–481
power supplies, 258–274
    AC power, 261–266, 422
    ATX, 269–273
    in computing process, 624
    DC power. *See* DC power
    defined, 54
    of laser printers, 501
    wattage requirements of, 274
power supply units (PSUs), 259
power-down mode, 429
power-on self test (POST), 219–222
power-saving modes, 269
PPM (pages per minute), 497
PPP (Point-to-Point Protocol), 581
PPTP (Point-to-Point Tunneling Protocol), 587–588
PR (performance rating) numbers, 165, 363
practice mode, for CD-ROM, 13, 652, 653
Presentation layer (OSI seven-layer model), 548
preset combinations, 235, 236
pressure roller, 501
Prevent Access to Command Prompt policy, 602
Prevent Registry Edits policy, 602
preventive measures, 631–632
PRI (primary rate interface) setup, 582
primary corona, 500
primary grid, 500
primary power supply, 501
primary rate interface (PRI) setup, 582
Principle of Least Privilege, 600
print devices, 507
print resolution, 497, 498
print servers, 506
print speed, 497, 498
printed circuit boards (PCBs), 239
Printer Browsing policy, 603

printer control language (PCL), 504
printer emulation, 508, 509
printers, 494–516
    connectivity of, 504–507
    connectors for, 50
    defined, 42
    installing, 507–510
    languages of, 503–504
    output from, 41
    troubleshooting, 510–513
    types of, 495–503
Printers and Faxes applet, 508, 509, 511, 512
printhead, 495
printwire, 495
private networks, 537
PRML (Partial Response Maximum Likelihood) encoding, 282
Processes tab (Task Manager), 117
processing, 41, 621
Processor scheduling settings (in Performance Options), 117
product keys, 353, 357
professionalism, 19–23
programming, 39, 207
programs, 146. *See also specific programs*
Programs and Features, 110, 112
Programs menu, 81
projectors, 424–426
Prometric, 8
proprietary form factors, 244
proprietary motherboards, 244
protective bags, 30
protocols, 534–535, 549
PRT-SCR (print screen) key, 503
PS/2 ports, 405
PSUs (power supply units), 259
public locations, 362
pulse code modulation (PCM), 441
PVR (Personal Video Recorder), 69

◼ Q

QDOS (Quick and Dirty Operating System), 88
QPI (QuickPath Interconnect), 173
quad words, 148
quad-pumped buses, 165, 189
quarantine (viruses), 611
Quick and Dirty Operating System (QDOS), 88
Quick Launch toolbar, 80, 82
QuickPath Interconnect (QPI), 173
QuickTime, 330, 443

◼ R

//R switch (Check Disk), 107
radio frequency identification (RFID), 599
radio frequency interference (RFI), 29–30, 265

radio waves, 468
RAID (redundant array of independent disks), 249, 300–305, 351
RAID 0 (Disk Striping), 302, 303, 305
RAID 1 (Disk Mirroring/Duplexing), 302, 303
RAID 2 (Disk Striping with Multiple Parity Drives), 302
RAID 3 (Disk Striping with Dedicated Parity), 302
RAID 4 (Disk Striping with Dedicated Parity), 302
RAID 5 (Disk Striping with Distributed Parity), 302, 303, 305
RAID 6 (Disk Striping with Extra Parity), 302
rails (power supplies), 271
RAM (random access memory), 182–199
    in computing process, 624
    as CPU memory, 147–148
    defined, 53, 147
    dynamic. *See* DRAM
    exabytes of, 168
    for importing video, 451
    and I/O addressing, 230
    of printers, 502
    and scanning images, 400
    and Second Life, 622
    static, 157
    for 32 bit versions of Windows, 71
    types, 188–194
    variations, 194–197
    video, 437–439
    Window, 438
RAM cache, 97
RAM interference, 162
RAM (random access memory) sticks, 53, 186–188, 194
Rambus, Inc., 189, 190
Rambus DRAM (RDRAM), 189–190
random access memory. *See* RAM
random access memory digital-to-analog converter (RAMDAC), 427
range (wireless networks), 561–562, 564
RAS (remote access services) server, 532
raster lines, 414
RCA connectors, 449
`Rdisk (x) ARC setting`, 383
RDRAM (Rambus DRAM), 189–190
read speed, 325, 332
Readme files, 509
Read-Only attributes, 126
read/write heads, 281, 283
ready to send (RTS) wires, 579
RealMedia, 443
real-time clock (RTC), 477
rear out connectors, 447
rear-view projects, 424, 425
rebooting, 371

Serial Advanced Technology Attachment power connectors. *See* SATA power connectors
serial communication, 577
serial connections, 504, 530
serial ports, 49, 579
Server System Infrastructure (SSI), 271
servers, 521, 531, 532
service calls, 628
Service Pack 2 (Windows XP), 101
service packs, 101–103, 373
services (ROM), 207, 538–539. *See also* device drivers
Session layer (OSI seven-layer model), 548
Setup Manager, 364–368, 371
S4 power state specification, 477
SFX12V power supply, 272
SGRAM (Synchronous Graphics RAM), 438
shadow mask, 415
shared directories, 342
Shared Documents folder, 69
shared files, 111
shared resources, 549
shareware, 653
shell size (DB connectors), 45
shielded twisted pair (STP) cabling, 526
shields (coaxial cables), 529–530
shift hot key, 90
SHIFT-DELETE hot key, 90
SHIFT-F10 hot key, 90
shipping computers, 483
Shockwave, 606
Shut Down System policy, 602
sidebanding, 435
signal-to-noise ratio, 446, 447
signatures (antivirus software), 610
SIMM (single inline memory module), 186
single data rate SDRAM (SDR SDRAM), 190
single edge processor (SEP) package, 173
single inline memory module (SIMM), 186
single-edge cartridges (SECs), 163
single-layer (SL) formats, 329
single-level cell (SLC) memory technology, 286
single-link DVI, 428
single-mode fiber optics, 530
single-sided (SS) formats, 329
single-sided RAM sticks, 194
single-word DMA (direct memory access), 288
Skype, 402, 453
SL (single-layer) formats, 329
slates (tablet PCs), 468
SLC (single-level cell) memory technology, 286
sleep timers, 478
sleeping state mode, 477

slimline connectors, 269
slimline form factor, 240
slipstreaming, of installation files, 370
Slot 2, 174
Slot A (Athlon Classic), 164
small computer system interface hard drives. *See* SCSI hard drives
small computer system interface (SCSI) IDs, 298–299
small-outline DIMM (SO-DIMM), 188, 193
S.M.A.R.T. (Self-Monitoring, Analysis, and Reporting Technology), 291–292
smart batteries, 475
smart cards, 599
Smart Recovery, 372
SmartMedia flash cards, 320
smartphones, 467, 472, 557, 558, 567
SMM (System Management Mode), 168, 476
SMTP service, 586
snapshot printers, 498
social engineering, 598
Socket 370, 173
Socket 478, 173
Socket 939, 171
Socket A, 164
Socket AM2, 171, 172
Socket AM2+, 172
Socket AM3, 172
socket services, 485
sockets, 153–154
SO-DIMM (small-outline DIMM), 188, 193
soft power, 242, 269, 270
soft power off mode, 477
SoftMenu, 213–214
software:
    authentication for, 598
    compatibility with hardware, 73–74, 340–341, 346, 349–350, 372
    compliance issues with, 597
    defined, 39
    installing, 109–113
    for Internet use, 574–575
    malicious, 603–608
    PC card, 485
    printer, 502
    removing, 111–112
    scanning, 398, 399
    and troubleshooting LANs, 546–547
    TV tuner, 455
    and vendor-specific certifications, 2
    video capture, 452–454
    wireless network, 558–559
software firewalls, 614–615
software licenses, 111
software methods, 303–305
software tracking systems, 483
SOHO networks, 614

solid ink printers, 502–503
solid-state drives (SSDs), 285–286
Sony, 321, 330
Sony Trinitron, 416
Sony/Philips Digital Interface (S/PDIF) connectors, 48, 449
sound, 440–444
    connectors for, 47–48
    hardware for, 444–451
    playing, 443–444
    on portable computers, 463
sound cards, 224, 439–440, 444–445
sound chips, 249
sound processors, 445–446
Sound Recorder settings, 441
sound-capture components, 441
Southbridge, 203, 210, 223, 245, 246
spam, 606–607
spare parts, 634
S/PDIF (Sony/Philips Digital Interface Format) connectors, 48, 449
speakers, 42, 444, 446–451
specialty input/output devices, 392
speculative execution, 161
speed:
    of ATA-2 hard drives, 291
    of CD-ROM, 324–325
    clock. *See* clock speed
    of CPUs, 242
    printer, 497, 498
    rewrite, 332
    spindle (rotational), 305–306
    of wireless networks, 561–562
    write, 332
spindle (rotational) speed, 305–306
splitters, 268, 269
spoolers, 507, 511, 512
spot color, 499
spread-spectrum broadcasting, 562, 564
Spybot Search & Destroy, 606
spyware, 603–607
SRAM (static RAM), 157
SSDs (solid-state drives), 285–286
SSE (Streaming SIMD Extensions), 164
SSI (Server System Infrastructure), 271
SSID (service set identifier parameter), 560
ST connectors, 529
stalled print jobs, 511–512
standalone role (networks), 344
standalone touch screen monitors, 406
Standard CMOS Features, 212, 213, 317–318
standard definition (SD) content, 424
standard parallel cables, 505
Standard SD cards, 320
Standard xD Picture Cards, 321
standards:
    for modems, 578
    for sound cards, 444–445
    for speakers, 448–450
    for wireless networks, 562–567
standby mode, 477

trackballs, 49, 465
TrackPoint device, 465
tracks, 284
tractor-feed paper, 495
Traits of a Tech, 19–23
transceiver ports, 557
transfer corona (printing), 501
Transfer Keys, 378
transformers, 483
transistors, 159
Transmission Control Protocol/
  Internet Protocol. *See* TCP/IP
transmit beamforming, 564
transparency feature, 78
Transport layer (OSI Seven-Layer
  model), 548
triads, 416
triggers (Task Scheduler), 105
Trinitron, 416
triple-channel memory, 194
tripping hazards, 482
trojans, 608
troubleshooting, 620–636
    and computing process,
        621–627
    keypads, 487
    LANs, 543–549
    local area networks, 543–549
    by PC techs, 620–636
    portable computers, 486–488
    printers, 510–513
    and tech toolkit, 632–634
    troubleshooting theory, 627–632
    Windows installations and
        upgrades, 371–373
    Windows installations/
        upgrades, 372–373
Troubleshooting, Repair and
  Maintenance (Domain 2.0), 644–646
troubleshooting theory, 627–632
    documenting problems, 632
    establishing theories of
        probable cause, 628–629
    identifying problems, 627
    testing theories to determine
        causes, 629–631
    verifying and preventing
        problems, 631–632
True Image (program), 342
TrueMotion VP6, 453
TrueType text, 504
trunk lines, 581
Trusted Computing Group, 217
Trusted Platform Module (TPM), 217
TSRs (terminate-and-stay resident
  programs), 611
T13 Committee (ANSI), 286, 293
TurboTax, 40
Turn off Automatic Updates setting, 103
TV tuners, 440, 454–455
TWAIN drivers, 399
Type I PC cards, 484
Type II PC cards, 484
Type III PC cards, 484

U

UAC (User Account Control), 111
UART (universal asynchronous
  receiver/transmitter) chip, 578
UDF (universal data format), 326–327
UEFI, 384, 385
Ultimate Boot CD, 612
Ultra DMA, 292–294
ultra mobile PCs, 472
Underwriters Laboratories UL 330 V
  rating, 263
Underwriters Laboratories UL 1449
  rating, 263
Uninstall/Change button, 111
uninstalling:
    programs, 111
    spyware, 606
    and troubleshooting LANs, 546
uninterruptible power supply (UPS),
    265–267
Unísono, 575, 576
universal asynchronous receiver/
    transmitter (UART) chip, 578
universal data format (UDF), 326–327
Universal Product Code (UPC), 405
UNIX, 536
unshielded twisted pair (UTP)
    cabling, 526
unsigned drivers, 400
Update Driver button (Device
    Manager), 115
updates and updating, 101–103,
    210–211, 373
Upgrade Advisor (Windows XP/
    Vista), 346, 347, 349, 350
upgrade installations, 341–342, 359
upgrade paths, 345, 348
upgrades and upgrading. *See also*
    Windows installations and
    upgrades
        and Aero desktop, 79
        drivers, 374
        issues with, 350
        preparation for, 350
        printer software, 502
        and troubleshooting LANs, 546
UPS (uninterruptible power supply),
    265–267
upstream USB ports and plugs, 44
U.S. Federal Communications
    Commission (FCC), 249
USB (universal serial bus) connectors/
    connections, 246, 249
        A, B, mini-B, 44, 45
        for bar code readers, 405
        external connections with, 44
        Hi-Speed USB, 286, 403, 485
        for LANs, 530
        for mice, 49
        for modems, 579–580
        for printers, 504, 506
        for scanners, 400
        thumb drives, 318, 319, 404, 634

for webcams, 403
        and wireless networks, 557, 567
USB Keyboard option, 393
USB (universal serial bus)
    keyboards, 393
USB to eSATA adapter plugs, 296
USBConnect Mercury 3G device, 567
Use recommended settings option, 361
User Account Control (UAC), 111
user accounts, 600, 601
User Advocates, 22
user data files, 343, 374
user information, 94
user interface, 75–90
    command line, 87–88
    Control Panel, 89
    customization of, 424
    desktop, 76–80
    login, 75–77
    My Network Places/Network,
        88–89
    Recycle Bin, 88
    taskbar and Start menu, 80–82
    Windows Explorer, 82–87
    Windows Sidebar, 89–90
user names, 360, 368, 598
user settings, 94
User State Migration Tool (USMT), 376
user-level skills, 12
users:
    access control for, 600
    communication with,
        543–544, 628
    educating, on preventive
        measures, 614, 631–632
    verifying system functionality
        with, 631
User's Files option, 86–87
USMT (User State Migration
    Tool), 376
utilities (tech toolkits), 633–634
UTP (unshielded twisted pair)
    cabling, 526
UXGA screen resolution, 463

V

V standards, 578
VA (volt-amps), 265
values (subkeys), 93
VC-1, 453
vendor-specific certifications, 2
versatility, 21–22
vertical refresh rate (VRR), 414
VESA (Video Electronics Standards
    Association), 47, 429, 432, 433
VESA Local Bus (VL-Bus), 226
VGA (video graphics array) inputs,
    422, 423
VGA (video graphics array) mode, 433
VGA (video graphics array) video
    cards, 427–429, 438
video and multimedia, 412–457
    input/output devices for, 392

LICENSE AGREEMENT

THIS PRODUCT (THE "PRODUCT") CONTAINS PROPRIETARY SOFTWARE, DATA AND INFORMATION (INCLUDING DOCUMENTATION) OWNED BY THE McGRAW-HILL COMPANIES, INC. ("McGRAW-HILL") AND ITS LICENSORS. YOUR RIGHT TO USE THE PRODUCT IS GOVERNED BY THE TERMS AND CONDITIONS OF THIS AGREEMENT.

LICENSE: Throughout this License Agreement, "you" shall mean either the individual or the entity whose agent opens this package. You are granted a non-exclusive and non-transferable license to use the Product subject to the following terms:

(i) If you have licensed a single user version of the Product, the Product may only be used on a single computer (i.e., a single CPU). If you licensed and paid the fee applicable to a local area network or wide area network version of the Product, you are subject to the terms of the following subparagraph (ii).

(ii) If you have licensed a local area network version, you may use the Product on unlimited workstations located in one single building selected by you that is served by such local area network. If you have licensed a wide area network version, you may use the Product on unlimited workstations located in multiple buildings on the same site selected by you that is served by such wide area network; provided, however, that any building will not be considered located in the same site if it is more than five (5) miles away from any building included in such site. In addition, you may only use a local area or wide area network version of the Product on one single server. If you wish to use the Product on more than one server, you must obtain written authorization from McGraw-Hill and pay additional fees.

(iii) You may make one copy of the Product for back-up purposes only and you must maintain an accurate record as to the location of the back-up at all times.

COPYRIGHT; RESTRICTIONS ON USE AND TRANSFER: All rights (including copyright) in and to the Product are owned by McGraw-Hill and its licensors. You are the owner of the enclosed disc on which the Product is recorded. You may not use, copy, decompile, disassemble, reverse engineer, modify, reproduce, create derivative works, transmit, distribute, sublicense, store in a database or retrieval system of any kind, rent or transfer the Product, or any portion thereof, in any form or by any means (including electronically or otherwise) except as expressly provided for in this License Agreement. You must reproduce the copyright notices, trademark notices, legends and logos of McGraw-Hill and its licensors that appear on the Product on the back-up copy of the Product which you are permitted to make hereunder. All rights in the Product not expressly granted herein are reserved by McGraw-Hill and its licensors.

TERM: This License Agreement is effective until terminated. It will terminate if you fail to comply with any term or condition of this License Agreement. Upon termination, you are obligated to return to McGraw-Hill the Product together with all copies thereof and to purge all copies of the Product included in any and all servers and computer facilities.

DISCLAIMER OF WARRANTY: THE PRODUCT AND THE BACK-UP COPY ARE LICENSED "AS IS." McGRAW-HILL, ITS LICENSORS AND THE AUTHORS MAKE NO WARRANTIES, EXPRESS OR IMPLIED, AS TO THE RESULTS TO BE OBTAINED BY ANY PERSON OR ENTITY FROM USE OF THE PRODUCT, ANY INFORMATION OR DATA INCLUDED THEREIN AND/OR ANY TECHNICAL SUPPORT SERVICES PROVIDED HEREUNDER, IF ANY ("TECHNICAL SUPPORT SERVICES"). McGRAW-HILL, ITS LICENSORS AND THE AUTHORS MAKE NO EXPRESS OR IMPLIED WARRANTIES OF MERCHANTABILITY OR FITNESS FOR A PARTICULAR PURPOSE OR USE WITH RESPECT TO THE PRODUCT. McGRAW-HILL, ITS LICENSORS, AND THE AUTHORS MAKE NO GUARANTEE THAT YOU WILL PASS ANY CERTIFICATION EXAM WHATSOEVER BY USING THIS PRODUCT. NEITHER McGRAW-HILL, ANY OF ITS LICENSORS NOR THE AUTHORS WARRANT THAT THE FUNCTIONS CONTAINED IN THE PRODUCT WILL MEET YOUR REQUIREMENTS OR THAT THE OPERATION OF THE PRODUCT WILL BE UNINTERRUPTED OR ERROR FREE. YOU ASSUME THE ENTIRE RISK WITH RESPECT TO THE QUALITY AND PERFORMANCE OF THE PRODUCT.

LIMITED WARRANTY FOR DISC: To the original licensee only, McGraw-Hill warrants that the enclosed disc on which the Product is recorded is free from defects in materials and workmanship under normal use and service for a period of ninety (90) days from the date of purchase. In the event of a defect in the disc covered by the foregoing warranty, McGraw-Hill will replace the disc.

LIMITATION OF LIABILITY: NEITHER McGRAW-HILL, ITS LICENSORS NOR THE AUTHORS SHALL BE LIABLE FOR ANY INDIRECT, SPECIAL OR CONSEQUENTIAL DAMAGES, SUCH AS BUT NOT LIMITED TO, LOSS OF ANTICIPATED PROFITS OR BENEFITS, RESULTING FROM THE USE OR INABILITY TO USE THE PRODUCT EVEN IF ANY OF THEM HAS BEEN ADVISED OF THE POSSIBILITY OF SUCH DAMAGES. THIS LIMITATION OF LIABILITY SHALL APPLY TO ANY CLAIM OR CAUSE WHATSOEVER WHETHER SUCH CLAIM OR CAUSE ARISES IN CONTRACT, TORT, OR OTHERWISE. Some states do not allow the exclusion or limitation of indirect, special or consequential damages, so the above limitation may not apply to you.

U.S. GOVERNMENT RESTRICTED RIGHTS: Any software included in the Product is provided with restricted rights subject to subparagraphs (c), (1) and (2) of the Commercial Computer Software-Restricted Rights clause at 48 C.F.R. 52.227-19. The terms of this Agreement applicable to the use of the data in the Product are those under which the data are generally made available to the general public by McGraw-Hill. Except as provided herein, no reproduction, use, or disclosure rights are granted with respect to the data included in the Product and no right to modify or create derivative works from any such data is hereby granted.

GENERAL: This License Agreement constitutes the entire agreement between the parties relating to the Product. The terms of any Purchase Order shall have no effect on the terms of this License Agreement. Failure of McGraw-Hill to insist at any time on strict compliance with this License Agreement shall not constitute a waiver of any rights under this License Agreement. This License Agreement shall be construed and governed in accordance with the laws of the State of New York. If any provision of this License Agreement is held to be contrary to law, that provision will be enforced to the maximum extent permissible and the remaining provisions will remain in full force and effect.